July 10. 1986

To our dearest

    This book is a

token of the memories which

you have shared with us.

    With great affection,

friendship & love,

      Doug & Marzi

LORD WILLIAM RUSSELL
AND HIS WIFE
1815–1846

Lord William Russell
and his Wife
1815–1846

GEORGIANA BLAKISTON

JOHN MURRAY

To the memory of
FLORA RUSSELL
1869–1967
and
DIANA RUSSELL
1874–1971

Printed in Great Britain by
William Clowes & Sons, Limited
London, Beccles and Colchester
0 7195 2242 0

CONTENTS

ILLUSTRATIONS

vi

Illustrations

John, 4th = Hon. Gertr█
Duke of   Leveson G█
Bedford   1719–179█
1710–1771

Francis, Marquess of Tavis█
1739–1767

Francis,   Hon. Georgiana
5th Duke of Bedford   Byng
1765–1802   –1801
                                              (1st wife)

Lady Anna = Francis,   William = Elizabeth   Adelaide = John   = Lady
Maria   Marquess   1790–1846   Anne   Lister,   1792–1878 Franc█
Stanhope   of   Rawdon   Lady   Elliot
1783–1857 Tavistock,   1793–1874   Ribblesdale   1815–1█
           7th Duke   1807–1838   (2nd w█
           of Bedford   (1st wife)
           1788–1861

                                              Georgiana   Victoria
                                              1836–1922   1838–1880

William,   John,   William   Rollo   Agath█
Lord Russell,   Viscount   1848–1933   1849–1914   1853–1█
8th Duke of   Amberley
Bedford   1842–1876
1809–1872

Hastings,   Arthur   Odo
9th Duke   1825–1892   1829–1884
of Bedford
1819–1891

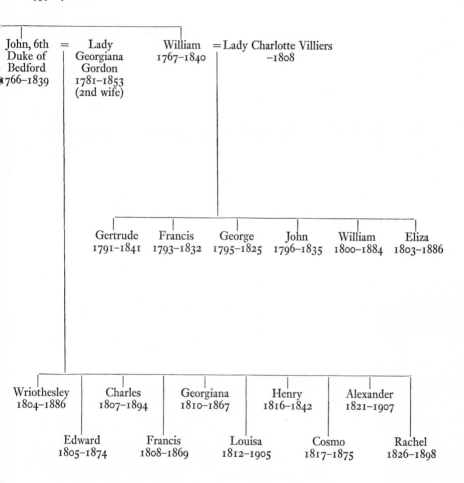

Lady Elizabeth Keppel
1739–1768

John, 6th Duke of Bedford 1766–1839	= Lady Georgiana Gordon 1781–1853 (2nd wife)	William 1767–1840	= Lady Charlotte Villiers –1808

Gertrude 1791–1841   Francis 1793–1832   George 1795–1825   John 1796–1835   William 1800–1884   Eliza 1803–1886

Wriothesley 1804–1886   Charles 1807–1894   Georgiana 1810–1867   Henry 1816–1842   Alexander 1821–1907

Edward 1805–1874   Francis 1808–1869   Louisa 1812–1905   Cosmo 1817–1875   Rachel 1826–1898

FOREWORD AND ACKNOWLEDGEMENTS

In preparing this book I have made use of papers that, with one or two exceptions, have not been published before. I have drawn freely on Lord William's diary, which is preserved at Woburn Abbey, and on three volumes of letters addressed to him, which were printed for private circulation between 1915 and 1920 by Herbrand, Duke of Bedford. Access to a collection of Russell family papers in private hands has also been invaluable. The Holland House papers and the Lieven papers, both in the British Museum, have provided material without which much in the lives of the William Russells would have remained obscure. Lord William's private correspondence from his legations in Portugal and Germany, preserved among the Palmerston papers, illuminates the official side of his life. The sixth Duke of Bedford and his sons wrote at length to each other about politics, but such matters, being considered beyond the scope of this book, have been generally omitted.

With regard to punctuation, the dots, dashes and underlinings with which Lady William Russell, apparently at breathless speed, strung together and emphasised her staccato utterances, can hardly be reproduced in print. In a general way, therefore, punctuation has been adapted to the printed page. The lavish use of capital letters, so general in the writing of that period, has also been suppressed. Erratic spelling has at times been corrected, for example in the case of Lord William's spelling of personal names, which was seldom right. Place-names, however, remain as they were written, and it will be seen how various at that time was the spelling of 'Stuttgart'.

On the accuracy of the spelling or phrasing of words or sentences in foreign languages, including quotations from dead languages – and a good many of such are penned by these highly cultured and cosmopolitan letter-writers – it has been necessary here and there, in the interests of sense, to make small emendations. Growing familiarity with Lady William's polyglot erudition, however tiresome it often seems as sentence after sentence fails to reach its end entirely in her mother tongue, breeds only respect for her genuinely broad and European culture.

Foreword and Acknowledgements

I have to thank Her Majesty the Queen for her gracious permission to quote from Queen Victoria's private journal. The Duke of Bedford generously allowed me to hunt amongst the exciting chaos of his private archives and my thanks are due to him and to the Trustees of the Bedford Settled Estates for giving me leave to print what I found. It is by the courtesy of the Trustees of the Broadlands Archives that the private letters that passed between Lord Palmerston and Lord William Russell are included in this book. Transcripts of Crown-copyright records in the Public Record Office appear by permission of the Controller of H.M. Stationery Office. For helping me with information I am indebted to Mr Brinsley Ford, Mr Roger Fulford, Mr Hugh Honour, Mr Hugh Murray Baillie and Professor E. R. Vincent. Finally I must thank Mrs Kitty West, who made many useful suggestions, and Mr Herbert Rees, who saved me from many unsuspected pitfalls.

PREFACE

Many years ago as a child I took a book from the shelves in my home and found that someone had written 'EAR' on the fly leaf inside. I was impressed by the boldness of the writing, and the singularity of the word, for had 'EYE' or 'LEG' been inscribed it could not have seemed stranger. Some time later my father gave me a silver box in three compartments, and on the lid of each was engraved in Gothic letters ЄЯЯ. He told me they were the initials of his grandmother Elizabeth Anne Russell, that she had been able to read in eight languages and had bought most of the books in the house. He could remember the smell of the cats who surrounded her, and the prickles on her chin when as a child he received her kisses. It would be but a slight exaggeration to say that since my early knowledge of her she has never been wholly out of my mind.

There was every encouragement to think about her, for although she had been dead for nearly fifty years she was constantly spoken of. Not only did her books line the walls of our home but we lived amongst an abundance of her possessions. It was hardly possible to ignore a person so acquisitive. Disposed about the house were carved and inlaid boxes in which she had kept her gloves and lace, and which still held some of her trinkets. Beads, talismans, coins, crucifixes and visiting cards were jumbled together in aromatic dust. Brass-bound trunks contained lengths of velvet and striped muslins. From desiccated cardboard boxes came gauze and ribbons out of which my aunts made themselves fancy summer hats. Rolls of Florentine marbled papers, crisp with age, were stacked at the back of cupboards where prints and drawings lay flat in heavy portfolios, rarely moved and never opened. We used her blank drawing books of hand-made paper for our sketching, and for fun we dropped hot red wax on our envelopes, impressing it with her seals that were engraved 'EAR' or 'Bettina'. Wherever there was a flat surface the ubiquitous 'EAR' denoted possession. Much of the nineteenth-century pine furniture had been brought back from Germany, where she lived for many years. There was a shelf devoted to Bohemian glass, some of it ornamented with a date and the initials of her sons, or with pictures of the Brunnen at Carlsbad. Curious feather pictures of birds, which had hung in her boys' nursery at

Stuttgart, now fascinated a later generation. In the attics stood vast deal chests bound with iron. They were numbered and had 'Lady William Russell' seared across their sides. In seventy-six boxes of varying size she had transported her belongings about Europe. An urgent application to her brother-in-law, Lord John Russell, for a Treasury Order to allow her bales to pass through the customs when she returned to England, and a letter from her husband directing her not to overload the postchaise, are evidence of the style in which she travelled.

From the books that had formed her library it was possible to trace a geographical pattern in her life, for wherever she went in Europe she bought books, and inscribed them with her name and a date in an emphatic hand. Her taste was for the ancient classics – not only in the original but also in translation to French, German, Italian and Spanish; next to the Gospels in Latin and Greek stood the Old Testament in Hebrew, for at the age of forty-three she took her first lessons in that language. Volumes of biography and history were acquired as they appeared from the presses of Paris, Leipzig, Dresden and Rome, providing a varied sustenance for her intellectual appetite. She made marginal comments in her books without inhibition. A brief note on a genealogy appears in an historical work, and a Portuguese proverb about bad cooking may be found scribbled in a book of French memoirs. On a page of Wingfield's *Tour in Dalmatia* she wrote: 'I celebrated my 9th birthday at Ragusa', thus giving us an unexpected biographical clue.

In attempting to trace the course of the life of this remarkable woman clues were necessary, since although many papers had been preserved much had been destroyed, perhaps at her direction or from filial piety. At different times she urged her correspondents to burn her letters and they seem mostly to have done so. When her youngest son died his widow destroyed his papers, so that the letters he received from his mother that made him, he said, roll on the floor with laughter, are lost for ever.

Two years after her death a small volume, privately printed, appeared in 1876 as a memoir by a friend, Mrs Annie Jane Harvey, but the tone of adulation in which it is written makes it of little interest. That she was generally acknowledged as very clever, beautiful and entertaining is apparent from the biographies of her contemporaries, but she was not universally beloved. Byron's flattering lines from 'Beppo' were often quoted by my family, but it was unknown to them that she considered he had abused her in a later poem. Her father-in-law declared she had a haughty and unbending nature, but he was fond of her in spite of the

xiv

Bern, March 2 Sunday 1828

Dearest John Miniken's as you will not many I conclude
you read Fénelon & find "que le joug *perpetuel* du mariage est difficile
à supporter, c'est un état de tribulation et d'afflyétissement très
pénible, auquel il faut se préparer en esprit de pénitence,
quand on s'y voit appellé de Dieu" — however come
& live with us, I will be a good sister to you, &
my children will love you & we will all coddle
you & amuse you ... nous ne sommes pas des
ennuyeux ... why should one always live so seeking
without any family friendships, & brothers, sisters, nephews
cousins &c &c — — When you are tired of le beau monde
think of me, as I have had so many years
sickness I shall be the most knowing &
sympathizing of all nurses — — You will see how
comfortable we shall be ... but do not consult
Lucretia Holland about it, she will ennuyer son
corazon simplicé by nature — — — in the mean while pendant
que tout cela se prépare let us write, your kind letter
of the 12th just reached me ... to Paris fate mio non
ho voglia di andare — — — nor to London ... I should
like much to pass the whole summer in Switzerland
I never saw it & have always wish'd it ardently,

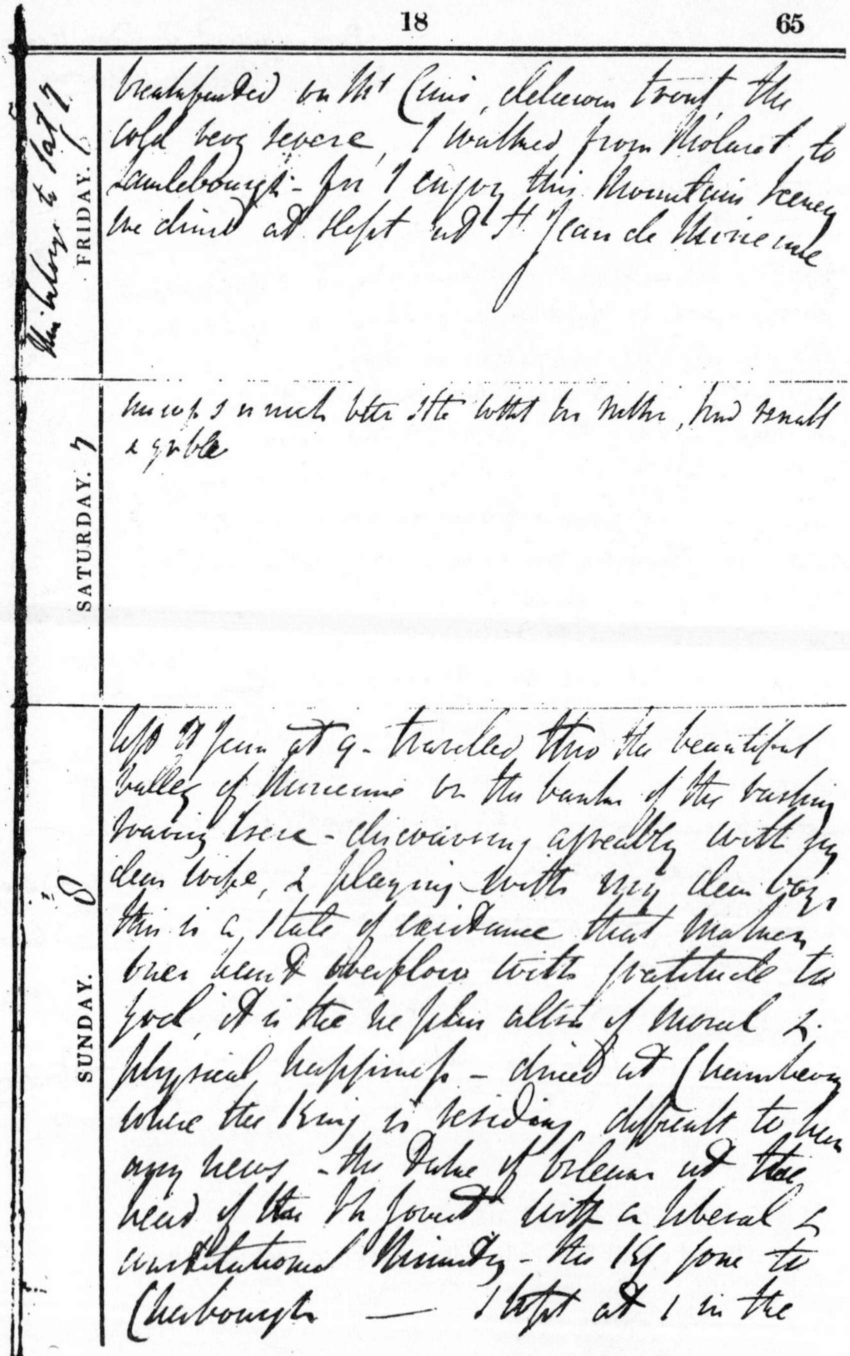
18 65

Thurs., Fri. & Sat. 7

FRIDAY. 6

Breakfasted on Mt Cenis, delicious trout, the cold very severe. I walked from Molaret to Lanslebourg — how I enjoy this mountain scenery. We dined at [illegible] and slept at St Jean de Maurienne

SATURDAY. 7

My cold is much better & the letter [illegible] rather [illegible]

SUNDAY. 8

Left St Jean at 9 — travelled thro' the beautiful valley of Maurienne on the banks of the rushing roaring Arc — conversing agreeably with my dear wife, & playing with my dear boys — this is a state of existence that makes one's heart overflow with gratitude to God, it is the ne plus ultra of moral & physical happiness — dined at Chambery where the King is residing, difficult to hear any news — the Duke of Orleans at the head of the Govt with a liberal & constitutional Ministry — the K. gone to Cherbourg — I slept at 1 in the

A page from Lord William Russell's diary

tracasseries she created in his family. Creevey hated her, and as a girl she offended Lord Glenbervie, who wrote tartly of her bad manners long before her marriage. Lady Holland had views on her selfish character and, despite their friendship, was ready to spread the malicious stories that caused a breach with Holland House in 1834. At the time of her great humiliation in middle age, Princess Lieven wrote that all the English women in Paris detested her and were not at all sorry for her. Lady William Russell's rigid morality may account for this ill feeling shown by ladies of easier virtue.

It may be doubted if she ever cared very much for her husband. There are no tender expressions of affection to be found in her surviving letters. The education of her three sons was the prime and principal occupation of her life, and her complacency at the success of her system she recorded in a letter written to Poodle Byng* in her old age. She was rewarded with the lifelong devotion of her children.

I have said that my great-grandmother was constantly spoken of in our family: her husband was rarely mentioned. This was perhaps on account of his lapse from moral behaviour, or because his sad and lonely end reflected ill on his wife and younger sons. In my youth he had no significance for me, and he was not associated with anything in my home, but, searching to know more about Lady William Russell, I found that her husband was no cipher but a man of distinction; his image appeared clearly from the books I read and the papers that existed. His diaries were preserved, as well as many of the letters he received, and government records disclosed his words and actions in the public service. Of the letters that he wrote to his family few have survived; they must often have given pain or aroused anger and were best destroyed. His unhappy faculty for provoking his correspondents will be seen in some of the letters printed here. The disappearance of the greater number from his own hand leaves us with a portrait seen as it were in a mirror; the reflection of the man appears in the answers to his letters, and it is usually easy to guess the substance of what he wrote. Grumbling at his father's extravagance, rating his brothers for lack of political foresight, wounding the feelings of his eldest son, who probably loved him more than anyone did, he seems propelled by a desire to hurt, and we find this humane lover of justice continually being accused of unfairness.

'Russell pens', wrote Lady Holland, with some truth, 'are small daggers not goose quills.'[1]

* See p. 68 n., below.

INTRODUCTION

Born on 2 October 1793, Elizabeth Anne was the only child of the Honourable John Rawdon, brother to the Earl of Moira. A soldier by profession, he had lost a leg at the battle of Brandywine in the North American war. With the wooden one that replaced his shattered limb he was reputed to beat his silly wife Frances, daughter of Joseph Hall Stevenson of Skelton Castle, Yorkshire. Bessy, as they called their daughter, was thus through her mother the great-grand-daughter of Laurence Sterne's 'Eugenius',* and on her father's side of Selina Countess of Huntingdon.† Although in her long life she was to show neither the demoniacal propensities of the one nor the evangelising spirit of the other, she may have derived much of her forceful character and remarkable intellect from these two forebears.

Captain Rawdon received the King's bounty for the loss of his leg, and was appointed a captain of Yarmouth Castle in the Isle of Wight, an employment he seems to have undertaken lightly since in 1797, when the French revolutionary armies were sweeping across Europe, he decided in a mood of Irish irresponsibility to take his wife and child to live abroad. His brother wrote curtly to him, and while refusing an offer of peafowl, plants and greyhounds, which Captain Rawdon was anxious to dispose of on leaving his house Bolney Court in Sussex, observed that although circumstances made his government of Yarmouth Castle a sinecure, invasion was menaced and every officer was ordered to the coast.

> Tho' for yourself you might slight the hazard of passing the sea to Hamburgh, it is a very different matter to expose your wife and child to be taken by a privateer. . . . How are you to get your wife and child thro' Germany? The roads are everywhere broken up by the transportation of Artillery & stores; and the reinforcements repairing to the Armies occupy nine days out of ten all the Inns and Post Houses. Horses for your carriage may not be procured for a fortnight together.[2]

* John Hall-Stevenson (1718–85) formed a club of demoniacks at Skelton, where the members indulged in 'heavy drinking and obscene jesting'. Laurence Sterne introduced him into *Tristram Shandy* under the name of Eugenius.

† Selina Countess of Huntingdon (1707–91) founded an evangelical sect known as Lady Huntingdon's Connexion.

I

Introduction

Captain Rawdon turned a deaf ear, and excusing himself on the grounds of his wife's health, crossed the sea. So far as we know, he never returned to England. The Rawdons travelled about Switzerland, Germany and Italy, finally settling in Vienna. Among their society were many Irish Catholics who, precluded by their religion from serving in England, had engaged themselves in the Austrian Army; such names as O'Reilly, Nugent, Dillon and Plunket were recalled by Bessy in later years. John Rawdon's closest friend was Lord Clanwilliam who had married one of the three daughters of Count Thun, the friend of Beethoven, the other two being the wives of Prince Razoumowsky and Prince Lichnowsky. In the aristocratic circles of Vienna were formed the earliest friendships of the Rawdons' child, and the foundation of her lifelong devotion to Austria was laid.

In 1800 Nelson accompanied Sir William Hamilton and his wife to Vienna. One of Bessy's earliest recollections was of being taken from her bed to become the unwilling partner in one of those 'Attitudes' with which the wife of the English Ambassador to Naples entertained society. We may wonder what terrible character was assumed by Lady Hamilton as she dragged the little girl about the room by her hair.

Her education was entrusted to emigrant French abbés, who were making their living as tutors while exiled from France. With them Bessy became proficient in Latin and Greek as well as in French and German. During visits to Carlsbad they also instructed her in astronomy and botany, and late in life she remembered with affection the good men who made her familiar with the bright star Aldebaran, *l'Œil du Taureau*, and showed her the yellow blossoms of *Millefeuilles* growing by mountain paths.

Receiving a handsome annuity from an uncle, Captain Rawdon, while bestowing on his daughter every advantage, was able to lead a life of comfort and amusement, and his taste for roistering company led Mrs Rawdon to confide to a minutely detailed diary the number of blows she received from her husband when he was drunk.

When the Peace of Amiens came to an end and war broke out again between England and France, Napoleon's decree against travelling Englishmen made Captain Rawdon a *détenu*; as an officer he was not interned but put on parole and, though free to travel where the French did not rule, he was not allowed to return to England. Establishing themselves at Venice, then part of Austria, the Rawdons remained there for five years, exchanging each summer the stench of the canals for the sweet

2

Introduction

air of Monte Berico at Vicenza, where Captain Rawdon hired the Palladian Villa Valmarana. In this beautiful house, decorated fifty years before by the Tiepolos with romantic paintings of the story of the *Aeneid*, and of Rinaldo and Armida, Bessy Rawdon's mind was imbued with a passionate love for classic tales and fables. Remaining all her life ignorant of English literature (except for the Bible), her whole thought, expression and utterance was coloured and informed by her intimate knowledge of classical legend acquired during the impressionable years of her youth in Italy.

One summer, there were in neighbouring villas other English families. Clives, Peploes and Greatheads added gaiety to the Rawdons' *villeggiatura*, and visits from travellers were made the occasion for parties and 'crowded suppers', and there was a ball for Bessy's twelfth birthday. Among the many visitors were three young men who became her lifelong friends: the future Lords Aberdeen, Kinnaird and Brougham. The first was returning from Greece, and taking her on his knee held her rapt with his tales of classic lands. When dancing the Monferrina with Kinnaird at London balls, Bessy Rawdon would recall the first occasion of their doing so at the Villa Valmarana. Henry Brougham, travelling regardless of Napoleon, and passing himself off as an American, had reached Italy by way of Germany, catching a glimpse of the Ogre himself at Cologne. He cannot have met Madame de Staël under the Rawdons' roof as Bessy stated in her old age, since in 1813 he disclaimed ever having seen her. Madame de Staël visited the Rawdons in 1804, on her way back to Coppet from Rome with her travelling companions Schlegel and Sismondi. There must have been talk of Benjamin Constant for Bessy asserted that he was of the party, whereas Madame de Staël's visit to Italy was the occasion for one of his rare escapes from her 'corybantic passions'.

When Napoleon invaded northern Italy the Rawdons went back to Vienna where the Captain died in 1808 and was buried in the same grave as his old friend Lord Clanwilliam. Summoned to return to England by her brother-in-law, Mrs Rawdon and her daughter embarked at Trieste in an English warship and sailed home under the auspices of Lord Collingwood, who had been directed by Lord Moira to offer them his protection. For the next three years they were to live with Bessy's uncle at Donington Park in Leicestershire and at his town house in St James's Place.

This powerful and magnificent nobleman was a close friend of the Prince of Wales. Described by a contemporary as being quite handsome 'if he would shave off the black whiskers that grow just under his eyes and

3

almost across his nose', he earned the devotion of his niece by his generous and affectionate treatment of her. He acted as host to the English Whigs and Irish wits, and for months entertained the entire French *émigré* Court. Beautiful and extremely intelligent, Bessy was well equipped at the age of fifteen to enter this brilliant society. She preferred the French-men to the cleverer English politicians, for they had courtly manners and were pleased with her for speaking their language as none of them could ever speak hers. In the company of the Comte de Lille and the Comte d'Artois (afterwards Louis XVIII and Charles X), the Duc d'Angoulême and the Duc de Berri, and the Versailles courtiers Gramont, Lorges, Damas, Blacas, Vaudreuil and Puy Ségur, she corrected the accent of her Viennese French and put a polish on her aristocratic manners. These 'old Dinosaurs of the *Ancien Régime*', as she called them, wore their hair powdered, with pigtails and *ailes de pigeon*. She recollected in later life that two old valets always stood behind the Duc de Lorges's chair and used to whisper to him: 'Monsieur le Duc, mangez de ce plat. C'est bon.'[3] They had been in the kitchen and had made it their business to find out.

The society of Lord Moira's intimates, Sir James Mackintosh, Lord Holland, Lord Grey, Curran, Grattan, Sheridan, Thomas Moore and Samuel Rogers, was better calculated to improve her mind. Her education continued under the surveillance of Mr Dalby, the chaplain: she was to be found reading with him in the library at Donington by those who came to fetch or leave a book. Thomas Moore, who liked to walk over from his cottage on the edge of the Park and use the library, may have found her there some days and stayed to sing a song. He wrote to his publisher: 'The title of "Merrily oh!" I would have as follows: "The Tyrolese Song of Liberty; a national air, arranged with English words, and dedicated to Miss Rawdon.'[4] Bessy thought he was like 'a clever little gnat singing about'.[5]

In due course she was presented at Court where she found favour in the eyes of the old Queen by talking German, a rare accomplishment in those days. Thereafter she was to be seen at London balls and was noticed by Lady Granville's sharp eyes. 'The dear Rawdon was pushing about, her shawl upon her arm and in her countenance "I will endure it no longer", the daughter very pretty, but her blooming little face quite lost in curls and nosegays.'[6]

> And waltzing females
> With unblushing face
> Disdain to dance
> But in a man's embrace.

4

Future generations ascribed to Bessy Rawdon the introduction of the waltz to London ballrooms, but this she denied. At Almack's the throngs were revolving and twirling before she grew up, and Lady Jersey (who waltzed till she fainted) was sending out invitations exclusively for waltzers, and 'waltzing lessons were given at 5 o'clock in all predominant houses'.[7]

Among those who noticed the particular quality of Bessy's beauty, remarked on by Lady Granville, was Lord Byron.

> I've seen some balls and revels in my time,
>   And stayed them over for some silly reason,
> And then I looked (I hope it was no crime)
>   To see what lady best stood out the season;
> And though I've seen some thousands in their prime
>   Lovely and pleasing, and who still may please on,
> I never saw but one (the stars withdrawn)
>   Whose bloom could after dancing dare the Dawn.
>
> The name of this Aurora I'll not mention,
>   Although I might, for she was nought to me
> More than that patent work of God's invention,
>   A charming woman, whom we like to see;
> But writing names would merit reprehension,
>   Yet if you like to find out this fair *She*,
> At the next London or Parisian ball
>   You still may mark her cheek, out-blooming all.[8]

It is on the authority of Samuel Rogers that we know that these lines from 'Beppo' are Lord Byron's tribute to Miss Rawdon. He knew her well since she was Annabella Milbanke's friend.

'Next time you see your friend Miss Milbanke', he commanded her one day, 'be so kind as to give her a hint not to send me any more of her foolish rhymes'.[9]

When nearly eighty, Lady William Russell spoke of the poet so: 'Lord Byron was Satan incarnate – talent – beauty – genius – wickedness – hypocrisy, vice – the quintessence, mind and body, of the cloven footed. But you looked in his face and listened to his voice and read his poetry, and his club foot and cloven foot were over looked.'[10] And again: 'He was not natural but I was struck with his remarkable shrewdness . . . I adored him, he had a magnificent head, a melodious voice and a very curious and dangerous "under look" with his beautiful eyes, but his shoulders sloped and altogether he had a mean figure . . . he always seized the first opportunity of sitting down.'[11]

Lord Moira's influence is evident in the Rawdons' introduction to the Princess of Wales, since he was employed by the Prince in his negotiations with his wife. They dined frequently at Kensington Palace. Distinguished in mind and in person, Bessy's merits as a companion for the heiress to the throne were apparent and she was chosen with Margaret Mercer Elphinstone to be attached to the establishment of Princess Charlotte. At the time of the furious disagreements between the Prince and his daughter as to whom she should marry, when the Prince behaved with calculated cruelty to the distracted girl, dismissing her household and ordering her to join him at Carlton House, a special plea was made at the instigation of Lord Brougham that Princess Charlotte should be assured of seeing Miss Mercer and keeping Miss Rawdon; but in the case of Bessy this was not allowed.

When the Princess of Wales saw her daughter deprived of her companions she tried to attach Bessy to her own person, having taken a great fancy to her, but was astonished to find that the mother had no intention of being separated from her child. Mrs Rawdon appears to have asserted her independence by arriving half-way through dinner at Connaught House and not allowing Bessy to be left alone with the Princess.

In 1813 Lord Moira was sent to govern Bengal. His house in St James's Place was sold and the lease of a furnished one in Hertford Street was taken for his sister-in-law and niece. Donington Park was shut up and it was naturally to her own relations at Skelton Castle in Yorkshire that Mrs Rawdon now took her daughter. Here they entered quite a different world. 'Foxhunters, rich squires, Yorkshire pies and brawn; eating, drinking, dancing, riding, shooting, jollity.'[12] All the squires had intermarried with their neighbours and were cousins: Lambtons, Lowthers, Brandlings, Chaloners, Wentworths etc. Describing her situation and starved intellect to her daughter-in-law years later, Lady William Russell wrote: 'J'aurais dévoré des comptes de blanchisseuse.'[13] The library at Skelton (the 'Crazy Castle' of his friend John Hall-Stevenson) had once inspired Laurence Sterne: Bessy Rawdon, seeking there, perhaps, a refuge from the hallooing foxhunting squires, found in it consolation for her bucolic existence. Reading in the fine library, she was confirmed in her taste for the classics that the paintings of Tiepolo in the Villa Valmarana had first inspired. She was not formed to become the wife of a jolly Yorkshire squire.

When Madame de Staël visited London in the winter of 1813–14 she would have found the Rawdons living in the house at the corner of Hertford Street; the little girl she knew at Vicenza, 'her little prodigy', had become a beautiful young woman. She must again have been struck by Bessy's distinction and intelligence for she conceived the idea of a match between her and her son Auguste, who had accompanied her, but nothing came of this project.

A lustre was added that summer to the London season by the arrival of the victorious Allied Sovereigns. As much in demand for her fluent French and German as for her beauty, Bessy was distinguished by the highest favour. The Emperor Alexander of Russia, that man of 'dubious gender',[14] carried a little spy-glass with which he surveyed the ladies at balls, and selected those he wished to dance with. At a ball at Lord Cholmondeley's, Bessy was chosen for a waltz and found him charming; it was remarked that he, the Czar of all the Russias, had stooped to pick up her fan, and he was seen 'leaning behind her chair at supper'.*[15] He thought her the most delightful person in London, and was at no pains to disguise his admiration.

At the end of that brilliant season and after the dissolution of Princess Charlotte's establishment at Warwick House, there was nothing to keep the Rawdons in England, and they set out for Paris and Rome. A letter to Miss Berry describes some of their adventures on the Continent and details the marks of distinction accorded them by the French Royal Family, now restored to their proper fortunes. In a second letter Bessy's reawakened affection for the Austrians and her innate Tory sentiments are revealed. Neither of these feelings was ever to be changed by her marriage into the Whig aristocracy.

Elizabeth Anne Rawdon to Miss Berry at 26 North Audley Street [PRP]†
Rome Jan. 4, 1815

I am so conscience smitten, so replete with contrition, so *pénétrée* that I do not know how to begin my letter, dearest Berrina. Only think of my being 4 months abroad without writing to you! I received your letter from Raith at Paris, it was dated the 14th August, the day we landed at Dieppe; I was quite enchanted with Paris, indeed with France & the French in general, I always loved the nation *hors de chez eux*, & find them as agreeable in their own country; I know this opinion to be somewhat in opposition to the

* I had not witnessed [a waltz] in any perfection since I saw the Emperor of Russia dance with Lady William Russell.' Castle (ed.), *Jerningham Letters*, ii, 183.

† Mary Berry (1763–1852) and her sister Agnes (1764–1852) had been the intimate friends of Horace Walpole. After his death Mary Berry edited his *Works* and she wrote several historical books. Extracts from her *Journals and Correspondence* were published in 1865. The sisters were sometimes known as Elderberry and Blackberry. Lady William Russell, quoting *Lycidas*, called them 'berries harsh and crude'.

greater part of Europe, but it is my fate to think so. We remained 2 months at Paris, intending to stay only 15 days, from thence we went to the South of France, Lyons, Marseille, Toulon, where we found a ship of war ready to convey us to Italy, by the orders of the Duc d'Angoulême, *Grand Amiral de France*. Our ship was commanded by a nephew of Massena's. He had instructions to put into every town on the coast we might wish to see, & to keep within shore during the whole voyage, which made it longer but more agreeable; we put into Nice, where we found the Chevalier La Cainea promoted to the ranks of Baron & English Consul. Lady Charlotte Campbell & the Glenbervies were not yet arrived to our great sorrow. We also visited Genoa, & at length reached Civita Vecchia, 40 miles from the eternal city, where we arrived the 7th of Novr. – before any of our *con-cittadini* who are at present too numerous to give you a list of. We stay here till after Easter, *poi* Naples, *e poi si torna in Francia, e poi Inghilterra*. The person who is to convey this letter to England is actually in the room & sets off this night, the post is not a sure method, so that this opportunity is most lucky. I have not time to write more.

God bless you. Love me & write to me. Mamma's kind love & mine to Agnes.

While they were at Rome Mrs Rawdon followed the fashion and had her daughter drawn by Ingres, and they made the acquaintance of Canova. Count Fiano's house, where they lodged, was one of the few to which the sculptor went, and they were soon on familiar terms with the great man. He allowed Bessy to chip at the marble of his statues and he inscribed a small picture of his studio to the 'amabilissima Bettina', and later gave them a copy of his portrait by Sir Thomas Lawrence. In Bettina's letters to him from England she sometimes made use of the old Venetian vernacular, recollecting it from her childhood. 'Mama vi demanda', she wrote, 'se vi recordate dei bei raggionamenti fatti vicino al suo sofà, sullo picciolo scagno? le vostre confessioni in somma? "tempi passati!"'* and she ended her letter: 'Addio, caro el mi sior Canova el me voggia ben, e ch'el me scriva per carità ma di botto. Sono in tanto la vostra affezionata serva ed amica Bettina.'†

Among other visitors to Rome that spring were the Duke and Duchess of Bedford. They had with them the Duchess's niece, Lady Jane Montagu, and the Duke's second son, Lord William Russell, who had served as aide-de-camp to the Duke of Wellington in Spain. The young soldier had once confided to his brother John that he thought his stepmother's niece

* 'Mamma asks whether you remember the good talk that went on near her sofa, on that little stool there? In fact your confessions? "Times gone by!"'
† 'Goodbye, my dear Signor Canova, say you love me and write to me, please at once. I am your most affectionate servant and friend Bettina.'

8

the most charming creature ever seen. 'Beautiful as the morning sun – with a temper more heavenly sweet than ever was known. I never met her equal. But she is destined for a Duke at least.' There had been a rumour that these two were to marry, but now she was spitting blood and was destined shortly for the grave.

The Duke of Bedford, who was forming a collection of sculpture for his gallery at Woburn Abbey, was about to buy from Canova his group of the Three Graces. In his Roman studio the little Duchess of Bedford danced with castanets before the sculptor, a lovely rival to those chaste marble figures, and it was perhaps here that William Russell was first attracted to the brilliant Bessy Rawdon, whose blooming complexion appeared in such contrast to the pallid face of the poor consumptive girl, slowly dying in the care of his stepmother.

After an adventurous journey described in a letter to Miss Berry, Mrs Rawdon and her daughter reached Naples where a revolution had turned out the King, Joachim Murat, and allowed the return of the Bourbon royal family. Napoleon's escape from Elba in March prompted Murat to attack the Austrians who occupied the north of Italy, but he was beaten back to Naples, from whence he fled to France, and Ferdinand IV was restored to the throne. Murat's wife, the ex-Queen, was Napoleon's sister Caroline.

Elizabeth Anne Rawdon to Miss Berry [PRP]

Naples, May 25, 1815

After such a length of time I have at last an opportunity of writing to England, but it required nothing less than the success of the Austrian campaign and the threat of a bombardment from the English, to bring about this event. I am still in enchantment at all these events after so many weeks of ennui & suspense we did not know how long this would last, I had the comforting idea of Naples being our prison for God knows how long, that it is a beautiful prison, I must grant, but let the cage be ever so highly gilt I am of so refractory a nature that I quite hated the place as soon as I thought I *must* stay in it – however six weeks have brought us in the Austrians as conquerors. I was charmed to see their honest old sauerkraut faces again with their sunburnt brown complexions and white hair & whiskers which was the effect the Neapolitan sun had produced on them, it had rather reversed the order of things and I had many battles to fight for my old friends beauty, especially as all the English here are Muratisti or what the Italian canaille calls *framassoni e Giaccobini*, which is their idea of all wrongheaded politicians.

I have found about thirty *amis de coeur* amongst Lord Exmouth's fleet

& the Austrians, so much for my present state of consolation. We have acquired the name of *le dame assassinate* at Naples, I never thought I should stand fire so well, or have any part of my dress pierced with cartridges, but so it happened; we were attacked by the *banditti* on the 1st of April (an agreeable *poisson d'avril*) coming from Rome to Naples, between Itri and Mola di Gaeta. I contrived to escape being shot by a lucky motion of my head, when one of the *briganti* levelled his gun at me but the ball went through my veil, they seem to have been particularly *acharnés* against my poor veil as it has three shot through it; had it been in France, I should have supposed it was a peculiar dislike to the *voile vert*, which they were so much shocked at the English ladies wearing. In the midst of our attack (they had dragged us out of the carriage & pursued us in the middle of the road) another carriage came up, with gentlemen armed, the robbers immediately left us to fall upon them; seeing myself free & mamma & the maid beside me, it occurred to me that the best thing that could be done would be to run back to our carriage and drive off, which we accordingly did. I have gained great credit for this manoeuvre *d'avoir pu ramasser mes troupes et faire ma retraite en bonne ordre*. When we got to Gaeta we sent 25 soldiers to the help of the other travellers, three of them were wounded with stilettos, our servant also, the surgeon of the Neapolitan regiment thought the wounds were mortal so that we had to remain two days in that place until they were pronounced out of danger and then proceeded to Naples. A few days after this a much more horrible attack was made on 4 English carriages, as all the men were wounded, and 3 gendarmes & 2 post boys killed on the spot. The roads all over Italy are so dangerous that we shall try to go as much by sea as we can, luckily we are very good sailors, for my own part, if there is a short road by land and a long one by sea, I prefer the long one, so much do I love a ship, *bien entendu* a man of war. Our plans are to sail from hence to Leghorn, as soon as we can, we then proceed to Florence and Milan, and go to England by whatever way we can. Ferdinand is expected in a few days with Admiral Penrose. Prince Leopold came in with the Austrians – the ex-Queen sailed yesterday for Trieste & as to Joachim nobody knows what has become of him, he came to Naples just before the Convention of Capua, and escaped to Ischia in an open boat, since that he is supposed to have got off in a Genoese *tartane* bearing English colours; our cruizers are in full chace after him, but I suppose he will have as much luck as his *cognato*. Whilst he was at Ischia he eat eggs in a Frenchman's house, and stood at the window with his uniform on, his host said to him 'Sire, on vous reconnait, deignez changer d'habit, et raser vos moustaches' he replied 'Non! je veux être pris en roi, si l'on me fait prisonnier!' This attachment to his moustaches is highly diverting. Although Ferdinand is an old ass and Prince Leopold looks like a young fool, yet there is something touching and respectable in seeing an old family return to 'what's their ain'. I exult at the issue of this campaign, in despite of my compatriots here – besides which I execrate upstarts, and when I saw the box full of them at the Opera, with all the first familys of Italy bowing to them & standing behind the chairs of the post boys sons, changing their lemonade glasses & helping them to ice, it made my blood boil, although thank God I am not a Neapolitan and have nothing to do with their servilities. The Queen is a pretty woman, all was *en grande tenue*, good manners, good representation, fine diamonds, pomp *et tout ce qu'il faut*, yet my Tory soul revolted, but I grow warm on this subject and will spare you any more effusions. Love to Agnese, mamma joins in every kind love to you both, dearest Berrina, if you will continue your friendship to me and think of me with as much affection as I think of you, I shall be very happy.

EAR

P.S. Lady Burghersh is just arrived from Rome, she has been attacked, & has brought a robber prisoner with her into Naples! – he proves to be a drunken hussar who took a fancy to the trade and after robbing 4 or 5 people, found a determined person in Lady Burghersh's courier, who mastered him. He is to be shot with a monk, who also turned footpad in the streets of Naples.

We have had cannon at the corner of every street, such shooting, such killing – but it is nothing to what we all feared and expected from the lazzaronis.

At Naples Mrs Rawdon secured an introduction for herself and her daughter to Monsignor Capecelatro, the venerable Archbishop of Taranto, to whose select salon admission was eagerly sought by intellectual and fashionable visitors. Notable for his learning, benevolence, and the multitude of his cats, this aged man, more dilettante than prelate, was captivated by the intelligence of the lovely English girl. He wrote to her for many years in a bantering style, addressing her as 'Mia saggia e bella Bettina', mingling Neapolitan news with enquiries for her intellectual welfare. '. . . avremo presto Amica Staël: quante questioni sono già in ordine sur l'Allemagne! Ma son sicuro che finiremo di accordo poiché io son debole a fronte del suo vulcanico potere. Parlatemi della vostra vita romana; Cardinali vi fanno la corte? Le belle arti vi danno nuova vita?' He would end a letter: 'date un abbracio alla Mamma nel nome del suo Pastore ed Amico' and he signed himself 'vostro vecchio Taranto'.*[16]

At a moment in June when Bonaparte and the Duke of Wellington were ranging their forces against each other in the north, the Rawdons left Naples by boat for Leghorn on their way to England, and Bessy's admirer,

---

* 'We shall soon have our friend Staël here: what a lot of questions there will be about *l'Allemagne*! But I am sure we will end in agreement as I am weak in face of her volcanic power. Tell me about your life in Rome; do the Cardinals pay you court? Do the fine arts give you new life? Embrace your Mama in the name of her Pastor and Friend.'

Introduction

William Russell, made his way to Paris. He was shortly appointed to the staff of his old general the Duke, who was, after the battle of Waterloo, Commander of the Allied Forces of Occupation. Headquarters were at Cambrai, and Lord William's duties kept him alternately there and at Paris, where he was noticed flirting with married and unmarried young women: 'Lord William with his demure look is a gay deceiver.'[17] During the next year he had opportunities of becoming better acquainted with Miss Rawdon since her mother took her to Paris to be dressed by Madame Hypolite. It was apparent that he did not wish to be forgotten by her when she was in England, and his anxiety is expressed in letters to her mother. There is something touching in his desire to know if the amiable Bettina 'is a Whig or a reformer or a Humian', since his future wife was never to show any interest in politics and late in life was rated by her eldest son for forgetting that the Russells were Whigs.

Lord William Russell to Mrs Rawdon [PRP]

Woburn Abbey, Sunday [28 July 1816]

From all the enquiries I have made about you there appears to be so little hope of my seeing you before I return to France, that I cannot help troubling you with a letter to clear my conscience of having delivered all the pretty speeches, remembrances, loves &c, &c, with which I was charged for you & your most amiable daughter. Those who loaded me most were M. de Tascon, M. Latour Maubourg, le Duc de Rohan, Madame de Coigny & many others, too innumerable to be named in a letter, put in their little packet which I leave you to arrange & in return desire a receipt in full for having laid at your feet my whole charge.

Are you fixed for ever in the northern regions, has our sun no charms to bring you south or must we make a crusade to deliver you from the hands of the Yorkshiremen?

Pray remember me to Miss Rawdon, or if she has not forgotten old times say Guillaume Tell salutes Miss Betsy. I am most anxious to know whether she is a Whig or a reformer or a Humian but be what she will tell her not to forget her friend & admirer

W. Russell

Lord William Russell to Mrs Rawdon [PRP]

Dover, Tuesday. [13 August 1816]

I have no merit in writing to you, as I frankly confess my object in doing so is to amuse myself, all my things having embarked, the trusty Grecian* not even having left me a book, & we are all assembled here to kill time till

* Lord John Russell's manservant, Pudar, was a Greek.

the Duke arrives. Our *bons mots*, if we ever had any, are all said, our Lady sleeps upon the sofa & the gentlemen are beginning to yawn, so I have no choice but to sit down & bore you. You may think it hard my preferring you for this purpose to all my other acquaintance but I know no one who will have more indulgence for my stupidity. So for the news of Dover. Lady Glenbervie & family have just started for London.* Lord Alvanley is here very ill, he is on his way to Calais. . . .

The dinner, the dinner, it is on the table so I give you joy of being spared a longer letter. Pray remember me most sincerely to the *bellissima, amabilissima Bettina* & believe me truly yours

W.R.

As the recipient of Lord William's anxious letters Mrs Rawdon may not have been pleased to see another suitor turn up in the person of his younger brother John. Did she perhaps urge her daughter in the absence of any strong feelings, to accept the elder as being one step nearer the dukedom? Displaying an unwonted diffidence, Lord John delayed his proposal too long, and the story goes that when he asked Bessy to marry him, she cried: 'You are too late, Johnny, I have just accepted William.'

'Did you ever hear', wrote Lady Granville, 'that Lord William was very much in love with Miss Rawdon, and they would marry if they had *de quoi*?'[18] When the engagement was made public in Paris she reported that 'Emily Rumbold was taken from a ball the other night in despair upon the news being announced, and there is a French married woman in equal sorrow'.[19]

The wedding took place in the drawing room of Hertford Street on 21 June 1817, and the honeymoon was spent at Woburn Abbey.

Lord George William Russell, who now considered himself the happiest man in the world, was the second of the three sons of John 6th Duke of Bedford by his first wife, Georgiana Byng, daughter of Viscount Torrington. He was born in 1790 and when he was eleven years old his mother died, an event that brought him close to his brother John, the future Prime Minister. They were educated together at a private school, Woodnesborough, and at Westminster. When he was sixteen he entered the Army as a Cornet and served on his father's staff when the Duke of Bedford was appointed Lord Lieutenant of Ireland in the Ministry of all the Talents. He became aide-de-camp to Sir George Ludlow the next year and was with him at the siege of Copenhagen. In 1809 he went with

* 'We found the inn at Dover crowded with travellers . . ., the Duke of Wellington's friends and suite, who were waiting for him. Among the rest Lord and Lady Worcester, Lord William Russell. . . .' Bickley (ed.), *Glenbervie Diaries*, ii, 195.

Introduction

his regiment, the 23rd Light Dragoons, to the Peninsula, where he was slightly wounded during a charge at the battle of Talavera, his horse being shot through the head, while every man and officer in his squadron was killed. Called on by the French to surrender he cried, 'Pas encore', and leaping on to another horse made his escape. At the battle of Barossa eighteen months later he was aide-de-camp to General Graham, later Lord Lynedoch, to whom he remained greatly attached all his life. He received high praise from his father for the accounts he wrote home of these two battles.

While on leave in 1812, he entered Parliament as the member for Bedford. It was perhaps during this time in London that he made the acquaintance of Harriette Wilson, who found him 'a gentlemanlike little fellow'. Returning again to Spain, he was attached to the Duke of Wellington's personal staff and took part in the victorious advance across the Pyrenees, being the bearer of the despatch containing the account of the battle of Toulouse in April 1814.

We may be sure he was in London during the summer festivities that year in honour of the visiting Allied Sovereigns, and he would have been among the young aides-de-camp, at Carlton House on 21 July, whose dancing the Duke of Wellington liked to watch, saying 'How would society get on without all my boys?' [20] He must have been too at the fancy-dress ball given for the Duke at Burlington House, when supper was served for 1,700 persons, and Lord Byron appeared dressed as a monk. 'Does he not look beautiful?' said Miss Rawdon, confiding her admiration for the poet to John Cam Hobhouse, who wore Albanian dress and had recently been favoured by Mrs Rawdon with 'a long inventory of her daughter's accomplishments while the charming Bessy was in the room'. [21]

When in the following spring Lord William was in Italy with the Duke and Duchess of Bedford, and much in the company of the Rawdons, the pressing mother had opportunities to bring her daughter's qualities to the notice of a more eligible young man than Byron's friend.

Women found him very attractive; his wit, gentleness and reserve delighted and intrigued them. He resembled in appearance his brother John, but he was more robust and better-looking; he had the same broad head, pointed chin and finely-cut nose. Like Lord John he was a great favourite at Holland House; the brothers aroused Lady Holland's latent maternal instincts and were always welcome in that Whig enclave. Hereditary shyness and a cold manner made it difficult for him to be friends with men of his own age; with Frederick Ponsonby* he shared memories of exploits and sufferings in the Peninsular War, but his other friendships were with those much older than himself. Lord Lynedoch (b. 1748), Lord Ludlow (b. 1758), Sir Robert Adair† (b. 1763), the Duke of Wellington (b. 1769) and Lord Holland (b. 1773) were the Duke of Bedford's contemporaries, but these were the men who received Lord William's confidence and affectionate regard. With his father he was wholly at ease, enjoying his company, tolerating his simulated indifference to politics, and, while viewing his parent's extravagance with impatience, he admitted that hospitality at Woburn was the most magnificent and luxurious in England.

Losing his mother while a child, he was cared for by his father's second wife, who was very fond of him and he of her until their relationship was upset by his marriage. Taking his cue from his wife he saw only the faults in his stepmother, and his coldness to her became the subject of her reproaches, though her letters to him remained stubbornly affectionate in spite of the rebuffs she received from him. In a letter to Lady Holland the Duchess wrote: 'Never was there a more warm-hearted, generous being than William, the poor fellow has suffered by his generosity [William, against her advice, had lent his stepbrother a horse for hunting], the country being deep and the rider inexperienced the horse *died* when it came home ... William has since become in consequence in manner what he always was *au fond*, quite kind to me.'[22]

To the suppression of his natural affection for the woman who replaced his mother might be ascribed the conflicting elements of his nature – its weakness and obstinacy. Disparaged from the first by his wife for lack of self-confidence, he was abused for using his own judgement. 'Believe the old Cock is sometimes right', he begged when a young married man.

'Tell me what to do. I tremble at the thought of doing wrong' is the cry of one who has been persistently found fault with.

Born a younger son, he resented the laws of primogeniture, which gave much to his elder brother and nothing to him. Lord Tavistock's precarious state of health was for many years a cause for uncertainty. In 1823 it seemed unlikely that the Duke of Bedford, victim of a stroke, would long survive. Should his brother also die, William would have found himself heir to his nephew, a boy with an indifferent constitution. The dukedom and the possession of Woburn, which he loved deeply, seemed

---

* The Hon. Frederick Ponsonby (1783–1837), son of the 3rd Earl of Bessborough.
† Sir Robert Adair (1763–1855), Whig diplomatist, friend of Charles James Fox.

sometimes almost within his reach, and it was not surprising that he allowed himself to ponder on such a possible change in his fortunes. But it was an unsettling situation for a young man who was naturally indolent. Happily an interest in politics, and his liking for his military profession, channelled his youthful energies away from idle contemplation of what might be. His dominating wife, persuaded to feel that she was not appreciated as she should be in England, without much affection for her husband's family, and with happy memories of her youthful residence abroad, was determined to detach him from those pursuits and interests for which she felt no sympathy: politics, hunting, and the Army. And while protesting her desire that he should excel as a soldier, she could not hide the fact that her own wishes would make it difficult for him to succeed. Neglecting first his duties as a member of the House of Commons, Lord William then resigned his prospects as a soldier and, shuffling off his responsibilities, was at liberty to live where his wife chose, which was not in England. His gentle disposition and his great love for her allowed Lady William to persuade him that it was better for their sons to be educated abroad. Deprived of occupation, Lord William fixed his hopes and thoughts on the upbringing and education of his sons, and the respect he had for his wife's intelligence and judgement in the matter united them in this object. At first, from a distance, he was able to discuss the problems of education amicably with his brothers, but their consternation at seeing him seduced from his country, without work, permitted a note of exasperation to enter their correspondence, and it became their aim, successfully achieved, to get him back into service. As a diplomatist Lord William regained some of the confidence and self-respect that had been diminished by his wife's contrariness, but he had lost the feeling of unity with his father and brothers and, as with most of those who live long abroad, his being outside the councils of the family induced a sense of injury and an inclination to cavil and dispute. Later, detached from his wife after a love affair at Baden-Baden, he was deprived of a settled family life, and the frequent depression of his spirits might be attributed to his deviation from the moral path as much as to declining health, for he was a puritan at heart.

The two principals in this book suffered through being married to each other. Is it idle to think that the nature of each, united to another partner, might have been developed to advantage? He, married to a woman such as Lady Jane Montagu, 'with a temper more heavenly sweet than ever was known', [23] or even to 'the poor and gentle Emily' Rumbold, might have been a happy man pursuing his chosen profession, fulfilling his duties with confidence, his lack of what he called 'animal spirits' passing unnoticed. His wife, however, is more difficult to assign happily to another. The selfishness of her character remarked on by Lady Holland makes it unlikely that she would ever have been quite contented. Today it would be assumed that much of her ill health was psychosomatic. Married to a stronger character than Lord William and the mother of a large family, she might with her practical and intellectual gifts have succeeded, in her early life, in casting about her an aura of domestic bliss. But unhappily her husband's indolence and want of self-confidence provoked her, and it was her contempt, harshness and lack of loving-kindness, that in the end produced the unexpected release of passion at Baden-Baden in the summer of 1835.

'J'ai deviné le bonheur conjugal',[24] Lady William confided to her daughter-in-law, but we shall see that for this 'maîtresse femme dominante au logis'[25] it was a condition that remained purely cerebral.

The thirty years covered in this book I have seen as a story with a beginning, a middle and an end – perhaps with a continuation. The reader will judge for himself the fault, and assign the blame for the failure of what had been a most auspicious marriage. Was it low spirits – or just lack of heart?

FAMILY AND FRIENDS

John 6th Duke of Bedford

The head of the family into which Bettina married was John 6th Duke of Bedford, in 1817 a man of fifty-one. He had succeeded to the dukedom on the death of his brother Francis, who was unmarried and died in 1802 at the age of thirty-six from an accident.

In Garrard's picture of him sitting under a tree in his park, we have the portrait of a shrewd, easy-going, thoroughly good-humoured country gentleman. Unpretentious in his manners, he was extremely shy, silent and reserved in society, but talked well when he was at ease and was 'respectable in debate' in the House of Lords.[1] Born and bred a Whig, he often said he meant to die one; in his youth he belonged to the radical society of the Friends of the People. His forebears had long resisted the power of the Crown, and his ancestor William, Lord Russell, lost his head in 1683 for complicity in the Rye House plot. As he aged, the Duke was fond of repeating that he knew nothing about politics and took no interest in them: an untrue avowal, and one that did not prevent him writing at length and with warmth to his sons on political topics of the day. He was an affectionate father, and a kind husband to his second wife, Georgiana Gordon, though he neglected his first, Georgiana Byng. At the time of his first marriage he was described as a young man who had '8 hundred a year with a disposition to spend 8 thousand'.[2] It was a disposition he retained all his life, though his means increased, for with the dukedom he inherited a prodigious fortune; the Russells having acquired by royal gift and prudent marriages lands in Bedfordshire, Devonshire, Cambridge-shire and Surrey, as well as the Bloomsbury estate in London. But his income was never sufficient for his needs; a taste for building, horticulture, agricultural experiments, and patronage of the fine arts taxed his resources to the limit. He had, too, a large number of children to provide for, and to please his wife he entertained with splendour, though it may be thought he was happiest when alone with his family. Owning numerous houses, he was never content to remain in any one for long. He was often hard pressed 'to raise the wind' for some new extravagance; mortgages were laid on his

18

estates and his agents were compelled to employ ruses to circumvent his demands, and so save something for the heritage of his eldest son, Lord Tavistock, who commented without rancour: 'My father had not the power or resolution to hold his hand when money was within his reach.'

Charles Greville thought the Duke uninteresting, weakminded and selfish.

> He is a goodnatured, plausible man, without enemies, and really, (although he does not think so) without friends . . . there are many who like Brougham pretend a strong affection for him, and some who imagine they feel it. Vast property, rank, influence and station always attract a sentiment which is dignified with the name of friendship. . . . The Duke of Bedford is a complete sensualist and thinks of nothing but his personal enjoyments, and it has long been a part of his system not to allow himself to be ruffled by the slightest self denial. He is affable, bland and of easy intercourse, making rather a favourable impression on superficial observers; caring little, (if at all) for the wants or wishes of others, but grudging nobody anything that does not interfere with his own enjoyments, and seeing with complacency those who surround him lap up the superfluities which may chance to bubble over from his cup of pleasure and happiness, while he alone drains it to the dregs.[3]

In spite of the truth of much of this indictment, it must be observed that Greville was not unwilling to 'lap up the superfluities', and having spent three weeks at Woburn – 'the house, place and establishment, and manner of living are the most magnificent I have seen. There is no place which gives so splendid an example of a great English Lord as this'[4] – found he was greatly put out at not being included in the next party to assemble there.

The Duke could practise small economies – it was noticed with surprise by a visitor to Woburn that, at a dinner served on plate, in a magnificent room, the marker of the Duke's tennis court was among the three or four men out of livery who waited at table – and where his own comfort was not concerned he could be practical as well as economical. 'The stage coach', he told his son, 'is not a dignified mode of travelling; but it is convenient, economical and saves a world of trouble – if your family is large enough to occupy the whole coach there can be no sort of objection, and I always adopt this plan of conveyance for my children, be they Lords or Ladies.'[5] When offering to house William and his family temporarily at Woburn in his own absence, he added the rider that he would only provide 'beef and mutton, cabbage and potatoes', the rest they must pay for themselves: 'I have what is vulgarly called run out in household

19

expenditure, the cause of it housekeeping going on at so many residences.' If the famous annual Woburn sheep-shearing was given up on account of the expense, because he had, as Lord Brougham suggested, overspent on the Duchess's *cottage orné*, the Duke did not check his expenditure on small embellishments of his property. A new maze laid out at Woburn, bells hung on his Chinese Dairy, armorial glass ordered for his windows, and the acquisition of rare heaths and cacti for his greenhouses, were interests he did not hesitate to gratify.

His father's self-indulgence was viewed by William with jealous eyes, and when at a distance and not sharing in the enjoyment of the outlay, he never failed to reproach the Duke for squandering his money on frivolities and hobbies – wax lights or 'cacto mania'. From his father's good-humoured rejoinders we may guess the content of his son's letters.

> I am happy [wrote the Duke in 1822] to hear that you have so good an *artist* in your Palazzo at Florence that you may indulge in the 'sensual and selfish amusement of eating', and in so spacious a house Lady William may possibly without much harm indulge in the 'selfish and sensual amusement of dancing'. The balls which you seem to criticize as expensive amusements were what is termed 'bread and butter' balls and cost a few pounds in wax lights, fiddlers and tea.[6]

The Duke's refusal to let William have a house on the Woburn estate, though seemingly lacking in affection, was doubtless prompted by good sense, for the strained relations prevailing between the Duchess and William's wife were hardly favourable for such a project. His excuses were various: 'It would be ridiculous as your rooms are always ready and you and yours are always *bien venus*', or: 'You are not cut out for a country gentleman', he would protest, conscious of being formed in that mould himself, for he liked to potter down the hedgerows with his gun, or, mounted on his pony, ride to see how his experimental grasses prospered and how his evergreen plantations grew. Happy in the open air, it seems he liked plenty of it in the house as well, for Lord Thurlow in July 'wore his hat at breakfast at Woburn on the pretext of fear of catching cold'.[7]

He was extremely fond of Lady Holland, and he took pride in having helped to re-establish her in society after her divorce from her first husband and her marriage to Lord Holland. He wrote to her regularly with what he called 'coeur ouvert' and 'plume coulante', discussing the topics of the day, his travels, his family, and his gumboils. She sometimes sent him a turtle from her property in Jamaica for which he thanked her in his characteristic way. 'The Turtle is arrived – 1000 thanks. I shall eat it tomorrow (today being my Banyan day) & I hope the *excess* will not prevent my going to town on Thursday & seeing you on Friday.'[8]

He was as frightened of steam vessels as she was of railway trains, but he had not her dislike of driving fast in a carriage. 'I came from Regency Square [Brighton] to Westminster Bridge in 4 hours and 50 minutes', he wrote to her in 1826, 'somewhat faster than you would like to travel.'[9]

A note of exasperation sometimes appears in his affectionate letters to his daughter-in-law, for her arrogance annoyed him, and he did not care for the attacks that were levelled at her by the newspapers at the time of Lord William's mission to Lisbon, when she was accused of meddling. He was always concerned for the good name of his children and it is clear that he thought Lady William should not have separated herself from her husband when he was appointed Minister at Berlin, in spite of the cause Lord William had given her for her defection. Perhaps for that reason she punished the Duke by keeping his grandsons away from England. Unhappily none of her letters to him have come to light. 'Latterly,' wrote Tavistock to Lord John, 'my father burnt all her letters unread.'[10]

At the end of her life Lady William gave her French daughter-in-law her considered opinion of the Duke.

'Mon beau-père était grand Seigneur (qualités et défauts), fort généreux, aimant la bonne chère et aimant à la partager avec ses amis. . . . Un peu Céladon,* mais pas avec les servantes, il n'était pas crapuleux, quoique gourmand et galant; fort libéral en politique. Sa femme était "coquette comme la lune", (et pis que cela) mais il était philosophe.'[11]

Georgiana Duchess of Bedford

The Duke's second wife, Georgiana Gordon, was as good-humoured as he was, but she also had to her advantage guile and high spirits. She was a daughter of the 4th Duke of Gordon and her scheming and ambitious mother, having married two of her elder daughters to dukes, hoped to do as well for her youngest. At one time there was a question of a marriage between Napoleon's stepson, Eugène de Beauharnais, and Lady Georgiana Gordon, and she was said to be much in love, but the difficulties of that match were insurmountable. Her mother then wished to marry her to the most eligible bachelor in England, Francis Duke of Bedford, but he, receiving a serious injury in the tennis court at Woburn, died in March

* A sentimental lover; a character in d'Urfé's *L'Astrée*.

1802. From his deathbed the Duke sent Lady Georgiana a lock of his hair and it was supposed he had meant to marry her, but in the absence of an engagement it was thought ostentatious of the Duchess of Gordon to put her daughter into mourning for him. Little more than a year later Georgiana was persuaded by her mother to marry the late Duke's recently widowed brother, John, who had succeeded to his title. She was twenty-two and he was fourteen years older. It proved a happy marriage and she had ten children. Affectionate and attentive to her husband, she was kind and dutiful to her three stepsons, Francis, William and John. William appears to have loved her dearly until his marriage, when his wife chose to find something almost improper in their relationship. Her audacious freedom of speech was thought by some to be too bold, but her merriness and high spirits, qualities that were lacking in the Russell family, did much – perhaps too much – to enliven parties at Woburn, oppressed by the shyness and silence of the Duke. Unrestrained, she would lead pillow-fights through the gilded rooms, overturning card tables, and pelting her guests with oranges and apples. There was blind man's buff under her auspices and what her stepson called 'no end of jolly rows'.

Sydney Smith thought her so attractive that he confessed: 'I am forced from time to time to read over my papers of holy orders to prevent myself from admiring her too much.'[12] When Thomas Moore stayed at Woburn he was elated by the splendour of the house and the condescension of the family, and after an evening of music he was made entirely happy when the Duchess expressed a wish that 'I could "transfer my genius to her for six weeks;" and I answered, "most willingly, if Woburn was placed at my disposal for the same time".'[13]

Her husband was very fond of her and made the study of her wishes an excuse for his extravagance. He built her a charming *cottage orné*, Endsleigh, above the Tamar near Tavistock in Devonshire, and bought for her a villa in Kensington near their friends at Holland House. In order that she might enjoy her native Scottish air, he rented the Doune near Rothiemurchus, transporting his children there every year in the late summer; and sea breezes were inhaled in the winter at Brighton, where he hired a house, sometimes two houses, to accommodate his large family.

The Duchess's three quiet stepsons recognised how great a contribution her vitality and gaiety made to the Duke's happiness, but they grew to mistrust her empire over him, and they thought her brood of children rough and ill-governed. Her conversation and boisterous spirits lacked for them the charm of rectitude and modesty, and they learned that she could

be an unscrupulous enemy and that she would lie, dissemble and pre-
varicate to achieve her ends. They were deeply attached to their father and
aware that their desertion could but do him harm. Sense and good
manners kept the peace for a time after William's marriage, but Bessy's
arrogant hostility and the Duchess's implacable dislike of her daughter-
in-law led inevitably to a rupture with Woburn.

In 1823, when she was forty-two, the Duchess met a young painter half
her age. Her long and intimate friendship with Edwin Landseer ended
only with her death. He was often at Woburn and some of his most
delightful drawings are of the Russells. The Duke was a complaisant
husband and Landseer and the Duchess were sometimes alone, except for
two servants, at Glenfeshie, a lodge she rented in Inverness-shire. It is
thought that, after the Duke's death, Landseer proposed marriage, and
that her refusal brought on the first attacks of madness from which he
suffered for the rest of his life, but Lady Holland's opinion was that 'the
fatigue and mental anxiety of having been on the *hanging* Council of the
Royal Academy where there are so many jealousies and bickerings . . . has
overset his nerves'.[14]

The Duchess gave birth to the last of her ten children in 1826.

The Marquess of Tavistock

The Duke of Bedford's eldest son, Francis Marquess of Tavistock, was a
man of great integrity but not much warmth of heart. 'Lord Tavistock',
wrote a contemporary, 'does not like company, but he does not like
solitude either. He is a good man – but not a happy man.'[15] He was highly
regarded for his vigorous mind and his political wisdom, and 'was entrusted with the secrets of both camps'. He constantly expressed himself
gratified by the course of events and by the esteem in which he was held;
it was an emotion from which he derived comfort but it was without
degree, for the good behaviour of the masses at the coronation of Queen
Victoria caused him no less gratification than being chosen to execute a
will or govern Ireland. He did not take the Lord Lieutenancy when it was
offered him, though he said he was ready to sacrifice 'my peace of mind,
my habits of life, pursuits at home, my health, and perhaps my life';[16] but
it was judged by others that he might sink under the heavy burden of
responsibility. His high sense of duty was becoming to a Whig aristocrat,
but for many years he laboured under the disability of wretched health,

and he drove himself mercilessly, whether it was in the interests of the public good or for private pleasure. His favourite pursuits were hunting, racing and shooting, but in the first two he was not fortunate, for in the hunting field he broke his bones, and at Newmarket he lost his money. 'He seems', wrote his father, 'scarcely ever to have a horse to run, and when he has he is beat.' He had his own simple establishment at Oakley, some twelve miles from Woburn; a charming house on the banks of the Ouse, where he had spent his boyhood before his mother died.

When he succeeded his father as 7th Duke in 1839, he applied himself with great energy to the gigantic task of putting right the affairs of the different properties. Rising at five, he would sit at his table trying to grasp the problems of his great inheritance. To his brother William, who was eager to give him advice, he wrote: 'You are little aware of the cares and worries and plagues I have had to go through . . . and were it not that it would be wicked to complain of my lot and not be grateful for it I should say that a man with fewer of these cares and responsibilities is a happier man.'[17] And he said he considered himself 'a well paid agent with an income of £12,000 working for those who had mortgages and settlements on the estates.'[18] But he had courage and took pains to do well. 'I hope to do great things if I live a few years, towards repairs and reforms.'[19] His efforts were crowned with success. Buying, selling, building, draining, he brought his properties round from the decay into which they had fallen, to be patterns of good management and prosperity.

He was married to Anna Maria Stanhope, daughter of the Earl of Harrington; they had great respect and affection for each other, but she does not seem to have been a woman of much intelligence. A story was told about her that when she was made a Lady-in-Waiting to Queen Victoria on her accession, 'she was desired by the Queen to go with her at nine o'clock in the morning somewhere. "To be sure, your Majesty, [answered Lady Tavistock] it is rather early but I will make a point of being ready."'[20] Involved in the Lady Flora Hastings scandal at the Palace, she was thought to have erred in judgement but was later exonerated from heartlessness. At Queen Victoria's wedding she appeared in a gown of scarlet and gold, which was considered 'very curious taste'.[21] As Duchess of Bedford she introduced afternoon tea-parties at her house in Belgrave Square, and it was supposed that abhorrence of his mother's social festivities contributed to her son's decision to withdraw from London society to the seclusion of a house at Kensington.

Lord Russell was the Tavistocks' only child. They were devoted to him although his early hypochondriacal tendencies gave them anxiety, and as he grew up it became apparent that he would never lead a perfectly normal life.

'Russell like all of us', said his father, 'has his merits and demerits, his good and his bad qualities – among the latter is a most extraordinary and morbid feeling of diffidence which makes him think that he cannot be useful or agreeable to anybody.'[22] Lord Tavistock had a great respect for his son's political opinions and often quoted them to others, but Lord Grey could get nothing out of the young man. '[Lord Russell] is the most impenetrable person I ever met with. More silent even than a Russell, it is impossible to get a word out of him, but he seems contented and good-humoured.'[23] Although for nine years Lord Russell sat in the House of Commons as the member for Tavistock, a letter he addressed to his father when he was twenty-nine is significant of the personal difficulties he encountered in public life:

'My dear Father,' he wrote, 'My digestion is so weak, it would I am persuaded be utterly impossible for me to attend and go through an Election Committee. I should fall into such a state of languor of both body and mind, as to be utterly incapable of attending to what was going forward. Waiting five minutes for a meal after my stomach is prepared for it produces this effect.'[24]

His father accepted his son's withdrawal from public life without recrimination and with some compassion. 'Russell', he wrote, 'reads and thinks deeply but does not reap happiness from his studies and reflections."[25] Lord Russell did not marry; as the 8th Duke of Bedford he was known as a recluse, who drove in a brougham with wooden shutters to its windows between Belgrave Square and Kensington, where he was reputed to keep two mistresses.

Lord Tavistock had no great affection for his brother William but he foresaw that William's son, Hastings, would reign at Woburn, and he did his best to prepare him for the position he must one day assume.

Lord John Russell

Lord John Russell was the youngest of the Duke of Bedford's three sons by his first wife. He was sent like William to Woodnesborough School and then to Westminster, but his stepmother saw that he was physically unfit for the rigorous life of that public school and he was taken away and completed his education at the University of Edinburgh.

As a very young man he travelled in Spain with Lord and Lady Holland, and he visited Napoleon during his confinement on Elba and talked with him for an hour and a half on politics and personal subjects. He reported that the great man pulled him by the ear as he got interested in the conversation, and that he made water freely in a corner of the room.

Lord John entered the House of Commons in 1813 as the Whig member for Tavistock, but as the Whigs were in opposition until 1830 those seventeen years allowed him time to travel and to study history, and he produced several literary and historical works. He then held office in successive Whig administrations, and was charged with the introduction of the Reform Bill of 1832. He became Prime Minister in 1846 and again for a short time in his old age. His high-minded Whig principles were much admired by his father and brothers, but there were those who thought that winds of criticism blowing in his own family would have been beneficial to him, and that in later years he was hedged from hostile opinions by the female adulation in his home.

Of diminutive stature and frail physique, he was never robust and his heavy colds were a subject of mirth to the readers of *Punch*. Cartoonists liked to depict him as 'Buttons', a tiny page boy, or as Jack the Giant Killer, a tribute to his political courage. B. R. Haydon saw a 'marked inflexibility of purpose about his head',[26] a vision that was supported by Sydney Smith's well-known observation: 'He is utterly ignorant of all moral fear, there is nothing he would not undertake. I believe he would perform the operation for the stone, build St Peter's, or assume (with or without ten minutes notice) the command of the Channel Fleet, and no one would discover by his manner that the patient had died, the church tumbled down, and the Channel Fleet been knocked to atoms.'[27]

His manner could be freezing, and he was reproved by his father for treating his political followers *de haut en bas*. Shy, taciturn, and extremely aristocratic, he lacked the common touch. His friendship with Thomas Moore, due perhaps to Moore's uninhibited admiration for the well-bred, is a notable exception to his lack of ease with his social inferiors.

He was often in love but did not marry until he was past forty. His attachment to Madame Durazzo, the wife of a Genoese nobleman, is frequently referred to in these letters, and he attended her in England, Paris and Genoa. It would appear that at some time Lord William also had been her lover. Another married woman, Lady Elizabeth Vernon, occupied Lord John's affections for a time, and it seems indicated by Lord William's inexplicit record of a 'curious conversation' with Lady Holland, that Lord John had a brief fancy for Mary Fox as a wife; an inclination that was probably snuffed out by her mother. It was his devotion to Louisa and Emily Hardy that ultimately delayed his marriage. His admiration for the two daughters of Sir Thomas Masterman Hardy was of long standing, and the snubs he received from these two young women were the current small change of London gossip. As early as 1828 Sydney Smith had written: 'I hear Lord John is to marry a daughter of the beautiful Hardy. She is a robust and energetic young woman. God send it may agree with John. I hope he will be fed up highly at Holland House before the Event and plumped out.'[28] Lady Holland thought he had been refused, and commented: 'It is a pity he has a rage to marry upon him, as he is so frequently repulsed and should as Binda says, be, as he would be in Italy, content to be Prelato or Monsignore of the family, as he is a delightful person in all relations but those of lover or husband; at least I should think so, and so do the young ladies.'[29] Four years later Poodle Byng heard that 'at last Lord John has been formally refused by the Hardy',[30] but early in 1834 it was said that he was 'bearing up manfully against the snubbing of Emily'.[31] Lord William's attempt in that year to bring the matter to a successful conclusion was a sad bungle.

In 1835, Lord John married Adelaide Lister, the widow of Lord Ribblesdale. She brought him four stepchildren and bore him two daughters, but died after the birth of the second. Two years later he married Lady Frances Elliot, a daughter of the Earl of Minto. Twenty-three years his junior, she had difficulty in bearing children, but the union was eventually blessed with three sons and a daughter.

If Lord John's political reputation does not now stand as high as it did, to many of his contemporaries, particularly in the middle and lower classes, his leadership was a source of inspiration. He was, with Lord Palmerston, responsible for the policy of promoting the unification of Italy, and he never ceased to press for better education, greater humanity in criminal legislation, and freedom of religious opinions. His second wife was a Presbyterian, and he adhered to the very low church.

His letters to his brother and to 'Bettina cara', as he liked to call his sister-in-law, are written with cool, dry humour; the true warmth of his affectionate nature was reserved until he had children and a domestic circle of his own.

27

Old Lord William Russell

Variously described as a 'zero'[32] and politically as 'an acknowledged driveller',[33] the Duke of Bedford's younger brother was an ardent Whig and sat for many years in Parliament. Widowed in 1808, he led in his later life an aimless existence travelling much abroad – 'the further he is from England, the more eager he always is about politics'[34] – and flirting with ladies he admired, such as Lady Westmorland and Lady Hardy. The younger Lord William and his wife found him a sympathetic friend, who understood their quarrels with the Duchess and shared their enjoyment of living abroad, but to some of his relations he was just a joke, and we hear of him as 'odd and absent as ever'.[35]

He had a trick of 'opening his mouth and putting his watch in it as he walked about the room'. 'Ah, you swallowed it in one of your absent fits', he was told one day when he had mislaid his watch.[36] In the last year of his life the Duchess of Bedford described him at Woburn as 'Old William, who chatters more and more to himself every day'.[37] He was murdered in his house in Norfolk Street, Park Lane, in 1840 by his Swiss valet, Courvoisier.

Hastings Russell

Hastings Russell is the only one of Lord and Lady William's sons whose character is clearly revealed in the course of this book. All his qualities are apparent in his letters. He was intelligent, honourable, warm-hearted and friendly, with a zest for manly pursuits. The battering his affectionate nature received from both his parents wrings the heart. He asked nothing better than to live at peace together with them and his brothers. After his mother's separation from his father he was, as a young man, her constant companion, and the duties which fell on his shoulders in the absence of Lord William were accepted cheerfully and discharged efficiently. Like his father, he would have made a good soldier, but circumstances combined to thwart him, and after his marriage he found it more practical to be a member of the House of Commons than an officer in the Guards. A shared passion for horses and hunting was the foundation of his affection for Lady Elizabeth Sackville West, but her character and intelligence did not match his own, and it may be doubted if he continued to find her interesting, or if she made him happy. Lady William never liked her, and compared her to a housemaid or an 'under teacher in a boarding school'. 'Elle me fait l'effet d'une mauvaise odeur',[38] she wrote with all the uncompromising cruelty of her forceful utterance.

The 8th Duke, upon his father's death in 1861, resigned into Hastings's hands the management of all the estates. Sarah Austin wrote to Guizot: 'I went to visit my dear young friend, Hastings Russell, at Woburn Abbey. It is very interesting to me, who love him, to see the care, the anxious thought & conscientiousness, with which he administers the vast *dominions* confided to his management. It is an oppressive charge.'[39]

He succeeded his cousin as 9th Duke of Bedford when he was fifty-three years old. He became President of the Royal Agricultural Society and was a pioneer of the Volunteer movement. He was wont to say that he knew what it was to live on an income of £200 or £200,000 a year.

Unsociable and cynical in middle age, preferring his mother's company to any other, he often wounded his brothers with his captious remarks. Unusually generous with money, he made them unexpected gifts, for which he did not like to be thanked and which were sometimes accompanied by caustic comments that embarrassed and displeased. Devoted to each other and using their childish names of Baba, Atty and Dodo, the brothers all their lives retained the foreign habit of kissing each other in greeting. After his mother's death in 1874, Hastings wrote: 'Life does not any longer seem worth living.'[40] A lifelong passion for firearms ended in a tragic climax. Sixteen years after her death he shot himself while suffering from influenza and an attack of the 'blue devils'.

Arthur and Odo Russell

The two younger boys, Arthur and Odo, remain in this book shadowy figures since their own voices are hardly heard, and it is only through the medium of others that we know anything about them in their youth. Young for his age, studious and shy, Arthur seems wrapped in his own thoughts, absorbed in the wonders of philosophy and natural history. In middle age he told his brother that he remembered taking Oken's *Naturphilosophie* to read in the sledge at Carlsbad: 'It made an impression I have never since got rid of.'[41] He became a Liberal member of Parliament, a philosopher and a *savant*. Indolent by nature, he remained almost wholly subservient to his mother with whom he lived until he married happily a French wife, Laura, daughter of the Vicomte de Peyronnet, at the age of forty. Lady William wrote under the picture by Kriehüber of her younger sons: 'The one has my soul and the other my heart.'[42] There is no doubt that it was to Arthur she apportioned her soul.

'Little grumpy Odo', as Lady Holland called him, had the most cheerful spirits of the three brothers and he busied himself in his own interests and those of others. We hear of him as a small child collecting seeds from the pine trees at Cintra for his grandfather to grow at Woburn, catching frogs in the ditches of Vienna and St John's Wood, keeping his own chickens at Potsdam, loving a little goat; and as a boy of ten running about Carlsbad looking for somewhere for Mrs Austin to live. Like his brothers he delighted in the power and penetration of his mother's intellect, and the tenderness he felt for her survived many trials engendered by her capricious nature. When he was twenty-five he complained of her 'coarse and insulting language' and wrote to his brother that 'Mama is ill from the conviction that she is cursed with three infamous sons'.[43] Benjamin Disraeli thought that Lady William had the three nicest sons in London. Odo had a distinguished career in diplomacy. Having served at Paris, Constantinople and Washington, he was for twelve crucial years the unofficial English Agent at the Court of the Vatican, and was on friendly terms with Pius IX. In 1870 he was sent on a diplomatic mission to Bismarck's headquarters at Versailles, and the following year he was appointed English Ambassador at Berlin, where he remained until he died at the age of fifty-five. He had married Lady Emily Villiers, the daughter of his chief, Lord Clarendon, and three years before his death he was created Baron Ampthill.

Mrs Rawdon

It was universally agreed that Bettina's mother was a tiresome gossiping fool: a burden that society had to bear. She tended to plague good-natured persons by demanding little favours, and, assuming the manners and caprices of a pretty woman, passed for one. Her remarkable likeness to her beautiful daughter (to whom she seems so near in age) is evident in Agricola's drawing, and must have been for her a matter of complacency.

When Lady Granville was contemplating the 'mingled pains and pleasures' of becoming Ambassadress at Paris, she made it clear that the presence of Mrs Rawdon and 'the laxative nature of the Seine water' were not among the anticipated pleasures.[44] On the other hand Lady Holland, who never suffered fools (certainly not female fools) gladly, confessed that she had 'always a sneaking kindness and liking' for her and often asked her to dinner. With few resources, Mrs Rawdon appears to have been an expert and industrious needlewoman, witness a letter from Lord Moira:

> Since Mrs Rawdon makes so valiant an offer of her exertions, I will have the moderation *only* to ask that she will undertake a Third Curtain, another Sopha, and two more chairs. Nothing in nature can be more reasonable than such a request. Seriously, however, it would vex me to have her work stowed away in a Bedchamber, or put into a Dressing Room where it would be spoilt with powder. It must therefore furnish the Drawing Room upstairs; to which end, she must toil and spin; because that room has three windows, and is in space 32 feet by 24. She shall take as much time as ever she pleases.[45]

In the pages of this book Mrs Rawdon may appear as the evil genius of the William Russells' marriage. Although her sole object in life was the welfare of her daughter, she was unable to resign herself to the bitter affliction of separation from her. Her foolish and selfish behaviour following Bessy's wedding is reflected in the letters Lord William was constrained to write to her during the honeymoon. Lady Granville predicted soon after the marriage: 'It is clear Lord William will not love Mrs Rawdon.'[46] She was right; he grew to hate her.

She has been represented as for ever making pecuniary calculations, and as too mean to set up her own establishment; but her indigent existence in hotels and apartments had the obvious merit of leaving her free to join Lady William whenever she was invited to do so, and we can assume that she was nearly always with her daughter when Lord William was not, and with them far too often when he was with his family. That she was generous in making gifts may be seen in the letters her grandson Hastings wrote her, but it was an embarrassing generosity arousing exasperation in the recipients by reason of its irrational exaggeration. Her grandsons were attached to her and she doted on them. We hear of her clutching their portraits enclosed in little cases while scrambling among the rocks in the Saxon Switzerland: she had a liking for talismans.

Lord and Lady Holland

Lord Holland was the nephew of Charles James Fox, whose principles he upheld and whose memory he revered. Travelling in Italy as a young man he met his future wife, Elizabeth Vassall, who had been married at the age of fifteen to Sir Godfrey Webster, a man much older than herself. Falling in love with Lord Holland, she abandoned her husband and returned to England with her lover. Webster divorced her, and she married Lord Holland, but not in time to legitimise their eldest son, Charles Fox, and it was the second son, Henry, who succeeded his father in the title. At first women were reluctant to visit Lady Holland, and she was not received in many houses, but the Duke of Bedford helped to re-establish his two friends in society, and Holland House at Kensington became the centre of a brilliant literary and political circle, predominantly Whig. Lady Holland's autocratic character made her an alarming hostess; she was fundamentally very kind, but her tart rebukes confused the timid, and her snubs enraged the bold. Lady Granville wrote of her 'ordering one about with the exigence of a child – too old to be scolded – too big to be taken away'. [47] If her asperity and sharp tongue sometimes drove indignant guests from her dinner table, her husband's amiable nature and cultivated mind ensured their return. 'I would not go to Heaven with Lady Holland,' said Ugo Foscolo, 'but I could go to Hell with his Lordship.' [48] 'Lord Holland is quite delightful', was Sydney Smith's opinion. 'I hardly know a talent, or a virtue that he has not little or big. The Devil could not put him out of temper. I really never saw such a man. In addition to this, think of his possessing Holland House and that he reposes every evening on that beautiful structure of flesh and blood, Lady H.' [49]

It was a long and very happy marriage, though Lady Holland ordered her husband about in a peremptory way and was extremely jealous of him. Lord Holland's failure to hold important office in Whig administrations was largely ascribed to the fear that his wife would in fact be the Minister. After Lord Holland's death a visitor to Holland House wrote of feeling 'the want of that soft protecting shadow which was thrown on one from Lord Holland's old chair, behind which one could no longer shelter oneself'. [50]

Motherliness was not one of Lady Holland's attributes, and she seems to have been a possessive rather than a loving parent; but Lord William and Lord John Russell evoked in her a feeling that approached maternal love, and expressions of tenderness and admiration for Hastings Russell often appear in her letters. He was indeed a favourite with all at Holland House. Lady Holland wrote from Ampthill when Hastings was seven years old: 'We have the Wm Russells & their delightful children. As to

32

Hastings he is without exception the most pleasing, promising child I ever saw, full of *sense* beside his acquirements, with all his father's courage, manliness & gentleness; not in the least spoiled, well behaved and tractable.'[51]

As the owners of Ampthill Park, Lord and Lady Holland were the neighbours of the Duke and Duchess of Bedford at Woburn as well as in Kensington.

Lord Lynedoch

Thomas Graham Lord Lynedoch, was born a Scottish laird and only became a soldier in middle life after the early death of his wife, the beautiful Mrs Graham, twice painted by Gainsborough, once as a housemaid with a broom in her hand.

He rose to be one of Wellington's generals in the Peninsular War, and William Russell fought under him at the battle of Barossa. Endowed with great physical energy, a rare sweetness of character, and perfect integrity, he was described as 'a man who had pleasure in doing anything for anybody'.[52] He had travelled much and was well versed in several languages, but he was 'not very intellectual'[53]; he liked farming, hunting and shooting. Younger men were astonished by his activity and the enthusiasm that took him by public conveyance to watch a prize fight, or brought him posting four hundred miles from Scotland to blackball a man he thought an undesirable member for his club.

'A Jewel of a Man', 'a wrapper up of ladies',[54] his devotion to the daughters of Sir Chaloner Ogle – Arabella Bouverie, Barbarina Wilmot (a blue stocking) and Sophia Asgill – prevented his re-marriage, since they were all married women when he first met them. He was undoubtedly in love with the last-named for twenty-five years, and we may read of him as the romantic lover at Woburn in 1812:

'We dispersed . . . through an enfilade of six rooms', wrote Lady Shelley, ' . . . Lady Asgill established herself in an attitude lying on the sofa with Sir Thomas Graham at her feet. In the next Lady Jane and Miss Russell at harp and pianoforte (both out of tune) playing the "Creation". Alas, it was chaos still.'[55]

At Cosgrove Priory Lord Lynedoch was the neighbour of the Duke of Bedford, and he acted as the Duke's second in his duel with the Duke of Buckingham.

His age was often the subject for speculation among his friends, amazed by his restless powers. When over eighty, he underwent a successful operation for a cataract on both eyes, which had hampered his enjoyment of the chase, since he had to be led across country by a groom. Of a noble appearance, he had 'milky, silk white locks', and in his ninetieth year, we are told, 'His head is finer than Jupiter's. It is like a grey, solid, war worn castle. . . . He is one of the men who make old age lovely.'[56]

William Russell felt for him filial affection, and Lady William, in propounding to him, in her letter of 24 February 1826, the problems of her husband's character, showed that she too regarded him with love and respect.

Princess Lieven

Dorothea Benckendorff Countess Lieven was the wife of the Russian Ambassador in London. Tall and thin, she was hardly a beauty, but her intelligence and her clever conversation, added to a powerful interest in politics, assured her friends and lovers among the statesmen with whom she passed her time in England and abroad. Metternich loved her at the beginning of her life, and she loved Guizot at the end of it. Lord Grey, the Duke of Wellington and Lady Cowper corresponded with her, and acting as a well-bred spy, she obtained information that was useful to her husband as a diplomatist, from the men who consulted and confided in her. Her interference in English politics determined Lord Palmerston to get rid of her, and by refusing to appoint an ambassador to St Petersburg acceptable to the Czar, he succeeded in getting Lieven recalled. He had been twenty-two years in England, and was made a Prince in 1826. Her husband's recall was a crushing blow for the Princess, and in great distress she accompanied him back to Russia in 1834. Lady William Russell's was among the thirty or so names of the ladies of her particular acquaintance inscribed on a bracelet offered to Princess Lieven as a token of regard and regret.

Bad health and the death of two of her sons served as an excuse for her to leave Russia the following year in search of distraction. She never returned or saw her husband again. Settling in Paris, she passed the last twenty years of her life there.

A great egoist, she was described by Greville as being 'beyond all people fastidious and equally conscious of her own superiority and the inferiority of other people'.[57] Susceptible to ennui, she admitted that even in the society of her most intimate friends she was often bored to death.

Part 1

BILLIKINS AND BETTINA
1817–1824

For the first two years after their marriage, while William was employed at the Duke of Wellington's headquarters, the young couple lived at Cambrai and at Paris, six months at each alternately. A child was born at Paris the first spring, but did not long survive. When the Allied occupation ended, Lord William went on half-pay and took a house in London whence he could attend the House of Commons, where, though he had been absent for much of the time, he had represented the borough of Bedford for the last eight years. In October 1819, a son, Hastings, was born in their house in Curzon Street. Nearly two years later Lord William decided to take his wife abroad, ostensibly for the sake of her health, but really, as he told Lady Holland, because the Duchess of Bedford's hostility made life in England disagreeable for them. They were away for two years, travelling in Germany and Italy. Their return to England in 1823 saw a temporary improvement in the relations of his wife with the Duchess, and six months were spent at Woburn, where Bessy unhappily had a miscarriage.

Duke of Bedford to Lord William Russell [WPP]

Endsleigh, 22 May 1817

My dear William,

You may always rest assured that I have no happiness in life greater than that of promoting the welfare of my children, and in proportion as I am able to contribute to this desirable end, I feel gratified. That you have every prospect of being happy with Miss Rawdon is a source of great satisfaction to me. I have never heard but one opinion of her merits, and I have told you before that in the little that I have seen of her, my own prepossessions are strongly in her favour. That she will improve them on our further acquaintance, I have no doubt, and with all the qualifications she has for rendering the marriage state happy, united to your own good sense and amiable feelings, I can have no fears on the subject. You ask my advice on your *ménage*, and I truly give it. Avoid all unnecessary expense in the first instance, and begin with economy. If you get involved in difficulties at the outset, you may never recover them; whereas, if you live

35

within your income for the first two or three years of your marriage, you will find the benefit of it ever after. You will not be rich, but with prudence and economy, you will have *de quoi vivre*, and all you have to do is to husband your resources. You have no expensive habits, but you are careless and thoughtless in money matters, and this you must endeavour to correct. If you have any debts still unpaid, let me know, and I will discharge them before your marriage that you may start clear. The advice I gave you before is upon the best consideration I can give to the subject, the most prudent. Continue upon the Duke of Wellington's staff and take a furnished house, or *appartement meublé*, as near Headquarters as you can. By this you will avoid all the expense of commencing with an establishment in England. With respect to the future, I will candidly own to you that I should feel a severe disappointment if you did not continue your professional views. As soon as a fair opportunity offers, I will purchase a Lieut.-Colonelcy in the line for you, which from the best military opinions I am able to obtain, is the most advantageous thing I can do, as it will afford you the best means of learning the soldier's trade, for you must know how to command a regiment, before you can command an army, but *de hoc et aliis aliter*. With regard to a post chaise, I believe the best plan will be to order one to your own liking, and then job it by the year. Coachmakers bills (besides the prime cost) are so enormously expensive for perpetual repairs. Sixty guineas per annum is, I believe, a fair price for a good post chaise, but I should recommend one to you which will serve for a travelling post chaise, and a town chariot, when wanted for that purpose.

And now respecting the wedding. I should certainly wish it to take place as early as practicable. Milliners and mantua makers in all these cases must be consulted for the bride's paraphernalia, as well as lawyers for the writings, but as soon as all these important personages are ready, the ceremony may take place, and you may then go to Woburn as long as you please, and till you are ready to go abroad. I am decidedly of the opinion that the marriage should be in church. Those sort of private marriages which take place in houses never appear to me to carry with them the sanctity and solemnity of the marriage vow. May I beg of you to communicate my wishes respecting the time of the marriage to Mrs Rawdon, and tell her that I am unwilling to trouble her with a letter on the subject, leaving it to you to explain my ideas. Say everything most kind and affectionate for me to Miss Rawdon, assure her that I feel most anxious to become better acquainted with her, and that I am already grateful to her for the fair prospect she holds out to me of so essentially contributing to your future happiness.

God bless you, my dear William, and
Believe me always
Your very affectionate father,
B.

Lord William Russell to Mrs Rawdon [PRP]

London, June 24, 1817.

My dear Mrs Rawdon,

Bessy is as well as possible. You are the constant theme of her conversation, & occupy her thoughts so much, that I shall become horribly jealous of you. Your absence seems to be the only barrier to her happiness which otherwise appears perfect, pray write to her, it will occupy you & delight her. Tell us your plans & projects. Adieu.

Ever affly yours
W.R.

Lord William Russell to Mrs Rawdon [PRP]

W.A. Sunday. [1 July 1817]

Many thanks for your letter as well as for the kind one you wrote Bessy which put her in great spirits.

As you have remained so long in England why should you not remain a little longer & come to us here, it would do your health much good & would delight Bessy. Think of this & arrange it, if you possibly can. You will find us quite alone unless my father should come down which he talks of doing.

I should have proposed this plan to you long ago, if I had not thought you would have left England, but as your health has determined you, & you have nothing to call you to Paris, I think you could not do better than to come here. Bessy will use her powers of persuasion with you so I will say no more on the subject.

I hope this cool weather does you good, you should endeavour to leave your bed.

37

Billikins and Bettina

Lord William Russell to Mrs Rawdon [PRP]

W.A. 17th [July 1817]

Upon my honor you use me most abominably. You allow me to marry your daughter & then you endeavour to seduce her away from me. Indeed I am obliged to watch her constantly to prevent her from getting into the diligence & going off to you – particularly on the arrival of your letters, so that I dread them so much, I am frequently tempted to burn them without giving them to her. But to speak seriously & to speak interestedly for it makes a great difference to me – the letters you write in this melancholy & violent style have a very bad effect upon both her spirits & upon her health. She becomes bilious & thoughtful. Today she told me you had written her a most *comfortable* letter & she has been quite happy & cheerful. Let me beseech you to endeavour to write always in this strain.

Certainly you must feel most acutely the loss of your daughter, but conceal your feelings from her as much as you can. Telling them to her can do no earthly good, & it makes her very wretched which I am sure is not your intention. Endeavour to make your letters a comfort & pleasure to her, & not a cause for weeping & repentance which they have too often been. What is done cannot be undone, therefore the best way is to bear it as well as you are able & strive to see joy & happiness where you now see only gloom & misery. So much depends on the way that we are determined to see the ups & downs of this world. Besides when you make Bessy weep, I take such an aversion to you, that nothing but my great affection & esteem for you makes me overcome. So, my dear Mrs Rawdon, let us sing '*Gaie, gaie mariez vous*,' without weeping.

Bessy is happy, I am the happiest man in the world & we will endeavour to communicate some part of it to you when we meet at Paris, which I hope will be in the beginning of August. As she tells you all that passes here I will trouble you no further than to beg my remembrances to Mde de Coigny & Souza whom you will probably see. We hear you are grown young, thin, fair & beautiful. Take care of your health & believe me

Your affte. *beau fils.*

The honeymoon over, the young couple set off for Paris where they remained too short a time to please Mrs Rawdon, but long enough for Lady Granville to report that 'Lady William is very pretty, very pleasing; Lord William looks quiet and pleased, but a little small between his accomplished bride and his *exigeante* mother-in-law who talks all the time as if Lady

38

William was dead. "From the time I lost my poor Bessy". It is clear Lord William will not love Mrs Rawdon.'[1]

Lady William never ceased to sigh at the dullness of Cambrai in spite of receiving those marks of distinction from the highest quarters which in later years Lord William accused English society of withholding from her.

Lord Palmerston, who made a tour in France at that time, attended a military review at the Allied Headquarters and was afterwards at a great dinner given by the Duke of Wellington to the Emperor of Russia and the King of Prussia, where he witnessed a curious scene. When the dinner was announced Lady Worcester, who from her rank expected to be led in by the Emperor, was passed by with a bow, and he offered his arm to Lady William Russell, the King of Prussia taking Lady Worcester. 'Alexander beckoned to the King to go first. The King refused, the Emperor insisted. The King was obstinate. The ladies looked foolish. The company expected a battle royal, when at last Alexander gave a vehement stamp with his foot, and the King . . . consented to take the post of honour and go first.'[2]

Lord William Russell to Mrs Rawdon [PRP]

Cambray 8th [August 1817]

No doubt you thought me barbarous & unkind in not granting the additional day you asked for, but when I say that I refused it on Bessy's account you will allow that my motive was good tho' you may not approve of the act. I say on Bessy's account because I knew she would require all her strength to make the journey to Cambray, & as you made no attempt to restrain or conceal your grief I was convinced that witnessing your tears & suffering for another day would so agitate & wear her out, that the journey would be too much for her strength & I have since been confirmed in my opinion by seeing that the agitation of leaving you & the sorrow of seeing your distressed state of mind kept her awake the whole of the first night, & she consequently began her journey the second day fatigued & unrefreshed, but thank God she arrived here very well, tho' she has been suffering since with a very severe cold, so I hope you will pardon what you call my impatience to return to Cambray, for I assure you that I considered nothing but Bessy's health, & the same consideration induces me to beseech you to put some check on your grief in her presence, for in her present situation it is very injurious to her. Indeed it appears to me that you have no cause to grieve when you see your daughter enjoying happiness & health & that you have the enjoyment of her society, of which you never know the value till the moment of parting. It is despising God's best gifts & tempting him to afflict you with some *real misfortune*, but

39

pardon me I am going further than I intended & perhaps further than I have any right, but again I say anxiety for Bessy is my excuse, so that believe me that all I do is for her happiness & if I knew how I could contribute to yours nothing I assure you most sincerely would give me greater satisfaction than promoting it.

Lord William Russell to Lady Holland [HH]

Cambray 25 Sept [1817]

... We are now established in our house & it is very comfortable – the *ménage* is admirably conducted & all is *couleur de rose* at Cambray. We avoid the officers with long waists, & their wives with short ones as much as possible. We shall probably be looked upon as uncouth beings, but life is too short to be passed away in making the agreable in such a place as this.

Mrs R is I fear still wretched & unreasonable, do you ever see her?

From this black garrison you can expect no news, but if you would tell me how the elections go on at Paris you would gratify me very much.

Lord John Russell to Lady William Russell [PRP]

Florence, Dec. 15. 1817.

I cannot determine whether I ought to begin my letter like young Dioscorous – Madame, *c'est avec raison qu'on vous appelle belle-sœur, puisque* ... or whether I should simply thank you for having written to Madame Albrizzi at Venice to procure me acquaintance at Milan. But the real object of my letter is different from either, being intended to ease my shoulders of the many *souvenirs, amitiés & adorations* which I am desired daily to convey to you. Amongst your friends Madame Appony makes many enquiries concerning you, & Fontenay begs leave to be remembered as *un des plus* I do not know what *de vos admirateurs*. The fact is as I was told the other day, I could not have done better than have got my passport signed by you, for your name has universal currency amongst those who know & those who do not. And the story of your robbery is now the crack story of the kind in Italy, & has not even been effaced by the petty larceny of Lucien Bonaparte's chaplain & cook, who were stolen one fine morning from his country house. . . . The conduct of Pauline,* is as you

* Princess Pauline Borghese (1780–1825), Napoleon's sister.

Billikins and Bettina

know not quite correct (to use Judge Adam's term) but as Cardinal Gonsalvi says, '*E vero un poco Messalina, ma è bella; bisogna scusarla.*'* The person who told me this desired me to keep it secret, but I think it ought to be published for the benefit of the R. Catholic church which by means of such opinions cannot fail to make many conversions.

Florence is a pleasant place enough without any distinguishing merit. There is also a want of fresh eggs in the market & of fresh beauties in society. The Italians are afraid of seeing their wives till they are married, & soon tired of looking at them afterwards. The only class who find their account in the arrangement are the old widows like the Duchess Sante & a Russian Princess who candidly owns she looks well at a distance.

Lady William Russell to Miss Berry [PRP]

Paris, March 22 [1818]

You have no idea of half the pleasure your letter gave me, to tell the truth I never could make out to my own satisfaction, the reason of my not having written to you on that occasion, which is now so long gone by, that I almost forget the date, *quoiqu'il en soit je me suis arrangée de façon que,* in a week or a fortnight perhaps, I shall assume a new character, in which the Lord assist & prosper me! I am frightened when I think of *quel terribil punto, mais il faut bien passer par là*, Lady E. Stuart† is *tale quale*; Madame de Broglie‡ said to her after her *accouchement* 'pray do you love your little shild very much? I had been reading about the feelings of maternity until I had mounted my imagination but I am quite disappointed, I do not like my little shild much.' *Ciò non ostante* she is going to produce another this summer. The Duke & Duchess of Bedford are to be at Paris in a few days. Lord Kinnaird is here, *fra mille quai*, & the Duke of Wellington looks horridly ill, *si dice* that it is not the present *combinazione* but love; that he declares he never knew the meaning of the word until he saw Mrs Paterson,§ & her departure for America *déchire son tendre coeur* in a terrible manner. He really looks mighty sick. They put people in prison every day, *e non vien fuori niente*; one man was arrested for having cut off

* 'It is true she is rather like Messalina, but she is beautiful, one must forgive her.'
† The wife of Sir Charles Stuart, the English Ambassador.
‡ Albertine Duchesse de Broglie, daughter of Madame de Staël.
§ Marianne Caton, widow of Robert Patterson; she married in 1825 Marquess Wellesley, the Duke of Wellington's brother.

his mustachios & leaving Paris the day after the *attentat*; this was a conclusion *à la Zadig.**

I hope to see you here if I live, my health is excellent & I have suffered nothing whatsoever from my situation, not so poor Lady Elizabeth, she coughs & looks very delicate. . . . My dear mamma is as you may believe *comme 'la mer (ou la mère) agitée'* as somebody used to call her. She has been very unwell this autumn & winter & is still thin poor darling.

And now farewell dear Berrina – remember me to Agnese & forgive such a *terre à terre* letter. God bless you.

A daughter was born to Lady William in April 1818 at Paris, but died when three months old.

Lord William Russell to Lady Holland [HH]

Dover 25 June 1818

As I am detained here I cannot employ my time better than by thanking you for your kind offer of Ampthill. When I am *de trop* at Woburn or they are tired of my society I assure you it will be a great relief to me to think that I have a place of refuge so near.

You will be sorry to hear that Lady William has had a relapse, & is by no means well, this makes me impatient to get her from Paris as soon as possible for I do not think the air agrees with her. We shall probably go in the first instance to Spa.

My father left Paris last Thursday – & was to meet the Duke of Wellington at Fontainebleau; these two forming a *partie carrée* with the Duchess & Lady C. Greville, have been in a vortex of pleasure & amusement. The Duchess proposed to end it by giving a dinner to the Duke of W. at Versailles. The Duke said no, *he* would give the dinner & ask for le Petit Trianon, & on asking for it, Louis le Gros Tyran said, *no, he* would give the dinner, *effectivement* the King paid all & the Duke took down his *société. Le peuple* said a great many sweet & sour things; on seeing the Hero's vain efforts to pluck some roses in the gardens for the ladies, they called out thro the *grille 'qu'il savait cueillir des lauriers mieux que des roses'*, then when the gendarmes pushed aside the people saying, '*Place pour Monseigneur*, they remarked *qu'il n'y avait plus qu'à arborer le Pavillon Anglais'*. At the Trianon when they wanted to come & see the sights like their betters, the guards told them, *qu'on ne laissait entrer que la compagnie*

* *Zadig, ou la Destinée* by Voltaire; Zadig drew inferences by close observation.

du Duc, upon which they said, *Vous pouvez donc nous laisser passer librement car il parait qu'il aime la mauvaise compagnie.*

Many other apt & witty things were said by this happy people, but I have given you the best of them. . . .

Lord William Russell to Lady Holland [PRP]

Paris 11 July 1818

I thank you for your very kind letter. Bessy is much better than she has been, but is still very weak & much afflicted – however I should not mind this, (for time would cure it,) did I not know that grief works upon her without appearing untill it breaks out in violent illness, & symptoms of this have once or twice appeared, however she has recovered, and I hope to do much by constant change of air & scene, for tomorrow we go by gentle journeys to Spa. Indeed the loss of our poor little girl is a most cruel blow – to me it was severe, but to her it was beyond what one can describe for she had attached herself to it most violently & indeed she could not have done otherwise for it was a common remark amongst people from its extreme beauty, to say it was too pretty to live, the blow too was still more unexpected from its good health, its constitution was so good that it resisted an attack for 6 days (an inflammation of the bowels) to which most children would have yielded in two. I talk to you perhaps like a foolish father, but it is your own fault for desiring me to write to you – & surely no man met with such a disappointment, returning with all the hope & pleasure that the idea of enjoying my home could give. I got a letter at Beauvais to say my child had been dangerously ill, but was recovering, soon after a servant met me to say there were no hopes, I got on his horse, missed the Doctor who had stationed himself to tell me all was over, & burst upon my house of mourning, & what a scene of affliction did I behold. My little child was in its cradle looking like a sleeping Christ, but her sparkling blue eyes were closed for ever, and her cheeks, when I kissed them, were as cold as ice, she had the complexion of her mother – but enough of this, it gives me pain to write it, & from your affection for me it will give you pain to read it. My consolation is that I have been of use to my poor wife & that is all that I desire.

I know nothing of my Father. I wish he was in England, for I do not at all like his travelling so rapidly in the heat, & I am sure he has no amusement in it.

Adieu, this is a melancholy letter but you will pardon it.

43

Mrs Rawdon, writing to Canova at this time, told him that Bettina Rawdon 'è molto felice col suo sposo, ma la povretta ebbe la disgrazia di perdere la sua bambina, il che la dolse moltissimo'.*[3] Bettina herself wrote to him some months later from Woburn where his marble group of the Three Graces was to be installed in a specially constructed alcove of the Duke of Bedford's sculpture gallery.

'Sono secoli cavaliere carissimo che non sento nulla di voi temo che la povera Bettina sia affato cacciato nel nero obblio. Eppure qui si parla ogni giorni di Canova e in qual parte del mondo non si parla di lui? Ma qui massimamente, in questo punto, che si aspetta le tre dive che hanno un bel tempietto di già preparato per loro. . . .'†[4] Countess Lieven was to say when she saw these naked figures that it made her feel cold to look at them, but at the time of her visit Woburn was under snow.

The termination of Lord William's service with the Duke of Wellington set him free to attend the House of Commons. He had taken a dilapidated house in Curzon Street and there Bessy gave birth to her second child, a boy, who was born in October 1819 and christened Hastings after Lord Moira, who while acting as Governor-General of Bengal had been created Marquess of Hastings.

Lord William Russell to Mrs Rawdon [PRP]

[London 1819]

You will be happy to hear that Bessy is much better – except that she tired herself with talking last night. She went out without me, & took advantage of my absence to stay up till 3 o'clock so she is pale & haggard today.

You have no conception of her success, & the admiration she meets with. Sir William Scott met her at Lady Holland's, & asked who that lovely creature was, for he could not take his eyes off her. Lady H. replied that the beauties of her face were not to be compared to the beauties of her mind. Her dresses have also great success, & she gives the *ton* to the fashions, in short whatever she comes out in, is reckoned the pink & perfection of gentility & all the milliners are ordered to copy it.

Pray give her all the encouragement you can about lying in, as she has all sorts of absurd fancies, & sits sometimes thinking & picking her lips,

---

* 'Bettina Rawdon is very happy with her husband, but the poor little thing has had the misfortune to lose her baby which has distressed her very much.'

† 'It is ages, dearest cavaliere, since I heard anything from you. I am afraid that poor Bettina has indeed been driven out into black oblivion! Yet every day we talk of Canova, and in what part of the world is he not talked of? But chiefly here, in this spot, where the three goddesses are awaited and have a beautiful temple ready for them. . . .'

Billikins and Bettina

till her mind is bewildered & her lips scarified. I shall take her into the country at Easter.

Lady William Russell to Lady Holland [HH]

Middleton,* Sunday [8 August 1819]

As you were so kind as to wish to hear how I bore the journey I write to announce my safe arrival & prosperous condition this day, I really feel quite well.

Lady Jersey is in great beauty & spirits, although she complains a little this day. We are a *partie carrée*, but the Duke and Duchess are expected & I believe Lord Grey also *viendra se désennuyer un tant soit peu*.

I hope your headaches & unpleasant feelings have subsided, & that we shall soon meet at the '*gloomy* Abbey'. This is a very *terre à terre* letter, but you cannot expect news from so remote a *département*.

Duke of Bedford to Lord William Russell [PRP]

Vienna, Nov 9 1819

I congratulate you on the birth of your son & heir and on Bessy's safety. I trust the next mail will bring us equally good accounts of her, and her progress towards recovery. I wrote to you soon after my arrival at this place and I have since received your Jobation on my absenting myself from England, to which I shall pay proper attention. I have not had a gun in my hand since I left England, but Esterhazy's *parade chasse* (for which I have been waiting) is now fixed for the 10th, 11th and 12th, after which we shall make the best of our way to England. I was invited to Prince Lichtenstein's *chasse* last week, but for reasons (good or bad) I sent my excuses. Pray tell Bessy with my love, that I think Wien the most detestable place I ever was in.

[*in the Duchess of Bedford's handwriting*]

My dearest Billy, I am delighted to have been wrong in my prophecy as to the sex of your child, and rejoice more than I can express that everything has gone on so well, and that your dear and amiable wife is safe, happy and comfortable. I always feel delighted when I have it in my power to prove the unalterable affection I have, from my first acquaintance with you, expressed and felt for you; the coldness of your manner towards

* The seat of Lord Jersey in Oxfordshire.

45

me, is always a subject of regret, particularly as I know it to be a great injustice to me, for if I have any merits, sincerity is one of the many. Pray thank Dr Gooch for his polite attention in writing to me, I do not write to him as my thanks are not worth paying for. . . .

Mr Gordon, just gone to England is a great loss to our society – he has taken charge of three German tragedies for Bessy, all the fashion here at present. I have got some more books for her which I will send when I can. By the time this reaches you we shall have left this hospitable town. I think nothing will prevent our being at Woburn by Christmas – when I hope you will join us. Pray write to Paris – *not a scold* either to me or to your father though that is better than nothing. *Embrassez la chère Bettina pour moi, de tout votre cœur.* Keep her laying as long as you can. I send a kiss and a blessing to my grandson. I am very impatient to see his little round chin. God bless you all. The Duke is quite well.

The year following the birth of their son was perhaps the happiest of the William Russells' marriage. Though not rich, their position was secure and Bessy's beauty and William's intelligence assured them a large circle of friends. At Holland House they were always welcome. Lady Holland recognised the merits of William's wife and received her graciously and even with affection. It was not till many years later that their autocratic natures came into collision.

Living in London on half-pay, the young couple were glad to go often to Woburn Abbey, where they had rooms that were always ready for them. William loved the house and park, he kept his hunters in the stables, and he enjoyed the company and conversation of his father and brothers. The shooting the Duke had been at pains to make the best in England. The American, George Ticknor, found William and Bessy in the party when he stayed at Woburn, and he described the last day of the shooting season: 'After the dinner cloth was removed in the evening the gamekeeper appeared in all his paraphernalia and rendered his account. 404 hares, partridges and pheasants had been killed.'[5] The Duke was proud of his game and liked to send pheasants to his friends in Paris, where they arrived, he told Lady Holland, 'en bon ordre . . . and are much admired for being gros et gras'.[6]

The parties at Woburn were large and brilliant, and if the Duke was shy and silent and his wife preoccupied with her large nursery, Bessy was ready to make herself agreeable to the guests, if not always to the Duchess. Lady Granville* has left an account of one of these gatherings; her cool

* Lady Harriet Cavendish (1785–1862), daughter of Georgiana Duchess of Devonshire and the 5th Duke. She married in 1809 Lord Granville Leveson Gower (1773–1846), son of the 1st Marquess of Stafford. He became the 1st Earl Granville.

Elizabeth Anne Rawdon, a copy of a lost drawing by Ingres

Lord John Russell

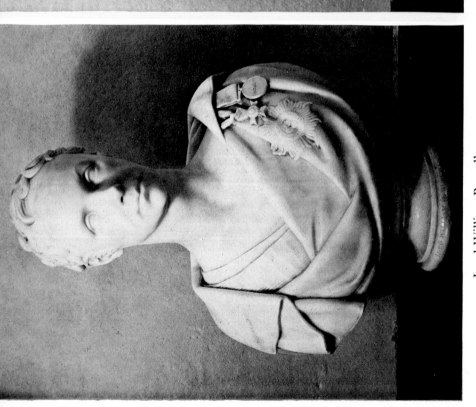

Lord William Russell

by R. Westmacott at Woburn Abbey

and witty appraisal of the scene must have established a bond of sympathy between herself and the young woman who viewed most of her husband's family with little affection.

'The Duchess has not yet appeared', wrote Lady Granville. 'She has seen *toutes ces dames*, but not me. You know I am not touchy, therefore I take the goods the gods provide me and swallow the affront with a grateful heart. It is very comfortable here, no more nor less. . . . In the evening the men play at whist or billiards, and we sit in the saloon all very well together, but Lady William Russell is the only one who really likes me, Lady Jersey* is too absorbed to think who is for or who is against. She sits netting and raving and it sometimes comes across my mind that she will go out of hers. Her countenance is become so stern and political that it affects her beauty. She occasionally stands up and gesticulates with unfeminine vehemence. Yesterday she seized Lord William by both sides of his coat, I believe what is called collaring a man, exclaiming, "Why should we have Germans to reign over us?"'

Lady Granville continued her account next day: 'We are new dealt every day at dinner. Yesterday I sat between Lords Thanet and Worcester. The former is very agreeable and we are becoming rather particular. Lord Jersey is cut short in all his sports by gout.

'Monsieur de Flahault† was the only new personage. His singing is enchanting and made yesterday evening more agreeable than former ones. The Duchess appeared. She was to me just what I wish her to be, uncommonly cold and uncommonly civil. . . . Lady William I like better every time I see her. . . . Punch‡ very entertaining, treating the Duke of York as if he was his *élève*. "Good God, sir, how can your Royal Highness say such a thing?" "Ah, ah. Well, I'm sure I don't, know. Well, Punch, well, I am very sorry."

'. . . I am not very much charmed here. I declare I do not know why I am not more. I think very few people as agreeable as Lady William. . . . I have a delightful room and find the day too short for all I have to do in it. . . . Why then do I count the days till I can go? Why do I feel that I shall not be able to refrain from screaming for joy when I drive off. It is no affront to Woburn. I do justice to its comforts, ease, splendour, and society. It is simply a strong, unconquerable wish to go, and I am inclined to say to everybody with the utmost sincerity, "Yes, it is delightful, only can't I possibly get away?"'

* Lady Sarah Fane (1785–1867), daughter of the 10th Earl of Westmorland, married in 1804 the 5th Earl of Jersey. She was a violent Tory. Always garrulous, her nickname was 'Silence'.

† Charles Comte de Flahault (1785–1870), reputed son of Talleyrand by his mistress Adèle de Filleul, Comtesse de Flahault. He married in 1817 the Hon. Margaret Elphinstone (1788–1867), daughter of Viscount Keith. He was Napoleon's aide-de-camp at Waterloo.

‡ Charles Greville (1794–1865) the diarist, son of Charles Greville and Lady Charlotte Greville. Nicknamed 'Punch'.

And she concluded the following day: 'We left Woburn yesterday having spent there a week of as much pleasure as is compatible with seeing it end without regret. The *locale* is itself a great source of enjoyment. So much space, so much comfort, such *luxe* and ease. . . . I believe it was being obliged to dress up very smart and sitting often at dinner between Lords Tavistock and Worcester. These were my grievances; my pleasures were Lady William's society, as much of Charles Greville's as shooting and whist allowed, Monsieur de Flahault's singing. The Duchess herself is very unwell and appeared but four times, and when she did very *souffrante* and out of spirits. Lady Tavistock did the honours with radiant good humour in a succession of dresses that looked as if they came out of an old masquerade warehouse'.[7]

Mrs Rawdon's absence from England and the freedom from her pressing attentions may have contributed to the William Russells' happiness during the year. The disconsolate mother was living in an apartment in the Rue de Provence at Paris, where Lord Glenbervie found her 'alone with her daughter's picture done by Ingres on her sofa by her. It is always there or on her chimney piece. Other people may call this an affected display of her concern for her separation from her daughter, but I think this a harsh and unjust judgement. But she is a silly woman and not sparing of her own gossiping and ill natured construction of the conduct of others.'[8]

Mrs Rawdon was not for long neglected by her daughter, who was always mindful of her parent's lonely situation. Henry Fox wrote of Bessy including her mother in her travelling arrangements that summer. 'I saw Lady William who sets off for Scotland tomorrow with her husband, mother, child, Terence, Horace, and a brood of puppies.'[9] Terence and Horace refer, of course, to Bessy's reading matter.

Frequent intercourse with Woburn had the unhappy consequence of revealing the latent hostility between Bessy and the Duchess, whose temperaments were incompatible. Twelve years separated them in age. The worsening of relations between the two women was distressing for their husbands. William had a bent for writing letters that offended, and his unhappiness increased the bitterness of his pen. The Duke, who had so much good humour that it was impossible to quarrel with him, wrote to Lady Holland: 'I know nothing of the Williams except from you – he seldom writes except to scold me for something I have done or left undone, so I am glad when I do not perceive his hand amongst my post letters'.[10]

The uncomfortable situation affected Bessy's health, and in the summer of 1821 William decided to take her abroad. They left England with their little boy in June and were not to return for two years. (It was at this moment that William began to keep a journal, which he did intermittently for the rest of his life.) They reached Calais after a calm passage of eight hours in the Packet and a few days later arrived in Brussels, where Lord William exchanged his 'rumble tumble for a barouchette in which Bessy and I travelled, putting Baby Bunting and his attendants in the post chaise'. Passing through Liège, where Lord William received 'many compliments

48

from the landlord, a coxcomical Frenchman, for my *beaux discours* in parliament', they arrived at Spa.

Lord William Russell to Lady Holland at Paris [HH]

Brussels 20 June [1821]

... You being at Paris was very near tempting us to go there, but prudence prevailed & we decided to retreat to Spa, which after all will not be much of a retreat, for their Majesties of Prussia, Wurtemburg & Holland are to be there, besides Royal Dukes, Grand Dukes & petty princes without end, so it will be a bad place for an invalid, & still worse for a poor man. I shall reconnoitre the position, & decamp if not to my liking. Yet there is a great charm in the society of kings & princes, especially when they condescend to speak to one which they do now and then in pretty watering places. We came here for two days but found so many old friends have remained a week to eat & drink with them. The Prince of Orange* is an *ancien camarade, et toujours le même.*

Bessy has been the better since she came abroad which makes me hope that travelling will do her good, she sends her love to you & Lord Holland. My boy is delighted with all he sees. He ruins me by stopping all the Savoyards & fidlers in the town, there is a perpetual concert going on under my windows, to the great discomforture of my neighbours.

What is John about? I fear his love† uses him very ill. Dont let him be made ridiculous. A Polish lady once told me that *chagrin* & love might always be destroyed by travelling post till hunger & fatigue got the better of it. If John is in want of such a remedy, let him try the road between Paris & Spa, I think it will be long enough – but mum not a word of this or I am a lost man. Lord Holland may cut his old joke & say if Russells dont speak, it is no sign of a quarrel.

LORD WILLIAM'S DIARY

[Spa] After dining at the Hotel d'Orange, lodged ourselves in the Hotel de la Ville de Bruges, a clean well situated house. We found nobody in the town but the Prince and Princess of Orange, and Countess Lieven, wife of the Russian Ambassador at London. She is a woman of quick discernment, and sound

---

* William, Prince of Orange (1792–1849), served on Wellington's staff in the Peninsular War. He married in 1816 Anna Paulowna, a sister of the Emperor Alexander of Russia. He became William II, King of the Netherlands in 1840.

† Madame Durazzo.

49

judgement, lively and easy in conversation, great knowledge of the world, and noble and elegant in her appearance and manners, but having little taste for anything but the society of the great or the agreable; to a person possessing either of these qualities, she can forgive the want of the other, but one or the other is absolutely requisite to be tolerated by her. She keeps up an extensive correspondence with the most distinguished persons in Europe and is supposed to give her husband great assistance in his diplomatic labors. She has a boy with her born the same day as mine.

Ever a prey to the torments of ennui Countess Lieven had written ten days before to Lady Granville: 'Envoyez moi donc les William Russells'[11]; but once they were arrived a cry of dissatisfaction reached London.

'Je vois beaucoup les Russells, ils sont bien, mais, mon Dieu, que je me suis gâté la vie pour être si difficile. Elle n'est pas ce qu'il me faut quoique de droit tout le monde doit la trouver charmante, il y a un petit brin de petite femme et puis tout n'est pas compris et puis il y a tout à coup un propos leste duquel vous avez l'air de douter, alors elle vous affirme positivement que c'est un homme qui le lui ait dit – au moins je ne citerais pas la preuve. Voilà ce qui pèse un peu avec son jeune et innocent et joli visage.'[12]

William, she thought, had ten times more *esprit* than his wife. In spite of her criticism she found them indispensable to her happiness and they were in one another's company on and off, for the next month.

Lord William Russell to Lady Holland at Paris [HH]

July 10 [1821] Spa

There was never any thing so kind as your offer, or so tempting, yet we must resist, I do it with difficulty & tell it you with pain.

I determined on leaving England, to sacrifice every thing to the restoration of Bessy's shattered health, & I believe the best chance is to keep away from capitals & remain as much as possible in these little watering places, for although the waters may not do much yet the regularity of the life, the quiet, the air & exercise does a great deal, besides when once in Paris how are we ever to get away? Its own charms are very great, but with you & Lord Holland & John & Allen,* & Henry† & your house & M.

---

* Dr John Allen (1771–1843). Engaged as a physician to accompany Lord and Lady Holland to Spain in 1802, he remained for forty years an inmate of Holland House, acting as librarian. He was Master of Dulwich College from 1820 until his death.

† The Hon. Henry Fox (1802–59), son of Lord and Lady Holland. Succeeded his father as 4th Lord Holland.

Honoré,* & your garden for my boy, I should never have power to budge, unless you turned me out of your house, which I am sure you would never do, no, I dare not even go near Paris, for fear of being carried down the stream that always sets that way – even you were hurried in to the vortex by going within ten leagues of it, & at Calais I felt the influence of the eddy. So once more thanking you most sincerely for the kindness of your offer we must decline.

I am surprised you should think John better at Paris than here, however if he is amused I will not entice him away, for that is as essential to him as mineral waters, & I have not much amusement to offer him here, yet every body writes me that he is looking pale & thin. He tells me he is coming here but my Father says he has ordered his horses to go to Paris, I suppose when the *wind* is N.E. he decides to come here, & changes as it (the *wind*) changes, & if the translations of his book† are published & you have an opportunity of sending me a copy, you would oblige me much by doing so.

There is not a soul here we know but Madame de Lieven. There is a King & Queen & half a dozen Princes still remaining out of dozens that have been here, at one time we had three Kings with us, our last King (Wurtemburg), a sharp smart little fellow, gives a ball & supper tonight. Last night I was talking to Madame de L. about her desertion from Holland House, when she ended by saying it was now a matter of no consequence, for it would not have been possible for her to have gone there after Lord Holland's attack on her Master.‡ I told her I thought she put the thing in quite a wrong point of view, for as far as I recollect the speech (& I have not much recollection of it) he made no personal attack on the Emperor, but was combatting the hypocrisy of his adversaries language, & showed it by [?mentioning] the manner in which the Emperor had been put on his throne. She would not allow this, & said it had made the greatest sensation on the Continent, every one having applied it as she did, & every one she met (particularly the grandees) asking her about it, & requiring an explanation. My object then in writing you this long story is to enable Lord Holland if he thinks it worth his while, to

* Lady Holland's cook.

† Lord John published in 1821 *An Essay on the History of the English Government and Constitution from the reign of Henry VII to the present time.* It was translated into French the same year.

‡ Lord Holland 'had been called to order by Lord Harrowby, and the interruption had the effect of a distorting of the sense of his words and caused them to be interpreted as a direct attack on the Czar'. Earl of Ilchester (ed.), *Chronicles of Holland House*, p. 10.

write me an explanation of his words (for mine may have been quite wrong) in order that I might show it to Madame de L. & desire her to write to the Emperor, yet it may not be worth the trouble for I have long suspected her & others of giving the Emperor a totally wrong & unfair impression of the words & acts & objects of the Opposition, therefore it may do but little good to explain away one phrase out of the hundreds that are misrepresented.

The Duke of Cumberland is just arrived.

Lady William Russell to Lady Holland at Paris [HH]

[Spa, 14 July 1821]

I too must add a few lines to William's long letter to thank you, dear Lady Holland, not only for your kind invitation, but for your excessive attention to Mama, who is as much *pénétrée* as myself at all your civilities.

The weather is so horrible here that the [?check] & constant damp & cold brought on my spasms as in England, which is rather disheartening as I felt so very comfortable whilst the sun shone & the bile went right. . . . *Faute de mieux* we frequent the royalties who are amazing bores, all but *Pépin le bref*, my *sobriquet* for Wurtemberg, who is grown short & thick like ye late Duc de Berry, & a dapper little King it is.

The Lieven is first fiddle & fiddles away with all her might & main, *ne se possédant pas de joie* but as usual pretending she is fatigued to death with it all; we see her eternally, she is certainly a woman of abilities; great *usage du monde*, great tact, excellent *ton de société*; *fort aimable et intriguant comme tous les diables*. We have examples of it even here, where one would think few opportunities offered themselves for the exertion of her talents in that line. You never quote so I do not fear telling you my mind.

So the greatest man that ever existed is no more!!* *Cela m'a serré le coeur!* Although I am accused by you all of being such a Tory, I grieve for the glory of mankind that not one genius should be left on earth. I take it philosophically not politically.

My boy grows charming, I adore him, we do nothing but play with him all day long & this mountain air has increased his colour & his flesh prodigiously. Goodbye. Ever your sincerely attached.

* Napoleon died 5 May 1821. He left Lady Holland a snuff box.

Lord Holland to Lord William Russell [WP]

[1821]

I can give you no explanation of my speech about Alexander – though I believe the papers exaggerated and I am sure Harrowby's interruption made the phrase more savage and possibly on that account more just than had I finished my sentence I should have made it myself. Whether Alexander knew of Paul's murder or not, I think he has done much worse things lately and I can say nothing about him which will please Madame de Lieven when repeated to her but this which I can say with great sincerity, that it will give me great pleasure to hear that he has conquered Constantinople and driven the Turks out of Europe. In Lancaster's and Bell's school the boy who has learnt to spell though under the instruction of him who can read without spelling, is teacher to the child who can neither read nor spell and so the Muscovite may civilise the Turk but if he breaks into the classes on this side the Vistula or at least the Elbe he can only barbarize and create confusion. Mme de L., who is a sensible woman and *not* a Russian, knows very well that the Czar and his subjects where they mix with the Europeans *ne font que jouer la comédie* and that even the anger of being accused of murder is as much an affectation of sentiment, to which they are utter strangers, as the religious horror or devotion of Talma in Oedipe or Hyppolytus. The historical fact is that Alexander *did* know of the intention of breaking in to his father's bedroom, and I can hardly suppose him so ignorant of the country he governs as not to have known the necessary consequences. At the same time I do not reproach him or the Russians with that act or that knowledge – still less do I reproach the Spanish army with revolting against Ferdinand 7th or the Cortes with deriving their power from that revolt. All I say is that as to the legitimate source of power Alexander has no more right to say the Cortes derive it from the crime of rebellion than the Spaniards have to say that he owes it to a murder.

Yrs V. Holland

This was intended for a postscript to my letter but absorbs the whole and is better than any thing I can say – the loss of the society of Madame de Lieven I really felt as a privation from what was a treat, as her conversation is extremely brilliant, her observations neat and pointed. I have always ascribed her withdrawing from any cause but that she assigned to Madame Flahault, because on the face of it there was falsehood, if politicks

53

and a dislike of hearing the King abused was to affect her associating with people, surely the latter was never heard in my house, and was the unwearied tiresome theme at Lady Jersey's, where she did go perpetually and the same people who came to me went to them only more frequently. No I humbly believe she was *purement* and *simplement* bored with me, and was unwilling from her good taste to tell my particular friends she thought me a bore, so flattered herself *en diplomate*. John is well and loving. We are all pretty well, love to Bessy Belle.

Lord William Russell to Lady Holland at Paris [HH]

Spa 26 July [1821]

Many thanks for your postscript. I wrote so long a letter to Lord H that I had no room for a postscript for you in return, so you must undertake to read a letter.

I am sorry he would not soften down his savage speech (for he is looked upon as a levelling, sanguinary, Monarch dethroning savage on the Continent) Lord H!!!! Those sort of speeches are so misunderstood & misapplied by foreigners – *mais c'est égal.*

I wanted to tell you that I have this moment come from dining with the Grand Duke Nicholas, where I sat next to a Comtesse Shouwaloff who told me (I wish you to repeat all this to Mr Moore) in talking about Walter Scott's novels & other English books, that the most beautiful poem in the English or any other language, was Lalla Rookh, that she had already read it ten times, & hoped to read it ten times more – that at Berlin they had got up a sort of tableau or scene out of it, in which upwards of two hundred persons walked in the procession, singing & dancing, & in the most magnificent dresses. The Grand Duchess Alexandrine was Lalla Rookh & other characters were represented by the 1st persons of the Court – by the description it must have been beautiful and magnificent. The Grand Duchess goes about with 2 copies most superbly bound & ornamented with gold, precious stones &c,&c. She has lent me one copy for I am ashamed to say I never read it, Mr Moore need not be affronted for I have never read anything. The Grand Duchess is making drawings from the procession, & these & others are to be engraved.

They have made a cloth at Ferriers the colour of which is called *Tombeau de Bonaparte,* & the *élégans* have made up coats of it. Is it true he has left you a snuff-box?

54

. . . Bessy still suffers much with horrible spasms. The weather is bad so we shall go away on the 1st. . . . Give my love to John – he is a lazy *vaurien* never to write to me. Remember me too to Holland the Savage.

LORD WILLIAM'S DIARY

Left Spa August 1st & reached Aix la Chapelle in 8 hours. The Prussians torment one here much about the passport, sending one from bureau to bureau for the sake of extracting one franc at each.

On the 2nd arrived at Cologne on the 3rd we passed through Bonn and so to Coblentz – a dirty town – afterwards we proceeded to Emms. It was so full we could find no place to lodge but in a cottage in the village ½ a mile from the baths. As we knew no one here we amused ourselves with riding about on asses, & enjoying the magnificent scenery.

On the 7th we went to Swalbach. Here we were accosted by a footman of the Duke of Cumberland, who begged we would join his dinner party as he had just sat down, but we endeavoured to excuse ourselves on account of travelling dress, dirt, etc, but in vain, in we went, and a most excellent dinner we found, made perfect by the exquisite politeness of the royal host & hostess. Countess Lieven was living there. With difficulty we got lodged, the town being full of Frankfort Jews, & after dining again the next day with our hospitable Prince, we proceeded to Schlangenbad 5 miles off, in a deep sequestered valley to which the sun rarely penetrates; there is no town here but a rambling, rumbling, tumbling palace built 150 years ago by the Elector of Saxe. In my life I never saw anything more gloomy, large rooms without furniture, long corridors only fit for ghosts. Our tempers were pretty cheerful or we must have sunk under it. We made an excursion through the Rheingau. On our return to Schlangenbad we found Madame de Lieven had arrived. A week afterwards the Duke of Wellington with his staff arrived on a visit to Madame de Lieven & we made another excursion to the Rheingau & Niederwald.

Lord William Russell to Lady Holland [HH]

Schlangenbad 18 Aug [1821]
. . . Your letter is written in very low spirits. I hope this may find all in a better state. What a sad thing poor Brougham losing his little girl. I feel for him with all my heart. God grant I may keep my little boy. Bessy is so fond of him, she would die if we were to lose him. But he is healthy, strong, full of spirits, & every thing I could wish. Lord Holland will not be able to say (as he does of the Russells) that he is like an otter, or that he never speaks, for he is handsome & jabbers like a magpie – he has all the quickness &

3*   55

esprit of his mother, & is quite a little prodigy. You will call this *les contes de Papa* – but one thing I can assure you of which gives me great pleasure as an Englishman & a father, which is that he is master of little Lieven & thumps him till he cries.

As you tell me John is gone in to Switzerland I shall not write to him. Where does he go afterwards? I shall be at Vienna about the middle of September where I hope to find a letter from you.

We are here in the most extraordinary place. *Figurez-vous* a large rambling scrambling gloomy palace built by an Elector of Hesse 150 years ago in a narrow dark valley in the middle of a large beech forest. Mrs Radcliffe * never imagined anything more fit to conceal banditti or to have ghosts flitting along the passages – but the merit of the place is in the baths, they are of the softest & clearest water, & have the art of making old women young – & when you lose that beautiful complexion you now have I advise you to come here. Ponsonby will tell you about them & us as he has been beautifying in them. . . .†

LORD WILLIAM'S DIARY

On the 29th August we went to Frankfort, & being lodged at the Hotel d'Angleterre, I received a fright which to my dying day I shall not forget – at least I hope not for it would be a want of gratitude for God's great mercy. My little boy 21 months old, was playing on the balcony & had run to the farther corner when I called to him to come in, instead of obeying me he squeezed himself thro the bars & ran as fast as he could along the narrow cornice or ledge about 6 inches broad. Never shall I forget the sensation of seeing him pass thro the bars & run from me, if I spoke or if he turned he must have fallen. God gave me strength to jump over the railings & to follow him. He had just reached the corner where the ledge recedes at a right angle with the house when I caught him by the arm & threw him into a window that was happily open.

Countess Lieven again joined us here & we spent two days very agreably, so much so that she persuaded us to give up our plan of going by Dresden & accompanying her as far as Stoutgardt where her brother is Russian Minister.

On the 2nd we left Frankfort.

At Heidelburg we found Madame de L. waiting dinner for us, which having despatched & the evening being fine we took a drive along the banks of the Neckar.

* Mrs Radcliffe wrote *The Mysteries of Udolpho* and other romantic tales.

† A gentleman while bathing at Schlangenbad was heard to remark: 'Monsieur, dans ces bains on devient absolument amoureux de soi-meme.' Head, *Bubbles from the Brunnens of Nassau*, p. 110.

Billikins and Bettina

The next day we arrived at Stoutgardt where in the evening we supped at Mr de Benckendorff a gentleman like, obliging, agreable man. His wife, whom they say is most accomplished, being very ill did not appear.

Our intention was only to have remained one day at Stoutgardt, but the Dowager Queen* having desired to see Bessy, & afterwards having asked us to dine at Louisborough caused us delay. Louisborough [Ludwigsburg] is a fine chateau, large & well furnished, the old Queen is the very image of her father, apparently, a kind, obliging woman, living upon English news, and remembering every anecdote she ever heard. She placed me on her left hand at dinner, & treated me with marked attention.

While at Stoutgardt I was taken round the Harar† of the King, the breeding & keeping horses are his great pleasure & expense. The mares are not on a large scale, but the horses are well chosen & brought from all parts of the world & I should think his Arabians are superior to any collection in Europe.

Having staid so long at Stoutgardt, it was thought right I should pay my court to the King. I had ½ an hour conversation tête à tête with the King. He talked well on various subjects, appears to have read much, to have just & liberal ideas, & in short to be a man capable of governing well a large country. His own is so small that he has no scope to employ his talents.

[They reached Vienna in the last week of September.]

Rooms were taken for us at the Müllenichen Haus, a dirty filthy place.

Here we were doomed to suffer a great loss & to undergo great misery. The little boy's nurse had complained of cold & bilious feelings, the day after our arrival she took calomel & thought herself better. At 5 o'clock on Wednesday morning Bessy was called up, & Dr Guppellini, supposed to be the best physician in Vienna, sent for. He treated her mildly but on Thursday as she became worse, we sent for Studenheimer to consult. He applied leeches & gave more calomel. On Friday she became still worse, the delirium increasing, & at night she became quite violent. Bleeding, blisters & ice were now applied but in vain. On Saturday she became milder and weaker & on Sunday morning at 5 o'clock she breathed her last. I never remember in my life to have spent five days so miserably – the lodging dirty & confined, the poor woman in one room singing & shrieking to the extent of her lungs, in the other the poor little boy fretting & pining to go to her, poor Bessy anxious & ill. May God spare me such a scene again.

* Charlotte Augusta Matilda, Princess Royal of England (1766–1828), eldest daughter of George III; she married Frederick William, Duke (subsequently King) of Wurtemberg.

† Lord Brougham, when visiting the Harar, remarked that the money spent on the stables would be more advantageously spent in building a university for the education of the nobility. Loftus, *Diplomatic Reminiscences*, 1st series, i, 78.

Billikins and Bettina

The poor woman was a most serious loss to us, she was attentive to the boy, mild and good, & thoroughly versed in the management of children, & the poor little boy loved her & regretted her so much. I have seen much of death, but I never saw anything so shocking or so unaccountable as the death of this woman, she was the gentlest & healthiest of beings. On Sunday I had prayers read over her body by Mr Bradford the English clergyman as it lay in the room. It was then removed to the church of St Stephens & buried in the Cimetière. Gordon,* who was kindness itself during all this time persuaded us to go to Baden, he took rooms for us in his house. Bessy, who had never slept since the illness of her nurse, was taken ill, I sent for Dr Frank. She is now, thank God, better.

Baden is a pretty place at the foot of the hills, about 15 miles from Vienna. The baths are sulphurous much like Harrogate. I got 4 days tolerable partridge shooting on Prince Trauttmansdorff's & Prince Esterhazy's estates, but I was astounded to see so little game.

On the 9th October we returned to Vienna & lodged in the Römischer Kaiser.

12 Oct. Went to Prince Metternich's party & had a long conversation with him in which he tried to persuade me that the Austrian Government is the best in the world. He dwelt much on the antiquity of their regulations, & said that because the base was solid, they never had been shaken in the revolutions that had convulsed Europe – that the French in their new mode of administration & code of laws have adopted most of their system.

[The Russells left Vienna at the end of October and arrived at Venice a week later.]

We lodged a few days at the Leoni Bianchi, but as the rooms looked to the North, we removed to better apartments in the Europa, at the débouches of the Canale Grande.

There are three houses always open, & in which strangers always meet with a welcome reception, viz., Madame Albrizzi,† Madame Benzoni‡ & Madame Micheli,§ author of Feste Veneziane, but the society is on a formal footing, & not very agreable to a person who is not perfect master of the Italian language.

* The Hon. Robert Gordon, English envoy at Vienna.
† Isabella Teotochi Countess Albrizzi (?1761–1836), a native of Corfu. Her salon was renowned. Byron called her the de Staël of Venice, 'a very learned, unaffected, good-natured woman, very polite to strangers, and I believe not at all dissolute, as most of the women are'. Ugo Foscolo had been her lover.
‡ Countess Marina Benzoni; 'one of the last of the old school of nobility; thoroughly profligate'. Thomas Moore, *Journal*, iii, 27.
§ Giustina Micheli (1755–1832). 'My deafness', she wrote, 'is an inestimable advantage in company; for with the stupid and gossiping I shun all communication . . . but I can employ my trumpet with sensible people.' *Cyclopedia of female biography* (1857), p. 545.

Towards the end of December the Viceroy* and Vicequeen came to Venice, they gave us a dinner & invited us to lotto parties once a week. He is a worthy man, the Archduke Renier, & she a Princess de Carignan.

Mrs Rawdon joined us on the 20th November from Paris. I went to Padua to fetch her, a desolate town with a fine cathedral. In Venice we did not go much into society. Madame Micheli, the best & most educated of the Venetian women, was so deaf that it was a penance to make her hear; the Benzoni was tiresome & dull, Madame Mocenigo an agreable woman with her *cavaliere servente*, Mr Foscolo,† an agreable obliging man, we saw now & then. Madame Albrizzi received every night, & is supposed to have the best society of Venice at her house; we frequently went to her opera box.

Duke of Bedford to Lord William Russell at Venice [WPP]

Woburn Abbey, December 17th [1821]

I yesterday morning received your letter from Venice of the 1st inst., and in a few hours afterwards, the Duchess was brought to bed of another *boy*. The birth was premature by some weeks, but I thank God both she and the infant are doing as well as possible. I gave her your letter first, with which she was much pleased. I am happy to hear from you that you have at length received all my letters, as it will show that I have not neglected you, though I am afraid I must plead guilty of having been idle of late about writing. All you tell me about your own happiness and domestic content is highly gratifying to me, and God grant you and yours a long, a very long, continuance of this. I never was at Venice, but I always thought it was possessed of a damp and unwholesome climate, however if Bessy and the boy thrive under it, what more can you desire? Politically speaking, I should think you would see enough to disgust you there, of despotic governments, and the odious John of the Austrians, and to see the once proud and flourishing republic of Venice, is now crumbling to dust; but Tavistock and John tell me you are become quite an *Ultra-Tory*. You were once accused of being a *radical*, so if the saying be correct that 'extremes often meet'. If one is true the other may be also. I trust, however, that every son of mine will act steadily, uniformly, and invariably

* The Archduke Renier (1783–1853) was viceroy of the Austrian provinces of Lombardy and Venetia. He was the son of the Emperor Leopold II.

† Probably Giulio, brother of the poet Ugo Foscolo. In a letter of 1825 to Lady William, Madame Albrizzi wrote: '... Luisetta Mocenigo se porte à merveille ... le très fidèle Foscolo est toujours son très humble serviteur et cavalier servente. Je crois que c'est le seul qui existe encore de cette chaste ridicule, et grace au ciel tout à fait disparue.' [PRP]

on the old Whig principles, and never lose sight of the solid rights of the people, the foundation on which our liberties and our Government rest. . . .

I have little information to give you in the shooting line. The Duke of York was prevented by his military movements and a sprained shoulder from coming. We had a week of some of our best coverts, and found the game lamentably deficient everywhere. Where we used to kill 140 or 160 pheasants, we killed this year form 40 to 50, with guns of the first calibre. . . .

I am much gratified by your kind attention in proposing to give me a work of Dannecker's. I was in his studio at Stutgard, and thought him a sculptor of great merit, though I think you rate him too high by comparing him to Canova. When you go to Rome, which I conclude you will do before the winter is over, remember me kindly to him, and tell him how much the *tre grazie* are admired, and even worshipped by our *cognoscenti* in this country. I hope to get my outlines of the Woburn marbles printed by the next spring, and shall immediately send him a copy. I have made some small additions to my collection since you were here, and one or two of exquisite beauty. I think you saw my Venus. If you meet with anything very good and *cheap* at Rome, buy it; but not without consulting some good judge, not Canova, for he is too jealous of good things going out of Rome.

While at Venice Lord William took lessons in Armenian from Father Pasquale Aucher, with whom Byron had also studied the language at the convent on the island of San Lazzaro.

'A very worthy man', wrote Lord William in his diary. 'Promised to publish his Milton.'*

With Mr Foscolo he made an excursion to see the Palladian Theatre at Vicenza, and he noted that among those he saw much of at Venice was Mr Hoppner, the English consul; a man with whom he was to become much better acquainted ten years later in Portugal. At the end of February the Russells, accompanied by Mrs Rawdon, made their way to Florence.

LORD WILLIAM'S DIARY

[Florence] Went to Schneidorff's Inn, which tho good does not merit its great reputation. It is besides immensely dear. We finally lodged ourselves in the

* Father Pasquale dedicated his translation of *Paradise Lost* to Lord William. It was published at Venice in 1824, cf. p. 504.

Seristori palace, an immense & most excellent home. I had three salons furnished in red, green, & yellow silk, a magnificent bedroom in red silk, excellent rooms for the boy, Mrs Rawdon, sitting & dining rooms for myself; besides a summer set of apartments on the ground floor. I found Sir Robert Lawley's servants in the house (of whom I took the lease) & his cook was most admirable. There were besides garden, stables etc.

They went to weekly parties at Madame d'Albany's, the widow of the Young Pretender: 'A cross illnatured old cat, speaking ill of everybody. Her house was crowded with vulgar English, & the rooms so small that it was very disagreable.'

Prince Borghese's palace was better suited for reception, and they went often to the house of the Austrian Minister, Count Bombelles.* 'He is a vulgar good humoured Frenchman, she a Dane, the famous Ida Brunn; coarse & frank, but clever & singing beautifully.'

Old Lord William Russell was also travelling in Italy, and the affection felt for him by his nephew and niece prompted them to make him a friendly offer.

Lady William Russell to old Lord William Russell [WP]

[Florence 1822]

I hope you will deign to accept of an apartment in our house without paying any part of the rent. You will oblige me most particularly, & you may be assured that it can be no additional expence whatsoever, as by getting all the requisites into the bargain, the house remains at the price we should have given for any other lodging that would have barely held us according to our present *ménage*. You need only desire your servant to lay in his own provision of candles, oil, tea, sugar etc., etc. for your own consumption, & get *his* share of the linen washed by your *blanchisseuse*; by which means you have your conscience perfectly easy about William's purse. You see I do not affect to be magnificent & make splendid offers as nothing can be more shabby than this proposal, *mais que voulez vous?* As to dining I need not say how happy we should be to receive you every day if the *fortune du pot* suited you, but I fear our hours will not agree till the weather

---

* Count Louis Bombelles was one of the sons of the Marquis Marcus Maria de Bombelles, a Frenchman of Portuguese Jewish ancestry. Count Louis like his brothers, Charles and Henri, had entered the Austrian service. Ida Brunn was well known also for her 'attitudes' in the style of Emma Lady Hamilton. "Comment ces gens se nomment – le mari est ni bon, la femme ni belle," was a witticism current in Vienna.

grows hotter, in which case you could make some arrangement with our cook about your cutlets later in the day. All our servants are on board wages except the two maids who eat up our remains.

I have now let you into all my family secrets, that you may be quite satisfied that my intentions are not beyond my means. Mr Rossi by a little coaxing will give the linen at least till Lady Lawley writes a thundering letter to deprive us of it. All her crockery & a fine palace for 50 sequins.

Duke of Bedford to Lord William Russell at Florence [WPP]

London, May 3rd 1822

I write one line in haste to say that I was under the necessity (not an agreeable one) of going out with the Duke of Buckingham yesterday in consequence of the censure I cast upon his political apostacy at the County Meeting at Bedford.* I escaped untouched. Your old friend, the General, accompanied me. I write only in the fear that newspaper reports particularly foreign reports, may alarm you unnecessarily.

More hereafter. Pray inform my brother.

Lady Holland to Lord William Russell at Florence [WPP]

May 14, 1822.

I plead guilty to all the charges, you flatter me by bringing against me. Sadly negligent have I been in writing, but the truth is that as the space widens between correspondents the difficulty becomes greater of communicating, objects appear so trivial for distant expectation that one at length becomes too fastidious for any topick and trusts too much to gazettes and family letters, however as you complain you shall have enough in future to remove at least the worst that of silence, but how far you will gain by receiving sterile or frivolous letters it will not be my business to ascertain. I shall only obey. I have at length been at Ampthill, a painful duty fulfilled and repugnance surmounted, not without cruel recollections and great anguish of mind.† Woburn of course, where both

* The duel took place in Kensington Gardens. They fired at the same time; the Duke of Buckingham missed and the Duke of Bedford fired in the air. Lord Lynedoch and Sir W. W. Wynne were the seconds.

† There were perhaps associations with her daughter Georgiana Fox, who died aged ten in 1819, and was buried at Millbrook near Ampthill.

Billikins and Bettina

my hosts were full of soothing and tender attentions; I never saw the place in greater beauty or abounding more in splendid comforts.

The Pavillion has been crowded to excess with persons of all parties enough to make the *distinction* the being excluded. Matrimonial schemes for the daughter of the favourite* have been the object in view, hitherto all have proved abortive, the last attempt has been upon Lord Gower† – floating dukedom in the vista, and other shadows of royal favor have not dazzled; the favorite's pleasing son Lord Francis has been trying for the modest unaffected heiress, Miss Sparrow, but without success; the favorite herself maintains her post firmly. She conducts herself well and in a favorable contrast to her haughty predecessor, she governs by smiles to all around, a better mode than by sneers and insolent speeches. Those who see her intimately observe the weight of favor on her spirits. She is overcome with the tedium of her life and scarcely conceals the oppression. She is however accused of being sufficiently alive to the goods of life and as the vulgar say of 'making hay etc., etc.' I hear the obsequious wheedling of Madame de Lieven to the long, lank Marquis is ludicrous, and though not overburthened with intellectual gifts still he has a portion of low Irish fun, which makes him see her drift and expose her to bystanders, there have been some comical scenes, too long to detail, between them at her own house.

John is living here nothing materially amiss with him, only occasional derangements from over fatigue and the bad atmosphere in the House of Commons; he distinguished himself considerably by his speech on Reform. Upon the chapter of the event in Kensington Gardens I shall be silent. It made me quite sick and bilious for 4 days altho' I heard it from the Duke himself the first intelligence. I thank you for the verses but cannot admire them nor do I thoroughly understand the Italian, which seems somewhat involved.‡ Now I have written this *galimatias* you must give me some sense in return. *Apropos*, one of the prettiest girls in town is Eliza Russell,§ so modest and innocently gay. I quite love her, and she is a great delight to both D. and Dss., the latter is invariably kind to her. How is your pretty boy? I hear of Lady William's beauty and *agrémens* from all parts.

* George IV's favourite at this time was the Marchioness Conyngham.
† George Granville Leveson Gower (1786–1861), eldest son of the 2nd Marquess of Stafford. He married in 1823 Harriet Howard, daughter of Viscount Morpeth, later 6th Earl of Carlisle. Lord Stafford was not made Duke of Sutherland until 1833.
‡ Lord William had sent Lady Holland some verses by Manzoni, presumably his ode to Napoleon, *Il Cinque Maggio*.
§ Old Lord William's daughter, who made her home with the Duke and Duchess.

63

Billikins and Bettina

Lord William Russell to Lady Holland [HH]

Florence 29 May 1822

... Your anecdotes of society are very amusing – but I am sorry to hear our friend Madame de L has so totally lost her *esprit* & good taste, for she had a prodigious stock of both, & I took a liking to her in consequence of finding a portion of good feeling tacked on to those qualities, ... for I have lately got a peep into diplomacy, at least deep enough to see that Russian diplomats as well as some others, are nothing more than spies, & that their great merit consists in being the first to report the tittle tattle of the Courts they reside at, so if the Ministers wont make love to the favorite, the Minister's wife must see what she can get out of the favorite's husband.

I cannot exactly tell you what our plans are, we are in a state of uncertainty & are rather cogitating a longer stay on the Continent. at least till Parliament meets next year. It has done Bessy so much good, another mild winter might finish the cure, & an English winter might undo all we have done – that is our best & strongest reason for remaining here, then there are a quantity of little ancillary reasons, domestic reasons, agreable reasons, prudent reasons, idle reasons &c,&c. If you did but know the worries that await us in our native land, pinches from poverty & pinches from our near & dear. Here we live in clover. This is the Paradise of small incomes. Imagine the Palazzo Seristori, as fine as any in Florence & finer than any in London, a cook who would dispute the palm with Honoré himself & various other luxuries for £100 a month, to say nothing of these lovely things that cost nothing – the climate & its attributes. It is almost too hot now. I cannot say what we shall do in the great heats. I have been to see Leghorn & the Lucca baths, we shall go to one or the other.

At Via Reggio I saw Princess Pauline, she is very ill, & told me she had given up all hopes of living. Her beauty is gone but her manners are perfect. Old Madame d'Albany is gone to Paris, she is grown so cross that every body was glad to get rid of her. Prince Borghese has taken up her Saturdays, which are agreable enough, his house is beautiful. Tonight he gives a splendid ball, at which my little dear wife (tho I say it who should not) will bear away the palm of beauty & of goodness unrivalled, & from her modesty unenvied.

Florence is dull enough, but we lead the life of turtle doves & know little about society. In English we have Lady Abercorn, Sandwiches, Georgiana Neville & others. *Old* Lord William lives in the house with us.

64

He appears such an unhappy wandering spirit that I was glad to offer him a home, but he is too restless to remain in it & wanders about from tavern to tavern without knowing why or wherefore. I quite pity him.

I went the other day to Leghorn & visited poor Horner's monument.* The medallion on it is strikingly like him, it had been all scribbled over by foolish & unfeeling Englishmen & Captain Fielding had the whole cleaned & put to rights which I thought a most kind act.

I am glad you think there is nothing seriously ailing about John. What are his plans? Does he go to his true & faithful love again. The shabby fellow never writes to me. Give him a scolding. How glad I am you have been to Ampthill, I hope we may yet pass many agreable days there together, & with your most good & worthy husband, whom I love honor & admire with all my heart & soul.

In June Lord William took his wife and boy to Leghorn for sea bathing, and a visit to Mrs Rawdon at the Baths of Lucca enabled them to escape some of the hot weather at Florence.

During the summer the Duke of Bedford was taken seriously ill at Endsleigh, his house in Devonshire.

Lord William Russell to Lady Holland [HH]

Florence 27 June [1822]

I am very grateful to you for having written to me so constantly about my Father, for tho your accounts were always very gloomy, they were a satisfaction to me from being the only ones I got for the first week, & without them I should have been left a prey to the newspapers. At last I have letters from my brothers, which have put me into spirits again, but certainly as you say much is to be feared for the future. I trust he will never go back to Devonshire. It certainly does not agree with him, & I think his health & spirits are better at Woburn Abbey than anywhere else.

By your letter you seem to think we shall go to England. It was my first feeling, but on second thoughts I believe it is better to endeavour to fortify Bessy's health by passing part of our next winter on the Continent, for unhappily the Duchess has taken such a hatred for Bessy & myself, & has so poisoned my Father's mind against us, that I fear our presence

* Francis Horner (1778–1817), Whig politician who died at Pisa and was buried at Leghorn.

gives him no pleasure. This is a great source of unhappiness to me, for you know how I love my Father. This is my real reason for not returning, but it is *entre nous* & I beg it may go no further, however if he should not get better, nothing shall prevent me from passing the winter with him. Bessy's health is so so. Our life is devoted to its service. We go to the Cascine at 6 every morning, breakfast at 8, study till 4, dine, Cascine from 7 to 9. Bottegone* & bed. Monotonous enough but not disagreable. My little boy is a dear little fellow, at least we think it, so much so that he breakfasts dines & lives with us as if he were 20 years old, to the horror & amazement of English mothers, whom Bessy says (& I think truly) adore their children – but cannot bear to have their children with them. Ward said my boy was so well bred, that if Lord Chesterfield had had such a son he need not have written his book. Here is a domestick letter for you – but you are good enough to interest yourself in my domestic affairs, so you will excuse it. Bessy's love.

On reading my letter over I fear by my way of expressing myself you may be led to think I mean to complain of my Father's coldness to me – not at all – nothing can be kinder than the letters he constantly writes me – but I mean my presence in England can give him little pleasure, as we are little at Woburn Abbey & in London he is never allowed to set eyes on us – but do not repeat this to anyone.

Lady William Russell to old Lord William Russell at Genoa [WP]

St Peter & St Paul's day
[Florence, 29 June 1822]

. . . I have just got your letter, my dear Lord William, & must say you seem to me to have the happiest knack of finding delightful abodes I ever fell in with! I am enchanted with the rampart house, & the account of the inn is excellent in its way. You discovered the Seristori for us, in short it is quite a gift, but why do you hurry off so? as you are so pleased with Genoa? is it because we are coming? – but I cannot tell you whether we are coming or not as Lord Lynedoch's long lost letter with details of the duel is arrived & Billikins is construing every line so intently I can get no rational answer from him – in short as to myself I am, as I said, charmed with your account of the house, its position, its view, its space, its price & so forth. As to an awkward approach it does not matter as we need not expect much

* A café renowned for its ices.

rain & moreover I am told nobody keeps a carriage *là bas*, which is pro-digiously oeconomical. . . . Where is Mr Hill?* (The *young* Pallavicinis are here) & where are the Durazzos & Brignolis, Lady Charlotte Lindsay? etc., etc., that form the foreign & national society of Genoa? Are there any gnats? You really have been so circumstantial that you will be surprized at my finding out more questions. The water being good is a great point – the vineyard to walk in for the boy another great point. Sea bathing agrees with him & his Papa – in short get us the refusal of the house & if you have a useful friend (not an ornamental one) who can tell one where to get knives & forks & *laquais de place*, recommend us to him.

By the bye is Mr Hill a likely man to lend one a house if he does not want it himself – or is he *à la* 'dog in the manger'? like the most of our country people? (*entre nous*). At an inn I dread infection for the child & noise for myself, so that *vive les remparts*! I am convinced it is admirable notwithstanding its want of elegance; if we move from hence it will be to Genoa & then we should land at the inn & then see your house, if it is not too much trouble send me the Italian paper about it, I mean the owners account of it if there is such a thing. Is it an apartment or an entire mansion? What a foolish letter I have written, pray forgive me & accept my best thanks for your kindness. . . . Mama at Lucca still. Thank you also for your promised account of the road. No news – the child quite well, and *lo sposo*, too. I am, or rather have been, very much the contrary from sleep-ing with open windows & driving about at night without a hat.

Lady William Russell to old Lord William Russell [WP]

Florence, August 15 [1822]
I am so charmed with the news of your son's marriage† that I must write to congratulate you immediately. I hope the next piece of intelligence will be Eliza's match. Why not to Mr Coussmaker, who will be Lord de Clifford? – a most ancient Barony which I prefer to a modern Dukedom. . . .

We were kept in great suspense about your brother's illness as for a whole week no letters came & we had only newspaper accounts, then came Lady Holland's gloomy dispatches, a cheering one from the good-

* William Noel Hill, English envoy to the Court of Sardinia.
† John Russell married in 1822 Sophia, daughter of Colonel George Coussmaker. She became Baroness de Clifford, her brother predeceasing her.

natured Poodle,* & a whole packet from Endsleigh of different dates with assurances of his recovery – and of course you heard constantly from Eliza.

We are still here as you see & all very well, the boy as fat as a *beccafico* & even poor I have a little flesh on my bones. We discovered after 3 months that the water we drank was poisonous, it had a *dépôt* of chalk & gravel enough to give one every disorder in Buchan's big book†; for the six weeks that I have taken to Santa Croce fountain I have not had one of my usual stomach uneasinesses & really since that period have visibly expanded. We are, alas, going to make a tour, by Parma to Milan & then to Genoa & through Lucca back to Florence – then Rome in October. We shall leave it before Christmas & be at home for the meeting of Parliament which we imagine to be in February, as it sat till August. This plan suits me exactly, I shall get quite well & never be cross or bored any more. You have no idea of the life we lead now – we never see a soul. . . . I am in the Cascine at 6 with the boy, drive & walk till 8½, Billy rides, – then home to breakfast. Dinner at 4, where we miss you still I assure you – drive out again at six, – a bath at 9, and sound sleep at 10. *Bella vita . . . bel piacere – io non so piu che bramare*‡, but you are no musician so you will not discover I am quoting one of Rossini's famous airs.

God bless you, my dear uncle, grant me some of your goodwill, you have lived long enough with me to see my defects. . . . *compatite li*,§ – and my qualities, if I have any. . . . *gradite li.*§

And now once more a thousand congratulations on your son John's good fortune, for I hear the lady is pretty & sensible as well as rich & *très bien née*, which I am fogram‖ enough to mind.

Lord William Russell to Lady Holland [HH]

Florence 24th August [1822]

I received your letter from Holland House yesterday, your account of my father was so uncomfortable that I decided to go to England immedi-

---

* The Hon. Frederick Gerald Byng (1784–1871), son of the 5th Viscount Torrington. Well known in London society as 'the Poodle' from his curly hair. He was a clerk in the Foreign Office and had married his mother's maid, by whom he had one daughter who died as a child to his great grief. He prided himself on having made an honest woman of the mother but never took her into society. He was a great gossip. Lady William, who danced with him as a girl, said: 'Il valsait sans accent, quoique anglais.'

† William Buchan's *Domestic Medicine* published 1769.

‡ 'A good life . . . as pleasant as can be . . . I could not wish for anything better.'

§ 'Have pity on them. . . . Be kind to them.'

‖ i.e. old fashioned.

ately, but letters from my brothers of a little later date changed my decision which was also much influenced by a great reluctance to leave Bessy & my boy. She wishes us all to return bag & baggage, but I am so convinced that her health will be essentially benefitted by passing the severity of the winter in Italy that I cannot resolve to take her from it. I fancy to myself arriving in London in a thick yellow fog (as I once did) finding a letter on the table in my house to say there was no room for us at Woburn (as I once did) or a letter to say they could lodge Bessy but not my boy (as I once did) & to crown all this the horrid spasms were to return to torment poor Bessy. I really think that if this very possible case were to happen I should in my despair leave England for ever. No, my dear Lady Holland, it frightens me & I dare not risk it. Notwithstanding the anxious longing I have to see my father (whom I love with all my heart & soul) after his terrible illness. In my eyes he has but one fault in the world – which is not loving & admiring Bessy enough, but it is natural he should be biassed by the feelings of his wife. Grievances are common to all families, & I tell you mine in the greatest confidence, relying on your never repeating them.

Here all is *couleur de rose* – a blue sky, balmy winds – all the luxuries of life within the compass of my purse. Bessy loved & admired by every body which adds much to my happiness, & indeed she deserves it, for I imagine no human being ever got so near perfection. She desires me to thank you for your kind offer of Ampthill & to say how much pleasure it would give her to accept it, should she go to England. Her health improves rapidly.

I have no news to send you from this. Most people are in the country or at Lucca Baths, where we are going & where there is much company, amusing themselves at the expense of M. Demidoff,* a Russian who gives balls & suppers, one of which was to have taken place on a Thursday, but the pious Queen sent *gens d'armes* to his door to seize anyone who ate *gras* on Friday morning. The [*torn*] same Demidoff also shocked her Majesty [*torn*] modesty by having a woman to wipe [*torn*] he came out of the bath & she ordered him to change the wipers sex. You see what a moral religious country I am living in.

You know Mr Shelley was drowned. Lord Byron has had a row at Leghorn. The Captain of his Yatcht [*sic*] Mr Tyrawley† hoisted a pennant

---

* Count Nicholas Demidoff (1773–1828) was the father of Anatole, who married Princess Mathilde Bonaparte.

† Edward John Trelawny (1792–1881), friend of Shelley and Byron. A naval officer of H.M.S. *Despatch* boarded Byron's boat at Leghorn and took away her pennant. Byron, who was at Pisa, wrote to Trelawny on 10 August 1822: 'I always foresaw and

Billikins and Bettina

in the presence of an English brig of war, which is contrary to naval etiquette, the Lieutenant of the brig, being shocked at the Yatcht's audacity sent a boat on board & hauled it down. When Lord B's captain reported the circumstance to him at Pisa Lord B said, if I had hoisted a pennant I should have defended it, but Mr T taking this for a hint set off to fight the lieutenant, but the Captain of the brig suspecting the business put the Lieutenant in arrest. Lord B then challenged the Captain – but he refused to fight, & has sent the whole proceedings to the Admiralty. Lord B goes to Genoa with his belle.

LORD WILLIAM'S DIARY

My father being ill with a paralytic stroke, I left Florence Monday 26 August at 4 a.m. with Albert, at 6 p.m. I was at Bologna, at 7 p.m. Tuesday at Alexandria, ½ past 5 Wednesday morning at Turin, kept there 4 hours as the Minister of Foreign Affairs was not up. At 5 p.m. at Susa, crossed the Mont Cenis in a beautiful moonlight night, stopped at Chambéry to sleep. 5 p.m. on Friday at Lyons, at 8 p.m. on Sunday I passed under the walls of Paris & at 11 p.m. on Monday I arrived at Boulogne. Went to London in a steam packet in 13 hours with a strong adverse wind. Found my father in a melancholy state of health, tho I hope not dangerous; his mouth distorted, the muscles on one side of his face unnerved & shocking to look at. Met Foscolo* at Woburn Abbey, an agreable man.

Lady William Russell to old Lord William Russell [WP]

Florence, Sept 21 [1822]

How can you suppose me to be such a *mauvaise tête* as to be angry at advice? I take it most gratefully & am willing to follow it when convinced. What provokes me & makes me furious is when people go whispering behind your back wondering why you *do* or why you *dont* so & so, etc.,etc., smirking up to you on meeting like so many Judases. All I detest is hypocrisy. I should like to have the talent without the pawpawness of Aretina – not to be the 'flagellum Principum' but the scourge of double-dealers. I assure you & I think you will believe it, that I am ready to do anything that is right as to our return home & that no selfish motives told you that they would take every opportunity of annoying me in every respect.'
Works of Byron, ed. Prothero, vi, 103.

* Ugo Foscolo (1778–1827), Italian poet and patriot, who lived in England after 1816. The Duke of Bedford's catalogue of the Woburn Abbey Marbles was prefaced by an extract from Foscolo's poem *Le Grazie*.

70

would induce me to decoy my husband from his country & family. We have not been very long abroad – just 15 months. My health is better & was wretched I assure you. An English winter in the *beau milieu* of my convalescence is not likely to contribute to its progress, but that cannot be helped; our purse is not overgrown but that must be endured, & *my* existence in your family is unpleasant which also is a cross that I must bear as cheerfully as I can. I cannot be foolish enough to repine with the *adorable* husband I am blessed with for my lot, thank God, is as happy as this world can make it, but I mean to insinuate that flesh & blood cannot always be so completely subdued by the spirit as to prefer a bad climate, bad health, narrow circumstances, cold relations governed by an artful *Regente* – to a quiet, peaceable happy domestic life – one's husband, one's child, one's parent always by one's side keeping the same hours, basking in sunshine. One's own sensations arising from bad health mitigated & daily obliterating – no tiny worries of an economical nature. This is a faithful picture you must allow – at the same time I declare to God I never urged Lord William's staying abroad, for he naturally likes it as much as I do, & if he did not it would entirely destroy *my* pleasure in any place whatsoever. Our intentions were as when you left us, to remain part of the winter abroad so as to be in England for the meeting of Parliament. This was before the Duke's deplorable accident. When we first heard of his illness it was by the newspapers, it made Lord William very uneasy but as it was immediately after that pleasant hoax of Mr Creevey's about Lord Hardwicke & the cricket ball & we got no letters from England Lord William did not think of setting off – then came several letters together, Lord Tavistock saying 'If my father grows worse & it should be necessary for you to come home you may depend on my letting you know.' I proposed our returning, when many considerations made Ld Wm prefer our original plan & that *he* should travel speedily to England & see his father, which he did. I could not with the child go *ventre à terre* day & night. Here I now am & have been 3 weeks as wretched as any poor woman can be & shall be so till the day I see my best comfort again – do not laugh at my conjugal tenderness. It is a proof of immense confidence my writing in such a style to you, my dear Lord William, so burn my foolish letter, it is written from the heart & immediately on receiving yours of the 6th when you had just seen my dear Billikin. Unworthy man, who did not appreciate that happiness as I would do. Alas! Alas! I am very nervous & my tiresome stomach not well, which is owing to the autumn; when the weather settles it will go off, as it is it is nothing like the past years.

I am annoyed at Lord John's letters, he accuses his brother of imprudence & impropriety in his correspondence with his father – he himself took huff at some political & literary allusions – so they are all in a state of affront, which I ought to be accustomed to as I never met with so touchy a tribe in my days on the score of the epistles. I never read Lord William's to his family as you may suppose. I only know that he takes great pleasure ever since I have known him in writing very long letters to his father & his brothers – & about a dozen rebuffs has he met with on the subject, he certainly is not much given to wound people by his conversation & therefore the whole concern is quite a mystery to me! He tells me he never recollects *what* he writes. I am sorry he should have occasional bursts of affection that overflow in him so constantly repelled poor fellow, & really cannot understand what is the matter. Lord Tavistock I do not include as he has more good sense & less vanity – *expliquez-moi cela?* I really am a second Lady Westmorland, so I will tear myself away. Pray forgive such a prosy production & commit it to the flames.

LORD WILLIAM'S DIARY

On the 19 September I left London with George Russell. Arrived Paris 22nd, lodged Hotel du Danube. Dined with Worcester & his new wife (shocking)* & Sir C. Stuart. Got to Brig on Saturday, found the town full of English who had been prevented from crossing the Simplon owing to a heavy fall of snow. Crossed the next morning, the snow 8 or 10 feet deep, went in a little cart with Sir C. Greville.† Arrived at Florence on 2nd October, Bessy's birthday, & found her & my boy, (thanks be to God) in good health.

[The Russells left Florence for Rome in October.]

At the gates of Rome we heard that Count Parisani had taken the Palazzo Sacrissanti on the Quirinal Hill for us. Count P. is an old friend of Bessy's, a worthy, obliging old man, devoting himself to her. She likewise found the Count & Countess Appony, the Austrian Ambassador, delighted to see her, Princess Czartorisky, an old Polish lady, & many others.

Lord William Russell to Lord Tavistock at Arlington Street [WP]

Rome Oct 24 [1822]

We arrived here last night, all in good health. I was in hope to have

* Henry, Earl of Worcester, subsequently 7th Duke of Beaufort, had married his deceased wife's half-sister.
† Major-General Sir Charles Greville K.C.B.

72

found a letter from you, but was disappointed, it is some time since I have had any account of my Father. I trust the next will be favorable.

You ought to come to Rome. I know nothing more delightful than one's sensations of entering this once famed city, formerly the abode of all that was great & good & accomplished on the earth, tho now the pigstye of all that is grovelling & corrupt. Fancy standing on the spot where Cicero denounced Catiline, fancy seeing the same columns that saw Brutus kill Caesar, & Horace getting away from the bore . . . St Peter's alone is worth the journey – but the journey is a great amusement, from Florence here by Perugia (the road we took) is perfectly beautiful, one continual garden, bounded by hills, watered by rivers, & strewed with antiquities. You drive along the banks of the Clitumnus where the white cattle were fed, you cross the Tiber, you go under 'Candida Soracte', in short you are delighted in mind & body. On our arrival at the gates we were directed to the Palazzo Sacrissanti. . . . (The air is the best in Rome, which I wished for the boy), the Pope is my neighbour, & from my windows I see the original of the statue erected in Hyde Park,* it stands on the Quirinal Hill.

Since writing the above I have received your letter & am delighted at my Father's success in shooting. . . . If you have got £50 or 100 to throw away I could buy you a quantity of pretty ornaments for Oakley in marble or *pietra dura*.

Duke of Bedford to Lady William Russell at Rome [PRP]

Hastings, Nov 21 [1822]

I have to thank you for a most kind and affectionate letter which I received in London, in my way from Woburn to this place, where I am come in search of that most desirable and most enviable of all blessings, health. Whether I shall find it or not, God alone knows, but the progress I have made since William left us is very slow – if I could persuade myself that it was sure, I should be content. At all events the old remedy *patienza* is always at hand, and to that with a grateful and cheerful mind I submit. I am not yet permitted to write, but I am determined that you shall have my acknowledge from my own hand, though it must be brief, and waste no time in preface. I am delighted to have so pleasant account of my little grandson, but you have no right to call him 'ugly' if he at all resembles the drawing William had of him.

* The statue of Achilles by Westmacott, erected in 1822 in the park at Hyde Park Corner, in honour of the Duke of Wellington.

Your paper *café au crême*, looks always alarming, and looks as if it had passed through the fumigating ordeal of the Office of Health.

Poor Canova! What a loss he is to the arts! And to you individually he will be a sad loss at Rome. His society was so cheerful, and the free and unreserved manner in which he always conversed on his art, was delightful. I trust you will be kind to the poor *abbé** for his sake. The loss to him must be irreparable. I never saw two brothers more attached.

Pray tell William I have had two very kind letters from him from Florence, and will write to him very soon. He is most generous and affte in so often thinking of me, but you must restrain his generosity, and not allow him to expend his 'little all' in presents to me. Those he names will be most acceptable, and tell him I shall write to him soon by my amanuensis on the *belle arti*, which are always interesting to me. As you were on the eve of departure when he last wrote, I trust I shall soon hear of your safe arrival in the Eternal City.

Our little author is here, reading to us every evening his proof sheets of his tragedy (Don Carlos). I hear by the bye, William has also commenced dramatick author.†

My eyes and head both tell me I must stop. The Duchess's love, mine to Billikins. I am glad you are pleased with the engraving, God bless you, ever your affte Papa.

Duke of Bedford to Lady William Russell at Rome [PRP]

W.A. Dec. 19, 1822.

Encore ce vilain café au lait! but it no longer alarms me, for containing only a most kind letter from you, there can be no plague in it; and if it really be *à la chemise de la reine Isabelle*‡, I can only say not that it 'speaks volumes', but simply quires, as to her want of *propreté*. I congratulate you on being so well, and earnestly recommend you to keep so, by staying at Rome as late as you can. Billikins is not likely to be wanted in the House of

---

* The Abate Giovanni Battista Sartori-Canova was the son of Antonio Canova's mother by her second marriage. The half-brothers were devoted to each other and after 1800 the Abate lived entirely with the sculptor.

† Lord John Russell published in 1822 *Don Carlos or Persecution, a tragedy in five acts*. It was in blank verse in imitation of Juvenal and went through five editions in a year. 'It has been perhaps more unfavourably criticised than any tragedy in the language.' Spencer Walpole, *Life of Lord John Russell*, i, 102.
Lord William had translated Monti's tragedy *Caius Gracchus*.

‡ Isabella of Castile, while besieging Granada, vowed she would not change her under linen until the town was taken. The siege lasted three years.

Commons till after Easter, and though March is March all the world over, I am sure that it is less detestable in Rome than in London. I cannot help wishing that you had named the Duchess in your letter. It is an object near to my heart that all misunderstandings should be done away and I cannot help feeling anxious, *most* anxious about it – should I not get over this protracted illness, it will smooth the pillow of a dying man on his way to the tomb, and should it please God that I am to recover it will render my remaining [*torn*] more cheerful and more [*torn*]. Do not write to me on this subject – *verbum sat sapienti*, and I leave it to your own judgement and feelings to act as you think best. The *surprise* on New Year's Day will at all events be most gratifying to me.

Lord William Russell to Lord Tavistock [WP]

Rome Christmas Day [1822]

I received lately your letter with your 12 reasons for not coming to Rome any one of which I think sufficient to deter you from making so long a journey, you are better & happier where you are & I should enjoy nothing more than to eat my Christmas dinner with you this very day. What a capital piece of beef you will have, what a turkey & what pies – if I get any beef at all for my dinner it will be baked dry as a coal. The Italian proverb says *qui sta bene non si muove* – & as you are *benissimo* I do not see why you should budge. I am just returned from a shooting excursion, we killed 57 woodcocks – we went to the house of a farmer in the low ground not far from the Pontine marshes. He had 1000 cows & 500 oxen & buffaloes . . . but all in a state of nature, you never saw such farming – fortunately they cannot exhaust the ground, they have but to scratch it & throw down the seed & up comes a magnificent crop in spite of themselves. The difficulty is to get it reaped, for the air is so pestilential in summer that the reapers die in the fields – but what is pleasant to see in that country is that every man who is not a pauper keeps his horse & his gun. They never walk & the chase being open to every body – no peasant is without his gun – perhaps this is the opposite extreme to our system, but certainly it is more pleasant to see these poor people enjoying their sport than cooped for months in a prison for killing a pheasant, snaring, night shooting &c,&c, is carried on with the consent of the proprietors. Yet game is plentiful & the market always full. The other day I shot a *chevreuil*.

I cannot tell you how happy it has made me to hear that Russell is to go to a public school – be it Eton or Westminster or elsewhere a public

75

school is what is necessary & is that which will add to his happiness hereafter & be a source of great satisfaction to yourself. I grant that the system
of education is bad – that a boy learns little, that there are many objections
to a public school – but it fits a boy to be a man – to know his fellow
creatures – to love them – to be able to contend with the difficulties of life –
to attach friends to him – to take a part in public affairs – to get rid of his
humours & caprices & to form his temper & manners – to make himself
loved & respected in the world – in short it is an essential part of our
constitution, & makes our patricians so superior to those of the continent.
I wish you could see how a young Roman nobleman is brought up – you
would not wonder at his turning out the being he is. Westminster feelings
will be much hurt at losing the Russells – but no doubt you have good
reason for preferring Eton & I can only rejoice that he is to have a public
education. I am fully aware the difficulties you have had to decide this
question – an only child is an anxious care – but his being an only child
makes public education more necessary, & I trust you will be rewarded for
your decision by seeing him improve in health & strength. A happy
Christmas to him Lady T & yourself, & many more which I hope we may
pass together with our poor Father in better health.

Lord William Russell to Lady Holland [HH]

Rome Christmas Day [1822]
  Will you ask Lord Holland to accept from me, as a Christmas offering,
& a token of my admiration esteem & love for him, & a proof that (tho far
distant) the first person who occurs to my thoughts as most worthy to
receive a work of Cicero's *De Re Publica* is himself. It has just made its
appearance, published with notes by Abbé Mai.* It is now on my table
but the difficulty is to send it to England before the London booksellers
get it but I will contrive the means. This letter is the *avant-courier* to announce it.
  What would I not give to be present at the exquisite dinner that will be
served up at ½ past 6 in Burlington St today.

> Where Honoré's most savoury bit
> Will be surpassed by Holland's wit

but I daresay you would be as well pleased to be where I am on the
Quirinal Hill – a brilliant sun, the works of Phidias, Praxiteles & the

* Angelo Mai (1782–1854), first custodian of the Vatican. Cardinal in 1838.

Billikins and Bettina

beautiful fountains before my eyes, & the cardinals in their antiquated coaches going to Mass. This is a delightful place & it has done so much good to Bessy's health & my boy is so well that I adore it – the only draw-back is the crowd of English who have turned it into a noisy watering place, fighting, squabbling, scandalizing & making themselves absurd. There are many pleasant foreigners, the Duc de Laval-Montmorency, an agreable man, has replaced Blacas. The whole house of Cavendish is here – Lord Carnarvon with the gout – Lord Kinnaird in high force, Lady West-morland in a piteous way, in the largest palace in Rome – the Duchess of Devonshire, the modern Maecenas as the Romans call her, & many others.

I hear John has written a tragedy. I shall, like you, believe in future, that every work without an author's name is his.

We shall leave this early in February for London, where I hope to produce Bessy in the same health & beauty she is in here. She is more admired here than ever . . .

Commissioned by the Duke of Bedford to buy antique marbles for the sculpture gallery at Woburn, William carried on, during that winter, an anxious correspondence with his father, discussing the merits of each proposed purchase. Fearful of being thought extravagant, he yet could not refrain from urging the Duke to acquire objects that seemed to him great bargains.

'Tho nearly all the antiquities of Rome are disputed and indeed much is buried in uncertainty', wrote Lord William in his diary soon after his arrival at Rome, 'I determined to make a tour with the ablest of the anti-quarians, Mr Nibby.' * With this distinguished and informed Italian, Lord and Lady William spent ten days visiting the sights of Rome.

LORD WILLIAM'S DIARY

Dined at a great dinner at the Duc de Laval Montmorency (French Ambas-sador) – Cardinals Consalvi, Doria, Albani – & all the *Corps diplomatique.*

The dissipation of Rome terrible – dined consecutively with Lord Kinnaird, Austrian Ambassador, Lady Mildmay, Mr Peploe, Lady Mary Stanley, Lord George Cavendish, Duc de Laval, Duchess of Devonshire, & Lord Carnarvon.

There are many clever young men among the English artists, Gibson, who is making a Mars & Cupid for the Duke of Devonshire, Messrs Campbell, Rennie, Wyatt, & a young Westmacott are promising sculptors; there are also several good painters, amongst them Mr Kirkup,† who is making a drawing of

* Antonio Nibby (1792–1839), Italian archaeologist responsible for excavations in the Forum. Author of a guide book to ancient and modern Rome.

† Seymour Kirkup (1788–1880). In 1865 at Florence, Kirkup presented Arthur Russell with two weak drawings of Lord and Lady William Russell.

Bessy for Lady Westmorland. She is also having her picture painted by Agricola*
(a clever young Roman painter) with her little boy.

Lady William Russell to Lord John Russell [PRP]

Rome, Monday 6 Jan. [1823]

Although you don't like letters, as you wrote to me last October, after an interval of two months, I will be indiscreet enough to molest you again *cognato carissimo* – the fact is I was tearing old papers & read over your last production full of kind expressions about henbane & coffee &c.,&c. I am proud to say I now scorn all such 'foreign aids', I sleep without rocking – eat without groaning, have lost my nervousness & my irritability, & am moreover less yellow & less skinny, which is of no great consequence you will say, but as indications of the great truths & important ones I have just mentioned. Your nephew is a youth of great promise – he speaks French like d'Alembert & English like Johnson, – neither lisps, stammers nor mispronounces, is quick, gay, passionate, goodhearted, gentle, ingenious, ruddy, bright-eyed, blue-eyed – fat, strong & healthy. I am as proud of him as you ought to be of Don Carlos, which Lord Kinnaird said he heard was faultless.

The winter is quite northern *physiquement* – *au moral* it is as gay as Paris the year of the great *explosion révolutionaire*, such dinners, balls, French plays, *ricevimenti* and operas as would do honour to London. 450 English expecting to be asked everywhere & to have the best boxes at the theatre, (there being but 33 such) resenting the Romans not turning out of theirs, expecting the Pope to interfere & get up the miracle of the loaves & fishes for them – 12 parsons with their reverend families parading about the Pincio, the Forum, and the Ambassadors routs. I saw their names on a list of chiavaris & the Hanoverian fogram who represents our country here – so my numerical information is correct.

We leave this in February, the first day of Lent 5 or 6 weeks (*au plus tard*) from this time, so if you condescend to write (but I shall not be huffy if you don't) do so immediately & it will just reach me. Your friends the Berry girls have taken possession of the Pincian heights where at noonday the oldest vociferates her jokes *aux échos d'alentour. Elle dirige, commande, observe, dispute avec une éloquence male.*

Is your *prétendue* Lady Elizabeth Grey to marry Lord Ancrum? We affirm it. The Dowager Lord William is here & acting the [*torn*] *amoureux*

* Filippo Agricola (1776–1857).

78

Lady William Russell

The Hon. Mrs Rawdon

from drawings by Agricola

John Russell, 6th Duke of Bedford, from a pencil drawing by Ingres, 1815

with Lady Westmorland,* who sometimes sits up from 9 till 5 in the morning with him *tête à tête*, & at others tells him he is 'like a bad nut, I crack you & find nothing in you'.

Duke of Bedford to Lord William Russell at Rome [WPP]

Woburn Abbey, January 28th 1823

. . . I write once more to that eternal city, principally to certify and confirm all I have said in my preceding letters, respecting the purchases you have made for me, and even to go a step farther by saying that if you exceed the limit I have allowed for purchases of good things by £200 I shall not quarrel with you. I look with hope to a good sarcophagus, and any other genuine sculpture of a good age. . . . Let me entreat of you to be particular as to history and authenticity of any works you may purchase for me, noting such in your memoranda without trusting too much to a frail memory. . . . You must endeavour to inspire Tavistock with a taste for the fine arts, that when I am dead and gone, the interesting pursuit may not be lost sight of at Woburn. It is not incompatible with those of hunting, shooting, or politics. . . .

P.S. Since writing the above I have received a most entertaining letter from Bessy with the new Cicero and the *Re Publica*. Pray thank her for both. I have not heard of any copy of this work having reached England. I shall show it to Lord Spencer this evening, who is here for the shooting finale.

LORD WILLIAM'S DIARY

We intended to have left Rome early in March, but the weather was so bad we did not get away till the 12th. On that day we set off at 11 o'clock. Count & Countess Appony, the Duc de Laval, Captain Fielding & Count Parisani came to take leave of us. Some went as far as the Porto del Popolo with us, & Bessy said her prayers in the church there. Countess Appony & Count Parisani prayed for her conversion, & a happy journey.

The prayers of Bessy's friends for her conversion to the Roman Catholic faith were not to be answered for thirty-seven years.

* Jane Saunders (1780–1857), eccentric and quarrelsome second wife of the 10th Earl of Westmorland.

4+L.W.R.   79

Returning to Florence the William Russells stayed there but a few days. At a concert given by Lord Burghersh, the English Minister, they heard Madame Catalani sing, and Velluti, the last of the great Italian *soprani*.

Moving on to Genoa a few days later, they fell in with Lord and Lady Blessington and Henry Fox. 'To my great joy', wrote this last in his journal on Good Friday, 'I found the William Russells on their way to England. She gave a delightful account of Italy, is quite miserable at going home, and keeps no bounds about the Duchess of B.'[13]

LORD WILLIAM'S DIARY

Our horses were ordered & the carriages packed to go to Turin, but Bessy not being well she preferred going to Nice by felucca. We therefore hired one for 12 louis & embarked the three carriages on board. We left Genoa on March 29th but did not get further than Savona that evening. The spring was breaking forth in all its beauty, the hills covered with olive trees & the plains with fruit trees in blossom, especially the almond; the sea smooth & blue. The next morning we embarked at 6 a.m., but the weather being calm we did not get further than Loana.

Gliding along on the sea with little wind, they made slow progress; sometimes they landed and putting their baggage on mules walked along the precipitous coast, re-embarking next day after a night at an inn. It was five days before they reached Nice. Passing through Cannes, Aix, and Avignon, they drove up the Rhône valley to Lyons and Paris. Leaving his wife there, William set out alone for London.

Duke of Bedford to Lord William Russell [WPP]

Woburn Abbey, Wednesday [1823]

I can only repeat that I am perfectly satisfied with the purchases you made for me in Italy. . . . I sincerely wish it were in my power to offer my house in St James's Square to you and yours, but you know how it is occupied, and I must reserve my own rooms, as in the present uncertain state of my health, I am liable to be called up to town at any time, at a few hours notice. You were certainly guilty of an imprudence in letting your own house for such a long term, but we cannot always have the gift of foresight.

The concluding sentence in your letter gave me great pain. Why should you suppose that the Duchess dislikes you? I can assure you that the very reverse is the case, and I think I know every feeling of her heart. She is ever anxious to show every possible kindness and attention to you, and your brothers, but her spirits are sometimes depressed, and this I think you may readily account for without any great stretch of imagination. *She* indeed, imagines that neither you nor Tavistock, nor John like *her*, and in this I am sure that she is wrong, but the feeling arises from an excess of sensibility, and I cannot blame her.

Lord William Russell to Lady William Russell at Paris [WP]

> Calais. Tuesday night
> 9½ o'clock. 1823

Whilst my bed is preparing, I write you a few hasty & sleepy lines to say I have arrived here in good health & without accident about ¼ of an hour ago – I stopt at the inn at Boulogne, intending to cross from thence, but after I had been some time there the man said he was uncertain whether he should sail or not, & proposed to me to take the packet to myself & pay 15 guineas, this I thought too magnificent so ordered horses, & came on here, too late for the gates but they opened them for me – the London packet does not sail till 12 o'clock tomorrow night, so I have decided to go in the vessell that carries the mail to Dover at 8 o'clock tomorrow morning – the weather is as fine as possible – there is a most excellent new inn at Boulogne, full of hot baths.

I long to hear how you have been dearest love, take great care of yourself – especially keep regular hours with regard to eating &c. kiss my pretty boy for me, & remember me to Mama. I leave you to go to my bed, so God bless you.

I will write again soon.

Lord William Russell to Lady William Russell at Paris [WP]

> Dover April 23. Wedy 1823
> 2 o'clock.

I am here about ½ an hour we had a tolerable passage, tho' much rain. Knowing you will be anxious to hear how I got over the water, I hasten to write a few lines whilst my luggage is searching & my dinner preparing – I have not yet decided how I shall go to London – I had made an agreement with a French courier to go shares with him in a post chaise but he has just sent me an excuse I fancy when he heard my name he took fright – I had for companions in the packet boat Mlle Anatole & 6 French Opera dancers – They did not look tempting but were amusing from their constant gaiety throut all misfortunes – Pray ask George Russell to bring over my coat – send to the tailor for it – My baggage is searched – I have to pay for 70 lb of books & the *jeu de margan* – but I do not know how much – The other things were passed quickly & civilly by the custom house – You will find in a little drawer of the salon of your hotel some letters of mine – You may either keep them or burn them – I hope your health is good – for God's sake take great care & see what regularity will do for you – for it got much shattered by the long journey – however I have no doubt that a tranquil mind & bodily rest will bring you back to what you were at Rome – I think your constitution has taken so favourable a turn, & that the foundation is so good, that if your mind & body are not worried & worn you will do well, even in this vile climate, pray keep to the plan you fixed upon when I was with you – & do not let any foolish trifles annoy you – How is my good little boy – I hope his cold is better, kiss him for his papa – . . . My love to Mama.

I have ate a good dinner of tough chops & a few grass – & am off for London in a hack chaise – it will not cost little more than the dilly with all my baggage – & I cannot wait.

God bless you, I will write from London.

I wrote from Calais.

Lord William Russell to Lady William Russell at Paris [WP]

St James's Square April 24th 1823

I am just come from the House of Commons, we had John's debate for reform, & made a good division, he spoke well, but feebly, I mean physically feebly – for he has a violent cold & looks ill – as for Tavistock it is shocking to see him, he is a perfect skeleton, I never saw a man so altered in my life, but the worst of it is, that the doctors disagree about his complaint, but Yeats thinks it is only disordered functions – nothing organic – tomorrow there is to be a consultation on him to which Abernethy is to be added, I shall be anxious to hear their report. Lady T. is looking fat & blooming but is terribly out of favor in a certain quarter, she tells me her treatment has been so sorry that she can stand it no longer – the devil is actively at work & full of mischief. I dread your coming into this nasty mess – before your health is good, & your temper proof against any storm, I fear a slight breeze would ruffle it, in which case you will be blown to sea in a week – *capite*? I got here at 1 at night, the ladies were at Almacks & did not come home till 4, Mrs Bennett & Eliza,* I mean, the house was lent to them from the amiable motive of wishing to keep out the family especially the older branch – but more of this when we meet – in the meantime I am glad the Bennetts profit, as they belong to our corps – the poor & needy – it is an ill wind as the proverb has it. In the House of Lords tonight I saw Lady Harrowby who was most anxious about you, Sandon wrote her word you were as handsome & plump as ever, so you must get up your good looks not to disappoint them in London. It is fortunate you were away this winter, the weak, the sick, the old, & the poor were all killed by the cold; so many deaths never were known. I have seen Lady Bath† who looks shockingly & coughs perpetually, she asked most anxiously about you, & offered us rooms in her house, I thanked her much but declined – as I think with the number of children she has it would be scarcely fair to encumber her, besides Lord Cawdor is in the house. The Ts. are come to remain – tomorrow I shall breakfast at Holland House, & then go to Woburn with Seymour‡ where I shall remain till Monday, & then return to attend the House of Commons.

I shall look out for a lodging for us in an hotel – but much as I wish to have you dearest love, I cannot press your return for the weather is horrible, a cold cutting wind, & a melancholy sun obscured by the fog & smoke – London is a dirty hole after Italy – where summer suns give light & heat where the wind woos you lovingly, here the sun gives neither light or heat & the wind cuts you in two. I saw Lord Forbes in the House of Commons he goes to Paris on Saturday – there is no one at Woburn Abbey but Lady Gordon,§ she has been in too great affliction to see any of her family, but thought she could support the tranquility of the Abbey, & the soothing language of the Duchess, I assure you it was not Rogers who told me tho' it looks like it – I found a most kind letter from my Father here, inviting me to go & see him, the last accounts of him are very good. God bless you dearest love, I am going to my lonely bed, & will finish this letter tomorrow, good night.

How did you & my sweet boy sleep – I hope well. I am going to breakfast at Holland House & will not close this letter till my return. Sweet Bess

* Old Lord William Russell's daughters. Gertrude, the elder, married in 1816 the Hon. Henry Grey Bennett, son of the 4th Earl of Tankerville.

† The Hon. Isabella Byng, daughter of the 4th Viscount Torrington, wife of the 2nd Marquess of Bath. She was Lord William's aunt.

‡ Colonel Henry Seymour married the Hon. Emily Byng, Lord William's aunt.

§ Widow of Sir William Duff Gordon who died 8 March 1823.

I am just come from Holland House, no news. I am off for Woburn from whence I will write again. Poodle Byng's mother is dead, mourning for us – God bless you darling, take care of yourself & love

Your affte & faithful husband

Love to Mama.

Lord William Russell to Lady William Russell at Paris [WP]

Woburn Abbey. Sunday. 27 [April] 1823

My disappointment was great dearest Bessy when I found the post of today brought me no letter from you, surely you can neither have written on the Monday or Wednesday, otherwise I should have got your letter today, what can have been the cause – it makes me uneasy & fidgety – but patience till tomorrow, when I shall certainly find a letter from you on my return to London. I came down here on Friday & found my Father much improved in his looks, his face has nearly recovered its form, but his complexion is changed to a ghastly sort of white – the pains in his head still continue at night but in the day he enjoys himself, & his spirits are good, he appears glad to see me, & takes great interest in the purchases I made for him at Rome – which pleases me as I dreaded his having been set against them by the Goths, the Duchess received me with the greatest affection, & appears anxious to please me, tho' evidently *génée* & constrained in my presence. She also talks of you as if she intended to be civil if not kind to you, expresses a desire to hear you sing &c – There is nobody here but Lady Gordon dressed like Lady Russell of melancholy memory.* She wept much when she first saw me, but has since appeared cheerful & the same as ever. The accounts of Tavistock are very uncomfortable – he has had a consultation of physicians, but it ended very unsatisfactorily both from their differing in opinion & from their being unable to determine the nature of his complaint – the functions are all wrong, & his food gives him no nourishment without their being able to discover the cause – he is certainly in a very precarious & alarming state – Yet he is in good spirits & confident about himself – I am glad you are not here, (much as I long to kiss your soft cheek,) for the weather is detestable. Yesterday it never ceased raining with a cold N.E. wind – today is better, tho' cold. I will not describe to you

* Portraits of Rachel Lady Russell, widow of William Lord Russell, who was beheaded in 1683 for complicity in the Rye House Plot, depict her in widow's weeds.

the miseries of last winter, you have already too much distaste for this poor foggy island – but they are something unheard of – the surgeons lost so many patients that they refused to perform operations – but no more of this . . .

How is my good boy, I feel very lonely without him & his dear mother, my thoughts & heart & happiness are all with you sweet Bessy, & I love you more than anything in the world. I am summoned to ride with my Father. God bless you.

St. James's Square – Monday morning. – I was near fainting when the stupid old porter told me on my arrival here there was no letter for me – but two minutes afterwards he gave me your dear consoling letter written on Thursday. God bless you for writing it & making me so happy, the account of yourself is as good as I could expect, a little more rest & care will bring you round, & I was much diverted by your account of the boy dear little fellow, but if the *bonne* has any cutaneous disorder which she could give to the boy, I would pack her off post haste – I have seen a good nurse like poor Davies whom I will write to you about tomorrow. Lady Gordon says she can give you an excellent Swiss *bonne* in about a year. I shall probably send my letter tomorrow to Sir C. Stuart – send for it – I shall be able to go for you in another week. Old Lynedoch says he will go with me. I am going to spend the evening in the Commons to hear a long debate. I have seen nobody in London yet – the weather is vile, you cannot come here till it gets better – God bless you pretty love –

I am your true, adoring, admiring, *faithful* husband

Lord William Russell to Lady William Russell at Paris [WP]

St. James's Square. Tuesday [1823]
I wrote to you yesterday by the post – I will send this today by the Foreign Office – you have been very idle about writing sweet love, as yet I have but one letter from you, & I have been nearly a week in England – if you knew what pleasure your letters gave me, you would not be so sparing of them – our debate was adjourned last night till today – we had no good speaking, McDonald was heavy & pompous, & the others the former without the latter – Lord Leveson Gower made his first Speech, & acquitted himself tolerably well – tho' it was more made up of words than matter – The Duke of Wellington has not been spared, some have been very severe upon him, indeed he appears to have been cruelly humbugged as well as

our friend Sir C. Stuart but politics bore you, so to go from public to private matters, I told you yesterday I had seen a nice looking nurse. I came to town by the coach, & having a cold chose the inside tho' it was occupied by a woman & child, whom I found out after some time to be a wet nurse of Alexander's leaving the Abbey, she appeared an excellent decent nurselike looking person – she told me she had been 17 months with the Duchess & was going to town in search of a place – I am sure you would have been pleased with her, she has two children of her own. Eliza tells me she is a most admirable person, but then you would not like to take anyone who had lived at the Abbey – I asked the woman if she was to be lodged in this house she told me no, . . . My Father told me I had done well to let my house – I said I intended to lodge in an hotel – he did not answer but looked annoyed – Bennett has said publickly, he will not remain in this house, unless we live in it, everything is given to them in preference to the sons, play, Opera boxes &c, but B. behaves very well about it. I have not yet had time to enquire about rooms in the hotels – but will do so tomorrow or next day – however I would not have you come home yet, the weather is odious, cold & black, it would certainly make you ill or melancholy. You neither gave me the mosaic for my Father, nor your banking book to be made up, I sold a horse yesterday but I cannot yet hear what he fetched. You never yet saw anything like the state of the family – quarrellings, intrigues, repetitions, misrepresentings &c. but I will reserve all the anecdotes till we meet, they are of all sorts, comical & disgusting, but I trust you will be able to hear them & bear them all with indifference, looking upon the calumnies & intrigues of that ill conditioned madwoman, as unworthy of your anger or consideration, & the intentions of those who repeat them as either mischievous or foolish, & consequently to be despised & let pass by – like the idle wind which you respect not – but I fear you will respect 'the wind' too much, whether it be the breeze of calumny, or the blast of Boreas – sweet love – I know you will have a difficult task to play – I know I am bringing you from the soft air, the sun, the charm, the indolence of Italy, to encounter the keen wind, the cold, the difficulties of England, & above all the differences, the intrigues, the wickedness that unhappily pervades my family. Nobody believe me, regrets or feels more than I do the sacrifices I cause you to make – it weighs upon my mind more than you imagine, for I know you to be a gentle, delicate, fine spun piece of texture whose mind is as ill calculated to encounter a difficulty or trouble, as your body is to resist the cold, & I frequently ask myself whether it is fair, too whether it is absolutely necessary to bring you from so much

enjoyment to so much worry – I believe as yet that it is my duty to urge you to live in your husbands country, yet if on this coming trial you again experience the sickness & worry you did before, if you again suffer in mind & body to that extent – I will leave Parliament & the Army, & go & spend & end my days in some southern climate with you – but for God's sake do not urge me too hastily to take this step, think what it is for a man to live out of his Country, to waste his life in nothing, to sit down a nonentity for the rest of his being. I need say no more than this, for your own intelligent mind will see the whole extent of its bearing – perhaps dear love, you may think I am taking up this subject too seriously & that it is uncalled for at this moment, but when I think how well & happy you were in Italy – how often you reproached me for bringing you away, & how little cheering the prospect I have to offer you in this country is, I cannot help thinking deeply & often on this subject – to me there is none more important – but I will bore you no longer, & only recommend you to cloath your body in furs & velvet – & your mind with indifference to those foolish trifles, that are so apt to make the summum of our happiness or misery in this world – after all we are not sent here to eke out our existence in pleasure or indolence, it is our duty to encounter, to contend with, to bear with the bad passions of our fellow creatures – to live in a perpetual state of trial, in short to act the parts allotted to us, with as much circumspection & care as a player would on the stage with a large & severe audience before him – so remember dear love your part in the great drama of life is to play the daughter in law of a wicked envious stepmother & your reward if you play it well (& no small one either) *will be to smoothe the pillow of a dying man* – to say nothing of contributing to a husband's happiness – So ends my sermon. I saw T. this morning he is rather better, yet I am not easy about him, he is cheerful & confident – How is my pretty good boy – Little Cosmo* is come out a prodigy of talent, he has the most wonderful memory ever known & repeats verses by the dozen, I suspect he is an opposition prodigy to ours, but we shall be beat out of the field without Mrs Rawdon to stand by us. I have seen nobody in London yet, but am going to sally forth now to make visits. The great news is that the Duke of Devonshire danced four times with Lady Elizabeth Conyngham at his own ball – some looked upon it as decisive.†
God bless you dearest love, I long to see you . . .

* Lord William's half-brother, aged six.
† The 6th Duke of Devonshire never married.

Billikins and Bettina

Lord William Russell to Lady William Russell at Paris [WP]

St James's Sq. May 1 1823

Yesterday & this morning I was very uneasy at not hearing from you, &
begun to fancy myself neglected, but today I have your letter written on
Friday – I cannot imagine why it is so long coming – today we ought to
have the letter of Monday – they must imagine you & I are conspiring, so
think it necessary to read our letters, but they will find us occupied in more
important matters, one another's love – Your account of the boy is delightful – Yeats says a little ink would take away the ringworm – I have not
mentioned it to anyone else – I have seen the Lieven, she adores me, & has
given me two *rendezvous pour jaser* – neither of which have I kept – tonight
I shall see her at Esterhazy's ball – the women adore me & make much of
me, but I cannot make out whether it is for my own *beaux yeux*, for your
sake, or because my Father & Tavistock are sick, & they forget the existence of Russell – Vanity attributes it to the first cause, truth to the second,
& knowledge of the world to the last – *qu'en pensez-vous ma belle* – In the
meantime I make hay whilst the sun shines – don't be jealous – I have a
most curious letter by todays post from the Duchess she wishes to be well
with us, you as well as I – & I have accepted the stretched out hand – &
squeezed it besides – you will perhaps allow your haughty, proud, unbending, unforgiving mind to disapprove of what I have done but you are
wrong, I will convince you of it when we meet – in the meantime put the
case by till that time, & do not brood upon it like a hen over her eggs – wait
till the old cock comes to assist – have more respect for him & believe he
does right sometimes – in the mean time I will send you her letter by
tomorrows courier – About this day week I will leave London tho' I am
by no means anxious for you to come here – the weather is horrible cold &
foggy – even Albert says he is quite *fracassé* by the *brouillard* – I came
from the House of Commons at ½ past 5 this morning & found my cold
so heavy, that I have kept my bed, & taken perspiring powders – Saturday
& Sunday I shall spend at Woburn – T. is much the same, the accounts
of my Father are so so – The post horn has arrived so God bless you,
kiss my pretty good boy for me, & believe me your true & faithful love –
how is Mama & her bile – give my love to her – The *bonne's* scaly arms
must be nuts to her. Adieu.

Billikins and Bettina

Lord William Russell to Lady William Russell at Paris [WP]

London. Friday, May 2. 1823.

Today I got your letter of Monday, giving but a melancholy account of your health – if you would walk more it would do you good – You would oblige me by keeping a carriage & going every day to the Bois de Boulogne – it would do you good & the boy good – it is a foolish & poor bit of economy not to keep a carriage – People will think I starve & stint you – pray get a carriage, it will not ruin me – Besides it is respectable – Your account of the boy pleases me much, & I laughed heartily at all you told me of him & Mama's head &c.

I have just had an interview with the Lieven she repeated all her former confidences – I fancy it is a relief to her to pour out her full heart. She adores you & will write to you, she means to propose to you to go to Ems. I have seen Dowbiggin * he has let our house till the end of July for 475 £ – he says the house is rotten, dirty, tumbling down & good for nothing, I am much inclined to take a new one & furnish it completely – he says it would cost about £1200 – I think I could manage the money without distressing us – with respect to our finances you cannot expect them to be flourishing after all our purchasing & travelling. But I have looked at the book & considered our ways & means, & I think by the end of June we shall be without a debt & without a shilling, many people would be glad to be in so good a state so don't fret.

I was last night at Esterhazy's ball, very brilliant, many enquiries about you, & a great desire to see you – tonight I dine at Holland House & shall perhaps go afterwards to Devonshire House, a concert, so you see I amuse myself – however I wish I was with you – this day week I shall set out for Paris – tomorrow I go to Woburn & return Monday – I enclose herewith the letter I spoke to you about yesterday, it is a curious production – yet if we must live in England it is better to be well than ill with her Grace – she has so many means of annoying us – which I should be glad to be rid of by a small sacrifice – don't destroy the letter – keep them till I come, the weather is better but foggy – John goes with me to W. A. tomorrow – & perhaps to Paris – Lady Holland has offered us rooms at Holland House till we get lodgings, she will write to you about it – I declined – there is nothing like being *fier* when you have not a halfpenny – the post is going – God bless you – kiss boy blue, love to Mama.

* Thomas Dowbiggin, of Mount Street, was an agent for general house business.

I have a letter from Laval. With a thousand loves to you – my cold is much better –

Yesterday I took James's powders & laid in bed, but today I am about again & quite well. Tavistock is much the same – tomorrow he sees Bailey again – I am not easy about him – God bless you. I gave Wrio* a Paris waistcoat – that caused the enclosed letter –

Duchess of Bedford to Lord William Russell [WPP]

[*enclosed with previous letter*]

Woburn Abbey, Wednesday. [1823]

My dearest Billy,

Your kindness in thinking of dear Wrio is most gratifying to me, for I assure you notwithstanding all you have heard to the contrary, that my feelings towards you have never varied. I have nothing to convince you but my word, of that you are a very good judge, if it is to be depended upon or not. The total change in Lady William's opinion of me, and her affection for me, is very mortifying, and what I sincerely regret, but as my conscience is perfectly free from having said or done anything against her her husband or her child, I can only trust time will convince her that she has been misinformed. You may ask those you have perfect faith in, if ever they heard me express anything but the strongest attachment to you, and the greatest possible admiration and liking for Bessy. Lord and Lady Tavistock, Lord John, Mr and Mrs Seymour, can and will I am sure vouch for the truth of what I have written. Lady Tavistock in particular knows how often to her I have lamented that all my attentions and wish to please Lady William had failed, and how much I took to heart everything I meant kindly, being received differently and differently stated. My prospects for a great length of time have been very melancholy. Probably, dearest William, I shall ere long be separated from you all and we may never meet, but I do swear most solemnly that I have to all of you, been a steady, true and attached friend, and that I am ready to face anyone who will bring any charge against me, either of speaking unkindly of you or of Lady William. Your father, if ever you will speak to him upon the subject, will state the same thing, he knows how often I have grieved over my unfortunate fate of never pleasing where I took most pains to do so.

* His half-brother, Lord Wriothesley Russell.

I add with sorrow that he has had two very bad nights, that yesterday was a very uncomfortable day to him, and that he is far from well today. God bless you my dearest William.

Lord William Russell to Lady William Russell at Paris [WP]

Saturday [1823]

I have hardly time to write to you yet I know you like to hear from me tho it is only a line. Yesterday I was at Devonshire House where a marriage was declared. Lord Gower & the 3rd Miss Howard – a marriage cooked up by Lady Granville, Stafford etc. I cannot find a lodging anywhere. Ould Greville says it is in vain to look for one. We must sleep in the streets, such is the hospitable reception one gets in one's own country. I have sent to know if Poodle Byng will let us his house – he has made a proposal which rather pleases me to take his house 4 months in the year – in which case we must take a country house – if this would not cost us more than our present house it would be agreable enough. I will see him to learn particulars. He loses $\frac{1}{2}$ his income by his mother's death.

Last night I got your letter by Bob Adair – he is the worse for his journey. I wish your health was better. The weather is now warmer so go every day to the Bois de Boulogne. T. is a little better. I have a kind letter from my father, saying all the Duchess tells me in her letter is true – poor dear man. Lady Gwydir tells me the hooping cough rages in London & that all her children have it. This is an objection to bringing boy blue too soon. . . . I shall leave this next Friday or Saturday. It will not be possible to spend my birthday with you as there is much business in the House of Commons. Johnnikins wants to go to Paris with me – but as he is a slow traveller he will retard my being with you some hours, which I shall be sorry for.

God bless you, pretty love, the carriage waits to take me to Woburn. You will be welcomed there whenever you arrive, but you must remain a couple of months in London to show your pretty face. God bless you. Kiss boy. Love to Mama.

Lord William Russell to Lady William Russell [WP]

St. James's Sq. Monday. 1823

I arrived in town this morning from W. A. & found your letter sent by Bradshaw, a thousand thanks for it but I do not like the account of your health, it is provoking that rest & cure does not restore you, perhaps fine weather may do something – it is gratifying to hear how well the boy is, but as for the *bonne* she appears to be a lost case – what will you do about her – The Duchess tells me the nurse I wrote to you about is perfect, careful, easy, attentive, good humoured, clean, intelligent &c. but you would not like the school she comes from. I shall leave this on Saturday for Paris, but where we are to lodge I cannot tell – the hotels are chock full – I shall enquire about Poodle Byng's house, you will not mind the old lady having died there – he has proposed to Tavistock to let me his house for four months in the year, he furnishing, cleaning, & repairing it – leaving his books &c. – this would be delightful if we had a country house for our home, & today I have heard of one. . . . I shall enquire into particulars tomorrow, but will do nothing without your permission as I know your aversion to the country – we could easily get the Curzon Street house off our hands & Dowbiggin says the roof, floors, drains, &c are in such a bad state that we cannot possibly live in it. . . . Lady Jersey begins her routs to night but I shall not go there – She has had a row with the Lieven in consequence of the latter making a bold attempt to make Mrs Canning take the precedence of other ladies as wife to the Minister for Foreign Affairs, I will tell you the details when we meet if you think it worth while to remind me of it. . . .

You appear to be amusing yourself at Paris with your Jules, your Henris, your Gabriels, your Augustes &c. – As for the Durazzo* she is certainly no beauty & to tell you the truth I was a little ashamed of her when I saw her at Paris – but you are too severe on her – I fear a little spite or lurking jealousy urged you on to see with jaundiced eyes – John-nikins proposed to go to Paris with me – but I thought he would delay me, so did not encourage him, at last he confessed it was to see Louise – I then advised him not to go, as I suspect she would rather not have him, for he checks her other flirtations, however you may be civil to her for she is a *bonne diablesse* – Old Lynedoch was at Woburn & made many enquiries after you & the boy, & hopes you will both spend the winter with him at Cosgrove, I gave him no hopes, knowing your horror of that place – he will perhaps go to Paris with me – Her Grace's fine letter had no result, she was cold & distant to me, I could not make her out, but she was playing some game too deep for my simplicity, as for my Father he was kindness

---

* Louisa Durazzo, née Brignoli, was the wife of the Marquis Durazzo, 'a little sulky disagreeable man'. Tributes to her charm and beauty are found in many contemporary memoirs.

itself, as he always is, & is much pleased with all my Roman purchases. . . .

I got the cloaths sent by Bradshaw – The taylor makes me too much of a dandy – & pinches me about the waste which I cannot bear for I like to be at ease in those parts – I am sorry you did not send me his account that I might compare it with the taylor here, however you may order me six white waistcoats – a brown morning coat – a blue coat made like a great coat, but to wear alone, & four pairs of light sort of summer pantaloons of a *quiet* gentlemanlike colour – I should also like to have a cloak, but he is not the man to make it – don't get me anything dandyish, I cannot bear being made a dandy of – enquire also about a whig for me. . . . Since writing this I have had two letters from you Nos. 6 & 7 & I am happy to hear your quack Doctor has done you good, your pains evidently come from nerves, which makes it as necessary to keep your mind as quiet as your body – I can find nothing like a lodging every Hotel is full – I shall see if I can make an arrangement with Poodle Byng.

You can go to Woburn whenever you please & they will be delighted to have you – but in the meantime we must have a *pied à terre* in London – for me to attend the House of Commons & for you to show your pretty face – Foscolo is going to give lectures on Italian literature, he begins tomorrow – I am already sick of this town the fog & smoke are detestable, the Society noisy, crowded, hot, & beginning late, about midnight – it will not be possible for you to attempt it – Mrs Bennett & Eliza come home at four & breakfast at one, what a waste of God's gifts . . . I shall probably be with you on Monday or Tuesday next & wish you to be prepared to leave Paris on the Saturday following –

God bless you pretty love, kiss my boy for me – & believe me your true, *faithful* & devoted Hub.

Mrs Henry Seymour to Lord William Russell at Paris [WPP]

12 May [1823]

I hear there is a very good sitting room and two bedrooms now vacant at Nerot's Hotel in Clifford Street. Lucy was there last year and found it very tolerably quiet and comfortable, and the sitting room is about the size of the drawing room in this house. Lord Lynedoch had also heard of it, and said he would write to you, but I fear it will be gone before your answer can be received by him. He has however hopes that Warren will be able to accommodate you in a short time. . . . I am quite sad when I think of the little pleasure Lady William can feel at returning to us all! Alas! Alas! That it should be in the power of any one person to destroy the comfort and happiness of several! There are so many, so very many in England, who, though they may not show it with so much demonstration yet who love and prize Lady W. quite as much as they can do in her dear Italy and Germany, etc. So many who would vie with each other to make her happy, and with whom I am certain, she would be happy to live, and yet that all should be destroyed by *one* being, it is really *very* cruel.

Good-bye dear William. Give her my affectionate love, and believe me always your very tenderly attached

Aunt

E. Seymour

I wish you would get me some *very* good perfume to put in some large sachets which I have made. I do not like musk.

Lady William Russell to Lady Holland [HH]

Paris, Monday May 12 [1823]

I shall of course have much pleasure in executing all your commissions to the best of my ability, but as I have 8 ladies to serve I shall be in good luck if I please them all.

What can I say about your proposal, I must look upon it as a fairy gift, to have all the *agréments* of Holland House poured upon my lap as if to welcome me back to England, if anything can make me anglomane it must certainly be such a piece of immense kindness, & I shall be like the old Stadtholder who thought London was lit up to celebrate his arrival. On the other hand I shrink into my shell when I think what it is to arrive on a visit off a long journey like Matilda Pottingen in the diligence. . . . a foreign *bonne*, untidy travelling habits English servants acquire on the Continent – heaps of packages, as we carry our little all in our only home, (our post chaise), moreover, I (to put you in the confidence of my wardrobe) have every article to make up here after 6 years marriage, as my *linge* & *lingerie* &c, &c, are all in rags, & my trousseau must be *renôuvellé*. I shall have to pawn my jewels to buy my shifts. *Voilà où nous en sommes*. I am afraid of inspiring horror & disgust, however as you are so very kind about it & seem to have anticipated all these drawbacks & made allowance for them – should we really be no nuisance, I would gladly avail myself of

94

your invitation for one week. My little boy travels with his own bed & sleeps in our room, & his nurse & my maid sleep together, so I hope we shall occupy no more space than when our numerical force was less. I hope then to be able to go to the country, as I am not well & incapable of much exertion.

Since I have been here I have done nothing but 'sigh & lament me in vain'. The sky is so grey, the clouds so black, the fog so thick, the blast so keen, the sun so dim, the society so insipid & *pour comble* the fashions so ugly, the hair frizzed up as it was 80 years ago, large hats drooping over the nose with kissing strings, as I am told they were called in days of yore, long waists, *des suppléments* to the stays, that is neck & hips made of tow or cotton where nature does not give them, no flounces but *entre deux* on the muslin & percale gowns. Bracelets the size of knight errants shields on skinny arms . . . *Blouses – demie blouses* &c, &c, &c. Yellow happens to be *fort à la mode* in every thing.

Henry Fox on his way back from Italy was taken ill at Paris. The news of his illness reaching Holland House alarmed his parents, and his mother despatched Lord Holland with Dr Allen to his bedside, following herself a few days later.

 The William Russells meanwhile went to England and established themselves at Holland House in the owner's absence.

Lady William Russell to Lady Holland at Paris [HH]

Dover, Tuesday June 6 [1823]

No words can describe our vexation & disappointment at having missed you! We met Lord Holland near Abbeville & from what he said thought we should just be in time to prevent you crossing. Your dear child is really in a most comfortable state, but it will make him so happy to see you & his father, that I reproach myself the regret I feel at not finding you here. As to minor concerns all your goods & chattels are safe through the customs house. I have bought everything you desired except a certain *fichu*. Now it appears by unlucky circumstances I have been too zealous in your cause as you would have had more contentment in purchasing your own things. *Mais que faire?* if I had not got all it would have appeared as if I did not like to load my carriage – on the other hand I have spent a preposterous sum – but as I told you before I will take whatever you don't want or like or change your mind about. Your *capote* would do for me, your *gros de Naples pélisse* can be cut down into my dimensions, it is always a useful thing. Nattier's flowers are to all tastes, even Mary's gown (if not too young) I can alter to my shape, as I have no ball dresses of my own whatsoever – so pray use no ceremony. * We avail ourselves of Lord Holland's kind permission of landing at your palace gate or we should be *sur le pavé*. Let us soon hear from you & issue out your orders. I have all your bills & receipts, & everything in my own name. I recommend my poor Mama to your kindness. Farewell dear Lady Holland.

LORD WILLIAM'S DIARY

4 June. Arrived at Holland House at 10 o'clock at night, cold and wet.

5 June. Went to London, heard my father had left the evening before for Woburn Abbey, supposed by the physicians to be in better health & having decided to rub in & take calomel, to endeavour to do away with the necessity of bleeding. Found Mrs Bennett & Miss Russell living in St James's Square. Called on Tavistock, found him looking thin, ill & out of spirits. My lady blooming & good humoured as usual. Attended the House of Commons.

6 June. Went to town, dined with Tavistock at 6, found him weak & low, advised his going abroad – which he apparently did not relish. Attended the debate.

Lord William Russell to Lady Holland at Paris [HH]

Holland House, Friday [1823]

I was much annoyed at missing you in France; by G. G.'s account you must have gone thro Boulogne whilst we were there – at Dover I received the kind message you left with Mr Payne – and took possession according to your orders of the old *château*. It looks melancholy without its owners, but I cannot tell you what a comfort it is to us, to be in the fine air, instead of a hot fusty room 10ft square in an hotel. My boy is rosy & well, running all day in the garden – & Bessy is as happy & comfortable as possible. Nothing can exceed the attention of your servants, & G.G. brought me a message from Calais to say I was to have a horse when I pleased. The only thing that discomposes me in all this is the fear of encroaching upon your bounty, for in these hard times it is unfair to put you to additional expenses, which I fear from the orders you have left must be the case. For instance I wished to put my servants on board wages, but you have desired the contrary. G.G. offered us your carriage horses – but they are too pretty to hack about, so I have taken a pair of jobs, & put them in your stable. The man bringing his own hay & corn & sleeping at the public house. You may

* The Hon. Mary Fox (1806–91), Lord and Lady Holland's daughter, had made her *début* in April.

find these details uncalled for, but as it is possible from the state of enjoyment we are in, that we shall remain here till you turn us out, I wish you to know what we are doing with your property. So tell me *con franqueza* when you wish us to depart. I have a very kind letter from my father, also from the Duchess begging me to go to Woburn, so we go tomorrow for a couple of days & return here. The things Bessy brought for you are safely arrived here. Mrs Rawdon can tell you all about them, colour, shape, stuff, price &c. John is in London, but speaks of coming to sleep here sometimes; he looks delightfully well. I wish I could say the same of Tavistock, he is shocking to see, tho his countenance & pulse have improved since I was in England. Halford * is very sanguine about my father & expects much from the new mode of treatment, yet I find him out of spirits about himself – in his letter to me this morning he says 'it is now within a few days of a twelvemonth since I was attacked with this illness, & I do not feel that I have within the last ten months made the slightest progress towards recovery.' This is gloomy indeed, but I think the Duchess depresses his spirits by always recalling his illness to his mind. How is Henry? When do you return? Bessy's love to you & yours.

Duke of Bedford to Lord William Russell [WPP]

Woburn Abbey, Tuesday [1823]

... With regard to your coming here when I go to Kensington, I can only repeat that my house *y todo che io tenge e la disposicion di V.M.*†, if you do not think you will be bored by such solitary confinement, but of this you must be the best judge. The paint is what I most dread, and I fear the corridor painters will drive you from one part of the house to another in succession, as it was left unfinished last year, and cannot be delayed another. ... Thanks for executing my commission at Paris about the Bréguet.‡ It is intended as a present for Dr Hunt as a mark of my gratitude for the trouble anxiety and care he took in drawing up the descriptions of my marbles, and moreover to compensate for the loss of his own, which became the booty of the London brigands, alias pickpockets. What I want from Falon is a lady's watch, as a *cadeau* to the Duchess on her 20th wedding day. I gave her one some time after my marriage, but it is a *warming* pan as compared with the present fashions. ...

* Sir Henry Halford (1766–1844), a fashionable physician.
† 'All that I have is at your disposal'.
‡ Louis Bréguet, a Paris watchmaker.

LORD WILLIAM'S DIARY

7 June. Went to Woburn Abbey, found my father so so, tho in tolerable spirits. Her Grace received us in her best & most cordial manner.

8 June. Rode with my father & Lord Lynedoch.

9 June. Rode to Ampthill with the Duke to see the Alameda made by Lord Holland for the inhabitants of the town. Opened some cases of busts &c. The mosaic head was much admired.

Tuesday. Returned to town.

Lady William Russell to Lady Holland at Paris [HH]

Holland House, Friday [1823]

Many thanks for your kind little note. Here we are in a perfect Paradise, the weather this day *se remet au beau,* the sky clears & begins to take on the *dolce color d'oriental zaffiro* – the birds sing, flowers perfume the air, my boy sports about like a young kid & Honoré gives us such sumptuous banquets that my stomach is quite surprized having been till now supplied with nourishment from a *traiteur's* basket. All your household are so attentive & polished that I am sure they pass their leisure hours in reading Lord Chesterfield & *l'Art de plaire.*

We have been to Woburn, the Duke's nights, alas, continue very bad, but he is cheerful to a miracle, especially in the evening when he is even gay. The Duchess was full of every kind of attention & *prévenance* to us all. They are not quite certain of the day they are to take possession of their new house. The Tavistocks are at the races, Lady Elizabeth Vernon went there with them, I believe. He is fearfully thin! but his countenance to me looks bright & his spirits seem as usual, I am told also that he entertains some hopes of being able to resume his hunting this winter. I hope you liked my doctor & that he treated Henry so as to make you perfectly happy about him. My love to him & to Lady Holland. Mary is lovely & universally acknowledged to be so, I never heard more encomiums on anybody's beauty. Thank you for your attention to poor Mama, she is very grateful & so am I.

Lord Holland to Lord William Russell at Holland House [WPP]

Paris, 9th June, 1823

Lady Holland is so hurried with one thing or another that she cannot write, but she as well as I are delighted to hear you are comfortable at

Holland House, and hope to be with you there soon. . . . *Vous vous moquez de nous* to be so scrupulous about the horses, for instance. You are much too delicate. It would do them and the servants good to take Lady William and the boy a quiet drive in the morning, and I hope on your return from Woburn you have done, and will do so. If, as I hear from others, Tavistock looks better than he did, I shall be easy, notwithstanding your account, for his complaint, however unaccountable, is surely of that kind in which, if there is a favourable turn, the cure is nearly certain. A gradual improvement of looks, above all, any gain of bulk or strength would, I think, be decisive, but I own I had seen none when I left England.

I am sincerely glad to hear such good accounts of your father, and to learn that Halford thinks better of him, but indeed, my dear William, he neither is, nor can be, in a state in which a reasonable man can take anything but a gloomy view of his condition, and my wonder is that he contemplates it with so much evenness of spirits and calmness of philosophy as he does, especially when I recollect that he was always liable to low spirits and that the disorder in most other people produces impatience and irritation. What there is therefore of melancholy in his letters I attribute to his sense of his true situation, to the disease, and to the lowering remedies, certainly not to the Duchess. She is despondent in her own mind and in her conversation with others, but quite the reverse with him, unremittingly attentive, and full of conversation, exertion and fun before him. Believe me, upon long, very long, experience, that the health, and in greater degree, the spirits of your father, as far as they are good are due to the Duchess, and if she does now and then worry any of you about trifles and *tracasseries* you will, I am sure, make some allowances for the painful and anxious attendance she has gone through, which is really enough to overcome the spirits of anyone much less disposed than she is wont to be mentally and by nature, to torment herself with foreboding calamities. Excuse me, dear William, for saying so much. Mrs Rawdon is very well, at least as well as she can be in Bessy's absence and the boy's. She is full of kindness to me and mine. Pray tell Lady William how sensible we are of her friendship in taking, and her dexterity in passing, Mary's dresses.

Yours in noise and hurry

From Holland House it was possible for William and his wife to enter into the gaiety of the London season and they were quickly re-established in society.

LORD WILLIAM'S DIARY

12 June. Went to town, paid several visits – Lady Harrowby, whom I found to be quite as I had left her, the room in the same state, & Montagu * in the same chair saying the same things. When people are absent for a length of time & have seen various & passing scenes, they are astonished on their return to their native place to find persons & society in the very place they left them.

Dined with Madame de Lieven, nobody there but Prince Esterhazy & the gentlemen of the Russian Embassy. The dinner good & gay & we avoided exhausting our spirits by leaving the table with the ladies. Went afterwards to the Duke of Devonshire's concert, where we met all our old acquaintances who appeared delighted to see us, & we were as much pleased as if they had been sincere.

18 June. Visited by Madame de Lieven – complained of Lord Holland's attack on the Emperor – said how much she regretted the impossibility of ever visiting or speaking to him again.† This all great humbug & nonsense. I never met a woman apparently so ingenuous, naive, & sincere – whilst she either propounds a falsehood, or professes a principle, which she inwardly laughs at. She told us with the simple innocent air of a girl of 15, that her liaison with Lord Grey was entirely owing to their both arriving early at Almacks, & finding nobody in the room, necessity threw them together.

Lord William Russell to Lady Holland [HH]

Holland House Wednesday [1823]

Last night I got a letter from you without date saying you hoped to be here on Wednesday (today). I hope it may be so, tho your servants rather doubt it, as they have not heard from you at Dover. However they are cleaning & preparing, & I hazard sending a few lines to Dover to tell you we are still in your hospitable quarters, which we shall evacuate with reluctance whenever we become M. et Madame de Trop. My Father is much the same, he has given up the mercury, dissatisfied with its effect. Tavistock so so, tho most people think him mending. I wish I could think with them. Russell is come home from Eton, with a return of his cold, glandular swellings &c, &c. We are a miserable family. Thank God my boy is well & healthy. . . .

I hope you have brought Henry back stout & well. Mary is in great

---

* The Hon. Edward Montagu, 5th Baron Rokeby (1787–1847). '. . . he propagates, almost creates gossip and scandal.' F. Leveson Gower (ed.), *Lady Granville's Letters*, i, 210.

† See p. 51 n.

beauty, & universally admired. Her gowns have not been unpacked, according to your wishes, tho there have been some brilliant opportunities of wearing them – & those brought by Bessy for the Ladies Ryder, have met with greatest success, which has probably excited Mary's impatience to eclipse them in acquired, as she already does, in natural beauty.

Tell Lord Holland they are going on rapidly & successfully with his hay & it appears to be a good crop – everything is waiting for your arrival to ripen & flourish, except the chinese roses – which have been most splendid but are now fading & disappearing.

The return of their hosts was the occasion for a renewal of the breakfasts and dinners that made Holland House so agreeable a centre. Henry Fox came back from Paris with his father and was pleased to find that Bessy's presence in the house relieved him from unwelcome tête-à-têtes with his mother.

'Only Lady William, my mother and me at dinner', he wrote in his journal. 'The former gave an agreeable and lively account of her winter at Rome. She is totally unlike anybody else I know. Her expressions are very peculiar and well chosen; she is accused by many of coldness and want of heart, I believe unjustly. She is certainly fond of William and of her delightful child. William is in my opinion by far the most amiable of the Russells; there is a warmth of heart and tenderness of manner that is delightful, nor is he at all deficient in understanding. His admiration and love for her is as great as it should be.'[14] He went with Lady William to a breakfast of the Duke of Devonshire's at Chiswick, taking with them his sister Mary, whose Paris dresses Bessy had adroitly smuggled through the Customs.

LORD WILLIAM'S DIARY

19 June. Went to Town. Attended the House of Commons. Waited to return to Holland House with Lord Holland. Supped with him at 3 o'clock. Although he had only returned from France this day & had made a long speech, he was lively & entertaining & agreable as ever.

22 June. Brougham* & Tierney† came out to breakfast at Holland House. The former is brilliant & amusing in his conversation, talking with the same ease on the driest law question, or the most trifling gossip of the day, but mischievous as a monkey. Tierney is sententious & sarcastic, but very agreable. To breakfast with 3 such men as Lord H., Brougham & Tierney, is the highest feast. . . .

Dined with the Duchess of Kent – a simple unaffected woman – her daughter,

---

* Henry Peter, 1st Baron Brougham (1778–1868), Lord Chancellor in 1830.
† George Tierney (1761–1830), politician, at one time leader of the Whigs.

the little Princess Victoria is fair, like the Royal Family, with pretty manners & voice.

25 June. Dined at Holland House. Lord & Lady Cowper, Lord Lynedoch & others. Lord Lynedoch was to go to Paris at 5 next morning, what fine vigour & activity in this old man of 80.* In conversation he said he wished to God he was at Cadiz at the head of 10,000 British troops. Went to Almacks where there was a great show of beauty & fine dress.

26 June. Brought Rogers back to Holland House. He had dined with William Ponsonby & having been ill placed at dinner was full of bad humour & spite – venting his venom upon Lord Dudley & Ward, who excited his spleen by being a Viscount & monopolizing the conversation.†

27 June. Sat up till 1 o'clock talking with Lord Holland who told me many singular & interesting anecdotes of Sheridan, whom he described as a man of splendid talents, wit & eloquence, but a slave to vanity, & never forgiving even to his last day, anyone who had wounded his vanity, & seeking repeated & the most calculated, cold blooded opportunities to be revenged, hating too most virulently anyone who had been of service to him or had lent him money, which he was fond of borrowing from those he disliked but never would take from those he loved. Whitbread‡ had conferred many benefits on him, he consequently hated him, tho they lived much together, & one day having supped together at Southill & retired to bed & met again at breakfast next morning – Sheridan said to Whitbread, 'I wish to tell you now what I have often thought, & what I thought last night, but would not say, lest you should think it said in anger or in drink, but which I now say after having reflected on it, slept on it, & reflected again this morning – You are mad. I have studied these matters much & you are mad, & another person who is mad is Mrs M. Angelo Taylor.'§

This is curious, Whitbread died mad. Let us see if Mrs M.A.T. will do the same. Lord Holland saw Sheridan a few days before his death in a state of dirt & misery not to be described, with bailiffs in the house. Lord Holland endeavoured to persuade him to sell the copyright of his works but could not get him to speak the truth about what he had sold and what he had not sold.

Leaving Holland House in July, Lord and Lady William went to live for several months at Woburn and for much of the time they were there they had the

---

* He was 75.

† Samuel Rogers (1763–1855), banker and poet, notorious for his sharp tongue. 'They tell me I say ill-natured things', he observed to a friend. 'I have a very weak voice; if I did not say ill-natured things no one would hear what I said.' Clayden, *Rogers and his Contemporaries*, ii, 125.

‡ Samuel Whitbread of Southill, Beds. (1758–1815), brewer and Whig M.P. He committed suicide.

§ The wife of the politician Michael Angelo Taylor was Frances Anne, daughter of the Rev. Sir Harry Vane.

great house to themselves. The Duke and the Duchess and their children were in Scotland from August to October, and in November went to a hired house by the sea. The Tavistocks were living at Oakley not far from Woburn, his wretched health still serving as a subject for speculation. From time to time Bessy and William went to town to stay in St James's Square, when they enjoyed the use of the Duke's private boxes at Covent Garden and Drury Lane theatres.

The Duke had lately bought for his wife a villa on Campden Hill that was only a stone's throw from their friends at Holland House. It was perfectly countrified and became the Duchess's favourite home.* Relations with her stepson's wife were more cordial from a distance, and Bessy in the absence of the Duchess was as happy at Woburn as it was in her nature to be. She was again with child and William had a scheme for buying a house in London; but in August she had a miscarriage, and her husband found he had no money for a house.

Duchess of Bedford to Lord William Russell [WPP]

Friday morn. [1823]

Tell Bessy, if I may presume to call her so, that her sliding commission is executing. I called yesterday in Arlington Street, where I found Tavistock and Lady T. together. I mentioned this that I may not appear to tell fibs, as I wrote in the morning that I had not seen her, but in a trio there can be nothing but common conversation. Your names were never mentioned, excepting by Tavistock who asked me if you stayed all the summer at W. My answer, I do not know.

I hear Lord Hastings is not the least altered.† His whiskers being grey astonish people, as his brows are as black as ever. I know nothing of the ball last night, beyond hearing my ladies come home at half past five, when I presume you were like a good country squire in your water meadow, *saving* your day as they call it in Devon.

Love to those who like to accept such a poor offering.

I hope Bessy is humane to my offspring.

Duchess of Bedford to Lady William Russell at Woburn Abbey [PRP]

Sunday [1823]

I have just heard a most excellent sermon the effects of which are to make me feel in charity with all man & womankind, to do unto others, as I

---

* Known successively as Campden Hill House, Bedford Lodge, Argyll Lodge, and Cam House. It has recently been demolished.
† Lord Hastings had returned from governing Bengal.

would be done by ... I have looked at the outside of Cavendish Square. I like the appearance much, & should have great satisfaction in being allowed to assist in your comfort, let me paper the quarter gallery, by way of something Duchess like, & magnificent, don't say I am stingy after such a distinguished mark of extravagance. I will speak to Kate, & do more, by going myself to any house likely to suit you. I yesterday went with the Duke to Devonshire House in the morning to see his Endymion.* Tierney says all the dandys are practising the attitude, but that it is not comfortable, tho' difficult to accomplish. Lord Jersey says he likes the dogs ears but, le Comte Lieven says, *vraiment*. Madame de Lieven *est très malade*, she's at Richmond. Lord & Lady Jersey go to Southampton tomorrow & on the 12th of Augt. everything most exquisite meet at Drummond Castle, all return to Lord Tankerville's, who I hear says, every body he meets exclaims I am coming this year to Chillingham!! he answers, the house is small & wretched, *n'importe*, they then all finish at Lord Grantham's, the men's hearts beating with delight at the thought of hunting, & the poor ladies, with theirs dying within them, at the thought of the long winter in the country. *Voilà une page de* gossip, not a word of scandal; I will try to see everything *en rose*, instead of *en noir*, but do you think I have any reason to be full of hope or of joy. . . .

Would Mrs Rawdon send me some pretty silks, or anything she likes for the morning, not made up. Lilac & straw color I am mighty fond of, & really here nothing is to be found but clothing *pour Les Anglais pour rire,*† *à propos*, I found Eliza just as you described, & have turned her out like a good picture, newly cleaned. Hippolite has cut off a pound of hair, & I flatter myself, your suggestions have been attended to, as they always will be, by a sensible woman like

Georgy Bedford

Lord William Russell to Lady Holland [HH]

[Woburn 1823]

Bessy got a letter from you this morning in which you say: do you ride, drive, read, sing or what do you do? This question looks as if your kind wishes followed us into our retreat, at least presuming so I will answer you in some detail, because you probably think she is pining for the pleasures

* By Canova.
† The title of a play given in Paris.

of the Capital & that I am yawning till the 1st September arrives. *Point du tout* – yet to prove to you the contrary I must give you a detail of our proceedings which is difficult because one day is like another – in a similar difficulty Miss Matthews said to Capt Booth*: then give me a description of your best day.

We rise then, Madam, the moment we wake – between 7 & 8 – but if you do not remember Amelia Booth, this will be all gibberish to you. About ten we appear at breakfast with two books which furnish us with conversation, for instance this morning Bessy brought the Bible enchanted with this passage – and he kissed his son & smelled the smell of his raiment & said look the smell of my son is as the smell of a field which the Lord hath blessed.† Bessy says this is taken from nature. We kiss little Hastings to prove it, & agree, we then listen with our ears & mouths open to all he says, & declare it admirable wit. We then repeat all the clever things he said during the morning – this passes away an hour – & puts me in mind that I must tell you one of his clever sayings. With a deep sigh he said to the maid – Oh if I could but breakfast once more at Holland House I should be so happy. She said why – he said if you were to hear all the beautiful things said by Lord & Lady Holland, & all the people at Holland House, when they are at breakfast you would not know where you were. But you will be bored with us by breakfast time so I will say no more except that it is impossible for any one to live alone with Bessy without being always happy, pleased, amused, instructed, gay & contented with himself – that she is happy too I can presume from her constant gaiety & good humour, however this long boring letter belies all I say, & looks as if I did not know what to do with myself. Pardon me it shall be ended.

... I *beg* you will not show this letter to your *neighbours* for reasons you shall know hereafter.

Lady William Russell to Lady Holland [HH]

13 Aug Wednesday [1823]

The prospect of seeing you on the 5th though not very near is very agreeable: why are you ill? It grieves me for verily I am mightily fond of you, *et quand je le dis c'est que je le pense car je suis singulièrement brutale sur ce sujet des antipathies.*

* Characters in Fielding's novel, *Amelia.*
† *Genesis* 27:27.

Billikins and Bettina

What shall I tell you that we do? We play with young 'small hopes' & think him the wonder of the world. I walk nearly as much as Captain Barclay,* amongst other feats I trudge home with an oaken staff & a dark lanthorn from Woburn town to Woburn Abbey at eleven at night, we amuse ourselves most forestally and shall be sorry when cruel fate puts an end to all our innocent pleasures. The Tavistocks are at the Seymours, & Russell, who is really a fine boy, less shy & more independent than he used to be – as to poor Lord T. I think him looking much worse than ever he struck me as being. This is all *entre nous* as it would be barbarous to make his father more uneasy than he already is, & useless to discuss upon my authority; he is more shrunk & shrivelled & languid but he says he feels better, has lost the pain he had after eating & has not lost flesh since he weighed last, all this *autant de gagne*, & most probably the Cheltenham doctor will profit of the favourable turn nature takes & get the entire credit of his cure. The poor Seymours are wretched about him, she loves him as a son. Lady Tavistock is not apparently alarmed; so much for the exact statement of facts.

Lady William Russell to Lady Holland [HH]

Tuesday morning from my bed [1823]

I owe you a hundred thousand thanks for a certain little book which I perceive you have given me by the *riverito nome di vostra eccellenza* being on the title page.

I am I confess disappointed at my little mishap. I was in perfect health, a blessing I had not enjoyed for some years, & on which my spirits so entirely depend that I confess myself a coward at the surprise or rather apprehension of any interruption thereof – so much for selfish feelings – then comes in a splice of maternity, for I wished for a daughter, & I cried bitterly when I saw my little foetus that would have been a rational & loveable little being. In short I am no heroine & have too thin spun nerves to attempt the character. I went out too soon, & was weaker than I thought & the air was so great a stimulus (I suppose) that when I came home I had an *accès de fièvre* so violent that it was frightful. In the night another with symptoms of lightheadedness, in which I said I know not what to Billikins

---

* Robert Barclay Allardice (1779–1854), known as Captain Barclay; renowned for his walking feats, which included walking one mile in each of one thousand successive hours.

who wrote for Woolryche.* I am glad he could not come. My fever returns more quietly – the Aesculapius says I have the ague, but having no shivers or transpirations I am aware it is all my eye. So I return to my bed where in God's name I must nestle for a few days & then begin the *routine de la vie* over again, with my bonny boy & my good husband. One is unreasonable to wish for an atom more happiness. Goodbye dear Lady Holland & millions of thanks for all your proofs of friendship.

Duchess of Bedford to Lord William Russell at Woburn [PRP]

[1823]

... *Je suis à vos ordres* to do anything, & wish I could say anything satisfactory about your dear father & Sir H. Halford's opinion, he says the disease in the head still exists, only kept at bay. He is going to make him try the French preparation of Bark, called sulphate of Quining, for tho' he is convinced no effusion has taken place, still all our attention must be directed to prevent it. This, my dearest Billy, is a sad history, as your own good sense must point out, that *bark & meat every day* would not be prescribed unless the constitution exhibited great weakness. His nights are very bad, last night a most particularly bad one.

The report of our going for the winter to Brighton is true, Halford says for the winter, it is the best climate for your father.

I hope Bessy will take care of herself, & as she has proved that she is not past childbearing, I hope for some time she will rest upon her *lauriers*. My kind love to her. I think we get on, tho' slowly, *de part et d'autre*; dear, then my dear Lady William, now come to dear Bessy, *je tremble de mon audace*. I wish you could have heard little Founchal† the other night describing & recommending the women who rub, *à la Grosvenor*. He says when they begin, or rather she begin, I was stupid, or vat you call it, she rub me, & I feel all over a little tingle sensation, quite a new man, oh it does me vast good & I shall take my woman where I go, they come live in your house, you give so much, & then deliver yourself of her. I cannot do justice to his bad English, but he was very amusing.

Adieu dearest Billikins
& Bettakina

* One of the Duke of Bedford's and Lady Holland's many doctors.
† Marquis de Founchal, a Portuguese diplomatist. 'Little hideous Founchal came in the evening, and told too many stories.' Earl of Ilchester (ed.), *Henry Fox's Journal*, p. 45.

Billikins and Bettina

Lady William Russell to Lady Holland [HH]

[Woburn 1823]

I disclaim any 'fancies about Rome'. Ld Wm, on my asking him what it meant, told me he had expressed to you a dread of any return of my stomach complaint, as he would in that case take me to Rome. I have no wish or no intention whatsoever to pass this winter anywhere else than where I am at present, if fate will allow it. I enjoy this quiet & liberty beyond anything & hope to be able to continue it; hitherto I am happy to say I have no threatening of my former dreadful sufferings, nothing ails me but the usual consequences of my accident. I had a miscarriage from an alarm on my cloathes being burnt off me at Cambray 5 years ago, & far from being cured in a fortnight I was several months debilitated & tormented by a low & intermittent fever. I have had scarcely anything else but bad health since I married, & should I feel that I was going to relapse, I should need no subterfuge to get into a milder climate, for without dragging Lord William away from his 'ties & duties' filial & parliamentary I could pass the bad season according as my caprice suggested either at Paris with my mother or at Rome with my uncle. *Pénétrez vous bien de toutes ces profondes vérités chère Miladi & surtout conservez moi votre amitié* which I appreciate. I am sorry the Duke suffers so much. Poor Lord Tavistock is worse off than him on that score, every body is full of solicitude about him but none can have the sympathy I have as everything he describes I have experienced & when I either see him, or his letters, I am ready to melt away with compassion & sorrow. As you say nothing of yourself I hope you are quite well; *c'est une bénédiction* how Woburn agrees with my boy. He is as ruddy as a peasant; when I look on him & think of London fogs, I tremble at the fate of Hagar & Ishmael.

My spouse wears a wig & is the very moral of old Greville in it. When he takes it off he is so like the Duke it is quite striking. He shoots partridges, hunts cubs with the young hounds, smokes segars & leads the most jolly life in Christendom.

Lady William Russell to old Lord William Russell at Florence [WP]

Woburn Abbey, Septr. 24. [1823]

When you and I parted we swore eternal friendship & vowed to write by every courier! It is now just 6 months ago & we neither of us have written a line! Suppose we begin? I really have thought of you five hundred times at least, & God only knows why I did not commit my thoughts to paper; however I accuse myself, as I ought to have been the aggressor, but – *passons une éponge sur tout cela.* How are you? I am very well indeed, after a slight indisposition I had a month ago, & am fat & jolly, ruddy & roughing it – not in an ecstasy of amusement, nor in a delirium of joy, but just in that sober state of satisfaction that a grey sky & damp air produces when it neither affects the lungs or the spirits. My Billikins is well & fattened by roast beef & plum pudding. My boy really a stout, healthy, rubicond boy, & amazingly popular. So much for my happiness – *car on peut être fort heureux sans s'amuser*, & to make up for the lack of diversion I read hugely, so you will find me a sort of a mixture of Lady Davy,* Miss Berry, Mariamia Dionizi – Hannah More† – Mrs Starke‡ & so forth. If it goes on much longer I shall write a work, car – *le moyen de contenir tant d'instruction*? It will all fly off like sky rockets the first opportunity. . . . I must tell you about Eliza. She is really *une jeune personne charmante – jolie comme un coeur, douce comme une colombe*, with a silver toned voice in speaking like an Aeolian harp, her complexion is grown beautiful, her hair raven black, her appearance altogether gladdens one with that purple light of youth – which *soit dit en passant* I am in a few days going to take my last leave of, as the 2nd of next month I shall be a certain age. I was born October 2, 1793. *Faites le compte*, it is a critical moment, but fortunately in this country we have *une seconde floraison* at about 40 which excites much applause – *quoiqu'il en soit*, when I go abroad again, I shall say 'on m'a mariée à quinze ans', which is the current lie of all the veteran ladies. But to return to more interesting things Eliza is fond of occupation, & does as much & as well as one can do without direction. Her pianoforte playing is so much improved I was surprized, she plays very well indeed, & a twelve months foreign tuition would make her quite a first rate performer. She has a pretty turn for drawing, & a good master would do wonders, she has a divine temper & a good heart, which expands more than I once thought it capable of doing. I want a *sposo* for her – something good – *una bella cosa*, but not *un'antichità*. Then I want to splice George to Miss Capel,§ who is smitten with him & confided it to me. She will have mints, & the run of

* Jane, Lady Davy (1780–1855), wife of Sir Humphry Davy. A prominent and lively figure in London and Roman society.
† Hannah More (1745–1833), authoress of improving books.
‡ Marianna Starke (1762–1838) wrote guide books to Europe.
§ Harriet Capel (1806–37) was the natural daughter of the 5th Earl of Essex. She married in 1824 Richard Ford, author of a *Handbook for Travellers in Spain.*

Cassiobury. He does not hate the young lady for he said she was 'a nice affectionate little thing' & likewise that he wanted a wife that would amuse him, now she is mightily lively, – a parched pea on a drum according to the elegant simile – & he is grown a *virtuoso* since he has been in Italy & beats time & looks languishing when he hears music, – & the little Miss plays on all manner of instruments remarkably well. I want to establish them in Russell Farm, *cela parait fait exprès,* – in the very domain of the Earl *papa suo.* Don't you think I am full of imagination & a most scheming woman? *che ve ne pare?*

So far I have written *de gaieté de coeur,* what remains to say is not of so pleasant a nature. Both your brother & Lord Tavistock are deplorably ill, tho the latter has begun a milk diet that seems to revive him a little. John-nikins is fat & flippant, dear little mannikin, & does not think small beer of himself as usual. If anybody purloins my letter they will think it is written by a barmaid from the elegance of the proverbs.

Addio zio carissimo, vogliatemi bene e quando non fate l'amore,* find time to write to me.

Lady William Russell to old Lord William Russell at Rome [WP]

Woburn Abbey, Nov. 19, 1823.

I was just beginning to think that poor *charme des gueux* was quite forgotten & that I was an additional proof of its being a misnomer, when your kind letter came to hand as the bankers say, this very morning; I shall have nothing but good news to give you to make up for the dulness of the epistle; *primo* Lord Tavistock is getting rapidly better, so rapidly that one does not know what to make of it for neither medicine nor regime has done it. He weighs more, he loses no more, he sleeps better, he has an appetite, his spirits are returned – that he must look lean & haggard for a long time to come is but natural, *mais voilà où nous en sommes après en avoir été quittes pour la peur* for everybody thought him dying, poor fellow; although he is by no means an agreeable member of society he is an honest one – a good Whig – a good sportsman, – a good landlord in perspective, & then with a father, a wife & a son to regret him, to say nothing of brothers really attached to him, – made it seem a melancholy business; I felt very sorry, God knows, tho not affecting to be frantic with grief as his demise would have made no vacuum in my affections, never having interchanged above

---

* 'Addio dearest uncle, love me, and when you are not making love, . . .'

a hundred words with him in my days, & having, of course, no ideas in common, or at least very few. Then the Duke has improved in his general health, though he has had some bad nights; the Duchess has had spasms, I only wonder she is so well, for give the devil his due she sometimes is 4 nights in the week up with him & the 24 hours round in apprehension of another stroke. . . .

As to our little selves we are like turtle doves upon an olive branch, all peace & harmony & quiet. We have been *tête à tête* since a few days after I wrote to you & shall be so till Xmas when the family return, at least we suppose & expect as much. Our boy is very healthy indeed, the English air agrees with him amazingly, as to myself I am in a state of constant contentment & my darling Billikins, blessings on him, is not bored with our solitude. He makes up for his two years absence in hunting & shooting, his father has given him a hunter & he is in great favour with 'Our Lady Of the Abbey'. *Moyennant quoi* we have the occupation of this noble mansion, which is mighty convenient in point of oeconomy, God help us; we are looking forward to the taking an unfurnish'd house, *ci vogliono quattrini** to buy chairs & tables, & this will perhaps enable us to succeed in so ambitious a project – as notwithstanding my grumblings & sermons Billy contrived to come home *sans le sou*. As we owe nothing it is no great calamity, but had it not been for this favorable juncture for the winter we should have been in a scrape. We go to town when Parliament meets; Johnikins is at Paris with my Mama, I say with her for they lodge in the same house. . . .

Johnnikins' 'belle Louise' is the object of his visit to Paris,† *cela va sans dire*, he wrote to me *gai comme un pinson* the other day, he owns that he feels another man when he crosses the Channel, with all his patriotism. You must know he has taken it into his head to be cynical & he yawns in an armchair & says rude things to look like Diogenes in his tub, so that provokes me sometimes. . . .

And now, my dear Lord William, goodbye & God bless you, you say a thousand things I don't merit, but I am obliged to you for putting up with my failings & making the best of me, write to me whenever you can *sans ennui*. . . .

During the winter the health of the Duke, of Lord Tavistock, and of Bessy
herself continued to figure largely in the letters the William Russells

---

* 'Money will be needed.'

† 'I hear John is an *élégant* of the first class at Paris and wears a cherry coloured underwaistcoat and two sardonyx pins.' Duke of Bedford to Lady Holland. [HH]

addressed to Holland House. A kerchief sent by Mrs Rawdon to Lady Holland from Paris got lost between the British Embassy and the Foreign Office; Lady Holland insisted it be traced. Bessy wrote: 'Mama is in fits about it . . . it must have been delivered to the porter who frequently steals things for which there is no redress as Sir Charles gives himself no trouble about either great or little matters.'[15] And she wrote again later: 'If you wish for another I will get it over my own way, but nothing larger . . . as what Mama sends me *now*, my winter furs, muffs &c. are entrusted to travellers & Boulogne smugglers.'[16]

Though anxious about his wife's health, William was happy. 'I am become a regular Squire Western', he told Lady Holland. 'My father has given me a brilliant horse & I only look forward to the days when I am to ride him.'[17]

Part 2

MILITARY YEARS
1824–1832

Since William could not afford to buy a house, Lord Tavistock proposed to him that he and Bessy should occupy a part of his own town house in Arlington Street. Tavistock expressed himself gratified at being of use to his brother, but, aware of the perils that might beset such an arrangement, he employed his wife to make a copy of all the letters he wrote to Lady William about it. (There was indeed a dispute about coals, when the Tavistocks behaved handsomely.)

Lord Hastings, Bessy's uncle, having returned from India, was made Governor and Commander-in-Chief of Malta, and William was offered an appointment on his staff, but in the meantime the Duke of Bedford purchased for his son a Majority on full pay in the 8th Hussars, and later in the year the command of the regiment, then stationed at Dorchester, was procured for him.* The Duke had written to his son: 'You are unjust in saying that I am "averse to come down with the money". It is the means that are wanting and not the will. . . . I trust however that I shall be able to pay for your Majority of cavalry. . . out of my income. . . . When the time comes for the purchase of a Lieut.Colonelcy we must consider the means of raising the wind.'[1]

The summer saw the outbreak of a storm that had long been brewing. Bessy was accused of incivility to the Duchess and was forbidden to go to Woburn, and William refused to go there without her. Husband and wife were not sorry to depart to Dorset. Lady Holland wrote to her son that 'Lady Wm is as ladies like to be'.[2] She reserved her observations on the 'tracasseries' in the Russell family for William.

Countess Lieven let Lady William know that accounts of the quarrel had reached the King. 'J'ai trouvé le roi bien instruit de vos démélés avec votre belle-mère et lui donnant tous les torts de l'affaire. Il a extrêmement approuvé la conduite de votre mari. Il me semble que vous êtes tous les deux rather in favour.'[3]

---

* To obtain a commission in the British Army, it was necessary to put down a sum of money. Promotion was gained one step at a time by sale and purchase of commissions. Those who could afford it rose in rank, the others remained where they were. Although the sum to be paid was officially fixed, evasions of the law were not prosecuted and a very large sum was needed to procure the command of a fashionable regiment. 'By going on half-pay, or by exchanging, at a price, into another regiment, wealthy officers avoided uncomfortable service abroad.' *The Reason Why*, by Cecil Woodham-Smith. There is an excellent account of the purchase system in this book, pp. 22–25.

113

After the birth of a second son, Arthur, in June 1825, Lord William took 'a sweet pretty rural retreat' in Richmond Park for six months while the 8th Hussars were at Hounslow. Then for nearly a year he was stationed at Brighton. The great improvement in the state of the regiment under his command was noticed and commented on by the Commander-in-Chief and by the King.

Lady William Russell to old Lord William Russell in Italy [WP]

Woburn, Feb. 12.[1824]

My dear Uncle Bil, nothing can be worse than procrastination so I will answer your letter of the 17th *à vue*. What shall I tell you? the Duke goes on as usual, Lord Tavistock mends, his wife in great affliction at her mother's death, poor soul! We are going to dwell in unity & amity as a foreign *ménage* in Arlington St., their house is too big & too dear so they let us half & unless I have more *cadets Roussels* we shall have room enough – so now I am going to grow uncommonly fond of Lord Tavistock, as I am in duty bound – not that I ever had a dislike to him, *c'est un galant homme, un honnête homme*, but he is not *aimable à tourner des têtes*. Rather like his ancestor in Grammont – '*taciturne à donner des vapeurs*,'* and when he does talk it is Hebrew to me as it is county interest, grazing cattle, capital sport, hounds & constituents, game & Ministers, and things of that import. So in short it is a firm between us and they have such an orderly, excellent set of servants & all their household in such apple pie order that I expect all the worldly comfort I have hitherto been a stranger to. Your little daughter is always pretty & good tempered & in great favour with our red faced Vixen, whom Heaven confound some day or other. Your son *le beau Franzis* (as Alava calls him) was here – *l'air plus conquérant que jamais* – he looks at women and says 'how do you do' even, with a voice & glance accustomed to subdue. He has added to his manly attractions whiskers of dimensions hitherto unknown – not moustachios – but *les favoris*, they are black, bright, curled, thick, & garnish the whole face, which gives him the look of a *joli Sapeur*. George was here too, he is a youth I like, he is rather in the languishing, sighing, soporific mood *pour le moment*. William is much improved, reads, talks very well, he shows that he has instruction, he pleased me, – as to poor dear Mrs Bennett you may imagine how I pitied

---

* C. E. Engel in her edition (1958) of the *Mémoires du Chevalier de Gramont* suggests that this silent member of the family was William Russell, son of Edward Russell, brother to the 5th Earl of Bedford. He was standard bearer to Charles II and died unmarried.

her!* I was glad to hear Sir John Aubrey had given them a house in Oxfordshire & furnish'd it as well as told him he had left them a legacy. . . .

I am always sick, I have never recovered my August mishap, which I thought was of no manner of consequence, when lo & behold when least expected I begin with a train of new complaints & opium, leeches, baths – *des diableries* of every kind! When summer comes I shall mend. We shall go to town as soon as our room is furnish'd – in March. Henceforth Arlington Street is the word – for letters, parcels or visits. My dear child is the picture of health, England & especially Woburn agrees with him most evidently; his spirits are inexhaustible & he talks as much as Lady Jersey & Lady Westmorland & Mama put together. My husband is also well & hitherto I have seen nobody amongst the *homines* I like better – but heaven knows what will happen in London – if I have good health *j'aurais des grands projets de conquête.*

I have written enough nonsense, perhaps you will think too much.

Lady William Russell to Lady Holland [HH]

Woburn Abbey, March 11 [1824]

. . . William will bless your eyesight in about three weeks, that is the period we have fixed for going to town. I am not impatient for my removal, I am lazy & very fond of Woburn. It agrees with my boy & he is fat as any of the old monks who inhabited the Abbey in days of yore. William too is attached to the place & happy in his father's society after 2 years exile. I cannot say I think favourably of the Duke, I should say *il baisse*, Lord Tavistock is as thin as a stick but evidently better if one can judge by eyes, complexion, spirits & the power of using violent exercise. Occult ailments I cannot pry into if there exist any.

As to myself I was injured by my drive which was *crève-coeur* to me as I enjoyed the air prodigiously, but the motion of the carriage reproduced the dragging muscular pain in my side & the threatening of the bearing down I have been tormented with which kept me so many months on my sofa & in my room greater part of the 24 hours which was thought such a marvellous occurrence & deemed so rude. My general health is very good, my amusements not varied *mais je végète tout doucement* thinking of the past & the future.

Our room in Arlington St is not yet habitable, as it does not merely

* She had lost a child.

require chairs & tables but must undergo a thorough repair of windows, doors, grates, ceiling, painting, all sorts of renovations that take time.

Mama will be beatified at having pleased you, she is really unrivalled in taste of every kind, dress, furniture, *étiquette* & all those minutiae. The *couturières & lingères & marchands* of every kind say '*ah, Madame, que vous avez du goût! on ne dirait pas que vous êtes Anglaise!*'

Duke of Bedford to Lord William Russell at Woburn [WPP]

London, March 22 [1824]

The system of depletion in various forms has been going on since I have been in town, but apparently without effect, as I have experienced no sensible relief, *mais tout au contraire*, as a Frenchman says on every occasion. I avail myself, however, of a cessation from uneasiness to say that as I have never spoken to you on the subject you mentioned to me, about Lord Hastings offer, you may probably desire to know my opinion. Lauderdale says Lord H. has accepted the offer made to him, so I conclude he is to have command of all British troops within the Mediterranean. At present they are confined to the island of Malta. However, having accepted the offer of Government, it remains with you to say whether you will accept his offer. Military Secretary would certainly have been the most desirable post you could occupy about him, but after that the place of first A.D.C. must be the most important, if not incompatible with your rank in the Army, but of this, you, as a military man, are the best judge, as well as whether you would like such a situation under Lord H. My opinion has always been that it is best for a professional man to pursue his profession, whatever that profession may be. Had they behaved well to you at Head Quarters, you would probably not have remained inactive since 1814, but you know my principle is never to ask any thing for my sons from official men, and I have often told my brother that I have done for his sons what I would never do for my own.

One subject, I am aware, may make you hesitate about accepting the offer, but the chances are that I shall be laid quietly by the side of those who have gone before me, at Chenies,* before your presence will be required at Malta, so you will leave England, your mind fully relieved from all anxiety on the score of my health, or, as I like to look at things always

* The burial place of the Russells in Buckinghamshire.

on the most favourable side, it is possible (though certainly not probable) that I may get better; you will then be equally relieved from anxiety.

I mention these things without reserve or affectation, because you must, of course, take them into your consideration. I give no advice, not feeling competent to do so, and this letter is for your eye alone; burn it when you have read it, or keep it, if you should wish to know hereafter what my opinions were. . . .

Tale-bearing, gossip, or some indiscretion on Lady Holland's part, perhaps, appears to have given Lady William an excuse to write an angry letter on leaving her father-in-law's house. The latent animosity between herself and the Duchess was released, and her rudeness had repercussions that caused a breach in the family, not easily healed.

Duke of Bedford to Lady Holland [HH]

C[ampden] H[ill] [1824]

. . . I retire from London with no weight on my mind, but that which, alas! relates to a part of my own family. I confess I cannot comprehend William's conduct to the Duchess he does not treat her with the common decency & decorum due from a man to a woman; much more from him to his father's wife. John has very good-naturedly undertaken to set matters right, but he does not seem to understand the question. Surely the Dss. cannot be expected to make an *apology* for an offence denied & not committed! Whilst William & Lady William continue to behave in this extraordinary manner, I cannot consent (painful as it may be to me) to go again to her before I leave town. I never name the subject to the Duchess. It has been one of great anxiety & vexation to her, & would to God she had been spared the pain of it from my own son! . . .

Duke of Bedford to Lord William Russell in London [WPP]

Woburn Abbey, Thursday [1824]

It was impossible that the Duchess could act otherwise than she did under accusations, so serious, as mischief-making, duplicity and falsehood, nor could Lady Holland do otherwise than deny what she must know to be utterly false and groundless. It is grievous, however, to hear that you and Lady William should consider such accusations as a subject for your 'laughter'. During the nine months that you were here, it was the constant wish of both the Duchess and myself, to make you and yours as comfortable as we could, and if we have failed in our endeavours, we can only lament it. As Lady William dislikes fetchers and carriers, and tale-bearers, the best thing she can do henceforward, when any of her soi-disant friends, come to her with stories against the Duchess, is to turn a deaf ear and not listen to them, and to him or her who brought her the story of her correspondence with Lord Holland, she may truly say, 'Ferdinand Mendez Pinto was but a type of thee, thou liar of the first magnitude!' and now I have done with this unpleasant subject and I trust for ever.

The Duchess has had a very bad night, and does not appear much better, but as the blister does its office well, I trust she will be relieved before the night.

Lord John Russell to Lord William Russell [WPP]

Thursday morning [1824]

Whether lukewarm or not, I am so full of the subject of your letter that I must instantly write to you. I cannot have advised one of two courses, both of which you think Lady W. ought to decline. I simply said that there was but one alternative, either not to quarrel at all, or if she did, to be prepared for the worst that a powerful, vindictive and unscrupulous enemy could do. Therefore I am not surprised nor ought you to be at what has happened. I felt it very acutely, but seeing what you wrote, and knowing what state you would be in, I thought it better to try and cool than to assist in exciting you. It is a bad piece of friendship to inflame an angry man when all that he does in consequence is at his peril and not at your own.

I am not at all disposed to find fault with your determination not to come to Woburn alone. But still, I think, that if sometime hence, my father should ask you to come, with Lady William, you ought to come, not to stay, but to pay a visit. In fact (putting out of the question all you say about venison and champagne which is to be had in any one of the 52 counties) it is very bad policy in us to quarrel with Woburn. Only suppose that T. and I were to do so likewise, as we might without being very quarrelsome. Do not you think my father would hear less truth? That he would do more unjust things? That he would lead a more unhappy life, and even that he might be led to do Tavistock a serious injury? In fact *she* throws stones at us to get back nuts and any expression of resentment on our part must strengthen her influence.

I only beg you to consider all this, not now but sometime hence, and make use of your solid judgement in your own case as well as in that of other people. You may call me lukewarm as much as you please, but I shall not cease to hold this language. All the stuff about Madame Durazzo is as you say a weak invention of the enemy to set me against Bessy, in which it totally fails.

Duke of Bedford to Lord William Russell [WPP]

Woburn Abbey, May 2nd 1824

It was my firm intention not to have said another word on the irksome subject which has formed a part of our late correspondence, but there are two expressions in your last letter which render some observation on my part imperative. Do not suffer any grievance you may think you have to complain of to 'rankle in your breast', but state openly and candidly what it is, and I will stake my existence that it will prove as groundless and untenable as the foolish story about the Duchess's correspondence with Lord Holland, which Lady William thought it worth her while to listen to, and to found a serious charge upon it. With respect to my use of the 'Pronoun, plural, "We"', it is dictated by no 'chivalrous and indulgent spirit', but a pure and simple feeling of justice, which I hope and trust will ever be the guide of my conduct to the last hour of my existence. The Duchess and I have always felt and acted the same towards you and Lady William, and I can venture to affirm from a thorough knowledge of the fact, that the Duchess's conduct towards you and yours has uniformly been kind, generous and affectionate, therefore she can have no 'sins' to lay to her conscience in that respect. I am unwilling to say anything which may appear in the least degree harsh, and will therefore content myself with observing that the Duchess has been abundantly tolerant and forbearing, and now let the matter drop, and be buried in oblivion. It has been the cause of too much worry, both to the Duchess and myself, and in my state of health I feel it to be more than my head will bear. . . .

Lord John Russell to Lady William Russell [PRP]

Longleat,* 20 August [1824]

I will endeavour to give you an answer which shall be more intelligible than my last to all your propositions. 1st. My notions of right and wrong are

* The seat of the Marquess of Bath in Wiltshire.

not confined to Whig & Tory but like yours to *coquine* & *honnête femme*. 2nd. I do not speak of the merits of the Duchess but of those of Lady Holland – constancy to her friends, & great kindness where many show indifference. I do not live with the Duchess so much as you do & never have been great friends with her. 3rd. I am not indifferent to your being turned out of my father's house. The truth is that being charged by William to warn Madame Durazzo against the Duchess I was obliged to tell her the story & she said, 'I am very sorry for him, he will be in such distress – pray write to soothe him.' This I tried to do, & with such success that if ever I see any body in a passion again I will blow the coals with all my might till they burn to pieces. It was a very shameful act to desire you not to come to Woburn, but I own I was not surprised at it. You must have known it was the Dss's will, & there could not be for any long time a doubt about her power. I suspect base hangers-on have contributed to enable her to attain her end. Binda* told the whole story to Madame Durazzo, much to the Duchess's honour & glory.

William could not have acted otherwise than he did, & you much mistake me if you imagine I said or thought so. What I said about hating on account of what you are falsely supposed to have said of Madame D. was evidently a joke. I never said I was employed as a mediator for you; nor was I, but I have been for others & hope never to be so again.

Madame Durazzo came into the whole thing *par hasard* as you say but will not talk of it about the world as Rogers is sure to do. I own I think it a great pity to make the world talk about our family quarrels.

Lady Holland be well assured is not likely to do anything but vex you & try to hurt you – as she now does the Lansdownes, most wickedly & cruelly. And now to conclude. I have a great love & even reverence for my father which nothing will shake. I am very sorry he is under the influence of a wicked woman, but I see some of my best friends under the influence of their wives & it is more their luck than their merit if those wives turn out to be well-principled & virtuous. Whatever you do, pray do not abuse my father to the world. . . .

* Giuseppe Binda was a native of Lucca and was for several years an inmate of Holland House, where he made himself useful in various capacities. The Duke of Bedford called him 'a foolish little fellow'.

Duke of Bedford to Lady Holland [HH]

Invereshie, Aug 22. [1824]

... Lady William wrote to me that William had had a bilious attack, & that she had saved him from a fever by sending for Hume. I do not wonder at your thinking him out of spirits – he has appeared to me to be so for a long time back. I have no doubt that he is annoyed. I wish *she* could be persuaded for the sake of the future peace & comfort of us all to make some advances towards the re-establishment of harmony. No one is more alive than I am to the comforts of a happy & united family, but I fear (*entre nous*) Lady W. is haughty & unbending in her disposition and unwilling to own herself in the wrong; but surely something like an acknowledgement of the impropriety of the very extraordinary letter she wrote on quitting Woburn, could do her no harm. If John has any influence over her, he ought to use it. 'Blessed are the peacemakers.'

Lord John Russell to Lady William Russell [PRP]

[Longleat 1824]

There is only one thing now I want to explain. Binda I concluded had got his tale from the Duchess. I only mentioned him to put you on your guard.

Her Grace brought me my father's letter; explained as a preface that you had sent word by William you would be at Woburn the next day without writing or asking my father beforehand. This I did not quite believe as my father had told me William was coming to Woburn, and my impression was that you were coming too. She then desired me to read his letter but gave no opinion any way.

We have been four days at Longleat.* Lady Bath was pretty well, and exceedingly kind. We had Luttrell,† Crabbe‡ and Moore there all very agreeable. Crabbe is very amusing from his mixture of cunning and simplicity. Moore is always delightful to me from his spirits and heart which overflow on all sides – upon the whole this is much pleasanter than the best dry wit, tho' the latter like dry Champagne is reckoned better taste

* Lord John was escorting the Durazzos on a round of country house visits. In Moore's *Journal*, iv, 235, may be found the only record of the complaisant husband's voice. When visiting Fonthill Abbey M. Durazzo exclaimed: 'un homme doit avoir le diable au corps pour bâtir une maison comme ça.'

† Henry Luttrell (1765–1851), a wit; the natural son of the 2nd Earl of Carhampton.

‡ George Crabbe (1754–1832), poet. He was rector of Trowbridge in Wiltshire.

than the sparkling. We go to Middleton tomorrow. Lady Holland is delighted with Mrs Rawdon who she says she has always liked. And so give
my love to Hastings and believe me yours affecly

> Beware of writing, sons, beware,
> For unexplained by tone or air,
> Without the means to soften down
> By foll'wing words the coming frown
> The slightest hint may sound severe,
> And dearest friends no longer dear;
> Causeless resentments turn the feeling soul,
> And waft a sting from India to the Pole.

Lord William Russell to Lady Holland [HH]

Dorchester Barracks, Aug 27 [1824]

... I could not find any lodging nearer than Weymouth, which is full
& dear. My officers are a wild, rollicking, gallivanting set, but good humoured & gentlemanlike, the men are all Irish – but they may be Dutch for
what you care so I dont know why I tell you so.

I never hear from my Father, his amiable virtuous wife has probably
estranged his affection from me; as she shows you the letters written in
confidence to her, perhaps you do the same, so I had better be silent.

Bessy, Mrs R & the boy are all well at Weymouth. I shall see them
presently.

Lady William Russell to old Lord William Russell [WP]

Weymouth, Oct 6. [1824]

By the bye I was 31 on the 2nd of
this month. *Tempus fugit*!! *Il m'en
coûte de l'avouer*!!

I went to town with Billikins not liking to trust him out of my sight, and
on my return found your letter from Middleton – then came yours to *him*.
He answered & I thought I might as well write later. I conclude as a good
courtier you did not write sooner for fear of getting into a scrape with my
respectable & praiseworthy enemy whom you bespatter with the name of
my friend. You should not offer her such an indignity. I am unworthy of

such an honor. I am glad you were happy in Scotland & sorry you would not *partager nos ennuis* here. It is a horrid place I must own – the climate exceedingly disagreeable even to me who like warmth & the sea, but the air is enervating, a perpetual sirocco – sea fogs as hot as the steam of a tea kettle, & then a monotony quite deadening. One walk, one drive, one view, all the houses looking one way, and instead of a marine smell one of pitch, tar, tallow, sea coal smoke & so forth. Dorchester is 8 miles off, a very melancholy town, surrounded by trees, like boulevards. Upon the whole it puts me in mind of some of the most melancholy country towns in the north of France. No houses to be let in or near it – & the barracks won't even hold the unmarried officers. *Quoiqu'il en soit, nous nous tirons d'affaire* & may be next year our quarters will be pleasanter.

My health is now perfectly good – all but the place disagreeing with me, but not making me ill. I walk as much as I can, but the weight of the atmosphere oppresses my breathing & benumbs my limbs so as to prevent its being a resource – & as to driving all the horses have been sick & are so still in various ways. My trip to town did me a deal of good; we were away five days & left the boy with Granny. He bathes & is very well indeed. As to our going abroad I hunger & thirst after it, but I suppose we shall be all *à la tantale* concerning that longing – I don't see a chance or a prospect beyond Paris, which I don't care about & only buy caps & bonnets in – which I now don't want. *Voilà, milord, où nous en sommes. . . .*

Lady William Russell to Lord Lynedoch [NLS]

11 October 1824

. . . William told you he would feel awkward in the neighbourhood of Woburn as I am banished *par contumace* from its precincts – but as everybody knows the affair and the Duchess is so crack'd I do not see why we should deprive ourselves of a pleasure on that account – so pray come and talk him over. You must know I was going down to Woburn in August on the Duke's going to Scotland and our going to Dorsetshire, to take leave till next year. William had some County business and went to Bedford a day before me – my horses were actually at the door the next morning, when the post coming in I received a letter saying he would be back that very day and I was to put off my departure, his father had written him a note begging of him to prevent my coming and he gave as a reason a string of words evidently dictated by the Duchess as I had heard them five hundred times from her own lips *à propos* to the Tavistocks and to myself whenever I or they had got into disgrace – 'that we could not command our affections but that a certain decorum and respect was due to her as mistress of the house etc., etc., etc.' in short that I had been rude and ungrateful as she had saved my life during my first lying-in at Paris and had rendered it pleasant ever after – *bref*, I was never to put my foot in the Abbey again. This was a great surprize as we had had no new disagreement and no explosion – having lived off and on in a sweet state of alternate discord and union for many months without any ostensible cause for either. As I was in the eyes of all London setting out for Woburn and was obliged to give a reason for not going the event became public – the party gone down to Woburn expected me, they were told I was not allowed to come – in short *cela fut un esclandre*. Lord John was there, wrote to me since several times with *des notices* on the subject and seemed to be amazed I had not expected it – which proves it was brewing some time. The Duchess told him and everybody that I had merely sent word by William the day before that I should be at Woburn to dinner, that the Duke thought it impertinent and forbid me the house etc. Lord John says he was aware it was an untruth as he had heard for upwards of a fortnight beforehand of this visit, but did not like to venture an opinion or deny a falsehood, in short it made a great fuss, but no quarrel between the Duke and his son as he has been in constant and active correspondence with him from that time to this about his regimental concerns. So I alone am the black sheep.

There is a candid statement of the whole affair and you will take the side you judge the fairest. Am I a vixen? *Je n'en sais rien.*

Burn my epistle when you have digested it.

Lord William Russell to Lady Holland [HH]

Weymouth 30 Oct [1824]

How can you be so mistaken about what you call the *tracasserie* in our family, thank God I am not on bad terms with my Father, I never had a quarrel with him in my life & he never was kinder to me than he is at the present moment. 3 or 4 months ago when Lady William was going at my request to Woburn Abbey, my Father at the desire of the Duchess forbade the visit saying Lady William was uncivil to the Duchess & that it was his duty to protect his wife, of course as it is his, it is mine & every other husband's, that being the case I cannot, nor will I enter the house of a woman, who turns out my wife on false grounds, not privately but before a parcel of foreigners. What do you mean by repentance? I have nothing to repent of. The person who acts must repent, not the person who suffers, it was an act of revenge & hatred on the part of the Duchess of Bedford towards Lady William. *Tracasseries* happen as you say in every family, but not such a public *esclandre* as this – a large party assembled at Woburn Abbey was made witness to it, I did nothing to cause it, I am not to blame for it, I do not repent of it, I did not give it publicity. I am on the best terms with my Father & hope I always shall be. . . .

Lord William Russell to Lady Holland [HH]

[Dorchester, 7 November 1824]

You are still mistaken. I bear no angry feelings towards anyone, I am neither revengeful or irritable, I forgive too easily, I bear malice towards no one, I am too happy in my interior, to look out for imaginary injuries. I am sorry I was, or if you will, my wife was turned out of my Father's house, & I daresay as the Vicar of Wakefield observes, there is much to be said on both sides, but I would rather not say my say & forget it all. *La Senora e muy loca,** tant pis* for those who live with her, & *tant mieux* for those who dont live with her, so I have nothing to complain of.

I daresay you meant well, so I forgive you all the abuse & calumny you have heaped upon me. If I go on in this way you will think I am drunk, tho I never taste wine or beer, but I am in good spirits notwithstanding I live in a lodging over a library in a gloomy street in gloomy Dorchester, we laugh, we talk, we abuse our friends, & that is all very pleasant. . . .

Lady William Russell to Lord Lynedoch [NLS]

Dorchester, Nov. 24 [1824]

A thousand thanks for your letter and all the details – you have been *trottant par monts et par vaux* most indefatigably. . . .

I believe I told you I was well pleased with Dorchester. I don't mean *ivre de joie* but it is preferable to Weymouth where I was aguish and ill – here I am quite well. As to the regiment I am much pleased at Lord William's getting it; I have for 7 years been urging him to do something.

* 'The lady is very mad.'

I hate idleness, it can lead to no good, & have ever discouraged the notions he had (I believe only vague ones, but still he frequently has talked of them to me) of giving up Parliament & the army. *J'ai jeté des hauts cris*, though for my own propensities nothing could have been more propitious as I confess I dislike England and I have lived since my marriage with such disagreeable human beings that I am rather prejudiced against the natives. I find them generally speaking unblushingly selfish, *peu touchés des maux d'autrui*; great dissipation & immorality with small cheerfulness (I might say none) & a kind of warfare to, *convenance* carried on that shocks me every hour of the day. Then I detest the climate & am unaccustomed to *les moeurs du pays*. I mean by *moeurs* not morals but modes of life, therefore it is entirely principle, and I have ever acted according to principle, that makes me forgo the gratification of my inclinations in living abroad – *il ne tendit qu'à moi* to break off this majority as he was more inclined to go to Malta (as heaven knows so was I) than into the 8th. I saw the advantages of the thing & entered into it *après un petit combat intérieur d'un quart d'heure* & a little lump in my throat. My object & constant pursuit since I married has been to *rehausser* Lord William in his own opinion, for he is too diffident, and from being kept like a frightened schoolboy under the thumb of an artful & vulgar minded woman for so many years – who wished to cow him, my task was not easy; the greatest part of her spite has been my weaning him from her. His intimacy & communications to her before marriage were of so extraordinary & degrading a nature according to my notions of decorum that I hardly conceived it possible that such could exist except between a stripling and a *complaisante* of the lowest kind. Every friend of his and people whose opinion I value (men not boys) have spoken of his judgement as you do – Lord Holland puts it above that of both his brothers even the *bel esprit* John – what he wants is confidence in himself & I do think that his present situation will lead to it – independent of its professional advantages. I, of course, wish to see him distinguished, & must prefer his present creditable employment to his lounging about London with Poodle Byng or George Leigh* – or Paris with Montrond† & Madame du Thé.‡ I have been in despair at his *désoeuvrement* hitherto, which has been greater in England than abroad, as here he actually did

---

* Lieut.-Colonel George Leigh, husband of Byron's half-sister Augusta.

† Casimir, Comte de Montrond (?–1843); the dissolute, unprincipled and intimate friend of Talleyrand.

‡ Perhaps a sobriquet for Madame de Coigny who was importunate for bohea tea. See pp. 232, 233.

nothing but hunt all winter & lounge all summer. Abroad he took a fancy to some employment such as learning languages & reading, which are mere pastimes & accomplishments but better than *oisiveté mère des vices*. I used ignorantly but with good intentions to want him abroad to apply himself to tactics & fortifications & the theoretical parts of his profession, but he said they were not his line. It is only to prove to you that *I* have never lost sight of his vocation as a military man.

Now these are points that I never talk of or breathed to a fellow creature. I write to you in a strain of seriousness which is my real train of thought, though not my usual style of conversation – I should be a fool to do otherwise. I know you love William as a father & will not take what I say *de mauvaise part*. I have not had fair play but that cannot be helped. Nothing but the extreme confidence & friendship I feel for you could induce me to write such a letter, but I am misrepresented because I scorn malapropos displays of sentiment & ethics.

I must release you from all this prose, which burn and do not take the trouble of answering. *Portez-vous bien – amusez-vous bien etc.*
Veuillez-moi bien.

Lord William Russell to Lady Holland [HH]

Dorchester 6 Dec [1824]

As you are so ill I will leave you in peace, but I intended to have attacked you for having accused me of being splenetick, which you now add to all the other bad qualities you accused me of before, certainly you use me very ill, for I am nothing but a *bon diable*, neither revengeful, malicious, envious, suspicious or splenetick.

I did not write (as I ought to have done) to thank you for your kind information about my Father's health, because I had little time, my mind being much engaged with the Regiment which I am endeavouring to improve.

We have made the acquaintance of your aunt Lady Susan O'Brien,* she is a charming, wonderful, gay old lady, but I am sorry to say she was much alarmed at the storm & has never been well since. Pray thank Allen for taking the trouble to write to me. Brighton appears as full as London in the full season. I wish we had been quartered there, instead of in this dreary melancholy town, where we are lodged over a bookseller's shop,

* Lady Susan Fox Strangways, daughter of the 1st Earl of Ilchester, widow of the actor William O'Brien.

better however than over a tallow chandler. We have a deal of knowledge at our feet ends, better than walking over *grease*. I know you like a pun, but I hope this sickness of yours is nothing of consequence; you should try change of air. . . .

That comical fellow John has disappeared from the face of the earth, I suppose he is lost in the delights of Genoa, happy fellow.

Lady William Russell to old Lord William Russell in Italy [WP]

Longleat, Jan. 2nd, 1825.
This moment I got your letter from Bologna of Xber 14. *Primo*, I thank you for it, *secondo* – I wish you a happy new year & *terzo* I relate to you our adventures up to the present day. I wrote to you from Weymouth, where I was sick & sorry; it is an aguish, nasty, noisy place which most people hate since the old King's days, but my ailments turned into nausea & so forth & now it is *une belle grossesse de 4 mois*. I shall be confined in May, please God, & am as well as possible & have been so these two months & more, all my qualms having ceased in the second month. One would think I was writing to Lazzerini by telling you such details, but I insist on your being interested in the fortunes of Bet & Bil, your nephew & niece. As to Billikins he is *colonel de houssards à moustaches*. He got the promotion for which he re-entered the Service & has the command of the 8th Hussars *moyennant une grosse somme d'argent* – the patronage of the Duke of York & the exertions of his friends – it is what I suppose his comrades term being 'a lucky dog'. In the meanwhile we are settled at Dorchester in a very clean, roomy, warm & comfortable lodging over a library & printing office – the town is reckon'd very dull – were it gay I do not know how it would profit us much for I do not suppose we should either enter into or contribute much to its festivities. *Quoiqu'il en soit* we live like Darby & Joan & very happy & contented I must say. *La signora madre* is on a visit to us & puts up with country quarters with great good humour, the boy is always in admirable health & we lead a jog trot quiet life that *quand on vieillit & que l'on est raisonnable* one is quite reconciled to; being all in perfect health & having no *contrariétés* we must needs be in good humour though the affair does not sound *folâtre* – the whole County are so civil to us, that *il ne tient qu'à nous* never to be in our lodgings; they are perpetually & repeatedly inviting us to their houses. Billikins has shook off all his Russell

128

indolence & slaves at his regiment, which was in a wretched plight & which he will gain great credit by putting into order. We are to be quartered at Hounslow next year I believe, which will exactly suit my *couches*, as marching with the regiment a great distance with 2 children (& perhaps 3) on my back would be inconvenient. How we are to contrive all our operations in Arlington Street I know not, but the Tavistocks have been good nature itself in giving us up an additional room to contribute to our necessities. She has had a horrid accident, poor soul, her cloathes having caught fire at Oakley & being cruelly scorched, but in no material way happily, still the pain is abominable.

We came here 2 days ago & return to Dorchester tomorrow. We have been coming to Longleat 5 times, I thought we should never achieve it. It is a beautiful place but the house is full of invalids – Greville *père** spits blood & keeps his room, Lady Charlotte is *souffrante* & never dines below, – Henry Greville is lame & on a *chaise longue*, – Alava† hobbles about on *béquilles* & though last not least Lady Bath was seized with a fit of the gout the day after we arrived. I heard of *le beau Guillaume's* love – *poverino, mi fa compassione!* The Duke writes that Johnnikins is coming home this month, – that his true love is good looking & lively I deny not – but she is a *coquine* which is rather a feather in her cap in our *coterie*. We honest women are mere twaddles.

I think I have left nothing untold – you are *au courant* of all our proceedings. Parliament meets in February, but we shall not leave our Dragoons till March, when the Assizes turn us out of our lodging which belongs to the judges. *Addio, Signor zio carissimo*, heaven knows when we shall meet as all *our* visions of foreign travel are vanish'd & absorbed in the realities of a professional pursuit.

Lord William Russell to Lady Holland [HH]

Longleat Jan 3 1825

. . . We have been here about a week, & so sick an assemblage of people were never got together. Greville *père mourant*, & everybody laughs,

---

* Charles Greville (1763–1832) father of the diarist; his wife was Lady Charlotte Bentinck, daughter of the 3rd Duke of Portland. Henry was their third son.

† General Miguel Alava (1771–1843) was a political refugee from Spain. He was a great friend of the Duke of Wellington with whom he had fought against the French in Spain. He became Spanish ambassador in London in 1834.

Greville *fils*, *le jeune et beau prêtre*,* lame, & everybody cries, but so is the world. Alava on crutches, & tho last not least poor Lady Bath confined to her bed with gout, cold & general suffering. We return to our garrison duties tomorrow. . . .

Old Lady Susan keeps us all alive by her gaiety & anecdotes of our grandmothers & their sweethearts, she is a prodigy & a most amusing prodigy. One day she amused us with the story of Lord Holland's birth, the wrapping him in flannel etc.

I am glad to hear we are to see John again, I thought he intended to become a Genoese patrician or *patito*.† I have not yet read his book,‡ nor do I understand with what view he has published on so hackneyed a subject as the days of Louis 14.

Bessy is well, & as you probably know *en famille*, as the Englishman said, 4 months gone.

Duke of Bedford to Lord William Russell at Dorchester [WPP]

Woburn Abbey, January 5 1825.

. . . You are very severe on John and his book, though you acknowledge that neither you nor any one else at Longleat had read it, and yet 'they hold it cheap.' I think the observations you make are not your own, and I think I recognise in them, the satire and malignity of that contemptible old woman, *le ci-devant jeune homme*,§ who is going out of the world, smashing and biting at all his friends, as he has done through life, and who, I believe, will die unlamented, unregretted by a single individual. I will tell you what John's object is in writing. It is to occupy and amuse himself, to amuse his readers and to add to his literary fame. The immediate object of his work is to prove that the stupendous event of our own times, the French Revolution, was not the work of the period in which it happened, but the result of a long series of misgovernment in France, during the preceding century; of the profligacy of the Court, and the baseness and corruption which spread from thence, over all her institutions and over the whole kingdom. He has done this very successfully

---

* Perhaps his good looks qualified him for the title of 'prêtre'. He does not seem to have been destined for the Church but for diplomacy. His *Leaves from the Diary of H. G.* were published 1883–1905.

† 'The *patito* or "sufferer of Genoa", is the *cavaliere servente* of Milan, the *cicisbeo* of Florence and Rome; but more serviceable and enslaved.' Lady Morgan, *Italy*, i, 252n.

‡ The first volume of *Memoirs of the Affairs of Europe from the Peace of Utrecht*.

§ The title of a play given in Paris. Appears here to refer to old Charles Greville.

to my mind, as far as he has gone, and I trust he will proceed with the same vigour as heretofore in the task. Let me recommend you to read the short review of the work in the Literary Gazette of last Saturday. It is from an enemy's journal, as it is Longmans paper and he is John's discarded publisher.

Lord William Russell to Lady Holland [HH]

Dorchester Jan 18 [1825]

I am truly sorry to hear of your continued & violent illness, Alava writes – *vous feriez pitié même à* Lady Caroline Lamb, however I hope you will soon get out of such a melancholy situation & be yourself again. If medicine can cure you, you have two of the first rate geniuses to administer it. I am sorry to hear Lord Holland has mounted the emblem of the gout, however I hope he will soon again display the white flag. It is very good of you to write to me in the midst of your sickness & with such disinterested views, for I can send you nothing in return for all your amusing anecdotes & news. We see nobody, hear nothing, know nothing of the world, it is a melancholy life for Bessy, the ornament & brightest flower of the brightest society of Europe, to be pent up in a small provincial town, but she is in good health, & consequently always gay, amiable, original & amusing. We shall remain a month or two more, for there will be nothing to do in Parliament, Ireland is all a bugbear. I have been so occupied in taming my wild Irish that I have not had time to read John's book, it is highly spoken of, Mrs Rawdon has read it & likes it. I have read Fouché's memoirs, but cannot believe them genuine, a man would be as great a rogue but none would proclaim himself such to all the world.

Lady William Russell to old Lord William Russell at Spa [WP]

Arlington Street
Monday, August 1, 1825.

From what I can make out of your letter, dear Uncle, I imagine I must direct to Spa, but you must indeed, like the man's excuse for bad spelling, have hit upon a deplorable *mauvaise plume d'auberge* when you wrote from Berne. I cannot make out half your meanings *dont je suis au désespoir* for I was otherwise delighted at seeing your ciphers again. As to your not writing I am not huffy about it only pleased when you do so far recollect me. I had good accounts of your daughter Gertrude* from Lady Bath, she thought her looks improved by foreign air & her child benefited – poor soul! I grieve most sincerely when I think of her cruel losses & many privations for some years preceding, though they were but trifles compared to her real distresses of mind. I thank God we are spared misfortunes & go on floating down the current of life smoothly & happily with the additional blessing of a second son; all of us are in health, I had what is termed an 'excellent time' and a quick recovery for I have been this fortnight past as if nothing had happened to me, & it is but six weeks since I brought forth. The baby's name is Arthur John after his uncle & his papa's old General. My boys have an uncle apiece as god fathers *et je vous retiens pour la prochaine fois.* William's regiment is at Hounslow, which will keep us all the year in or about London, he still fags most assiduously & I am glad he has occupation.

I take it for granted that your thousand & one fair correspondents keep you *au courant des affaires de la société;* having passed one month in my room & having been early in the spring kept at home with attacks on my chest, I have been out but little & upon the whole judged the world to be flat. Not that I was at all *ennuyée* but I was as well or rather better amused at home, *les plaisirs n'étant pas vifs;* our house is delicious & our Simpson & Co. flourishes admirably, only the birth of Prince Arthur will oblige us to part company unless they build, which Lord Tavistock talks of & Lady Tavistock *dis*talks of, – we ought to have terms for the Italian *parlare & sparlare.*† As to my feuds as you call them, *non c'è niente di nuovo.*‡ It remains as it was this time last year when the social war broke out. You, being a cautious personage, although in the thick of it, never expressed an opinion, & heaven forfend that I should attempt to draw you from your neutrality. I look upon you all as the little mediatized princes of the Rhine between two great belligerent powers, though as Whigs you act a corrupt part – for I represent liberty & independence against oppression & power – but Whigs are all tyrants at heart, witness Lady Jersey at Almacks. William has letters from both his brothers saying he could not have acted otherwise & Lady Holland assures him they both blame him to her. I have kept the whole correspondence to my infinite & daily satisfaction, not that I

---

* Gertrude Bennett, usually referred to as 'poor Gertrude', was now living at Viareggio, perhaps driven there by poverty. She wrote herself of her 'evil destiny' and before her death in 1841 was mentally unbalanced.

† *Parlare* to speak, *sparlare* to speak ill of.

‡ 'There is nothing new.'

132

mean to publish or appeal to the public in manuscript, but I have during my 8 years matrimony doubted my own senses about many things – they appeared so discordant – & now I find like the Duchesse du Maine '*que c'est toujours moi qui ai raison*' and that in your family without being any one of ye *Le Menteur* of Gresset – forget what you have said – want energy to speak your mind, attach not sufficient importance to your words from an indifference to all but personal facts – & thus in political & family business many a rub must be excited, – elections – correspondences & public meetings have testified to the truth of what I advance, so in future I shall take care, not of what I say (for I am too valiant not to wish to be answerable for my words) but of what I believe. Little Johnnikins always repeats everything he hears to our disadvantage (to keep up our spirits) & on either of us exclaiming 'dear me, why didn't you contradict,' he laughs violently & answers, 'Oh, *I* said nothing.' which is being a useful & a faithful friend. Last year he wrote to say he wondered I was surprized at being turned out of Woburn Abbey as I must have seen it had been long the Duchess's object. Now admitting this *I* cannot be blamed & the event was not an accident of *my* provoking but *prédestiné. Voilà où nous en sommes.* . . . We have *Loulou** & the *Mofskis* here running about like rabbits & the old fellow near dead of it.

Mama passed 7 months with us at Dorchester & Weymouth, since which she has been at Brighton & is now in town on her way to Berne, where she means to be *en pension*, we endeavour to prove to her it is a folly, but she will, so I give up Paris. . . .

Duke of Bedford to Lord William Russell [WPP]

September 8th, 1825.

Whilst I regret that we should be compelled to think & feel differently on the unpleasant subject we have recently discussed, I agree with you that any attempt at explanation must be perfectly useless. In every other respect, your letter has given me the most heartfelt satisfaction, and I cordially thank you for it. Let everything on so painful a subject be now forgotten, and completely blotted from our memories. What I have said with regard to myself is the settled conviction of my mind – others may think differently, but I feel that the vital powers languish and decay, and the lamp of life is glimmering, and must soon be extinguished. May you

---

* Probably Louisa Lady Hardy and her daughters.

and your wife and children enjoy every blessing that the world can afford, is the sincere and anxious prayer of your truly affectionate father.

Lord William Russell to Lord Tavistock [WP]

Richmond Park Farm, Sep 15 [1825]

I doubt whether my father understands my plan or agrees with me. He says 'he is acting upon the principles I propose, with the exception of keeping Millbrook & being less hard upon poachers (under the existing odious system of game laws)'. When I was at Woburn the other day, I saw no symptom of acting upon my principles being commenced, I am all for keeping all partridge land, consequently am for keeping Millbrook, but without allowing compensation to the farmers, & as for being less hard upon poachers I am decidedly for keeping poachers off & punishing them if they take my game, in my opinion the laws are not at all to blame, & I very much doubt whether Mr Wortley's bill would not have created a still more odious law than the present, the evil is in the abuse of the law, not in the law. Who ever heard of the odious game laws 20 years ago, nobody complained of them till the game was collected in such quantities, during a time of distress, that the poor could not resist taking it, & the prisons were consequently filled with them. The only change I wish to see in the law, is to make game saleable because then the rich fundholders, merchant bankers &c. will do that legally which they now do illegally with impunity, & the fair dealer will compete with & undersell the poacher in the market. *Now* the peasant working for 8 or 9 shillings a week with a wife & 8 or 9 children sees a fat, tame pheasant come daily to his garden to eat his potatoes, temptation is daily before him, he resists a week, the Devil urges him on, nobody is looking, rent day is near, money short, he takes up a stone, kills the pheasant, gets 3 shillings for it, it is bought by his landlord's banker, who gives a dinner to the landlord himself, who finds his own pheasant delicious. The poor peasant pleased with his success & 3 shillings knocks down another, the keeper is behind the hedge & takes him to prison – the banker goes on encouraging others to knock down pheasants & is never punished. I do not mean to defend the peasant, he acted illegally, but I would not put temptation in his way by having *tame* pheasants, my game should be wild as game.

I am decidedly for landlords having game on their estates, & a strong law to protect that game, nor do I think that allowing poachers to intrude at all leads to popularity, but as Liston says *Wicy Warsy*. . . . To condemn a practice because it is foreign is certainly absurd, but when it is foreign, odious & injurious then it may be condemned. My father says he is the only one of his family who likes battue shooting because he is infirm, now I never saw him do otherwise than retire from the contest, & shoot the stray game that went back to him; what much better sport he would have by going out with 3 or 4 guns on a fine day for 3 or 4 hours especially in November. It is evident my father writes under feelings of soreness & disappointment, nor am I surprised at it. He gave in to the fashionable amusement of the day, & with great skill, talent & expence succeeded beyond everybody, Woburn shooting was everything, there was no *bassesse* the fashionable world would not commit to shoot at Woburn & dance at Almack's, those two things were the ne plus ultra of fashionability. My father naturally enough was proud of his creation, & the admiration it inspired, those days are now gone by, everybody has the same quantity of game, the fashionable are surfeited, pampered, insolent & tired of shooting (ourselves too it must be owned as bad as any) like lazy overfed footmen; the Duke has not observed this change in public opinion. He is out of humour with us & the law & contemplates the destruction of his creation with regret. I feel for him, & instead of wishing to give the tumbling fabric an hastening kick, I wished to point out a method of preserving it, & making it useful with less expence. I fear he has not taken my suggestions in good part, I am sorry for it, they were well meant. . . .

Lord William Russell to Lady Holland at Paris [HH]

Richmond Park Farm, 16 Oct [1825]

You will perhaps be surprised that this letter is not dated from Ampthill, but Henry Webster* is so happy there, I would not for the world disturb him, & it is so seldom younger sons get into the mansions of their Excellencies that they should not give up possession without cause, tho I must in justice say you are an exception to the system of excluding that proverbial race. Selfishness is the ruling passion of the nobles of this island, to possess several houses & to keep them empty is their great delight, & a feeling peculiar to this country. In my daily & wearisome rides to Hounslow, I pass by the villas & palaces of my dearest friends, the wet streaming down the walls for want of fire, & my daily reflection on passing them is on the pleasure (inexplicable to me) of keeping them empty. Mr Simond in his travels talking of Osterly says, I should be so glad to get someone to

* Lady Holland's son by her first marriage.

sit under the shade of my trees, to smell my flowers etc. But to return to Ampthill. You are very good & very unlike your neighbours to offer it to us. . . .

Duke of Bedford to Lord William Russell at Richmond [WPP]

Paris, January 1st, 1826

I am very sorry to hear that you are distressed for the sum of £1000, but from the statement you have sent me of the cause of your embarrassment, I can very easily understand it. At all events I am thankful to you for this mark of your confidence in communicating to me in the first instance your wants, before you have recourse to any other means of raising this sum. If it is in my power to assist you, I shall most readily and cheerfully do so, but I have my doubts on the subject. The same post brought me Adam's* statement of ways and means for 1826, which is not very encouraging. At Christmas and the New Year, I like you, *et tout comme le reste*, have many heavy bills, and as I shall have some operose and expensive work going on at Woburn this year, in repairs, painting etc.etc. together with some improvements within the Abbey, as well as out of doors, I am obliged to economise as much as possible. I think, however, I have hit upon a means of raising this £1000 immediately, and will write to Adam on the subject by this post. To him I refer you, and if my plan is not feasible, he will, I am sure, point out some mode by which your wishes may be accomplished. . . .

Lady William Russell to Lord Lynedoch at Cosgrove Priory [NLS]

[24 February 1826]

I am afraid you will think me affronted at your joke so I write to swear I am not so one bit, but it is a subject on which Ld Wm is sore as he dreads henpecking amazingly from its being in the family; I have *des gentillesses* said to me on this score by all relations and friends from the moment I married till now so that I am quite hardened against the charge; we have all our weaknesses, & I should say Ld William's peculiar one was that of such a dread of being led that he will not be advized, & any insinuation of the kind annoys him to death – as to his manly pursuits I take it for granted Lord Tavistock held forth with his usual eloquence on the

* The Duke's auditor.

sublime subject, but pray open your eyes & see whether I prevent his hunting – he is constantly absent when there is anything of moment in the House of Commons & always because he is hunting. His elder brother writes volumes to him on the abuse of his constituents & all the gossip of the *canaille* of Bedford which he sucks in like mother's milk & babbles out like an old woman to Lord William; who is now at Woburn hunting and there is much going on in the House & many enquiries made after him – he was at Cosgrove – when Lord John & Mr Seymour & others could not believe he could be there, there being such interesting things going on in the Commons – his Major comes gallopping after him all in a sweat & at a non plus from his sudden & frequent flights – he goes at least every ten days & I never really urged his return, so I do not know what I am to do, unless I *monter en croupe*, & hunt with him to shew my conjugal love.

Had I the power you attribute to me I should most undoubtedly make use of it to cut down his stud to the standard of a poor younger brother, he has from 11 to 16 horses & 5 men in the stables, our indoor establishment consisting of one footman who is his *valet de chambre*, his under butler & my *laquais*. Judge, for you know our income. Then from his hereditary delicacy of constitution, the example of his elder brother & the opinion of physicians I do not wish for over exercise. From our small fortune – his being a member of Parliament which necessitates a town residence – and his regiment which entails a country quarter we cannot have a hunting box & dedicate our lives to that fascinating pursuit – therefore I think his friends and well wishers ought to be satisfied with his free agency; he has given up none of his former friends – he has not given up his profession – he is not gone out of Parliament & he does keep hunters. These are undeniable facts, therefore with common candour & common veracity nobody can say that his wife has made him give up anything – duties or amusements. I equally keep up with the greater part of my old friends in which he does not control me or indeed in anything for I am as free an agent as he is, & I do not see that there is any violent coercion on either side.

Both my children have been very ill, the baby dangerously so of a sort of croup – the physician came 5 times in 24 hours, as you may judge. I have been nowhere this fortnight, they are quite convalescent now, indeed Hastings is well.

I have made an *exposé* of facts that you can argue from – & I repeat that though the subject led me on, I vow I did not take fire at your *plaisanterie*, nor is it that which made me so diffuse, but your answer to Lord William's letter, which made known to me his having let out his annoyance, which he heretofore kept in when the everlasting subject was broached.

Goodbye my dear Lord Lynedoch, I am pleased with the idea of Brighton because it is healthy for children, & there are plenty of clean houses & good medical advice, besides the being near London when Parliament meets & a part of the year some of *my* friends come there.

Lady William Russell to Lady Holland [HH]

Brighton [1826]

I am more obliged to you than words can tell, but I will not hamper you with any chiffons for me, I mean to be parsimonious for some time to come.

I hear the best accounts of the Duke of Bedford, his sons are all delighted with his looks, I wish I could say as much of your Johnnikins, he looks dreadfully. He came here to get rid of a horrid cough but took it back with him. Lord Tavistock too has been the worse for the east wind. London generally upsets him. My boys are well. Mamma has gone to Berne, her project of three years hatching *vient d'éclore* & I hope to God she will find the whole thing what she thinks & expects.

Brighton at first disagreed with me, but now I am as well as ever, I never have any of my former ailments now. I hope you will tell me the same of yourself, though if you forsake Brighton I shall not see you for ages, not meaning to budge from my quarters the whole twelvemonth. William will I daresay fidget about a little as he is wont, he is at Epsom today & the Elections will of course call him away. Of Woburn I do not think as the Duchess will be confined late in the year & then go to the Highlands – then autumn comes & the journey to Nice for the winter, at least she said all this to me, it may be changed; I thought her looking ill & immensely large, but in violent spirits.

Duke of Bedford to Lord William Russell [WPP]

London, Thursday [1826]

I am much afraid I shall not be able to *raise the wind*, at present, to accommodate you to the extent you require, as I am very short of cash and much pressed. John, too, has a prior claim, as he has never received any assistance from me. He has somewhat exceeded his income and got involved in some difficulty, out of which I must extricate him as soon as I can.

The latter part of your letter to Adam gave me some uneasiness. It is when you talk of quitting active service from inability to go on with it. I think after the credit you have gained in forming an excellent regiment out of a very bad one, you ought not, in justice to yourself, to think of going again on half-pay, nor ought you, in fairness to me, after the large sum of money I have paid to obtain for you the command of the 8th.

You ought now to be in possession of a very fair and reasonable income, including your pay as Lieut.Colonel, and you should consider how many officers there are in command of regiments, with scarcely any private fortune, and little to live upon beside their pay and appointments . . .

Duke of Bedford to Lord William Russell [WPP]

Endsleigh, July 20 [1826]

I assure you I have not misunderstood you. Last year you wished to borrow £1000 to relieve some pecuniary difficulties, and I was fortunate enough to be able to accommodate you, by borrowing this sum from my Sinking Fund. This year you wished to borrow an additional £500, and Adam told you the truth when he said that I could not command that sum, small as it may appear. The fact is that John is under some pecuniary difficulties from having lately exceeded his income, which I must deliver him from before he goes abroad, probably about the amount of the same sum, £500. He wrote to me about it when I was at Paris, but not having the money, I have not mentioned it to him since. Be assured that I meant to give you no 'lecture', in the invidious sense of the word, and all I said was dictated by the purest notions of affection and regard for you. I had no thought of reproaching you, for it would have been undeserved, and had no feeling but that of regret at not being able at the moment to accommodate your wishes, and had I ten times the sum at my disposal, it should be yours. You will probably say that with my income I ought to be rich, perhaps I ought, and if I spend my income in any way that is reprehensible, and even exceed it, there is no one to blame but myself. In all you say your reasoning is perfectly correct, and your encomiums just, but I think you are a little bit hard upon John. He has many expenses. A ready furnished lodging in London; much travelling; his servants, horses etc., to keep and he is remarkably generous and gives much. His literary labours add something to his income but not as much as they ought. You say he is cheated, and he probably is. In pecuniary matters I daresay the *Punica fides* is not more sacred with the modern Greek than it was with the Old Roman! . . .

Lord William Russell to Lady Holland [HH]

Brighton A[ugust] 10 [1826]

You were right in supposing we enjoy ourselves in Brighton, as indeed we do at most places, having light hearts, nice children & few cares, but there is no pleasure without alloy; that I might have my portion Bessy has been very ill, with a bad bilious attack, I believe from catching cold after drinking the Carlsbad waters, which she does at six o'clock every morning. She is now much better if not quite well. Lord Lynedoch has drunk the same waters for 5 weeks & leaves us tomorrow much restored in health. He goes to Northamptonshire & then to Scotland. He will be over to breakfast with you some morning.

Many thanks for your kind invitation to Ampthill, we should like it much if we could surmount all the difficulties in the way of so long a journey, such as want of money, the children, tho I should like to take the liberty of bringing Hastings – but if I see a possibility of moving towards the end of the month, you may depend upon us.

I never heard of your accident at Windsor Castle & regret to hear that you are suffering from it. Brighton no doubt would do you good.

With respect to society this is a singular & not unpleasant place, we have people from London fresh & fresh every day. Some stay a short time, some a long time, all are in search of pleasure, health & amusement, & sometimes look for them in my house, the consequence is, my weekly bills are doubled & we shall be obliged to escape to the Continent to avoid the butcher & baker. Indeed I believe Bessy never sees the steamboat leave the Chain Pier without longing to get into it & leave her cloathes & servants to themselves . . .

The care and thought given to the education of their sons by the William Russells made them consider sending Hastings to Hofwyl, a school in Switzerland founded and directed by Fellenberg, a disciple of Pestalozzi. The school was much visited by the curious and those interested in the system.

Lord John Russell to Lady William Russell at 18 Arlington Street [PRP]

Berne. Aug. 26. [1826]

I have seen your mother, & your school. Mrs Rawdon looks quite plump & rosy; the wholesome life & air of this place seem to agree with her, the dulness does not overcome her – *que es mucho* –. For me I have been going thro' a round of entertainments ever since I came, but that is owing to the quantity of English who after seeing the glaciers are anxious to have a tea-party, which perhaps in their hearts they prefer.

As to Hofwyl I have spent some time there, & am greatly inclined to approve of the school from 7 to 14. The boys are made perhaps rather too rough for good society, & therefore when they get near manhood I should take them away. But they have excellent health, are very happy, & learn besides Greek & Latin, any science, language, art or trade you chuse to have them taught. In fact Fellenberg spends £1500 a year upon some thirty professors; a magnificence of course above any common school-master. If you sent your boy here you must come in the summer to see him. He does not like the boys to go home, & he rather amused me by telling me that he had once 3 sons of a grand seigneur from Silesia who did not at all care for their parents but by dint of being kept away from them 8 years filial affection became so strong in them that they quite longed to see their father & mother, & on their return were models of sons. 7 or 8 years old is decidedly the best age to begin, & consider what a thing it is to have your son well & happy from that time for 5 or 6 years. Our own private schools are abominable.

I leave this in a few days, to see some Alps; but I shall not cross 'the reverend face of that tall pile.' . . .

Lord John Russell, who had represented Huntingdon in Parliament since 1820, lost his seat at the election in April 1826, and went abroad, visiting Geneva, Genoa, Florence and Rome. There was some fear that he would not return until the following May. Lord William wrote to him in November: '. . . You say you cannot think why people should wish you to come home to Parliament. . . . If you feel any ambition (which you have not), if you give up the charms of Genoa (which you cannot), if you would renounce the dinners & tea tables & gossips of Rome (which you cannot), and dangling after ladies (which you cannot), there is a noble field of utility opened to a states-man.'[4]

Lord John Russell to Lord William Russell [WPP]

Paris, October 6. [1826]

. . . Thanks for your advice, I was coming home, but my father has advised me to go to Italy for the winter. So I shall march for Rome in a few days, Lady Holland being in this instance *véridique*. Pray write to

Genoa. I hope Lady William received my lecture on Fellenberg, I think he would do for Hastings very well. I suppose you know I am coming into Parliament. I am to be brought in by Lord Fitzwilliam . . .

I have no doubt the Duke of York will die, and the Chancellor be d——d, and that the rats will fly to Canning to cut his cheese. But why should I go home for that reason? I shall enjoy the spectacle at a distance. All sorts of absurd rumours about Canning's negotiations here. I believe he has come entirely to eat truffles and improve his French. He is in high good humour and very popular with the people here. They say we owe to him our station in Europe.

Pray, when you go to Woburn look at Nina, and see that my Father does not shoot her. I believe he thinks old horses are game, as the Duke of Cumberland did pigs.

I have given up my lodgings, and have nothing in England but a secretary who is no use to me. I intend to return in March, April or May, and stay at home all the rest of my days.

Lady Bath to Lord William Russell at Brighton [WPP]

Naples, Nov. 24. 1826.

Altho' you probably have heard directly the sad accounts of Lord Hastings' illness I must write you word of his arrival here at Baia in the Admiral's ship but so ill I fear there is no hopes of his lasting many days. I need not tell you how cordially I share in the affliction this will be to Lady William, nor how much I feel for Lady Hastings. . . . Pray let me hear from you dear William how Lady William bears the misfortune that awaits her in the loss of a kind affectionate relation* – and write me a great deal about yourself. I hope you go on prosperously altogether? how are your dear children? . . . Wherever I go I find people full of the souvenir of Lady William. I talked much of her and heard much of her from the dear old Archbishop of Tarentum here, he calls her always his *chère Bettina* and says he taught her Greek, he is the finest and most delightful of old men and for affection for him I even nursed his cats tho' not with pleasure I confess!

* Augustus Hare in *The Story of my Life* tells of a dream Lady William had before the news of Lord Hastings's death reached England. Meeting him in a great hall, she embraced him and said 'Uncle, how terribly cold you are.' He answered: 'Bessy, did you not know I am dead?'

Francis Russell, Marquess of Tavistock, 7th Duke of Bedford

Princess Lieven, a print from a portrait by J. Lucas

Georgiana, Duchess of Bedford, an engraving of a portrait
by Landseer

... I hear that the floods have destroyed the cascade and a great part of Tivoli, that the river has taken another course and that Lady Westmorland is riding about the country to find it – at least this is the story told here ...

Lord William Russell to Lady Holland [HH]

B[righton] Feb 18 [1827]

Lord Egremont is much better, I believe quite out of danger. I saw Mrs Canning yesterday who appears comfortable about C. & expects he will be able to go to London on Saturday. H. M. is in bed with the gout in both feet. Grim death strikes at illustrious victims, princes, ministers & bishops are all called upon to surrender. We smaller fry have also had a pinch from him, but escaped his clutches this time. I have been in bed with fever & Lady William is still in bed with cold &c., but considerably better. I am happy to hear that you are convalescent. The severity of the weather is frightful. Nothing was ever known to equal it at Brighton.

On dit that the *Marquise de Maintenant** will soon become the *Marquise de Ci-devant*. Who is to be *Madame de Dorénavant* nobody yet knows. Lady Copley is mentioned.

In the summer of 1827 the Hussars proceeded to Ireland and the Russells followed. A pause of two weeks at Cheltenham to drink the waters allowed William and his father to exchange characteristic letters. It may be inferred that William's was written with his usual want of tact. He continued on his way to Ireland alone, and we can only guess that the fault for which his wife punished him by remaining behind was a flirtation, a piece of wanton extravagance, or some incompetence. She followed with the children a few weeks later and put up as best she could with Army quarters. It is surprising to find Lord William writing at this time of his wife's contented disposition, for after two months in barracks she became determined to leave Ireland and join her mother who was settled at Berne. Making her health an excuse, Lord William asked for three months' leave of absence to accompany his wife to Switzerland. He sacrificed his professional interest to his wife's fancy and it was perhaps the crucial mistake of his life. Their faithful old friend Lord Lynedoch joined them before they left Ireland, and with him and the little boys they made an excursion to the Giant's Causeway. The prospect of having to spend in the future a whole year with the regiment in Ireland did not serve to raise their spirits.

* Lady Conyngham.

Military Years

Duke of Bedford to Lord William Russell [WPP]

June 22nd 1827.

I very much regret your going off without my seeing you, but I will not fail to look at Lord Holland's ground for building, with him, on the spot. . . .

Pray do not give yourself the trouble of writing to me about politics. You know I dislike the subject, and I assure you I have never heard your political conduct maligned or calumniated by anyone.

Lady Jersey told me you had been to see her at Osterly, and had explained your political faith to her, but she has neither maligned or calumniated you, to my knowledge. You know she likes talking, but I assure you all I have heard from her tho' warm, has been with most perfect good humour.* However you have just as good a right to your opinions as she has to hers, or I have to mine. At Holland House I own I hear a good deal of language which I would willingly avoid hearing, and the last time I dined there, old Holland, Jack Allen and John were so violent that I got up and walked out of the room, but I must truly do the justice to say I have never heard anything violent of you. . . .

Duke of Bedford to Lord William Russell at Cheltenham [WPP]

Campden Hill, June 29, 1827

. . . The waters I am sorry to see do not seem to agree with you, as they appear to have stirred your bile without removing it, and I regret that it should all be reserved with splenetic bitterness, against the most noble, high-spirited and upright statesman, Lord Grey.† He dined here yesterday with Lord Lynedoch, who I am happy to say heard Lord Grey's speech and highly approved it. I also had the satisfaction of hearing it, and a more clear, manly, honourable, and direct exposition never came from the lips of man. It delighted his friends and confounded his enemies. *You* cannot understand it. You may probably have read it in that honest and impartial paper the 'Times'. You will not allow us unfortunate peers the advantage of honour, which has been given to us by custom from time immemorial. A Peer delivers judgement upon his honour, and not on his oath, however, you will have the satisfaction of hearing that we are about

---

* 'Lady Jersey has been meddling sadly. I only care as it affects the Duke of Bedford; but she has done mischief between him, his sons and brother.' Earl of Ilchester (ed.), *Lady Holland to her Son*, p. 64.

† Charles, 2nd Earl Grey (1764–1845), Prime Minister 1831–4, had refused to co-operate with Canning.

to be purified by the infusion of seventeen good and virtuous men, and among them those temperate statesmen, Mr Lambton and Lord Sefton; though I suppose you think, with the 'Times' and 'Morning Chronicle' that we are so incorrigibly bad as to be past improvement. You say you have tied yourself to the tail of that great fish, Lord Holland. I wish you joy! He will swim you into foul waters. I have always loved Lord Holland for his *private* virtues, his good heart and social qualities, but as a politician, I have long thought him shabby and dirty, and always void of that essential quality in a statesman – judgement.

Lord William to Lady William Russell [PRP]

Dublin, July 31 [1827]

I feel so wretched, so gloomy all alone, I know not what to do with myself. My thoughts are incessantly with you and my boys. I am sure this is a punishment to me for all my transgressions & want of kindness to you – indeed dearest Bessy, I love you with all my heart & soul. I hope that when we meet again we shall part no more – pray dont worry & fret yourself. I am so sorry to know you are not well & cannot sleep, however you have the babble of the children to divert you, & I have nothing, but am tormented by dreary disagreable thoughts. Dearest Bessy, pardon me. I am not so bad as you believe me to be, & with the help of God I will be better. How I wish we could live in peace & harmony together. I wish for nothing in the world besides you & my boys.

I called today on Lord Anglesey, who asked me to dine with him, & I refused (being engaged to General Dalbiac). In this I fear I was guilty of a breach of etiquette, he being the King's Viceroy. Lord A. was very kind to me & entered largely into his views of the Government of Ireland, which in my opinion are directed by sound sense & judgement. I hope he may be allowed to pursue them, for altho' this country is now perfectly tranquil, one false step may produce a civil war, the greatest of all evils. God avert such a calamity from Ireland.

I left off here to go to dinner. Mrs Dalbiac is a lady who has been in all quarters with her husband, talking of the delight of this & that quarter. I met there a Mrs Grey, wife of Col. Grey – she has six children & marches about with them, a very nice little woman & knew you formerly at Mr Brandlings. I confess I felt annoyed at seeing all these officers with their wives & children & feeling I had not mine, but the fault is my own. You have punished me severely but deservedly – dearest Bessy, forgive me.

I hear of nothing but praise of my regiment. All the great authorities say it is the best in Ireland.

Lady Holland to Lord William Russell [WPP]

Ampthill, 19 September [1827]

It is difficult to be here without perpetually thinking of you, Lady William and dear little Hastings, and many times have I been on the point of telling you so, and requiring in return some account of yourselves, but Lord Holland has really been very unwell with gout and an obstinate cough, which though it did not alarm, yet made me uneasy, and my unlucky privilege is upon such occasions totally to unfit me for even the exertion of writing. Besides I have been much tormented by a very obstinate cough, which has lasted too long, and will not yield unless I try a blister which is now the remedy under consideration. The weather has been most unfavourable, cold, windy and raw, so that the whiskey* has not played its part among our pretty drives and walks. You know of course your father is deriving benefit from Leamington and the Tavistocks are to be with him instead of Chatsworth and Doncaster. John has been here some days. He represented you on the race-grounds, where Tavistock was victorious. Said John is remarkably well, all the better for the sea breezes and the company at Ryde. . . .†

Rogers has been quite friendly and really amiable. Nursing and soothing us during our solitude and sickness, at a pinch his naturally good heart always peeps out. He likes his friends but in sorrow and adversity.

The only news in the county is the visit of Lady Tavistock to Mrs Whitbread.‡ It is only a proof among many of her extreme good nature, and she has made a worthy man most happy, and by taste and condescensions raised herself in the estimation of everybody. . . .

At the *Exposition de l'Industrie*, just before Charles X left Paris, he admired a gun, the gun-maker was enchanted and offered it as an *hommage*

---

* A whiskey was a small pony carriage.

† 'The world say Lady Elizabeth Vernon, who has occupied him at Ryde all the summer is the attraction. How odd that all the Russell family should have been in love in succession with her.' *Lady Holland to her Son*, p. 68. Lady Elizabeth Vernon, daughter of the 2nd Earl of Lucan, was the wife of George Vernon, who added Harcourt to his name.

‡ William Henry Whitbread, eldest son of Samuel Whitbread, made an unsatisfactory marriage as a young man. It has been said that the gravel of the Southill drive was never disturbed by callers during the first Mrs Whitbread's lifetime.

to H.M. *Merci mon ami il me serait inutile, je me tiens toujours de fusils Anglais.* You may judge what a story this has made against him in Paris. . . . Give my best regards to Lady William. I hope her accounts of Mrs Rawdon are good and that Baby keeps his beauty.

Lord William Russell to Lady Holland [HH]

Dundalk Barracks, 19 Sep [1827]

It was most good natured of you to write me so long & interesting a letter which was doubly welcome in this *triste* abode. Imagine an enclosed square of a grey stone, at the end of a dirty town, with a starving ragged population, surrounded with marshes, on the banks of a tide river, leaving nothing but mud at ebb tide. Add to this a sky the colour of the stone, & you have the picture of our dwelling place. For my part I am accustomed to such places, but for Bessy it is a trying situation, however her *gaieté de coeur*, her spirits, her contented disposition carry her thro more merrily than many who are in merrier places, yet I confess it grieves me to see the most brilliant, the sweetest flower of Europe on such a dung-hill – her health too is not good, she has had two more such attacks as the one she had after dining at your house. I am not easy about her.

We leave this soon to go to Berne to see Mrs Rawdon, & hope we shall find you in London *en passant*. We remain the winter & spring abroad & then return to Ireland to spend a whole year *en garnison*. As for politics we hear little about them but regret to hear my family is divided & violent. . . .

Lord John Russell to Lady William Russell [PRP]

[1827]

I am sorry you are going off in the steam kettle, without my seeing you. Some books which I wished to see here, before I finish my own, prevented my going to town. But be sociable and go to Paris: send Mrs Rawdon the money that would have carried you to Berne, and all will be well . . .

We are all together by the ears about politics. As you do not care about them, so much the better for you, but I suppose when your boys grow up you will be glad to find yourself on the ministerial side.

The Russells stayed but a few days in Paris on their way to Switzerland, but Lady Granville had occasion to comment that Lady William 'will not come out of an evening. She is prettier than ever, a tower of Babel, tall, unbending, and gifted with tongues.'

Duke of Bedford to Lord William Russell [WPP]

Woburn Abbey, October 22 [1827]

I got your letter from Dover and am sorry to hear that Lady William knocked up at Sittingbourne, as this is but a bad beginning of a long journey to Berne. To break down after 40 miles of easy travelling on good McAdam roads. I trust those from Calais to Berne, certainly not on the system of McAdam or the Mayor of Bedford, may cause no serious interruption of your progress. Here we have had an abundance of rain, but the weather is very warm. On the subject of my little grandson Hastings, it is difficult to know what to advise. As he is eight years old, you should certainly be *thinking* of school. I was sent to school myself at seven, and therefore sent you and Tavistock to old Moore's at the same age, though without sufficient reflection for it is certainly too young. Nine is perhaps quite time enough, as you think Hastings' constitution delicate, with his fine manly mind, it will require much consideration where to send him. A small school with a few boys like Mr Everard's or Mr Robert's would probably be the best for him in the first instance. Of Fellenberg's I know nothing, but from general reading of his system, but you will have an opportunity of looking closely into it, and making ample enquiries, whilst you are in Switzerland. I have a dislike in general to home tutors, and think it a bad plan for boys. They ought if possible, to be removed from home, and associate with other boys at a certain age. . . .

Having joined Mrs Rawdon at Berne, they remained there all the winter. Lord William returned to England by himself in February to attend Parliament; his constituents were dissatisfied with his prolonged absence from the House of Commons, and he was needed to vote with the Whigs on Catholic Emancipation. Provoked by several adjournments of the debate, he left London again for Switzerland before the Catholic question was carried. This ill-considered behaviour drew from his brother John a good-humoured rebuke.

His wish to live in England appears in his project to employ Blore to build him a house on Lord Spencer's estate at Wimbledon.

Lady William Russell to Lord John Russell [PRP]

Bern, Jan 9, 1828

Dearest John, I wish you *il buon capo d'anno* with heart and soul, do not think that the said heart is cold nor the said soul worldly if I have been such

148

a tigress as not to write to you. You sent me a dear little letter, kind and affectionate and full of brotherly advice, which I did not take as is usually the case. You said do not go to Bern but send your Mama the journey money and bring her to Paris, but after all *you* gave up Paris yourself. *J'aurais été bien attrappée* therefore had I staid there for your *beaux yeux* and only had Madame de Dino's to shine upon me.

This is a woful place but life jogs on, and inasmuch as my mother is here it is better than Dundalk. Your brother has a great zeal for his M.P. duties and goes off in 8 or 10 days, a most mournful journey. I beseech you, dear John, seriously to take care of his health and write to me about him and often about other things besides – do spare me a few moments tho' I deserve it so little.

We intended going together to Paris in February, but as Parliament meet sooner I really dread the cold and scorn Paris, atrocious as Bern is. I shall therefore remain with my two little men who are well; Hastings tortured with Latin and other puerile accomplishments, and your godson leading the happy joyous life of infancy, without even an alphabet to plague him.

I come away from here in April or thereabouts, but we have no house in London, and no money, I believe, so I must give up the pleasures of *la capitale* and my only perspective is Dublin and the 8th Hussars when the session is over – June or July.

Do write me a line *pour commencer* when you receive this, and then on his arrival, and then when you have any political potion to communicate. I am discreet in my demands. Give my love to Lady Bath – and pray tell me family matters as much as will enter into one of your paragraphs – talk about the Cross and Crescent* like a red cross knight *à tort et à travers*. I am much interested in the concern tho' like Sir Roger de Coverley I am of opinion that much is to be said on both sides. Give me a glimpse into futurity as to *when* I shall see you, *how* and *where*, for you wrote such vows of never leaving England again that it made my hair stand on end.

Mama sends you her best regards even her love if you will accept of it, she is full of gratitude at all your kindness to her – and so would I be if I could but think you were my affectionate brother as I am your affectionate sister.

* Lord John Russell had written an 'Historical Discourse' on *The Establishment of the Turks in Europe*. 'It is a mere compilation of extracts from other books. I was sorry to see his name to it for 5 shillings.' *Lady Holland to her Son*, p. 81.

Lady William Russell to old Lord William Russell in London [WP]

Bern, Jan. 17, 1828

Why did you not step across here cruel uncle who are as bad an uncle as the uncle of the Babes in the Wood! I got your letter from Milan to-day. . . . Geneva, Bern, Paris – all at hand. I suppose however you got my long prose from Dundalk in September which I directed as desired to Florence. If my spirits could stand *that* they would stand Bern. You know I carry my happiness about with me. *Vous l'avez vu de près*, you have discuss'd it with Lady Westmorland when sane, – so she is worse! Poor soul! And dear unhappy Gertrude! My heart bleeds for her, – as to William it really was nonsense, I wanted to answer his note immediately & Lord William prevented me, I know not why, – however, I am glad of his young & innocent marriage* – may it be happy! or at least may they think themselves so. I always protected it when the sager members thought it a folly. Do not think his notions overstrained, they coincide with mine. *Je ne suis pas démoralisée* maugre those I live with – to say the truth dear Lord William I have long thought like Lady Foley & have quoted her opinion – of her own beauty saith she 'there *may* be prettier women than I – I don't deny it – only *I* never saw them', now I say 'there *may* be very honest people, but hang me if I ever met with them.' Yet I sigh for honesty – adore integrity, worship virtue – pant for excellence – groan for the truth – & am reckon'd harsh & austere in my expressions, told I expect heroes & heroines instead of men & women. *Oimè*!!

When shall I see you? I believe you are my friend though you are so prodigiously neutral. My boys are well, this place is healthy, cheap & dull. I stay a couple of months longer with my mother to wait for the long days & fairer weather instead of going to Paris in February as I originally meant. In London we have no house, & shall have none; as long as the Dragooning lasts we cannot afford both. We have a house here with everything for ten louis a month – £8, – & masters *à 30 sous*. I shall pass through London in summer on my way to Ireland but not partake of the Season . . . *j'ai tant vu le soleil*! Pray write to me politicks & all, nothing will come amiss to me, in my widowed state I shall require amusement so it will be kind to write & you *are* kind, you cruel uncle.

What has Eliza in her head & heart? – still *le beau* Cradock? I confess she is a very pretty little girl, but I never felt uneasy as to sentiment

* Old Lord William's son married in 1828 Emma, daughter of Colonel John and Lady Charlotte Campbell.

blanching the roses of her cheek, she seems sweet tempered and sensible, but I scarcely know her, & she is unnaturally cautious for her age, *elle ne se livre pas, elle ne s'oublie pas, point d'abandon, – point de jeunesse?* except in her appearance. As to me *j'ai les yeux creux & le teint blême, venez voir cela!* My poor dear Mama is, thank God, well, fat & strong, full of her energetic affection & generous sentiments. She had been very alarmingly ill in autumn; I am so glad we came to her! Our journey here was most disastrous, we did nothing but overturn & break down, it has almost sicken'd me of posting which I am generally so fond of. I have occasionally my spasms; here there is a very good doctor. My said spasms are not bilious after all & they give way to the soothing foreign treatment of baths & emollients, better than to the irritating system of mercury & violence which are not good for a chronic complaint, tho' admirable for a terrible kill or cure case of fever etc.

So poor good Auguste de Staël is dead! I regret him! The Corps Diplomatique at Bern detest the Bernese & all the Swiss, they are at daggers drawn. The said Corps is *assez bien composé* – the French Ambassador is a first rate man, in every sense of the word, talents, *honnête homme, bon père, bon époux, bon voisin, – homme aimable, homme d'esprit,* we are all wondering *ce qu'il vient faire dans cette galère,* however he was offered, as the papers say, the *affaires étrangères,* & now he is going to Paris to put the new ministry *en train,* who cannot help themselves much like their neighbours and natural enemies in Gt Britain. You may have seen him in Rome with the D. de Laval, when we were all there together, – Monsr. de Rayneval. As to *our* Algernon Percy* – the least said the soonest &c., &c., *vous le connaissez aussi.* Run over to Paris at Easter, probably I shall be there then. Goodbye now, this is enough to prove you live in my memory. Mamma's best regards & thanks for your recollection of her.

Lord William left Berne on 2 February and travelled rapidly to England. Capable and practical, his wife had prepared for the contingencies of his long and fatiguing journey.

[A note by Lady William Russell] [PRP]

You will find in the carriage for your use on the journey

a tea-pot

Lump sugar – in an eau de cologne box

---

* The Hon. Algernon Percy (1779–1833), English Minister at Berne, son of the 2nd Baron Lovaine.

Powdered sugar – in a tin box

Lemons

a drinking glass

a bottle of Epsom salts

2 teaspoonfuls to a dose

Seidlitz powders a box to make an effervescent draught with lemon juice & sugar

Biscuits – in a paper parcel

Black tea – in a tin canister

2 pots 1 of raspberry jelly & 1 of apricot jam

a terrine with a veal & chicken pie

straw flask with Marsala

2 napkins – a red case with a tumbler – a green vase!

a little green flat bottle with riga balsam for cuts

a bottle of raspberry vinegar

a bottle of rose water

a bottle of eau de cologne

Lord William Russell to Lady William Russell at Berne [PRP]

[1828]

... indeed I wish we could never separate again. When I look at all the little packages & comforts you have put up for me, I feel all your goodness & kindness to me – but no more of this, you don't like it.

My head aches much so I will go to bed. Kiss my dear little boys for me, & pray take care that Arthur never is left alone near the fire, he would surely burn himself.

I trust your health is better. Make yourself robust for the spring. I read your little Fénelon occasionally & like it much. God bless you & the boys.

Lord John Russell to Lady William Russell at Berne [PRP]

Grosvenor Square. Feb. 12. 1828

I postponed answering your letter, my dear Lady W. till I could give you some account of Billy of Berne, who has arrived here after much fatigue, looking well, & very 'dapper', a word that has come into use for the benefit of Don Miguel.* Not that William is in any other respect like that constitutional, but rather dangerous Prince.

* Claimant to the crown of Portugal, who had been in London.

I think you do wisely not to leave the place you are in, tho' it be the glaciers, at this chilling season. We have snow the last two days, after a January that was more like summer, or the imaginary season spring than winter. When you are moving towards Paris let me hear from you, for I may project a journey to that capital . . .

Many people are in town – my father and the Duchess arrived yesterday evening. Lady Jersey is again in opposition, & quite delighted at all her old friends being out. All the other ladies take their separate parts, more or less violently, but generally, as women should do with their husbands or lovers, or something between both.

I am not going to be married as you think I ought to be, & am getting too old to enter into that happy state. My occupations fill up my time pretty well, but I will not deny that a man who marries happily is much happier than any body else. But the reverse! & the irrevocable nature of the connexion are most alarming.

Tavistock had two bad falls out hunting, but is getting well.

There are some excellent novels come out. The *Red Rover* is the best, *Herbert Lacy* is very good. I hope you like the *Promessi Sposi*. Your friend old Greville is now very great; as he is quite for the Duke of Wellington.

Duke of Bedford to Lady William Russell at Berne [PRP]

London Feby 15 1828

I waited to thank you for your letter, till I had seen William, and could give you some satisfactory intelligence of him. On my arrival in town I found he had preceded me by a few hours only. He is, I am happy to say, looking well in health but this after a tedious and fatiguing journey. Dr Yeats told me that you had written confidentially to him, somewhat un-easy about William's state of health – be assured I shall not betray his confidence in me, tho' at the same time, I think all uneasiness should be removed from your mind – and now to the immediate purport of your letter. I feel satisfied from your description that the Hofwyl establishment would not do for Hastings, moreover it is removing him to such a distance from his native land that in that alone it would be objectionable. I am quite convinced that you do everything that a mother can do (and how few mothers can do as much) in his present tender age; but the difficulties are what to do with him when he should be removed from under your immediate eye – my own opinion is in favour of a *small* private school in a healthy situation by the seaside – a private tutor at home is a great hazard – how difficult it is to find one you could entirely approve! particularly a foreigner. I do not wish you however to abandon the idea altogether and Switzerland is entirely the best place from whence you can direct your enquiries. Hastings is not an ordinary boy, he has great capacities, and his disposition, as you describe it to me, will require great nicety and delicacy of management. With regard to his learning, if he is to remain at home for two or three years longer, I will venture to say that you will find no tutor so capable of instructing him as yourself. A public school in England is one of the greatest evils I know of, but I fear in some respects it is a necessary evil, with our habits of public life, our free Constitution and the habitual intercourse of men of all professions....

LORD WILLIAM'S DIARY

28 Feb. [London] Breakfasted with Rogers, weak & vain old man. Long & curious conversation with Mrs Grundy [the Duchess]; appears sore & out of humour, complains of her husband, declares she knows nothing of her future prospects or of her children's. Dined with Russian Ambassador.

1 March, Saturday. A melancholy letter from Lord Lynedoch dreading the loss of his eyesight – & anxious to find a suitable husband for *his adopted child*, Miss B. What an excellent noble good man – I pray that he may recover his eyesight. Dined with Lord Gower. English dinners are too long & formal to be gay. Found Lord Holland alone reading Herodotus in Greek.

2 March, Sunday. Read Fénelon's letters, full of excellent practical wisdom & true piety. St Paul's epistles to the Romans & Corinthians, nothing can exceed them in beauty & piety above all his modesty & diffidence of himself. Read the story of Esther in the Bible. Ahasuerus is a weak Prince, sacrificing his feelings & Ministers to his love of Esther; she after gaining her object becomes cruel. How inferior is the language of Racine in his play to the language of the Bible.

4 March. Went to Oakley.* Family out, strange reception.

5 March. Oakley. *Tutti alla caccia.* Read Bolingbroke's State of the Parties; fine style of writing, forcible language. Cobbett on the alarming state of the country – finance & poor law. Charles & Chester *sempre bebendo.*

6 March. Presided as foreman of the Grand Jury. Returned to Oakley – alone.

7 March. Grand Jury from 10 till 11.

'I wish someone would take William in hand and thrust him forward a little', wrote the Duke of Bedford to Lady Holland. 'His talents are quite lost to

* Lord Tavistock's home in Bedfordshire.

the public. He went to our Assize and in Tavistock's absence took his place as foreman of the grand jury and gave universal satisfaction by the manner he conducted the business. I know Lord Holland has a good opinion of him, why wont he take him in hand?'[5]

Lady William Russell to Lord John Russell [PRP]

Bern March 2d Sunday 1828

Dearest Johnnikins as you will not marry I conclude you read Fénelon and find '*que le joug perpétuel du mariage est difficile à supporter, c'est un état de tribulation et d'assujettissement très pénible, auquel il faut se préparer en esprit de pénitence, quand on s'y croit appellé de Dieu*'. – however come and live with us, I will be a good sister to you, and my children will love you & we will all coddle you and amuse you. . . . *nous ne sommes pas des ennuyeux*. . . . why should one always live so selfishly without any family friendships of brothers, sisters, nephews, cousins &c &c. When you are tired of *le beau monde* think of me, as I have had so many years sickness I shall be the most knowing and sympathising of all nurses you will see how comfortable we shall be, but do not consult Lucretia Holland about it, she will envenom your *corazon sinfiel* by nature.* In the meanwhile *pendant que tout cela se prépare* let us *write*, your kind letter of the 12th just reached me, to Paris *frate mio, non ho voglia di andare*† – nor to London. I should like much to pass the whole summer in Switzerland. I never saw it and have always wished it ardently, here I am *et cela serait bien bête de m'en aller* after *m'être morfondue* a whole winter in this execrable town, to go and racket about two capitals I know by heart & do not value fourpence. *Convenez-en*. I want too, to dedicate some of my time to Mama. I have been ten years now a drudge of a wife, tramping after a regiment of Irish Dragoons for 4 years, so I want my fling & wish for glaciers instead of ices in ballrooms, & mountains & green valleys instead of lights and small talk. One never sees enough of it, so suppose you come *here* instead of to Paris & let us have an Arcadian summer together. . . . *pensez-y – cela me sourit*. Nothing can be more detestable than Bern, but it is better than Dundalk or Dorchester.

Hastings has masters and profits, I assure you he latinizes very genteelly. I only regret that he should begin so early, all sensible people particularly teachers say that if boys begin Latin at 11 or 12 they would learn

---

* 'Your heart faithless by nature.'
† 'To Paris, my brother, I have no desire to go.'

more in 2 years than they now do in ten, but it is one of the stupid tributes one pays to custom and prejudice. So here the poor boy is having begun at 7. I potter on with him – and fill my dull brain with other people's ideas having none of my own, make my poor mother very happy, go to bed at 10 & so life glides on *coulant comme l'eau sous les ponts. Labitur & labetur!!* If it only would not carry away with it all one's illusions, there is the rub!! the most legitimate, alas, in the middle of life melt away as the early ones did at the dawn.

I have seen Hofwyl – but I told you that. I have heard from your father, he had just been cupped and was going to be bled, I do not like that! Poor dear old man, God preserve him! When I am away from you all I grow sentimental & am fond & foolish. When we are all together we squabble and find out each other's peccadilloes with a microscope. If I stay in Switzerland the summer as I wish, I shall come home to England in September *senza dubbio* – if I do not I shall be at Paris in April, but as there is no moral duty in *faisant ses Pâques à Notre Dame* & I prefer the Helvetic Confederation, the odds are that I shall do as I wish – which I daresay you think ladies pretty generally do. In the midst of all the interest of politics & Society, a letter from a *Parentela con el U** from a country town in Switzerland cannot have much zest – however receive it as a testimonial of affection and pray write often to tell me I live in your memory. Love to Lady Bath into whose face I can never more look after stealing her book! Tell me all about our Daddy for I have taken fright about him. Why will your elder brother break his bones & benumb his faculties by such a foolish pursuit? Half those exertions in a better cause would 'move mountains!!'

Viva VmD mil años hermano – tu cuñada muy aficionada

Ysabetha†

Your dapper brother in the shape of Satan shews me all the kingdoms in the world to tempt me, he wants to take Charles Cavendish' house off his hands at Paris . . . and buy Dowager Lady Liverpool's in London, one in the Rue Faubourg St Honoré the other Mayfair looking on the Park opposite the Londonderrys. He has no eyes for Chamounix or Grindelwald, and I have taken a pastoral turn. Do come in summer, come with him . . . *gravissons les rochers, grimpons les montagnes, parcourons les vallées . . . vamonos!*

I have had so much of the trumpets & barracks, let me hear eagles &

---

* 'From a kinswoman with your Honour.' (Lady William's Spanish has gone astray.)

† 'May you live a thousand years, brother in-law, Your very affectionate sister-in-law, Elizabeth.'

see chalets, and have my mother's company instead of the Quarter masters
... just till the autumn. *Suis-je raisonnable?* Once more God bless you.

Hastings Russell to Lord William Russell in England [WP]

[Berne 1828]

Be so good my Dear Papa as to send or bring me a little pocket sun glass. I have formed such projects for shooting. I rode two hours lost in a wood. I was obliged to get off more than once from the steepness. We go from the frigid to the torrid zone. Atty cried this morning for you. I will send you in my next letter a bunch of violets for the weather is so hot that we sit with open windows and without fires. I make great Progress in latin and I begin to waltze with music. Do bring me the Pony by the Rhine. Mama says she will meet you half way and we will bring your Arab and you and I will ride back to Bern. I hope the two horses wont bite each other. Goodbye wapsy write me as many letters as you can. Your affectionate little son.

LORD WILLIAM'S DIARY

8 March. [Oakley] Rode with Lord Lynedoch, found him old & broken, & out of spirits at the prospect of losing his sight. Spent the day in all the silliness & gossiping of a country house.

9 March, Sunday. Breakfasted at Woburn Abbey with Charles, Georgiana & Louisa; the 1st short & awkward, the 2nd thin & graceful. Both appear quiet & good. Went to London with Charles. Quiet dinner with the Duke of Bedford, agreable & magnificent, sat between Lady Stuart & Rogers; she is agreable & good natured he agreable & ill natured. Could not sleep for toothache.

10 March. German lesson. Dined with Lady C. Greville. Old Greville sour, gossiping, ill natured, *il figlio, piano, blasé,* spoilt, out of humour with himself & the world. Those who seek happiness in the world are always disappointed, when the fever subsides listlessness & *ennui* predominate.

11 March. Long & singular conversation with Mrs Grundy*; accusations of falseness against Mrs Tavy.† Protestations of sincerity, friendship: *mi pare loca.*‡

14 March. Up all night with toothache, went to Nossac who relieved me.

16 March, Sunday. Rose at 6 with toothache; read some chapters of St John –

* *i.e.* the Duchess.
† *i.e.* Lady Tavistock.
‡ 'She appears to be mad.' Lord William mixed Italian and Spanish here: 'loca' is Spanish for 'mad'.

Fénelon's letters. Lesson in German. Dreadful letter from Bessy overwhelmed my spirits.

Lord John Russell to Lady William Russell at Berne [PRP]

Grosvenor Square March 18. 1828

Many thanks for your letter from Berne, which could not have been more agreable if it had been from the gayest place in the world. Your project for the summer is a very agreable one, & only wants what many other projects do, that it should be practicable. William seems to be due to his regiment before the autumn, & alas, Bridgesomething will hardly be a more agreable place than Dundalk. But the military glory is immense, & William will be perfectly qualified to take a part in the last war that England will ever wage, which it is very likely will happen in our time.

This war between Russia & Turkey excites less talk than you would expect. Mr Pitt & Mr Fox would have spoken sixteen hours apiece upon it, but nobody now seems disposed to talk five minutes upon it. A question of mine on the Test & Corporation Acts, & which is really important excites much more interest. We are always very domestic in our politics. . . .

I am living still at Lady Bath's but quit it in a day or two. She is so kind that nothing can exceed it. But I must go back to my independence. As to Switzerland I confess I have not at this moment much inclination to *grimper*. I want to make books, but not such books as is made by walking hills.

I think you must come away in July, at least if the regiment is to be kept, & that is quite necessary now. Lord Anglesey has begun so well in Ireland that I trust you will be quiet there next winter. And you may go to see Killarney & *grimper les rochers* of paddyland – why not? But pray let me know what you do, for whatever it is, there is a fair chance of my doing the same. I have half a mind to go to the Pyrenees. But that might be after or before.

Our London life contains no novelty. We have our champagne as usual well iced, & our hearts almost as well. Less private quarrels than last year, & hatreds subsiding into a pacific indifference. It would not amuse you to come here. Still a house in London is perhaps your best way of having a home – parliament always lasts four months, & if you do not like London you had better have a house within ten miles of it – perhaps that would suit you better. Paris is, I hope, out of the question . . .

Write again. William seems at present uncertain what to do – he does not know how to chuse between the plumed troops, neighing steeds, & Desdemona.

Mrs Rawdon had better come nearer home, or move on to Italy, where you can go & see her from time to time, or you may get on the staff in the Mediterranean. But perhaps William has not yet rank sufficient. Great talk of reducing your pay in the finance committee. They think soldiers are too rich.

LORD WILLIAM'S DIARY

20 March. Went with Dowbiggin to see some houses near St George's Hospital; promised the refusal of one.

25 March. Visit from Yeats who said my liver was torpid.

28 March. [Woburn] Went with my father, Georgy & Louisa to Bedford races, afterwards dined at the ordinary, & went to the fancy ball. The races cold & tiresome, the dinner bad & disagreable; a clergyman disgraced himself & his holy profession by singing a filthy song. The ball hot, & crowded & dull. These days of pleasure to others are days of ennui & suffering to me, but it is necessary to sacrifice oneself occasionally.

29 March. Having slept & breakfasted at Dr Hunt's – a worthy good clergyman – rode to call on Samuel Whitbread, who is very ill, inheriting that dreadful disease scrofula, from the Greys, & having sacrificed his health to fox-hunting, & neglected his duty as member for Middlesex. Called on Lord Ludlow; Lady Charlotte Ludlow dangerously ill. The old veteran lives alone growling at the world, but his sister's illness has cast him down.

30 March, Sunday. Commenced reading the Bible with an intention of reading it thro, 2 or 3 chapters a day. Mr Blore,* an architect arrived. He builds you an admirable house for £2500 in the Gothic style.

2 April. Mr Blore told me he could build me a good house for £5000. Recommends some land of Lord Spencer in Wimbledon Park.

4 April. Went to Oakley. T., Lady T., Russell, *bello buono giovine.* She lives entirely in her room, *dolce far niente, oh che piacere.*

5 April. Returned from Oakley. Lord William Russell arrived & his son William. We sat down to dinner 7 Russells & talked incessantly.

6 April. Sunday. Went to church – our service is too long, it exhausts the attention. Mr Roy drawls dreadfully. Read, wrote, walked & dined. Lord William & son, John; politics is the only subject on which Englishmen talk with pleasure, & eagerness, & it is the most important affair of life except for religion.

---

* Edward Blore (1787–1879). He built Abbotsford for Sir Walter Scott.

Military Years

Lord John Russell to Lady William Russell at Berne [PRP]

W. Abbey. Ap. 7 [1828]

I have received your letter dated Lady Day, & being quarter day it ought to have given you a more lively prospect of *quattrini* than you seem to have. William says if he could stay a couple of years abroad he could economise. I suppose when the regiment is done with that plan will be adopted. In the meantime he is gone today to Laleham* to meet his old Commander & our present premier. Perhaps he (the Duke) will, what is called at Newmarket, let him into a good thing. He likewise talks of going to Ireland, to see the dear regiment. I suppose he will occupy himself for some time longer, & when it fails you will find yourselves none the richer. I am but Job's comforter you will say. Indeed as for living in this country without being rich, except as a bachelor, I know not how it is to be done. Far be it from me to presume to give any opinion with respect to the education of Hastings, as you have given the subject such deep attention, but I should say, if you have a tutor let it be a foreign one, for an Oxford tutor costs you £500 a year, for which you get two dead languages, & a smattering of theology – very dear for the money it must be owned.

Lady Jersey has another girl, which she wanted, & the Duke of Wellington will be the first person to see her, as soon as she sees anybody. With premiers & pretty children at command what can she desire? Lord Holland was at Ampthill the day before yesterday, but hurried back to St Alban's to the Verulam arms, & to the arms of his wife. So we did not see him. The Catholic question comes on the 29th. & William may go on the 1st. of May – & then I & his constituents have done with him. When Lord Hill† & his regiment may want him is a matter with which I have no concern. Tavistock is gone to Newmarket. As for my going to Switzerland it is doubtful still. But I shall certainly think myself entitled very soon to a holiday. Old Greville is just what he was. My father very well. After all is not Ireland as good as Switzerland, except for a month in the summer? Parliament begins again next week; what a pity that you have no sense of its importance! I dare say however you will be in time an eager politician. Those grey hairs you speak of betoken wisdom.

Give my love to Mrs Rawdon, & the boys. I had a letter yesterday from a Scotchman at Ayr, begging permission to call his son after me on account of my public conduct. There's for you! Addio, carissima.

* The Earl of Lucan's house near Chertsey.
† The Commander-in-Chief.

Lord William Russell to Lady William Russell at Berne [PRP]

Woburn Abbey April 7th [1828]

I have received no letter from you since I last wrote, dearest Bessy – I am in a state of fidget & nervousness lest they should go astray.

I pass my time here much in reading & reflecting, I hope beneficially, at least I think so, & indeed I feel my mind is adopting different views & sentiments. However not to torment you about my worthless self, I will go to a more interesting subject, the dear boys. I think much of them, their present & future state, education, prospects in life &c. Nothing can be more unsatisfactory than the system of education in this country, unless it is the nonsense people talk about it. You know pretty well what that is, so I need not repeat it, among other things that manliness of character cannot exist without school education, what can be more false. My two brothers are here Henry & Cosmo. They are forward in classical learning, but in everything else they are little savages, with minds not elevated above the grooms. This disgusts me with schools, besides you may remember the dirty tricks & language they taught little H at Brighton. As for their father & mother, they scarcely know them. Beyond all doubt the greatest blessing a child can have is an attentive mother, the greatest misfortune is to have no mother, or a negligent, or foolish or vicious mother. The mother forms the child's first principles, & if they are well grounded, they never desert him thro life.

I do not mean to pay you any idle compliments, dearest Bessy, but why should I conceal the truth, I see nobody so attentive to their children as you, nobody so fond of them, nobody so capable of instructing them in the studies they should pursue, the moral duties they should perform, the good & noble & pure feelings that should animate their little breasts. This makes me desirous that Hastings should remain under your care, till we see that home is pernicious to him. I mean the indulgences he meets with, or, what is more dangerous, always feeling himself the first object. We must watch this, not blind ourselves by our love of him, but be firm & send him to school if it is really to his advantage. In the meantime, I would make that sad day as distant as possible by making home as profitable as possible, by a constant & regular pursuit of his studies, for which purpose you must secure a good tutor. He will be so much under your eye, we shall not run the risks of others. I confess (& God forgive if it is vanity) that I am most anxious that our sons should be conspicuous in the world – I mean as scholars & statesmen.

I should be glad if you could induce H. to study the law, of course I mean eventually, for even if he should not like the profession, the study of it leads to a knowledge of the institutions & constitution of his Country, as well as to the power of speech. It is idle to prophesy but I think I can see sufficiently into the future to believe that our financial difficulties, our extravagance & luxuries, the ignorance & faulty education of the nobility, the industry & activity of the lower orders will bring about an attack upon our institutions, a convulsion in which the nation may sink, or rise, regenerated. Should that happen, men of honor, talents, courage will be wanted at the helm of State, & I should feel proud & gratified, if I had educated my sons to be useful to their Country. They bear an illustrious name, but a name that want of education to the young men, or from the spurious blood, that a vile woman has thrust into it, may sink to insignificance, if not to something worse. I should be proud & gratified if my children could uphold it.

Never were children so blessed in a mother, and that may do everything. Some, indeed most, of the greatest men in the world were educated by their parents & never went to school. The greatest people that ever lived were the Ancient Romans, especially during the Republic. Who reared the Gracchi? Cornelia, & had a monument erected to her honor & virtue as a mother. Julius Caesar was educated by his mother, Aurelia, Augustus by Atia, Agricola by Julia Procilla. These men were not effeminate, their fame has handed down to posterity the names of their excellent, virtuous mothers. Under the Emperors it was the fashion to leave children to servants & Tutors, but losing the mother's care they grew up less learned, less virtuous. A school is much the same sort of education. Tacitus, in giving the preference to the system under the Republic, to that pursued under the Empire, says, the youth went forth into the world with all the advantage of home discipline, his mind expanded by the fine arts, impregnated with science, fortified by principles of morality &c. His father then takes him to the Courts to study oratory.

Tacitus also expatiates, & Julius Caesar does the same in his commentaries, on the advantages of keeping them from women till 20 years of age.

These Romans were great men, we are figurines compared to them, then why should we say that their method of educating children was erroneous & ours perfect – the conclusion is unjust & untrue. However I do not want to set my face against the common approved form of our country, that would be folly. I merely wish to avoid its extreme errors, & profit by its advantages. Of course I say nothing of all this in the world, it would only bring quizzing & ridicule on the poor boy. I say he will go to school when he is old enough & strong enough. The worst part of home education is that boys must be *made* to learn, severity is necessary to secure persever-ance, & here perhaps you may fail. . . .

LORD WILLIAM'S DIARY

7 April. Went across the country to Laleham. Duke of Wellington came to dine, looking well but thin. I endeavoured to make him talk on military discipline, on which he has clear, sound, but peculiar notions, but he prefers telling gossiping stories to the ladies, probably as a *délassement* after his labours.

9 April. I had been to see the palace of the late Duke of York (Oatlands), the scene of his luxurious sybaritical life, it inspired me with no one gratifying feeling or reflection. To-day I went to see St Anne's, the beautiful & modest retreat of Mr Fox. The whole place inspired me with feelings of love, admiration & veneration for the memory of that friend of freedom & the human race; the very seats where he had sat I looked upon with the same respect & awe I had formerly viewed the antiquities of Rome. I remembered the greatness of his public life, & forgot the failings of his private life.

16 April. Went per coach to London.

18 April. My father returned to town from Ely, & was attacked with a fit of apoplexy in his carriage. He was immediately bled & cupped & was better in the evening. The Duchess also ill.

20 April. Went with Mr Blore to Wimbledon Park. He says he can build me a house with 4 rooms on a floor, stable, coach house etc., for £5500. My father rather better. Remained at home & read Fénelon's life.

25 April. Went to Boyle farm* on a visit to Mr & Lady G. de Ros, who live in the smallest cottage in Lord H. Fitzgerald's kitchen garden, where they appear most happy & comfortable with two little children.

29 April. Catholic Question put off to the 9th, very tiresome, for it delays my departure for Switzerland.

Hastings Russell to Lord William Russell in London [PRP]

[Berne 1828]

I have written three times to you dear Papa without telling you that I had a double tooth pulled out. He lugged at it twice. I send you some vio-lets but write me a satisfactory answer about my Poney.

Atty wants Papy to come and so do I. We are going to the Donau Weibchen. I have been looking over the newspapers to see what the Oakly

* At Thames Ditton.

hounds have been about. Pray Papa tell me the sport and how Uncle Tav's broken bones are. I must complain of your laziness.

Dear Papsy this letter has been long in hand. I have had so much *lessoning* so dont be angry this being my fourth letter. I have got your note. The fencing master asks after you daily. I do the Assaut like another Angelo.* I am glad my Poney is fat and well as he will bear the journey better for I hope you mean to bring him though you have never given me a direct answer.

I have translated the Bible from latin into english. How is Grand Papa. Give him a kiss from me and my love to *Cosey*. How is Lord Lynedoch. Tell him I wish he would come here and travel with us so goodbye dear Papa

Lady William Russell to Lord John Russell [PRP]

Bern, Thursday May 1st 1828

I never felt more anxious & fretted in my life than I do now about your poor dear father! pray dear John write me one line regularly merely as a bulletin. I dont know if this luckless event will detain your brother or whether your father will be sufficiently recovered to remove his uneasiness & allow him to have set out. I am going out of Bern for we begin to suffocate & the double windows being removed the noise is insufferable. I shall go only a few miles off to refresh the children and myself after six months captivity in this Ark. Direct always Bern. God bless you.

Tell me how long Parliament will sit? till July? or far into July?

Lord William Russell to Lady William Russell at Berne [PRP]

[London] Thursday May 8th. [1828]

This, dearest Bessy, is the birthday of your poor husband. He is 38 years old – two thirds of an average life are over. I pray to God that those years which He is graciously pleased to allot me in this world, may be spent in sincere repentance for the past & such an anxious desire to lead a life of goodness, as may induce Almighty God to pardon my past transgressions, & assist me to atone for my sins by upholding me in my intentions.

But you, dearest Bessy, what am I to say to you? Alas, this is a black

* Henry Angelo, a famous fencing master.

page without hope. Nothing, no nothing can restore your confidence, your love – God have mercy on me.

I am melancholy as night, no wife to kiss me, no little children to bring me presents & wish me joy. Nobody here, even knows it is my birthday.

Today the call 2 comes on, the debate may last 2 nights, I hope to get away on Saturday though & to find a letter from you at Paris, to tell me, what to do & where to go. Write to me also *poste restante* Belfort – Lucerne & Zurich they say are beautiful places, & excellent schools, especially at the latter. Madame de St Aulaire went there to bring up her children.

I have been putting back the books & locking up the bookcase, it is really lamentable to see how filthily dirty the books are & spoilt – they should be cleaned by a bookseller. I fear I shall not be able to bring you many things for I have nothing but a small portmanteau, the Berne one went to pieces, & was too big for the mail.

My father gets better every day. He is much pleased with your letter, continue to write to him. William marries Miss E. Campbell on the 17th. I have given him a pair of saltcellars. Write to congratulate him, for he thinks you have not forgiven him for the Goodwood gossip.

C. Cavendish & Hare go with me as far as Paris. God bless you, dearest Bessy & my dear boys. I am most impatient to see you all but nervous to the greatest degree, pray be merciful to me.

LORD WILLIAM'S DIARY

9 May. Adjourned debate renewed – & adjourned again.

10 May. Left London at 6 a.m. with Colonel Hare, too late for the Calais Packet; got on board the Margate Packet, & caught the Calais Packet. Arrived at Calais at 8 o'clock: left it at 10 in the Mail.

18 May. Rejoined my family at Berne – who were thanks to God all in good health, the boys grown stout & tall, & delighted to see me.

Lord John Russell to Lord William Russell at Berne [WPP]

Hotel Aubin, Rue de Rivoli [Paris]
May 20, 1828.

Dear Brother,

Forasmuch as you tarried long in the city of St Paul, working with the faithful, and did not tarry yet a little while, to deliver the Gentiles out of bondage ye are greatly blamed. Some of the brethren said, Where is our brother William that in this day of strife he wrestleth not with us? And others said, Perchance he is gone with his wife, and unto his offspring, little remembering the council, and unable to remain with us as yet two days to see the righteous exalted, and the pride of the intolerant laid low! Verily this is much weakness and it shall be remembered to him in the synagogue, and in the day of the election, when he shall ask again to be named an elder, and the people shall say, 'Is not this he who turned his back in the day of battle, and fled from before the face of the Inglisite, and the Peelite, and the Orangite, and took refuge in strange lands, where no man could find him? And shall not the Milesian cry Shame! and the Pharisee rejoice in his heart?' This is part of the epistle of John to his brother William when he fled into the land of Goatian, and sojurned with strangers in the mountains.

There was indeed a great outcry in London, upon your departure. And if the question had been lost by one I think you would have found it hard to stand against the clamour. For my part I never was more surprized than when I found you were gone. You are so much the more bound to be there next time ...

Yours affect.,

John Corporatus.

LORD WILLIAM'S DIARY

19 May. Went to Thun, the environs of which are beautiful. The weather was fine & I enjoyed myself in walking about with Bessy & the boys, admiring the beautiful scenery of the lake with the Alps in the background.

22 May. Little Arthur, who is not yet three years old has seen Cader Idris & the Devil's Bridge in Wales, walked on the granite Causeway in Ireland, & yesterday went to see the glaciers of Grindelwald in the Oberland. Wet day, walked about the valley, & taught Hastings to load a gun & fire at a mark.

23 May. Heard the Catholic Question was carried by 6 votes, & that Don Pedro had renounced his sovereignty of Portugal in favour of his perfidious brother Miguel.

31 May. At Interlaken. Hastings translates the Bible with great ease – the difficulty is to fix his attention & to make him apply, but he is young, 8½.

2 June. Went to see the very fine waterfall of the Giesbach on the lake of Brienz, & dined under a tree to the great delight of the children.

4 June. Returned to Berne.

Military Years

Duke of Bedford to Lord William Russell at Berne [WPP]

London, May 27, 1828.

... Yesterday I received yours of the 18th from Berne, and will not fail to announce your arrival to all the family, except John, who is, God knows where. He went off a fortnight ago for Paris in great haste, but nobody has heard anything of him since. He is always mysterious and may perhaps be gone to Genoa. I agree with you in all your philosophising, and moral reflections, not upon the *amor patriae*, but the *amor abire patriam*, which seems to be as predominant a feeling in Switzerland as with us.

I am just going with Mr Blore to see your ground at Wimbledon, and select a site for your house, if you are determined on building (with Lady William's consent and approbation) and have fully considered all the expenses of building, furnishing, etc. I have got Lord Spencer's proposals, which are very fair and liberal. It will make a complete villa. 10 acres of land at 55 guineas per annum, ground rent certainly very moderate.

Love to Lady William. The Duchess is a little better, but Dr Clarke says not with child.

'This day we are married eleven years,' noted Lord William on 21 June, 'God grant us health to enjoy this happy state for a long continuance.' They had been joined at Berne by Lord Lynedoch, 'old and broken and very blind'. He went with them to look for a house at Lausanne and they found one 'called Bellevue on top of the hill which Bessy decided to take'. Making all together an excursion to Chamonix, the brave old soldier despite his eighty years walked with Lord William and guides up La Flégère to view Mont Blanc. Some verses scribbled on an inn wall were noted with amusement by Lord William.

> In questa casa troverete
> Toutes les choses que vous souhaitez,
> Vinum bonum, coctas carnes,
> Horses, couriers & harness.

Due to his regiment in Ireland, he settled his wife, who was again pregnant, in the pretty house at Lausanne in the middle of July and left for England with Lord Lynedoch in the old General's carriage. The roads were execrable, the rain incessant; they travelled much by night. 'Poor old Lord Lynedoch, supposed to be 82 years of age, never appeared fatigued on the journey.' In London he consulted Fitzroy Somerset* and the Duke of

---

* Lord Fitzroy Somerset, 1st Baron Raglan (1788–1855), Secretary at the Horse Guards.

Wellington about his military prospects, and wrote to his father about going on half-pay. On 1 August he re-joined his regiment near Dublin. 'What can exceed the ennui of a mess?'

Lady William's state of health may be taken as the reason for her not to accompany her husband to Ireland, and it is evident that another pregnancy was unwelcome to her. In a contrite letter to his wife Lord William wrote of 'his fatal sin' and his regret for his lack of self-restraint.

It was becoming apparent that domestic happiness and a soldier's profession were not compatible. In a brief moment of enthusiasm he considered joining a French expedition to fight the Turks in the Morea, but, the Duke of Wellington counselling him against this, he decided to give up the 8th Hussars and to go again on half-pay.

Lord William Russell to Lady William Russell at Lausanne [PRP]

Newbridge. Augt. 2d. [1828]

I cannot tell you, my dearest Bessy, what a weight oppressed me at finding myself again in barracks & thinking that had it not been for my own brutality you & my boys would have been with me. Then I should have been quite happy here.

In your life you never saw so strange a place, an enormous straggling pile of building something like a German Palace, the nearest town 5 miles off. The Commanding Officer's house is excellent, plenty of rooms & quite separate. Last night I found prepared, & slept in our great bed, the two pillows placed as if you were to lie by my side – oh Bessy how wretched it made me. Not a soul slept in the house besides myself & the silence in the night, only interrupted by the tread of the sentry, was awful. Today I have given it up to Lord & Lady Brudenell.* I found her in Dublin in great distress, the only house beside this was offered to them for 30 gns a week! & she is frightened to death, the owner of the said house never stirred without a policeman at his heels with a loaded pistol. He has since taken fright & gone off to England. What a Country to live in. If Ministers dont play their cards well, there will be an awful rebellion here. At present all is very tranquil.

I arrived last night to dinner & have to go thro that tiresome proceeding again today & every day till I can get away. . . . What a life to lead – it is a sort of monastic life without the hopes of futurity. Yet when I see these

* James Lord Brudenell (1797–1868), later 7th Earl of Cardigan. Commanded the Light Brigade in the Crimean War.

fine men & horses, with spirited youths to command them, when I think how much they are my own creation, how I have toiled to bring them to perfection, it goes to my heart to give them up. There is an unaccountable & irresistible pleasure in the pride & pomp & circumstance of war that is very delightful, but the details are tiresome & disgusting. One of the soldiers has written me a congratulary poem on my return which I will send you. . . .

Pray tell me what I shall do with all the things, plate, linen, platters, wine, furniture – shall I sell them, shall I give them away. Pray write & say for I tremble at the thought of doing wrong. If I sell them I shall be mean, if I give them away I shall be foolish & heedless, if I keep them I shall be stupid, this is always my poor fate, so send me peremptory orders in writing & they shall be obeyed.

As yet I have only received two letters from you. It is dinner time so I will finish this tomorrow.

Sunday 3d. I have been occupied this morning in looking into various details, clothing, messing, stables, dinners &c &c. & am much pleased with the state in which I find the regiment, it is in high order, the little Major has been diligent & obedient & all have been zealous, but all this you dont care about.

The weather is of the old Irish sort, rain, rain & rain. This consoles me for your not being here, for the damp might have disagreed with you, tho the soil is dry . . . I got no letter from you this morning. Lady B. arrived last night & is established in my house in barracks. I long to know your projects that I may form mine upon them. The chief question is where do you lie in, for that must regulate all other movements. In all this consider yourself & not me. Places are much alike to me – time flies on, at Paris & London as at Lausanne & Newbridge. In a few years it matters little whether one has been amused or not. Indeed it is better not to have been amused for amusement distracts one's thoughts from that on which they ought to rest, Eternity. Thank God mine are regular, & every day becoming more obedient & more sober. I have now but one source of discontent, the absence of you & my boys – but in a very little while I hope we shall be again together in cheerfulness, I hope, dear Bessy, & content & gratitude to God, for we owe it to his goodness & mercy to us. I regret the affliction & mortification my fatal sin has brought upon you, but to me it has been the cause of much good, in opening my blinded eyes upon my own weakness. I may be stupid, obstinate, morose, harsh, disagreable but I think & hope I can never again be wicked.

169

Military Years

LORD WILLIAM'S DIARY

9 Aug. The daily & dull routine of a barrack life; however, I have plenty of books, & amuse myself tolerably considering my family are away from me.

14 Aug. Made a speech to the regiment on their disgraceful drunkenness. Went to Carton,* a fine place comfortably furnished, but I covet none of their fine possessions – mighty dull.

20 Aug. Incessant rain; re-established the fencing school, but the officers prefer billiards & lounging about to manly & gentlemanlike exercises.

22 Aug. The Russians have arrived under Choumla, the French are going to occupy the Morea without I fear the consent of England.

23 Aug. Received a letter from Fitzroy Somerset to say the Duke of Wellington approved of my going to Greece with the French army. Wrote to Bessy about it.

Lord William Russell to Lady William Russell at Lausanne [PRP]

[Newbridge, 23 August 1828]

... I will walk round my room, reflect & then tell you my decision.

I have decided to accept. I can always throw it up if *you* dont like it. At all events it will enable me to get away from this, where I am bored to death & melancholy beyond description. If no other good comes of it, I shall at least see you & my boys on my passage thro Switzerland, & I hope take you on with me to the south. Be prepared, packed, in marching order – get the axle tree of the post chaise strengthened.

Tomorrow I shall go to Dublin to ask leave to go away. My next letter will be from London, but write an answer to this by return of post. I shall not be easy till I know your opinion & wishes. But keep it all a rigid secret. Write as mysteriously yet intelligibly as you can. Send your letters under cover to Madame Appony, tell her to forward them to London unless she hears from me. If I set out immediately for Paris I will write to her to keep them for me, but write one letter by the common post to London & say *I approve.*

Given leave to go away, Lord William dined for the last time at the mess. 'Felt melancholy that I should probably not dine with them again, & half inclined to make them a leave take speech.' On his way to London he found his brother John at Cheltenham, and the Duke of Wellington, who advised him not to go to Greece. While waiting to hear if Lord Sefton would purchase his commission, he went to Woburn with his father and Eliza Russell.

* The seat of the Duke of Leinster in Co. Kildare.

'What a delicious place this is, every comfort, every luxury, every amusement is contained within it – yet how little is it prized by its owner.' Invited by Lady Cowper* to join a large party at Panshanger he wrote of the agreeable days spent there. 'Walked, drove, sauntered about & passed the day in all the pleasant idleness of a country house. Lady Cowper is a charming woman, without the common female fault, detraction. Lounged on the lawn talking with Lady Cowper & Madame de Lieven, two clever women.'

Receiving 5000 guineas from Lord Sefton for his commission, his spirits rose high. On 28 September he left London for Dover – 'having previously settled my money matters, placed £2000 in the Duke of Bedford's hands, paid my debts & having money beside. This is a vast comfort.'

Duke of Bedford to Lady William Russell at Lausanne [PRP]

London, Sept. 26 [1828]

I write only one line by this mail to say that Mr Adam has seen William and is much pleased by his candid and explicit statement of his affairs. He has paid Mr Green of Bedford his loan of £1000, and he (William) has lent me £1500! so this is safe, and I trust you will prevail upon him not to draw this, till it is actually wanted for his next military promotion. The sooner you can persuade him to give up the arrangement of his affairs to you the better. I am sure you have a much better head than he has, but this perhaps is paying you no extravagant compliment.

Lord William Russell to Lady Holland [HH]

London Sep 26 [1828]

I regret much that I shall not see you again before I go. If the Packet had sailed on Sunday I would have gone by Brighton to have got a glimpse of you & Lord Holland, my political leader, the only statesman now left who has the great noble manly views of Mr Fox. You must take care of him, not only for your own sake & all our sakes, but for the sake of England. But Brighton is a nasty unhealthy place in the month of September – and Ampthill, poor Ampthill, its oaks & its lawns, its splendid avenue, & gay garden, its airy rooms, & healthy air, its Alameda & good roads, what has poor Ampthill done to be deserted for such a stuffy, stinking, dusty, noisy, unhealthy place as Brighton. Lord Holland had better give me Ampthill &

* Emily Lamb (1787–1869), daughter of the 1st Viscount Melbourne, wife of the 5th Earl Cowper. After his death in 1837 she married Lord Palmerston.

take my regiment in exchange, then he can live in country towns, & I can live like a nobleman at my ease.

My father is remarkably well, full of his new house.* I start on Sunday for Lausanne & then for Florence to winter spring & summer, & then to winter spring & summer again; perhaps I shall settle at Lucca with Binda *bueno*, Binda *bello*.

Lord William passed two days in Paris, then travelled rapidly till he reached Lausanne at 10 o'clock at night on 6 October.

LORD WILLIAM'S DIARY

6 Oct. Had previously sent on a courier to announce my arrival to Bessy. The inn keeper told me nobody was in the house. I would not believe him, ran up to Bellevue alone, knocked & halloed in vain. The wind blew, the rain poured, the darkness impenetrable. I almost broke my neck & came away with a heavy disappointed heart.

7 Oct. Up early to enquire for Bessy, heard she was at Berne, could find no letter at the post, went to Bellevue, found the old woman who said the servant & carriage were gone to Geneva. Ran down & caught the steam boat – ran to the post, a letter but no information, found the courier at Sécheron, he knew nothing. Déjean† said she came the 10th – full of perplexities & disappointment.

8 Oct. Remained at Geneva in hopes of a letter, get none, sadly disappointed. Went to Ferney to see Voltaire's house & garden; the rooms as he left them. Heard many anecdotes of him.

9 Oct. Went in the steam boat to Lausanne in search of Bessy. No news of her. Lord Meath told me Bessy was at Berne.

At Berne he found his wife and children. His half-brother Wriothesley was with them. He led them all back to Lausanne and then to Geneva, where, dining with Lady Elizabeth Vernon, they met Charles de Bonstetten,‡ 'a clever, lively, agreable man, 84 years of age'. Lady William having chosen to be confined at Florence, they set out to cross the Alps into Italy at the beginning of the winter. Lord William was constrained to write in his diary: 'The passage of the St Bernard by Bonaparte is a trifle compared to putting a family of women and children in motion.' They went over the Mont Cenis to Genoa; another week saw them at Florence where they were again ab-

* No. 6 Belgrave Square.
† The inn keeper.
‡ Charles-Victor de Bonstetten (1745–1832), Swiss writer who had known Rousseau and Voltaire, and was a friend of Madame de Staël.

sorbed into the society that amused itself with plays at Lord Normanby's,*
and operas written and produced by Lord Burghersh.† After looking at
many houses that were 'gloomy, dirty and dear', they hired one in the Via
dei Bardi. The decline in Lord William's spirits may be noticed; gloomy reflections punctuate his journal. Idleness did not make him happy and the
presence of Mrs Rawdon in his house did nothing to cheer him.

Duke of Bedford to Lord William Russell at Florence [WPP]

Brighton, November 3rd 1828

I received your letter on the subject of your imputed remissness in not
having attended the Mayor's dinner at Bedford. I think your justification
ample. I was certainly to blame in not having mentioned it to you, but in
fact my head is good for nothing. When the health of the members was
drunk, Tavistock or the Mayor ought to have made your apologies, particularly as you wrote them to the latter. The thing is over and there is no
more to be said. With regard to your going out of Parliament I can see no
necessity for it whatever. If any unforeseen event should occur so as to
prevent your future attendance, it will then be time enough to think of it,
but I suppose there will be nothing to prevent your coming over after
Lady William *est relevée de ses couches*, and there is seldom business of
much importance till after Easter.

Duke of Bedford to Lady William Russell [PRP]

Brighton Decr. 8 [1828]

10,000 thanks for your amiable and entertaining letter. With regard to
Wrio, I can only say thanks, a thousand thanks for all your kindness to him.
On his religious principles, I have written more fully to William; all I can
say is, heaven guard him from the Calvinists, Methodists, and Evangelicals, unfortunately so much the fashion now, amongst our young clericals,
but more so amongst our young females, for they are the weaker sex,
(excuse my saying so to *you*) more alive, more susceptible, and more
enthusiastic than ours. It is the aggregate of all these feelings which forms

---

* Constantine Henry Phipps, Viscount, later Marquess of Normanby (1797–1863),
author of several novels. Ambassador at Paris 1846–52.

† John Fane, Lord Burghersh, later 11th Earl of Westmorland (1784–1859), English
Minister at Florence: he married, in 1811, Priscilla, daughter of the Hon. William
Wellesley-Pole, later Earl of Mornington.

the foundation of that religion, of which so many of your sex are now enamoured. I most anxiously wish that Wrio should steer clear of this sect; but don't imagine that I want him to be a gay and pleasure-hunting parson – quite the reverse, he must direct his vessel between the Sylla and Charybdis of the Church and endeavour to be a good, pious, moral and benevolent divine without folly or fanaticism; not one of our Pharisees of old, (of which there are too many) assuming to be so much better than us poor publicans and sinners. I like earnestness and real piety in religion, as much as any man, and God forbid that I should throw cold water upon it at any time. *Au reste* Wrio is thoroughly amiable and if he falls into good hands is sure to do well, at all events, he will never be a hypocrite. I could not resist writing these few words in answer to what you said.

We have all the world and his wife here (Lady Jersey always excepted) tho' with the exception of the Hollands I have seen but little of them. Lord Holland is uncommonly well, and Miladi equally so, except when the *entrées* are too tempting to be philosophically (I will not say religiously) resisted. That loving couple Lord and Lady Ellenborough* have been here, but are gone and have left the heir apparent. My Lord comes occasionally to see him, as he says he is foolishly fond of him. . . . John has left *his love* and is gone to Holkham. . . .

With best wishes for a *petite fille* rather than another *gros garçon*.

Lord John Russell to Lord William Russell at Florence [WPP]

Holkham,† December 14 1828.

I have nothing more to say on the subject of your concerns. I confess it is not easy to make all things square. What immediately presses is that you should attend Parliament. . . .

You would like the shooting here, it is very wild, with a number of dogs all running before one, no pheasants stopped and an infinite number of rabbits. The only inconvenience is that the shooters are as wild as the dogs, and one runs a chance of being shot every minute. I shall go to Althorp, Middleton and Woburn before the session commences. It is certainly the jolliest part of the year. My father is pretty well and her Grace very much so. Tavistock still complains of his collar-bone and I want him to give up the fox with a small 'f' to the Fox with a large one. But it is not likely.

* Edward Law, 1st Earl of Ellenborough (1790–1871), married 1824, as his second wife, Jane Digby. Divorced her in 1830. Their son, born 1828, died in 1830.
† The seat of Thomas Coke, M.P. for Norfolk.

Woburn Abbey, from an aquatint

Lord John Russell and Lord Holland, painted and engraved by
H. Hughes

Give my love to Lady William and the boys. I don't envy you Florence, 'the common sink of London and of Rome'. . . .

No new scandal, the gourmands are obliged to hash up the old.

LORD WILLIAM'S DIARY

17 Dec. [Florence] Bonstetten told Lady E. Vernon that Bessy had a *netteté* in her expressions, a *justesse* in her ideas that put him in mind of Mde de Staël.

21 Dec. Mrs Rawdon's birthday. Age? Won't tell.* Gave her the boys' picture. God forgive me if it is a sin not to go to church, but the difficulty of getting a seat, owing to the aristocratic arrangements, the length, repetition & coldness of our prayers – the gossip & malevolence of the audience, make me feel that my appearance there would be a vain & empty parade, useless to myself & others, displeasing to God from the little fervour I should put into my prayers, & the little good I should bring away.

25 Dec. Children's ball at Lady Normanby's. Little Hastings in great delight.

26 Dec. The weather hot & damp – it is impossible to feel well in such weather; when the body is oppressed, the mind is oppressed.

28 Dec. Sunday. Went to the Calvinistic church – an excellent sermon on living in the fear of God.

30 Dec. The mornings of this month were employed in study – restoring my Latin. In the evening I read some amusing book, & the time slipped rapidly & pleasantly away & brought me to the end of another year.

31 Dec. All the past year is mine no more
    The flying hours are gone.

Lord Tavistock to Lord William Russell at Florence [WPP]

Oakley, Dec. 22, 1828.

It always gives me great pleasure to receive a letter from you, especially when it contains such good sound English sentiments as I found in the one I have just got from Florence. To confess the truth my own feelings upon the subject of home and country are so strong that I cannot trust myself to say what I think of those who for the sake of their own ease, or convenience, or pleasure desert her in her utmost need. Montrond told me t'other day that after the taste he had had of England, he was not fool enough to live out of it if he could help it. If these are the feelings of a Frenchman

* She was fifty-four.

what ought to be those of an Englishman. We have had hitherto a charming winter – altho' hunting and shooting 3 or 4 times a week, I have never been cold, wet thro', only once, and the storm which wet me lasted about 5 minutes, and was succeeded by a beautiful sunny day – when it rains in Italy does it hold up in this way? I have Lord Collingwood's authority (a pretty good one) for saying there is nothing like the climate of England after all, but there are a set of discontented spirits, who will allow no merit to their native country. Let them pass their days abroad 'unwept, unhonoured, and unsung'. I have no patience with them. Are we sent into this world merely to enjoy ourselves? to discharge no duties? – to pass our time in ease? – to degrade ourselves into selfish and sensual beings? – making no exertions for the good of others and spending what we have among those who care not for us, our families or our country, so long as we spend amongst them those resources from whence we derive all the comforts and enjoyments we possess?

We have had some pretty sport lately, but my nerves have been so much shaken by my falls of last year, that I have not been able to crowd to the forward cry. I never had the hounds and people so good – my Turf career has been a most unprosperous one. . . .

Duke of Bedford to Lord William Russell at Florence [WPP]

Woburn Abbey, December 29th 1828

We will talk about Hofwyl for Henry and Cosmo when we meet. I understood you and Lady William to object to it on the ground of the boys usually there, not being of the same class and station in life as our own boys. I think this a material objection. I do not mean in an *aristocratical* sense, or that I should wish the boys to be nobles or allied to nobility, but that they should be possessed of those feelings and principles and characters which belong to gentlemen. Bad habits and bad principles acquired at school in early life, will too often remain. But we will discuss all this when we meet. I have not heard from Wrio for some time, but I hope he will when this letter reaches you, be tending his steps towards home, to enter upon his new career, and that he will pass some little time with you and Lady William at Florence, before her *accouchement*. I have told you before that I am convinced no persons are more capable than yourselves, of instilling sound religious principles into him and removing from his mind those errors with which I fear he is too much imbued. I may say to you in

176

confidence that I cannot feel easy about him. He is thoroughly amiable, and has high principles of honour, which he will always call into action when he suffers himself to reflect, but he has a weak mind, and is too easily led by designing people, less honest and upright than himself. Among them I reckon the Evangelicals, the Calvinistick Methodists, and all that class of the over righteous, who assume to themselves a superior sanctity and contempt for the doctrines of others, like the Pharisee in the Scriptures. These are an increasing and a very dangerous sect. Wrio has recently written a letter to Eliza which makes me unhappy. It is a rhapsody about 'Grace' etc. etc. and full of the Methodistical cant, though not so in his view of it I am persuaded. He tells her that she must not hide the talent entrusted to her under a bushel, but must enlighten the whole house by it, thus constituting her a Missionary to my whole family. Poor girl, all this bewilders her head, and has totally changed her character. She has given up plays etc. by Wrio's advice. Can you think this right or wise, or judicious at her age? He ends his letter by telling her that Providence has sent a Prussian A.D.C. to some Prussian Prince, to comfort him with religious conversation in the midst of the vanities and follies of Rome. This, in my humble judgement, borders a little on blasphemy. Here she is beset by female friends of this sect who do her infinite mischief. One of them gave her what she called a religious book, which she, in the simplicity of her heart, gave to me, and I found it full of impiety, blasphemy and obscenity. I will not name the lady, but Wrio knows her for I wrote to him on the subject several weeks ago.

There is evidence in Lord William's diary at this time that he found his wife increasingly difficult to live with, and that he apportioned some of the blame to himself.

LORD WILLIAM'S DIARY

It is sad, provoking, and degrading to feel the insuperable influence of constitution on our actions; all the books that ever were written on moral conduct, all the wisdom of the sages & philosophers can find no remedy for this – it is in vain to chalk out a rule of conduct, if nature has not given you the constitutional means to act up to it; a man with low spirits should retire from the world as necessarily as a madman is confined, but if he is bound to live with a person of a haughty, violent, malignant, irritable, discontented temper what is he to do, to yield will be of no service to him, he must suffer and a dreadful state of suffering it is – & if he has animal spirits he may command himself like a ship is commanded by a rudder, which in a calm would be like an ungovernable log, his reason would be a rule of prudence, his religion would make it a duty, his love would make it a pleasure, he would feel that he was the wisest & the strongest & he would yield to the weakest, that is in part, he would not irritate by a misplaced opposition, he would not try to stop the impetuous torrent but to change its course, & weaken its violence. Reason has no influence upon distorted passion & anger, it only inflames it, he would then rejoice in his noble conquest over himself, & pity the miserable sufferer, but without spirits, alas! alas!

La Bruyère says:– Il faut en France beaucoup de fermeté et une grande étendue d'esprit pour se passer des charges et des emplois et consentir ainsi à demeurer chez soi, et à ne rien faire. Personne presque n'a assez de mérite pour jouer ce rôle avec dignité ni assez de fonds pour remplir le vide du temps, sans ce que le vulgaire appelle des affaires. Il ne manque cependant à l'oisiveté du sage qu'un meilleur nom et que méditer, lire, parler et être tranquille s'appelât travailler. This is applicable to England also.
Nous devons travailler à nous rendre très dignes de quelque emploi. Le reste ne nous regarde point, c'est l'affaire des autres.

With the New Year a theme was introduced into the family correspondence that was to recur for the next twenty years. Tavistock and Lord John Russell were aware that their brother was being seduced from England and that his natural obstinacy and his loyalty to his wife led him to assert reasons for his desertion that were false. They wished sincerely to get him back into the service of his country and to ensure that his sons were brought up as Englishmen. They assailed him with reproaches for living abroad and absenting himself at a moment of great political importance. As a member of Parliament his vote was needed to help carry through the Bill for Catholic Emancipation; but his concern for his wife's situation kept him at Florence until after the birth of his third son. He went alone to England in the spring, and no doubt the representations and efforts of his family induced him to take the command of the 90th regiment, which was then stationed in Corfu. Having settled his affairs in England, he returned to Florence and in the summer removed his wife and children to the cooler regions of Switzerland until it was time to take up his military command.

LORD WILLIAM'S DIARY

1829 – 1 Jan. The first of the year found me with Bessy, Hastings & Arthur & Mrs Rawdon lodged in Casa Leblanc,* Via dei Bardi at Florence. Thanks to

* Alexandre Leblanc (1793–1866) was making his drawings of Florence at this time and it was presumably in his house that the Russells were lodged.

God in sound health. May the end of the year find us equally well & equally happy.

2 Jan. There is so little variation in my mode of life that I scarcely think it necessary to write down the daily events. Each day resembles another & altho I neither live in the midst of amusement or excitement I live in a state of calm content, to me much preferable. Soon after 7 I get up – by 9 a.m. dressed & have breakfasted: remain in my room till 1, reading or giving Hastings lessons in Latin. Walk, visit, drive till dark, dine with my family at ½ past 5, generally spend the evening with them, occasionally go to a ball or play, thus time flies swiftly away, innocently employed, & pleasantly passed.

Lord John Russell to Lord William Russell at Florence [WPP]

Woburn Abbey, January 8, 1829

. . . Your perpetual complaints of the injustice with which your wife is treated in this country are totally unfounded. If you both like better to live abroad and find, what is true, that your income is nearly doubled, well and good. But do not give a false and mistaken reason. People here have the same opinion of her as those abroad, but if it is not said by a man with a name half French and half German, if it falls from some such common, vulgar name as Rogers, Moore, or Brougham you think nothing of it. As to receiving in your own house in London and giving dinners that is not to be done with less than five or six thousand a year, as you well know, nor is there any homage or court paid to any one in this country. The Duke of Wellington and Brougham mix in Society as equals, and never think of claiming more deference than other people. But after all where in the world was talent and power of conversing ever more proved than it now is in England? . . . There are but few people here and the shooting only begins on the 20th, when the Duke and Lady Jersey come. The report you have heard about me is not true.

Lord Tavistock to Lord William Russell at Florence [WPP]

[January 1829]

I have this moment received your letter. . . . First let me return to you all the compliments of the season, and secondly, let me assure you that my remarks in my former letter with regard to a foreign residence, were not intended as personal, for I could not intend to censure those who are induced to quit England on account of their children, or from the feelings of duty. Certainly, every man deserves praise who makes sacrifices of any kind for the sake of others. It appears by your letter, that I have been mistaken with regard to the motives of most of those who live abroad. I know and see so little of them that I have no right to give an opinion against yours, but I had fancied that their objects generally were not quite so patriotic and disinterested as you describe them. My imagination had even pictured to itself many a Tory squire, who after having supported all the wars which have led to our present fallen state, who, after having voted with Pitt and his successors, for all their ruinous and wasteful measures, and after having railed against us for years and calling us Jacobins, Revolutionists, and Radicals, for having protested against those very measures which have at length driven him abroad, after having filled many a bumper to the 'Land we live in', and those that don't like it dam'em, let 'em leave it!! Looking in triumph at the same time at all the 'democrats', and winking at his loyal friends, I had fancied such a man running from his country in her utmost need, after having been instrumental in bringing her to her present state. My illiberality had even gone so far as to fancy your great Herr, Lord Normanby, winning thousands at Doncaster to spend them in scenes and theatres abroad, after having with anti-national feeling, done his utmost to write down everything that is English and cry up all that is foreign, but it seems I have been quite mistaken, and I must now look upon all these gentry as 'serving their Country' upon Italian soil. Well!! Thank you for having given me such enlarged notions. We old English codgers get sadly narrow-minded by living so much at home. Now to be serious. Montrond's opinion is I daresay, good for very little, but with regard to yourself and your children, permit me to make one observation. There is no subject upon which an argument may not be raised on either side, but you and I fight for truth not for victory. Recollect then that habits and tastes are formed when we are young, that we return to old associations with greater delight than to those which are of recent date. Be careful therefore, that whilst you are saving your own pockets you are not doing so at the expense of giving your children a preference to foreign countries. *Verbum sap.* I need only instance for examples, male and female, the Duke of Hamilton and your own wife. I am sure she will forgive me. Now to defend myself. You return, I perceive, to your old charge about my subscription to Lord Byron's monument. Far be it from me to defend his character or to approve of his long residence abroad, but having formed early habits of intimacy with him at Cambridge, and having consequently been placed upon the Committee by other college friends, I did not feel myself justified in taking so strong and decided a part as to withdraw my name, joined as it was with

Lord Lansdowne's and many other good men. I paid my tribute to his talents and public services in the cause of general liberty, not to his private virtues. However, I don't tell you that I did right. I am liable to err like other people. Perhaps I did wrong, very wrong, but I am satisfied that my motive was neither base nor selfish. By subscribing I paid no court to power, and it would have been more convenient to me to have spared my money. However, I am no better after all than other people, and very far from satisfied with myself. I did not know till very lately that Lord B. had abused you and Lady William in one of his latter poems. . . .*

* The student of *Don Juan* will not be surprised that the William Russells felt they had been mocked in some stanzas of Cantos 13 and 14. The characters of Lord Henry and Lady Adeline Amundeville bore enough resemblance to themselves to have irritated the originals and amused their acquaintance. Countess Guiccioli, in her memoirs, recorded that Byron told her he was studying Lady Blessington as a model for Adeline.

Canto XIII

XIV

Chaste was she, to Detraction's desperation,
    And wedded unto one she had loved well –
A man known in the councils of the Nation,
    Cool and quite English, imperturbable,
Though apt to act with fire upon occasion,
    Proud of himself and her: the World could tell
Nought against either, and both seemed secure –
She in her virtue, he in his hauteur.

Canto XIV

LV

At sixteen she came out; presented, vaunted,
    She put all coronets into commotion:
At seventeen, too, the World was still enchanted
    With the new Venus of their brilliant Ocean:
At eighteen, though below her feet still panted
    A Hecatomb of suitors with devotion,
She had consented to create again
That Adam, called "The happiest of Men.'

LVI

Since then she had sparkled through three glowing winters,
    Admired, adored; but also so correct,
That she had puzzled all the acutest hinters,
    Without the apparel of being circumspect:
They could not even glean the slightest splinters
    From off the marble, which had no defect.
She had also snatched a moment since her marriage
To bear a son and heir – and one miscarriage.

Duke of Bedford to Lord William Russell at Florence [WPP]

Woburn Abbey, January 19, 1829.
A thousand thanks for your affectionate felicitations in the new year, which I return ten-fold to you and yours. My own days are nearly numbered, for although I have only just entered my grand Climacteric, and 'the days of men are three score and ten,' disease and infirmities have made such ravages on my constitution, that I am not what you represent me to be, and the refrain of my song must be like that of Partridge 'non sum qualis eram'.

As to politics, all I can say is *nous verrons*, I am not so sanguine as you in thinking we may all come together again. Party (I mean honest, conscientious party for good purposes) received a severe blow in 1827 from which it will not easily recover. I cannot after this, with any confidence, connect myself with a political party, and I know Lord Grey feels the same. As to Lord Holland, he is an excellent man, and I have a very sincere affection for him, but he is totally unfit to be the head of a party, being entirely without judgement or discretion, and this I have thought for the last 22 years. . . . John is gone to Exeter to attack an infuriated mob of parsons and blackguards. I have a commission to trouble you with, i.e. to send me home three dozen of the light Genoa straw-bottomed chairs. They are made at some place near Genoa, but I forget the name of it.* They should be all of one pattern. . . . No truth in John's marriage, though they say he is much in love.

Lady William Russell to Lord John Russell [PRP]

Florence Via de' Bardi 1532
January 25 1829.
Would you take care of the enclosed, they are money concerns therefore I recommend them to your care. I do so because I want you to pay what I have just recollected I owe the London University & have written to Child to that effect. Tell me what book to give; would *Crusca* be the thing? as I am here? or are they provided therewith? in short direct me.

I was annoyed when I saw by your last letter to your brother what he had written to you, were it true, it would be so foolish as to require the utmost concealment, but it is insincere – *n'appuyons pas*. Our first

* Chiavari was celebrated for these chairs.

coming abroad was purely & simply & naturally a visit to my mother whom I had not seen for two whole years. We were in winter quarters on the north coast of Ireland in barracks, which 'ye Gentlemen of England who live at home at ease' probably cannot give yourselves the trouble to sympathise in. . . . however winter being a totally idle time for the military, it was chosen instead of summer as a visiting period for Switzerland. We had positively no intention whatsoever of remaining beyond 4 months & I actually only took clothes for that season (I am now expecting the remainder of my wardrobe from England by long sea). When the time came the bad French roads, the Swiss snow, my mother's tears & my children's red noses, made me prefer a Bern stove to Paris followed up by London, & your brother went back alone. Since that *de fil en aiguille* we have stayed on 14 months, – *now* my wish is to remain a couple of years for different reasons Oeconomy chiefly predominating, certainly not pleasure. Thank God, *j'ai l'esprit de mon âge* beyond even what I see in women 10 years older than myself, – & I feel *nel mezzo del camino* [*sic*] *di nostra vita* so well acquainted with *ce qui en vaut l'aune*, that I do not run after or post after *des succès de société*. I have had more than my share & more than my *due* & feel myself on all occasions as little like 'Q in the corner' wherever I may be, & whenever I can conquer my laziness as to going out, as possible. Dear John, I carry my pains and my pleasures about with me – woes if I have any, like the stricken Hart – the arrow sticks. . . . My health is miraculously improved by a Swiss doctor, I have quite lost my spasms of so many years standing & my pain in my side. At the present moment expecting to be confined in 3 weeks, the most robust of my sex may be allowed to ail without being sickly. This is a vile climate – I had forgotten it. I have such rheumatics of every sort as make me tremble to move out. But the world wags on merrily. Such balls, such vivacious vulgarity, such plays, Operas & dinners, as would make London & Paris envious; I partake but modestly of these social enjoyments, as I tell you from rheumatism & laziness. Hastings is very *répandu*; there are about 30 English children, who give fêtes to one another, this is a new world to him, and he goes out with his Papa with uncommon airs and graces, and returns home to his ould mither with wonderful accounts of his *soirées*. Poor little boy he is sadly pulled down & tormented by an odd thing which is his second teething, he has changed all his teeth at once, and his double & treble and single all shedding & cutting at once which makes him so pale and so thin that were it not that he is not ill I should be quite unhappy. Your godson is prosperity itself, I think he is somewhat the

image of an 'infant Alvanley' and Hastings perhaps 'the infant Rogers'.
I do not like the comparison *ni au moral ni au physique* either way. As I
hope you take interest in your nephews, I wish to comfort you with the
assurance that Hastings neither learns to play on the guitar nor dance the
Tarentella nor even speak Italian – he is all Latin & riding & fencing
and the most male the most *propriaque maribus* pursuits imaginable. He
does not speak broken English nor broken anything, which is what I see
English parents [*cut off*] . . . say nothing, because we all think our goslings
eaglets.

Goodbye dear John write to me & tell me you have some affection for
me, I hope your letter may find me alive. I am told that the excruciating
operation of nature we are particularly born for, is less agonizing in these
southern climes than towards the polar regions. *Juno Lucina facit opem*
more willingly – *nous verrons*. In the meanwhile I hope it will please
God to spare me to my poor little children, I only care for life for their
sakes Heaven knows!

LORD WILLIAM'S DIARY

3 Feb. Sprained my knee, having walked far into the hills on a cold frosty
morning, & lost my way. I got on a wall to look about me & jumping down on
some ice my foot slipped & I fell & could scarcely walk home.

4 Feb. Rode with Cornwall to Caffaggiolo to see his race horses; a curious sight
to see Newmarket jockeys training in the midst of the Appenines. The cold very
severe.

5 Feb. My knee much worse, laid up with it.

7 Feb. Sunday. Confined with sprained knee. I did not find my confinement
tedious for I borrowed of Mr Leblanc Larcher's Herodotus which I read with
great pleasure. I put it down with regret & took it up again with delight. I like
his simple gossiping way of relating great acts.

20 Feb. At 4 a.m. Bessy in labor, at ¼ past 12 a boy born.

22 Feb. Sunday. Bessy going on as well as possible.

24 Feb. Letters from Lord Holland, my father & John urging me to come home

Lord John Russell to Lord William Russell at Florence [WPP]

Half Moon Street, Feb. 6 [1829]
. . . You much mistake me if you think I wished you to come away before
Lady William's confinement (which however I did not know anything of
till very lately) on the contrary I thought having once got to Florence

matters here were so uncertain that you ought not to be pressed to come home. . . . Nor indeed should I say it was necessary at all were it not for the town of Bedford, which is falling into a state of great discontent at the nullity of their member. Your leaving England the day of the Mayor's feast made him (the Mayor) angry with the family – and my father finds it difficult to keep up his interest – these things I beg you to ponder.

I cannot comprehend why it should be expedient or useful to bring up your son at Florence. The most necessary thing is to have the ideas and habits of the country he is to live in, which I presume is England. Our education too is greatly improved of later years, and there are some I believe very good schools. . . .

Give my love to Lady William. Tell me if she does not intend to come nearer this way in the spring. . . .

Lord Holland to Lord William Russell at Florence [WPP]

11 Berkeley Square, 10 Feby 1829

You will hear from the papers and your other numerous correspondents the curious events and unexpected prospects which have opened upon us at the meeting of Parliament. Wellington and Peel now they have decided upon the admission of Catholics are in earnest and mean I believe to accomplish it. The frightful bill which precedes and the many foolish ones which are expected to accompany and clog the measure are manifestly adopted to save the honour and gratify the prejudices of some who would not be converted without them. Even if these catch some converts the struggle will be a very hard one in the Commons. All our strength is required and painful as it is to say so to a man so far off, nay unpleasant as it will be to Lady William, I must acknowledge that your presence will be most useful. I have been asked to press you. I am tickled with the notion that my wishes would have weight with you – but annoyed at being the channel of unpleasant advice. Yet my zeal for this the greatest of political causes outweighs all other consideration and I must acknowledge that you ought to come and that we all hope to see you. . . .

Pray give my love to Lady William. She will hardly be in charity with me for pressing you to come but indeed you must.

Duke of Bedford to Lord William Russell at Florence [WPP]

St James's Square, Feb. 10, 1829.

The newspapers (which I conclude you see at Lord Burghersh's) will inform you of everything that has passed, & is passing in Parliament. The time is now arrived when every friend to civil & religious liberty should be at his post from day to day – we are in an awful crisis, and the times are more pregnant with interest than at any period of my publick life of more than 40 years duration, I trust therefore you will lose no time in getting home as soon as possible. Every day from this period to that when Catholic Emancipation may be finally carried, or rejected will be of importance in Parliament – the Brunswickers* both in & out of Parliament are numerous, active, bitter, malignant & persevering – they are resolved on upsetting the Duke's administration, & with it every hope of peace in Ireland – nothing can follow such an event but civil war & rebellion. It is of the utmost importance that you & every one who thinks as we do, should be at his post. John says he wrote to you a few days ago that you need not come till Easter, but his opinions you know are ever varying, fickle & inconstant as the wind. I hope your co-Whigs now at Florence will come also, but with them I have nothing to do – about you I am very anxious.

Lord William Russell to Lord Holland [HH]

Florence, 24 Feb 1829

I received your letter yesterday when Lady William was in the 3rd day of her confinement, but the moment I think her quite safe, I will set off for England. You are right in thinking you have great influence over me, *politically*, no one except my good brother has more. When Aeolus let loose the

Luctantis ventos tempestatesque sonoras

which scattered & shipwrecked the Whigs, you were the plank to which I stuck – in the first place there is magic in the name of Fox, in the next place I like your views on our foreign policy. England should be the terror of the ambitious & the scheming, & the asylum of the oppressed, & that I think is your notion. Then in civil & religious freedom & all that concerns our domestic policy, we go hand in hand together. I liked Canning because he lifted us out of that foreign mud in which we had been grovelling ever since the peace, & because he was a friend to Ireland. In these two great virtues were swallowed up all his little vices. It does not do to look at a Minister with a microscope.

I wrote to Lady Holland to tell her I had got another son. Mother & child have since been going on as well as possible, have the goodness to

---

* The so-called 'Brunswick Clubs' were founded to resist Catholic Emancipation.

tell this to my Father, for I shall not have time to write to him. I cannot say exactly when I shall be in England, for I cannot leave Lady William till she is quite recovered. You will feel that I could not come away before with any comfort to myself, but I will not delay. . . .

I have been passing a very pleasant winter here, not in my usual amusements, but in an amusement quite new to me, reading, and I have found the greatest pleasure in it. I am ashamed to say my Greek & Latin are too far gone as to be of no use to me, but I found a library here with excellent translations of the old authors, & I have just finished Larcher's Herodotus in which I delighted. In short my head is so full of Greek wars & Roman quarrels, & my heart so full of my three sons, that I shall obey your call with regret, however [*paper torn*] is great & urgent, & I will be at my post.

Lord John Russell to Lady William Russell at Florence [PRP]

London. Feb. 20 [1829]

I hope by this time all the dangers, & most of the inconveniences you allude to in the latter part of your letter will be past. But for the southern climate of Florence, I doubt if Juno Lucina likes it all that better than Brighton or Hastings.

I do not doubt that you went abroad meaning to stay four months – & I wish you had done so – I trust even now that you do not intend to stay two years, for the only rational object of it, the education of Hastings, will I am sure be better conducted in England – not at a public school perhaps, for unless his disposition is altered he does not want that, but among the habits & customs of England. I am very sorry you did not execute your plan of taking a house, at Brighton, which really suited you quite as well as any foreign place could do. London I do not believe would. William ought to come up now & then to town for a vote, but it would not often be necessary, & then he could join you the next day, instead of waiting here to vote upon two measures six weeks asunder. I assure you if he does not alter his ways, my father will have to spend several thousand pounds to keep his seat for him at Bedford.

I am afraid you do not care enough about our politics to be aware what a mighty triumph we Whigs have had upon the Catholic question. The Tories keep their places with an entire new set of opinions. Ireland is to be pleased & not coerced – in short the whole thing stands on a new footing. With regard to individuals nothing is allowed except that we are all grown older, some are strengthen'd in virtue thereby, some in vice, but none have changed their characters. As for me I am tired of my old ways, & should like to be settled quietly – but of that I see no prospect. . . .

Our Catholic Bill will be finished I hope before the end of March, & then we have nothing of importance to do till Easter.

Lady Holland to Lord William Russell at Florence [WPP]

6 March 1829

I am much gratified by your kind attention, and so are all you have named. As you do us all but justice in believing we rejoice at the safety of your 'dear Bessy', the race of Russell is so good that it cannot be too numerous. It is the best tribe we have. I write, though convinced this letter will not reach you, who will be on this side of the Alps, which I am afraid is necessary, as there will be a finale all support necessary. The Duke of Cumberland has played old Nick at Windsor, and if they knew where to turn, doubtless another Government would be formed, but that seems impracticable.

Lord Holland to Lord William Russell at Florence [WPP]

London, 10 March, 1829.

In the first place thanks and congratulations for the intelligence of a third son and Lady William's well doing. I think it a better race than the Atridae and there cannot be too many of them. As you do not mention Hastings and his brother, I conclude they are well and perfecting themselves *nel bel idioma del favellare Fiorentino.** You are very good about my politicks. You at least describe what they are very accurately. The Whigs are covering themselves with glory by their unaffected and disinterested support of the Government. . . . So that if this letter finds you still at Florence you need not on the ground of the Catholick question put yourself to the trouble and expense of the journey. I say thus much in fairness not in the way of advice. You best know the other motives publick or private which might induce you to return. Your father certainly thinks that the electors of Bedford dislike your absence. Your father's health

* 'In the beautiful Florentine tongue'.

continues visibly as it was, but the return of attacks are somewhat more frequent, his care of himself we all think rather diminishes and there is no denying that his strength is somewhat impaired and must be more so by the frequent recurrence of disorder and medicine.

I envy you your studies – they are everywhere delightful and I know not why Tuscany seems to me to give one a relish for poetry, oratory, art, and all kinds of refinements. As to the loss of Greek, grammarians have made of late years such short cuts to the knowledge of languages, that it is easily recovered. . . .

Having christened his little boy William Odo Leopold, Lord William set out once more for England; his half-brother Wrio went with him. Snow was falling on the Mont Cenis and lay twelve feet deep. 'Had two men hold up the carriage, escaped narrowly some overturns.' In London he noted that he had a warm reception from the Duchess and a cold one from his father.

LORD WILLIAM'S DIARY

17 April. [Oakley] Tavistock spit blood a month ago, some say from the throat, some from the lungs; he is in a precarious state & much worried about his hounds & the conduct of his neighbours.

19 April. With John in the coach to London. Saw Fitzroy Somerset, always kind & obliging; settled to take the 90th. With John to dine & sleep at Holland House. Lord Holland & Allen defended the conduct of the Spaniards in their conquest of Mexico & Peru.

22 April. Dined with the Duchess of Kent – all the great Whigs. Curious conversation with Sir J. Conroy – he spoke of their gratitude to us for having visited H.R.H. in former days. The little Princess less pretty; her education much *soignée* & superintended by her mother.

23 April. Dined with Lord Essex at his new house in Belgrave Square. Bad road, no post goes there.*

25 April. Called upon to pay 1314*l.* for the 90th; think it my duty to take command of this regiment.

2 May. Went with Lord Lynedoch to Newmarket; the poor old man is very blind & rather broke, *mais toujours le même.*

4 May. Saw the Duke of Richmond's horses & others. There is a great attraction in this place, the beautiful horses, the fine air, the spacious heath, the interest, the society, all unite to seduce one to the turf. I fled from temptation.

---

* Lady Holland described the new fashionable quarter of London as 'that swamp called Belgrave Square'. Earl of Ilchester (ed.), *Lady Holland to her Son*, p. 87.

Duchess of Bedford to Lord William Russell [WPP]

Wednesday morning [1829]

Wriothesley and Eliza are to be married, and I feel anxious, my dear William, that you who have been so kind to him, should be one of the first to be informed of it, by his mother, who is steady in her affection for you. Pray write for me to Lady William, I am unable to, for though it is an event I have long expected, it fills me with such a mixture of feelings that I am quite nervous.*

God bless you.

Lord John Russell to Lady William Russell at Florence [PRP]

Halfmoon Street, May 8 [1829]

Before I answer your letter I must speak of Wrio's marriage with Eliza. I hope you will think as I do that it is an excellent arrangement; indeed it seems so natural as to be almost inevitable. Wrio always was in love with her, and would have been very lonely in his parsonage, but now with a pretty wife, and a good house that requires alteration, and a certain quantity of duties that are agreeable to perform to a man of kind heart, and a nice comfortable country about him, I think he could not fail to be happy. I am quite sure at least that this moderate draught of slow engagement gives a better chance of happiness than the dram drinking of our men of pleasure who when they are not intoxicated are in low spirits and ready to hang themselves!

As for books you need not give any to the London University, it is quite hoptional. You will be glad to hear our institution flourishes, and next year we hope to have it really like a place of education – this year has been chiefly for amateurs.

I have great thoughts of going with William to meet you, and after that following my own conceits on the Continent. In a few days I must settle, as I believe he only stays a fortnight more. By the way said William has become strangely absent and forgetful – as much as I used to be, – but I hope I am nearly cured.

As for Juno Lucina, we have here Lady Francis Leveson who in four or five days was quite well and is indeed a wonder of a woman. Perhaps the season was favourable to the interests of Popery, and the birth of children.

* They were first cousins, and of their three children one was mentally deficient.

We care little about the new Pope. The Duke has settled that matter for us, and we care neither for Pope, Emperor or King. He is beyond doubt a great man, and as the article is rare we are going to put up his statue. As for Otho or Odo I think both names will look ridiculous in the Morning Post, so I have no choice. If you must have an Emperor, why not Napoleon, and he and Arthur can fight the battle of Waterloo with pea-shooters.

Those who have seen my father in town gave very good accounts of him. My belief is that he is growing prudent, and I think if he is prudent he will outlive all his 3 sons of the first brood. He has a constitution of iron, and he is a peer, which is favourable to long life. Tavistock is still weak and subject to complaints on the chest. Love to all your boys.

LORD WILLIAM'S DIARY

8 May. Lord Lynedoch made me a present of a horse, which reared & jumped & almost had me off.*

9 May. Dined with the Duchess of Bedford with 3 of her sons.

13 May. Holland House. Family party; she is very obliging & he is always agreable & instructive.

14 May. Rogers came to breakfast – the society, library, house, garden, *bonne chère* & hosts make Holland House a most agreable *séjour*. Fitzroy Somerset took me to dine with Brudenell – 4 of his beautiful sisters. Lansdowne House; Lady Jersey took me there. These large parties are miscalled society.

17 May. Called on the Duchess at Campden Hill. Went to Lady Salisbury's. Duke of Wellington cold. The Duke of Cumberland hit the Duke of Sussex† saying 'How are you?' The latter said to me 'He's drunk by God' – & would give 10gns he was gone from the country.

Duke of Bedford to Lord William Russell [WPP]

Endsleigh, May 16. 1829.

I shall certainly (*Deo volente*) be at Campden Hill to dinner on Thursday next, and hope you will dine with me at 7 o'clock, that I may have the pleasure of seeing you for at least a few hours before you go. John wrote to me some time ago, that he was going with you and meant to pass the

* A troublesome horse; in July Lord William wrote, 'The same horse given me by Lord Lynedoch, altho' he had been from London to Florence & from Florence to Milan nearly knocked me off again.' And the following year at Rome Charles Greville complained: 'Rode . . . on a confounded high going old hunter of Lord Lynedoch's that he gave William Russell.'

† The fifth and sixth sons of George III.

winter in the Mediterranean. Today I have another letter from him to say 'it is not quite settled.' You know he is the most uncertain little fellow that ever lived, and there is no depending on his plans from one day to another, however I think it is unreasonable to expect that such a fashionable man should leave London and all its attractions, in the month of May! As to his love, she has never been otherwise than cruel, at least so her mother told me last autumn. I have no doubt that the young clerical couple will be happy – they deserve it, and I think have every reasonable prospect before them, to make them so. . . . As to Tavistock, I am in despair about him. I wrote to him as strongly and affectionately as I could to urge him to do what you suggested. He answered me shortly (and I think irritably) 'that there's no use in it', as Jenks and Thackeray (of Cambridge) who he could only have seen for a quarter of an hour, are agreed! I wrote also at the same time to announce Wrio's marriage to him, and to this he does not say a single word, good, bad, or indifferent. This is so unlike himself, that it annoys me. I have no doubt that his Newmarket concerns worry him. He seems scarcely ever to have a horse to run, and when he has he is beat! I suspect these Newmarket jockies are an over-match for his unsuspecting nature. This is all for you alone, and something more confidential than the letters between the Duke of Wellington and Lord Anglesey.

Lord William Russell to Lady William Russell at Florence [PRP]

London. May 18th. [1829]

Dearest dear Bessy, first let me tell you that I love you with all my heart & soul, altho you write me such shabby short letters & by the 1st post I got none which made me uneasy till Normanby told me he was in the same state, so we consoled ourselves by attributing it to the post & not to our wives, tho probably the latter were to blame, but in this noisy, bustling town nobody wears the face of grief above a minute, tho black clothes are worn six months for everybody.

I have now paid off all bills, & we stand clear of all debt, that is a comfort that many of the rich would envy us, & afterwards finding my purse full for the first time in my life, I have emptied it into the lap of the person who most deserves all my superfluities, a person I love, a person I esteem, a person who deserves to be rich, who is economical yet generous, who brings up her children well, who loves her husband, who is the model of all goodness, all taste, all knowledge, all virtue, in short who I have long wished to assist. Dont be jealous, dont be angry, & accuse me of depriving you & my children of their right – but first let me tell you what will perhaps make you very angry, before I gave away this money I wished to know if you had plenty & went to Childs to enquire what balance you had in hand. I found £450, so you are rich, & I determined to give away £600, but I am in a giving humour & have given Wrio my copy of the Transfiguration for a wedding present. I think pretty magnificent for a younger brother, but to return to my other gift. I have plagued you enough & will a plain unvarnished tale relate. I placed £600 to your account at Childs & desired him to buy you an exchequer bill for £1000. If I had placed it in the funds, you could never have touched it without my consent & signature, they may fall & your interest would be diminished. The exchequer bill is your own & you can do what you please with it. It brings you 3 per cent interest, consequently encreases your income 30*l.* a year. You will have to pay about 40 or 50*l.* premium for it, which I have now paid for you, & which Government will pay you back when you sell it. It will be a comfort to me to think you have £1000 at your command in case of any difficulties that may raise hereafter.

I shall not mention it to a soul, & I would strongly advise you to keep it a profound secret, even from your Mama.

I hear the foreign postman's knock. My heart beats violently & I am all of a sweat.

Never was I more disappointed. On the 20th I gave a long letter to that beast the Poodle detailing all the Zante plan * to go by a Courier & you have never received it.

What am I to do. I cannot leave London in this uncertainty about your movements. . . .

[end of letter missing]

LORD WILLIAM'S DIARY

20 May. Went to Hounslow with Lord Brudenell to see the new cavalry manœuvres. Dined with Lord Hill, & a quantity of old generals in stars. They are not Bayards or Bonapartes.

22 May. Went to Campden Hill – conversation with the Duchess – complained of want of settlement on her children – in violent spirits & good humour – *mi pare loca.*†

* The 90th Regiment, of which Lord William had obtained the command, was stationed in the Ionian Islands, then belonging to the British.

† 'She appears to be mad.'

24 May. Holland House. extraordinary conversation with the hostess, objecting to John's marriage with Mary.*

25 May. Went to see Mr Barry's beautiful drawings of Asia minor & Egypt. . . . House of Commons till 12 – sugar duties – very cold. Letter from Bessy objecting to Zante.

28 May. Confined to bed in the morning with cold & cough. Wrote to Green at Tavistock's desire to propose to resign Bedford. T. is shortsighted in his policy. At home sick, but amused with new school books for Hastings.

29 May. Dined with *Padre mio* & John, French play, Lord & Lady Holland; her commentaries on Bessy's letter to Duke that he should recall us from exile & educate Hastings.

31 May. Campden Hill. Drove the Duke & Duchess to call on Hallam† at Richmond Park – he enjoys his retreat after the labors of the Courts. Sir A. Wood had just left – formerly resident at Zante he now occupies my former cottage. Ill with cold & cough. The cousins are cold lovers.

2 June. Set off with John for Dover; bad cough, weather hot.

3 June. 4½ hours passage to Boulogne. Slept at Montreuil. Very good inn at l'Europe. Read 1st vol. Schiller's 30 Years War. Most interesting & admirably written.

4 June. Slept at Beauvais – delicious weather, agreable journey enlivened by John's varied conversation, & by reading the life of Burns.

5 June. Arrived at Paris, my cough worse, John gave me sal volatile & mindererus for it.

6 June. Shopping, visiting etc. Margaret [de Flahault] still abusing everybody, clever unamiable woman.‡

7 June. Thank God I leave Paris today, detestable place.

Lord William Russell to Lady Holland [HH]

Florence 20 June [1829]

It would be an act of ingratitude in me to enjoy the society of my family, & forget how agreable you made the *séjour* of England to me, when I was without them. I assure you I shall always remember with pleasure the days & hours I passed this spring at Holland House, & your unvarying kindness to me. I had a most agreable journey with John, but as soon as the little

---

* Spencer Walpole's *Life* (i, 156) refers to this passing fancy of Lord John's.
† Henry Hallam (1777–1859), lawyer and writer.
‡ '. . . (She) has not a single diplomatic fibre in the whole of her dry anatomy.' Princess Radziwill, *Dino Memoirs*, iii, 252.

dog found something better he left me, or rather I left him to enjoy himself at Genoa – where he has found *de quoi*! Madame Durazzo's house, where he is domesticated, is most delicious, such a view over the marble town, & blue sea, such air, so soft, smelling of cypress, orange flowers & figs. Such sunset, succeeded by such a moon, fancy what this was to our pores still closed with a London north easter, & our noses still smelling the smoke. Such *beccaficos** too, so fat. How could John resist all this, when the lady bid him stay.

To go to more domestic scenes, I found Bessy the very best of nurses, grown fair & fat, handsome of course, & the baby doubled in size with nothing but mother's milk. Hastings & Arthur are two of the sweetest boys that ever were – the one sharp, clever, full of observation, thin & delicate – the other fat, good-humoured, passionate, decided, but incapable of learning ABC, yet both of excellent nature – & I have no doubt will be ornaments to their country & family in their respective ways. Certainly were I Duke of Bedford & had such a daughter in law as my wife, I would not let her waste her sweetness in a colony. She is a remarkable woman – I know not such another – but you must pardon me, I am in all the ecstasy of getting home, & worrying you with my feelings, but I have nothing else to tell you.

Florence is always Florence, just as you left it, & I have seen nobody.

Lord John, who joined his brother and sister-in-law at Florence at the end of June, was with them on and off until October. Visiting Lady Ashburn-ham's beautiful villa outside Florence, Lord William commented: 'the air was soft & dry & fragrant with orange blossom, but I would rather live in a small farm house in England'.

To get away from the great heat of Florence in July, they moved north to the lake of Como; Lady William was often ailing and the children were pale and languid. Moving on to Switzerland, they were joined by old Lord William, and with him visited the falls of the Rhine at Schaffhausen. In September they went to Berne and lodged at a *pension* in the Grande Rue.

Lady Holland to Lord William Russell at Florence [WPP]

Holland House. 3rd July [1829]

I was very much touched and pleased at your remembering me in the midst of all your domestick happiness. It is gratifying that you should find a nook to remember an absent friend. It must have been delightful

---

* A dish of little birds.

to find Lady William so well and so surrounded, tho' I hope she will not continue her maternal duties too long, as she is not overstrong and the exhaustion in hot climates is greater than in these latitudes. Take care of this. Little Hastings too is a forced plant and will not be the better for relaxation. I cannot but hope something may turn up for you in England. Your description of John's attractions to Genoa are quite sufficient to justify his stay there. What a glorious, poetical, yet exact account you give of them, but the lady you do not describe. She is I fear quite altered physically.

... Your father, Mr Hamicks considers to be in a very alarming state, and although he does not say it, he evidently is not satisfied at the mode of treatment which Halford pursues. *Au reste* the Duke is tolerably cheerful, and looks at times well, but the double vision perplexes and vexes him a good deal. He was to have gone yesterday to Woburn, but remains for another bleeding, and goes on the 6th. It is alarming when another attack is impending that he persists in going without a medical attendant. The Duchess is very attentive and miserable about him. ... Tavistock has recovered completely and is looking quite well again. He has a fine constitution to rally from severe attacks. ...

We are told our dear Henry is to be in England this month, the last letters were however from Palermo. ... Dear boy, did he know how much we longed to see him, and how very unhappy his father has been at his prolonged absence, he would not delay, but you, as all have since the days of Adam, will find affection does not ascend in the degree it is felt by elders.

Duke of Bedford to Lady William Russell in Italy [PRP]

Ryde, Aug 24 1829

Your letter from Milan reached me a few days after my arrival in this island. 10,000 thanks. I wish we could have had a little of your Italian heat, either in this island or the island of Great Britain, but it has not yet reached us. I never remember a more cold, wet, damp and uncongenial *soi-disant* summer than we have experienced. I hope you may have something like fine weather during your *séjour* in the vicinity of the Alps, and I anxiously hope that you may fall in with my poor brother, and comfort and assist him. I am afraid that he is *very* ill, but I am in daily expectation of hearing more authentic particulars from his physician at Munich.

I had a letter from your William from Como. ... You and John seem to have been playing at the double game of hide and seek, and cross purposes. You say you have been waiting for him at Milan, Como etc. – he says he knows not what has become of you, nor where to look for you. You say you are *not* going to Geneva – he says you *are*. By the time this reaches you I hope all these mysteries will be cleared and you will all be comfortably together. London gossip says that *la Belle à Gênes* complains of Johnadab, and says '*je ne suis plus rien pour* Lord John!'

LORD WILLIAM'S DIARY

8 Sept. [Berne] John arrived unexpectedly from Genoa. Percy called on us full of form.

10 Sept. Lord William went away. What a strange mode of life, neither respectable nor useful; we could not persuade him to stay.

12 Sept. Dined with Percy our Minister; priggish house, furnished like a lady's.

14 Sept. Hastings reads Virgil with tolerable ease, French admirably, German well; besides this he has a great deal of general instruction & very good sense. We rode full gallop for two hours.

20 Sept. Went with John to Fellenberg's*; met there Baron de Gerando, who has written an admirable work on morals, self-improvement etc. Fellenberg is well intentioned, excellent man, but diffuse & prosy in his conversation, tho his improvements are good – he has a new institution for the Department de la Linth – he has plans too for improving the condition of the poor, but he is thwarted by the sovereigns of Berne, a narrow selfish set. John does not get on well with these good people.

21 Sept. Rain, constant rain. John read us part of his 3rd volume of History – Voltaire & Rousseau – which is excellent, sound ideas on government, a pure morality.

22 Sept. Rain, rain – the Splugen stopt & many bridges destroyed on various roads.

26 Sept. Rogers came to pass the evening with us; the old dog is satirical & false – & so occupied with others' affairs that his time is spent in prying into their weaknesses.

27 Sept. Rogers went off rather huffy, having collected good stories, but I will frighten the old curmudgeon when I see him. The Duc de Laval Montmorency called on us on his way to England as Ambassador; he is a warm hearted man.

1st Oct. George & Mrs Lamb dined with us.† Long conversation on education

---

* Philippe Emmanuel Fellenberg (1771–1844), Swiss founder of the school Hofwyl.

† The Hon. George Lamb (1784–1834), youngest son of the 1st Viscount Melbourne. He married Caroline St Jules, natural daughter of the 5th Duke of Devonshire and Lady Elizabeth Foster.

in which G.L. reprobated our school system tho he thinks children should be taken from their parents. Why is it necessary that this unnatural act should be, & why is it beneficial, the fault must be in the parent.

Lord Tavistock to Lord William Russell at Berne [WPP]

Oakley, 18th September [1829]

... With regard to Bedford, I have nothing more to say to you. My informants have been Palmer, Dr Hunt, and Green. Whatever you may think of the former, you will not suspect either of the others of being un-friendly either to you or to me. They have a notion that you do *not* attend your duty with assiduity, and that you are wanting in proper respect and attention to the Corporation. These are unpleasant reports to me as well as to yourself, but I give them to you because I think it right that you should know exactly what is passing. You are quite mistaken if you think that I consider your attendance at the Mayor's feast as of no conse-quence to your political interests; far from it, I never was more annoyed than at your leaving England last year on the *very day of the dinner*, and your not coming from Cassiobury on a former occasion when you were expected, and actually waited for. However, all this matters very little now, the town will probably be lost to us whenever a general election takes place and the County perhaps, even before that time as I shall hardly feel myself justified in staying in Parliament* unless my health should greatly improve in the course of the present autumn. ...

Lord William Russell to Lady Holland [HH]

Berne Octr 4 [1829]

... You advise me to settle at Brighton; I desire nothing better, nor does Lady William, but alas, how are we to do it, without getting into debt & retiring again exiles to the Continent, & even here I am obliged to pinch & screw to make two ends meet, but 'vogue la galère' with my 3 nice boys, I am content to be anywhere. Hastings, Arthur & Odo, tell Mr Allen the names are essentially English.

John, I am sorry to say, has left us, he is a delightful companion. I think he is determined to be married to somebody, but I tell you this most confidentially, for I dread his taking a rash step, which may embitter the latter part of his life – which we should all lament, consequently we are all

* Lord Tavistock sat in Parliament for the county of Bedford.

interested for his sake & our own in his choice, at least if he is determined (as I believe he is), to make a choice. You are one of his oldest friends, & if you see his course well-shaped can encourage him, & if ill-shaped can check him. Indeed I know nobody whose happiness is so likely to be influenced by marriage as John – a foolish woman would thwart his fixed habits & make him wretched, but he is kind-hearted, easy, gentle, with a manly mind, & agreable society that would make any sensible woman happy – but I have given you this hint in the *strictest secrecy*. Rogers appeared here like an apparition for a few hours & amused us exceedingly with the history of his adventures at Splugen, where he was turned back by the destruction of the road. . . .

Lord John Russell to Lady William Russell [PRP]

Neufchatel, Saturday night [1829]

Here I am at Neufchatel, but as for the lake I have seen nothing of it, having set out so late. I believe after all I shall pursue my journey to Paris. It is not worth while to cross the Alps to be caught in a cold journey in December, and if I went to Genoa, I am sure I should stay there till March. Very pleasant but wrong.

It is painful to part, and to have my affections so far off, but I believe I have decided for the best.

What a storm we had today!! Give my love to William and the boys. I am so sorry to part with you all that I am quite sad. And the dulness of the journey thro' France by myself is not likely to put me in spirits. Happy the Duke of Buckingham (and Chandos) who past thro here for England accompanied by Madame Bonaparte Wyse.*

Lord William Russell to Lord John Russell [WP][6]

Berne Thursday Nov [? Oct] 7 [1829]

We miss you very much in our domestic circle, however I did not like to press you to stay for I knew you ought to go to England, & that your duty & inclination were at variance. You have done right to yield to duty & will have your reward. You would have been a great comfort to Lady William at Genoa, but then you must either have gone home in the midst of winter, or have given up your labors in England which are very

---

* Laetitia, daughter of Lucien Bonaparte by his second wife.

important – for much is to be done there, in improving the morals & the knowledge of the people. . . .

Our weather is worse than ever, I fear the Alps will be impassable. Bessy too has been ill, but is now better, Heaven knows when we shall get to Italy. These domestic cares are unknown to you, however I hear they do not frighten you from wishing to engage in them. You are quite right – there is no happiness like that derived from wife & children, it makes one indifferent to all other pleasures – but then 'beware' don't tumble headlong into marriage. Remember when once in, you can't get out & if it don't suit – it is 'Hell upon Earth'. You are a man of settled pursuits & habits & must have a wife that will take interest in them, a gadding, flirting, dressing, ball-going wife would be the Devil – nor would one of the new-light ladies be quite the thing, a little good sense, a little money would be better, not too young either, in short look before you leap is the advice of an old stager & your sincere well wisher.

Again marshalling his family and household Lord William crossed the Alps by the Simplon pass and descended into Italy. 'Hastings & I rode; he is wild with spirits when on horseback; the fine air & wild scenery also contributed to cheer one. . . . All the people shouted when they saw him on his little pony.' Their destination was Ancona, the port at which Lord William was to embark for Corfu. On arrival he went on board the steam boat, but the courier from England not arriving, and the quarantine laws preventing him from re-joining his family, he saw them daily across the bars of the *Sanità*, until he took his final leave of them. His wife then went with her little boys to Rome where she remained for the next nine months.

Once more Lord William was an active soldier but commanding an infantry regiment. The four weeks he spent in Corfu were happy ones. His diary recorded his delight in the agreeable climate and the beautiful scenery; the blue sea, the clear air and the view of the Albanian mountains. His regiment was in good order and his military duties were light, allowing him to go for long rides with his brother officers through the olive groves. Sir Frederick Adam, the High Commissioner, was civil and kind, offering to lodge Lord William's family should they join him. There were dinners, concerts and balls at the Palace and there was a tolerable Opera. Allotted a house that was scarcely habitable, he took a small lodging where he sometimes dined alone and read Cicero and Suetonius. Observing the cheerful contentment of the officers' wives and families, and pondering on the intransigence of his own wife, he was provoked to remark on happiness being less with the rich than with the middle orders of society.

The time passed quickly enough with a field day or two, an inspection, a parade. He won the approval of his General, and when his regiment was set to build fortifications he applied for and was granted two months' leave to visit his family. He paid his farewell calls on the General's wife, Mrs Woodford, and on Lady Adam, a handsome but ill-tempered Greek. His friends came to see him embark in the steam boat; he was accompanied by five Captains who were bound for England. They were all drunk. After three days' horrible rolling he was once again in the lazaretto at Ancona. Before he left Corfu Sir Frederick Adam had offered him the post of Resident at Cephalonia.

Released after seven days from his quarantine, he posted rapidly to Rome where Lady William had established herself with her sons during the period of her separation from her husband. Before he rejoined his wife Lord William realised that he would never persuade her to return with him to Corfu and that it was unlikely she would consider accompanying him to Cephalonia, though there were many ready to assure her that the climate was excellent and she need not fear for the health of her children. Reluctant to discharge her duties as the Colonel's lady, she was equally determined not to play the part of Resident's wife in a small and distant British possession. On Christmas Eve, one week after his arrival in Rome, Lord William wrote to Sir Frederick Adam refusing the post.

The last day of the year found him thanking God for all his blessings and commending the excellence of his dear wife. 'Few children were ever blessed with a mother so good, so attentive, so kind, so wise.'

Lord John Russell to Lady William Russell in Italy [PRP]

Halfmoon Street, Nov 7 [1829]

Carissima Cognata, on my arrival here two days ago, I found your letter from Milan. No doubt I should have enjoyed the journey with you very much, and Genoa at least as much; but that is over. If I had staid this month at Genoa I should have left you in a solitary state in December, so far you are better at Rome. I trust the eternal city and the remembrance of Curtius and Cato will *retremper votre âme*; or in other words, that you will see a number of friends there and amuse yourself. Solitude is very bad for the morale, and reasoning every day for a month about Corfu &c. has the worst effect both on the perception, and the disposition. Macdonald* here says William's coming home in the spring would be fatal, but that the regiment will be one of the first to come home. If I knew what you wished, or if *you* knew what you wished, I might use some influence to hasten that period, but I do not feel confident that you might not be much more provoked with Colchester than with Corfu. If you would really like it better I will speak to Fitzroy Somerset – for next year be it understood, for this is doomed. Macdonald says Corfu & Lady Adam puts the case in

---

* Sir John Macdonald; adjutant-general at the Horse Guards.

a totally different light, and must be disagreeable – you are quite as well not to go. But never allow William to quit parliament, army &c., which in his last letter to me he again talks of. Bedford will be quiet this year. If I had any influence with you I should say this – give up all thoughts of parliament this year – settle between Corfu and Rome as you best can with credit, for William must not lose his military reputation; come to England in August next year, and contrive to have the regiment here for the next winter so that William may vote in every important question that comes on.

Tavistock says with regard to the Mayor's feast, that he should no more have thought of asking him to stay for it, than to dine with him if he were staying with him at Oakley – it was a matter of course. Between ourselves a gentleman of common sense, who has represented a boro' for 15 years ought to know what is required and expected. . . .

My father comes to town today – only think how strange; he missed Tavistock by going out of town the day T. arrived and will not see him till the spring. T. seemed a little mortified; I am sorry I shall not see him either for some time. I imagine he is settled at Torquay.

I was very happy at Berne, so I made no sacrifice. You will see Russell at Rome. Pray put him in the way of opening his understanding to the wonders of Italy. He is very well disposed. I will get the book for Arthur and shall be delighted if I give him thereby a taste for literature – but if he has it ten years hence it will be quite soon enough – he has a fine fallow understanding.

Lord John Russell to Lord William Russell at Corfu [WPP]

Woburn Abbey, Nov. 27th [1829]

I am happy to hear from my father of your arrival at Corfu tho' I have no letter myself. Gossip there is little or none to write. But a bad letter grows good directly as the square of the distance it travels, – so here goes. We have all the world just arrived – the Duke of Wellington, Fitzroy Somerset, Rosslyn, Aberdeen and last not least the Duchess herself, who has come from Scotland on purpose. . . .

Depend upon it the Bedfordians will be quiet enough this year, if you appear in good time next. Our politics are as unsettled as ever. My father of course persists, but Tavistock says he must as yet keep aloof. Poor fellow, he must keep aloof the greater part of the session. Every one says he looks very ill, but he is pleased with the climate of Torquay, and tho' he has been ailing has had no fresh discharge from the lungs. It remains to be seen what is his strength of constitution.

Lord Holland as usual is very eager, and holds opinions that other people do not hold, but which I think to a great degree very wise – he thinks our commerce with Russia of the greatest value to us, and cannot bear its being risked by frothy articles in newspapers. . . .

Much obliged to you for your advice about a wife. I am not bent upon marrying, and if I do, it will be somebody I like, and then all caution goes for nothing. Addio.

Duke of Bedford to Lord William Russell at Corfu [WPP]

Woburn Abbey, Dec. 17, 1829

I have by this morning's post received a letter from William Adam, enclosing an extract of one from his brother Sir Frederick Adam, in which he says you are gone to Rome, and is in hopes you will bring back your wife and children with you to Corfu. He writes in terms of great commendation of you and seems much pleased with your society. I sincerely hope you may accept Sir Frederick's offer of the Residency of Cefalonia. . . . Lady William will I am sure cheerfully content herself with such society as the Cefalonians afford, and devote herself for one year to the exclusive education of her children.

I cannot make out that John wants a wife – in my opinion he is much better without one – he is cut out for an old bachelor, with all his little enjoyments about him, and would be bored to death as a Benedict. Lady Holland seems to suspect that he has renewed his intercourse in Addison Road,* tho' this is but bad authority, all I know is that he frequently applies for my box at the theatre for Lady Hardy. The Duchess joins in best love to Lady William, and I am ever your affectionate father.

Lord John Russell to Lord William Russell at Rome [PRP]

London, Dec. 22nd [1829]

I am glad to hear of your going to Rome, and hope Lady W. will agree to the Cephalonian plan, tho' at what season she is to go there, I cannot well perceive – at all events she will have a good house there, and Edward

---

* Lady Hardy, whose daughters were admired by Lord John Russell, lived in Addison Road.

says, a finer climate than Corfu. Pray tell her I wrote to her long ago (directed Rome) but fear the *red hats* have made her forget me. I trust to hear more from her when she gets among the *red coats*. Part of your letter was exceedingly imprudent; it had been opened somewhere, and a wafer stuck on each side of the seal, but I trust the openers were Italians, who cared little about the society of Woburn – however as I know what you think of it all, there is no need of writing it, except for the benefit of the post-office clerks. . . .

The newspapers for want of anything else speculate on where our Premier* shoots – wherever it may be he shoots very ill. At the old Abbey he staid three days, and talked of his campaigns with great gusto – he says he has not read Napier, but it is evident he has – he gave me his own account of the passage of the Douro very well. He had been reading Bourrienne's book. I ask'd him if he did not think the *second sight* of Marengo curious. He said not very; he was sure to find the Austrians near the Po; *au reste* he told a story of N's saying to Brede who in 1809 commanded the army in Germany, and hoped he had not spoiled N's plan. 'Plan de campagne – je n'en ai jamais – je tombe sur l'ennemi par tout où je le trouve.' Not true for he often had a plan. . . .

Love to the boys and brat.

LORD WILLIAM'S DIARY

The first of January 1830, found me at Rome with my excellent wife & three dear boys, Hastings 10 years old – a sweet child full of kind, warm, affectionate feelings and great spirits, but his bodily health & strength are not equal to the activity of his mind – his information is considerable for his age, & he is passionately fond of reading, but I doubt whether his application will ever be sufficiently strong to overcome difficulties, so as to be a good scholar, at present I see no chance of it, but he is young.

Arthur is four years old, a fine stout manly boy, but he is beginning to shoot out of his stubby fatness into length & thinness, he has no disposition to read and will not learn his alphabet.

Odo is nine months old, healthy & thriving under his mother's nursing. God grant that these dear boys may all be in health at the end of this year & their dear mother to bring them up.

Resuming social habits that had changed little from those of 1823, the Russells
entered into the festivities of the Roman season. That Bessy was in great
beauty was a source of satisfaction to Lord William.

* The Duke of Wellington.

Military Years

'I see nobody in society to be compared with my dear wife, for beauty, grace, elegance, manners & conversation, she is the most brilliant in society as she is the most domestic & simple at home, attending to her *ménage*, her children & her various duties. Who so learned, yet who so modest? She is the paragon & the perfection of women. God bless her & preserve her for all our sakes.'

He was now in his fortieth year and the melancholy that sometimes descends on a man at that age becomes apparent in his journal. He had not the same zest for the entertainments offered, and found the little operas at Princess Zénéide Wolkonsky's, and the theatricals at the Russian Minister's, Prince Gargarin, more agreeable than the parties (that he compared to Vauxhall) full of English. The great balls at the foreign Embassies were his detestation. 'I am too old for balls, they don't amuse me; they make me sad when I gaze on all that thoughtless beauty, & reflect that soon they will be the dwelling place of worms.' An increasing misanthropy led him to make sour comments on many of the persons who formed his and Bessy's society. Lady Lovaine,* whom they saw much of, was 'snobbish, sour, scandalous, & ill natured'. Her daughter, Louisa Percy, who was to become one of Lady William's lifelong friends, 'has her natural good qualities spoilt, – all abroad about religion – does not wish to be mixed up in heaven with thieves, yet she will steal away a reputation & call it no theft.' Lady Westmorland was 'crazy, cunning, envious & malicious. Why must people be always occupied with their neighbour's affairs. She is clever, quick & eloquent & it is sad to see a mind like hers so perverted & overthrown.'

And of Lady Holland's son, Henry Fox, he wrote: 'Why is he not in Parliament instead of dangling after old women?' In general he found the young English bachelors in Rome without vice or virtue – 'they drink no wine & are a poor effeminate set'. When Lord Tavistock's son, Lord Russell, spent some weeks in Rome, his uncle had an opportunity of studying the character of the delicate young man who stood between him and the dukedom. 'A nice good young man, but little in him – pity he is not more brought out, directed, & better educated.' And finding him one day 'natural, unaffected & true', on another he complained that he was stand-offish. '*Je le plains, pauvre garçon,* – it is a sad fate to be placed in a great station without the powers necessary.'

The impatience with which he viewed the weaknesses of others was significant of his dissatisfaction with his own life, and of a growing un-certainty about his future. The tension that arose later in the year between the William Russells is as yet hardly apparent, but the frequent praise accorded to Lady William by her husband in his journal is a tribute to her virtues as a mother, and not to her excellence as a wife. The re-iterated

* Louisa Stuart Wortley Mackenzie; wife of Lord Lovaine, who succeeded his father as 2nd Earl of Beverley in 1830, and his cousin as 5th Duke of Northumberland in 1865.

praise suggests the action of a person who holds a talisman and incants to ward off fear and disaster.

Among their new acquaintance was the American novelist, James Fenimore Cooper, who was travelling in Europe with his family. He found the Russells congenial company, and Lady William lent him books to read. Returning Moore's life of Lord Byron to her, he wrote a note to accompany it.

'I hasten to return the book, Lady William, which I have read quite as closely as it deserves. Do you not agree with me in thinking it, in good honest English, a catch penny? . . . little as I like the book my gratitude for your politeness is quite as great as if it had been better. Very respectfully your serv. J. Fenimore Cooper.'[7]

Fascinated as ever by the classical remains of Rome, still largely unexcavated, Lord William spent hours walking about the city alone, or riding with his friends or with Hastings. His affection for his eldest son was increasing and the long gallops he took with him in the desolate Campagna were compensation for the evenings spent in crowded rooms in Roman palaces.

'I know nothing more delightful than riding about Rome with the little fellow, the pleasure of teaching him to ride, pointing out to him the great monuments of antiquity, & occasionally losing oneself in reflection on the ruins & their founders, is not to be described.'

Reading occupied many hours of his day, and his struggle to master a language in which his wife was proficient led him to study the Bible in Italian.

The house in which the Russells lived at this time had been inhabited by Byron during his brief visit to Rome in 1817, and was sometimes shown to the public. A young Englishwoman recorded that, without knowing Lady William, she passed through the rooms as a tourist; her guide paused and pointing to an ornamental bed said: "That was Byron's bed." A little boy playing on the floor looked up and, pointing to a cradle, said: 'And that is Odo's bed, and there is a flea in it.' This young woman, who married the Vicomte de Peyronnet, became the mother of Arthur Russell's future wife.

Lord William Russell to Lady Holland [HH]

Rome Jan 9 [1830]

It gave me very great pleasure to hear of you yesterday from Henry Webster, who I can tell you is in the highest force with the best cook in Rome 'faisant le magnifique' wearing several orders, talking several languages, & the idol of the ladies. It is a pleasure to see a man in such enjoyment of existence. He is a practical denial of all the doctrines of the philosophers, I really wish the rising generation would observe & imitate him, I am sure they would be happier than they now are with their rigid abstinence from wine &c.,&c., at all events they might catch some of his gaiety, frankness, good fellowship.

What can I tell you of Rome, to me it is not what it was. The Duchess of Devonshire, Gonsalvi, Laval, Appony, Kinnaird, Bartholdy, Canova, & many others with whom we used to live are gone to the other world, or to other countries, & we have found no substitute for them. You would not know Rome, it is so changed, such good hotels, such good shops, such good lodgings, such good dinners, it is more like Paris. Poor Falck* has had a very bad gout – we saw him much before his illness, & to see him is to like him. I dont know (except Lord Holland) a more agreable man. We have several young sprigs of nobility here, but they are all very quiet. Russell was disposed to admire a pretty little Spanish lady, but probably he did not kindle so quickly as Spanish eyes desire (*oyos matadores*) so she gave the preference to young L. Bonaparte, whom the indignant husband caught & cuffed & kicked downstairs, & has packed off his poor little frail wife to be shut up in a convent in Spain for life. Thus has tragically ended the little innocent *amour*, of which Russell might have been the hero, still it is as well not to be kicked by an enraged Don. . . .

I shall not go home but return shortly to Corfu, leaving my family here, for the sea voyage, climate, are not good for a sucking teething child.

Do you remember your conversation at the Théâtre Français with my father, when he gave a grunt, or as Lord Holland said a grant. Try again & see if it is a grunt or a grant, for we want very much to settle at home, & now that Tavistock has sold his house, we have no place to put our books, pictures & valuables in. The weather here is dreadful. Yesterday a heavy fall of snow with thunder, you had better keep Henry with you. This is a miserable, idle, gossiping place for young men. I want to hear him thundering in the Senate.

Duke of Bedford to Lord William Russell at Corfu [WPP]
Woburn Abbey, Feb. 3, 1830.
. . . Since you went to Rome from Corfu, all your friends have been most anxiously expecting to hear something from you on the subject of the offer Sir Frederick Adam made you at Cefalonia, and I need scarcely add that all have been very anxious that you should accept it. We have not

* Baron Anton de Falck (1776–1843), Dutch Minister in London.

heard a syllable from you on the subject, but a recent letter from Sir Frederick to his brother, says that Lady William has declined it. I deeply regret this, but as I suppose you have decided on the best judgement you could find, it is useless for me to say any thing on the subject. I was sorry to hear your children had been suffering from coughs at Rome, but if it was the whooping cough, it is an unpleasant complaint well over.

I regret to hear that you have been put to any inconvenience by the removal of your goods and chattels from Tavistock's house in Arlington Street, but he has convinced me that you have no cause whatever for complaint, I regret therefore that you have been writing to him on the subject, as it annoys him and vexes him; and his mind being in a very irritable state the natural concomitant of the complaints he labours under, these little annoyances seriously affect his health. As for me you well know that I have no house to give you wherein to stow away your goods. Many thanks for your information respecting works of art at Rome, but I have no money to throw away on such things, the times are very hard – the distresses great, and I must save every shilling I can scrape together, for positively necessary expenses. The 5000 stucco casts you mention would be no very great expense, and such might probably tempt me. . . .

Returning to Corfu at the beginning of March, Lord William made the journey by way of Malta, where he spent a week with the Governor, Frederick Ponsonby, his old friend of Peninsular days. Seduced by the good society, the large parties, handsome dinners and easy living, he concluded that this was truly the 'Pays de Cocagne'. Hookham Frere,* a voluntary exile, slowly drinking himself to death, gave William dinner, who found him lively and agreeable 'but not the man he was – but who is?'

Before he left the island William paid a pious visit to the tomb of Bessy's uncle, Lord Hastings, but felt he 'might have better mourned a better man'.

During the two months he spent with his regiment in Corfu he was much concerned with the horrible drunkenness of the soldiers, lecturing them on the errors and dangers of their indulgence in strong liquor. 'The men drink 3 quarts of wine after working, besides their rum, having 10d a day to spend & wine 3d a quart. This is a most disgusting waste & employment of money . . . it is very disgusting that whilst our peasantry are working for 4d & 6d a day, the soldiers & sailors are living in a beastly state of drunkenness. This sets one against the possession of Colonies with all their concomitant evils.'

He was again captivated by the beauty of the island; the almond trees were in flower and the figs were budding. In the hot weather he would

* John Hookham Frere (1769–1846), diplomatist and author; he retired to Malta in 1818.

walk out at half past five in the morning with a volume of Montaigne in his pocket, and sit reading under an orange tree. He was always glad to get away from the troops: 'Muster. To escape drum & fifes, I rode out alone. What a lovely country; I passed over the gardens of Alcinous & rode along the brink of the sea where Ulysses was shipwrecked: what scenery, what delicious weather. Under the enormous olive trees the grass & fern are as green as in England, then the paths lead over wild crags covered with myrtle, gum cystus, laurestinus & various beautiful plants – the sea of a deep blue beneath, & the Albanian mountains beyond.'

He made an expedition to Zante while the hills of the Morea were still covered with snow. 'Took in several passengers at Argostoli, we had the appearance of a steam boat going to Margate. Strange to see the English all over the world. At midnight I sat on deck as we passed Leucadia, Sappho's Leap, & thought of Virgil's & Lord Byron's description of this voyage; the brilliant stars, futurity, & my family – how the mind wanders & is lost on such a night.' Later on, in May he sailed on board a warship as far as Corinth, passing Ithaca, Missolonghi, Patras and Lepanto, noting with excitement the classical names of antiquity associated with each promontory and plain.

Granted further leave, he returned early in June to Malta, where he hired a small schooner to carry him to Italy. Eager to rejoin his family, his patience was sadly tried by the contrary winds that delayed his journey. 'Felt so melancholy I could have drowned myself.' His mental anguish was soon aggravated by seasickness, and in seven days they made little progress. Becalmed off Catania, violent winds soon obliged them to lie under the rugged desolate coast of Calabria. Wrapped in his cloak, Lord William mused on his past while he listened to the Maltese sailors singing their wild Arab songs. He prayed to God that his remaining days on earth be spent in happiness and goodness, and that his boys might be virtuous and happy men. Employing in his journal a form of contracted phonetic spelling, not easily decipherable, and which he used increasingly in times of emotional stress, he made resolutions about his treatment of his wife. In an endeavour to raise his spirits and banish his worries he read the plays of Sheridan and recorded his gratitude for the laughter they provoked.

LORD WILLIAM'S DIARY

22 June. Becalmed all night off Stromboli. This miserable burning rock.

23 June. A breeze sprang up at 9 a.m. May I never forget the reflexions of this day. Calm.

24 June. Calm.Calm.Calm. Patience. Patience. Patience.

At last on 29 June, fifteen days after leaving Malta, they decided to run into Naples, where he landed and, hiring a carriage, hurried on to Rome, which

209

he reached in two days; but Bessy and the boys had left in the steam boat on the 24th.

Lady William Russell to Lord Lynedoch [NLS]

Rome, March 22, 1830.
The time now approaches when you promised a visit to Rome, I still cherish the hopes of eating our Pascal Lamb together. I am here with my mother & children, all thank God quite well, till the middle of May when I move northwards in quest of cool shades for the summer & when I expect Lord William who left Rome with Captain Hamilton of the Navy for Naples a fortnight ago nearly; and embarked on Captain Popham's ship the *Infernal* for Malta – he was longing to see Malta & F. Ponsonby, & also desirous of avoiding the Ancona passage & above all the steam boat of which he has no agreeable souvenirs going or coming; a King's ship will take to Corfu, but he will be condemn'd to swallow a third time the Ancona affair, lazzaretto & all; however *pour les beaux yeux de Corfou que ne ferait-on pas*? It is a charming concern altogether & a most eligible residence for a family – so convenient, so healthy, so near, so economical, & so agreeable above all & *comme il faut* in all ways. I hope to grow vastly intimate with Lady Adam & add her to my list of dollies which is pretty numerous as it is, from connexion & circumstance.

When Lord William is *quite perfect* in his profession I want to live settled somewhere to educate Hastings till the public school time – that is my look out in life, *chacun a le sien*, & for a *mère de famille* I suppose it is the right one. After Hastings comes Arthur & then Odo – at proper intervals, so as not to interfere with one another in their education. I hope you approve of the name I selected; Thomas, begging your pardon, was not romantic enough nor William either & Leopold was too much so – so I took refuge in the middle ages & the family annals & found the first Norman adventurer of the Roussels who came over with the Conqueror was Odo de Roussel, so here is his name revived, good man, 800 years after an ungrateful forgetfulness of his posterity. . . .

The slender Percy is here too, I mean the *Honorable Algernon* our Plenipo in the Alps *auprès des* Cowherds.

Our Roman society has been peculiarly quiet & agreeable, not one quarrel has been got up the whole season, which was universally attributed to the absence of Lady Westmorland, she arrived here however a fortnight ago & set us all quaking, but hitherto no disturbance has arisen. . . .

Lord John Russell to Lady William Russell at Rome [PRP]

Holland House, Ap. 16 [1830]

We have not written to one another for a long time – it is difficult to keep up a correspondence which is once broken, so I beg you will write from time to time, & I will answer.

The great event of the day is Mary Fox's marriage. She is to marry Lord Lilford, a gentleman of about 28 years old, a peer with an estate, not I believe very large. I do not know him by sight, he is reckoned some-what of a fop. But she likes him very much, & her spirits quite boil over. It appears Lady Holland prevented the match last year by her interference, but this time it has gone better. This is all very well. For my part I am very well satisfied to see her well married, & have never given any further suite to what I said to you last year. . . .

What are you going to do? I suppose you will leave Italy in June; I am told your children look delicate. Hastings may, but not Atty I hope. Give my most tender & avuncular love to them. I will order your money to be paid to the London University, which at the present writing, is not making such progress as it ought. Yet the course of lectures there is excellent.

I wish we were all settled in England. If William will give up his regiment which is the best thing he can do, you may come & live in Sussex, with great comfort, tho' not splendour, and come to London for two months in the year. Depend upon it the sooner you are settled in England the better.

This is the last advice of your affectionate brother.

As you have not gone to Corfu this year, I hope there will be no question of it any more.

Duke of Bedford to Lord William Russell at Milan [WPP]

Belgrave Square, June 25 [1830]

Since I wrote to Lady William this morning I have received your letter from Corfu. I write only one line to stop you coming to England, in case you had thought of it. Your coming into the new Parliament is quite out of the question. You must stick to your profession where you are doing so well. John stands for Bedford (at my request), where your standing would have ensured a fierce and expensive contest. You would have been beaten and I should have lost the Borough. More in detail by the next mail.

Lord John Russell to Lord William Russell at Milan [WPP]

Brooks's, June 25. 1830.
I received today your letter from Corfu. My father has I believe written to you what he has done about Bedford. The representations were so general that you could not be brought forward again with credit that he determined you should not stand. The choice of a successor for a long time hung between Russell and me, but at last my father settled that I should stand. As your fate was fixed I could do you no harm by accepting. But I stood out with my father that whenever you came to live in England, he should bring you in the first opportunity. I do not think it was possible to do better, but I leave you to the accounts you will receive from my father and Tavistock, Mr Hunt, Green, Whitbread, Lord Ludlow, etc., etc. All agreed that it would be folly for you to stand for Bedford again. . . .

The King will be dead in a very few days. A disease in the lungs has reduced him to a miserable state. I will write again.

Duke of Bedford to Lord William Russell at Milan [WPP]

Campden Hill, June 28, 1830.
I wrote to you very shortly, and in haste, by the last mail. Since which the demise of the Crown* has taken place, and a dissolution of the present Parliament may shortly be expected. You will not be called upon, for any senatorial or representative labours, as your standing again for Bedford is wholly out of the question, for the most substantial reasons; and the same reasons would operate against my proposing you for Tavistock, where the electors are not at all disposed to submit to a non-attending representative. It was the universal opinion at Bedford, amongst friend and foe, that you could not offer yourself for that Borough, without the certainty of a contest, and the strong probability of a defeat, in which case I should have lost the Borough for ever, for I never could have attempted it again – there was but one universal opinion, both in the Corporation, and in the town, as to your non-efficiency as a member, and it would have been childish and absurd in me not to have yielded to that opinion. John is anxious that I should bear him harmless in your estimation as to the whole of the transaction. It was to comply with my wishes that he has come forward, and I think his popularity will ensure a quiet and secure election. When

---

* George IV died 26 June.

you are disposed to resign your active military duties, for those of a civil character, I have no doubt that we shall be able to find you a seat in Parliament if such should be your wish; but at this moment I think it would be most inadvisable – for two duties are incompatible – as a soldier you are universally well spoken of and esteemed. Sir F. Adam writes to his brother that he has never met with a young officer, who has so just a notion of the profession, and of military knowledge of duties as you have.

I am sorry that Lady William has such a dread of the climate of the Ionian Islands for her children – especially as I hear of many having been there without suffering from it, many healthy young English children still running about those Islands – but we have done with this now. I heard there was a prospect of the 90th going to Malta next year, and I wrote to Lord Fitzroy on the subject. . . . I have also written to Lord Hill to make you one of the King's A.D.C.'s in the event of a Brevet promotion, stating fully and without reserve your claims and services. . . .

Lord William caught up with his wife at Genoa, but it was not a happy reunion and his journal, using the cryptic abbreviations he adopted under stress, recounts a succession of quarrels and reconciliations. The presence of Mrs Rawdon, the great heat of the summer, and the letter he received from his father telling him he was not to stand again at the next election, but that his brother John would take his place at Bedford, were trying aggravations at this time.

They crossed over the Alps to Geneva, and Mrs Rawdon did not rejoin them until December. Lady William was 'suffering dreadfully from nerves', but the cultivated society of Geneva made the next few months pass happily enough, and in September Lord William asked for a further six months' leave of absence and was granted it.

LORD WILLIAM'S DIARY

3 July. Bunzen & Parisani had letters from Bessy. Thank God they have all arrived safe & in good health at Genoa. As soon as I can get my passport I shall be off. Started before 5 p.m. Travelled all night.

4 July. Travelled all night.

5 July. Breakfasted at Pisa, saw Binda at Lucca preparing for his wife's confinement. Called on poor Gertrude at Viareggio, & supped at Massa – travelled all night.

6 July. Arrived at Genoa at 8, & found my dearest wife & boys in good health. My most grateful thanks are due to God for this great mercy.

7 July. Nothing can be more gratifying than the affectionate warm hearts of my dear boys, God bless them.

8 July. Saw Mde Durazzo, obliging good natured creature.

9 July. A letter from my father to say I was not to be returned for Bedford – this is hard. Another from John to say he meant to replace me – this is cool.

11 July. Tk H bth. fry of A. sys O is slfsh bst pr by trmbld sdly [Took H to bathe fury of A* says O* is a selfish beast poor boy trembled sadly]. Read my feelings & longings from 14 [th] to 29 [th]. So end all human joys & hopes – in disappointment, but I must not be discouraged. Satisfied with O. Called on Madame Brignoli at Albaro.

12 July. [Genoa] Almost failed – it is very difficult, God help me. Bilious & headachy. . . . Again wrote to my father.

13 July. Dined with the Durazzos, pretty house, agreable dinner. I shall fale, crge crge [courage courage].

14 July. Went with the boys to bathe in the sea. a nt snsblty flng. lt O b reklss hdlss gy thghtlss nd lgh. wnt D– bgn tdy, o fr anml sprts. a sys o slky. [have not sensibility, feeling. let me be reckless, heedless, gay, thoughtless and laugh. won't do, begin today, o for animal spirits. A says O is sulky.]

16 July. Boys began to learn to swim by being put in deep water with a handkercief round them, Atty not in the least alarmed.

18 July. Went to see the Brignoli Palace, what fine pictures; the Vandykes at Genoa are superior to those in England; he there found the people rich & ignorant of painting, & consequently took less pains. Read in the papers Bessy appointed Lady of Bedchamber to the Queen.

21 July. Went to the theatre, illuminated for the King & Queen of Naples,† very handsome, Madame Durazzo's box, who is always friendly Crowds to see the old King – strange curiosity, when will men fly to see an honest & a virtuous man. Mud pleases man.

Lord Tavistock to Lord William Russell at Geneva [WPP]

London, July 5th [1830]
    John has desired me to inform you that he went to Bedford yesterday to ask our friends there to release him from his engagement to them in order to accept an invitation from Huntingdonshire, where he would have had an easy conquest, and to take Russell in his place. But he found the enemy (Mr Polhill) already in possession of the field and intended to steal a march upon us. Under these circumstances it was thought John should

* 'O' here appears to signify Lord William and 'A' his wife.
† Francis I of Naples and his Queen were returning from the marriage of their daughter to the King of Spain at Madrid. 'The King has the features of a man of eighty and he is not even fifty-four.' Acton, *The Last Bourbons of Naples*, p. 39.

not lose a moment in canvassing the town. An express was sent to Whit-bread, so he and John and Polhill were hard at work all yesterday. It is well that my father decided upon his standing in your place, for we should have had no case at all with you, and must have abandoned that seat altogether. As it is we lose the choice of Hunts and Middlesex for John, which is provoking and has made our friends abuse you, especially as they are out of sorts at being obliged to put up with Hume for Middlesex. In Hunts too, there is great disappointment and not a little soreness, and added to all this vexation, John has been forced to do that which he naturally dislikes. If you had come over for a short time all this might have been avoided, but there is no use in complaining now. . . .

May I wish Lady William joy of her appointment? By the bye, I was desired to inform her, and you, that Harrow is now the best school. A Westminster man is head master.

Lord John Russell to Lady William Russell at Geneva [PRP]

Bedford. July 4 [1830]

Here am I, standing in William's shoes, & very pinching shoes they are. A Tory candidate has started, in the person of Mr Polhill, who relies on his money & beer to bring him in. I was canvassing all yesterday, & shall be all tomorrow. We are likewise to have a contest in the county against Tavistock. So you will see how impossible it is I should get to Geneva. Nay even in the autumn, instead of partridge-shooting or Swiss lakes we are to have the regency question & Civil List. No one can say in the present state of affairs, what may happen next, and whether we are to have a regency of the Duke of Cumberland, the Duke of Sussex, or the Duchess of Kent is quite in the air.* In the meantime they have appointed you Bedchamber Woman, which to me ignorant of events, conveys no meaning, but I understand the chief duty of the office is to wash the Queen's knees. I should have thought you might have looked higher.

I am sorry for my own part that I was chosen to stand for this place; I should have preferred going to my old constituents of Huntingdonshire, who have been very anxious for me to stand again, my old opponent having resigned.

Tavistock is much better than he was, but not yet well. The Duke of Wellington seems to have the confidence of the new King, but his ministry is very weak in the Commons. I am told your regiment is to stay abroad till

* In the event of William IV dying before Princess Victoria was of age.

October twelvemonth. We may have a revolution before that. By the by it seems not unlikely in France. The maxims of Louis Quinze do not agree with the Charter. We are here only too abundantly supplied with all things; corn, cotton, men, women & children.

I hope William has joined you. He will come into Parliament again when he wishes it, or soon after.

LORD WILLIAM'S DIARY

22 July. [Genoa] Severe heat.

23 July. Bessy bilious attack.

25 July. Thermometer 84 in the rooms. Reading Valmont, these books on virtue are true & excellent, but they go too far when they say all happiness depends on a practice of virtue, no doubt it gives a pure conscience which goes towards giving happiness. I find it very easy to be virtuous in all great actions, to be generous, disinterested, pious, charitable, devoted cost me nothing, but these occasions seldom occur, I want a manual of happiness in little things of which life is made up, domestic grievances, worries & annoyances; a bilious habit, & adieu happiness, not all the virtue of Socrates will bring it. Long walk with little H. He is an amusing idle boy, yet so good, not one bad thought, God bless him.

26 July. I shall fale, hve nt niml sprts. [I shall fail. Have not animal spirits.] Thermometer 82.

27 July. Worse & worse. sd scne a sys O hve bd hrt, o prncpls slfsh mlgnt topd & htes mi. ts impssble I gve up, mst fle – sprts nt qual t he drdfl tmpr all rslutions useless. hpes O my b bst th m rgmt ftn & lng. sd,sd,sd. Gd hlp m,Gd hlp m [sad scene A says I have a bad heart, no principles, selfish, malignant, torpid & hates me. It's impossible, I give up, must flee. Spirits not equal to her dreadful temper. All resolutions useless. Hopes I may be absent with my regiment often & long. Sad, sad, sad. God help me, God help me]

28 July. Called on Madame Durazzo. agreable & good-humoured – oh what a charm is good humour.

Lady William Russell to Lord Lynedoch at Varese [NLS]

Genoa, July 28, 1830

It was really too hot to write when I last received your letter, so as William told me he was going to pen you off one I deputed him to answer your questions – however it does not seem certain that he has done so.

The sea is milk warm & Hastings & Arthur learn to swim from a famous teacher here, an old boatman who walks & runs in the element like a

Triton. Till October it is not cold *à l'anglaise* & in Italy nobody bathes but in July & August taking the benefit of sea water by absorption & not by immersion. Hastings had been ordered Italian sea bathing two preceding years for something he had the matter with him, so I profitted of my delay here waiting for Lord William, & not being certain how long I was to wait I gave the boy warm sea baths to prepare him, *dans une cuve* & then the open sea, & now swimming. The heat grows suddenly tremendous; Italy is always horrible in summer *on a beau dire*, it is like nothing else. General Woodford writes to William from Geneva that the weather is chilly, we are going there ultimately, but there are so many disagreeable people there that I have lost my Swiss ardour *pour le moment* & capriciously dread the place. I should prefer Lucerne or perhaps Germany, any northern mountains, until the torrent of English began to *s'écouler* somewhat, & one could have *des coudées franches*, but yet I am steady to my preference for a Swiss summer for my children & avoiding a whole year round in Italy. The houses here are as everywhere else on the Continent difficult to be got & dear unless you take them by the year. We could only get this single one for a month & give 500 frs for it; it is small and inconvenient but well furnished & with a divine view & a pretty stuffy garden next door to Mr Hill's delightful mansion. I think this place beautiful & don't regret my accidental residence as I think the sea baths will tell hereafter notwithstanding the vapour baths we have endured for some days. Yesterday, or rather last night we had a furious storm & all day today wind & rain which has cooled the air, I am therefore able to write you all this rigmarole. I wish I could see you for I have a hundred things to consult you about & tell you of – pray answer by return of post.

I cannot tell you how I admire Genoa. I have been here 5 times but only for a few days each time & now it appears quite new to me. If you dread the heat step into our *campagne* at Geneva & then give it up to us in as many weeks as you like.

God bless you, dear Lord Lynedoch, this is a long letter all about nothing at all, but I am always sincerely your affectionate friend.

There are no accommodations for sea bathing & a bathing machine was never heard of. People bathe in the harbour which is not scrupulously clean – there is no shore & but two gates by which we can get down to the piers to step into the boats, they are miles apart & not opened but by an order from Government till 8 which means 9. The vicinity of one of these piers makes the fortune of this lodging house & induces *inglesi* to take it.

We got a ukase to have the gate opened at 5 which makes the guard very cross at having their slumbers disturbed; I believe out of revenge they throw their fleas on us, for when we return home we are swarming. I don't swim like fat Miss Talbot, but I go with the boys to superintend & put my modesty in my pocket as I am a *vieille maman*, but it is more the morning breeze & the row in the boat than maternal tenderness that carries me so far. I could not stand the oppression & languor of the day were it not for those couple of hours, & walking is impossible even so early.

LORD WILLIAM'S DIARY

29 July. [Genoa] Repetition of yesterday very sad. Tri tmng shrw [try taming shrew].

30 July. Old scene. mtl rprochss [mutual reproaches] Lady Tweeddale wrote to say she has taken us a house at Geneva.

1 Aug. Rcnclition [Reconciliation].

2 Aug. Trrbl scne abt 5 – sd sd sd – I have not spirits for it.

3 Aug. The boys finished their course of bathing, Hastings has made great progress in swimming, but he is too anxious. Arthur has no fear but will learn nothing. Madame Durazzo took me to call on M. del Negro, who has a beautiful house with magnificent views. The moonlight scenery of Genoa is lovely.

4 Aug. Heard I was made King's A.D.C. – *tant mieux*. Set off at 7 p.m. fine moonlight, travelled all night.

7 Aug. Breakfasted on Mont Cenis, delicious trout, the cold very severe, I walked from Molaret to Lanslebourg – for I enjoy this mountain scenery. We dined & slept at St Jean de Morienne. m wf s n mch bttr stte wtht hr mthr, knd rsnabl & grble [my wife is in a much better state without her mother, kind reasonable & agreeable].

8 Aug. Travelled thro' the beautiful valley of Morienne on the banks of the rushing roaring Isère – discoursing agreably with my dear wife, & playing with my dear boys. This is a state of existence that makes one's heart overflow with gratitude to God, it is the ne plus ultra of moral & physical happiness. Arrived at Geneva at the Campagne Baumgarten at St Jean at 8 p.m.

10 Aug. The children up at daylight, enchanted with the garden & grounds, pretty view of the town, lake & Rhone, but after Italy it is difficult to be pleased.

11 Aug. We have a nice clean modest house, on a hill over the blue waters of the Rhone, & commanding its junction with the Arve, a little alley of trees then a vineyard & sloping lawns from which they are taking a second crop of hay. The boys are happy as boys can be full of health & liberty, in short if this could last it would be perfect happiness.

13 Aug. Lady Westmorland & Charles Sheridan visited us, also Lord & Lady Haddington, Lady Tweeddale, General & Mrs Woodford, Sir C. Lamb & Lady Montgomery, Lord Eglinton &c., &c.

14 Aug. Took Hastings to bathe in the Rhone – it was cold as ice.

15 Aug. Sunday. Went to hear M. Mallan the famous Calvinistic preacher, who has delighted so many English, his doctrines were to me odious, & his language rhapsody.

16 Aug. Wet day. Bessy suffering dreadfully with nerves.

17 Aug. Lord Lynedoch arrived whilst we were at dinner, unexpectedly; he came from Varese to pay us a week's visit, he is very blind & grows more infirm, but his energy, his love of society, the lively interest that he takes in all that goes on are wonderful – he is an excellent old man.

22 Aug. Sunday. Dined with Lady Westmorland & went afterwards to a blue party at Madame Klustine's, a Russian – but I hate blue people.

26 Aug. Lord Lynedoch left us, poor old man; I fear I shall never see him again,* – I hope his end may be without pain & suffering.

Lady Holland to Lord William Russell at Geneva [WPP]

August 16 1830

I was much pleased at seeing again your handwriting and rejoice that you are with your charming family, and on *terra firma* once more. . . .

You must not overrate any influence I ever had with your father. When he was very ill, and wanted nothing but silence, I was a comfort, but now that he is, thank God, quite well, his habits are more gay, and throw him into various and more sprightly society. Nevertheless I have ventured a suggestion about you that he may or not adopt. . . .

Your description of your children is comical. Hastings I know is charming, and the little second if he is so like you, bids fair to be a general favourite, and is I daresay with Mama. Is Hastings tall and strong? Mr Allen dotes upon him, and so indeed do we all.

Duke of Bedford to Lady William Russell at Geneva [PRP]

W.A. Aug. 16th. 1830

I write only half a dozen lines to acknowledge your kind letter from Genoa on the eve of your departure from hence, and I thank you (which

* He lived another fourteen years.

I do most cordially) for all the kind things you say of me personally. It is curious that your appointment in her Majesty's household has not been notified to you officially. The King mentioned it to me when I had an audience of him at his levée – since when it has been gazetted. . . . The only doubt among the speculators has been whether you would not think it *infra dig.* for a person of your rank to be a Bedchamber *woman.* I see one of the election attacks on John was that his brother's wife was Bedchamber woman to the Queen! Of course you, and wiser heads than mine will decide this knotty point.

Pray, give the enclosed to William. I am sorry he is so *entêté* about Bedford. Everyone concurs in the opinion that he would not have polled 200 votes – he seemed displeased with me, too, for laying his professional claims before Lord Hill, as entitling him to be A.D.C. to the King, but he will come right on all these points in good time. Your duty as a good wife is to set him right. . . .

Lord Tavistock to Lord William Russell at Geneva [WPP]

Carton, Ireland

August 18th [1830]

Well, my dear William, the election is over, and we have lost not only the seat at Bedford, but the seat at Huntingdon, too. Poor John's is a hard case. He might have been returned without difficulty for two counties, but now, alas, instead of having as you prophesied 'a quiet berth for life', he 'avowedly, (as Althorp says) the most popular man in England has been defeated in the place of his natural connection'.

. . . One of the most active and zealous of his Hunts friends observed, 'Oh, if you want him at Bedford, and have no other member of the family to put up there, I have nothing further to urge, for no man is your friend who would advise you to let Lord William stand again!! At a Corporation dinner not long ago, your health was passed by in so marked a manner, after my father's had been well received, that it was observed upon by many strangers who were present. I mention all these matters because you appear to fancy that you might have stood again with a fair prospect of success, and because I wish to set your mind at rest on the subject, and to show you that my father could not have acted otherwise under the circumstances of the case. . . . I wrote to Charles Bailey, who having been always your Agent, and having no prejudices on the subject, appeared to me to be the person most qualified to give a good opinion on the subject.

I received his answer this morning in these words, 'Having had an opportunity of ascertaining pretty accurately the public feeling in regard to Lord William, I have little hesitation in saying his almost total absence from his parliamentary duties has caused such a sensation in the minds of his constituents, as in case he had offered himself again for this Borough, his success I conceive, would have been almost entirely hopeless, and that Lord John was the person best calculated to remove that impression and give the cause the best chance of success'. . . . I write all this to you as a reasonable being, although other members of the family say it is useless since you do not suffer reason to enter your mind on this subject.

LORD WILLIAM'S DIARY

1 Sept. [Geneva] Letters from T. and John, still harping on Bedford; they have mismanaged but it is nothing to me.

12 Sept. A very kind letter from Fitzroy advising me not to give up my regiment.

15 Sept. Hastings does a lesson in Latin every day with me. Arthur will not learn his lesson.

17 Sept. Most beautiful weather. The Duc de Laval & Mons. Manerbes called on us; the former met Lady Westmorland for the first time after their famous quarrel,* she showed every disposition to reconciliation.

19 Sept. The Durazzos & Duc de Laval dined with us. . . . Madame D. is alarmed at going to Paris.†

22 Sept. Dined with M. & Madame Fabre,‡ beautiful house, excellent library with Canova's statue of Venus & Adonis, superb dinner. Sismondi,§ M. & Madame Naville, Lady Westmorland & several other agreable people. These Genevese are full of instruction & acquirements, but rather pedantic, & too fond of disputing.

28 Sept. Received leave of absence for 6 months.

2 Oct. Dear Bessy's birthday, God bless her & send her many more.

---

* Lady Westmorland had quarrelled with the Duc de Laval on account of his having received Lady Blessington in Rome.

† A revolution in France had turned out Charles X and put Louis-Philippe on the throne.

‡ Guillaume Favre (1770–1851) sometimes called Fabre. A Swiss, who, as well as owning an immense library and many works of art, was the author of some learned books. Sainte-Beuve called him 'un dilettante d'érudition' but had to concede that his writings were extremely dull. *Causeries du Lundi*, xiii, 246.

§ J. C. L. S. de Sismondi (1773–1842), Swiss liberal historian and friend of Madame de Staël.

Military Years

Lord John Russell to Lady William Russell at Geneva [PRP]

Middleton, Oct. 11. 1830

I have received, my dear sister, your letters that were sent here. I conclude you have accepted, after all, the womanship for I understand matters of etiquette are to be softened, & I suppose you have had some explanations on that head. After all it is as well, as you like it, & it will not put you out of your way. My father seems to have adopted a line of neutrality on the subject.

It was too late in the year with an autumnal parliament before me, to make a journey to Geneva. I fear my affections will not carry me near so many miles of posting as they did some time ago, by which I see I am getting old. You give some tolerable reasons for not coming to England, but that one of not having a house is stale. Where have you a house? At Berne? Rome? Geneva? I conclude by what you say that you are not going to Corfu; I should never have thought you would have disliked it so much. After all the post of Resident for William would have been far more honourable than that of Woman for you. But that is all over, & when this winter's campaign is over, I imagine the regiment will come home.

Tavistock has been unwell again, but is better – he is going for the winter or part of it to Brighton. I do not expect he will stay in Parliament beyond this year; any exertion is dangerous for him, & had there been a contest for the county this year, I do not know what might have been the consequence.

We are going to have Talleyrand,* Madame Dino,† Princess Esterhazy and the Duke here tomorrow. Belgium is in a sad uproar; otherwise things are going well. English politics are in rather an odd state, as usual. The session which is going to open will however clear the air, and then we shall know what we are to have. Do not expect primogeniture to be abolished – very well for now, but had it taken place one hundred years ago you and William would have had only about £300 a year.

Let me know where you wander to.

* Prince Talleyrand (1754–1838) had arrived in London as French ambassador.
† Dorothea (1793–1862), daughter of the Duke of Courland, was married at the age of fifteen to Talleyrand's nephew and heir, Count Edmond de Talleyrand-Périgord, created Duc de Dino by the King of Naples. She bore him two sons, but it was a marriage of convenience only, and in 1815 she accompanied Talleyrand to the Congress of Vienna to do the honours of his house there. It was the beginning of a relationship that lasted till his death. She was granted the rank of ambassadress in London.

Military Years

Duke of Bedford to Lord William Russell at Geneva [WPP]

The Doune, N. B., Oct 16 1830

I have been a long while without writing to you, and I take some shame to myself for my neglect for I have no reasonable excuse to offer, beyond that of idleness, which is no excuse at all. On my first arrival here I received a letter from you which I ought to have answered immediately, but I have put it off from post to post, and it now lies before me, staring me in the face, and reproaching me with my neglect. In that letter you said that you have heard that I was 'offended' with you, this, like most things we hear, was one of the lies of the day – perhaps I may have expressed myself a little hurt at some words in your letters about the representation of Bedford, but beyond this, believe not a word you hear, and be assured that so far from being offended, my real and sincere affection for you has never suffered one moment's diminution. I shewed your letter to John, but to no one else – however, in future as it is your wish I will shew them to no one. On Bedford I can say but little beyond what you already know – the Borough is gone, and for ever, unless when I am removed to another world where there is neither strife nor bitterness, the Bedfordians should think better of their past conduct, and wish to renew their connexion with my family – whether the fault has been mine, or yours, or John's, it is now quite useless to enquire into – *l'affaire est faite*. . . . With regard to the favour you ask of me for a place to stow your goods and chattels in, till you return to England, I really know not where I can find one, but I wrote to Adam on the subject, and if we can find a place we will. . . .

LORD WILLIAM'S DIARY

2 Nov. The papers full of sad news – a cholera morbus marching thro the southern provinces of Russia to Moscow; Antwerp in flames, – the Duke of Wellington pelted by the people, a change of ministry in France that may bring on war. The Prince of Orange & his family gone to London. The wrath of the Deity seems to be let loose on us.

4 Nov. Lady Westmorland put Bessy in a tableau as the Virgin & Child (Arthur), very beautiful.

5 Nov. Went to M. Fabre's party; heard of the change of ministry in France at which everyone made a long face, even Sismondi, & Fabre took ether at the fall of the funds.

6 Nov. Beautiful weather. Passed the day in the way I like best, alone with my dear wife & boys.

13 Nov. Strange news from England, the King advised not to dine in the City – threats of plunder & massacre etc.; the Ministers very unpopular, the funds fell 3 pr cent. Party at Madame Klustine's where everybody asked me if I was not alarmed at our revolution, especially Sismondi. What is ambition & public service when the Duke of Wellington ends by being hissed & hooted.

15 Nov. Letter from John saying my regiment was to return home, if so we must go to Paris, I am sorry for it. Letter from Tavistock, spitting blood again.

Lord William Russell to Lady Holland [HH]

Geneva Nov 14 1830

It was very good of you to think of me & send me a little English news, which in these anxious & awful times is what we seek for most. We are all well, thank you, & packing up to return to Italy, with great thoughts of passing the winter at Lucca, where Binda promises to find us a good house & his society will be a great inducement to remain there.

I was indeed sorry to hear of Lord Holland's illness, not only for his own sake & for yours, but also for the public sake, for in these days we are in want of all our public men, especially of those who resemble Lord H, for he is always English, straightforward & above all bold, & it is his courage that I particularly admire & like, which in these days of panic & terror is a great virtue. I hope soon to read one of his manly speeches in the papers, in the meantime nothing has given me greater pleasure than to see Lord Grey himself again, I hope to see the end of his career as brilliant as the beginning, & then the last 3 years will be forgotten & forgiven. Nobody speaks like him & his views are sound & liberal, but one thing I don't understand, which is whether John has given the Reform motion to Brougham, if he has, well & good, but if Brougham has taken advantage of John's temporary absence from Parliament to bring it forward, I must say in the mildest language I can use, it is uncourteous, unwise, impolitic, vain & presumptuous, but the strongest language I can use, & which suits my feelings, but is unfit for a letter or a lady's ears. Yet I can hardly believe B capable of such conduct. . . . It is a sad thing we should be obliged or even inclined to look to such a leader to steer us thro our difficulties – but enough of politics, yet on what else can one write. . . .

I am pleased to think that John is with you & so well, now that he has lost Lady Bath your house will be his home. I want to see his name in the House of Commons. . . .

The Russians are here in crowds, having been sent away from Paris – lest they should get corrupted. Poor innocents!

If any of you had any faith at Holland House I would recommend the homeopathic system to Lord H. It has done wonders but faith is necessary.

The Duke of Wellington's Ministry having been defeated in the Commons, the King sent for Lord Grey, and the Whigs returned to power after forty-six years of Tory rule.

Lord John Russell to Lady William Russell at Geneva [PRP]

Burlington St., Nov. 26. [1830]

*Bettina cara, il mondo e rovesciato; siamo tutti noi radicali divenuti ministri, e cortigiani di palazzo. Io son Pagatore Principalissimo; ho sette milione di libre esterline di pagamento a fare, e ho una casa bella, gentile, comoda, que ester a sa disposicion de V. M.** In plain English I am *for the present*, Paymaster General of the Forces, and have got *for the present*, a very nice house at Whitehall, next to the Horse Guards. Now if you were coming to England immediately I should be most happy to lodge you and William & the children. There is plenty of room for you all. But I am afraid your abominable plans of Italy will come in the way of this & every thing that is good. But if you do come pray make up your mind directly for I have plenty of offers of tenants.

I cannot write to you on public matters, but with an official reserve, which is so hateful to me that I prefer saying little or nothing. We put on our flag, Peace, Economy & Reform. I trust we shall keep to these good & fair words. Neither foreign nor domestic affairs, however look promising. The labourers have risen & are carrying on a servile war against the gentry with various success. The Duke of Richmond has been distinguishing himself as the Pompey of the country.

Lord Holland is slowly recovering. The King behaves better than it was possible to expect. I wish you all health & happiness wherever you may be, as Lord Eldon said, & am your affectionate brother.

* 'Bettina dear, the world is overturned; all we radicals are become ministers and courtiers of the palace. I am Paymaster General. I have to make payments of seven million pounds sterling, and I have a fine, beautiful, and comfortable house [*then lapsing into Spanish*] which is at your disposal.'

Lord William Russell to Lady Holland [HH]

Geneva Dec 7th [1830]

Nobody will tell me anything about the new Ministry – perhaps you will have compassion on me. There never was a more anxious time, the difficulties of the country never were greater and our safety hangs upon the wisdom & firmness of the present Ministry; whether it is a thread or a cable is what I want to know. I like the general composition of the Ministry, tho some of the details puzzle & displease me. Why has not Lord Holland an efficient place. Why has not John an efficient place. I see my father has got the Garter. I rejoice that he has got it from his old friend Lord Grey & not from his new friend the Duke of Wellington, but I would have given it to Lord Brougham, the riband is faded & wants fresh dyeing – *capite?* I dare not say more to you Aristocrats. . . .

Duke of Bedford to Lady William Russell at Geneva [PRP]

London, Dec. 10, 1830

I was about to write to you as you desired to the care of your banker at Genoa, when a letter from William informed me that you had given up your Italian project, and remained at Geneva. As Lord Hill tells me that William's regiment may be expected home in two months, I imagine we may look to see you in old England about that time. John tells me that he has offered you his official house at the Pay Office, which is an excellent house, and a delightful situation, as your own official duties will commence I imagine, on your return to England. I hear your Royal Mistress has commenced, not a parliamentary, but a petticoat reform, amongst the ladies of her household – she insists on their not being *decoltée* in the extreme, or so dressed, or rather undressed that she may be able to pass her fan under their naked shoulders. I think she is quite right, but *you* do not need this admonition, for I have always seen with pleasure your costume marked by propriety and good taste – I may add good sense, for ladies should always leave something for the imagination. . . .

Looking forward to your return to England when we have got rid of our fogs and frosts, I will only add *hasta la vista.*

Lord William Russell to Lord Holland [HH]

Geneva Dec 29th 1830

If you have the gout you may chuck this letter into the fire, or give it to John Allen to tell you the purport of it. The fact is I am rather bit by these

226

new ideas that are floating in men's minds, & if you were Minister of Foreign Affairs,* which I *very, very* much regret you are not, I might perhaps bother you with my crude notions, & leave them to you to digest, but as it is I will only put it to you for reflection, whether you do not think the mode of managing our foreign relations may not be placed upon a different system. Hitherto they have always been conducted with a view to war. Duplicity, want of confidence, ambition, avarice and all the bad passions have formed the hinge upon which those important matters have turned, but is it totally impossible that sincerity, openness, frankness, love of peace and order should govern men's minds, & that nations should treat with each other like man & man? If ever there was a time, when such a desirable, noble object might be accomplished, this is it. . . . If Mr Fox were alive – or as they say here, if Mr Canning was alive, we should see the most glorious epoch in history. Peace & good will directing nations, but I hope to see it brought about by you & Lord Grey. Perhaps you will think this one of the Utopian schemes of Geneva, in fact we are all camelions, & whilst at Corfu, I thought only of parades, field days, courts martial, as the highest effort of human nature, now I think of liberty, peace, order, law and the amelioration of mankind as of higher importance. But of this I am quite convinced, that an extraordinary change is taking place in men's minds, from which will spring extraordinary good.

I should like to see England start from its lethargy & take a lead, as it is, like a bad hound, we are lagging behind.

These theoretical, speculating, reading, discussing republicans, look upon our aristocracy, as the most ignorant, prejudiced, selfish, idle of the human race. . . .

Instead of returning to Italy the William Russells moved to another hired house
   at Lausanne.

LORD WILLIAM'S DIARY

30 Dec. Left Geneva to my great regret, for we had passed some happy days there, & I like it much. Dined at Nyon, & arrived at Lausanne. The roads slippery as glass. Drove my char & H. rode. Our house called Villamont, too large & dreary. I hate to be over housed.

31 Dec. Deep snow, walked about with Hastings. Shops full of people buying new year's gifts. I regret Geneva.

I am not very well & very melancholy; I regret to begin the new year so ill –

* Lord Holland was Chancellor of the Duchy of Lancaster.

but I have to thank & do thank God from the bottom of my heart for all his mercies to me, for allowing me to pass many happy days with my family. especially with my dear boys, who are all that I could wish. God bless them. Hastings is a dear boy, manly & affectionate, Arthur too & little Odo. God bless them all & may they grow up good & honest men, it is my only desire in living.

In the spring of 1831 the Russells began to move towards England; it was imperative they should be in England for the Coronation. The Duke of Bedford and William's brothers were concerned at his protracted idleness and Bessy's obvious reluctance to return to England. Lady William and her sons had been away for four years; Odo, now aged three, had never been to his parents' native land. They reached Paris in April, and while her husband went backwards and forwards between the capitals, Lady William remained in France with the boys. Lady Granville, who was now the English Ambassadress at the Court of Louis-Philippe, remarked that she was 'really beautiful – grown into a very large woman, brighter and clearer than anything I ever saw'.[8]

Thomas Moore, warmed by the friendship of the aristocracy and happily aware of its condescension towards himself, described in his journal William's arrival in June at the Pay Office in Whitehall, which was Lord John's official residence as Paymaster of the Forces.

'While we were at breakfast Lord William was announced as just arrived from Paris. I begged Lord John to let me give him up his room (the bedroom I occupy being that Lord W. always sleeps in); but he said "No, no, you shan't be disturbed; he shall have Pudar's" (Lord J's servant) "room; it's a very good one", and immediately ordered Pudar to get it ready for him. The meeting between the brothers highly characteristic; so quiet, but at the same time so cordial.' And a few days later Moore wrote: 'Breakfast with Lord John and Lord William; very agreeable. The latter proposed that we should go together to the Duchess of Bedford's *déjeûner*. The day fine, and the assemblage of pretty women in these green flowery grounds (Camden Hill) very charming.'[9]

Lord John, always zealous for the happiness and good name of his brother, made proposals for diplomatic employment, but it was not till the late summer that an opportunity arose of directing Lord William into the service in which he made a career for the next decade.

Duke of Bedford to Lady William Russell at Lausanne [PRP]

Woburn Abbey, Jan. 6, 1831.

The last foreign mail brought me your kind letter. I will begin by wishing you and yours a happy new year in the good old fashion, with many to come, and then proceed to tell you that I have given orders for £200 being paid annually into Child's to *your account*, for Hastings education, Which I hope William will not think argues any distrust of *his* prudent management of this little educatory fund.

I am glad to hear you are to be at home in the summer, though I was in hopes that it would be a little sooner, as I hear John has offered you his house at the Pay Office (a most excellent house) and I was in hopes that you meant to come and embellish the Court of your royal mistress, particularly as you are no longer a simple 'Woman,' but are to form part of the *appanage* of the drawing room. If you are grown as fat as you say you are, and if his present Majesty had the same taste for corpulent ladies as his late Majesty of blessed memory, you might aspire to the honour of succeeding Lady C. as favourite sultana, but I believe you are not ambitious, and will be well content with being Bed Chamber Woman to *her* Majesty.

Pray tell William that I have not answered his political questions, but leave that to the Paymaster General of the Forces; as I am no politician but simply a bystander and looker on, and derive all my political knowledge from the same source as William viz. the newspapers. . . .

You must excuse my bad writing, as I have disabled my right shoulder shooting, and cannot hold my pen without difficulty. I trust however your being able to decypher this *griffonage*, and that you will always believe me your *très affectioné beaupère*

Love to William and my blessing to your numerous progeny.

Lord William Russell to Lord John Russell [WP]

Lausanne Jany 14 [1831]

. . . I have no wish whatever to be Minister in Switzerland nor do I wish you to ask for anything of any sort or kind for me, but I certainly think we pay high for our diplomatic services, & are hardly served for the money – certainly great reforms would be desirable in that department, especially to introduce a system of simplicity & truth, – lying & intriguing can never serve any cause.

Our villa at Geneva was too cold, we were obliged to leave it, & could get no house in the town, owing to the Tyrant of the North having ordered all his subjects to leave France, lest their pure minds should get corrupted, & Princesses came pouring into Geneva in shoals, hiring all the houses. I in my own person must be in England in March, probably my family will remain here a little longer. I will tell you in the greatest confidence that my intention is to give up my regiment. Country quarters in England don't suit us, & I can see no good in going on with it. Tell me if you see any objection to this scheme. . . .

Duke of Bedford to Lord William Russell at Lausanne [WPP]

Woburn Abbey, February 24, 1831

. . . The Times is more mischievous than usual yesterday, particularly on the Game Laws. Those Strand and Fleet Street statesmen and legislators know nothing about the matter, and wish to prevent country gentlemen having any rural amusement, but they may drive them all to Cobbett's Wen, hence their tirades and *ad captandum* writings about the country and Game Laws. They do not seem to know that the Game Laws are wholly repealed, and that there is only one solitary Act of Parliament now, for the preservation of game. Poaching has diminished here considerably, and will shortly be nearly at an end, if gentlemen will give the new law fair play. I am sorry you do not like the *battues* here. I do what I can to amuse my friends, and if they are dissatisfied, I am sorry for it. Tavistock has never said one word to me against them. If he dislikes them he has only to say the word and I will discharge all my keepers, and allow the labouring poor to come through the woods and plantations with their guns and their snares till there is not a head of game left, poaching will then be at an end because *ex nihilo nihil fit* and there will be nothing to poach, but I will venture to say that the labourers will become ten times more demoralised than they now are. I do not know how you define beaters. I have always supposed it to be by beating the woods with men and dogs to drive the game up and to this I can see no objection to people who are fond of shooting though you think it like 'shooting rabbits and pigeons out of a cage', I have never heard anyone complain of the tameness of the shooting at Woburn. In these days of change and luxury since the lapse of half a century, I believe you would find it difficult to get gentlemen with their double barrel guns and detonators and copper caps to come down to you for the pleasure of toiling all day through a wood, for the chance of a stray shot at a woodcock, hare or pheasant, nor would you persuade a gentleman with his red coat and top boots and white corduroy breeches to come down with his four or five hundred guinea horse to follow a pack of slow deep-toned hounds, picking out the scent of a fox or hare for three or four hours. The times are changed and we must change with them. As soon as the Strand and Fleet Street gentlemen have destroyed shooting, modern fox-hunting will soon follow, and it is certainly the more barbarous and indefensible amusement of the two.

Duke of Bedford to Lord William Russell at Paris [WPP]

Endsleigh, May 11, 1831

Many thanks for your letter – the triumph in Bedfordshire seems to have been complete, and every thing as it ought to be. John was unanimously elected for this county yesterday.

With regard to your going on half pay, I can have no interest in the matter but your own, and if your military friends, Lord Fitzroy and Macdonald approve, I can have nothing to say against it. You will then be an idle man with nothing to do, and I suppose you would not dislike being in Parliament. John's being a double return, he will of course give up Tavistock and I think there would be no difficulty whatever in getting you elected in his place. I have had many applications on the subject, as you may suppose, but you are my first object; though it must be on one condition, viz. that you are not running over to Paris or elsewhere, while this great question is pending, but you must be at your post day and night, till the Reform Bill is safely through the House of Commons. . . . As soon as your decision is formed on this matter, let me know. And now you must let me give you a little advice about Lady William, which I trust you will take as it is meant in good part. I think she ought to attend her duties in the Queen's family, or resign the situation. I know that the Queen has said she only gave her so long a leave of absence, on the plea of your regiment being abroad, that plea no longer exists – *verbum sap* – have you taken any steps about my horses which have been waiting for you at Portsmouth for the last fortnight? If you think my girls are shabbily dressed, you should make Lady William send them some better dresses from Paris.

Hastings Russell to Lord William Russell in England [WP]

[Paris] 1831

We are now in our new house and like it very much. You know that we have got our driver as coachman. I have got a carrotman hwo passes every day whith a cartikin. The coachman gives the horses hay morning and evening and straw all day long corn 3 times a day but his own horses *4 times*. I think and should like to know if a little green feeding would not do them good and purge them a little as it is spring. The coachman and his horses have most curious names for he is cald Flander Timothee and they Peckin and *brave homme*.

I ride poney every day in the *Champs élisé*, but it is in vain to try to make him gallop right.

The day before yesterday we went to dine with the Richmonts hwo is going 30 laegues off and makes as much row as if she was going 300. When her great big magnitising came in, he set to kissing her and squaeked *bonjour maman*. Yesterday I and Atty went to dine with lord Granard we have dined with them 3 or 4 times and Atty would never spaek.

Tell me what the fifth weel behind the cannon is.

Habemus a dancing master and an english latin and greek master *imus venimus videmus* the german play . . .

Duke of Bedford to Lord William Russell in London [WPP]

Endsleigh, May 22, 1831.

. . . If you are going to Paris immediately send to my tea dealer, for a pound of black tea such as he is in the habit of sending me, and take it to old de Coigny from me.

Duchess of Bedford to Lord William Russell at the Pay Office [WPP]

Monday evening [?1831]

You ought to have come in, for I presume I am not the first lady you have visited in *robe de chambre*. This was my reason for being denied to the world. I assure you, my dear William, that I most sincerely regret having seen but a glimpse of you. My heart is warm and affectionate by nature, and has always been true and faithful to you, in both feelings. You do your father injustice in thinking he does not love to see you. He is most anxious about all that concerns you. I left him quite well on Friday morning. I am most grateful to Bessy for her attention to the girls, and am sure her taste will please me.

With kindest love to her, and every kind wish for your health and happiness, till we meet again, I say God bless you.

Had I known this morning you were going tonight to Paris, you should have carried some souvenirs to your children, whom I hope you will find all well.

I am dead with the heat.

Duke of Bedford to Lord William Russell at Paris [WPP]

Woburn Abbey, June 6, 1831.

Old Coigny* is really too bad about tea – she is the most importunate mendicant I know, and will lose nothing for want of asking. She is constantly writing to me for tea (which I send her) and to Lord Jersey at the same time. I am convinced she has hoards of tea. I always tell her she can get it just as good in the Place Vendôme, but I believe what fails in convincing her of this is that she must pay for it! Talleyrand says that she hides all her gold in pots of *confiture* and puts currant jelly over it. It would be a good trick if you could buy her a pound of Bohea tea in the Place Vendôme, and tell her you received it from England. . . .

Duke of Bedford to Lord William Russell at Paris [WPP]

London, July 5, 1831

. . . You are not cut out for a country gentleman. I should imagine a town residence in this neighbourhood (Belgrave Square) would suit you best. You would have room for your goods and chattels, without having any store rooms, and Lady William would be near her official duties at St James's and Windsor. . . .

I wish you would get me a model, to a scale, of the *Carousels*† they use at Paris, in the *Champs Elysées*, and the *Guingette* gardens, with the chairs for the ladies and mock tunes for the men to run at the ring. Chenu will pack it up and send it over to me.

Duke of Bedford to Lord William Russell [WPP]

London July 15, 1831.

. . . You are wrong in saying that I 'would not have you for a tenant', if Seymour had relinquished his residence at Woburn. I told you that I did

---

* Louise de Conflans d'Armentières, Marquise de Coigny, was known in French society for her wit, her meanness, and the ugliness of her voice. When she died in 1832, gold was reported to have been found in her mattress, her petticoats, under the floors, and in her sofa cushions.

† Roundabouts.

not think the life of a country gentleman exactly suited your tastes and habits, and wished to dissuade you from it. I think your plan of Brighton far better, and if you can get a good and cheap house there, you cannot do better than establish yourself for a time. You remember Kemp Town. I imagine the houses are cheaper there than at the west end of the town, tho' it is now dignified by the *séjour* of some of our great aristocracy – Duke of Devonshire, Marquess of Bristol, Lady Jane Peel etc., etc. It is an excellent winter residence – the air is healthy and good for your children.

I shall be happy to give you house room at Woburn Abbey *en attendant* and beef and mutton, cabbage and potatoes, but I cannot be at house-keeping for you, and your establishment must be on board wages. I have what is vulgarly called run out in household expenditure, and Stagg* says the cause of it is housekeeping going on at so many residences. I daresay he is right. . . . Reform goes on well, as far as John is concerned, but the conduct of the Anti-Reformers is violent and atrocious. I firmly believe the object of many of them, is to kill John by wearing him completely out – there is no iniquity too bad for them. Give my love to Lady William and tell her I will write to her by the next mail. The girls received two splendid ball dresses lately.

Duke of Bedford to Lord William Russell at Paris [WPP]

London July 27 [1831]

. . . That sly old fox Talleyrand is too much for us. He generally goes every evening to Holland House, late, when every one else is gone, and sucks Holland's brains for an hour or two before he goes to bed.

Your sarcasm about the Duchess's 'splendid fête, and the £1000', was misplaced, as your sarcasms usually are. You saw about the Duchess's Thursday evenings here – some eatables supplied by my own *maître d'hôtel*, cook and confectioner, without the aid of any Gunters or Jarrards, and a few bottles of wine from my own cellar. This on the night of the fête, with the addition of £20 or £25 for fireworks and a few lamps in the shrubs, with a band of music for the young folks to dance, was the whole of the additional expense. I hate grand dinners and never give them, so these fêtes (so called) cost about the same as ten or twelve dinners, for which you have hauled me over the coals!

* The Duke's steward.

I conclude the Queen will require all the Household to attend her at the Coronation.

My love to the Bedchamber woman.

In the previous year Belgium had risen in revolt against Holland to which she had been united by the Powers at the Congress of Vienna. England and France supported a separation of the two countries and in July 1831 Leopold of Saxe-Coburg accepted the Belgian crown. The indignant Dutch invaded Belgium, and France warned Prussia that in the event of aggression on her part a French army would be sent to assist the Belgians. A European war seemed imminent. The Whig diplomatist, Sir Robert Adair, was sent on a special mission to Brussels, and William Russell was appointed to go with him. In the account Lord William gave his wife (who remained at Paris), of the critical day when he carried a flag of truce to the belligerents, there is evidence of how much he enjoyed being actively engaged in an undertaking that was part military, part diplomatic.

Duke of Bedford to Lord William Russell [WPP]

London, July 29, 1831

I must begin by telling you that Adair starts on his mission to Bruxelles on Sunday morning and is very anxious to have you with him as his private secretary. Lord Palmerston has received your name in a very flattering manner and says 'the choice is excellent and he is sure you will be highly useful', I trust therefore you will not hesitate in accepting the offer, particularly as you once told me there was nothing you would like better than accompanying Adair on a foreign mission. You are now an idle man, and have nothing to do, so how can you employ your time better? Adair says it is 'a *very confidential* situation in which he wishes to place you', and thinks you may be of great use to him with regard to the state of the surrounding armies, French, Prussian, and Dutch – in short you will be his war adviser, opposed to that able man General Belliard. I feel confident that you will give your whole attention to the importance of the subject, and not think the appointment *infra dig.* in the present critical state of Europe, particularly of that part of the Continent. You will soon be able to reach Bruxelles, and join Adair in the very outset of his diplomatick mission. As I have suggested this appointment to Adair, I trust you will not hesitate to accept it.

235

Military Years

Lord William Russell to Lady William Russell at Paris [WPP]

Brussels, August 15 1831.

I am just come in from Louvain, where I left the King, but as he returns to Brussels this evening and the war is over, my mission is at an end.

The events we have been engaged in were of great consequence, on their result hinged the peace or war of Europe. Adair, as I told you, attached me to the King's person, the morning after joining him he sent for me between 6 and 7.

Adair had arrived with a letter from Sir Charles Bagot at the Hague, giving hopes of an immediate conclusion of peace. The King said he wished me to go to the Commander in Chief of the Dutch Army with a flag of truce, carrying a letter from Adair with Sir Charles Bagot's news, and to propose a cessation of hostilities till such time as something definitive could be concluded.

The King conducted me himself out of the town towards the outposts, and when the balls began to fly about us I begged his Majesty to go no further, but let me proceed with my trumpeter and white flag.

The trumpeter was so frightened he could not blow, the white handkerchief of my Lieutenant of Dragoons so dirty it was not recognised, so I had to pass thro the balls at some risk, and had the pleasure afterwards to hear a Dutch officer say, that had he known it was a flag of truce he would have fired grape at me, so exasperated were they at being stopped.

At the Dutch outposts I found the Prince of Orange, who received me with the greatest cordiality, and kissed me twice. His brother, Prince Frederick, was with him and was also very kind. The Prince of Orange had just had a horse killed under him. He was driving in rapidly the Belgian outposts, and highly elated at the success he promised himself from his attack, no less than the taking of Louvain. To be checked in his victorious career was wormwood to him. I felt for him with all my soul, but what could I do, my object was peace, not war.

He kept walking his horse on whilst his troops continued attacking, so when I thought he had reflected enough on my letter I urged him to order a cessation of the firing.

He said, 'My dear William, I never was so *contrarié* in my life, Louvain must be mine in a few hours, I have sent a corps round the town and shortly expect to hear its guns open on the Brussels road; Leopold and his army must be my prisoners.'

I urged to him the slaughter and massacre of taking a populous town by assault, the inutility of it, for the French were close on his left flank and he must have them 'sur les bras' the next day. At length he said if Leopold would evacuate Louvain he would retreat.

I told him that I could not make such a proposition to King Leopold, but proposed that he should order the firing to cease, or either receive or send an officer to treat with Adair. He consented to this in the handsomest manner, though evidently under strong feelings of irritation and disappointment. Indeed it was hard for him, the cup dashed from his lips just as he was going to enjoy the delicious draught of revenge.

I then took leave of him, and he gave me his A.D.C. to carry his orders to the Duke of Saxe Weimar, who commanded the corps that had gone round the town, telling me to come back to him. The A.D.C. was in considerable apprehension at being murdered by the populace of Louvain, and insisted on having a strong escort.

I saw Adair in the town and told him to go to the King, and that the Prince of Orange had consented to receive him. I forgot to say that the Prince of Orange had said he would not treat in any way with the Belgians. The only ground on which he could consent not to advance was the near approach of the French troops as he had no quarrel with them and did not wish to go to war with France, that as I assured him they were near he believed me, but that was not sufficient for his officers, and that his A.D.C. must have occular proof of their presence, consequently I left him charged with two missions, one to stop the advance of the Duke of Saxe Weimar, the other to show the French to my Dutch officer.

We galloped with our escort as hard as we could go to the Montagne de Fer, a hill on the Brussels road commanding Louvain; when we got there we could neither see nor hear anything of the Dutch troops. The Dutch A.D.C. said he knew their line of march and that we could cut across it or meet it. As luck would have it we could get no tidings whatever of it, the peasants knew nothing, nothing had passed through the villages. We galloped up to every hill, yet nothing could we see: at last I felt convinced that the column had been stopped, and began to feel comfortable when a peasant told us that some Dutch troops had passed by a wood he pointed out; we galloped up, got traces of them, and at last fell in with the tail of the column. We urged on our horses, outstripping our escort, for we heard the cannon begin to fire at a distance. It was the most anxious time I ever passed, the Dutchman and I were both well mounted, he was as eager as I was. We kicked and spurred over fields and ravines

Military Years

till the poor devils could not stir, when fortunately we fell in with a Dutch officer, so my A.D.C. sent him on to order the firing to cease till we arrived which we did a few minutes afterwards. My A.D.C. delivered his orders and then presented me to the Duke of Saxe Weimar,* who would not return my salute but rode up and down in a paroxysm of rage, saying amongst other things that he was 'honteux d'être beau-frère du Roi d'Angleterre'. I let him storm on, feeling that any angry reply might cause an attack on the town, and I believe that he felt disposed to strike me, for he sent an A.D.C. to order me and my escort to retire to the rear, but I felt that my message had a right to provoke him and I felt the necessity of conciliation, so I said nothing.

Having at length brought him to obey his orders, I set off with my A.D.C. for Brussels to enable him to see the French troops. I also procured him an interview with General Belliard, who desired him to tell the Prince of Orange that an attack upon Louvain and the King would be considered an insult to France and followed by an immediate attack upon his troops. At the same time he gave us two French officers to go with us, as a sample to show the Prince, one an A.D.C. the other an old *chef d'escadron*.

We had some difficulty in traversing the Dutch outposts, so that we did not get to the Duke of Saxe Weimar's quarters till midnight; he was in bed but had not slept off the fumes of wine – in short he was dead drunk. He came out and positively refused to let us pass through Louvain, though charged with a pacific mission to the Prince of Orange, which is contrary to all rules of civilized war, but my old *chef d'escadron* was a match for him, treated him in his own coarse language, and told him he was drunk.

My mission being finished I took leave of my Dutch A.D.C. who behaved admirably and promised me to be with the Prince of Orange by daylight, and I returned with my two Frenchmen to Brussels pretty tired as you may suppose.

Now I must tell you what happened at Louvain in my absence. Adair went to the Prince of Orange and after much difficulty persuaded him not to attack the town, and also persuaded Leopold to evacuate it, and it was definitely settled that it should be given up next day at 12 o'clock, which was an admirable arrangement for Leopold's army was good for nothing, disorganised, and without generals or officers, besides not very brave, and all the Civic Guards whose exploits have been drilled into our ears for the last nine months, ran away as hard as it could go, such a *débandade*, such a

* Duke Bernard of Saxe-Weimar (1792–1862), general in the Dutch infantry. His wife was the sister of Queen Adelaide.

sauve qui peut I never saw, not even in Spain. . . . So you see this was a most eventful and anxious day. . . .

I returned to Malines to join the King, who thanked me much for my zeal in his service, and treated me most confidentially. He has much more *caractère* than I should have given him credit for. Nothing could surpass his courage, calmness and activity under very difficult and dangerous circumstances. . . .

Lord John Russell to Lord William Russell [WPP]

Whitehall, Aug. 23, 1831.

You have done very well for us in Belgium; I only hope others may contribute as much to the preservation of peace. The Government have taken up your quarrel with the Duke of Saxe-Weimar, and have written strongly requiring a reprimand to be given to him. I trust this measure will satisfy you, and that you will consider it as taken out of your hands. Such was the unanimous wish of the Cabinet today. . . .

Lady William arrived in London with her children in time to attend Queen Adelaide at her coronation in Westminster Abbey on 8 September.

The Duke had written to Lord John: 'Lady William must make her choice between the Pay Office and Belgrave Square when she comes; at the latter I doubt whether she will find anyone capable of even boiling a chicken. I shall send her a carriage horses and footman.'[10]

Lady William chose the Pay Office.

Hastings Russell to Lord William Russell at Brussels [WP]

[8 September 1831]

JOURNAL. Thursday

Got up at a quarter to 8 & saw several regiments go bye. The infantry regiments came first, and then the horse guards, then the blues, the scotch grays, and lastly the lancers. It was then about 9 o'clock and Lady Holland came; I went down to see her she spoke a great deal to me and invited mama and me to dine at Holland house tomorrow she had a room to herself and we had one to she seemed very much pleased with us all and came up in the drawing and rote a letter to grandpapa she said that she had written to him about us (mama came down to see lady Holland) then mama was ready to go to court and I went with her to the door of the palace and then came back and dressed.

I will tell you some of the particulars before the procession, when mama came there she was let in with the other attendants into a private room to the Queen Princess Leven who was outside imagined a charming way of getting in she pretends to faint and asks to go in Lord How anounced her saying that she was fainting and wanted to come in. (but I made a mistake it was after the ceremony in the abbey.) The Queen got up and smoothed the sopha when in stalked mother Leven sat down pouf by the Queen and set to talking another thing happened in the abbey lady Sophia Lennox fainted and while they were holding her up she shot a Cat all over herself and everybody. Then came George Leven and a little girl called Bulow, I cant say much Leven or of the Bulow.

The Procession was very beautiful first came guards and then carriages and guards between each carriage then the watermen carrying water lillys dressed in red the Kings household the Beefeaters the King and Queen in their state carriage and guards they were very much cheered. Then I went to dinner and when I came back the Levens were gone; so Butty* Odo Arthur and I went to see the procession go back.

Mama came back and dressed to go to dinner then I went with Dade † and Atty to see the Illuminations. They were very fine before the admiralty but before the other houses there was only A and R and W R. (before the admiralty there was this) GOD SAVE THE KING. W.R. IV. A.R. RULE BRITANIA. then at the top there were 2 flags all in coloured lamps and a + with a serpent going up it and a crown at the top then I went home and to bed.

Goodbye dear papyo my Journal does instead of a letter.
P.S. Odo ran into the room where uncle Jon was and called out o Papyo! and then he was so ashamed that he ran away and almost cried.

I have put the pages wrong so I wis number them.

Friday.

I got up rather late then I went down to breakfast then I wrote to you till dinner time then I read my booky till I went out with Dady to order a bath for mamyo I am now come home again and going to dress to go to Holland

---

* Mrs Butler, the boys' nurse.
† Girardet, Dade, or Dady: a manservant; 'a stupid old Swiss . . . whom Lady William engaged in her service while you were in Greece', wrote old Lord William to his nephew.

house. I think I saw 3 of the 8 hussards in the street tell me if it is possible. Remember to send me my Pistols which are in the green shooting things as soon as possible.

Lord William Russell to Lady Holland [HH]

Brussels Sep 15 [1831]

It gives me the greatest pleasure to know that you have discovered the charms of my boy. I never boasted his good qualities to you because I thought you would set it down as a father fondness, but now that you have found them out yourself, I may say that a more intelligent boy, with a sweeter disposition does not exist in the world, he is besides noble-minded, honest & true. I was hurt that my father could not give up one days grouse shooting, to see such a daughter in law & such a grandson after 4 years absence, but, *mum* as you love me. This in the strictest confidence. I too am getting acquainted with *your* boy* & like him more & more every day, but what delights me above every thing is to find him an excellent Whig – & a real Foxite, worthy of the great name he bears. . . .

Lady Holland to Lord William Russell [WPP]

Holland House, September 20 [1831]

Though not being well, I cannot resist thanking you for your letter, and all the kind gratifying things you say of Henry. It gives us both heartfelt pleasure to hear commendation of him from you. I am not without hopes of seeing Lady William and that dearest of children, Hastings, here for a few days. Well may you be proud of him, for with all the playfulness of childhood, he has solid essential qualities, and as you say a most perfect temper and disposition.

Depend upon my being *mum*. You have known me too long to suppose I would risk giving pain to my old and dear friend, but you must be a little fair. He was on his way to join his young ones, and had allotted only a month for the whole excursion, and he was persuaded on his return to town he should find your family.

In October Lady William went into waiting on the Queen at Brighton. It was generally thought that when her term of duty was done she would join her

* Henry Fox was also attached to Adair's mission.

husband at Brussels, but she showed no inclination to leave the south coast and Lord William was content to come and go on visits to his family. In view of her reluctance to move, the Duke of Bedford was prompted to urge his daughter-in-law to spend at least Christmas Day at Woburn. 'Remember that 4 years absence demands some little extra effort of fiílial duty.'[11]

Duke of Bedford to Lord William Russell at the Pay Office [WPP]

The Doune, N.B., Oct. 20, 1831

Many thanks for both your letters since your arrival from Bruxelles. As probably neither you nor Lady William require *fourneaux* for various *entrées* during your excursion to Woburn, I should have imagined that Stagg could have continued to serve you with roast and boiled, from the servant's hall fire or some other part of the house; but I suppose he thought your foreign habits could not put up with such fare. However if you have been prevented by the state of the kitchen from going to Woburn, I shall regret it.

Lady William Russell to old Lord William Russell at Florence [WP]

Woburn Abbey, Oct. 28, 1831.

By my calculations you must be now at Florence, happy in the society of Gertrude. I hope you did not lose my bandbox *par distraction* by the bye, & that she liked its contents. I received your letter from Bern in London where I arrived the 6th of September with William who joined me from Brussels at Calais. On the 7th I unpacked & waited on the Queen, on the 8th I was in attendance for 15 hours, 12 of which I stood pretty well for a beginning of Court duties. Then William having gone back to Belgium, as a gay young widow I plunged into the vortex of dinners & parties, – lived as much with Tories as with Whigs, heard them all *déraisonner* equally, thought like Sir Roger de Coverley 'that there was much to be said on both sides', & amused myself uncommonly after my 4 years of domesticity – however the damp & going out at night gave me 3 short but sharp returns of my old spasms, but I am none the worse, – the boys are thank God prosperous. William came back the 8th of October – the 20th we came here with John the Reformer & in a few days we are going to see Wrio & Eliza – the Druid & the Druidess, then we meant to go to Brussels till my Court attendance recommences with the Drawing Rooms the 24th February but lo! the Queen has called me into waiting at Brighton till the 15th of December, so thither I repair with my children, & my hubby goes back to Adair & King Leopold, where I shall join him before Christmas, please God, the wind, weather, politics & cholera admitting. So now you have my memoir & a programme of my movements. . . . Russell having given up Parliament owing to his headaches, the sitting up bringing them on, your brother & Tavistock proposed to Lord William his seat – but he declined & your son Francis is put up or brought in, which ever is the technical phrase. He has been dying to be in Parliament these many years, so I hope it will agree with him. Let me hear from you, dear Lord William, & tell me all about your health & Gertrude & her children. . . .

Duke of Bedford to Lady William Russell at the Pay Office [PRP]

W.A. Monday [20 December 1831]

Your letter to the Duchess under John's cover, arrived this morning, and I took the liberty of opening it trusting it might be to announce your speedy arrival – I saw you talked of coming in Jany. and then immediately re-sealed the letter and forwarded it to the Duchess, who is now on her road journeying homewards by easy stages, on account of her invalid who is still very weak. I trust you will reconsider your decision, and be here earlier than you talk of – this week or the next at latest, but I really think after 4 years absence from the 'roast beef of old England' you ought to eat it on Christmas Day, in the hall of your forefathers – at least your husband's. On your arrival in town you will have found a letter from me, if it is not lying *perdue* on the Paymaster's table. Let me hear soon, and that you are coming soon – *hasta la vista*.

We do not know if the William Russells spent Christmas at Woburn, but Henry Fox, who was one of Sir Robert Adair's secretaries, makes it apparent that Lady William was expected in Brussels at the end of her service with the Queen, for he wrote to Lord William: 'The new house is comfortable – smells of dinner and is rather desolate – we have all felt lowspirited since we came into it. We are not allowed to smoke in the Chancery lest Lady William should perceive any traces of smoke when she comes.'[12] Sir Robert Adair also hoped for her arrival. 'Tell Lady William that since my occupation of my house I have found no inconvenience from cold, or damp or bad smells etc., except indeed from the abominable *smoking of segars*, which I should hope her influence would put an end to.'[13]

In February Lady William, still in England, was seeking, it seems, a possible escape route from Brussels and enquired of Sir Robert, 'What is the earliest time for the waters at Aix la Chapelle?' [*][14] Her husband was also playing truant and at the beginning of March Adair wrote again to him.

'You say nothing about coming here, and perhaps the quarantine regulations, while they continue to be so strictly enforced may make Lady William hesitate . . .' [15] But the prolonged absence of his secretary could not be ignored and at the end of the month Sir Robert wrote: 'I don't know what to say about your coming here except that you must now seriously consider with yourself how far you mean to make diplomacy a profession. . . . I have just had a despatch from the Foreign Office calling upon me to state the periods during which my attachés have been absent from my mission, and for what causes, and whether with my leave or without it.' [16]

Lord John's efforts on behalf of his brother were renewed; it was imperative that employment should be found for William in circumstances and surroundings that were not wholly unacceptable to his wife. Lord Palmerston, the Foreign Secretary, was co-operative and on 24 May 1832 Lord William accompanied by Colonel Hare [*] and Major Badcock[†] sailed in the *Britannia* for Lisbon on a special mission.

[*] Richard Goddard Hare was a connection of Lady William's through the family of Earl Ferrers. He fought in Spain with the 12th Regiment of Foot, and had been attached while there to the staff of General Graham, Lord Lynedoch. While in Portugal in 1833, he heard that he had inherited a fortune of £10,000 a year from Sir Thomas Clarges Bt., a distant relative, whose name he then added to his own. Attaining the rank of Major General, he died at the age of 78 in 1857, having married, in 1848, Lady Clarges, daughter of Sir Thomas Buckler Bt., M.P.

[†] Major Benjamin Lovell Badcock, son of Thomas Stanhope Badcock, served with the 14th Dragoons in Spain. In 1840 he assumed by sign manual the surname of Lovell only. He was the author of *Rough Leaves from a Journal kept in Spain and Portugal* (1832–4).

Part 3

DIPLOMACY

Portugal 1832–1834

When Portugal was invaded by the French in 1807, King John VI and his family took refuge in Brazil. Returning to his own country after fourteen years, he left his eldest son Dom Pedro as Regent of Brazil, and brought with him his third son, Dom Miguel, whose education it was said had been so neglected that he could neither read nor write. Encouraged by his mother Queen Carlota, a sister of the King of Spain, who urged her son to put himself forward as pretender to the crown of Portugal, Dom Miguel three times tried to overturn the democratic government that had been established at Lisbon during his father's absence in Brazil, and which the King had accepted on his return. Twice pardoned by his father, he was, after the third revolution, banished, and went to live in exile at Paris and then at Vienna.

John VI died in 1826, having appointed a Regency with his daughter the Infanta Isabella at the head of it. Dom Pedro, electing to remain Emperor of Brazil, renounced his rights to the throne of Portugal in favour of his daughter Donna Maria da Gloria, a child of seven, and confirmed his sister Isabella in the Regency during the minority of the little Queen. He sent the Portuguese a Constitution and, hoping to dispose of an obvious danger, offered his daughter's hand to her uncle, his brother Dom Miguel, a man of twenty-four, promising him the future rank of Regent. To those who desired an early return of Dom Miguel to Portugal this arrangement was not acceptable, since owing to the youth of the bride it demanded patience. Troubles very soon broke out; deserting troops crossed into Spain and, proclaiming Miguel as their King, prepared to invade Portugal. A reactionary Spanish Government, eager to support absolutism and backed up by France and Austria, encouraged the deserters without regard for Spanish promises of neutrality. The Portuguese Regency under Donna Isabella appealed to England for help, and Canning in a speech of brilliant dexterity, in view of England's policy of non-interference in the internal affairs of other countries, announced to the House of Commons that troops were about to embark for Portugal.

A British squadron had been sent to the Tagus in 1824, affording no more than moral support to King John VI of Portugal at the time of Dom Miguel's revolt. It was still at the mouth of the river, and the arrival of a contingent of English soldiers at Lisbon assisted the Spaniards to remember their forgotten promises, while the invading bands were dispersed by Portuguese troops. Nearly two years later the serious illness of the Regent, Donna

245

Isabella, led the Emperor of Brazil to decree that their brother should be Regent in her stead, and Dom Miguel arrived in Lisbon early in 1828, having passed through London on his way from Vienna. He swore to maintain the Constitution and made many promises of good behaviour, but, his adherents persistently urging him to make himself absolute King, he forgot his oath and was readily persuaded to accept the crown offered him by the newly convened Cortes.

Upon this act of usurpation the British Minister and the troops were recalled. In the north the inhabitants of Oporto declared for Dom Pedro, and Dom Miguel sent a force to blockade the town and attack the Constitutionalists.

The Tory party in England had been in favour of recognising Dom Miguel as King, but the fall of the Duke of Wellington's Ministry in 1830 brought in the Whigs with Lord Grey as Prime Minister and Lord Palmerston as Foreign Secretary.

The murders and horrible cruelties sanctioned by Dom Miguel and the crowded state of the prisons in Portugal filled with political offenders of all classes, encouraged the Whigs in their support of Donna Maria. Outrageous acts of oppression against British subjects determined the Government to send Mr R. B. Hoppner as Consul to Lisbon with instructions to demand redress, which this energetic gentleman was successful in obtaining. The French residents were also subjected to tyranny and wanton acts of cruelty. A French squadron appeared in the Tagus under the command of Rabaudy, who obtained no satisfaction for the demands he was instructed to make. Later in the summer the reinforced French squadron captured the whole of Dom Miguel's fleet, the Admiral declaring that he made war against the tyrant and not against the Portuguese people.

A revolution having driven Dom Pedro from Brazil, he now arrived in Europe anxious to sustain the cause of his daughter. Collecting a force in England and France, he sailed for the Azores, which were loyal to Donna Maria, and awaited the moment when he might hazard an attack on the coast of Portugal. His fleet was commanded by an English naval officer, Captain Sartorius.*

Adhering to their policy of non-intervention, but observing the anarchy prevailing in Portugal and apprehensive of an extension of the civil war when Dom Pedro landed, the English Cabinet determined at this juncture to send Lord William Russell to Lisbon with the object of observing the movements of the Spanish army. A disputed succession in Spain presented a further hazard in the situation, since the pretender Don Carlos gave his support to Dom Miguel to whom he was bound by marriage as well as by opinions. Arriving as a refugee in Portugal, he wandered about asserting his claim to the Spanish throne.

* George Rose Sartorius (1790–1885). For his assumption of the command of Dom Pedro's fleet in 1831–3, his name was struck off the Navy List, though he was later reinstated, and he was made K.C.B. in 1865.

'Spain', Lord Palmerston instructed Lord William, 'will be quiet provided we keep our promise of neutrality.' 'It is also very important', he wrote, 'that Admiral Parker* should not proceed to actual hostilities for the protection of our subjects till all other means of obtaining redress . . . shall have failed.'[1] He warned him in a private letter that there might be 'complications of affairs which may throw upon you a most unpleasant and difficult responsibility. I am however convinced that you will judge rightly, if the case should arise, and that at all events you will act according to the best judgement you may be able to form, we will bear you out in anything you may do.'[2]

Lord William and his staff arrived at Lisbon on 2 June and were met by the English Consul, Mr Hoppner, who for six months had been and still was charged with diplomatic duties in the absence of an English Minister.

Richard Belgrave Hoppner, who was the son of the portrait painter John Hoppner, had begun his service as a clerk in the Foreign Office. He spent eleven years as Consul at Venice, where he was intimate with Lord Byron. We have Lord William's testimony, in a letter to Lord Palmerston, that he was clever and zealous, and probably the difficulties of his position at Lisbon led him to deserve as well some of the other epithets applied at the same time. The sympathy and respect felt at first by Lord William for his countryman evaporated under the strain of events and a divergence of political opinions.

Dom Pedro landed near Oporto in July 1832 and captured the town, Dom Miguel's forces withdrawing towards Lisbon. Pedro being unable to obtain any decisive advantage, the war dragged on till the following year, during which time the Tories continued to urge the Whigs to acknowledge Miguel.

Lady William with her mother and her children arrived in Lisbon at the end of the year. They occupied for some time the beautiful house at Larenjeiras, a league outside the town, belonging to the unfortunate Baron Quintella, who had been proscribed by Dom Miguel, and who was saved from imprisonment or death by taking refuge with his wife in an English warship under the assumed name of Mr and Mrs Smith. Later Lady William moved out to Cintra. During the few months that Lord William occupied the post of British Minister at the court of Donna Maria, they lived in the Pombal palace, a fine house overlooking the Tagus.†

Lord William's humane feelings were outraged by the misery he saw around him, and his conviction that the neutral policy pursued by the English Government was wrong, coupled with the responsibility of his position and his anxiety to do well, made it a trying time for him, and he directed officially and privately a flow of urgent appeals to Palmerston for British intervention. Appealed to by the wretched people round them, the Russells gave refuge and assistance to the persecuted, regardless of the side

* Admiral William Parker (1781–1866) protected British interests in the Tagus during the civil war.

† It now houses the Lisbon picture gallery.

to which they adhered, thus falling foul of the English Consul, a violent partisan of Dom Pedro's cause. A change in the fortunes of the war placed in Hoppner's hands certain captured papers suggesting a lack of discretion on the part of the Russells. He transmitted them to London and his action had a painful sequel when Lord and Lady William returned to England the following year. The Russells' infatuation with Cordova, the Spanish Minister, was to have unfortunate repercussions for them. Deprived of the educated company they were accustomed to and contemptuous of the poor quality of Lisbon society, they were led, not surprisingly, to rate this cultivated if somewhat devious gentleman higher than he deserved.

The success of Dom Pedro's arms placed his daughter Donna Maria on the throne of Portugal, and William Russell was ordered to present his credentials as English Minister to her, but Lord Palmerston, having for some time promised Lisbon to another diplomatist, begged Lord William to take the post of Minister in Wurtemberg instead.

The Russells returned to England in April 1834, and engaged in an angry correspondence with Ministers and with Lord and Lady Holland, regarding the captured documents.

LORD WILLIAM'S DIARY

1 June. Arrived off Rocha. – Put into quarantine. Admiral Parker came alongside, we had some conversation thro the port hole, like him much, met him again at the *Parlatorio* & had a long conversation with him, he is no partisan. Dined with the Admiral. The Admiral & I settled our plans in case of being called on to act *dubito vigorens.* Saw the Consul Mr Hoppner at the *Parlatorio,* violent partisan, much jealousy between those two authorities. I am the bone of contention. Called on Viscount Santarem,* a little insignificant man covered with stars, told him my instructions, found him very civil. Madame de Lemos (Juramenha), Beresford's† woman, waiting at the door with her son to see him, she is the life and soul of Miguel's party. Saw several of the Ministers going to the Council at Caxias, what a set, Bastos, an old lawyer, the only one of energy, he was in a *seja*‡ with 4 mules & two dragoons. The Council did not break up till 7, they must be in a stew. Dined with Hoppner, met Mr Duff there, a merchant with a star, if the merchants take to these follies, the aristocrats must find out some other tinsel to bedaub themselves with.

10 June. Lodged at Reeve's hotel. Several arrests in the preceding nights, especially ladies. Met at Mrs Hoppner's a Donna Anna Camara, threatened with arrest, how wonderfully these southern ladies keep up their spirits under their

* Manoel-Francisco de Barros y Souza, Viscount Santarem (1790–1856), Dom Miguel's Prime Minister.

† William Carr Beresford, Viscount Beresford (1768–1854) had commanded the Portuguese army during the Peninsular War.

‡ 'litter'.

calamities, ours would sink under them, she gives a most deplorable account of Lisbon, never did I hear of such an atrocious Government. Dined with old Brown,* aged, almost doating. Magnificent dinner. Princes and potentates may boast their power, but I know nothing like the power of wealth in a merchant. Met Mr Brandt the American Minister, a *soi-disant* liberal, but these Yankees are playing a slippery part. They have a frigate & a corvette in the river.

11 June. Badcock set off, quite delighted, especially with his dress.† Drove out to Belem, Brown's *quinta*. Not a house is altered, improved or cleaned since I first came here 23 years ago. The same dirt & filth exists. Miguel is in his *quinta* & amuses himself by making the batteries fire.

13 June. Aspettare e non venir ‡ is sad work, wish this was over that I might get home. Went to the English burying ground, how many of my poor country people who came in search of health have laid their bones in this foreign land, it is a very beautiful piece of ground uniting the beauty of the eastern burying grounds covered with cypress to the gaiety of the French, full of flowers. A monument to Fielding § is in preparation, the English having been shamed into it by the French. Took a long drive but the roads are detestable. Drank tea with Mrs Hoppner.‖ Miguel came twice towards the town to look at a new battery, he was huzzaed & caressed by the soldiers. He has two grooms behind him with long sticks to beat the people who don't salute him.

14 June. Dined with Mr Duff. Baron & Baroness Quintella, poor people, she talked of her children & her eyes filled with tears, what horrible & detestable tyranny.

15 June. In the morning I went to see Quintella's children & took them on the terrace that the poor mother might look at them.

16 June. The Portuguese Government has put patrols of 3 soldiers on my house & Mr Hoppner's, probably to prevent persons taking refuge in them. Dined with Mr & Mrs Hoppner, Sir Thomas Troubridge, who sees things well, *mais fat.* Called on Mr Duff & saw his guest. Badcock returned, the *petit imbecile.*

17 June. I grow impatient. Delicious weather. Drove to Larengeras, Quintella's villa. He has a pretty theatre lighted with gas, a great innovation in this barbarous country. Dined with old Brown, all the magnificence of a rich merchant, but he is sick & feeble, & what is wealth without health. Drank tea at Mr Duff's, & saw there the poor Quintellas. *La famille D. est bien ennuyeuse.*

* 'Native' Brown; a merchant who had been a friend of the Duke of Bedford when he was in Lisbon in 1814.

† Badcock was sent to Elvas and Badajoz to ascertain if any Spanish troops had entered Portugal.

‡ 'Waiting and not coming'.

§ Henry Fielding (1707–54), author of *Tom Jones*, died at Lisbon.

‖ '... a pleasing woman, a Swiss, full of animation and good humour'. Erskine (ed.), *Letters and Friendships of Anna Jameson*, p. 42.

Diplomacy

18 June. We are getting the Admiral into better trim, my presence here has given rise to better language & supported Hoppner who will be the *diplomate*. Went with him to call on Rabaudy, commander of the *Melpomene* frigate, gentleman-like & kindhearted man, has given refuge to 4 Portuguese. Our Admiral is much blamed for not being equally kind. A guard placed at our door & an order issued to protect the English.

20 June. Dined with Mr Lucas. 24 persons. Magnificent dinner. He has a nice house & pretty daughters. Mail from England, letters & good accounts from dear Bessy & the children. Given the rank of Brigadier in Portugal. Reform Bill received the Royal assent.

21 June. Corpus Domini processions etc. The puritanical republican Yankees fired two salutes for a Catholic saint. Curious.

22 June. Moved to the house of Pinto Bastos at Junqueira, the poor man having fled, his son an intelligent man, they are rich merchants. Regret my hotel, its fine view & fine air. On my return from drinking tea with Hoppners, Mr Phillips sent me a note to say a vessel had arrived at Algarve which had seen Don Pedro's fleet half way from the Azores. 80 ships. This is delightful news. I have hopes of seeing this scoundrel kicked out & the prisons thrown open.

24 June. Feverish night, got up most anxious. Alas, alas, the whole report is false, hope deferred maketh the heart sick. Went to church, one of the neatest I ever saw. Bought a necklace of *minhas novas*, a sort of diamond, for Bessy.

26 June. Went to the reading room at Lisbon, a fine establishment but few books. – at Geneva all books, at Lisbon all is sacrificed to dancing.

28 June. Started at 5 o'clock for Cintra, the scenery is very beautiful but the houses are neglected, in short the whole country is going to ruin. Rode up to the Cork Convent, the monks appear very happy & contented people but they have no library, no garden & no apparent occupation, they were very civil. From that we went to Collares. Met Don Miguel opposite the Palace of Queluz. Hare made him a low bow which he returned, he is a small pale man, covered with hair, & rides well. Quantities of courtiers in *sejas* were going to the Palace.

1 July. I never thought to see out the month of June without Pedro making his appearance. My patience is wearing out. Went to church.

3 July. Wrote by the *Viper* to the Admiral & by the *Echo* steam vessel to Palmerston & Bessy &c. Dined with Mr & Mrs Gould, a grand dinner, 24 persons, each had some story to tell of the tryanny of the Government. The merchants are splendid fellows.

4 July. Decided to send Badcock by Badajoz to Salamanca. Called on old Brown who is doating. Mr Lesseps,* the French Consul, & Viscount Manuel the

---

* Jean-Baptiste de Lesseps, sole survivor of La Pérouse's expedition to Kamchatka in 1788. Uncle of Ferdinand de Lesseps, the pioneer of the Suez Canal.

Spaniard dined with me, he is more enlightened & liberal than Spaniards usually are. The *Viper* came in & brought me a letter from the Admiral to say the expedition had sailed on the 27th, the force including sailors does not amount to 8000, they go to Oporto. Another from Palmella* to explain & to beg of me to join them at Oporto. How can I do this it is contrary to my instructions, however I will do what I can.

5 July. Mr Waring told me the curious anecdote of Don Miguel having pursued us from Queluz with a blunderbuss to shoot us, he maintains it is a fact. The man must be mad.

6 July. Young Duff came to me to say he heard his house was to be searched, & that his father wished to put his daughter on board ship; went to Duff who said he expected his house to be searched & wished to place [Quintellas] in safety, I offered my house. They wished me to get them an asylum on board the *Romney*, which I did. Donna Anna Camara & several ladies taken up, the Government is a mixture of cruelty, imbecility & ignorance.

8 July. A long letter from the Admiral about the Quintellas being on board the *Romney*. *Le bon homme* acts up to the letter of his orders & not up to the spirit.

Letters written by Hastings to his father during the summer give an account of day-to-day events in London. Riding daily with his young aunts, Georgiana and Louisa Russell, Hastings shows that he is aware of the love affair between Louisa and Lord Abercorn, and he makes his own shrewd comments on what he calls his 'chaperonage'.

'What's in the wind about Abercorn and L.? I don't twig but I know that she has ridden alone with him to Richmond Park on his arabian while I rode another way with Georgy. We rode to Putney Bridge, Wimbolton Common and the Park by Hammersmith. . . . We met a quantity of chaps. Abercorn of course.'[3]

Several masters had been engaged to teach Greek, Latin, and the use of the globes. Monsieur Drocourt 'the French chap', who remained as tutor to the boys for fourteen years, is heard of for the first time.

Hastings Russell to Lord William Russell at Lisbon [WP]

[London 1832]

Dear Pappy today I rode with Lord Lynedoch we went to Holland house and saw Lord Holland and Henry Fox who all asked after you Lady Holland was driving in her Poney chaise and Lord Greys brother and his Wife were walking beside her he said that you were the fittest man

* Duke of Palmella (1781–1850), liberal Portuguese statesman who became Dom Pedro's Prime Minister and was later ambassador in London.

that could be sent and then they told him who I was. Then Lady Holland said what a charming agreable excellent man you were. Lord Lynedoch agreed and said that from the first moment he knew you he never had occasion otherwise for a minute then we went away and met General Upton the first thing he said was were is our *friend* William has he sailed and Lynedoch Introduced me to him.

goodbye dear Papyo Mammy wants my letter to send.

Hastings Russell to Lord William Russell at Lisbon [WP]

[London 1832]

Dear Papyo Mama did not send my letter by this post because it was not quite reddy so I will send it you by the next. As I have not written to you this week I will tell you the whole story of it at once.

This week the Dutchess weent to Woburn with the Duke Abercorn and Louisa *soli*! to make him pop the question but he did not though everybody in town beleived he had. so when they came back after 3 days every body said I wish you joy on your marriage some of them rather sourely.

Rio and his wife came to stay with G. while the rest of them are at Woburn. I rode 1 day with Rio and G. and the other days with G. alone.

The other day as we were riding in the park we saw a Lady run away with: the horse ran up rotten row then he tried to leap over the rails but caught with his hind legs and fell over the lady who was much hurt.

goodbye dear Pappy. Mama wants my letter please write to me.

P.S. we are going to Tunbrige wells tomorow.

Hastings Russell to Lord William Russell at Lisbon [WP]

[London 1832]

we have been to Tunbrige wells I dont remember anything wonderfull that we did there and what we saw I will tell you when I see you. . . . Today I went in the carriage with mamy, who is quite well. We went to see Lord Lyendch who has been Couched and is doing as well as can be. but we dont now if he will see.

Nikie exercised the poney today. Today I rode with Uncle Jonn to Richmond Park for he was going to Richmond.

Dear Papy I hope you are well and that you mean to come back to us soon. Lord Lyendoch has had his bandage removed and he sees quit well: goodbye dear Papyo.

Lord William Russell to Lord Palmerston [PP]
Private
Lisbon, July 9, 1832.

... the very kind way in which you say that whatever errors I may commit in the difficult situation in which I may be placed, you will support me, this added to the very handsome manner, in which you fought my battle against that ruffian Saxe-Weimar & the procuring me the Brigadier-ship makes a large debt of gratitude due from me to you – but I believe I am doomed to be shot by a ruffian in authority, for I have written my brother John a most curious story of Don Miguel galloping after me to shoot me, which story I have since traced to come direct from Donna Isabella the Regent, so it is true, ask my brother to show you the letter.

LORD WILLIAM'S DIARY

10 July. A French frigate came in with orders for Rabaudy to go home. All the ladies cried at this, he is much beloved, whilst our poor Admiral from taking neither side has not a friend.

13 July. The *Viper* had a shot fired at her by Belem Castle & the Commander detained a prisoner on board. Wrote to Santarem to say I could no longer discharge the duties of my mission & should go to sea in the *Viper*, he replied & said they did not want to interrupt our communication. I said he did for the Commander was detained on board, he had him released, I said I would stay, he said he was glad of it.

14 July. Went to call on the Quintellas on board the *Romney*, they little know what a responsibility I am taking on my shoulders for their sakes.

15 July. A very quiet day & got the morning for reading a treat I have not had for some days.

16 July. Capt Richards of the *Asia*, came to me with despatches & a letter from the Admiral to Viscount Santarem, very good, demanding an apology & that the Governor of Belem Castle should be dismissed for the insult to the *Viper*. Took Capt Richards to Hoppner who accompanied him to Santarem, Hoppner insisted on the apology being put in the Gazette which S. refused, & a violent scene took place, wrote to Admiral to tell him I thought Hoppner was right. A letter from Hare on board the *Stag* off Oporto. Don Pedro was organising his corps & intended to advance in a few days. Richards was to return at daylight in a boat the Admiral being at anchor in Cascaes Bay. He keeps fidgetting about the Quintellas but his notions on neutrality are absurd.

18 July. Wrote a letter to the Admiral to chide his tardy ways, hope it will not affront him.

19 July. Heard that Don Pedro was anchored in Cascaes Bay, he has only a frigate, 1 corvette, 2 brigs – the Portuguese have a ship of the line, a frigate & 3 corvettes. Two poor women came to me for charity, one the wife of Colonel Cheria now in Elvas prison. Her son was hanged. Poor things, how little we know of this misery in England. Called on board the *Romney* where Duff asked me about getting off the Princess Sa [?Sarmenta]. Offered my house & services. Packet came in & brought me two letters from Bessy. Thank God they are all well. One from Lord P. requiring an explanation about Badcock having gone into Badajoz without a passport. What stuff & nonsense at such a moment too. Sartorius came down with his fleet & blockaded the Tagus.

20 July. Went up to Duff's house, from which I saw very close under me four fleets. The French, English, Pedro's & Miguel's, the former with a frigate blockading a 74.

21 July. Heard the Portuguese fleet was to go out to attack Sartorius. Went to see it but it did not take place, & I believe never will. Rabaudy went out & gave a Royal salute to the flag of Donna Maria. Why has our Admiral allowed the French to show him the example, that Frenchman has borne away the palm & done his country much service.

Lord William Russell to Lord Holland [HH]

Lisbon 21 July [1832]

My letters make you so angry that I am almost afraid to write to you, tho I fear this will also put you into a furious passion – for it is to urge you & your colleagues to *withdraw your support* from this horrible contemptible animal at the head of this country, to acknowledge Donna Maria, the legitimate and lawful Queen. The interest of England requires it, humanity requires it, justice requires it, honor & good faith require it – but all these have ceased to have any weight with you since you became a Minister. . . .

I know that all I say will make you very angry, but if it saves the lives of these poor creatures cutting each other's throats, & dying in loathsome prisons, I don't care.

LORD WILLIAM'S DIARY

24 July. No news. Melancholy as night. Dined alone, went to call on Mr Brent. On my return found Mlle d'Avilez who had taken refuge in my house in the garden, asked her in to tea. Her father is a distinguished General, 4 years in prison, without trial or charge against him, her mother two months in prison, & her little brother & sister dispersed about, poor thing. *Viper* came in – rather a cross letter from that old ass the Admiral, what a foolish old woman it is to object to take off the Princess.

28 July. After dinner the *Viper* arrived with despatches from England. No hopes of recognition, these half measures are cruel.

29 July. Wrote a very strong private letter to Palmerston & a public despatch, I fear I shall offend them all. I can't help it, but no private interest shall ever make me shrink from acting in the cause of humanity & justice. I would rather be re-called than remain here a quiet spectator of these horrors, without the power to aid the sufferers.

31 July. Dined with Captain Matthieu on board the *Bellona*. Hoppner, Lesseps, 3 Portuguese refugees, & Leroy, who is full of fun, cleverness & vivacity. They say he is the image of Napoleon, a very good & gay dinner, the French have the art of making dinners agreable.

1 Aug. No news; talk of rising &c., but all talk. Montalegre* came to fish, he seems low, says it is the heat, but I believe it is political cold, he has told them in Madrid that Pedro has not a chance, disagreable to be proved a fool, Pedro in my opinion is sure to win.

2 Aug. Dined in the *Romney*. What odd people, I never could be in love with a Portuguese, they shock one cruelly at times.

3 Aug. Heard in the morning that Don Miguel's fleet was going out, went to Mr Duff's, it was a beautiful sight. Admiral Sartorius was under weigh standing to the westward under easy sail, he had nothing with him but a steam vessel which he apparently despatched to collect his fleet, for we afterwards saw a frigate & corvette standing to the southward, he was followed by the *Don John* a 74, *Pss Real*, a frigate, 3 corvettes & 3 brigs. After watching them anxiously for some hours they got out of sight. What a moment for Portugal. Much, perhaps all will depend on this action.

4 Aug. The telegraph announced that Don Miguel's fleet had taken 2 ships from Sartorius. Men riding about to announce the news, which was spread to being the whole fleet; on my return from Campolide I found the town illuminated. Went to Hoppner, the two French captains & all in consternation, tho all pro-fessed not to believe the news.

5 Aug. The whole thing turns out to be a vile & impudent lie. Very unwell with cold & headache.

6 Aug. Letter from the Admiral to say the fleets were opposite each other 20

---

* The Spanish Minister.

leagues out at sea. Went on board the *Romney* to bring away Mr Smith, alias B[aron] Q[uintella].

7 Aug. Bad cold & cough, took a sweat. Drank tea at Hoppners with the two French Captains.

8 Aug. Montalegre wrote to tell me Pedro's troops were defeated, how that fellow enjoys giving me news he knows will annoy me. *Viper* came in, a very angry letter from the Admiral at my remonstrating against his keeping those poor devils on board the *Royalist* on ship's provisions. He is an old ass.

Lord Palmerston to Lord William Russell [PP]
Private

Foreign Office, 12 August 1832

... With respect to the escape of Portuguese people by means of the *Viper* great delicacy should be used; it would be inhuman to drive people back to be put to death and therefore in cases of real personal peril you must use your discretion. But it would not be consistent with our understanding with the Portuguese Government to allow the *Viper* to bring out of Lisbon people who merely want to go and join Don Pedro's army. ...

LORD WILLIAM'S DIARY

11 Aug. The apathy and cowardice of these wretched Portuguese disgusts me, they deserve to be slaves. Went on horseback to Campolide. Dined with Hoppner, quite bent down with despair.

12 Aug. This day year I was engaged in making peace between the Belgians & the Dutch. I wish I could make peace between these wretched people, headed by the brothers.

16 Aug. The liberal party in very low spirits. Mrs Hoppner wept with vexation. Called at Duffs' to keep up the spirits of the Smiths. I don't despair of the good cause.

Lord William Russell to Lord John Russell [WP]

Lisbon Aug 17th [1832]

I yesterday received your letter of the 4th. I regret very much that you are so bound to Spain, or rather by Spain that you cannot assist the good cause in this Country. I am no statesman. & am guided more by my feelings than my head so as you are in the *galère* & cannot get out, it is useless for me to ask, '*que diable allait-il faire dans cette galère là.*' Here I am your servant & must fight your battles which is no sinecure. Yesterday a lady abused the English Ministry with such violence to me, that she burst into a flood of tears. The Miguelites pretend to despise you, & old Montalegre laughs at you, this comes from neutrality. However I don't despair, Pedro is not Napoleon, and Sartorius is not Lord Cochrane, still I am convinced that men fighting for their freedom must beat the wretched slave; the smallest trifle, the least daring would give a different turn to events. If Miguel succeeds is he to be allowed to butcher the whole country at his pleasure?

Anxious as I am to get away, I believe it would be imprudent to recall me at present, for I am constantly called upon to settle disputes with Spain, & being on very good terms with Montalegre I can do so, with greater ease than others, besides the Constitutional party has great confidence in me, & the Miguelites respect me, so I cannot leave this without detriment to the good cause.

Duke of Bedford to Lady William Russell [PRP]

W.A. Tuesday [1832]

I shall be happy to see you and yours, baggage wagon, cavalry and all, whenever it suits your own convenience.

I have this morning a very pleasing letter from Lord Abercorn asking my consent to his union to Louisa. I hasten to communicate this event to you and to assure you unaffectedly that it gives me the greatest satisfaction. Pray communicate it to John.

Poor William I fear is not in a very good humour at Lisbon; he writes a furious tirade against the government that employs him. He writes one to me equally furious, against the law of primogeniture which gives Woburn, Endsleigh &c. to me and no house to him!

Lord John Russell to Lord William Russell [WP]

Sunday 22nd [1832]

Your impatience is not wonderful – but it is not founded on those calm considerations which must guide us. I fear you will not like the instructions we send about the *Viper* but depend upon it they are just. Do not let Hoppner get hold of you, for he has more passion than judgement. I have no time to say more. Your wife & children are well at Woburn.

The fleet will probably stay two months longer. Till then, having accepted a post, you must stand sentry there. Our session is over, thank God.

Lord William Russell to Lord Palmerston [PP]
Private

Lisbon, 26 August, 1832.
. . . You take my outpourings very goodnaturedly. . . . Poverty, terror, anguish of mind & body are always present on one side, on the other cruelty, lying, & all that is mean & contemptible. My person shunned like the pest, all houses shut against me, everyone, even the English merchants (whose purses never suffer without their crying loudly) open mouthed against the English Government. When I turn from this I look on our magnificent Fleet which could put an end to their horrors . . ., besides the strong feelings of Hoppner, & want of feeling of the Admiral require a medium. I assure you I never abused the privileges of the *Viper*, beyond saving a poor devil's life now & then, however I now take them in to my own house & if the police come for them we must fight – 'pro aris et focis'. like Charles XII at Bender.

Duke of Bedford to Lady William Russell [PRP]
Private

Nuneham Park, Thursday. [1832]
If the Hollands go to Woburn on Saturday, (which I have no belief they will) I must rely on you for taking care of them till I return, which will be on Sunday evening, not to dinner, for I dislike travelling on Sunday during church time if I can avoid it; but don't say this to Lady Holland for she will not comprehend it. You must begin by ordering all the flowers out of the living rooms into the south corridor, where they will not offend her.

I am very sorry that William has written to Lord Palmerston asking to be recalled – it is in the first place wrong during an important pending mission; and secondly it shows a capriciousness and fickleness and unsteadiness of purpose, which will make any government unwilling to employ him in diplomacy. I have not mentioned this to any one, and think the less said about it the better, though as he has written to Lord Palmerston it will of course be discussed; but I should advise you not to speak of it to any one, particularly to the Hollands, who (*entre nous*) have always their own game to play.

In England Lady William was preparing herself for the journey to Lisbon. Until late in October it was uncertain when she could get a passage in a warship, or indeed if she would go to Portugal at all.

Lord John Russell to Lady William Russell at Woburn [PRP]

Endsleigh Sept 23 [1832]

It is very odd, but I am so busy here that I have no time to write all my letters – but then I write about a dozen a day, which I never did before. . . .

I believe you may go out on the *Britannia* after all – but you may be kept cruising for some time if there is quarantine. However William is responsible for that if he wishes you to go.

If you & the children were here I should be quite contented here – the place is so very beautiful.

I do not think the bread bad at Woburn, but the water is not good. Here the water is excellent, & the bread too, I think. But I am partial to this County, & shall continue so, if they re-elect me.

Lord John Russell to Lady William Russell at Woburn [PRP]

Bowood Oct. 7. 32

I have received two letters from you & one from William, mainly concerning your voyage to Lisbon. It is no light matter to go among such barbarians in the very heart of their barbarism, trusting to the chapter of accidents. Yet events of late are rather in favour of the continuance of the war at Oporto, & tranquillity at Lisbon; therefore of your going. I cannot however finally advise until I see my colleagues in London. In the meantime what had you best do? I rather think you had better come to the Pay Office, as the 10th is so near, & the 20th not far off. I shall go to Holland House for a few days on Tuesday or Wednesday, but you can come when you like. I do not think I shall be able to tell you any thing decisive till Friday.

I will write to my father about your going to Endsleigh; I do not imagine he will object, but my own advice is that when you know the ship is ready for sailing, & she is intended to go, you get on board with your children. To Endsleigh with your return will consume 8 or 10 hours – more than the Captain may like, polite as he appears to be. . . .

Lord John Russell to Lady William Russell at Woburn [PRP]

H. H. Oct. 10 [1832]

Your case is extremely confusing. I do not believe there is any desire to recall William, but you may have a dismal and disagreeable expedition. To make things worse Graham is in a fidget to get *Britannia* to sea. Telegraph has ordered the gallant Rainier to get ready with all haste, and Graham says she may be ready the 15th. If you are to go therefore I think you had better make yourself ready to come to town on Friday with the chickens. There will be no need of staying in an hotel at Plymouth. What I meant was that you should get on board and make yourself comfortable, and in 24 hours you will be sure to sail. I do not advise going from London by steam, but from Portsmouth you might do it very well. It is a bold affair however to take yourself and the children.

Lady William Russell to Lord Palmerston [PP]

Woburn Abbey Friday October 12 1832

My dear Lord Palmerston,

I have received the large parcel safe and sound by this morning's post & return you many thanks. You have no apologies to make for writing concise notes, it is I who am conscience stricken at having bombarded you with so many letters, my great consolation is the air of consequence it must give me at the Woburn Post Office.

Your sincerely obliged

E. A. Russell

[*endorsed by Lord Palmerston*: Lady William Russell has received her diamonds.]

Lord John Russell to Lady William Russell at Woburn [PRP]

Oct. 12 [1832]

Another change over the spirit of your dream. The Admiralty have heard that the *Britannia* came out of dock on the 9th & will be ready for sea the 16th. She certainly goes to Lisbon, but it is likewise certain that the Government are very anxious she should go out as soon as possible, as some other ships are coming home from the Lisbon station.

It is for you to decide. If you are to go out, this is the best opportunity possible. William leaves no discretion with me but as to the mode of your reaching the *Britannia*. He will be mortified if you prefer Paris & your mother to Lisbon & your husband. At the same time it must be owned there is some inconvenience in being so long on board a ship, & that Lisbon is not a pleasant place to rest in, if the Portuguese war should terminate unfavourably to Pedro.

I must urge at all events your coming to town tomorrow. A steam packet goes on Sunday morning from the Tower to Plymouth, but I suppose that will be too soon for you. I conclude the Admiralty would give you a few hours more to reach Plymouth at my request than they would otherwise give. You shall see Graham & Hardy upon it yourself when you arrive in town, & I will send Pudar with you, if you think he can be of use.

'Lady William was to leave town yesterday', wrote Lady Holland to Henry Fox on 19 October. 'She is to sail in the *Britannia*. The worst part of her expedition is the necessity of quitting the great ship of war to be lowered into a steam vessel in the open sea, as the *Viper* is the only vessel, a sort of Cartel, which Miguel's govt allow to enter the Tagus. Like you, she hates England so much that she would go anywhere. She has neither kin nor home, or anything to bestow affections upon, or very much receive them from others, from her selfishness of character. Her children are charming. Perhaps it is unlucky for Hastings to become such a wanderer, but he is a delightful boy, full of good dispositions & kindness of heart.'[4]

Lord William Russell to R. B. Hoppner [FO 63/389]

Lisbon, October 15 1832.

Sir,

The Corporal of the police patrol stationed about my house last night killed my porter by shooting him through the head in the most wanton and ferocious manner without the man having given him the slightest provocation. If one of my servants is thus deprived of his life while doing his duty within my own courtyard by the very men who are ostensibly stationed there for my protection, I can no longer consider my own life, nor the lives of those dependent on me in safety, I therefore request you will inform Viscount Santarem that I have called upon the British Squadron to enter the Tagus, explaining to him that it is solely for the protection of British residents, and not to interfere in the contest going on in this country.

In the absence of Admiral Parker, who was temporarily at Oporto, Lord William addressed himself to Captain James Hillyar. With his official demand for the ships to enter the river he sent a private letter in which he wrote: 'I therefore take the whole responsibility of calling in the Fleet upon myself, the executive part must depend upon you.'[5] Hillyar on receiving these instructions answered at once that he was informing Viscount Santarem of what was about to occur and that he was sending off to the Admiral. 'I think', he wrote to Lord William, 'that it will be prudent to wait his reply before I enter the Tagus, for should our entry be resisted, I do not think the ships under my orders are adequate to the forcing of the passage of the Tagus up to Lisbon, or retaining our position there.'[6] Perplexed, he excused himself again next day. Deeply disturbed, Hoppner and Russell addressed the reluctant Captain at some length. Hoppner wrote, unwisely as it later appeared: '... When H.B.M. Government ordered them [the ships] to quit the Tagus they certainly never contemplated so long a duration of the present contest in the country. I do not doubt therefore that they will be glad of a reasonable pretext for commanding them to their former position in the river, and the outrage now committed on Lord William Russell affords such a pretext as no one can cavil at. I might still allege other reasons but I deem these sufficient.'[7] And Lord William expressed with feeling his dismay at the Captain's hesitation.

Captain James Hillyar to Lord William Russell [FO 63/397]

Caledonia in Cascaes Bay,
17 October 1832

My Lord,

After giving your Lordship's and Mr Hoppner's letters my most serious consideration, I have decided on complying with your wishes and purpose entering the Tagus as soon as the wind permits, and the pilot will take charge of the ships, which he declines doing while it remains in the present quarter.

Brought up in the school of prompt and implicit obedience to every order of my superior officer I have my doubts whether I am not deviating from the path of strict duty, but the case seems urgent and I shall be most happy if it meets the approbation of my superiors, and conduces to the protection and comfort of H.M. subjects at Lisbon, in whose anxiety I most cordially sympathise.

Captain Hillyar also wrote that day to Admiral Parker, sending him all the correspondence. ' . . . I have felt that my situation is peculiarly delicate from the nature of your orders not to enter the Tagus except under particular circumstances to which has been opposed the importunities expressed in the accompanying documents. . . .'
  The Admiral for his part thought fit to send off the whole bundle of letters to the Lords at the Admiralty. He accompanied the packet with his remarks on the excellence of Captain Hillyar's conduct.

Lord William Russell to Lord Palmerston [FO 63/384]
Lisbon, October 18 1832.
  An event has occurred here which has induced me (after consulting with Mr Hoppner) to call upon Captain Hillyar to enter the Tagus with the ships under his command.
  The circumstances which led me to take the step are these. On Sunday last (14 Oct) at 9 o'clock p.m., my porter was sitting on a bench outside the gate of my house, his accustomed post, when three soldiers of the police guard, who are stationed near the house ostensibly for my protection, came up and asked him what he was doing there, he replied that he was doing his duty, waiting the return of his master, they then insisted on searching his person, to which he submitted, then after using very abusive language to him they drove him into the courtyard with their bayonets, and as soon as he had entered shot him dead, the ball passing through his head and striking the wall near the door. After all the enquiries I have made, I cannot learn that the soldiers received the least provocation to commit such a wanton murder on one of my servants, within the gates of my own house, indeed the man was of a gentle harmless disposition, incapable of giving offence to anyone. I cannot therefore look upon it in any other light but a premeditated insult to me. . . . The *Caledonia* and *Revenge* are now entering the Tagus.

Lord Palmerston to Lord William Russell [PP]
Private
F.O. October 29, 1832.
  We have approved your decision calling in the Fleet & have ordered it to remain in the Tagus. But pray contrive to get on better terms with Admiral

Parker, because your difference with him is a little embarrassing to me, as other members of the Cabinet of course lean to him as I do towards you. I cannot quite say that the instruction he left with Captain Hillyar was at variance with the instructions given by me. . . . I think you were perfectly right in urging Hoppner to call in the ships & that Captain Hillyar exercised a very proper discretion in complying with the call. But Hoppner used an unlucky word in his letter to Hillyar which if the correspondence were to be produced before Parliament might give rise to criticism. He should have talked of a 'good reason' and not of 'a reasonable pretext'. . . . If Hoppner's letter had been a despatch to me I should have asked him to send me another copy with that one word changed, but as it is the Cabinet wish me to put upon record a remark upon that expression. . . .

Lord William Russell to Lord John Russell [WP]

Lisbon Nov 9th [1832]

I am happy to find that the entrance of the Tagus is approved of, but regret that my letter was disapproved of. Parker was an ass to send it home & make a long story about it. The fact is I am the most indolent & apathetic of God's creatures till roused, when my feelings overpower me, I am a sort of savage. Parker is a well meaning man, & we are the best of friends.

My family are still in quarantine & I think will do very well here, I am glad they came out. . . .

Lord John Russell to Lord William Russell [WP]

Nov 16 [1832]

I am delighted to find that all your family arrived safe. It is very well for November to be no worse. I am glad too that the streets of Lisbon are quiet.

I am a bad person to lecture on official decorum, and caution, but you must bear in mind that private letters are not to be written by a gentleman 'entrusted with a confidential mission' as if you were writing to your father or your wife. As a plain particular Parker is rather punctilious, but as a servant of Government he is in the right. The King recommended to Lord Grey to give you a caution on the subject. On the whole however I think you have done admirably – quite right in bringing in the ships, &

right also in leaving the affair to take its course, & not using the force of the British fleet to obtain some extravagant reparation, as many or at least some of our dips would have done. . . .

Lord William Russell to Lord John Russell [WP]

Lisbon Dec 4th 1832

I only yesterday got your letter of the 16th, in which you give me a gentle admonition for my letter to Captain Hillyar, & say that the King desired Lord Grey to *caution* me. I suppose Lord Gy delegated the duty to you, & that you have modified the word, which ought to have been *admonish* me. Now I don't mean to defend my letter, but if I had not written that letter our ships would not have come into the Tagus, they would now have been tossing about to their great peril & damage, or in Vigo bay (quite useless). Admiral Parker would have written one of his silly letters to Viscount Santarem, Santarem would have written one of his lying excuses – have laughed at the Admiral, & the English would have been robbed & insulted as usual. All these evils were avoided by my unfortunate letter, for which I am to be rebuked. The fact is Captn Hillyar ought never to have sent it to the Admiral, the Admiral ought never to have sent it to Sir J. Graham, Sir J. Graham ought never to have laid it before the Cabinet. Now, my dear John, let me ask this favor of you. If ever you find the Cabinet displeased with my services, take upon yourself to get me recalled. I believe I owe my employment here to your kindness, against the opinion & wishes of Lord Palmerston, Sir J. Graham & perhaps Lord Grey. My wish is to be of use, & I neither seek for honor nor emolument, therefore if I am not of use get me recalled. I have done my best to uphold the honor & power of England, to protect my countrymen & to make known the liberal & honorable feelings of my Government & I may say successfully, therefore you need not regret having sent me here. My task has at times been a very difficult one, & always a painful one, & made more difficult & more painful by the narrow views & petty jealousies of Admiral Parker – & I am obliged to share in the odium of all his proceedings, of which at times I very much disapprove. His unpopularity here is great, amongst all classes except the Miguelites, Santarem ridicules him, old Native Brown says he is a d——d S of a B, & a Tory, & will not let him into his house. However it is my duty to live on good terms with him & I do so – but he has been a most unfortunate choice for this command. . . .

My family is well, but Bessy is out of humor with the country etc. & I almost wish she had staid at home, & Mrs Rawdon is a terrible burthen, poor woman. If it was to do again, I would not have brought *in* the Fleet or brought *out* my family, but I am a great fool.

Duke of Bedford to Lord William Russell [WP]

Woburn Abbey, Christmas Day 1832

I have sent you for your Christmas cheer at Lisbon, a Stilton cheese, and a good large *pâté de faisans aux truffes*, and the same for Edward, * which I request you will convey to him on board the Nimrod, as soon as you have an opportunity. . . .

None of Lady William's letters to her brother-in-law at this time survives, since she directed him to burn them when read. It may be inferred that they were full of complaints and abuse of the persons around her. Her lifelong Tory sentiments make it a matter of no surprise that her opinions, freely expressed without regard for her husband's position, drew forth the criticism of the English newspapers and their accusation that her husband was completely dominated by her. Lord Brougham wished that Lord William might be recalled, finding him under the thumb of 'that cursed woman'.[8]

Lord John Russell to Lady William Russell [PRP]

Whitehall Jan. 16 [1833]

Your letters are so entertaining that it requires some courage to burn them. However I will execute your orders thereupon. What you say is, I have no doubt, quite true. The business of an Admiral however, is to look punctually to his orders; a Dip. especially on a special mission, is more concerned with the general spirit of his instructions. However I am glad that you have 'mis du coton', & trust all will end smoothly between our high functionaries at Lisbon. Palmerston, you may depend upon it, will give William all the support possible, and S. Canning is a likely fellow to join in his views rather than in those of the Apothecary at Madrid.† . . .

You will see by my letter to Billy that the Duchess is very ill. My own belief is that she has got over the worst – still it has been a serious attack, and will leave her very weak.

* Lord Edward Russell was serving as a naval officer in the *Nimrod*.
† Henry Unwin Addington was envoy extraordinary at Madrid; his cousin Henry Addington, 1st Lord Sidmouth, was known in politics as 'The Doctor'.

I have no time to write any more. Give my love to the boys. Your future prospects must depend on future events. This is as clear as an oracle. We had a great dinner yesterday at Lord Grey's where the new Duchess of Sutherland dined.

When Montalegre, the Spanish Minister, was recalled to Madrid his place was taken by General Cordova,* whom both the Russells found cultivated, intelligent and civilised. If Lord William invested him also with qualities that he had not got, honour and good faith, it was because he was anxious to find these virtues in a man who flattered him with his confidence and declared himself eager to settle the Portuguese question. Cordova's duplicity was ultimately revealed, but the Russells could not foresee what scandals would arise from their friendship with this ambiguous gentleman. An example of the Spanish Agent's use of brightly coloured writing paper was enclosed in the next communication to Lord Palmerston.

Lord William Russell to Lord Palmerston [PP]

Private

Lisbon, 25 January 1833

I am like a man who *knows* there is a large diamond under the ground where he is standing, & having no tools to get at it, begs everyone who passes to assist him, but they laugh at him & declare the diamond only exists in his imagination. I *know* that a pure liberal patriotic feeling exists among a large & the best part of the community here and I cannot make it apparent – so I must adopt the two words in the mouth of every Portuguese – *tomorrow*, and *patience*.

M. de Cordova dined with me yesterday, he is as decided a Miguelite as Montalegre, we have gained nothing. The two enclosed notes will prove to you, that I live on the best terms with the Spanish Agents.

Duke of Bedford to Lord William Russell [WP]

Baron's Court,† Feby 2nd 1833
. . . My keeper at Endsleigh informs me that you had given orders to be supplied with pheasants from home once a week. I regret that you did not

* Luis Fernandez de Cordova (1792–1840) served in the Spanish army and was ambassador to Prussia from 1827 until he went to Lisbon. In 1835 he returned to a successful military career in Spain during the civil war there, but incurring the enmity of Espartero, he died a refugee in Portugal.

† The seat of Lord Abercorn in Co. Tyrone.

communicate your wishes to me, as there are but few pheasants at Ends-leigh, and I wish to encourage them in the woods, which cannot be done if the coverts are disturbed every week. I should have given instructions accordingly. . . .

Lord William Russell to Lord Holland [HH]

Lisbon Feb 15 1833

I must trouble you with a few lines on three things – first to congratulate you on the marriage of Henry * (if you like the marriage), 2ndly to ask you if amongst your Spanish acquaintance you know M. Cordova, the Minister here, & what sort of a man he is. Thirdly to tell you as an admirer of Fielding that no monument is yet put up to his memory here, one was begun, & was stopped for want of funds. Whilst all Europe is subscribing to Sir Walter Scott, a very superior English writer (in my opinion) is left without a stone over his grave. This is a national disgrace.

I know how much you like Fielding's writings, as well as your neighbour the Duke of Sussex, so amongst us I think we might repair this neglect.

We are all well, & as happy as people can be in the midst of this misery, & join in love to Lady Holland.

Lord John Russell to Lady William Russell [PRP]

Feb. 22. 1833.

I am glad you write so much, & am very much amused by your letters, which I put in the fire as commanded.

I am a bad correspondent, & worse during the session of parliament, but I will write when I can. Our new house is very tiresome, as indeed the old was, but does not keep such late hours. We have numbers of practical men of business, very fair & moderate men, but not shining or genteel. This is what I always expected, & indeed wished, but it is not lively.

The Duchess is rather better, but her lungs are certainly affected, & it will take her a long time to recover. It is as you say, she would now be a loss to her children, & I must say I should be very sorry to see her illness take a bad turn.

Our master is come to town, & has a *levée* today. The splendour of his

---

* Henry Fox married, in 1833, Lady Mary Augusta Coventry, daughter of the 8th Earl of Coventry.

reign is past, but if he is prudent, he will still be popular. Her Majesty always contrives some way of putting herself ill with us plebeian world.

The spring brought no great change in the situation. Dom Pedro's supplies were reported to be exhausted and it seemed probable that after all Miguel might win.

Lord William Russell to Lord Palmerston [PP]

Private

Lisbon, 16 March 1833

M. de Cordova has made a long despatch out of a conversation that took place between himself, Viscount Santarem & me. I have not seen it and am convinced that he is not capable of putting words into my mouth that I did not use, but in case it should be quoted to you, I wish to tell you it is the mere *bavardage* of diplomacy & means nothing, for I told them that I was only here to observe the military proceedings of Spain. . . .

Duke of Bedford to Lord William Russell [WP]

London, March 25 1833

. . . You were served right about the stinking pheasants for not applying at once to the fountain head – how could my people at Endsleigh be supposed to know any thing about packing & sending game to a distance. If you had written to me you should have had as many pheasants as you please quite fresh – at all events you have had more good *pâtés aux truffes*, to regale the noses and stomachs of your Portuguese with. You have heard a good story of 100 doz. of peaches at Endsleigh, but like many others it wants the simple ingredient of truth – it would be sending coals to New-castle indeed, to send preserves to Lisbon, which is the very land of *con-fitures*.

Duke of Bedford to Lord William Russell [WP]

W.A. April 7. 1833

. . . Thanks for your flowers – the *Diosma Ericoides* is a very fragrant plant, but a greenhouse plant with us, as it will not stand our climate – the only botanical hint you gave me was incorrect – the yellow flower was not *trifolium* but an *oxalis* – the leaves are trefoil, but the flowers are totally dissimilar to the trifolium tribe, the *oxalis* is in English the cuckoo bread.

I hope things are going on well in the Cabinet now, but I know nothing. John comes here on Wednesday but he never tells me any thing.

. . . When you come home, any seeds or plants, natives of Portugal will be acceptable.

Lord John Russell to Lady William Russell [PRP]

April 9 [1833]

My dear Betty, you must be heartily tired of your Portuguese pilgrimage, & I see by William's letters that he heartily wishes it over. But we cannot neglect for that 'the sacred duty of neutrality'. Pedro must be allowed to play his pranks till his money is out, and then I daresay he will be glad to compound the matter.

In the meantime we are all ill here. A single day struck down Palmerston, Graham, Althorp, P. Thomson, Peel, and your humble servant. It is a sort of epidemy called the *grippe*, and like the cholera comes from Russia – it is a sad pity Muscovy ever was admitted into the good society of Europe! by and by we shall get from them the leprosy, the plague and God knows what beside.

I dined yesterday with the Lievens, who are an exception to all rule against the Russians. Talleyrand was there very agreable and easy. He was bitter against Mme de Staël who he said was very ugly when she cried – *elle pleurait comme une Genevoise*. Ld Holland has got the gout. M. Dedel the ague. The Dss. still very unwell – so we are all confined in this free-born climate as Lady Holland calls it. . . .

How comes it that Leopold has given William his order?* He must write to our King to ask permission to wear it. Fox's marriage is never mentioned by his parents. The brides of last year, Lady Lincoln, Lady Sydney, & Lady Newark are all the ornaments of our parties, & are very fond of their husbands, which gives unspeakable disgust. You had better write to Palmerston for anything you want great or small. Very likely he won't give it to you. I am going to Woburn tomorrow for 1–2–3–4–days of holiday & then work till August at least.

* The Order of Leopold of Belgium (1st Class).

Diplomacy

Lord Palmerston to Lord William Russell [PP]

Private

F.O. 2 May 1833

... Do not place too much confidence in Cordova, it is evident he is a mere tool of Zea's* and that all his boasting about the acts of liberality, moderation or grace which he would obtain from Don Miguel are of no more value than the twaddle which I have so often been doomed to listen to from Zea on the same subject & which was only meant to humbug me & to lead me on by expectations which he cared little whether he should ever be able to realise. . . .

I do not mean by this that you should be in any degree less cordial with Cordova than you have been, but place no confidence in him. . . .

I own I should much rejoice at the triumph of rational & liberal principles in Portugal because the Arbitrary governments have chosen to make the Peninsula the arena & Pedro & Miguel the champions for fighting the fight of the conflicting principles which agitate Europe and the success of the genius of evil in Portugal would be not merely a triumph but an encouragement.

We do not mean to leave you with less than the *Asia* & a three decker in the Tagus. . . .

Miguel's Government must come to terms about the Oporto wine question, & permit our merchants there to export their wines . . . paying duty to Miguel, and without enquiring whether they also pay duty to Pedro who has joint command of the river.

If you see Santarem tell him this is a serious matter upon which we shall stand no nonsense & that he had better give us an early as well as a satisfactory answer. Our merchants are growing clamorous and if he is contumacious they will halloo us on to measures of violence against Miguel which we shall not be sorry to be urged to have recourse to.

Duke of Bedford to Lord William Russell [WP]

Belgrave Square, May 3. 1833

... I have sent your dried flower to Forbes this morning, but I doubt whether he will be able to make anything of it, as there are no leaves on the stalk. I would ask you to send me a collection of ranunculus roots, but I fear I should be able to make nothing of them, without you could send the

* Viscount Zea Bermudez, the Spanish Prime Minister.

10+L.W.R. 271

climate with them. I have more than once imported *les belles ranuncules de Portugal* but have never succeeded in getting either size or colour. I always used to admire the gay assemblage on the verandas, of beautiful ranunculi & glazed tiles, with their scriptural stories, and legends of saints – the whole together made a brilliant appearance.

. . . Give my love to Lady William and tell her I hope to write to her soon *tout de bon*. She will say I have been a long while about it. Your bairns now will begin to feel the heat, and stench of Lisbon, but Cintra is always cool and fresh. John tells me that she means to come to England next month. If she comes to Plymouth or Falmouth, I hope to give her the accolade at Endsleigh. If the Duchess is well enough to move we shall probably go there this month, but she is much thrown back by a severe attack of the prevailing influenza, and her cough and sleepless nights are as bad as ever.

Lord William Russell to Lord Palmerston [PP]

Private

Lisbon, 4 May 1833

. . . M. Cordova has procured the release from prison of one lady, the wife of General George d'Avilez, who is now in my house. . . . I have been overwhelmed with abuse here by the ultra-liberal party for associating with Mr Cordova, but I think you will approve of it when you see what a link he is to me, to communicate with the Portuguese government & recommend humane & moderate measures, which I do rather as a private individual than as a public agent, & as Mr Cordova knows that as long as England withholds her acknowledgement from Don Miguel, all his labours are in vain, he endeavours that I should not paint the devil blacker than he is. Of course I never allow him to meddle with English affairs, (which he would willingly do if not checked). . . . I have thought it right to give you this explanation of my intimacy with Cordova because the newspapers & others have accused him of making dissensions amongst the English & French agents, & between Hoppner, the Admiral & myself, in which there is not one word of truth. . . .

Duke of Bedford to Lord William Russell [WP]

Endsleigh, 29 May 1833

I will enquire the price of the water engines we use here for our gardens, and then if you please I can send you one by sea from London to Lisbon.

Diplomacy

It would not be worth while to make a model for so small an implement, nor would a Portuguese be probably able to make one from the model – we understand these things better in England than anywhere. My roller that you mention, is nothing but a cast iron garden roller, with a box over it to carry off the turf that is mown – so it does two operations at once – rolls and casts away, but there is no watering attached to it. It is drawn by two burros * in boots. If you like I can send you a boot, and any Portuguese shoemaker can boot these patient animals – when I was at Cintra, Madame Guildenmeister (the Dutch Consul's wife) had a lawn of about a quarter of an acre, which was sown with camomile and other seeds which gave a fragrant smell to the turf as you walked over it; but the best seeds your friend can sow to get a good turf, are the Dutch clover (*trifolium repens*) and the yarrow (*Achillea millefolium*) which latter never burns and is always green, with the Dutch clover it will *mat* into a close turf. I am glad you have got Quintella's *quinta* at Larengeiras but nothing equal to Cintra in summer in point of coolness – I am amazed at Lady William not admiring Cintra . . . .

Duke of Bedford to Lord William Russell [WPP]

Endsleigh, May 30. [1833]
My birthday present to you consists, I believe in my good wishes and warmest affections, and I have no recollections of having sent any other. My labyrinth in the pleasure ground at Woburn is finished, and a very pretty thing it is. I have planted it with the usual *charmille* of hornbeam but I shall take your hint and put in some roses and honeysuckles to climb round the hornbeam which will have a pretty effect, and *égayer* the *ensemble*. Our English ladies walk in good waterproof shoes so there is no chance of their getting wet, even in our damp climate. Your Portuguese shoes would soon be wet through. You must bring me some Chinese bells and shew me how they are hung to produce a sound. . . .†

Lord John Russell to Lady William Russell [PRP]

June 13 [1833]
I am very glad, my dear Bessy, to find by your letter of the 1st that you took my refusal so well. I think upon third thoughts you indeed agree

* 'donkeys'.
† The palace at Bemfica near Lisbon was hung with glass bells that sounded in the wind.

with me very much in the end, so you and Hoppner must jog on together, if not lovingly, on terms of civility.

Nothing very interesting here to you. I am glad you are out of Lisbon, as I expect to hear that the contest has been carried on and decided in the streets of that town. I imagine the Portuguese care very little about it, provided we do not insist they should be clean. . . .

I am very sorry you are not to be here in June.

Lord Palmerston to Lord William Russell [PP]
Private

F.O. 14 June 1833

. . . I daresay all you tell me of Cordova's personal character is perfectly true, but I judge the diplomatist and I know who he is employed by. Remember all the fine things he promised to accomplish for us by changing & liberalizing the conduct of Miguel's Government & see whether he has fulfilled any one of the expectations he held out. On the contrary Miguel's Government becomes more intractable instead of more docile, & shapes its course not according to Cordova's advice but according to the number of ships we have in the Tagus. . . . With all possible respect therefore to M. Cordova, I shall wait till I see some results from his fine speeches, or letters however well written, before I attach any value to the language he is instructed to hold.

Lord William Russell to Lord Palmerston [PP]
Private

Lisbon 17 June 1833

. . . Cordova is still at Coimbra . . . he is now as decided an enemy to Don Miguel as we could wish. I know you believe that this is all acting on the part of Cordova but I assure you that he is sincere. I have told Hoppner that I would answer for his sincerity, but he chooses to persevere in his first impressions, however you will one day know that I was right.

Three weeks later he made his last protestation of faith in the Spaniard. 'I must repeat again & do so more sincerely because you are prepossessed against him, that my friend Cordova has conducted himself like an honest and enlightened man.'[9]

In July, Captain Charles Napier,* replacing Sartorius in the command of

* Charles Napier (1786–1860) K.C.B. 1840; admiral 1858. He wrote *An account of the War in Portugal*. To avoid the penalties of Foreign Enlistment he went out under the name of Carlos de Ponza.

Pedro's fleet, proceeded to attack and destroy all Miguel's ships in an action off Cape St Vincent. Lisbon was rapidly evacuated, Donna Maria proclaimed Queen, and Lord William was directed to present his credentials as Minister at her Court. Those who had lately been the oppressed became the oppressors. Refugees again resorted to the Russells' house and they found themselves abused for their humanity and for their kindness to all sufferers without regard for their political creed. For some time there was a danger that the Frenchman, General Bourmont,* who was in command of Miguel's army, would recapture Lisbon.

'Does Mrs Rawdon fear the usual consequences that follow a city taken by storm?' asked Poodle Byng in a letter to Lord William.[10]

Lord William Russell to Lord Palmerston [PP]

Private

Lisbon, 25 July 1833

... As for my friend Cordova we have got him on the nail, & can smash him when we please like a wild goose (which he is). He went over to see the fight, disembarked in the midst of the flight, was made prisoner, well beat, & carried before Villaflor,† who knew him, treated him kindly & sent him back. We have every right to accuse him of a breach of neutrality in being in the engagement, & I shall not let him off on easy terms. I have told him that I should make a formal complaint to you.

Lord Lynedoch to Lady William Russell [NLS]

Stratton Street. 28 July, 1833

I need not say how delighted I was to receive your letter, tho' it began by a severe scolding, aggravated, unfairly, on your part, by a charge against me of breach of promise of attending you to Lisbon – now to reply to such a charge I can only admit that, when you made me so flattering a proposal, my answer was, that nothing could be more agreeable to me, should circumstances allow of my absenting myself from this country – now certainly no such favourable circumstances ever did occur as to enable me, by any exertion to leave this part of the world.

A proof of this, is that I had waited impatiently for a release of parliamentary duties to have the operation on my eyes performed by Alexander,

* Comte Louis de Bourmont (1773–1846); he conquered Algeria for the French in 1830.
† Count Villaflor, Duke of Terceira (1790–1860) commanded the land forces of Dom Pedro.

and it was not till towards the middle of July last summer that I was able to settle a day with him for that purpose. A month's confinement was the necessary consequence of this, you were by that time quite out of reach, & business of the utmost consequence to my private affairs, made my going into Scotland an imperative duty. I was detained there till the beginning of this year, ever since my return to the south I have been obliged to be at the call of duty in parliament, & being in daily expectation of hearing of your landing in Britain as you should have done under all the circumstances of the case. But with all your admirable qualities & talents (which I will not attempt to enumerate) there is a spirit of adventure at bottom in your character, which twists your judgement to its purpose & stifles the calls of reason to other duties – then you detail me gravely all jarring propensities & ask me to tell you to what sect you belong. However you may detest tyranny in the abstract you are certainly not liberal – you hate & would shoot out the 'profanum vulgus' as much as the parasite Horace wish'd to do. You must then stop the march of intellect, by stifling education. It is no longer possible – and if attempted, it will only hasten the fall of despotic governments. This is my firm belief. There are mad ultras however who wish to bring on the struggle in the vain hope of replacing things as they were.

On 2 August Mr Hoppner wrote privately to Lord Palmerston that 'such was the precipitation with which Don Miguel's ministers fled from Lisbon in the night of the 23 ult., that it did not occur to them to destroy or carry off, their official & private correspondence, which has accordingly fallen into the hands of Don Pedro's government. I have been allowed the hasty perusal of the contents of one of M. de Santarem's portfolios & even to retain a few letters and papers found therein. These I have now the honour to enclose conceiving they may not be devoid of all interest to your Lordship, as well as extracts from the remainder as I had time to make while they were in my possession.'[11]

Among the documents he enclosed were several letters from the Spanish Agent to Viscount Santarem. They revealed Cordova's wholehearted devotion to the cause of Dom Miguel, his intimacy with Miguel's Prime Minister, and the current use he made of Lord William Russell as a source of information. One of these letters was written on bright green paper. Lord Palmerston, more astute (or better informed) than his Agent, wrote to Lord William that one of the intrigues with which Cordova was charged by his government was to set by the ears 'le consul et le commissaire'. That Cordova relished what he had successfully contrived will be seen in his letter of 23 June that Palmerston showed Lord William when he returned to

England.* Malice must be suspected in Hoppner's selection of papers he sent to his chief. The name 'Russell' introduced into the margin of Cordova's letter as a source of information, if compared with the name as it appears in despatches written by Hoppner, suggests that he was indeed prompted to this act of spite by his dislike of Lord William and his wife, who had found it impossible to bear him out in his violent partisanship for Dom Pedro. The storm that blew up when the Russells returned to England was centred on these letters from Santarem's portfolio. Lord William, who had placed his confidence in the Spaniard, felt himself to be not only a fool but a man who might have unwittingly injured his country's interests; and his chaste, if impetuous, wife was ridiculed for an imaginary love affair.

Lord William Russell to Lord Palmerston [PP]

Private

Lisbon, 7 August 1833

... Pedro and his *canaille* are playing the deuce. . . . The moment he heard that Lisbon was taken off he came. I went to see him on arriving – his head was turned with success – & his manner (not his words) towards England & France was as insolent as possible. I afterwards dined with him, & a more offensive dinner I never was present at. He gave the precedence to Hoppner to mark his preference of revolutionary principle to mine, it was evident that neither the King of England, his Minister or his Navy were in any favor with him. . . .

Duke of Bedford to Lord William Russell [WPP]

London August 7, 1833

We have no intelligence from Lisbon the last two days, but I trust by this time everything is peaceably established there, Donna Maria da Gloria on the throne *de facto* as well as *de jure*, and you will immediately be appointed here, and accredited there minister plenipo – to her most faithful Majesty. Lady William must console herself for the overthrow of D. Miguel's usurpation, by assuming the dignity of *Madame l'Ambassadrice*. I omitted in my last to answer your question about your Spanish horse. If he is as you represent him, I will take him with pleasure at 37 *moidores*, and if you will tell me what this is at the present rate of exchange, I will pay the money to your account at Child's. You must find some means

* See pp. 310, 311.

of sending him to London. I hope he is not too high – 14½ hands is the size I like, but if he should be more than 15, I cannot get on without difficulty. Was the old Spanish horse I gave Brown, alive at the old gentleman's death? if he was, I hope they will shoot him, and not allow him to be beat about in a Lisbon chaise. I see Lady William's friend, the pheasant pie Spaniard, has been making a fool of himself, and getting himself taken prisoner in a rhodomontade escapade for D. Miguel.

Lord Palmerston to Lord William Russell [PP]
Private

F.O. 12 August 1833.
I presume you will have presented your credentials and therefore I write to Hoppner to tell him that his functions have ceased. We cannot have at the same time a Minister & a quasi Minister & he could not drop down to only a Consul, after having so long exercised higher functions. . . .

Lord William Russell to Lord Palmerston [PP]
Private

Lisbon, 16 August 1833
. . . Allow me to thank you most sincerely for the confidence you have placed in me & the kindness you have had to appoint me to this special mission. I will discharge my duties of it to the best of my abilities, and I will request Hoppner to continue the important affairs relating to commerce till he hears from you. He is a man of the most impracticable temper I ever met with. Sour, suspicious, malignant, vain, irritable, envious, heartless & false, but clever & zealous. He has an amiable wife & two children & for their sakes I hope he will receive the rewards he so justly deserves for the assiduity & ability with which he discharged his duties here.

You will find Parker's opinion of him to be the same as mine – the old Admiral on further acquaintance I have found true & honest as a British sailor, with the soundest judgement & great firmness. . . .

Can you tell me without inconvenience how long you think I shall remain? I ask the question on account of private arrangements. I have lived as a Brigadier with military economy but as a Minister it would be necessary to take a larger house, give a few dinners etc.,etc. Expences I would not enter into if it was your intention to replace me soon. . . .

Diplomacy

Duke of Bedford to Lord William Russell [WPP]

Nuneham, August 20. [1833]
I accept your Chinese ducks for my menagerie with thanks. Edward will bring them home, if he is coming, which I trust he is, for he still complains of his health. I am sorry that the pheasants eggs came to nothing, but it was not my fault, for they were sent off fresh – probably the sea water in the packet destroyed them. Your satire about the Campden Hill breakfasts is misapplied in the present instance, as not a single strawberry or cup of tea has been given them this year. Economy and retrenchment have been as much the order of the day with us, as with Joseph Hume, and the House of Commons. . . . You are aware that very little port wine is consumed in my house since I discontinued it in the Steward's room – not more than a pipe in two years. If you could send me so small a quantity as a pipe or two, I should be glad of it. *Bucellas* is seldom drunk in this country, and I am amply supplied with as much as I shall ever want, by a present from old Native* some time since.

Lord John Russell to Lady William Russell [PRP]

Aug 23 [1833]
. . . Hoppner is before this time removed from his brief authority. No doubt he has done much mischief, but it is likewise true that Miguel's people have been long intriguing to get him removed & it was not desirable to give them a triumph. I do not believe he has given up William's letters to Pedro's Ministers. I believe on the contrary that they gave them up to him. This is at least what appears in the face of our accounts. You will rejoice if Bourmont returns to Lisbon. . . .

Lord William Russell to Lord Palmerston [PP]
Private

Lisbon, 26 August 1833
. . . My brother John sent me a note of yours in which you say you have promised Lisbon, but will employ me elsewhere. I am ready to serve when & where you please – and care not how soon my successor arrives, for this is no bed of roses, & Hoppner has stuck a great many thorns into

* See p. 249 n.

it, by having made himself an Agent of Don Pedro's & encouraged our consuls to do the same, that is the reason we are not let into Vigueras. There is a low democratical French party here who had got Hoppner completely into their hands. He is gone home in this packet to ask you for something, let me advise you to send him to Poland or Petersburgh.

Shall you keep me here this winter? I ask on Lady William's account, who has been driven away from Cintra by the guerillas.

Lord John Russell to Lady William Russell [PRP]

Aug. 29 [1833]

I have received your 'voluminous letters'. It is really time that you should learn to be a Whig, for it is not useful, decent, or respectable to malign the Government under which your husband is acting, and the leaders under whom he has always acted. But it appears that you think Toryism more genteel, it may be so – but baser hearts than those which often 'lurk beneath a star' I do not know.

Palmerston will let you know in his own time when William is to return. I rather think you may as well come away for the winter, but you will see. Now Hoppner is come away I hope you will take some chicory *tisane pour rafraîchir le sang*, and get into good humour again.

Papa is gone to Leamington, the Duchess to Scotland, I am going to Ireland, and we have all got holidays for five months. I think if you do not come home this winter to live in England you ought to give up your place about the Queen, which is a sinecure – but of that hereafter. I long to have a good talk with you.

Lord Palmerston to Lord William Russell [PP]

Private

F.O. 30 August 1833

... You exhaust upon Hoppner all the epithets which the language affords, but you do him great injustice; of all the things which you say, those which describe a little irritability of temper & sensitiveness of character are alone deserved. It was one of the political intrigues with which Cordova was charged, to set you and Hoppner by the ears, & he seems to have succeeded pretty well; judging at least from your letters, for from Hoppner I have had no ventings.

I hope you & Admiral Parker will get on good terms with Pedro & his Government; you both of you coquetted with the Miguelites & it was not surprizing that at first Pedro should have shown a preference for Hoppner, but all that is now over.

Lord William Russell to Lord Palmerston [PP]

Private

Lisbon, 7 September 1833.

... I beg of you to understand that I do not hold here the language of my private letters to you, which are intended to let you behind the curtain. ... I do everything to uphold the Government & make it respected. Pedro & I are the best of friends. ... Pedro wants to found his government upon the support of the middle & lower classes. This might do if they were as virtuous & well educated as they are in England, but here they are very little less corrupt than the nobles. Many of my friends who I thought the purest patriots have turned out to be mere hunters after place & money. Pedro always receives from 9 till 10. I go there sometimes as a duty. The last night I was there I found three merchants' wives, & half a dozen unwashed citizens, not one person of family. This will not do in this aristocratical country. ... perhaps when the Empress comes she may alter all this.

You *taquiner* me for having coquetted with Don Miguel; with him personally, *never*, but I always was for an amicable arrangement & Donna Maria, & now regret more than ever that it could not have been brought about. I have seen more human misery in the 15 months I have been here, than in all the rest of my life. Fathers, sons, brothers, wives, sisters tearing each other to pieces. If I could have guessed what I was to have gone thro when you first gave me the appointment I would not have accepted it for any rank or salary you could have offered. ...

Lord John Russell to Lord William Russell [WPP]

Endsleigh, Sept. 16, 1833.

I think you could not give me a better proof of what I said than by telling me that the Whigs have not so much the character of gentleman as the Tories. Compare the two administrations. Lord Grey you admit was a perfect gentleman – full as much as the Duke of Wellington. Althorp next to Lord Grey is the most perfect gentleman I ever saw, and it is because he is so much a gentleman that he has such complete command over the House of Commons. What was Goulburn? a mere clerk. Melbourne is a thorough gentleman. Peel, tho' a very honest man is no gentleman. Now Lord Brougham, whatever else you may say of him, is quite as much a gentleman as Lyndhurst. And even our worst are superior to Herries, who according to Lord Dudley was 'no gentleman'. With all this I do not mean to deny that the Tories are generally gentlemen. The Whigs and Tories in fact are parties of gentlemen. The Radicals are not. You must be strangely prejudiced not to see this. It is the constant reproach made to us by the democratic party that we are aristocratic. I thank God we are too much so to do anything mean or dirty. As for Lord Holland, poor man, he meant well all the time, but persuaded himself that you did not wish to stay at Lisbon – no doubt his wife suggested it – and this is his fault – he is lax in his principles, but I never knew him do an ill-natured thing to anyone.

Lord Palmerston to Lord William Russell [PP]

Private

Windsor, 21 September 1833

... I can assure you that whether I *taquiner* you or not, we are all very much pleased with you & think you have acted extremely well in very difficult circumstances. I have no doubt that your judgement of Pedro is perfectly correct.

Lord John Russell to Lord William Russell [WPP]

[September 1833]

You are quite wrong to be angry with Lord Howard.* It was not his fault but 'an untoward event' that he should be named to succeed you. He is a gentleman and a man of his word – and by no means bit by Hoppner, who is now low enough with every body. Come home yourself – even if you leave your children at Lisbon, and return for them. It will do you a world of good to state your own honest and plain tale to put down a whole crew of critics.

I have another reason for wishing you to come home, which I cannot at present mention – it concerns, however, your future destination.

* Charles Ellis, 6th Baron Howard de Walden, later 2nd Baron Seaford (1799–1868) had been appointed to succeed Lord William at Lisbon.

Diplomacy

Duke of Bedford to Lady William Russell [PRP]

W.A. Oct 4, 1833.

I have long been intending to answer your amiable & entertaining letter of the 6th ult., but my good intentions have been as often frustrated, as it is probable that we may now have the pleasure of seeing you here soon for your master (Lord Palmerston) tells me you are to be in England soon after Christmas. I will not now enter into any of the details of your despatch and more especially what regards newspapers, for I have a thorough contempt to them all, and would therefore most strongly advise you not to dirty your fingers by entering into any controversial disputations with these gentlemen. I believe Tories and Radicals have abused you equally, and the only portion of the press, which is exempt from scandalous and degrading proceedings, is that which belongs to the Whigs, so I hope you will at least do us that justice. Your account of your reported Love is very amusing, and from what you say of him, I suspect his *tendresse* was excited rather by the *pâté de faisans aux truffes* than by your own personal charms. By the by, I hope William received the last I sent him.

As they could not find a slipper small enough to match Cinderella's glass one, so in an inverse ratio, no saddle could be found large enough for the dimensions of her most faithful Majesty, and I rejoice to hear that they were successful when they came to yours. . . .

Looking to your arrival towards the end of the year or the beginning of the new one, I shall kill the fatted calf for your return, and cover up my best tables, that they may not be ruined by the profusion of ink you throw over them.

Lord Palmerston to Lord William Russell [PP]

Private

F.O. 4 October, 1833.

I have at length settled my arrangements about the mission at Lisbon, & Howard de Walden will be there in about a month's time. The result of this transfer will be to make Studgart vacant, & if that post would be agreeable to you, I should have great pleasure in offering it to you. . . . The King of Wirtemberg being himself a soldier would be pleased at having a military man at his Court & Lady William would probably find Studgart not a disagreeable residence.

Lord John Russell to Lord William Russell [WP]

Elm Park, Oct. 13 [1833]
Palmerston tells me he has offered you Stutgardt. I hope you will accept it, as I think it will do very well for your family, & you will be of great use in watching the progress of the Liberals of Germany. I shall be glad that you are rid of the dirty Portuguese. . . .
The Pay Office is open to you day and night.

Among paragraphs that appeared in *The Age* during September were these: 'Hoppner's Hop. People are inquiring we hear, why Mr Hoppner, late Consul at Lisbon, has been recalled; the real reason, we understand, is as follows: – Lady William Russell and Mrs Hoppner could not put up their horses together, and Lady Russell vowed she would not stop a moment in Lisbon if the saucy Swiss was not sent about her business so Hoppner and spouse – hopped.'
'Lord William Russell is recalled from Lisbon, at his own *pressing* solicitation; the *urgency* of some *private* affairs requiring his immediate attention in this country. Lady William was, we hear, most anxious to visit – Cordova.'[12]

Duke of Bedford to Lord William Russell [WPP]

London, Oct, 21, 1833.
The radical press continue to attack Lady William and yesterday I hear the *Age* which you know is a Tory paper, had a violent article against her; but as this is a *respectable* paper which I make it a rule never to look at, I know nothing of it – pray give my love to her, and tell her I have received her long letter, which I will answer very shortly. She defends herself with eloquence, and with some vehemence, against the attacks which have been made on her, and in her defence of herself, I must own she does not spare the Whigs, for whom she appears to have a natural hatred. . . .
. . . As Lord Palmerston has offered you Stutgard I suppose you will accept it – it is a good beginning for a diplomatick career and they say the present Court is very agreeable – only let Lady William steer clear of the Duke of Cumberland and all German intrigues, for I daresay, that though Stutgard is far removed from Berlin, he extends his salutary influence over the whole circle of the Empire. . . .

Diplomacy

Lord John Russell to Lord William Russell [WPP]

Althorp, Oct. 27, 1833

You have done right in accepting Stutgart, but I think you are mistaken when you say that it is intended to put you on the shelf. Lord Howard, it appears from his brother's account, had long wished to be sent to Lisbon before all other places, and at some time or other got a promise of it from Palmerston. When P. said he could not offer you Lisbon permanently you professed you had no wish to remain there, and pressed to know when you were to come away – so that every thing that has taken place has been in regular course.

I shall willingly assent in obtaining your wish to stay till the urgency of the military question is over. Some paragraphs in the *Globe* may have annoyed you; they did me, and I shall endeavour to find their source. However both Lord Grey and Palmerston are entirely satisfied with your conduct. As to Stutgart it is a place where you may learn all the sayings and doings of Germany, of which I know little, and of which we have no good reporter. In doing this you will fit yourself for other and more important situations; and for my part I shall always be ready to do what is best for you. . . .

Love to Lady William – she treats all my advice with contempt.

Duke of Bedford to Lord William Russell [WPP]

Woburn Abbey, Oct. 31, 1833.

I am sorry to have given you any offence by the foolish paragraphs I cut out of the newspapers, it was not my intention. When I see the names of any of my own children, or my near connexions in the papers I take in, I naturally read the article, and I sent you them, from the best and purest of motives, that you might see what an ill natured and gossiping world was saying of Lady William simply that you might put her on her guard. I was told that she was continually abused in the *Age* (which I believe is a Tory paper, but I have never seen it). I refused, however, to look at it – there let the subject rest – I have done with it. . . .

Duke of Bedford to Lady William Russell [PRP]

W.A. Oct 31 1833

I received your long and argumentative letter on the subject of your position at Lisbon, Portuguese politicks &c.&c., in due course, (in the mercantile phrase) and now take up my pen to answer it, though it must be very briefly, for I have neither taste nor leisure for politicks. I am an old man, and no politician, and shall be well content to be laid on the shelf, till my last hour comes, be it sooner or later. You defend yourself with much eloquence, and with some warmth; but you have a right to do so where you think yourself unjustly attacked. My advice to a woman is never to meddle with politicks. I have given this advice over and over again to Lady Jersey (who is the warmest female politician I know) but I fear she does not attend to my advice – however we never communicate on politicks – what I am far more anxious about, is the welfare of your children, and I cannot help feeling that it is quite time now, that Hastings should go to school. He is a delightful boy, and you must excuse me for adding, that he is too old to be under the guidance of a Mama, or what is vulgarly called 'tied to his mother's apron strings'. Turn this in your mind.

I cannot recommend to you at this *triste* season of the year to go to Endsleigh – *dans la belle saison*, you must some day or other come and see it – however at present we have no female servants there, to receive you. The housekeeper and *Cakie* (as they call her in Devonshire) i.e. kitchen-maid, are with the Duchess in Scotland.

Have you fixed any time for leaving Lisbon? As I have heard Lord Howard is going very soon, and that the military question is settled, I suppose you will all come away together. I regret to hear from William that Odo has got the scarlatina, but I trust it will prove but slight.

Stutgard will I daresay be a pleasant residence, as I am told the Court is agreeable, and of course you have nothing but the Court in such a little place as Stutgard – avoid politics as you would plague and pestilence, whether German or English.

Duke of Bedford to Lord William Russell [WPP]

London, Nov. 13, 1833

I assure you no one can more sincerely rejoice than I do, in any thing that can tend to your comfort, and to your professional honour, whether civil or military. Nothing can be more flattering to you than Lord Palmerston's conduct, and I learn with pleasure that both he and Lord Grey are completely satisfied with the manner in which you have fulfilled an arduous and difficult mission. I regret that Lady William should have made herself the object of vulgar newspaper animadversions, but as she has been equally the subject of Radical and Tory abuse, I trust it may be a lesson to her in future, never to run into that dangerous course to a woman, political contention. When she goes to Stutgard, let her be what she ought to be, neither Whig nor Tory neither Austrian nor Italian, but simply the English Minister's wife, giving grace and dignity to her station, and lending a charm to the society of his house, which must always make her loved and respected wherever she may be – this is the advice of an old man, not quite superannuated, but nearly so. . . .

I will have some pies made for you and sent to Lisbon. . . .

'I much regret Mrs Rawdon went to Lisbon,' wrote Lord John to his brother, 'people attribute to her much of the evil.'[13] Princess Lieven wrote Lady Cowper a malicious account of the stories going round London, in which she blamed Lady William for interfering in Portuguese politics and 'for showing especial favour to Mr Cordova. . . . This Cordova is very handsome and intelligent. His papers fell into the hands of the Pedroites at the taking of Lisbon, and among them were discovered little green and pink *billet doux* which contained a mixture of politics, literature and other matters, addressed by Lady William to the Spanish Minister. . . . It is the Hollands who are most excited about the affair, and since Lady Holland is the only one who has talked about the affair, omitting the amorous side of it which she condones, no harm has come of it all, apart from her saying of Lady William that she thinks her imperious nature and love of domination very difficult to forgive. . . .'[14]

Duke of Bedford to Lord William Russell [WP]

W.A., Nov. 19, 1833.

Your game pies will be sent off today to Falmouth, to be forwarded to you by Messrs Fox. – viz. 1 of pheasants only – 1 of pheasants and partridges mixed – both *aux truffes* they are in Wéry's *grand talent*, so I hope they may be acceptable at Lisbon, and I am rather glad that Cordova is not there to partake of them – in Alava's well known phraseology 'c'est un coquin de la premier classa'!

The *Spectator* (the best written of the radical papers) goes on abusing Lady William, and now has got to you. On Sunday last, he says you are 'perfectly incapable, and completely governed by Lady William and that Lord Palmerston never could have employed you, but because you are my son' – what have you done to offend the editor? I suppose he has been at Lisbon to pick up news and you did not ask him to dinner. . . .

Diplomacy

I hope you will not forget my mendicant requests, and treat me as a common beggar without noticing them. Portuguese ranunculi and carnations – particularly the yellow – to these I would add a bag of the incense – the same as old Brown used to send me – the best I ever had. Addios! Love to Lady William and your bairns.

Duke of Bedford to Lord William Russell [WPP]

Woburn Abbey, December 7 1833

You attack me most unjustly (as you are too apt to do) which I trust I shall be able to prove in my defence. Your official seal went some time ago, and is now in all probability in the Bay of Biscay, or in the Tagus. You did not tell me that you wished it engraved on steel, so I had it cut on a fine red cornelian with a bloodstone handle. As soon as I knew your wish to have an Inchings Park cheese, I sent for one, but was informed that Mrs Bennett had ceased making them. The moment I knew you wished to have pheasant pies, I directed Mr Wéry to put forth all his talents to make two super-excellent ones and the enclosed will prove that they have at least left Falmouth, and if the *James Watt* has not delivered them into your *garde-manger*, the fault is not mine, so let me in future beg of you to be a little more just in your attacks, or you will be but a bad negotiator in diplomacy. . . .

Give my love and blessings to your boys, and tell Odo I am delighted to find that he is collecting acorns for me in the Penha Verde gardens, that I will sow them and make a plantation with the produce, and call it Odo plantation. I wish you to send me the acorns of all the genus *quercus* or *ilex*, natives of Portugal, as I am now about to form an *arboretum*, and the genus *quercus* will naturally be my foundation, and pray do not forget a collection of the *ranunculi*, and carnations and *picotées*. Gardening is my hobby horse, and chief occupation and amusement so you must forgive all this trouble.

Duke of Bedford to Lady William Russell [PRP]

W.A. Dec 18. 1833.

I have received your long tirade against newspapers and their calumnies and falsehoods. You must excuse me for saying that I think you are throwing away your eloquence, as they are utterly beneath contempt.

As for myself, neither my health nor my inclination fit me for such discussions, so I beg they may be dropped for ever.

[*endorsed by Lady William*: He cut out all the abusive paragraphs in the Sunday papers & sent them to me expressing his sorrow at my having made myself an object of political abuse & hoping it would be a lesson!!! to me.! upon which I answered as may be supposed drawing his attention to the recent lies about other people just contradicted 'on authority' & therefore wondering he should not suppose the newspapers might be equally mistaken about me. This is the sensible answer to my answer.]

Lord William's natural touchiness led him to imagine an intended slight in the appointment of Lord Howard de Walden to succeed him at Lisbon. Accepting and then declining the post of Wurtemberg, he voiced his irritation to his brother John who answered: 'It is rather hard I must say when I endeavour to do everything that may make your life useful & honourable that you should express feelings so different at one time & another. Lady William is at least on this occasion more reasonable.'[15] Lord William wrote to Palmerston in December: 'I therefore resign it [Stuttgart] . . . but should you hereafter have any mission where I could be of use, & do not think me utterly incapable I shall be glad to have active employment . . . & when these Portuguese imbroglios clear up, you will know whether my views have been as erroneous as they are reported to have been, & by that judge whether I am fit to be employed in diplomacy.'[16]

Lord John Russell to Lord William Russell [WP]

W. Abbey, Dec. 31 [1833]

. . . If Ld Howard arrives, I advise you to tell him all you know of the state of affairs, and to come away *directly*. Don't suffer anyone to say that you staid to the injury of the British Ministry. I hope you will not in the end refuse Studgart. But at all events first see Lord Grey, who is very much hurt at the notion that you should consider any slight is put upon you.

LORD WILLIAM'S DIARY

1 Jan. 1834 Broke forth with the brilliant sun of an English spring, the air was balmy & serene – nature & I were in harmony – sunny & pleasant, my little children carolling & singing like birds on a tree, but no rose without a thorn, & my thorn is – Discontent about nothing is painful to see, & requires patience to bear. My windows from Pombal house look over the broad, beautiful & silvery Tagus, the *Asia* in front, with the proud standard of England floating listlessly over its waters, the *Revenge* & *Donegal* higher up, merchant ships of all nations scattered about & boats plying to and fro adding to the liveliness of the scene.

Went to Court with my civil & military suite. The Ministers of France & Sweden formed the whole *Corps Diplomatique* both of them alone, unsupported, & with my suite & about 20 naval officers, England cut a slendid figure. The young Queen looked fat, good-natured & suffering, the Empress by her side looked like a pretty chambermaid full of youth & spirits. The Emperor looks the soldier, but I can discover no intelligence in his face. Called on some merchants – on Palmella, gouty, corrupt, scheming, ambitious.

2 Jan. Another beautiful day – we had a fire. Me to the Princess Isabella's quinta at Bemfica – walked about the garden, sat with the windows open, ate, drank, danced – in short picnic'd the day away. The Infanta Donna Anna was the Queen of the party, gay, affable & pretty but rather noisy. The Duchess of Palmella the model of wives & mothers, the Duchess of Terceira the model of a soldier's wife. Marchioness Frontiera who shewed us her ruined house with perfect composure. There is something striking in the self possession and tranquil manners of the Portuguese, I know no women who are such perfect ladies. The party teaed & supped with me in Lisbon.

7 Jan. Gave a dinner to the pretty little Marchioness of Bellima, & a party in the evening, but the Peds & the Migs will not amalgamate just yet, however the English Minister's house is the place to try it in.

8 Jan. Took a long ride into the country with my own little Hastings, it is a pleasure to have his ingenious mind & gay disposition to fall back upon from the folly & deceit in which I live.

10 Jan. Violent storm. Rode with Hastings to Larengeiras. Who would have thought that when we lived in that beautiful place it would soon have been torn to pieces with cannon balls. and the destructive propensities of soldiers. Happy is the country that knows not civil war.

12 Jan. The Duchess of Terceira dined with us, her husband being at the army, she is an excellent amiable woman, Marchioness Frontiera, a lady of some acquirements & Marchioness d'Anjega who has been three years in prison, whilst her only daughter was separated from her & died in another prison – how horrible.

13 Jan. Went with Admiral Parker, Richards & Fanshawe to the village of Costa – a strange distinct race of fishermen, living in straw huts, on the sands – fine men.

14 Jan. Dined with Quintellas, magnificent dinner, but cold, uncomfortable & badly cooked. Excellent good people both of them & the most grateful I have met with. Assembly ball, hot, stinking, vulgar, tiresome.

18 Jan. Went to the English Catholic College – good primitive people, happy people too. Next day to the English nuns – are they happy, they say so, but if they are it is the happiness of the grave. Got away from the bores & took a delicious ride by myself – no companion but my horse. What delicious weather – what beautiful scenery – what a pleasant state of mind. Contemplative life without sun or scenery is melancholy.

26 Jan. Bessy & children went to Cintra – hot weather.

28 Jan. Rode over to Cintra, found the little children better & enjoying themselves much. Went with Hare to call on Don Pedro, found him alone with the Empress. He talks well, his future views on Portugal are good – but he wants better advisers. The Empress is natural & amiable.

Went to Mrs Gould's ball – very pretty. The Admiral bored me to extinction about a libel in a Portuguese paper. *Le cher bon homme.*

30 Jan. Letter from Friere to tell me the Duke of Terceira was attacked at Valle. *Diable, s'il est battu. Dieu nous préserve.* However I don't think he will be & this horrible war may end. Dined with the Yankee Consul Hutchinson. Splendid, no Republican simplicity – substantial luxury – *ainsi va le monde.*

3 Feb. Very kind letters from Palmerston & Lord Grey begging me to take Stutgard – I presume I must.

Lord Palmerston to Lord William Russell [PP]

Private

F.O. 10 January, 1834.

. . . I am sorry to infer from your last letter & from what I hear from other quarters that you look upon the execution of the diplomatick arrangements respecting Lisbon, Stockholm & Stuttgardt, as a measure which may be considered by the public as implying dissatisfaction with yourself. You know that this arrangement is the result of arrangements antecedent to your credentials, & which was made known to you at the time when those credentials were sent to you. Its completion could not longer be delayed without much inconvenience & I can have no hesitation in declaring at any time what has been its cause. I should very much regret your finally refusing Stuttgardt & I cannot but think that your doing so would rather tend to produce the impression which you wish to prevent. In consequence of your letter to me, accepting that appointment your nomination to it has been formally published & communicated to the King of Wurtemberg. If now you should decline it, people will naturally ask why you do not go; & why another is sent thither in your stead, &

Diplomacy

all sort of reasons may be imagined for the change. The appointment is in itself honorable, & in the present state of Europe important.

Pray consider the matter well & let me have your decision upon it, on full reflection.

Sir Edward Disbrowe* to Lord William Russell [WP]

Brighton, January 1834

... You will find Stutgard a quiet but very comfortable residence, the King and Queen extremely civil and even kind, but whether you will see much or little of them will depend on a thousand circumstances over many of which you will have little control. He is clever and occasionally fond of talking politics. At Court you will be occasionally invited to dine at 5 o'clock, probably the only persons besides the daily attendants, at other times all the Ministers are invited together. Balls at Court occasionally, these will probably be increased in number as the Princesses are coming out. On all these occasions you will have an opportunity of speaking to the King on any subject, I am sure Lady William will like the Queen. ...

The people of the country are very civil to all the foreign ministers, a German Court cannot be without a certain degree of [?formality] but I think them a hearty good sort of people, and was always very much pleased with them. ...

I strongly recommend you to take my house without delay, there is no other, and no chance of another to be had. It is very convenient, 34 rooms including a large ballroom, price 170*l.* per annum, and perhaps with pictures hired a little more. I have done a great deal to it. It was a new house when I took it. 8 stall stables, standing for 3 carriages in the yard, kitchen out of doors, yard to yourself – a house at the end of the town, the best end and among gardens. In winter the residence is wholesome, in July and August abominable, but you are in the middle of the Baths, and at Baden Baden you are not considered out of bounds. ... You will need a filter, it is indispensable, the water is so bad. The country is I believe known to Lady William and yourself. Wood is dear, tea, coffee and wine must come from Francfort. Game, meat, and bread are cheap. You will get some tolerable shooting if you are fond of it. ... I will conclude by strongly recommending 2 footmen who were in my service. ... My English coachman is anxious to return to Stutgard, and wishes to be

* Late Minister at Stuttgart.

292

recomended. He is honest, cleanly, and took very good care of my horses, he speaks German, French and some Italian.

LORD WILLIAM'S DIARY

14 Feb. Lord Howard arrived – thus ends my mission. Have I fulfilled it as I ought to have done, with diligence, good faith, sincerity, honor, integrity – I believe I have – then I quit it without regret. The question with me has lost its interest – there is so much injustice & party spirit, & so little patriotism that it disgusts me – no one can accuse me of want of diligence.

20 Feb. I remained in charge of the Mission in consequence of the Emperor being too ill to receive us. I invited to my house all the best Society of Lisbon to introduce them to Lord Howard & likewise gave him the best information on every subject – afterwards he may choose his own friends & take his own line – but if he is wise he will adopt my friends as well as my policy. . . .

8 March. Had my audience of leave at the Ajuda Palace. Said a very few words to the purpose, my successor made a long speech – *mais à quoi bon* if you dont mean to do anything. Pedro tolerably civil, but he has neither manners, thoughts nor soul, *c'est un pauvre sire.*

Went the same day to Cintra – the weather beautiful, the spring bursting forth in every direction.

9 March. Went up to the Moorish castle with the boys, a strange wild delightful spot. What a joy, what a comfort to get rid of the weight of representing England, & away from the base intrigue, lies & follies of Lisbon, I enjoy my personal freedom & the freshness of the air.

Lounged about the house of Montserrat, the ruined residence of Mr Beckford, how beautiful – the weather like July in England. The Goulds & Mr Walsh joined our party & dined with us – with some midshipmen. An express came to say that Bessy's leave take of the Queen was put off till Friday, *tant mieux* – I hate to think of Courts when I am in the midst of fine scenery.

18 March. Numbers of people came down for the Duke of Terceira's birthday – we sat down 40 to dinner. – The Infanta Donna Anna, & most of our Lisbon society. Afterwards there was a pretty ball, when all the ladies gave him crowns of laurel to commemorate his victories. Bessy gave him a crown of olive & told him she hoped he would give peace to his country. It was done in good taste & pleased him, he told her it was the height of his ambition.

21 March. Took leave of Don Pedro, the Queen & Empress. They were all going to bed at ½ past 9 & came scuttling back. I never saw such a Court or such manners otherwise *des bons gens.* The following days were passed in packing up & taking leave.

29 March. Left Lisbon. My house was filled with persons who came to take leave – Mortier & the French Legation – the Duke of Terceira. Admiral Parker & the officers of the Navy attended us on board the *Lightning* & went as far as Belem with us. This was friendly and flattering to me. They went off in the Admiral's barge & the crew gave us three cheers.

[The William Russells landed at Plymouth on 11 April and went to stay for three weeks at Endsleigh, the Duke's house near Tavistock.]

[Endsleigh] The scenery is pretty and the house delightful, but I don't think the air good. *Caro mio padre*, Wolryche & Edward make a *triste* society.

25 April. The quiet & repose of this place is very enjoyable after the noise, bustle & confusion of Lisbon.

26 April. The Duchess arrived – what spirits, what a woman. Badcock arrived from Portugal. Took him with us to London.

[At a party at Lady Grey's a few nights later Lord William found 'all the diplomatists'.]

Madame de Lieven received me well with more kindness than any one; she is always true & constant to her friends. Old Talleyrand was there & questioned me much about Portugal. He said that Don Pedro was *un fou*, which had made my position most difficult. Old Rogers acted the *diable boîteux* & gave me an account of all that had scandalously passed & was passing during my absence.

Had interviews with Grey & Palmerston, the first was most anxious to get information about Portugal – the latter appeared informed to his own satisfaction, tho I thought him very ignorant of the real state of the country.

The angry correspondence initiated by Lady William on her arrival in London with Ministers and with Lord and Lady Holland had more than a little justification. Publicly abused in the newspapers and taken to task by her father-in-law for interfering in Portuguese affairs, she was conscious that if she had allowed her political bias to appear in her conversation her interference had been confined to acts of compassion towards those unfortunate persons who had suffered a reversal of fortune and were oppressed. She had also been mocked for an imaginary love affair, and the impugnment of her chastity roused the fury of this virtuous woman whom Byron had once derided for her lack of passion.

There can be little doubt that Lady Holland had talked, repeating with embellishments what she heard from her husband who had seen the papers from Santarem's stolen portfolio. That the Hollands felt uneasy about their indiscretion is apparent. Their letters to the Russells were carefully drafted, Lady Holland employing her husband to compose her reply to Lady William's attack, and it is impossible not to feel that in spite of the good humour and the pained expressions of vexation, Lord Holland had something to conceal.

Receiving negative answers from Lord Althorp and Sir James Graham, Lady William addressed herself also to Don Pedro's Prime Minister, the Duke of Palmella, who certified on his honour that in the intercepted letters that he had seen there had been no reference to herself.

Applying also to Lord Palmerston, she received a typically brisk answer.

Lady William Russell to Lord Holland [HH]

Army Pay Office
Sunday morning, May 4 [1834]
There is a story of which I want to find out the *foundation*: of which this is the *misrepresentation*. That letters of mine written on pink, blue & green paper were *intercepted* & given to *Ministers*, read & talked about, & as my Lisbon informant expressed himself, 'an unfair use made of'. Besides this individual, *others* & all people of *sonorous* name & even *official* names recently come across the Bay of Biscay, told me much tho' not all on this subject for it was a sort of ghost story, everybody had heard it but nobody had *seen* the pink, blue & yellow ghosts in question. The Duke of Bedford had written me enigmatical innuendoes & the Duchess informed me at Endsleigh that he had been *very much annoyed* as he was told by   that a political correspondence of *mine* to *Cordova* was in the hands of *Ministers*. Notwithstanding the absurdity of the story & the impossibility of the fact, I am compelled to take notice of it, & mean to ask everybody likely to have been mixed up in the transaction until I have achieved the Herculean labour of *coming to the bottom of it*, – as *something* must have given rise to the report, mutatis mutandis such as *names*, *contents* and other trifles usually altered during the 'propagation of a lie'. I appeal to your authority & beg you will give me a clear answer, as to whether there *is ever was* or ever *supposed to be* letters or notes in my handwriting or *transcribed*, to any man, woman or child, sent to *you* or *yours*, for any motive or by any usance whatsoever, since I have been away these 18 months.
Yours, dear Lord Holland, very sincerely
Elizabeth Anne Russell

Diplomacy

Lady William Russell to Lord Holland [HH]

[May 1834]

Many thanks for the precision of your answer. I wish'd to put the matter out of the possibility of any equivocation. The Tale of the Tub or rather tale of the Club was that Lord Tavistock wrote to his father that at Brooks's nothing was talked of but a correspondence of *Lady* William's with Cordova, which had been intercepted & was at the F.O. That people at Brooks's had it from Holland House & that Lady Holland had seen & read it & knew it to be mine from the pink & yellow notepaper which was quite Lady William's *own*.

Now what affected the Duke was its being political. Lady Holland's hints of its being amorous were too uncertain to afford him any consolation & I believe he thought there would be a second trial & beheading in the family, from hence came the paragraph in the *Age*, which was said to be *verbatim* words uttered at a dinner at Holland House, but as to all that, I quite rely on Lady Holland's well known kindness & candour & am sure it was 'des méchants qui ont dit cela'. All I wanted was to annihilate the statement of any such letters of mine existing & I think the story not creditable to Ministers, & if they are *believed* to buy & read anybody's *private* correspondence – above all a lady's. Consequently all parties are the better for my inquiries.

By the bye I gave away a great deal of colour'd paper to various people at Lisbon as well as tooth brushes, nail brushes, hair brushes, Bramah's pens & other English rarities much coveted by foreigners, & amongst others to little Cordova, who is neither so great a rascal nor so great a wit as you suppose. He cannot *spell*, so if the letters were well spelt they were not his whatever the colour of the paper may be.

Santarem's private correspondence stolen & sold was *pro bono*, you got it stale I assure you. Everybody's notes & letters in his house were read by midshipmen, assistant surgeons, lieutenants of Marines, English tradespeople, Portuguese clerks, in short it was the most blackguard affair you can well conceive.

Pray burn this letter that when your private correspondence is stolen, I may not shine in it. My love to Lady Holland. I will call on her today, but I felt more tired yesterday than the day I arrived.

Diplomacy

Lord Palmerston to Lady William Russell [PRP]

F.O. 5 May, 1834

I hasten to give you a categorical & I trust satisfactory answer to your inquiry. No correspondence of yours either on political or any other subject was at any time sent to me from Lisbon; and except the notes which you have honoured me with, once or twice, about parcels, passages, & so forth, I have never seen any production of your pen either on pink, or blue, or green or any other coloured paper. The report therefore which has reached the Duke of Bedford is pure invention, utterly destitute of any foundation whatever.

A good many letters from various persons found in Santarem's portfolio after he bolted from Lisbon were sent to me, but your name is only once mentioned in any of them, and simply as having in conjunction with Lord William undertaken to apply for a passage for Mr Lemos in the next packet. All these letters were shewn by me to Lord John last summer when I received them.

LORD WILLIAM'S DIARY

7 May. Dined with the Lievens & had no one but Dedel, the Dutch Minister, an agreable man. They are all on bad terms with Palmerston – I am not surprised at it. She told me she wished me to go Ambassador to Petersburgh – this is probably from the fear that Prince Lieven may be recalled unless we name an ambassador.

Passed some days in the vortex of London Society which is one constant whirlpool of heartless & rather dull dissipation. The most agreable dinner was at Roger's where I met Bobus Smith, Sharpe & Creevey & the conversation turned on English literature with anecdotes of authors etc., highly interesting & amusing. They all agreed in thinking Gulliver's Travels the cleverest book ever written, but a book that ridicules the ambitious efforts of mankind is sure to meet the approbation of clever men living in retirement.

With regard to a possible appointment to Petersburg, Lord William had expressed himself with some bitterness to Princess Lieven who repeated what he had said to the Duchess of Dino.

'Nothing could be more splendid or fortunate for my career, yet if Lord Palmerston thought of me I should refuse. What he wants is not an enlightened and truthful agent, but a man who will distort the truth to suit his prejudices. If you display any independence, whether of language or of opinion, it irritates him. His one thought is how to get rid of you and bring

297

about your ruin. When I was at Lisbon my views did not agree with his, so he attacked my wife's reputation, and if I were to send him any information from St Petersburgh except what he wanted to receive, he would simply say that I had been bought by Russia. . . . No gentleman can in the end do business with him.'[17]

Lady William Russell to Lady Holland [HH]

Pay Office, Monday 12 May, 1834.
Lord Holland, Lord Grey, Lord Palmerston, Lord Althorp & Sir James Graham having assured me that there is no sort of foundation for the story you are accused of having set about as to there being intercepted letters of mine, will you tell me where you picked it up? or whether you picked it up at all and never said any such thing? I wish to close the business & it now rests with you, or must I follow it up & ask Hoppner as well as write to Lisbon, for I shall never let it drop till I make out the origin of the invention, unless it ends with you by your denying having said it, which I shall rest satisfied with.

Lady Holland to Lady William Russell [HH]
[*draft in Lord Holland's handwriting*]

[1834]
Your questions are so easily answered that I will not demur to being a witness in a cause with which I have no sort of connection good bad or indifferent – so be assured I never heard of any intercepted letters of yours & I hope I need not add that I could not invent or repeat what I never heard. I believe Ld H has already told you what the amount of his knowledge in the matter was & he certainly knew & told you to the full as much as I know or can recollect.

LORD WILLIAM'S DIARY
12 May. Went to the Levee, was ushered into the King's Closet, he was civil but not cordial, asked me some questions about Portugal – he said he considered Silva Carvalho a great enemy to England – I said I did not so consider him, & we parted. I afterwards went to his ball but he did not speak to me. I suspect he has been prejudiced against me by some Court intrigue.
18 May. [Woburn] Prince Talleyrand, Duchess of Dino, Lord & Lady Sefton, Lord Ossulston & others arrived. Here is another aged statesman, Talley, too

old I suspect for the exigencies of his employment. Has France nothing young in body & fresh in intellect to send to this Court. The Duchess of Dino is a clever, handsome, & accomplished lady – but of dissolute manners; the honesty of Talleyrand & the chastity of the Duchess will not exalt France in the estimation of England.

20 May. The Lord Chancellor Brougham arrived – if this man's judgement & steadiness were equal to his talents, he would govern the country – but no one has confidence in him, he is flighty – wayward – tricky & not over honest – entertaining in society beyond anyone, tho' rather controversial, peremptory & vulgar. He is always ambitious to shine as a man of the world, a sort of *roué* – but his manners are bad, his wit forced & his stories bawdy, he cannot get the easy drollery of Alvanley, or the sarcastic gentlemanly humor of Sefton, yet he is always aiming at it. He met my brother John with some awkwardness, having lately played him a scurvy trick by getting the Registration Bill out of his hands & giving it to his brother. He rattles away in French or even German, speaking both ill, but never at a loss, never abashed.

Lord Melbourne arrived with uncouth manners. He has much good sense, & great nerve, I think him the ablest of the Ministers for practical purposes. What a beautiful, delicious place Woburn is at this season of the year.

John's speech on the appropriation of Church property had created great alarm amongst the Ministers & they were in constant confabulation. It will probably lead to a break up. John need not have thrown the spark into the barrel of gunpowder. We all went over to Ampthill. At dinner sat next the Duchess of Dino, clever & instructed, but rolls her eyes dreadfully.

'A little breeze was stirred up', wrote Charles Greville, 'by Johnny Russell making a declaration without any necessity that he was unable to agree to the appropriation of Irish Church property, and that he might feel obliged to separate from his friends upon it. This disgusted his colleagues and a Cabinet sat to decide whether he should go out or not, and they very unwisely settled that he should not stir.'[18]

'Johnny has upset the coach', was the comment of a member of the Cabinet. The ensuing dissension among the Ministers led to the resignation of Lord Grey and the fall of the Government. The King asked Lord Melbourne to form a coalition but, this proving impossible, the Whigs carried on.

Duke of Bedford to Lady William Russell [PRP]

W.A. Tuesday [1834]
You asked me last night whether I was angry with you for what you said about Lady Holland. We had just sat down to our whist party, and I could

not enter into a discussion on such a subject, at such a time; but I will freely confess that I was much hurt at what you said, and my feelings entirely corresponded with those of the Duchess who expressed them with warmth. Lady Holland has unquestionably her faults like all other people, for who is there without them? But she has been uniformly kind to me and to all my family. She certainly has been so to you, and I could not but regret to hear you speak of her as you did, and especially before a stranger like Miss Eden. Lady Holland has not been without her share of misfortune in life, whether by her own fault or not, it is needless now to discuss, but she has expiated her error over and over again, by her unremitting affection towards Lord Holland. That she has been received into society is most fortunate both for her and for Lord Holland whose life and happiness so much depended upon it. The Duchess gives me a credit which I do not deserve, in saying that I essentially contributed to that event. I certainly did all in my power to restore her to that which she had lost, but my power was inconsiderable, and it was to my late brother that she was more indebted than to me. He was warmly and affectionately attached to Lord Holland. She has certainly shown her gratitude, by her constant kindness to me and all my family. It was therefore with pain that I heard her so severely censured in this house, and by one of my own family. You asked the question and I have answered it openly and candidly. William tells me you have had a bad night and are very unwell today. I will therefore not aggravate your indisposition by sending you this note till you are better – it requires no answer.

LORD WILLIAM'S DIARY

21 May. Returned to London. Suffering violently from headaches & ringing in the head for which I consulted Quin.*

26 May. Went to Holland House.

28 May. King's birthday; attended him as A.D.C. to the parade & guard mounting. Went to the Drawing Room – very full & brilliant. Dined at a great diplomatic dinner at Lord Palmerston's. Sat next to Sir Stratford Canning with whom I had been in correspondence at Lisbon during his mission to Madrid. . . . Afterwards we went to a full dress party at Lady Grey's. So ended the tedious birthday – I would rather hunt butterflies than go through its fatigues.

30 May. Children's ball at St James's Palace; took my 3 little ones, to whom the King & Queen were very attentive. The Duke of Cumberland attacked me furiously, I think he was drunk or in a high state of nervous excitement.

* Frederic Quin (1799–1878), the first homoeopathic doctor in England.

3 June. Went to Richmond on a visit to poor Princess Lieven, whose distress at leaving England is not to be alleviated. She is a great loss to society & the Prince's recall has been brought about by the *gaucherie* of Lord Palmerston.* Seftons, Cowpers & Charles Greville were of our party.

4 June. Rode to Claremont† with John & his Hardy party. I had not been there since the lifetime of poor Princess Charlotte, & was made melancholy by seeing her rooms, favourite walks &c., just as she had left them. Claremont is pretty but to me a dull place. I do not covet it as a residence. Entered into a correspondence with Lord Holland on my Portuguese mission.

Lord William Russell to Lord Holland [HH]

[1834]

I am sorry to trouble you about myself, but when calumnies have been actively spread, it is natural that I should endeavour to place facts on their true foundations & according to John's account you have misstated a fact. You told him the other day in conversation that the letters written by Cordova & transmitted to the Government in England were seized by, & sent regularly thro the Portuguese Government. Not at all. They were *stolen* by a servant of Viscount Santarem & carried to Mr Hoppner & by him sent to the English Government. Palmella himself told me that he never saw them, & that they never passed thro the hands of the Portuguese Government. What was in those letters I cannot tell for they were never shown to me – but a most infamous use was made of their supposed contents to calumniate Lady William & myself, & the calumniators with the cowardice which belongs to that contemptible race have now shrunk away, & dare not repeat before my face, what they whispered behind my back.

I am so young a diplomatist, that I know not whether it is permitted to steal the private correspondence of another diplomatist & transmit it to Government, but this I know that if the service of Government requires such dirty proceedings, it would be more decent in the members of the Government receiving such correspondence to keep it sacred amongst themselves & not allow its contents to be hawked about in public, & more fair in them, should it contain any allegations against an agent employed to make them known to him & call upon him to justify himself, instead

* By refusing to appoint an ambassador to Russia acceptable to the Emperor Nicholas, Lord Palmerston had secured the recall of the Lievens.
† Near Esher in Surrey. Princess Charlotte died there in 1817.

of trusting them to the credulity & malice of the public – besides which you cannot fail to see what embarrassments may attend a Government so acting – suppose only that Cordova had been sent Minister to London (& it was on the cards) how would you have excused yourselves to him for having made public his *stolen* private correspondence – If there was anything in that correspondence that accused my conduct or judgement, the manly & friendly part would have been to have called upon me to justify myself – but that is another question, into which I will not enter. I will content myself in stating the fact as it happened – & I repeat, & if you doubt, am prepared to give proof of what I say, that the letters written by Cordova to Viscount Santarem transmitted by Mr Hoppner to the English Government were *stolen* by a servant of Viscount Santarem (the said servant being a spy employed by Mr Hoppner) & carried to Mr Hoppner & sent by him to Government and as far as I can learn the cause of my recall from Lisbon!!!!

You will thank me for stating the fact as it happened so I need not apologise for the length of the letter.

Lord Holland to Lord William Russell [WP]

Thursday [5 June 1834]

Your letter I own vexes & hurts me – I believe I should be less annoyed if on self-examination & recollection of all I can remember about the gossip concerning these letters I could find any one thing to reproach myself with, for then I should only have to acknowledge it & express my contrition. But really I *cannot* – and it seems to me that you & Lady William are hurt and angry with me without any reason at all. It is true indeed that I told John for I thought that the letters I had seen were the property of the Portugueze Government, & I supposed, tho' on what authority I forget, that they had been seized at Santarem's on the evacuation of Lisbon. The matter seemed to me at the time so indifferent that I did not much attend to the mode in which they came into the possession of the person who shewed them to me – but I must in justice to Mr Hoppner observe that he was neither the person who shewed them to me nor the person who gave me the impression of their being seized in Santarem's house. Of this I am confident for with the exception of a letter & interview with him about his pension I have not seen or had any intercourse with him since the letters came to England and certainly not asked or learnt any thing about them from him. So far as to the manner in which the letters came into the hands of the English Government where John tells me they are still likely to be and you say they came through Hoppner and a servant of Santarem's. Now as to the letters themselves – In the first place those I saw were very few and very insignificant. The sum and front of them, as far as I recollect, I told Lady William when she asked about them. In them there was nothing that would have justified much less that required either a friend or a Minister to seek for that solemn explanation which you say would have been friendly and manly, but which *ne vous déplaise* I must say on my judgement would have been both 'impertinent and ridiculous' for what were the only facts which by possibility could regard you or Lady William? and what was the extent of comment which ingenuity could raise upon such facts? 1st. The colour of the paper of one letter (which contained nothing of importance) indicated it to be of English manufacture – from that it was natural perhaps to conjecture that it came from Lady William and it was possible to infer from a diplomat using it in official correspondence, that he the said diplomat was disposed to take credit for being on terms of familiarity with the English Mission. I have been also reminded of what till Lady William's letter to me I had utterly forgotten that there were two other letters from the same person, in one of which your name or Lady William's was quoted per margin for a piece of intelligence and the other probability of Hoppner's early removal from Lisbon mentioned as likely to occur in consequence of a misunderstanding between you and him – all of which perhaps tended to prove that Cordova availed himself of his familiar intercourse with you and your family to *vanter sa marchandise* with the Portuguese Government of Miguel but surely was not of sufficient importance to require much investigation or enquiry and still less to warrant one in calling upon you for a justification. There was in truth neither suspicion, charge nor story about them in the minds of any who saw those letters. Nor really should I have imagined six weeks ago enough to furnish the material of a *tracasserie*.

The other part of your letter, if there were any foundation for it would certainly require a defence from me – but indeed my dear William, my defence is easy, for your suppositions are entirely groundless, groundless I believe as they affect others, groundless I am sure as they affect me. You seem to imagine, 1st. that you were recalled from Lisbon on account of these letters or the calumnies founded upon them, and 2ndly. that I urged that recall. I venture to assure you that the first supposition is groundless because Palmerston when I expressed my surprize at the report of your recall and asked him about it answered me that he had told John at the time of sending you out your credentials to be presented on a contingency, that if you did so, you must not expect to continue there long, for tho' he had not promised, he had long destined another for Lisbon – with respect to the second – I think I learnt your recall from report and I certainly neither expected nor knew it till after it had been sent and John was apprized of it. When Howard had been named and I think gazetted, but at any rate when his appointment was known, I certainly plead guilty to the charge of advising Grey and Palmerston to hasten his departure, for I did think the continuance of a Minister known to be recalled at a Court in the circumstances in which Don Pedro's then was – was inconvenient to the public service and I had heard that you yourself considered it as irksome which appeared to me a very natural feeling. Had I imagined that your wishes were the other way, I should certainly never have expressed my opinion as to the necessity of dispatch, though as I told John in a letter to Woburn on the subject that circumstance which would have suppressed would not have altered my opinion.

Now, my dear William, I do not feel that in any part of this transaction nor in any other that I have acted in any way inconsistent with my un-altered and unalterable regard and affection for you or done or said any thing to prevent my signing myself

Your sincere friend
Vassall Holland

P.S. If your letter was *long* mine is *longer*, if yours was *wrong*, I trust and hope mine is not *wronger*. I heard of these very letters at Lisbon long before the few I saw were shewn to me and while writing this letter I re-collect that a Portugueze told me they would be published in the *Chronica* or the English papers – I have written in a hurry and at length and with many interruptions and conversations – for I was unwilling not to say and to appear to say all that occurred to me at the moment.

Lord William Russell to Lord Holland [HH]

Friday morning [1834]

I must trouble you with another letter because you still appear to doubt the accuracy of my statement of the seizure of Santarem's letters. Previous to the seizure of the voluminous correspondence (which would have required waggons to carry away) Santarem's servant *stole* the private correspondence of Cordova & carried it to Hoppner. The first passed into the hands of the Portuguese Government & some of it appeared in the newspapers. Letters from Zea, Asseca, Saraives & the Duke of Wellington – the letters stolen by the servant never went into the hands of the Portuguese Government, but were disposed of by Hoppner, the most interesting were sent to the English Government. This is the fact as it happened & if you doubt it, I am prepared to prove it by the testimony of Palmella & others. A most infamous use of this correspondence, & it is of importance to me to make it known by what foul means it was got at & to learn whether it contained any accusation against me. I am happy to hear from you that there was nothing which could authorise the Government to call for an explanation & nothing appears against me except being intimate with Cordova. Now so far from thinking that wrong, I did all in my power to cultivate & encourage that intimacy, & feel convinced that it enabled me to discharge my duty much better for the public good than if I had always been wrangling with him like Hoppner. . . . The coloured paper was given to Cordova by Lady William. Was there any crime in that? I am forced to harp upon these trifles because there is a mystery in my recall from Lisbon, which I have never been able to penetrate, the only thing clear is that I was sacrificed to a cabal, to the cry of a pack of ravenous demagogues who knew that I should keep a strict eye upon their iniquitous proceedings. That the Government should not have upheld me against this cabal, is to me incomprehensible or was I recalled because I would not make myself a partisan in the Portuguese contest?

Hoppner made himself a partisan & received a piece of plate from the demagogues & *canaille* of Lisbon. Was that becoming in a British Agent? Lord Howard made himself a partisan & you see his fate – insulted by the very party whose interests he espoused.

You say that you knew nothing of my recall – all that I know about it is this – Lord Palmerston on sending me my credentials, told me that he had given the Mission to another without naming him. Supposing my successor to be in London I wrote to say that the position of the English Minister was surrounded with difficulties & that the sooner he arrived in Lisbon the better. He did not come. The democratic party raised a cry against me – it was essential to my character & reputation to make head against this party, & show that my conduct was honorable & judicious. I wrote to Lord Palmerston & asked to be allowed to remain till the end of the war, & to John to urge the same request with Lord Grey. Both consented. Soon afterwards (I believe by very next mail) I received a letter from Lord P. to say that Howard would succeed me *immediately*. An express was sent to fetch him away from Sweden, & the public disgrace was put upon without any reason being given, or of my having been able, up to the present moment to discover the cause of the sudden change in the minds of Lords Grey & Palmerston. I wrote to John to intercede for me – he did – but in vain, he was not listened to. Happily for me the delay in Lord Howard's arrival was so long that the uprightness & wisdom of my conduct at Lisbon appeared manifest to the respectable Portuguese gentlemen & to the English merchants & I received from them the most flattering testimonies of their friendship & esteem, & the letters that I receive from Lisbon speak of my recall as a calamity to the Portuguese nation. It was besides an act of cruelty to the suffering persons to whom I had extended my protection – so it is not to be justified on the grounds of public good. I felt the harsh conduct of your Government so keenly that I refused Stutgardt being determined to accept nothing at their hands, but a most kind letter from Lord Grey, for whom I have the highest regard afterward inclined me to accept it, however if you are to pursue the same policy on the Continent that you have pursued in Portugal, if you are to stir up rebellion by your agents, & put one unprincipled faction against another – to support the *canaille* in robbery, the democrats in overturning the institutions of the State, I am not the man to be employed in your service. Look at Portugal; you have deluged it with blood for two years, you have lost every friend in the country, & you have put a puppet on the throne, with a fool to govern her, where neither will remain two years – but this is another question.

A few more words about myself, & I have done. I will not conceal from you, that what has hurt me most in all this business has been your conduct towards me, for whether it was active hostility as I had been led to believe, or whether it was indifference, as it now appears to have been from your letter, it was not such as I thought I had a right to expect from one who had been for so many years the intimate friend – I will not say of myself – but of my father. However indifference is better than active hostility, & I have gained so much from writing to you so I don't regret it – it would besides take a great deal to alter the regard & affection which I have always had for you, & which I was fool enough to have thought reciprocal.

306

Diplomacy

Lord Holland to Lord William Russell [WP]

6 June [1834]

In answer to your letter which I assure you hurts me excessively & which I am quite sure I do not in the slightest degree deserve, I shall only write one word to set you right in point of fact. I do *not the least doubt* the accuracy of your information as to the method of obtaining the letters, but neither can you doubt the correctness of my assertion that I never heard of it & supposed that they were seized at Santarem's on the evacuation of Lisbon, till John told me otherwise. Nor can you I think dispute the correctness of my observation that as far as regards any part I had or you suppose I had in any of these transactions, the way the letters came into the hands of the Government can be nothing to the purpose.

With respect to much of the other part of your letter & especially Hoppner, I can only assure you upon my honour that it in no way whatever has any relation to anything *I* did, said, or thought. Hoppner may have done all you imply & if he did he certainly deserves the censure you bestow upon him, but I am guiltless of knowing what he did or doing more than receiving an old acquaintance with civility & hearing his report of things in general, in which there was no other complaint of you than general expressions of regret that after an entire agreement you had ended by differing. It appears by your letter that you knew of the appointment of your successor before I did, & indeed before I even knew of such an intention – for though Palmerston communicated it to John, he never mentioned it to me till it was done. You had too on hearing of a successor said that the 'sooner he arrived the better' I believe I heard that you had said so – but I am sure that the sum affront of my offending is that on hearing the same thing I made the same remark. I never heard of your expressing a wish to stay till Lord Howard had been sent for & I think gazetted.

Now as to the word *indifference* which you quote from my letter of yesterday. I forget in which part of it I used that word but I am quite confident that it could not be applied by any misconstruction of my meaning to indifference about your welfare, comfort, feelings, or honour. If by some strange oversight it is placed so as to be susceptible of any such perversion, I do conjure you to obliterate it from your memory, for I assure you it has conveyed a meaning to your mind the very opposite of that I feel or intended to convey. I write with terrible length & with some agitation & hurry because it vexes me to know you are discontented or angry with me & after reading your letter over & over again, I see you are so but really know not for what. I certainly do not suspect the causes of your recall to have been those you describe, but if they were I must appeal to your justice whether one who knew neither of these causes nor of the recall itself till it was sent out, can be in any way responsible for them or can be otherwise than surprized at being reproached with them.

Not satisfied by the answers she had received and with a suspicion that she was named in a secret correspondence as well as in the captured papers sent by Hoppner to Lord Palmerston, Lady William returned to the attack. When Palmerston showed Cordova's transmitted letters to Lord William, it was made clear that her name was not, in fact, involved.

Lady William Russell to Lord Holland [HH]

16 June [1834]

I wish to ascertain clearly & positively whether my name *was* or was *not* in the correspondence clandestinely shown to you by a Portuguese & not officially transmitted to your colleagues? I thought the question was at rest after the explicit & satisfactory answers Lord Palmerston & Sir James Graham were so obliging as to write to me, but it is revived by the avowal of the smuggled letters, & although it may be convenient at present to gloss it over as a mere *tracasserie* and attempt to laugh it off, *je n'y entends point raillerie*, I cannot alter the circumstance of my name having been falsely, indelicately and unfairly brought forward some months ago, but the misrepresentation of the supposed contents of documents privately read & publicly talked of, but I have a perfect right to enquire on what grounds? And whether any other evidence than the word 'Russell' *en marge* interpreted *Lady William Russell* in your conclave, exists?

I am sorry to give you so much trouble but you will I am sure not regret an opportunity of speaking the truth & obliging me.

I wrote this note several days ago & was wondering why I got no answer, when I found it in my bureau drawer this morning.

Lord Holland to Lady William Russell [PRP]

16 June [1834]

I much fear you will not think anything I can answer either clear or positive. But first I must observe that no correspondence was ever shewn me by any Portuguese. 2ndly, that none was shewn me by anybody, clandestinely or in the Cabinet. You say you have had answers from Palmerston & Sir James Graham which you state to be explicit & satisfactory. I cannot give any more so than the latter – for he was in truth the only person who shewed me any letters at all & he did so with the most friendly intention, to prove how little foundation there was for stories said to be going about at Lisbon & in London but which I for one never heard distinctly from any body. I concluded from his shewing me these specimens of the correspondence that the whole had been transmitted to the Admiralty or the Foreign Office from the Portuguese Government – for I then supposed, but William now tells me erroneously, that they formed part of the papers seized at Santarem's on the capture of Lisbon. I was led into this mistake from having heard of the correspondence from a Portuguese long before I saw them & as I believe long before they came to England. Graham shewed me only three or four & I read I think only two or three. Your name was in none of those I read nor as far as I recollect was it said to be in any of the others by any person who professed to have seen them. I saw & read that on coloured paper – & whatever comment the colour might give rise to the contents were certainly too insignificant to furnish any. On your earnest enquiry on this subject, of which I never knew said or thought much & possibly recollect still less, I was reminded that your name or William's was on the margin of a letter as the authority for news quoted therein – I do not recollect whether in the hand of the writer or the receiver of the letter. – Indeed I am not very confident that I saw it.

What you mean by conclaves or interpretation I really do not comprehend or even grasp. I have been told that the whole correspondence is at the Foreign Office. If so I daresay Palmerston would shew you the whole – I really only saw a small part of it & that very late in the day. The talk about them was long ere that forgotten. I heard very little of it & am sure I neither contributed to nor repeated it.

Now, my dear Lady William, will you be offended if after answering so many questions I venture to ask you one. To what good purpose can all these enquiries into foolish & unfounded reports tend? Excuse me for saying so much.

LORD WILLIAM'S DIARY

18 June. The Duke of Wellington gave his annual Waterloo dinner. It is strange how his political feelings have absorbed his military feelings – this is a political not a military dinner. Does the Duke forget that his own military reputation was made in Spain & Portugal, that his genius shone forth there, & that at Waterloo he displayed none, not even foresight. Does he forget that his soldiers & officers laid the foundation of his reputation in the Peninsula & inspired & cemented that mutual confidence in General & Army which enabled him to win the battle of Waterloo, yet he has decorated the Waterloo Army & forgotten the services of the Peninsular Army. He remembers the anniversary of Waterloo & forgets the anniversaries of Talavera, Salamanca, Victoria etc.

20 June. Rode with Hastings to Streatham to see Wrio & his wife. Good people, great saints – but I can never believe in real sanctitude till I see it imitating the Apostles, preferring poverty to riches – can a man act fairly by two flocks? Why not give up Streatham or Chenies? Mammon says no. Went to the Queen's ball. Bessy ill & could not go: mixed, brilliant & full.

21 June. Our wedding day – 17 years are we married, & may we live together 17 more to see our dear boys swimming fairly in the stream of life.

22 June. Lord Palmerston showed me the famous intercepted letters of Cordova's upon which the calumnies against Lady W. were founded, her name appears in them merely as an agent of good, but I will make the authors of these falsehoods eat their own dirt, swallow their own lies, there is not one that I will not make ashamed of himself, & I will trace it up till I discover the villain who wrote *Russell* in the margin to fix some false information on me. The fact is we live with cads & rogues, & their efforts will always be to reduce chaste women & honest men to their own level – which is only to be done by calumny, to refute it it must be boldly met. I wrote a letter to Lord P. that will sting him. Lord Holland has behaved in all this in an unfriendly way. Lady H. like a d——d bitch.

Cordova to Santarem (*on green paper*) [PP]

[1833]

Mon cher Vicomte,

Dans la crainte de ne pouvoir pas aller vous voir ce matin, ce que je tâcherai de faire ne fut ce qu'un instant j'ai l'honneur de vous prévenir que Lady Russell a écris hier soir à l'Amiral pour lui demander le passage de Mr Lemos dans le paquebot prochain. Lord William m'a promi de lui en parler aussi demain. Celui ci m'a dis qu'il est aller vous voir pour vous demander un petit service en faveur du Maitre de sa maison qui m'a paru tout à fait insignificant. Il m'a prié de vous en parler de sa part et je tâcherai de le faire aujourd'hui mais je lui annonce votre visite pour dimanch ou Lundi et alors il ne manquera pas de vous en parler lui même.

L'affaire est de peu ou pas du tout d'importance et j'espère que vous ne laisseriez pas échapper la bonne occasion qui vous êtes offerte pour obliger à la fois cet pressant Agent, ainsi que l'Amiral y Ladi Russell dans l'affaire de Madame Zeal. Il m'a parlé d'une communication de Lord Palmerston qui nous regarde et que je regarde comme tres bonne. . . .

Tout à vous
Cordova

Cordova to Santarem [PP]

Mardi matin 23 juin [1833]

. . . Je me suis assuré de que nous n'avons rien à craindre du côté des Anglais par les déclarations que j'ai fait hier soir à Lord William Russell, au surplus et le cas échéant, je ne manquerais pas de lui addresser pour réclamer l'observance de la neutralité réciproquant promise entre nos cours respectives. Je peux vous assurer que Russell se trouve pas mal disgracié auprès de Palmerston qui en écoute plus Hoppner dont les rapports flattent et trompent les espérances et les project de ce Ministre. Il s'en suit de tout cela une guerre à couteau tiré entre le consul et le commissaire, que j'espère faire tourner à l'avantage de celui ci et au rappel du 1er pour peu que les événements répondent à mes espérances.

Lord William Russell to Lord Palmerston [PP]

Pay Office Whitehall, 23 June 1834

As there is not one word in the letters you were good enough to shew me yesterday that inculpates Lady William, or even explains the foundation of the infamous calumnies so industriously propagated against her, I need not trouble you more on that subject, but as you have read private letters of Cordova's carefully selected by Mr Hoppner & given to him as he *says* by the Portuguese Government but stolen by a servant as *Palmella told me* – it is but fair towards that much abused man Cordova that you should read the other letter of his which may place his character in a better light than you now view it. I am also desirous you should read them on my account because it is right that you should know that a person employed by you on diplomacy, though convicted of indiscretion, is a man of honour and a gentleman, for it appears by Cordova's letters that he received information from a source, which some malevolent anonymous person has fixed upon me, by writing *Russell* in the margin of the letter. Now it is very probable that I did give him that information (& very immaterial whether I did or not) for Cordova & I were military men & treated each other more with the frankness belonging to soldiers than the distrust of diplomatists – the only passage lacking of truth in Cordova's letter is his assertion that you and I were on bad terms, which I can only account for by having told him that I had recommended an adjustment of differences in Portugal, but that my opinion was disapproved of by you and my Government – which he exaggerated into being ill with you. The letters I send you and which I beg you to read are selected out of many. You will see by them that I never spared him when I thought him tripping. You will see the whole explanation of the conduct of his Government as well as his own – the truth of which has since been apparent by despatches made public &c. You will see that the information he gave me was of more value than anything I gave him – for upon that information (that Bourmont was marching), I forced Don Pedro to fortify Lisbon & saved the capital and the Queen – & you will see that my friendship with Cordova for which I have been so censured enabled him thro me to alarm the whole Spanish frontier & prevent Don Carlos from entering Spain. I dont present Cordova to you as a pure & perfect character – but few men placed in the situation he was could have their private correspondence brought to light & come equally pure out of the fire.

I send six letters & request of you to return them, & if at the same time you would allow me to show Lady William the letter in which *my* name & not hers is put in the margin, you would oblige me.

LORD WILLIAM'S DIARY

27 June. The Duchess put off her Woburn party that was to have been given to Madame de Lieven, on the pretext of Louisa's approaching *accouchement*, but in fact, *la chère dame n'aime pas la bonne compagnie.* Dined at Lady Harrowby's, a farewell dinner to the Lievens. Old Talleyrand told me that he wished me to go Minister to the Hague. This is the 2d time that he has spoken to me on the subject.

1 July. Went with Lord Lynedoch, Calvert & Gibbs to Maidstone, we embarked at the Tower in a steamer with 200 citizens going to Gravesend to amuse themselves. This easy & cheap exit for the Londoners renders their lives less irksome & more healthy. Old Lynedoch is an extraordinary man, 88 years old, yet full of vigor, energy & spirits. When he dies the mould in which he is cast will be broken. At Maidstone Fremantle shewed us the method introduced by Colonel Head of drawing by the lasso which might be made useful on service.

3 July. Returned to town to dine with the King, a farewell & most melancholy dinner given to the Lievens previous to the final departure from this country after a residence of 22 years, & a serious loss they are. He is honorable & gentlemanlike, she is the cleverest woman I ever had the pleasure of being acquainted with – she has no great instruction, her ideas are formed & expressed in the clearest language. Palmerston has got rid of her because he is afraid of her, & he is right but that does not diminish our loss.

4 July. Called on Madame de Lieven. In came the Duke of Cumberland. I sat him out. He was in high good humour, but attacking Lord Grey & the Ministers.

5 July. Went to Woburn where my father was alone, he was in excellent health & spirits & I enjoyed 3 days with him very much.

9 July. Left Woburn Abbey – at Barnet saw the morning paper, foretells a change of Ministry. Arrive in London, Lord Grey in the Lords, Lord Althorp in the Commons had resigned their seats from some misunderstanding with Lord Wellesley about the Coercion Bill. Went to a ball at the Duchess's at Campden Hill.

10 July. Great anxiety & consternation in the town, went to Brooks's met Ebrington who was evidently puzzled to know what way to view the question, & how to act. Advised his seeing John & we walked together to Whitehall, met Lady Holland pale & haggard with the apprehension of being ousted.*

11 July. Nothing known, reports flying in all directions. Brougham trying to give himself the air of being charged to make a Ministry to which he has no pretentions. Saw Madame de Lieven, said it was *pitoyable de voir ce pays bouleversé par des bêtises.* Dined at Lord Grosvenor's – *l'avare.* We suffered Bülow, Dedel, Bacourt,† watching like mice & curious.

12 July. Nothing known – the King remains shut up at Windsor with mere twaddlers. Melbourne sulky, Brougham intriguing, busy & meddlesome, Holland anxious to remain in on any terms, Ellice & his co-partners intriguing to get in Durham, the Grey party huffy, John calm, waiting for events. Went to Brooks's, Albemarle knew nothing of the King, the Radicals striving to get themselves in. Disgusted with the whole scene, order a chaise & go off to Woburn Abbey. Whirled down to Woburn in 4 hours & politics whirled out of my head. Found the Duke & Landseer *tête à tête,* not bitten by the frenzy of London, but quiet & almost indifferent.

13 July. The fresh air, the sweet flowers revived me, but amidst all the beauties

* 'To us who could hardly keep afloat, the loss of *upwards* of £3000 a year is calamitous indeed.' Earl of Ilchester (ed.), *Lady Holland to her Son,* p. 151.

† Respectively Prussian Minister, Dutch Minister, and attaché to the French Embassy.

of Woburn Abbey I most admire the oaks, I could look at them for hours with increasing pleasure.

14 July. Enjoyed myself at Woburn. My father was cheerful & in excellent health. Landseer enthusiastic about the scenery, animals &c.

15 July. Returned to town. Melbourne has made a Ministry.

16 July. Talleyrand, Duchess Dino, Dedel, Clanricarde & others dined with us. Old Rogers very biting, thinks the *Times* the first of oracles. Saw Lady Grey, very sore & discontented.

Letter of entreaty & *amende honorable* from Lady Holland.

20 July. Called on little Mrs Gould & went to see Landseer's pictures, his animals, especially his horses are beyond praise, true & excellent. Dined in consequence of Mylady's letter at Holland House. I confess my weakness for this house – I may say the house, rather than the inhabitants; formerly my affection was for them but I have been obliged to remove it to inanimate things, that is the library, the ancient curious dining room, the garden etc., all connected with associations of days gone by. Lord Holland amuses me, I love him as I do a child, he is guileless & gay but he has no heart, & the heart & nothing but the heart attaches. My Lady is kind & obliging & entertaining, but, but – no more of this, they are not my friends & I regret it. 3 Cabinet Ministers. Lord Carlisle was gouty & dull, a good man tho', John soporific, & old Holland, gouty & gay, shouldered his crutch & showed us how affairs were managed. Alas, alas, where are these people's children? Old Creevey was present, he & Denison told us anecdotes of Fox & days gone by, very interesting.

Meeting the William Russells the previous day at dinner with Lord Essex, Thomas Creevey had written in his diary: ' . . . we had Rogers and Miss Rogers, Lord and Lady William Russell and another or two. I have never seen a woman that I hate so much as Lady William Russell, without knowing her or ever having exchanged a word with her. There is a pretention, presumption and a laying down the law about her that are quite insufferable. . . .'[19]

Lord William Russell to Lady Holland [HH]

[1834]

Lady William is out, so is Hastings, but both are engaged tomorrow & on Monday we go to Tunbridge Wells, but I shall be very happy to dine with you tomorrow, & will bring Hastings should he not be engaged. With respect to the rest of your letter I will not enter into the subject you have touched upon – it is painful & disagreable & might lead to a lengthy correspondence which had better be avoided – but as long as Lady William is under the impression that the stories put into circulation against her issued from or even passed thro' Holland House she cannot look upon it as a friendly house – that impression (false I sincerely hope) once dispersed I trust our former friendship may be renewed.

At the end of the month Lord William was prostrated by an attack of scarlet fever. When he got better they all went to Tunbridge Wells, where Lord Lynedoch paid them a visit.

Lord William Russell to Lady Holland [HH]

Tunbridge Wells, Aug 5th [1834]

Many thanks for your kind enquiries – the fine air of this place has bettered my health. . . . I have additional proof in my last letter from Lisbon of Hoppner having stolen Santarem's correspondence. Our friend turns out a most disreputable character. What do you think of his giving poor Madame Santarem's love letters to a female enemy – the gratuitous malice of the man shows the malignant nature of the man. He had an object in injuring me – but why destroy for ever a poor woman whose sole crime was being frail in the flesh. I believe I shall be obliged to do what all the world does – publish.

Is it true we are going to lose old Talleyrand? I suppose he is too aristocratic for the present order of things.

LORD WILLIAM'S DIARY

11 Aug. [Tunbridge Wells] Dined with the Duchess of Kent, sat next to the little Princess Victoria, who has good manners, appeared anxious to please, & except being rather short of her age appears as far as one can judge of so young a person at a formal dinner, to have all the requisites to fill the great station for which Providence has destined her; her fate is not an enviable one. Promised her a parrot & sent her a monkey.* The Duchess of Kent is a good well-meaning body governed by Sir J. Conroy in whom there is no harm.

20 Aug. Failed in negotiating a matrimonial alliance for Johnikins.

'I know you have no object in view but my happiness', wrote Lord John to his brother; 'that however would not be obtained unless I could contribute to the happiness of the person in question. Now *I* have no reason to think that

* Princess Victoria wrote in her diary on 30 August: '. . . at ½ past 9 Mr Hastings Russell brought me as a present a dear little Brazilian parrot . . .'.

Miss Hardy has for me any more regard than our long acquaintance & intimacy necessarily occasion. Yet I will not refuse your kind offer, only do not lose me a friend in trying to gain me a wife.'[20]

There had always been some doubt as to which of Sir Thomas Hardy's daughters Lord John preferred and Lord William may be excused if in proposing for Louisa he made an error. Lord John met with a firm refusal and it seems that Emily was Lord John's choice though she was of a most unsuitable size. Sydney Smith once spoke jokingly of her as being seven feet high.

'I wish William had never interfered', the disappointed suitor wrote to Lady Hardy, 'but as it is I am very miserable.'[21]

A letter from Mr Meaghers the British Vice Consul at Lisbon had confirmed Lord William in his belief that Hoppner had acted in an unfriendly way towards him.

'... Respecting what your Lordship hints about the letters found at Santarem's and sent to Hoppner I can positively state that a great number of those were brought here by Pinto, the day after Santarem and his colleagues quitted Lisbon. Of this fact I am an eye witness and what is more Dominick Duff told me that he and William Hoppner were employed for several days in copying some of these letters, consequently the interpolations your Lordship alludes to may be easily accounted for – there were I am almost certain, amongst these letters some of the correspondence of the Spanish Minister with Santarem. . . .'[22]

'I am glad', wrote Lord John to his brother, 'you have further proofs of what one could indeed doubt no longer; viz. that Cordova's letters were obtained by very vile means. Are you equally sure that the word "Russell" was written by young Hoppner?'[23]

LORD WILLIAM'S DIARY

28 Aug. We went to Woburn Abbey, to me always the most enjoyable of all places, yet so little enjoyed by its owners. After passing 10 days, to the great delight of the children, we returned to London & passed our time in purchasing furniture etc, for Stutgard, & taking leave.

I passed two days at Panshanger,* the place is beautiful, the house most comfortable, the fare luxurious, & the company most agreable, yet there is something very unsatisfactory in the English country house life; it is gossip & nothing but gossip. Ask yourself on going to bed how you have passed the day – the answer is most pleasantly, – but how? – in gossiping. Ask yourself the same question the next day, the same answer. Two days you are in a state of delusion – the third the nothingness of your existence breaks upon you, & the fourth you are devoured by tedium & ennui.

From that I went with John to Woburn Abbey, – & a delicious drive we had,

* The seat of Earl Cowper in Hertfordshire.

one of those fine autumnal days so enjoyable in England – with much talk on the state of the country. Passed two very pleasant days with the Tavistocks, John & Russell. I always enjoy these fraternal parties.

Duke of Bedford to Lord William Russell [WPP]

The Doune, October 11, 1834

I have just got your letter of the 5th from Woburn Abbey. I had heard nothing of you for some time and your last letter being a P.P.C.* I concluded you were by this time in *Deutschland* on your road to Stuttgart. I had received two previous letters from you, which I take blame to myself for not having duly acknowledged, and trust for your forgiveness. Be assured that you have not in the slightest degree 'incurred my displeasure', but there was nothing in your letters requiring an answer, except one question, (which I will answer presently) and to say the truth, I thought it was just possible that I might hear from Lady William before she went, but she still perseveres in her unaccountable silence, the cause of which I am at a loss to conjecture. I have not heard from her for months. She wrote to me to announce your illness, which naturally gave me some anxiety and uneasiness. I then wrote to her to enquire more particularly about you and how you were going on, but she never answered my letter or took the slightest notice of it, and had it not been for the kind attentions of Dr Yeats who wrote to me twice I should have known nothing of you. I have since learnt that Lady William has been at Woburn Abbey, but only from other sources as she has never had the common courtesy to write a line either to the Duchess or me, to say that she was going there, or that she was going to leave it. No one understands *les bienséances du monde* better than Lady William, and I really think she would have behaved with more civility to a common inn keeper, than she has done either to the Duchess or me. . . .

Wurtemberg 1834–1835

They left London in the Government vessel *Firebrand*. Relations with Holland House were spoiled and Lady William had again given offence at Woburn. Lord William was debilitated by his attack of scarlet fever and sore from the passions engendered by the Cordova affair. Their journey to Stuttgart was made disagreeable by very cold weather and irksome delays. They

* *pour prendre congé.*

317

embarked too late to get over the flats at the mouth of the Thames and the night was spent anchored off the Nore. At Rotterdam there was so little water in the Rhine that they had trouble in finding a ship to go up the river, and were delayed five days. Three more were spent in freezing cold at Cologne; Lord William wrote in his journal: 'We remained two days to recruit & start the baggage, the sl scn [usual scene] alas, alas, it is sad work & now hopeless. . . .'

On 2 November they reached Stuttgart and took possession of the house that had been secured for the British Minister. Lord William's predecessor had recommended it, and the secretary of Legation, Henry Wellesley, had advised his new chief to hire furniture (a common practice in Germany at that time, the dealer taking it back at the end of a lease), but to bring his own carpets and chintz from England. 'Let me pick up servants' beds etc. for you at sales, nobody thinks of furnishing their houses but with the commonest chintz.' . . . [24]

A letter from Lord Palmerston written in a friendly and characteristic style reached Lady William soon after her arrival, hoping that she would find the appointment agreeable to her. 'I am sure it cannot fail of being so to everybody there. But after having been so much accustomed to sieges and battles and having sat in batteries as ladies do here in side boxes, to see armies engaged, how will you be able to sink down to the tameness of a peaceable life with no more animating amusement than sham fights.' [25]

When Lord John wrote to his brother that he would be useful in Wurtemberg observing the progress of the liberals in Germany, he did not suggest that the post was one of prime importance, and Lord William had himself stated that he was being put on the shelf. Germany was a federation of sovereign states, with a representative body, the Diet, that met at Frankfort. Towns were small, there was little economic development or new industry, and there were as yet no railways. In the south, constitutional liberty was replacing the despotism that still existed in northern Germany, but the forces of monarchy were continually struggling against revolution. A period of reaction had followed the failure in 1831 of an insurrection in Poland and had for the moment driven the symptoms of restlessness beneath the surface. At the time the Russells arrived in Germany, it was not incompatible in a country with a highly educated middle class to have laws that still permitted malefactors to be broken on the wheel. The Russell boys remembered in later life having heard from their coachman an account of such an execution that he had witnessed at this time. It has been conjectured that the Thirty Years War put the civilisation of Germany back by two hundred years.

The slight importance of his mission and the dullness of his employment left Lord William time to dwell gloomily on English politics, and his correspondence with his brothers was long and acrimonious. He held that his opinions were more truly Whig than theirs and they accused him of apostasy.

'I shall be glad', wrote Lord John, 'when you have arrived at the end of your reveries. I am not going to lead or to follow a revolutionary party in this country; the people are quiet and well disposed, but they see no need of using an almanach of 1795, when they can have one of 1835.' [26]

The King of Wurtemberg had been married to a sister of the Emperor Alexander of Russia, and by this marriage he had a daughter Sophia,* the high-spirited girl so much admired by Lord William. That he aroused tender feelings in her is supported by the legend that she sometimes slipped notes under the door of his room. She married in 1839 the son of his old friend the Prince of Orange and became subsequently Sophie, Queen of Holland. She maintained for forty years an affectionate correspondence with Lady William Russell and remained a great friend of her three sons until her death.

The King of Wurtemberg's third wife was his cousin Pauline.† She is the Queen who figures in these letters and who also became the devoted friend of Lady William; her letters dwelt sadly on the indifference of her husband the King, the difficult character of her stepdaughter, and eventually on Lady William's own unhappy situation.

For a time we lose sight of Mrs Rawdon; it would seem that she went to Berlin, where she had a friend, Countess Pauline Neale, and remained there until she was able to join the Russells in the summer for the season at Baden-Baden, where Lord William lost his head and fell passionately in love with a Jewish woman, to the astonishment and outrage of all who knew him and saw it happen.

The sadness he felt on the last day of 1834 he ascribed, as he had done on the first of the year, to the inordinate discontent of his wife. He had detached himself from his interests and affections in England to live abroad at her wish, depriving himself of the company of his father and brothers, losing his seat in Parliament, and giving up a career in the army, but the sacrifice had not promoted her happiness. She was forty-one, out of humour, and contemptuous of his appointment to a small and dull German Court. His misanthropy was increasing and his spirits were often low. His affection for his irritating wife was vanishing and they were united in little but their concern for the education and welfare of their sons. His journal expresses his disillusion with his life.

LORD WILLIAM'S DIARY

19 Nov. Dined at Court, the King is a man of talent & cultivated mind, but spoilt by being a King. First by the adulation of a parcel of flatterers who surround him, secondly by the foolish etiquette of a German Court, which forces him to act a part, & limits his intellect from having full play, for instance his own family always sit next to him, & such like absurdities. I went after to drink tea

* Princess Sophia of Wurtemberg (1818–77).
† Pauline (1800–73), daughter of Duke Louis of Wurtemberg.

at Meyendorff's* without looking at my papers, & he put Galignani into my hands, where was announced the resignation of the Ministers. John was talked of as leader. The *Times* scouts the notion yet I see none more fit, barring health.

Dissensions among the Whigs and the elevation of Lord Althorp, on the death of his father Lord Spencer, to the House of Lords, gave William IV a chance to dismiss the Ministry. In the absence of Sir Robert Peel, who was abroad and who was immediately sent for, the Duke of Wellington became Premier and Lord John Russell succeeded Althorp as leader of the Whigs in the House of Commons. It was usual for diplomatic envoys to offer their resignations when the government that had appointed them went out, and William Russell was for some time in doubt about what he ought to do. He was not asked to resign and the Whigs returned to power the following April.

LORD WILLIAM'S DIARY

28 Nov. [Stuttgart] John advises me to resign, Hare not. I shall take my own time & do nothing hastily. Haste brings repentance.

30 Nov. By letter received from Mrs Rawdon at Berlin it appears that the Prussian Court asked that I should be sent to Berlin. This is strange – strange that the Court should have asked for me & strange that Palmerston should have kept it to himself.

3 Dec. Mais allons cultiver notre jardin. I can neither delay nor direct the storm so why should I trouble my head about it, I must look to myself & my own duties & my first is to educate my children & today Dec 4th Hastings went to attend the lectures of the gymnasium under Professor Schwab.† The 4th class had just commenced with the Odes of Horace. He came back pleased and finding it easy.

21 Dec. I shall hold my place (if permitted) if not I shall resign, not sorry to get out of a very disagreable profession.

25 Dec. For all God's blessings I am most grateful, my heart & conscience are sound, my dear children well & good. Had an interview with the Queen to announce the Duke of Gloucester's death, on which solemn occasion, I was seized with such an irresistible desire to laugh that I fear the Queen perceived it. I am not fit for Courts & their silly ceremonies. Letter from Tavistock, very angry with my political creed – but he & John are blinded by faction.

Should the Duke displace me, I can retire to private life without one single regret, a little out of pocket perhaps, but what of that, I know how to economise,

---

* Baron Peter Meyendorff (1790–1863), the Russian Minister.

† Gustave Schwab (1792–1850), poet and man of letters. He directed the Academy at Stuttgart. Mrs Trollope wrote (*Vienna and the Austrians*, p. 29) that he was doing for Swabia what Walter Scott had done for Scotland. Lady William had a great regard for his character and gave his daughter a grand piano when she married.

so does my wife, & my children will be better for being brought up with simpler habits. That which would annoy & perplex me most is what the world would call good fortune, diplomatic promotion.

26 Dec. Hard frost. Small places are like men with small minds, all is etiquette, littleness & affronts – really life is too short to be always on the *qui vive* about one's Ps & Qs, so I must take my chance, if they are affronted it is their affair not mine.

31 Dec. Here I am arrived at the last day of the year, & as I began it in peace & contentment, so do I end it, full of gratitude to God for his great mercies to me, & for all the blessings that he has showered upon my unworthy head. But for one unfortunate cause, the same that ruffled the perfect smoothness of the 1st day of the year, I should have gone thro without a care or a sigh, but alas, how one little thorn can make one's pillow uneasy – however I don't complain, there are large sets off against this one failing & it becomes me to see the bright & not the dark side of the affairs of this wretched & mysterious existence.

LORD WILLIAM'S DIARY

1 Jan. 1835 The first of the year found me at Count Beroldingen's* ball, merry making – alas I go thro' the forms but merry I never am. The cares, vicissitudes & intention of life, with its mysteries & its doubts, keep my mind constantly oppressed, from which it never rises by any natural elasticity. The first of the year found me H.M.'s Minister at Stutgard, neither an active nor a useful employment. Went to Court, arrived late. The King very civil, talked politics. Queen & Princesses very civil.

3 Jan. Sharp frost. Took a long walk on the hills with Hastings. I delight in getting out of the human stink and human gossip of the town, the air is purer on the hills & my thoughts freer. Bessy ill.

4 Jan. Sunday. Took my children on the hills to slide. Punished for walking with me, this is bad feeling. Went to see Don Juan – a very moral piece for Sunday evening, as good as a sermon.

5 Jan. Out shooting near Louisburgh with the Royal party. Prince Jerome de Montfort† out, this hopeful youth would have been a King had Bonaparte lived.

8 Jan. What a detestable climate. Dined with the Meyendorffs. M. passes for a very clever man, so he is, speaks all languages well, knows all things, but the mould of his mind is small, he will never be a great man. She is a good little creature,‡ stiff manner, & seeking to be agreable & respected by exposing & laughing at the little foibles of others. Went to bed rheumatic.

* The Foreign Minister.

† The son of Jérôme Bonaparte by his second wife, Princess Catherine of Wurtemberg.

‡ Daughter of Baron Hogguer, former Dutch Minister at St Petersburg; her mother was Russian.

9 Jan. Cold & rheumatic. Rheumatism is the appanage of old soldiers, the reward for the toils of their youth. Wellesleys* dined, they tell me he is in terrible *mauvaise odeur* with the Court.

10 Jan. Heavy rains. Hastings begins Polybius at the Gymnase under Schwab. Letter from Tavy, very severe & condemnatory on my politics, but people who live in a clique get dreadfully narrowminded & personal. Wrote my defence.

Lady William Russell to Colonel Hare Clarges [PRP]

Stuttgardt, January 10 1835

... There never was a greater contrast than this place & Lisbon in bad & in good. All the people one has to deal with are well born, well bred, well meaning, well mannered, well educated – but the dullness & dreariness is leaden – the climate desperate. My pursuits are twaddling after the boys, lessons & masters, who are, I must say super excellent here, & solacing myself in the evening at 6 by a German play, which is over at 8½. I then come home to a cup of tea & a book & read till 11 or 12. When I am asked out I always get the toothache & have brought myself to such a pitch of perfection on this point, that it now really comes on whenever an invitation appears. ... To say the truth this is a two-penny half-penny mission such as our political friends think good enough for one, & one's political enemies not worth taking from one. I pity poor William for he really must be bored to death. ...

LORD WILLIAM'S DIARY

14 Jan. Confined to the house – no great evil in winter & in such a place as this. Read Madame de Staël's *Germany*. A remarkable, clever book & as far as I can judge her opinions & views are most correct. The Germans are deep thinkers but they don't bring their thinking to bear fruit. They make no progress in practical science, they have few writers on the nature of government.

16 Jan. Heavy as lead. Life is a load without animal spirits. Fine day. Walked & rode to shake off my gloom, but in vain. Meyendorff dined. All diplomatists pull each other to pieces, *c'est leur métier*.

17 Jan. Still heavy & sad. Got on my horse & plunged into the forest. The motion, the air, the absence from the stink of men, revived me. Ball at Court – but as I neither dance nor play whist, nor make love, & politics are not talked I

---

* The Hon. Henry Wellesley (1804–84), son of the 1st Baron Cowley; he was ambassador at Paris 1852–67, and was created Earl Cowley. He married in 1833 Olivia Cecilia, daughter of Baroness de Ros and Lord Henry Fitzgerald.

am *déplacé*. The young princesses pretty & full of gaiety & nature. Handsome supper & so we parted.

20 Jan. Beroldingen's ball. The Queen & Princesses there. Took Hastings, he was frightened & bored, but his manners are very distinguished & strike everybody – especially when he was presented to the Queen.

22 Jan. Meyendorffs & Wellesleys dined. Her ball pretty & gay. All balls & all societies are alike – blue, red, green & white gowns, toques, hats & feathers & turbans, stars & ribbons, whist & ombre, the same music, the same speeches, the same ennui. *Vogue la galère* we must go thro with it. Princess Augusta told me that Madame de Lieven was going to Italy. What, bored so soon. There is no living long in England without getting a taste for its free air.

27 Jan. To dine at Court. All the Dips present. Foolish form, boring, ridiculous; filthy dinner. Sat next to Madame Beroldingen, handsome & agreable. The King would be a clever, agreable man in any society, but he is a slave to silly form & stupid *entourage*. His daughters are pretty & distinguished looking, the Queen has evidently bad health. He seems anxious about his son's education.

Lord John Russell to Lady William Russell at Stuttgart [PRP]

Brocket Hall, Jan 25, 1835.

I am glad to find that education proceeds so well at Stutgart. I thought Germany would suit you for that purpose, and as a godfather I am much better pleased to have my godchild in the moral air of Germany than among the dirty and despicable Portuguese. I read lately the service of baptism and was alarmed to find how much I had taken upon myself in several instances. Either the dissenters are right in objecting to godfathers, or they ought not to be such mere forms of speech as they now are.

I begin to have my doubts about public education. But the parents who bring up their children at home are specially bound to see that they do give them an education which shall have as much of the merit as is possible of a public school. In general the parents who have departed from the common rule have been fanciful, projecting people, either too strict or too lax, too much insisting on study or too little.

Your German authors certainly will not succeed in England by dint of their euphonious names. But I should like to hear whether the library lack of the country is changed in substance, as well as in names. It was to be expected from any school of which Goethe was a founder that the whole would soon evaporate in mysticism and truths so profound that no one could see to the bottom of them.

The report of the day is that your former mistress is *enceinte* – or as Lady Chesterfield has it, *en famille*. I leave it to you to find out the truth.

LORD WILLIAM'S DIARY

28 Jan. Rode with Mrs Wellesley, she is one of those people who please everybody, always good natured, good humoured, gay and merry without *morgue* or envy – but also without any of those noble feelings of our nature which form the real charm of character.

29 Jan. Sharp frost. Hastings skates very well.

9 Feb. My spirits grow so depressed that I know not what to do with myself. It is the disease of my mother coming on me I fear – alas, I have not a friend on earth to whom I can confide my sadness. Letter from Tavistock, he is triumphant & severe on me, so I have written him a civil & sorrowful truce from political discussion. He is blinded by party zeal & old prejudices.

10 Feb. Long walk *solus*, my delight. Read Blackwell's Court of Augustus, more amusing than the Court of Wurtemburg. Servants stealing my corn. What an annoyance. Better as Horace says to have no corn.

11 Feb. Sharp frost. Rode my new horse. They are never perfect to a man of my age.

13 Feb. Dreadful cold & headachy. Went to Anna Boleyna, pretty music. The Germans have a natural taste for music. I have none – nor for anything else – except quiet repose. I hope the next world will be one of repose.

20 Feb. Continue to be confined to the house with cold, fever and low spirits. Life is a troublesome affair even with health, especially for me who has not a friend on earth. I hope I shall find one in Heaven or wherever I am destined to go.

3 March. Ball at Court. Princess Sophia with whom I had much conversation is extraordinarily clever, but looks consumptive.

5 March. Went to the Riding School to see the Carousel* practised by Prince Frederick & others. When Beroldingen came in & told us that the Emperor of Austria was dead I never saw such consternation. B. tore his hair, the Duke of Nassau grew pale – it must be confessed that it is an alarming event.

7 March. Heavens how time flies. 66 days, why I dont remember to have gone thro 66 hours, this at least proves that I know not ennui – no, I am as happy as the day is long, God be praised. All within is calm, & looking at my boys grow in intellect is a never ceasing pleasure.

8 March. Snow. I never was in a more detestable climate.

* A form of jousting.

12 March. Meyendorff & Hohenlohe, just returned from Paris, dined with us. Conversation turned as usual on the little faults & failings of our friends, exaggerating & bringing them out as much as possible – & when they have cut a man to pieces, they say he is a *parfait honnête homme*, thereby passing a perfect *éloge* on him without intending it. Diplomatists dare not talk politics – they are ignorant of religion & morals – they despise literature & *les beaux arts*, so they take refuge in scandal.

14 March. Dined with the W[ellesley]s: A large party in the evening. A party of people with whom one has not one idea in common is to me the most painful of punishments.

17 March. Constant rain. Profited by it to walk alone on the hills. How I love being alone.

18 March. Requiem for the soul of the Emp. Francis. Mozart's fine music.

21 March. Dined at Court. The Master is clever, but the confined & flattering society in which he lives has cramped his ideas, besides he has been much deceived by Russians purposely. The Mistress is violent in politics & not over-wise, otherwise a good woman.

28 March. Rode with Meyendorff to the Solitude,* a fine airy, solitary position, that I should prefer much to the stinks of Stutgard. Went to a farm beneath kept by a young industrious clever man who was feeding his cattle on composition stuff, having no hay owing to the drought. This might be a fine country in active hands, but the people are stupid & lazy.

30 March. John announces his marriage with a widow & 4 children – bold man, I hope he may be happy.

31 March. Long walk alone. Schwab dined. He says all Germany is in a state of fermentation.

Lord John Russell to Lord William Russell at Stuttgart [WPP]

Queen Street, March 21, 1835.

I am delighted to find we agree so well in politics after our polemics, and I am not disposed to ask, *à qui la faute*, though no doubt you will naturally distribute all the blame to me, and I to you.

But there is another event, which makes me less disposed to dispute about any thing. I am going to be married, and who to? To a widow with four children, this you will perhaps think does not sound well, but she is a charming person, full of good qualities and merits. She was married young and is now about eight and twenty. But I have not told you her name, it

---

* An eighteenth-century rococo palace.

is Lady Ribblesdale,* the sister of Mr Lister who married Theresa Villiers, so now you know all about it, and the remainder shall be told another day. Give my love to Bessy, and tell her I hope she will write to wish me joy.

Bessy wrote at once: 'My dear Johnnikins, my mother who knows everything announced to me your marriage three months ago from Berlin. Perhaps you did not think of it yourself at that time, but she positively did, and named the lady; and yet she is not a Scotchwoman and has not the gift of second sight. So I am saved the trouble and emotion of surprise. My boys are very much astonished, and the two little ones will not believe in the four children. That is a joke, they are sure.'[27]

    It was Lady Holland's opinion that Lady Ribblesdale's size was 'more suitable than Emily Hardy's to the stature of her *prétendu*'.[28]

Lord Tavistock to Lord William Russell at Stuttgart [WPP]

London 9th [April] 1835.

... He [John] is to be married on Saturday – to lead the House of Commons – and to stand a new election – pretty well for one man. ... No one knows what is to happen. Lord G. and John are at issue about the Radicals, which is our main difficulty, and may prevent a satisfactory arrangement. We went yesterday to be introduced to Lady Ribblesdale his intended – she is pleasing and rather pretty but not a great beauty, in my judgment. None of our friends or family know anything of her – she has lived in a totally different society. Lady Jersey asked at a great dinner at Chesterfield House tother day who she was? – on which Punch answered from the other end of the table – 'who is she? – why a devilish pretty woman.'

LORD WILLIAM'S DIARY

3 April. Terrible row among the servants, confound the whole race. What a plague they are, yet it is a plague to be without them. These small things worry; it is foolish to be worried by them yet we are tied to the earth by small things & cannot escape from their fangs; perfect liberty is the chimera of the insane.

9 April. Buried myself in the woods to get out of the stink of humanity.

---

  * Adelaide Lister (1807–38), widow of the 2nd Lord Ribblesdale. Lady Hardy wrote: 'She was a pretty little goose of a woman, but very fond of Lord John and he grew much attached to her.' Gore, *Nelson's Hardy and his wife*, p. 179.

11 April. John's wedding day. I hope he may be happy, but I fear he has laid the foundation of a few plagues, which he was formerly exempt from.

18 April. Snow. Called on Lady A[nglesey],* who is like all English fine ladies, & her daughter the same, gossiping & full of the affairs of others.

20 April. Dancing in all the public houses but these are not a gay people, heavy like their air & their beverage. Lady Anglesey in our box to hear Anna Boleyna.

21 April. Lady A. & her daughter dined with us. I cannot imagine how she could either by her conversation or her beauty have caused the father of a large family to abandon his wife & children & live in adultery – it is a fine lesson for the young & the passioned to look & reflect on a woman grown old & ugly in sin. Were I such I should shut myself in some dark hole & not walk about a living lesson to warn the young from vice.

22 April. Rode with Meyendorff & Hastings round the King's Harar, an immense establishment, but he breeds too much from Arab blood, or rather Eastern, for I doubt whether he has a real Arab in his stable – he has however some clever young horses.

23 April. My spirits are low beyond bearing nor can I bear it much longer. I have a distaste to life, a longing to be gone in hopes of something better which gets the upper hand of me. I feel that I have not a friend upon earth – it is a sad, sad feeling – but it consoles in dying. My poor mother was the same.

24 April. Reproached, blamed, scolded, reproved, lectured. My very kindnesses thrown into my teeth, & this incessantly & never ceasing makes life but a wearisome burthen, however it is a burthen that I must bear, so courage – failed again but better.

28 April. Melancholy as midnight. This grows upon me – I inherit from my poor mother – that & consumption. She died of broken spirits & broken health & I am doomed to share her fate.

Lord William Russell to Lord John Russell [WP]

Stutgard Ap 29th [1835]

Whatever you do let me beg of you not to ask Palmerston for anything for me neither directly, nor indirectly, don't even name me to him – he has his own coop of favorites to which I don't aspire to belong – nor have I nous enough to comprehend his policy, nor have I activity enough to

* Lady Charlotte Cadogan, daughter of the 1st Earl Cadogan. She married in 1803 Henry Wellesley, 1st Baron Cowley, from whom she was divorced in 1810, when she married Henry, 1st Marquess of Anglesey, whose first marriage had been dissolved by the laws of Scotland, his wife then marrying the 6th Duke of Argyll. Lord Anglesey had eight children by his first wife and ten by his second. She was the mother of Lord William's secretary of Legation.

meddle as much as he likes – so as a favor I entreat of you, not even to name me to him. I don't want money, I don't want diplomatic rank nor diplomatic honors, & am very well here untill my services are necessary elsewhere. Then employ me where & how you please.

You are more useful to Ireland where you are,* otherwise I should have been glad to see you at the Foreign Office – & I would have given you some hints as to our diplomacy that would have put it on a more useful & respectable footing. On the Continent the conservatives look upon you as a most dangerous & detestable democrat but they would have preferred you to Palmerston, who gives them all the stomach-ache.

You have no time to read more, so goodbye & God bless you, & aid you in the great & glorious work you have undertaken.

Give my love to your wife & tell her not to interrupt you by over-fondness – tho you had but a poor honey-moon.

I think you ought to pay the Catholic Priests. Ireland will not be quiet till you do.

LORD WILLIAM'S DIARY

1 May. The first of May ushered in by rain & thunder. Great dinner at Fontenays to celebrate the fête of Louis Philippe. The Dips drank to his health with sour faces.

3 May. Went first to Carlsruhe, a melancholy, but dreary looking town as stiff as a German Court. Up the fine vale thro which runs the Rhine, thro Rastadt famous in military & diplomatic history, to Baden Baden, a most beautiful watering place.

4 May. Sallied forth with the early morn to see the place & hire a house. Found my old acquaintance Col. Synge, who has built a cottage & resides here. Took an apartment. Went over the hills to Gernsbach, a beautiful drive, to see the castle of Eberstein in the valley of the Mourg, a delicious house fitted up by the Grand Duke in an old ruin. The scenery magnificent & lovely, there is nothing so delightful as the burst of spring in a pretty country.

5 May. A fine wild drive thro the Black Forest to Wildbad, a dreary bathing place, & from that to Stutgart, all the better for a most enjoyable drive thro magnificent country.

8 May. 45 years old. Presents from my dear little boys. God bless them & make them as good men as they are children for no man was ever blessed with better sweeter children.

* Lord John was Home Secretary in Lord Melbourne's administration.

328

15 May. Went with the Wellesleys down the Neckar to Gatsfeld, the salt bath. A pretty rich country.

16 May. Went to see the Castle of Hornberg, an old castle of the Teutonic Knights, lately repaired by a brewer, who has fitted up some delightful rooms to let. Wellesley has taken some. I would willingly do the same *mais* to do what I like is a pleasure that never happens to me. Dined at Heilbronn & returned.

18 May. Read Silvio Pellico's *Prisons*. A most interesting book. Indignation at the Austrian Government, pity for the sufferers, & admiration for the patience & fortitude of the author fill one's breast by turn.

21 May. Dined at the Rosenstein with the King & Queen. I delight in the Princesses, they are so gay, so natural, so well brought up. The 2nd brood is also very promising. The Queen has a very pleasing countenance. The Palace is a creation of the late Queen's, a woman with a vast mind for the good & the magnificent.

22 May. Letter from poor Madame de Lieven which I answered. What a blow she has received.* These blows often fall on those who are absorbed in worldly grandeur & vanity. It would appear that God wished to called them to a sense of what is due to himself. They are awful blows.

Lord John Russell to Lady William Russell at Stuttgart [PRP]

Wilton Crescent, 24 May [1835]

My dear sister, I have received your letters, and your beautiful present to my wife, and one of your cases which has been transmitted to Paris. Adelaide will write herself to thank you for the present, and I will take care and duly burn your letters.

Palmerston says he should not like to offer Dresden to William, as it is no step at all, and he wishes him to be in some place of active employment. I think he is right. As for masters you will find them all over the Continent, and need not be uneasy on that head. I think you must both be sick of Stutgart by this time, tho' after the dirt, bustle and blackguardism of Lisbon I can imagine that cleanliness, quiet and gentlemen are very agreeable. I will write again when I have time. . . .

LORD WILLIAM'S DIARY

27 May. Heavy rain, heavy air, detestable climate.

28 May. (King's Birthday) Did not give my dinner as I ought to have done – can't be helped.

* Two of her sons had died within a short time.

1 June. Ball at the Rosenstein at 11 a.m. in honour of the Princess Sonderhausen née Oehringen, married three days. I polonaised with her, with the Queen, the Princesses & others. I am enchanted with the Princess Sophia. She has the great soul of her mother; told me she envied Lady Hester Stanhope, this is romantical, but a romance in a young mind that may be refined into something useful.

2 June. There lives opposite to me a pretty Polish girl, an exile. She has three little pots of flowers on which she bestows the greatest attention & care, watering & giving them air. What is this but nature breaking out, & bestowing that love on inanimate things that she is destined to bestow on her offspring. I daresay that she would not exchange her three little ugly flowers for all my beautiful flowers, exchanged once a week without my ever knowing it. It is beautiful to watch nature in her smallest vagary.

To get away from the disagreeable summer climate of Stuttgart Lord William had hired lodgings at Baden-Baden, and there the whole family went at the beginning of June. Princess Lieven was on her way there, too, from St Petersburg. Overwhelmed by the death of her two elder sons, she made an excuse of her health to get away from Russia. From Berlin she wrote to Lord William: 'Il me faut du monde, de la distraction, seule mon état est affreux', and she begged him to take an apartment for her at Baden and to join her there as soon as possible. 'Je serais trop malheureuse d'y être seule pour commencer. Vous ne savez pas ce que c'est pour moi l'isolement dans ce moment! C'est affreux. . . . Adieu, mille tendresses à Lady William. Nous avons pleuré en nous disant adieu, je pleurerai bien en la revoyant! Quant à la politique nous en parlerons.'[29]

Her letters to her husband in Russia told him of the happenings at Baden-Baden, and of Lord William's reckless behaviour that was witnessed by the fashionable society assembled there for the summer season. She wrote to Prince Lieven every two or three days telling him of the arrival and departure of her friends and acquaintances, of her daily occupations, of her wretched health, and with an abandon that seems self-indulgent she dwelt on the paroxysms of tears that overcame her when she thought of her lost sons. She gave an account of her conversation with the foreign diplomatists who came to the spa and divulged to her husband the opinions on European affairs that had been confided to her. William Russell was less ready than other men to reveal to her the secrets of his profession, and she complained of the trouble she had in getting anything out of him. He was often irritated by her inability to leave politics alone, but he liked to discuss with her the problems of his future employment. Painfully aware of his disabling shyness at a tea table, he was happier in *tête à tête* conversation with friends at the baths than in the drawing-room of the Princess, where he felt he cut such a poor figure.

Mrs Rawdon had joined her daughter for the summer and her irritating presence, the excessively hot weather, and his own bitter dissatisfaction with himself, may have combined to precipitate the folly of her son-in-law.

LORD WILLIAM'S DIARY

6 June. Bessy and the boys went to Baden.

8 June. Off at 4 a.m. Drove my own horses to Freudenstadt at the head of the Black Forest & the valley of the Mourg. Some of the road very pretty. A day to me of great enjoyment tho alone.

9 June. Drove down the beautiful valley of the Mourg & breakfasted at Swentzenburg, a pretty spot. Thro Gernsberg to Baden, found all well, & the Princess Lieven arrived in great sorrow. Drove with her.

11 June. Yesterday & this day passed in all the idleness of a bathing place, which I detest. Heat intense.

'Les chaleurs sont si fortes', wrote the Princess to her husband, 'qu'on ne peut pas voyager le jour. Je fais de longues promenades le soir avec les William Russell en calèche dans les rochers, les forêts, car c'est ici, comme en Suisse, superbe. Ma meilleure ressource c'est les Russell, mais ils n'ont pas beaucoup d'esprit – tu sais que je suis gâtée, ah mon Dieu, oui bien gâtée, ce qui fait que sous tous les rapports ma vie est bien finie, bonne à rien à personne.' She found William Russell 'bien bon enfant et naïf comme un Anglais.' 'Pour mes promenades en calèche', she added, 'je prends toujours une femme et deux hommes.'[30]

Lord Tavistock to Lord William Russell at Baden [WPP]

June 13, 1835

. . . I never see anything of John now. When he is not engaged in the House of Commons, or his Office, or with his wife, he is at some party or ball. I am provoked with her for taking him out so. When he took the lead of the party he promised me that he would live for it. The only good of his marriage was the chance it gave him of now and then passing an evening at home, but she is evidently bent on going everywhere and will destroy him I fear. However she is now fortunately confined to her sofa, and is likely to produce a 'little John'.

I have not seen the Hollands this year, but I hear much of a quarrel she has had with John, in course of which, she is the aggressor, and has behaved ill. She was very rude to Lady John. But I find I am getting into gossip and must hold hard. My father continues to mend. . . .

LORD WILLIAM'S DIARY

12 June. The poor Lieven takes interest in nothing but politics & always politics is a bore. Left & slept at Carlsruhe.

13 June. Off at 5 & drove my own horses to Stutgart, very delicious.

15 June. Countess Beroldingen gave a breakfast at ½ past 8! Dined with Madame Meyendorff. My health gets worse & worse & my spirits go with it.

16 June. Returned to Baden & wrote to Palmerston to ask for leave of absence; also my despatch on the state of opinion in S. Germany. Found Madame de Lieven much better.

17 June. Drove with Wessenbourg & the Lieven to the Favorite, an eccentric palace built by an eccentric Margravine, whose kitchen & chapel divided her care. She punished herself in the latter for the crimes she committed in the former, for she cooked herself.

19 June. Madame de Nesselrode,* a clever agreable woman, her daughter, Madame Creptowich, naive & gay. The day passed in the lounging, gossiping & idleness of a watering place. Drove to the Cascade. The children in ecstasy.

21 June. The English have assembled a flock round a pastor. The church first serves the Catholics then the Lutherans, then the Anglicans. This is indeed toleration & must be acceptable to God.

22 June. Began to drink the waters by the advice of Dr Gurggert. Met at the source M. de Heeckeren, Dutch Minister at Petersburgh & with him had some interesting conversation on the Dutch question. The Princess of Orange† arrived & lived in our house.

24 June. Passed the day as usual, & ended as usual by drinking tea at Madame de Lieven. Letter from Palmerston to offer me Brussels. Declined.

The news that Lord William had been offered Brussels was passed on the same day to Prince Lieven by his wife, with her comment that she would prefer William to be appointed to Berlin. She added that she would be careful not to say so to Lady Cowper, for it was a principle with Palmerston that a diplomat who was desired by a Court was the very one not to be sent.

'Lord William est venu me demander conseil. Palmerston lui offre Bruxelles, mais il trouve cela trop mauvaise compagnie – du moment qu'il a ce sentiment là je lui ai conseillé de refuser, ce qu'il fait ce soir.'[31]

Among the multitude of English, Germans, Russians and Poles who could afford to spend some weeks at a fashionable watering place were people from all levels of society. Princess Lieven was at pains to tell her husband that she received those Russians who were *convenables*. During the three months she stayed in Baden there was a flow of visitors to her salon. Less *convenables* than some, and rather a burden to a woman who knew herself to be European rather than Russian, were Prince Lieven's nieces.

'Ta sœur, bon ami, et ses pauvres filles sont hélas, la risée de Baden. On les prend pour Dieu sait *quoi* tant leur extérieur est étrange, c'est terrible,

* The wife of Count Nesselrode, the Russian Foreign Minister.
† Anna Paulowna, daughter of the Emperor Paul I of Russia.

on court après. . . .' 'Je commence à deshabiller l'une de tes nièces, c'est à
dire à lui ôter ses diamants et ses diadèmes afin de pouvoir la mener avec
moi à la promenade.'[32]

LORD WILLIAM'S DIARY

28 June. Took a ride alone. I grow every day more fond of solitude.

1 July. Met the King of Wurtemberg walking with his two daughters. They,
the daughters, appeared delighted to see me. He took the opportunity to tell
Bessy that he would never consent to the marriage of his daughter with the Duke
of Orleans. He, the King, is always reserved & apparently afraid of me.

6 July. Visited the Princess of Orange who received me very graciously. The
evening passed at Madame de Lieven. I pity her, she is so forlorn, & regrets her
embassy as much as – alas, alas, poor human nature. How I hate myself in a
salon.

7 July. My father approves my declining Brussels, this pleases me.

8 July. Dined at the Queen of Wurtemberg's, 10 miles off; a good woman, it is
the fashion to abuse her, but I prefer seeing people's merits to their faults,
especially the humble & oppressed. I should be good for something if nature had
given me the means.

9 July. Went to Madame de Lieven, where I found Madame Nesselrode,
Creptowich & Jerome Bonaparte. I am good for nothing in a salon.

10 July. Wrote to Pater by common post. The little Dino who I meet at the
source every morning at 6, made his *éloge*.

11 July. Letter from Palmerston saying he would give me whatever I pleased.
Answered by return of post selecting Germany.

Lord William Russell to Lord Palmerston [PP]

Private

Baden, 10 July 1835

. . . You say 'tell me frankly what your wishes are.' Frankly then I tell
you without wishing to disturb your arrangements I should prefer remaining for the present in Germany, because I wish to unite as far as I can my
private views with my public duties, & I find Germany furnishes better
than any other country the materials of education for my children. Stockholm is too distant to please me, Stutgart is a complete *far niente* & not a
dolce far niente. Brussels would have been a more active post, but the
expense that would have been put upon me by the thousands of English
who pass through & reside in that town alarmed me. . . . Should Munich
become vacant I should like very well to go there.

Diplomacy

17 July. Great heat. Falck took my place in my morning drives with Madame L., a great relief, for tho a clever woman her everlasting politics are tiresome, besides my compassion for her has ceased. She cares mighty little about her children, more about her Embassy.

18 July. Went to Gernsbach with Princess Lieven, Duchess Dino, Countess Creptowich (Nesselrode's daughter), the Falcks, General Schopping, Prince Jerome Bonaparte. An odd mixture but clever & agreable people. We never got to the Chateau being exhausted with the heat. Bessy joined us at 4 o'clock.

19 July. Violent thunderstorm. They are grand in these mountains & clear the air deliciously.

Telling her husband all she knew, Princess Lieven wrote: 'Palmerston a été blessé du refus de William Russell du poste de Bruxelles, il lui écrit pour lui demander ce qui lui convient. Comme John Russell est le véritable premier ministre il faut bien faire un peu de cour à son frère',[33] and a few days later she wrote: 'William Russell demande par la poste d'aujourd'hui la place de Berlin. John lui écrit qu'il serait un imbécile de ne pas demander tout ce que bon lui semble. William l'a pris au mot, et Palmerston, qui le déteste sera bien forcé de faire sa volonté.'[34]

There were also those who made it their business to advise Lord William on purely personal matters. From another part of Germany Mrs Wellesley took it upon herself to issue a sly warning to her husband's chief:

'I must write you a few words of caution, dear Lord William, don't flirt *too* much with the Duchess de D. It is safer to fly from danger than to brave it, so do come here as soon as you can tho' I am afraid we shall appear very stupid after your great *Dips* with bright eyes.'[35] And from England the Duke of Bedford put his son on his guard against the ladies: 'I think Palmerston's letter to you will convince you that he is not your *enemy*. You must take anything those amiable *diplomates Mesdames de Lieven et Dino* say of Lord P. *cum grano salis*, for they are both at daggers drawn with our Foreign Secretary.'[36]

Duke of Bedford to Lady William Russell at Baden [PRP]

Campden Hill, July 17 1835

Accept my best thanks for your amiable letter, which I received yesterday. I sincerely hope that the Baths of Baden Baden may be of service to you both. As for me the hospital for incurables is the only fit place for me, for I do not see the slightest chance of my ever getting better, however, I shall if possible again try the bracing air of the mountains of Scotland – the only difficulty in the way is how to get there. We have here an aereal ship constructed by a Frenchman which is going to Paris and back, and I believe 10 or a dozen adventurers have already taken their passage on board – such is John Bull universally! I think there cannot have been two opinions on the propriety of William's decision respecting Brussels, at least, amongst his real friends; and I only hope that it will make no odds (as the servants say) with Lord Palmerston, when anything better turns up. My own opinion is that Berlin will be the proper place to send him to when Adair retires – all I can say is, let Lord P. eschew Sir George Shee! We have plenty of rumours here, *on dits*, and gossip of various descriptions, but I will not enter on them, nor anticipate any of the evils with which we are threatened, 'sufficient to the day is the evil thereof' – let William stick to his diplomacy, and look neither to the right nor to the left, in serving his country to the best of his ability. At home we are in the 'midst of Faction's storms', but I anxiously hope and trust that John is steering a safe and easy course through these storms – certainly with a most powerful and most factious party opposed to him, he 'enacts more wonders than a man', and well deserves the *sobriquet* the Tories have given him of Jack the Giant killer. There are some of William's politicks which I own I do not quite understand, but as I am a retired politician, and merely a looker on, I do not attempt to argue these points with him. . . .

I daresay you enjoy the natural beauties of Baden Baden. I believe all those badens in your part of Germany, have their peculiar charms. I remember in my time (more than half a century ago) the *dolce far niente*, with a proportionate admiration of sausages and *sauer kraut*, were the chief delights. Remember me respectfully to your two ex-ambassadresses of London, Mesdames de Lieven and de Dino. All the dislike I ever had to the former, as an *intrigante* &c., have vanished into thin air, in the contemplation of her severe afflictions, and I can feel nothing to her but pity and respect. . . .

I suspect John will survive the disfavour of your Wurtemberger King, and not be the worse for it. I believe he (the King) is what we call in England a *rat* i.e. he was a radical, but is now the reverse.

Addios! *Me voici au bout de mon papier, et peut être, de mon Latin.* . . .

LORD WILLIAM'S DIARY

22 July. My health is wonderfully improved. I owe it to training & simple diet. Health is a great blessing – but I feel morally & physically the effects of the scarlet fever.

24 July. This week was passed in bringing about my cure. Excursions, drives, walks etc. The climate is perfect & the place beautiful. So many are running at the ring of pleasure, that they have not time to observe one's motions, consequently one's life is most independent, social & secluded. The poor Lieven alone *gênes* me. I cannot neglect yet I cannot pity her, she serves as a fine moral lesson, more instructive than any homily. Went to bl & spk to rbcc. [Went to ball & spoke to Rebecca.*] Swarms of English of all sorts.

27 July. Madame de Lieven put into my hands the letter she received from Lady Cowper – but what does it prove? What everyone knew that a lover is preferred to a friend. It has put her into despair.† Madame de Lieven is a sad picture of human vanity.

28 July. Long conversation with the Duchess Dino about the letter; she views it as I do. Concert at Madame de Nesselrode. *Mais que suis-je, bon à rien dans un salon.* My health gets daily better.

Sir Robert Adair had been appointed to a special mission at Berlin but, aware that William wished for the post, told him he did not mean to remain the winter.

Lord John Russell to Lord William Russell at Baden [WPP]

July 22, 1835.

I have received your letter and spoken to Palmerston who is quite ready to agree. He and you and Adair may now settle the matter among you, and I only hope you will grumble a little less at all that is done by the Ministry you serve.

We are all well. Love to Bettina cara.

* It has not been possible to establish with certainty the identity of the lady with whom Lord William fell in love at Baden-Baden. Princess Lieven and Charles Greville named her as Madame de Haber, and it seems probable that she was Henriette, eldest daughter of Baron Salomon von Haber, a well-known Jewish banker of Carlsruhe. After the death of her husband, Jacob Marx, in 1830, she kept house for her father, and in 1838 she made a legal application (which was refused) to revert to her maiden name; she, perhaps, already used it when at the age of thirty-nine she met Lord William. Two of her brothers married Beyfus sisters, nieces of Baron Amschel Mayer Rothschild, which may have given rise to the legend propounded by Countess Rzewuska that Henriette de Haber herself was 'Rothschild's niece'. She died in 1871. Her Jewish birth was perhaps sufficient reason for Lord William to refer to her privately as 'Rebecca'.

†'Would you believe it, my Lord', wrote Princess Lieven to Lord Grey, 'Lady C. has written me a letter filled with what she deems good reason for preventing my coming to England! And she cites as the most cogent of these, Lord P[almerston].' Le Strange (ed.), *Correspondence of Princess Lieven and Earl Grey*, iii, 139.

Diplomacy

Lady Holland to Lord William Russell at Baden [WPP]

Holland House, 24th July [1835]

I heard with great concern both from F. Ponsonby and others that you were complaining of your health. I had suffered for some months from various ailments, let me have the satisfaction of knowing how you are – the report of Lady William and the dear boys is highly satisfactory, pray remember me to them even to little grumpy Odo.

Your father is recovering his general health, his calm, sweet, temper enables him to bear with composure, if not fortitude the great annoyance of his eye which is drawn down upon his cheek so that he has not the power of closing it night or day and the tears excoriate his cheek, it is most distressing to see, however he continues to amuse himself and beguile the long hours better than some who tho' not so afflicted, are yet more overcome, but health is a sad chapter for me. . . .

Of Politicks you must hear enough, only at this moment the Ministry are supposed to be in a *moment de crise* as the Lords are half mad with theology and topicks of ecclesiastical policy more like the polemics of other ages than of this. So we cannot calculate upon their rashness – in the case of them turning out the Ministry we must look to Messrs Hume, Wakely and such gentles for statesmen, it was remarked that the Bishops were surprized at finding Lord Melbourne such an able and learned adversary upon the subjects they chose to make prominent. It is rather singular how skilled he has always been in Church controversy, he is as conversant with it as Lord Holland who you may remember is very subtle and learned. Addio.

The more Lord William was troubled by the violence of his feelings for Madame de Haber, the greater pains he took to conceal the passion he felt compelled to record in his journal. Contracting words and writing illegibly, he sought to disguise his excitement and anguish.

LORD WILLIAM'S DIARY

29 July. So are we constituted of fl & bl ver which we have ncontr [of flesh & blood over which we have no control] & thus we go thro life struggling, fighting, resisting, yielding. It will be a happy day that puts an end to the chances & vicissitudes to which we are exposed. Those who wish to live are formed of other materials.

30 July. This is certainly a beautiful place with a very delicious climate. It is

337

strange to see how many English live in a state of complete *désoeuvrement*, discharging their duties, moral, correct, indulging in no vice but that of detraction, & spending soberly & methodically the gains of their father. It is a sort of vegetation, above the oyster, but below the dog.

31 July. Prince Jerome de Montfort told me that an infernal machine had exploded at Paris, by which the Duc de Nevers & others were killed. I carried the news to Madame de Lieven, where I found assembled the Countess Nesselrode, Duchess of Dino & others, the consternation was great.

1 Aug. The Duchess of Dino left us, giving me a little souvenir. She is a clever well informed woman, with one fatal sin, but Heaven knows what misfortune or what temptations led to this, & Heaven shall judge her, not me.

5 Aug. Letter from the Duchess of Dino which I answered to Berne.

7 Aug. Letter from Adair to appoint me at Frankfort. Good God what a fool I am.

Lord William's appointment with Adair took him away from Baden for several
    days.

LORD WILLIAM'S DIARY

12 Aug. [Baden] This is the anniversary of my famous day at Louvain, as well not to see the Princess of Orange.

13 Aug. The King of Wurtemberg and daughters arrived, met him at Madame de Lieven's. He was *causant* & very agreable.

14 Aug. Bessy & the boys went to Stutgart.

16 Aug. To Gernsbach. What a delicious day, what scenery, how I enjoyed myself, & yet I ought not to have done so. How little can I control or mask my feelings, & how much does one's happiness depend on them.

17 Aug. Good God where am I. Worse & worse.

18 Aug. Drove to the Hoop. What scenery, what air, what calm enjoyment, what a congenial mind; so ends all happiness.

19 Aug. Bessy & the boys returned whilst I was out walking. All in good health, thank God. My heart & feelings have been upset & have taken a peep into happiness that will make the rest of existence a blank. From kindness, goodness, sympathy, gentleness to harshness & vexation.

Princess Lieven to Prince Lieven [LP]

6/18 août 1835 Baden Baden

... Lady William Russell est allée passer quelques jours à Stoutgard, elle revient aujourd'hui. Son mari, le tranquille Lord William a fait en attendant des farces, mais telles que tout Baden en est etonné. Il s'est livré à une Juive et se donne en spectacle avec elle. Je ne sais ce qui en adviendra car il a l'air un peu égaré. Il vient tous les jours chez moi mais avec la mine d'un fou. . . .

Princess Lieven to Prince Lieven [LP]

20 août 1835, Baden Baden.

Lady William Russell est revenue de Stoutgard fort ignorante de tout le scandale arrivé durant son absence. J'espère qu'elle continuera dans cette ignorance, mais à Bade c'est un cri universel et un grand étonnement de ce tranquille et froid Lord William: à la manière anglaise il s'est si peu gêné qu'il se promenait en voiture avec cette femme. . . .

Princess Lieven to Prince Lieven [LP]

10/22 août 1835. Baden Baden.

. . . Le nuage matrimonial n'éclate pas mais il grossit, car ce pauvre homme est par trop innocent & le jouet d'une première venue qui l'affiche avec une impudence inconnue dans ces régions-ci. . . .

LORD WILLIAM'S DIARY

26 Aug. I can do nothing, write nothing, I am absorbed body & soul.

28 Aug. It is strange perhaps sad that after all my efforts to arrive at a high state of moral perfection – in an instant I succumb, & return to old tastes & old habits. God have mercy on me.

29 Aug. What a beautiful walk, how I enjoy wandering alone thro the woods, every tree, every flower is a companion to me & the whole one vast temple of beauty. Perhaps a friend would increase the pleasure but it is long since I have found sympathy in the human race.

30 Aug. What a day of delight. Conffn of passion.

1 Sept. This time last year I was at Woburn Abbey. Would I were miraculously back there.

2 Sept. Dreadful, fearful scene. I don't think there exists on the face of God's earth a more unfortunate unhappy being than myself, nor do I ever expect to find repose on this side the grave. My most fervent prayer to God is to be taken out of the arena, where I make so bad a fight.

3 Sept. Worse & worse. This world is a mass of vice, hatred & envy. Hypocrites sheltering themselves under their cold, cautious natures to destroy the more open & less prudent. How I hate & despise them, that Meyendorff is a dirty dog, & his wife a dirty bitch.

Princess Lieven to Prince Lieven [LP]

3 septembre 1835, Baden͵Baden

... L'explosion que je crains est arrivée. La pauvre Lady William est dans les larmes. 18 années de confiance et de bonheur sont détruites. C'est un triste spectacle. Le pauvre homme est fou. A 50 ans prendre un amour violent pour une femme perdue, dîner avec elle en public, se promener avec elle! Ce qu'il y a d'horrible c'est que cette Juive a un furieux amour des duels, et qu'elle travaille déjà à entraîner Lord William dans une querelle qui aurait cela pour dénouement. Toute la société et je dois dire les Nesselrode à la tête redoublent d'égards & d'empressements pour la femme et montrent une grande froideur au mari. Il n'en voit rien, il n'en sait rien, il ne sait plus même ce qui se passe en Angleterre. ...

Lady William Russell to Lord John Russell [PRP]

Baden, Sept 3rd [1835]

Would it be possible to know the period of our removal to Berlin? Lord Palmerston has never given the least hint of the appointment, but from what you wrote & everybody says & writes from England the affair is indubitable. Our odious Stuttgardt house is up the 1st November, 8 weeks hence. To renew the lease? ... to pack? ... or not to pack? are questions worthy of thought & foresight. You are always so good-natured that you will not be annoyed at such trivialities, especially since you are become a family man and can now enter into the importance of such matters.

It would be most desirable to leave this part of Germany soon, but it is not from avidity to pounce on a new place – I cannot explain – but you will trust to my reasons – & give me some dates as soon as you can. The Baden waters did your brother infinite good – douches – vapour baths & waters; we have had enough of it now, but Stuttgardt is aguish.

Here we have seen myriads of remarkable people. Nesselrode & his dame – I like them very much, good people in every way. Zea Bermudez & his dame also good people. Dino & Lieven, Bacourt & Fagel & Wessenberg &

more – the two dear Falcks – also good people. I walk & talk & never go to the rooms – tho' I live next door to them & see from my window the *Hoi Polloi*. The country is lovely, the walks, drives and views are interminable & variety beyond all description. We are a ten hour drive from Stuttgardt between breakfast & a late dinner & 15 English miles from the Wirtenberg frontier. My boys are thank God well.

Pray write and pray enquire and pray love your old faithful sister.

Lord William's encounter with the angry Duke Bernard of Saxe-Weimar before Louvain in 1831 now had a sequel.

LORD WILLIAM'S DIARY

4 Sept. Met Bernard of Saxe Weimar – addressed him, said he would receive anyone. Sent Colonel Sandilands. Saxe Weimar appointed Heeckeren & made a very satisfactory apology, so ends this matter. Met Saxe Weimar at the Salon & shook hands with him. Melancholy as night.

5 Sept. Went in the evening to Stutgart, travelled all night.

Princess Lieven to Prince Lieven [LP]

5 septembre 1835, Baden Baden.

... le duel a été demandé par Lord William. Il a accosté le duc Bernard de Weimar à la promenade pour lui demander satisfaction de ce qu'il l'a insulté il y a cinq ans devant Louvain lorsque Lord William y avait été envoyé pour arrêter le combat. Le Duc a accepté & appelé Heeckeren pour être son second. Celui-ci a agi en homme d'infiniment d'esprit & après bien des pourparlers il a fini par démontrer à Lord William qu'une insulte dont il n'avait pas demandé raison depuis cinq ans ne devait pas être fort grave, qu'au surplus il avait cinq semaines qu'il voyait le Duc Bernard tous les jours, et qu'il paraîtrait étrange, et un peu capricieux de s'en aviser aujourd'hui, que l'insulte faite par le Duc au roi d'Angleterre avait été éclaircie dans le temps et que le Duc n'avait jamais songé à l'insulter personellement – bref l'affaire est arrangée à moins que la Juive ne veuille la réchauffer, car tout ce qu'elle aime c'est le plaisir d'un duel pour quelque cause que ce soit. Le pauvre William est positivement fou, il a demandé hier à sa femme le divorce; elle lui a dit que jamais elle n'y consentirait. Tu seras bien étonné d'apprendre tout cela de cet homme si

Diplomacy

réglé, si tranquille, si bon. Il maltraite ses enfants, enfin je crois que cette femme lui a donné un breuvage qui lui dérange le cerveau. . . .

LORD WILLIAM'S DIARY

6 Sept. Stuttgart. Found Lord & Lady Grosvenor; he has the largest property in England, but his near economy is perfectly disgusting.* Avarice is I believe a counter-weight that Providence places upon great riches. Thank God I have no love of money. Cut Meyendorff.

7 Sept. Lovely day, lovely drive, thro a lovely country ending with the most agreable dinner.

8 Sept. No rose without a thorn, no pleasure without pain. I can drink deep of the beauties of nature till I am drunk with happiness – alone too I can do it, but if I could find another of a sympathetic taste the pleasure is augmented. The valley of the Mourg will never be effaced from my memory.

9 Sept. Again I went thro the most beautiful scenery. What a day of joy.

Moving away from Baden towards France, Princess Lieven was no longer a witness of the drama, but from Paris her letters to Petersburg noted new aspects of the affair.

Princess Lieven to Prince Lieven [LP]

7 septembre 1835 Strasburg
. . . J'ai le cœur déchiré en quittant cette pauvre Lady William Russell. Quelle position que la sienne, & quelle sera encore sa destinée. Son mari après avoir manqué un duel avec le Duc Bernard de Weimar a couru à Stoutgard pour se battre avec notre Ministre Meyendorff, qu'il accuse de tous les commérages de Baden. Ce pauvre William est fou, il veut se battre n'importe avec qui. Reconnais-tu cet homme si calme, si doux? Ce que c'est que l'empire d'une belle coquine! Je suis partie avant de pouvoir apprendre ce qui se sera passé à Stoutgard. Le Meyendorff sera bien surpris. Ma pauvre amie ne sait pas un mot de tous ces challenges à droite et à gauche. Elle est à Baden dans les larmes, dans les angoisses. Madame Nesselrode a comblé Lady William de marques d'intérêt dans cette triste circonstance, mais quelle humiliation pour cette femme

* Richard Grosvenor, Viscount Belgrave, later 2nd Marquess of Westminster (1795–1869). He married in 1819 Lady Elizabeth Leveson Gower, daughter of the 1st Duke of Sutherland.

jusqu'ici si heureuse. Je crois son mari fou, il n'y a pas d'autre explication possible, il a fait des choses incroyables publiquement et devant sa
femme. . . .

LORD WILLIAM'S DIARY

10 Sept. The morning was bright & beautiful yet the sun looked false, peeped
out & retired. Drove down the valley of the Mourg, but in the evening black &
heavy clouds announced a storm. Regained my home at 10 – & what a home,
bad, bad, bad, bad.

11 Sept. The storm burst amidst thunder & lightning. It is a question, whether
this life is more tolerable with all the passions set in motion bringing their fatal
consequences or to go thro it motionless as the oyster.

13 Sept. Rainy melancholy day, left alone in my own house, found consolation
from one of the gentlest minds I ever met.

16 Sept. Lady Davy; she fatigues one with her gossip, her stories of this & that,
what care I what others do & say. However I bore with her.

18 Sept. Violent rains set in. This place full of English not venturing to go on
or turned back from Italy, *tant mieux*, there is no harm in checking the idle
pleasures of this idle gentry. There is something awfully grand in seeing the
fléau de Dieu, the cholera at the gates of Italy, & penetrating like Atala with slow
& stopless step, the inhabitants quaking at its approach.

21 Sept. Dined with the Duke of Argyle & his illegitimate daughter.* He has a
fund of good humour & contentment about him, otherwise his existence would
excite my compassion.

Lady William Russell to Princess Lieven [LP]

[1835]
J'avais deviné le duel absolument comme vous m'en parlez – quoiqu'il
m'avait avoué qu'une dame lui avait dit 'comment? vous vous êtes laissé
insulter de la sorte!' et que cela ne lui avait laissé ni paix ni cesse depuis –
enfin la tête n'y était plus & n'y est plus & je suis abimée, abreuvée
d'amertume!

Lady William Russell to Princess Lieven [LP]

[1835]
Ma bonne amie, tournez sur le danger de cette abominable coquine,
car la famille croit que c'est une petite aventure leste (fort désagréable pour

* 'I cannot help thinking she must be his daughter – she is so *very ugly*.' Lord
Sudley (ed.), *The Lieven–Palmerston Correspondence*, p. 95.

l'épouse) mais qui terminera comme les amourettes du père avec Lady Elizabeth Vernon et Lady Sandwich!! et nullement comme un scandale sérieux & fort dangereux.

Princess Lieven to Prince Lieven [LP]

1/13 septembre, 1835 Paris.

... je trouve ici deux tristes lettres de cette pauvre Lady William Russell. Son mari l'a quitté pour voyager avec cette abominable Juive, elle ne sait où ils sont allés. Elle suppose que cette femme veut la pousser à bout pour amener le divorce & épouser Lord William; elle est résolue à tout supporter avec résignation pour l'amour de ses enfants ... mais enfin cette femme m'écrit des lettres à fondre le cœur. Elle n'a que sa religion et elle en a beaucoup qui la défende du désespoir. ...

Lady William Russell to Princess Lieven [LP]

Stoutgard, le 16 sept [1835]

Il est temps, ma chère amie, que vous me rendiez service d'écrire à mon beau-frère. Il n'en résultera rien que ma justification. C'est à dire des preuves que ce ne sont point des transports jaloux ni des soupçons injurieux & que ce n'est point moi qui l'ai compromis par un esclandre mais son imprudence – il ne s'agit nullement de l'accuser de quoi que ce soit – uniquement de détailler ce dont tout Baden a été témoin, rappelez-vous, chère, que ce ne sont pas de ceux qui entendent à demi mot & qu'il faut parler fortement, c'est à dire, dire la pure vérité. La publicité du scandale – le regret extrême que cela a causé par la bienveillance & la bonne opinion qu'on a toujours bien voulu nous accorder, l'étonnement que cette conduite a produit après deux mois de séjour pendant lesquels nous étions inséparables (on a commencé par se retirer de votre société). Parlez de l'horrible créature telle qu'elle est & de la conviction que la liaison n'est innocente par la corruption même de l'aventurière si connue, si méprisée. Si je vous rappelle ces choses, chère, c'est que malgré votre amitié & votre zèle, malgré vos bontés immuables pour nous, vous avez voyagé – vous êtes à Paris ou à Valençay – vous êtes entourée de personnes et occupée de nouvelles qui doivent nécessairement affaiblir les douloureuses impressions des derniers tristes jours que nous avons passés ensemble. Je vous envoie comme vous me l'avez demandé un billet qui vous autorise à cette démarche. Vous ne parlerez *à personne* – cela reste entre vous, mon beau-frère et moi – & cela nous sera d'un immense secours. . . . C'est le seul moyen de le tirer de Baden & de faire cesser ce scandale. Mon beau-frère ne vous citera jamais, vous pourrez en être sûre.

Je suis ici avec mes enfants depuis le 12 – mon départ a été inévitable. J'avais comme vous le savez tout emballé; à son retour, jeudi la nuit, pendant qu'il soupait, je lui ai dit mon intention de quitter Baden – que toute ma société était partie, c'était vide, triste, le temps pluvieux, point de meubles, les soirées longues & sombres. Il a beaucoup discuté les agréments du lieu, l'ennui de Stoutgard &c. – enfin les événements du lendemain ont été tels que je lui ai dit que positivement je ne pouvois rester en tiers. Je l'ai supplié de rompre l'affaire en partant avec moi – il s'y est refusé – et m'a dit faites ce que vous voudrez, allez-vous-en avec les enfants, moi je reste, j'ai loué l'appartement jusqu'au 1er octobre – j'y resterai le plus longtemps possible – je déteste Stoutgard, j'y resterai jusqu'à ce que j'aille à Berlin. Là-dessus il sort – fait seller un cheval – descend au rez de chaussée faire une visite –s'y montre à la fenêtre. On amène une calèche de louage – mes enfants et moi à la fenêtre – la dame se met dedans, me regarde avec son lorgnon – part, et mon mari sort de la cour à cheval & suit la calèche (pour me prouver qu'il ne voulait pas être contredit). En partant il dit à mon fils, dites à votre mère que je vais faire une très longue promenade & que je ne retournerai que fort tard dans la soirée, qu'elle aille à Stoutgard si elle préfère, moi je n'y viendrai que plus tard, je lui ferai savoir quand.

Alors, chère amie, je n'avais qu'à partir. Voilà ce qui est arrivé à la porte de ma maison, de celle de Chabert – devant les gens – les curieux, enfin vous connaissez le local. J'ai donc commandé mes chevaux de poste et deux heures après j'étais en route. Il m'a depuis écrit qu'il ne voulait pas être tourmenté ni sermonné, qu'il irait à la revue des troupes près de Heilbronn, qu'il retournerait à Bade & qu'il ne viendrait ici que le plus tard possible, parce qu'il voulait encore prendre des bains & que l'air lui convenait pour sa santé mieux que Stoutgard. Voilà donc, chère amie, un pauvre homme qui se prend par obstination et il faut tâcher de le tirer de là le moins tard possible – car tout ce que le public européen a vu sera sujet de conversation. Ce qui s'est passé dans mon intérieur je vous le dis à vous seule – et vous voyez où nous en sommes. Cette créature veut l'afficher pour le compromettre et s'accrocher à lui; il ne s'en doute pas & croit que c'est un petit *flirtation* passager aux Eaux. Hélas! Enfin me voilà bien tristement, bien tranquillement – espérant tout. Dieu merci, la petite Belgrave est ici; je m'occupe de ses arrangements pour l'hiver, cela me distrait, je lui trouve des meubles et des maîtres, des traiteurs & des laquais. Je vous embrasse, ma bien chère amie; quand mon beau-frère saura ce qui a été public, il saura à quoi s'en tenir & tirera son frère du bourbier en l'envoyant quelque part. S'il ne savait que mon histoire il croirait que c'est une brouillerie jalouse que femme et mari arrangent ensemble & il le laisserait là – cette femme le traînant dans la fange – ce qu'elle fera infailliblement. Prenez garde que l'odieuse Flahault ne m'entende pas nommer. . . .

Je reçois votre chère lettre. Vous avez l'air de m'aimer & de me plaindre. Vous écrivez donc & vous parlez de votre amitié pour les deux frères qui vous engage à dire à l'un en confidence le danger de l'autre. Vous ne parlerez de moi que pour dire la vérité, c'est que je n'avais pas l'air de m'en douter. La fête du roi de Wurtemberg est le 27, il ne veut pas venir; la Volksfest le 28, il ne veut pas venir; Lord Grosvenor ici, il ne veut pas le présenter. Enfin il me semble que c'est bien le moment pour une amie d'intervenir puisqu'il ne s'agit point de querelles de ménage – mais de carrière & de réputation. Ne perdez pas de temps & écrivez-lui fortement. Il faut le tirer de la fosse par les cheveux, c'est un délire. Pardon si je ne parle que de moi! L'événement est si triste! Je vous conjure de ne point me nommer *à qui que cela soit*!

Ma mère sera ici ces jours-ci, & vous pouvez m'écrire sous couvert à son adresse, seulement ne vous servez ni de papier ni de cire noire ni de votre cachet avec vos armes & faites mettre l'adresse par Mlle Mentzingen*: . . . Dites: 'No time should be lost from what I hear now and from what I have seen myself, in getting your brother away.'

Cela ne vous compromet pas ni moi.

Princess Lieven to Prince Lieven [LP]

16/28 septembre 1835 Paris
. . . J'ai eu hier une triste lettre de Lord John Russell. Il se réfère à moi pour apprendre si son frère est devenu fou, et ne veut rien faire sans que mon témoignage corrobore les tristes et désolantes relations que lui transmet Lady William, laquelle écrit vraiment que cette diablesse de Juive l'a ensorcelé par quelque breuvage, il paraît que toute la famille est consternée. . . .

* Princess Lieven's niece and companion.

Je ne doute pas que Lord John ne tire de suite son frère de là. Cette femme est une horreur. Elle est accusée d'avoir empoisonné son mari Haber mort il y a deux ans. Elle a voulu assassiner un de ses amants, enfin c'est une femme digne de la potence, et qui veut devenir Lady Russell. Elle veut pousser à bout ma pauvre amie pour lui faire demander le divorce. Jamais elle ne le demandera, elle aime trop ses enfants pour cela, mais quelles humiliations que celles qu'elle endure! Et elle si calme, si sensée, si grande dame . . .

LORD WILLIAM'S DIARY

25 Sept. Went once more to Ebersteinberg. What a view, what a beautiful ruin, & on the top of the highest tower I sat an hour & gazed & gazed. Left for Stutgart after dining.

27 Sept. Arrived at Stutgart. What a chill, what – I tremble whilst I write. *Du sublime au ridicule il n y a qu'un pas.* Dined at Beroldingens to celebrate the King's birthday. What tiresome stuff.

28 Sept. The feast of the people, pretty & well imagined races. The Court, Grosvenors etc. The Duke Bernard pointedly civil to me. I did right to send him a message. Nothing like an explanation.

29 Sept. Races. The King in high force. Melancholy as midnight. The Duke Bernard renewed his attentions, & astonished all the fools who gaped & were astonished & disappointed.

30 Sept. Awful scenes. It cannot last.

2 Oct. My letters all opened & some stolen. This is infamous, disgusting, horrible, must have redress. Some sin openly, some clandestinely, some thro passion, others thro cold calculation, which are most vile? The world protects the hypocrites.

Lady William Russell to Princess Lieven [LP]

Stoutgard le 3 oct. [1835]

Ma chère amie, je vous suis reconnaissante au delà de toute expression! J'avais écrit à mon beau-frère & lui avais dit de vous écrire – cela vous épargnait tout embarras, mais vous aviez déjà eu la générosité de lui écrire. J'ai eu deux lettres fraternelles & affectueuses, malheureusement il ne peut pas venir – il me plaint mais je ne demande pas la pitié mais du secours. Je voudrais tirer mon malheureux mari du bourbier par les cheveux. Je pense à sa réputation, à son avenir si profondément malheureux si cette créature ne le lâche pas – il aura honte de revenir auprès de moi, il regrettera ses enfants & il me regrettera quoiqu'il me déteste pendant que le délire dure.

Il est revenu le 27 pour la fête du roi, nous avons été ensemble partout pendant ces trois jours. Je me tue pour sauver les apparences & je n'en puis plus; je commençais à avoir une lueur d'espoir qu'il en était peut-être dégoûté & que nous serions quittes pour de l'argent. Hélas, n'en pouvant plus chez lui il est parti à cheval seul à 5 heures du matin m'ayant crayonné un mot pour me dire qu'il reviendrait le soir. Il est minuit & il n'est pas encore de retour. Voilà que la vie de Baden recommence et les rendez-vous de cabarets. Je suis si honteuse & si malheureuse que je ne sais pas ce que je deviendrai. Il est sûr qu'elle se vante de l'épouser & qu'il a dit qu'il l'aimait éperdument et qu'il l'épouserait un jour. Veut-on m'empoisonner? On dit qu'elle a empoisonné son mari – il est mort très subitement mais il était étique. Ce qui est certain c'est que l'on me provoque au divorce – ce qui n'amènerait pas le mariage quoiqu'avec ses idées juives allemandes vous comprendriez l'inepte intrigue.

Dieu sait ce que je vous écris, vous aurez pitié de moi et de mon style, je marche toute la journée pour pouvoir dormir la nuit & avoir le calme nécessaire et un maintien décent. Je vous demande pardon de mon égoïsme et vous supplie de ne point montrer ma lettre et de vous défier de la Granville et de la Flahault en ce qui me regarde. . . . Mon humiliation et ma peine sont si profondes que je n'ose point regarder en avant. Je vis au jour la journée en tâchant de lutter contre ces terribles événements. Je vous embrasse et désire vos lettres quelque courtes qu'elles puissent être.

Lord John Russell to Lord Palmerston [WPP]
Private

Endsleigh, October 4th 1835
I have private reasons for wishing that William should come home before he goes to Berlin, and I shall be much obliged to you if you will direct him to come to England without loss of time.

Lady William Russell to Princess Lieven [LP]

7 oct mercredi [1835]
. . . Je suis bien malheureuse & je me décourage. J'avais dans les commencements beaucoup de force, maintenant je m'affaiblis; il me

menace à chaque instant d'une séparation me disant qu'il remercie Dieu que cela sera bientôt – mais il n'explique pas – il est comme fou. Mon beau-frère m'a écrit deux lettres affectueuses me plaignant, et mes enfants aussi, et m'assurant de son affection – mais il ne bouge pas, et toute la famille est si timide & si inerte que je ne puis les tirer de leurs fauteuils. Ils ne s'alarment pas, ils sont seulement 'very sorry' pour moi!

Figurez-vous qu'il est parti seul à cheval samedi matin à l'aube du jour, m'écrivant de ne pas l'attendre à dîner mais qu'il reviendrait le soir. Il est revenu *lundi* à dix heures du soir ayant passé trois jours & deux nuits dehors sans linge!! tous ses valets passant la nuit sur pied pour l'attendre. Depuis cette équipée nous avons dîné ensemble à la Cour, nous dînons chez le Prince Schönburg – nous avons eu les Capels & [*illegible*] à dîner chez nous – imaginez ma triste mine & mon pauvre coeur. Je tâche de dire que l'orage passera mais peut-être que la foudre tombera sur moi – enfin je perds la tête comme j'ai perdu la paix et le sommeil. Ne parlez pas de moi à Paris mais parlez de moi à mon beau-frère pour lui dire que je n'ai point poussé à bout son frère, que je me suis tu, que j'ai fait l'aveugle, que je me suis tenue tranquille, car ils tâcheront de m'inculper & ils me diront que ce n'est rien & que la Juive était belle & que c'était dans l'ordre. Je voudrais leur faire comprendre combien cette créature est dangereuse – pas moyen – ils croient que c'est une fantaisie qui passera. En attendant il a une telle haine contre moi que cela m'écrase. Ecrivez-moi souvent & si vous avez quelque chose à me dire d'intime, mettez sous enveloppe de Wellesley; Honble Henry Wellesley, Secrétaire de Légation &c. Plusieurs personnes mettent des lettres sous son enveloppe, il n'y aura rien d'extraordinaire.

On nous mande que nous irons à Berlin de suite, mais à quoi bon si elle nous suit ou me précède, puisque quelquefois il me dit qu'il ne veut pas que j'aille à Berlin – et d'autres fois qu'il compte quitter la carrière. Je ne sais pas à quoi me tenir et je deviens sotte et bête, comme un enfant qui a peur d'un spectre, car il n'a plus sa tête.

Lady William Russell to Princess Lieven [LP]

le 15 [oct. 1835]
Très chère amie, Lord William part pour Londres, vous le verrez sous peu à Paris. Mon beau-frère après avoir *bien réfléchi* à ce qu'il me mande,

trouve mieux qu'il aille en Angleterre. Palmerston lui donne un congé *at the request of Lord John* – ce qui est fort habilement conçu.

Enfin il y a de quoi se donner, comme Alava, à tous les diables possibles si l'on n'était déjà livré à eux. Chère amie je veux croire que tout se remettra mais tout va bien mal. Je ramerai comme un forçat & en silence pour empêcher le mal futur, mais il faut empêcher cette créature d'aller à Berlin. Le pouvez vous? et que je ne sois point nommée. Il est tellement démoralisé qu'il est vraiment brutal avec moi, il me traite comme Wellington traitait sa femme; c'est qu'il faut gagner Waterloo pour faire cela de bonne grâce – & moi de mon côté je ne suis pas la Duchess de Wellington. Enfin patience. Je sors, je me produis en public avec lui – nous dînons à la Cour, nous allons au spectacle, nous donnons à dîner – et je vous jure qu'il n'y a ni soupirs étouffés ni élancements d'yeux vers le ciel – ce n'est point mon genre & je n'ai point de vocation à être victime, ainsi donc il ne peut pas se plaindre que je le compromets par mes gémissements en public, mais je gémis, chère amie & je brûle et j'étouffe et j'ai honte & je ne sais quelquefois où donner de la tête. J'espère en Dieu que l'Angleterre, la politique, la chasse peut-être, la campagne, les ennuyeux frères, la belle Abbaye, le danger de la Patrie, les discours d'O'Connell, les mensonges de Brougham, le remettront dans son assiette naturelle, et que nous redeviendrons honnêtes gens. Et alors je pourrais vous écrire autres choses. Pardonnez-moi et *brûlez-moi* et ne parlez de moi ni à mes amies ni à mes ennemies. Mais ne manquez pas, ma très chère, de me détailler tout ce que vous verrez en lui & tout ce que vous entendrez sur son compte sans miséricorde. Je ne puis rien savoir de pis que ce que je sais déjà. Dieu fasse que cela cesse. Ecrivez-moi de suite en recevant celle-ci & brûlez-la – et puis écrivez-moi quand vous le verrez, ce qui devrait être le 21 de ce mois car il devrait arriver le 20 à Paris. Je vous embrasse. Je suis aise que votre liseuse réussisse, elle a un air doux & digne outre qu'elle est belle. Je suis heureuse que vous aimiez ma bonne Madame Appony,* elle est excellente & puis très comme il faut. Madame de Broglie† est mystique avec beaucoup de noblesse dans le caractère et point de charlatanisme ce qui est rare dans ce genre d'exaltation. Marguerite [de Flahault] n'est ni bonne, ni mystique, ni noble, ni exaltée, ni douce, ni digne, c'est une justice à lui rendre. Pour le charlatanisme la Granville vous en offre sous les formes les plus séduisantes.

* The wife of the Austrian Ambassador at Paris.

† Albertine, wife of the Duc de Broglie and daughter of Madame de Staël. She was a fervent Protestant.

Diplomacy

15 Oct. Good God what a day, another such a one and, and –

16 Oct. Dear Hastings' birthday – gave him my blessing, & left for Paris, arrived at [*illegible*]. From violence, hatred, anger, fury I fell into the opposite. Great God if it is a crime to prefer pleasure to pain, have mercy upon me.

17 Oct. Oh I breathe again & dare not write my feelings.

19 Oct. Days to be blotted from my existence, but alas, alas, it must not be.

20 Oct. Went to Strasbourg, bad cough & cold.

24 Oct. Arrived at Paris. Called on Madame de Lieven. Delighted to see each other, at least it appeared so, but all is false in the great world. Lady Granville came in, then Madame Appony, & these three ex & in Ambassadresses, who hate each other, kissed & complimented till I could have vomited.

26 Oct. Long conversation with Marguerite de F[lahault]. Talleyrand trying to break up the English Alliance because Palmerston kept him waiting & Lady H[olland] was rude to the Duchess of Dino, *ainsi va le monde*. Dined at Lord Granville's, he has no influence & no opinions.

27 Oct. Long talk with the Duchess Dino, almost said that Talleyrand would never pardon Palmerston's rudeness. What great effects from little causes; he is breaking up the Alliance. Walked with Madame de Lieven, dined with the Goulds & went to the Variétés, afterwards to Madame de Lieven, where I met Thiers, a clever man.

29 Oct. Letter from John which I answered with the greatest indignation, then calmer. Dined at Flahaults', much magnificence. but no amusing conversation, the Nations don't amalgamate in society.

30 Oct. Had a long interview with Leopold King of the Belgians, he is as he always was temporising, cunning & slow & wishes me to espouse his interests in Prussia.

Princess Lieven to Prince Lieven [LP]

28 oct 1835 Paris

... Hier j'avais pris le bras de William Russell pour me promener aux Tuileries, c'est un bon excellent homme, je suis fâchée de conspirer contre lui, mais aussi pourquoi est-il devenu fou. L'affaire commune a été très publique et l'idée de divorce aussi, et Lady William est détestée de toutes les femmes anglaises; n'est plainte par aucun. Voilà l'injustice du monde. J'espère que cet horrible esclandre n'arrivera pas, mais John est bien endormi. William ne veut pas aller en Angleterre, il préfère rester à Paris et faire son affaire par lettre.

Diplomacy

Lady William Russell to Princess Lieven [LP]

[Stuttgart 1835]

Je ne pourrai jamais oublier, chère & parfaite amie, toute la sincerité, la délicatesse, la pure amitié que vous avez montrées à cette triste occasion. Je n'ai pas voulu vous écrire de plus tristes détails. Hélas, il est parti d'ici le 15 & a passé 5 jours à Baden & 2 à Strasbourg avec l'infâme Juive & a logé dans cette même maison Mesmer dont le maître est un si abominable et si honteux coquin que certes la Princesse d'Orange ne devrait pas s'y rendre l'année prochaine. Il s'est montré en public avec elle bras dessus bras dessous partout sans pudeur, sans regret – enfin je vous assure que je ne suis pas sûre de sa tête. Mes rapports avec lui sont les plus cruels & les plus gênants du monde. Nous sommes comme toujours en société, nous ne sommes jamais seuls qu'en voiture & alors il met la tête à la portière et j'en fais autant. Il est à toute occasion injuste & même brutal quand il en trouve moyen. Il a demandé un autre appartement & vous comprenez que cela ne me convient que trop tant par précaution de santé que toute autre considération. Enfin je suis vraiment martyrisée. Si les frères avaient voulu agir cela aurait déjà cessé – le rappeler & puis non pas le sermonner comme un écolier, mais le garder là & se donner un peu de peine pour le tirer de la fange, mais le point d'honneur chez eux, hélas, n'est pas vif. Ils ne connaissent point le sentiment d'indignation – ils sont paresseux, flasques, peinés pour moi comme des femmes entre elles pour les douleurs de l'enfantement, mais ne sachant ni agir ni secourir. C'est pitoyable & je suis au désespoir. Enfin Dieu merci il est à Paris, il a dit, il a écrit même qu'il n'irait pas en Angleterre. Maintenant il me mande qu'il y va le 12 je crois. Dieu fasse qu'on l'y retienne. Il ne s'agit pas de le mettre aux galères mais de le *garder à vue* jusqu'à ce que cette fièvre animale soit passée & puis je recommencerai ma tâche quelque pénible qu'elle sera toujours & pour la vie; mais il est rigoureusement nécessaire de le distraire & l'éloigner. Si ma vue l'importune, ce qui est fort naturel, il faudra qu'on l'aide à éviter ma présence pendant quelque temps – je ne lui parlerai plus du passé – mais la tête n'y est pas pour le moment & il n'y a point d'autre manière d'agir. La distraction & l'éloignement & puis un autre poste. Mon pauvre beau-frère a été si mou dans cette circonstance qu'un eunuque du Shah de Perse aurait montré plus d'énergie. Ah mon Dieu, ce n'est pas seulement mon sort mais celui de quelques millions d'hommes qui se trouve entre ses faibles mains.

Il n'est point nécessaire que je vous recommande le secret sans réserve de mes communications. Vous avez gardé un silence si généreux & si admirable sur les tristes événements de Baden que je sens pouvoir vous écrire & à vous seule. J'écris à mon pauvre mari froidement et sèchement des détails de ménage & les projets de Berlin. Je ne sais que lui dire – je ne veux pas le quereller & il ne veut pas se raccommoder!!! Je suis désolée d'avoir occupé la société pendant quelques moments aussi désagréablement – je suis reconnaissante de l'intérèt que l'on veut bien prendre à un aussi déplorable événement. Il y a toujours réaction & je m'attends à ce que l'on trouve à redire à ma tenue plus tard – c'est inévitable! Mon mari a toujours été plus aimé que moi, on l'excusera, surtout les hommes, mais je ne désire pas qu'on le blâme, seulement qu'on oublie & je voudrais pouvoir aller avec lui nous cacher quelque part provisoirement. Je le répète, il faudrait que sa famille trouvât moyen de le tenir avec eux et de l'occuper. . . .

Adieu, ma pauvre amie, nous sommes toutes deux bien malheureuses! Mais Dieu aura pitié de nous. Brûlez mes lettres je vous en conjure.

Hastings Russell, who had received his father's blessing on the anniversary of his birthday, was now sixteen; henceforward the responsibility for his mother, brothers and his grandmother was often to fall on his young shoulders, in the absence of his father. He bore the burden with characteristic sweetness. His letters to Lord William are full of humour, good nature and good sense, and if they sometimes express impatience with his grumbling and contradictory parent, he quickly checks his irritation with a joke. Not the least of his concerns was the charge of the horses and the servants.

Hastings Russell to Lord William Russell at Paris [WP]

Wednesday. Oct. 28. 1835 [Stuttgart]

You bid me write to you and as Mamma has an inflammation in her eyes I will try to manage it though I have so much to do that I have only time to eat, drink & sleep.

The weather after having been bitter nipping cold as in Siberia is now so muggy & heavy that we have all the windows open, and no fires.

The horses are all physick'd & bled being stuffed up & lazy & their blood is thick & black; there were even the German scraggy fleet horses grown so sluggish & lazy from stuffing & heavy air that I think they will all have apoplexies. People feel the same, the clouds are brown, grey & black & you may fancy you see the air creep lazily along. The town goes on as

usual; everybody this year complains of the play, the best singers &
players are sick & it is reckon'd exceedingly tiresome & the diplomacy
grumble. Mamma has not been since you went as she has had the Lumbago
which Ludwig cured with vinegar & mustard poultices; now her eyes are
bad, but she has had no toothache as yet. She bids me say she got last
night your note from Bar le Duc & begs you will let her know what you
learn about Berlin so as to pack your things. They will be long going,
enquiries must be made for the conveyance, & the packing itself will take
long she says you would like to have some books there on arriving &c &c.

The Wellesleys hemale & shemale say you told them you should *not* go to
England at all – I thought Lord Palmerston sent for you about Berlin?
Let us know your movements, Mamma says you told her you should be
back in 3 weeks.

Nothing can exceed the Puffendorfs gratification at Wellesleys being
surchargé d'Affaires. She is full of young and always sick. I mean the
female Puffendorff. Fontenay says: *qu'elle vomit son vénin et son fiel tous
les matins dans un bassin ce qui l'épargne au prochain*. He & his wife & his
tiresome little child dined with us at 2, they told Mamma they wished to
dine early with her & bring Charles, Fontenay was very funny but both
parents could scarcely eat from terror at the repartees of their son who is
the vulgarest little brute I ever saw & has all the names, words & oaths of
French footmen.

Mamma begs you will let her know your motions & locomotions as
every body bothers us to death with questions & we look exceedingly
sheepish not knowing what to answer & the Wellesleys answering the
contrary from us.

Since I wrote this it has turned quite cold they say it is a fall of snow in
the Black Forest. The fever does not diminish, people die more & more
every day but we dont mean to die any of us till you return so no more at
present from your dutiful son till death.

LORD WILLIAM'S DIARY

1 Nov. [Paris] Palmerston says he will answer me by the next post. What folly.
Went to Baroness Delmar, my old flame.* My heart beat at seeing her. She is a

* Emily Rumbold (1790–1861), daughter of Sir George Rumbold, Bt.; she married
Ferdinand, Baron Delmar, a converted Prussian Jew. 'She is a good girl,' wrote Lady
Granville in 1817, 'and she has tried all Europe for a husband.' Leveson Gower (ed.)
Lady Granville's Letters, i, 124. 'A more striking picture of splendid misery I never
beheld . . . she feels her marriage to have been humiliating and is ashamed of herself
and her husband.' Earl of Ilchester (ed.), *Henry Fox's Journal*, p. 284.

good creature & most attentive to her husband who is going blind after having built the most magnificent house in Paris.

2 Nov. Went to Lady Granville's, who is *ennuyeuse et haineuse*, a sort of family clique, disagreable enough. The Talleyrand dinner had failed, all hatred & the little Dino out of humour. Thus is the great world; is it any sacrifice to leave it, none to me.

3 Nov. Long rigmarole with Madame de Lieven about intrigues etc.; says our Ambassador is null, & the dupe of a trick. Dined with the Austrian Ambassador Appony. Went to Lord Granville's & with him & Lord Canterbury to Court, long conversation with the King, also with King Leopold; introduced me to his Queen,* ugly little woman. The Queen of the French a most amiable, good excellent dignified woman. *La Reine et la bonne femme.* Madame de Lieven's; made the acquaintance of M. de Barente & the Russian Ambassador, Count Pahlen.

4 Nov. Dined at Baron Delmar & sat next to my old friend & love Emily – formerly the poor & gentle Emily, but now the rich yet still gentle Emily. She is evidently not happy. Her husband is blind for life, melancholy & irritable, & the trouble of representation is rather a weight than a pleasure to her. Poor Emily, I pity you – a better creature does not exist.

Lady William Russell to Princess Lieven [LP]

[Stuttgart 1835]

Je reçois régulièrement toutes vos lettres, très chère amie – que vous êtes compatissante & quel tact dans votre compassion!!! & que je vous suis reconnaissante & que je voudrais pouvoir exprimer ma reconnaissance avec votre éloquence! C'est du fond de mon pauvre coeur bien navré, bien brisé que je vous remercie. Je n'ai plus mal aux yeux. J'ai écrit trois fois à mon mari & à cette heure il aura reçu mes lettres, il vaut mieux que vous ne lui parliez pas des miennes; je vous écrirai, j'espère, sous peu sur d'autres sujets moins odieux mais pour le moment vous comprenez que j'ai l'âme & le cerveau remplis de ces horreurs. Je n'ai nulle distraction, ma vie est aussi triste que monotone. Cette tranquillité & cette monotonie me convient, mais cela fait que je ne puis penser qu'à mon malheur; je n'y pense pas avec aigreur, j'espère, & Dieu sait que mon coeur se fond devant vous – car votre amitié est touchante. Hélas, chère amie, mon pauvre mari est un être dominé par les circonstances, voilà pourquoi il est criminel à son frère de ne pas se prévaloir de sa situation actuelle pour l'arracher à ces abominables entourages... cette créature est à Baden, si on

* Princess Louise d'Orléans, daughter of Louis-Philippe.

l'en sépare pendant trois mois, il apprendrait sa mort même sans émotion, mais si l'on les laisse ensemble il sera comme le chevalier des Grieux courant après Manon Lescaut. Outre cela le chagrin que cela me cause nécessairement j'ai si honte de cette affaire que si l'on m'avait surprise *moi* commettant un vol je ne saurais l'être davantage. J'irais en Amérique si l'on nous y envoyait volontiers. *Vous* ne m'y oublieriez pas! Que le bon Dieu vous conserve & vous console, ma pauvre chère.

Hastings Russell to Lord William Russell [WP]

Stuttgardt, Nov. 5 1835

I am so unaccustomed to a serious letter that how to collect my mind sufficiently to answer your sudden & unexpected question (as you say you are impatient for my answer) about the choice of a profession I really scarcely know, when I read over the catalogue you put under my eyes – especially as I never remember your speaking to me on such a subject, & I should say that it required some months consideration & an opportunity of judging between different careers before I could positively fix on one.

All I can say however as to predilection (which is not the result of my judgement) is that as long as I can remember anything since I was a child of seven or eight years old I have wished to be in the Army; & I can not say that I have ever varied from that prejudice if it be one, for it is not the fruits of reflexion but merely a preference I have felt to that profession over all others.

I have often heard you say that you hurried into the Army before your education was finished merely to get away from school & that you much regretted it. I am in no hurry to leave a happy home as notwithstanding my age & want of experience what I hear & what I read & what I feel makes me certain that a good education is the best & only foundation for any career whatsoever. I should therefore not wish to enter thin, pale, beardless & boyish into a marching regiment in time of peace – but complete my studies & then chuse my profession which I still think will be the Army after all. You tell me also to consult somebody here – I could only consult my own countrymen on such a subject & here there are but two neither of them in the Army but luckily both men of birth Mr Wellesley & Lord Grosvenor.

I recollect hearing frequently last year Mr Wellesley ask you whether you did not mean to give me a year or two of college as a start in the world – (though he is against school & means to bring up little William at

356

home) & talk of the good result. I often heard this discuss'd & it appeared to me you were all of one mind on this subject & indeed that Oxford was the favourite & I remember that my Mother always said that Cambridge or Oxford would depend on which was the best at the time I should enter, as they varied & had their ups & downs. The age Mr Wellesley mentioned was 18 or 19. This year Lord Grosvenor who has been much with me & look'd over my books & sat over some of my lessons, made the same question to my Mother as Mr Wellesley did last year & was of the same opinion & being also an Oxford man gave his preference to that University – he added 'that it would be scarcely fair to put a young man suddenly into the Army without a little previous College life', he said 20 was full time enough for the Army & a couple of years at Oxford till that time would be of the greatest service.

This is what I have been in the habit of hearing over & over again last year & this from the only two Englishmen here, before you desired me to consult anybody.

With regard to my Mother she is very anxious I should chuse entirely for myself so as to have no after regrets & act quite on feeling a vocation for some particular career, but her desire has always been ever since I can recollect anything that I should be sufficiently studious to chuse the Law as leading to every thing great & honorable in England; & she said lately that she would wish me at all events to attend a course of jurisprudence at Berlin which both Falck & Nesselrode recommended to her as an ingredient to every liberal education.

Lord Grosvenor has taken down a list of the books I have read hitherto & am farther to read on classical & general History – for his boys – & he told Mamma that most of them had been recommended to him by Wilberforce but he found her collection more complete and that he regretted not having had time to follow up Wilberforce's directions on that study. Mamma has a letter Uncle John gave her several years ago from Dr Parr to Grandpapa about John's education, the course is the same as Wilberforce's. Lord Grosvenor says he will shew me Wilberforce's letter. Mamma has also one on the same subject of the Bishop of Llandaff about Lord Euston's education given to her by his daughter old Miss Watson. Mamma says she has never form'd a system from these letters but is not sorry to find that her notions as to a course of reading coincided with these Reverends.

Professor Schwab seems very much satisfied with what he calls my general knowledge as to ancient history & classical information; so that I

357

may hope that I have not mispent my time up to my present age & I certainly shall not slacken as I feel every day more & more the importance of study.

With regard to Parliament & public speaking the Army would not prevent that any more than the Law would & I hope that I may hereafter look to public life as my occupation. Diplomacy I always felt a positive aversion to. The Church I never thought of as a profession but I do not feel myself unqualified for it by any means. The situation of clerk in an office I am totally ignorant of in every respect & therefore never thought of it either & cannot say anything about it for or against.

I have answered every point of your letter which I have read over & over again & I hope you will be satisfied with what I have said. My earnest wish is to finish my education & then to chuse a profession which I have every reason to think will be the Army as it has always been my preference; should War take place in the interval I should wish to enter the Army sooner & go immediately on active service, if Peace continues I would defer entering till I have completed my studies & should at that period, as you apprehend, wars have entirely ceased & the Army become mere idleness & dissipation then of course I should chuse another profession, but I venture to doubt of the possibility of everlasting peace as it appears never to have been the state of the world since the Creation.

LORD WILLIAM'S DIARY

5 Nov. Called on Lord Granville who is *boutonné comme une rose*. Dined at the Duc de Broglie's.* 40 covers. He is a clever man, honest too, but has bad manners & a supercilious smile. She is very pretty & very agreable.

6 Nov. Dined at Madame Graham's. Lord W. Bentinck, whose simplicity astonishes the French, & Lady Charlotte Greville. To the Opéra Comique & to Lady Granville's, whose house is not kept up with any splendour.

8 Nov. Dined at the Tuileries. Took Princess Mary† to dinner. It is not possible to see a more amiable, united family, especially the Queen.

9 Nov. Went to the Duc de Broglie. She has an angelic face, but is sometimes insolent & not over wise. She is a saint. He is clever but pedantic & sarcastic. To Lady Granville, the usual set. Letters from Bessy & Hastings. The latter don't quite please me. Answered.

* Achille Charles, Duc de Broglie (1785–1870), Minister of Foreign Affairs and President of the Council.
† Princess Marie d'Orléans, daughter of Louis-Philippe.

Diplomacy

Stoutgard, Lundi 9 nov. [1835]

Chère amie il n'y a que vous qui puissiez m'aider, car ici je suis entourée de malveillants, d'ailleurs j'observe un silence absolu donc il faut que j'écrive à Paris pour avoir des renseignements sur l'Allemagne. Ne vous adressez ni à Buol ni à Meyendorff pour cause l'un est beau-frère de l'autre – mais Moltke & autres à Carlsruhe – pour savoir officiellement par la police positivement & absolument *où* cette femme se rend. Il y a fort long-temps qu'elle annonce son départ, tantôt pour Berlin tantôt pour Paris, puis Francfort & Vienne. Il est donc à presumer qu'elle pourrait aller à Londres puisqu'elle ne nomme pas cette ville. Elle a parmi ses autres séductions une faculté, dit on, de mentir, tout à fait miraculeuse. Ce qu'il y a de sûr maintenant c'est qu'elle quitte Baden le 15, que cet infâme vieux Kuppler, le maître de la maison rose Mesmer l'annonce en offrant son appartement au rez de chaussée. C'est aujourd'hui le 9, vous recevrez ma lettre le 12, si vous faites écrire de suite on pourra prendre des informations promptes et sûres; et on pourra continuer à suivre sa route & savoir avec quel passeport elle voyage (car j'ai mes soupçons) & sous quel nom, si elle a ses enfants avec elle &c. Tout cela est très facile à savoir sans que mon malheureux nom y paraisse – mais je désire que cela soit non pas comme si *vous* vous y intéressiez, mais par les moyens que vous savez comme affaire de police, car je ne voudrais point de faux rapports & de 'on-dit'. Très chère, vous comprenez combien je serais rassurée si je la savais casée pour l'hiver là ou elle ne pourrait pas nuire. Elle se vante publiquement 'de le tenir et de ne pas vouloir le lâcher'! Vos informations seront donc officielles et comme double report la Duchesse Dino pourrait savoir de Kramer son médicin ce que la Juive devient car il a l'honneur de soigner ses maladies secrètes. . . . Cette affaire n'est ni oubliée ni même assoupie; j'ai lieu de tout craindre & il n'y a pas d'autre moyen au monde qu'un éloignement complet & un départ subit. Si la famille voulait comprendre cela!! J'irais au bout du monde rejoindre mon pauvre mari si on voulait seulement le faire partir de suite. Ne croyez point que mes craintes soient exagérées.

Vous avez été si compatissante, si sincère, si exacte, si délicate, si parfaite dans cette affreuse circonstance que je suis sûre que vous agirez sans me nommer!

Elle a voyagé sous mon nom à Strasbourg, et dans les petites auberges de campagne on les a vus. Ils étaient Milord et Milady. Il y avait une femme de chambre, c'est à dire sa servante, *un enfant*!! Ah, mon Dieu, mes pauvres enfants! Un enfant, ce qui est vrai, car le plus petit restait en arrière dans la maison ou j'étais délaisée aussi, point de domestique, *ma* calèche verte!! & un certain gros portefeuille énorme sur lequel en grosses lettres se trouve le nom du possesseur pour garder l'incognito. Enfin la tête n'y était pas j'en suis sûre, j'en suis désespérée plus j'y pense, & au duel & à tout plus je me sens mourir de honte, de crainte vague, de désespoir pour l'avenir – enfin vous comprenez mon état.

Faites, chère amie, promptement les démarches nécessaires. Mon beau-frère se réveille, il voit le danger, et qu'il ne s'agit plus de me plaindre mais d'agir, Dieu merci, & Dieu fasse que cela ne soit pas trop tard. Figurez-vous que lors du second voyage à Strasbourg cette dernière fois le 21 & 22 octobre, son valet de chambre a reçu ses ordres lorsqu'il montait à Baden sur le siège, de rester en arrière & de le suivre par la diligence le lendemain au soir; quand cet homme arrive à l'auberge de l'Esprit à Strasbourg, on lui dit 'Monsieur est ici, mais Madame vient de partir avec les enfants'!!!

LORD WILLIAM'S DIARY

10 Nov. [Paris] Dined at Talleyrand's. Lieven, Boehm, Guizot, Thiers, Molé, Mignet, Pasquier, Gérard. The most remarkable men of France, but alas what are these men? Their minds are stored with knowledge – but they have none of them that firmness of character which constitutes the real dignity & utility of man. They have written & spoken in favour of political liberty, they have arrived at power & they have crushed it. What is to be thought of such men?

12 Nov. No letter from Palmerston. I am at a loss what to do. Letter from Tavistock; disagreable. Answered it as I ought. I detest meddlers – if they push me I will give the whole thing up. Bitter cold. Out of humour.

13 Nov. Called on my old friend & —— Madame Durazzo, alas what wrecks old Time makes with the human form divine – she is a friendly good creature. Went to Opéra Comique & Lady Granville's, a sort of English sect, tiresome enough. It is strange how people go on like horses in a mill, doing & saying the same things.

15 Nov. Letter from Palmerston to say I am to go to Berlin. Saw Lord Granville, *bon de rien*. Decided to return to Stutgart.

18 Nov. Left Paris.

Diplomacy

Lady William Russell to Princess Lieven [LP]

[Stuttgart] 21 novembre [1835]

Ma chère amie, tout cela est de l'hypocrisie je suis fâchée de vous le dire. Cet homme n'a pas d'entrailles. Les lettres que je reçois sont brutales et grossières. C'est un esprit renversé, démoralisé, dépravé pour le moment; l'esprit se remettra peut-être, le coeur jamais (sauf un miracle). Enfin j'attendrai, je ferai tout mon possible pour y tenir, mais je n'ai point d'espoir, je l'avoue, et tout ce que la famille a fait paraît être exprès pour pousser leur malheureux parent dans l'abîme d'où il s'agissait de le tirer. Ils ne se soucient pas de le voir, cela les gêne – c'est un peuple craintif & paresseux. Ils sont moralement sourds et aveugles. Enfin je resterai à mon poste tant que je pourrai & je ne l'abandonnerai qu'à toute extrémité – mais ceci n'est pas un cas ordinaire. Dieu fasse que j'aie tort! Je suis pénétrée de votre amitié & de votre droiture; je le suis aussi de la délicatesse de Bacourt. Il ne le saura jamais, mais je lui garderai un sentiment d'estime inaltérable pour toujours.

Les lettres et paquets arrivent à Mesmer par la poste constamment. La Juive l'attend à Baden, ou ira le rejoindre comme de coutume à Strasbourg; il a écrit de Paris à son frère, qui me le mande '*that he had taken the lady back to her family, where she is to remain*'!!!! C'est la dernière lettre que je reçois de Devonshire datée le 4 novembre – comme pour dire je m'en lave les mains, c'est une affaire finie, consolez-vous, il n'est point nécessaire que mon frère aille en Angleterre. Comme il n'avait point l'enlevée à ses parents, je ne comprends dans aucun cas la nécessité de ramener cette brebis égarée dans son bercail de Francfort, et je ne conçois pas l'inéptie de mon correspondant. Quoiqu'il en soit voilà un mensonge dans toutes les règles. La Juive est là où elle a toujours eté (elle y était hier le 20) disant qu'elle part – et je me remets à vous chère amie pour savoir où elle va. Vous pouvez compter sur mon calme. Je mettrai une grande et douloureuse patience à cette terrible opération morale qu'il faut que je subisse. . . .

Il m'écrit qu'il revient de suite mais ne nomme pas le jour; que Palmerston l'envoie à Berlin de suite & puis il ajoute qu'Adair n'est pas encore averti & que cela ne sera probablement qu'à Noel. Ainsi n'ayant pas reçu de nouvelles de l'Angleterre je ne sais pas à quoi m'en tenir pour le moment. Vous me le direz & ne manquez pas de me mander le jour de son départ de Paris. Il a renvoyé son valet de chambre & en a pris un autre, c'est à dire il lui a donné un congé pour aller voir ses parents – afin que ce voyage de retour soit fait avec mystère. Cela au moins est plus décent quoique aussi désolant que le départ d'ici & le scandale des 5 jours à Baden (du 15 au 21).

Chère amie, faites adresser par la petite & cacheter en rouge, je ne veux pas que votre écriture & cachet sous l'adresse Wellesley soit reconnu – la petite Wellesley est rusée & bornée, son mari est borné & têtu. Nous sommes très bien ensemble, je ne vous parle que de leurs caractères & non de leur procédés. Vous m'écrirez ouvertement par la poste, papier, écriture, cachet à vous appartenant, des choses insignifiantes, nouvelles de Paris & de Berlin – mais quand vous avez quelque chose à me dire qui regarde la Juive ce sera comme je viens de le dire. Vous comprenez chère que si la Juive va à Berlin je n'y vais pas & que si je l'y trouvais je m'en irais – ce qui ferait bien plus de bruit que de n'y point aller du tout, et je voudrais éviter cet éclat, car très positivement je ne veux pas être en tiers. Je m'en irais dans ce cas fatal en Angleterre & alors il pourrait opter entre sa maîtresse et sa femme ; je souhaite que les choses n'en viennent pas là, et il faut tâcher de l'empêcher.

Demandez à l'Ambassade *où* il se fait envoyer ses lettres après avoir quitté Paris – Strasbourg – Baden – Francfort ? ou bien à Stoutgard ?

Duke of Bedford to Lord William Russell at Berlin [WP]

London 24 Nov 1835

On my arrival in London yesterday on various matters of business (principally health) I was much disappointed to find you had left Paris, and were actually gone to Berlin. I was in hopes you were coming to England, and that I should see you at Woburn soon – I assure you I wish much to see you, for I cannot help feeling that my days are numbered and that my time in this world of trial and sorrow is not likely to be of long duration – if you should however come to England after you are fairly installed in all your dignities at Berlin, it will give me very great pleasure to see you once more, and I'm sure you will be equally welcomed by the Duchess, write to me as soon as you can, when you have arranged your plans, and let me know what they are. I return again to Woburn immediately.

Princess Lieven to Prince Lieven [LP]

27 Nov 1835 Paris

Je continue de recevoir de tristes nouvelles de cette pauvre Lady William de Stoutgart et aujourd'hui son malheur est connu de tout le

monde. Elle a pris des informations sur les projets de la Juive et elle
apprend qu'elle aussi ira s'établir à Berlin auprès de Lord William, ma
pauvre amie a pris en conséquence la résolution de ne point s'y rendre. Je
ne sais que dire de ce projet. Je conçois bien comme affaire de cœur il soit
naturel; comme raison, cela est mal jugé, car la brèche demeurera alors
sans remède, et si ce n'est à elle-même c'est à ses enfants qu'elle doit
songer – le mari ne le lui pardonnerait jamais cette défection. L'éclat de
cette séparation nuirait à sa position sociale et politique même et certaine-
ment il ne tiendrait pas longtemps à ce poste sans sa femme. Elle m'écrit
des lettres à faire pleurer, lui m'en écrit des plus gaies, et voilà comme va
le monde.

LORD WILLIAM'S DIARY
21 Nov. Strasburg. Bitter cold but warmed by a good dinner.
24 Nov. Nedab. [Baden] Found Mrs R. Horrible woman.
25 Nov. Arrived at Stutgart.
27 Nov. Dined with the King & took leave, & a most tender one of Princess
Sophia, who is a charming girl, & will do honour to any throne in Europe.
1 Dec. Dined with Meyendorff, he is so false I cannot bear him.

Prussia 1835–1841

Lord William left Stuttgart the next day and travelling by way of Frankfort,
  where he stayed two nights, reached Berlin. He found there a despatch from
  Palmerston desiring him to go to England as soon as he had presented his
  credentials. He found the King of Prussia "an old soldier of few words and
  awkward manners, but an honest man. He told me my antecedents were
  in my favour and hoped I was not a *brouillon*.' Lord William was received
  also by other members of the Royal Family, and sometimes he sat with
  the Duchess of Cumberland and her son. 'The poor blind boy makes my
  heart ache',* he wrote. 'My impression is that altho' these people were very
  civil they have strong prejudice against my name, party and opinions.'

Princess Lieven to Lady William Russell at Stuttgart [PRP]

10 dec 1835 Paris
Chère chère amie,
  Je suis bien inquiète de votre silence. Vous ne m'avez pas donné signe
de vie depuis le retour de votre mari. Il m'a écrit pour annoncer son

* The Duke and Duchess of Cumberland's only child, Prince George, became blind
after an accident in his early youth. He succeeded his father as King of Hanover in
1851.

départ pour Berlin le 2, mais il ne vous nomme pas et je suis donc à ignorer encore si vous êtes partie avec lui; si vous le suivez; quand? . . . Tout le monde me demande de vos nouvelles avec tendresse. Je suis triste, bien triste, le mauvais temps me détend les nerfs. Je pleure comme à Baden, comme avant. Ah, la vie n'est que des larmes.

Lord William Russell to Lady William Russell at Stuttgart [PRP]

Dec. 21 [1835] Berlin.

This is the last letter you will receive from Berlin. I leave tomorrow for England, & these are my last instructions. You will remain at Stutgart till the middle of February – before that you cannot be lodged here otherwise than in a bad inn, besides the cold is not bearable & would kill poor little Atty. The air is so rare that I cannot sleep, & I have slept in a battery whilst the cannon roared.

When you set out I would advise you to travel slowly, going by Munich & Dresden to see those places & to arrive here when the weather is softened & the violent gaiety a little abated. In the meantime send here whatever furniture you can spare so that it may arrive towards the end of January or beginning of February with each case numbered & a list sent to me of their contents so that I may know what to open. Above all send the Mohez carpet. Don't send any plate unless to go to England by Hamborough. I should like the horses to meet me here on my return from England but not to arrive before me. We must combine this afterwards, you should not allow Nicholson to keep 2 German *helfen* – one is amply sufficient. The two German horses might draw the *fourgon* here. Send me my brass bed, for I cannot sleep in these horrid German beds. Sell the big coach, it is falling to pieces, & don't overload the post chaise so as to break or damage it.

I have not heard from you for 8 days. Write to England & give me all your commissions. I shall be back about the middle of February.

Lady William Russell to Princess Lieven [LP]

[Stuttgart] 23 dec 1835

. . . J'écris à mon beau-frère & réponds à ses questions. Il est très fâché comme de raison de notre malheureuse histoire, mais il ne peut pas encore bien comprendre pourquoi tout le monde la connaît!! Concevez-

vous cela ? Il me mande d'un air étonné que toute l'Angleterre en parle! et
puis me dit – il faut que cela soit votre mère!!! Vous savez, chère, que ma
pauvre mère a été d'une innocence parfaite et complète & vous le direz,
j'en suis sûre, en esprit de justice si jamais il s'agissait de l'inculper. Ils
voudraient arranger une histoire de jalousie excitée par les révélations,
d'une mère &c.,&c. Enfin cette pauvre mère a toujours eu l'imagination
tellement frappée de l'idée que les eaux de Baden lui avaient monté à la
tête comme elle en avait vu 3 exemples, pendant que nous étions là. L'un
d'une veuve de général qui s'était jetée à l'eau devant sa porte. Là où
Blucher demeurait & les gens même de Blucher avec la femme de chambre
de ma mère l'ont secourue – et puis on a saigné et purgé cette femme qui
huit jours après était tout à fait raisonnable. Ensuite le domestique d'un
russe dont tout le monde parlait & qui est mort dans deux jours à l'hôpital
– et puis un inconnu sans domestique à l'auberge qui est devenu fou à
la suite des eaux & s'est coupé la gorge. Enfin tout cela avait tellement
effrayé ma mère que malgré son indiscrétion naturelle elle avait plus de
terreur que de colère dans les commencements & elle ne pouvait rien
savoir que ce que le public entier lui apprenait. Enfin ma chère, ils sont
embarrassés & voudraient bien pouvoir dire que c'est bien dommage que
j'aie su,&c. Je vous en préviens en cas que vous entendiez quelque chose
de semblable & que vous puissiez rendre justice à une pauvre femme âgée
tout à fait nulle dans cette abominable affaire. Enfin je me tue de répéter
à mon beau-frère – il avait perdu la tête, il faisait des choses si scandaleuses
qu'il insultait le public – la société, il ne s'agissait point de moi seule,
mais de son fils de seize ans qui n'est ni aveugle, ni sourd. C'est pour cela
que je vous en supplie de le rappeler pour le tirer de l'abîme. Vous avez tardé
à le faire, le mal par là a empiré; comment voulez-vous que l'on n'en
parle pas quand plus de 3 mille personnes en ont été témoins? et que la
Juive voulait l'afficher et lui se laissait faire comme un écolier. Enfin, ma
bonne amie, je vous ai dit que toute cette famille était dure d'oreille
moralement et qu'il faut leur dire les choses fortement et bien crier pour
qu'ils croient. S'il y avait un incendie ils laisseraient brûler la maison avant
que d'y porter du secours & même attiseraient le feu. Voilà comme ils font
politiquement! Voilà où nous en sommes en Angleterre. Mon pauvre
mari m'écrit de Berlin avec moins de violence & aigreur. Son coeur n'est
pas touché, ni sa conscience, mais la tête revient un peu je crois. Il
m'écrit sèchement mais avec peu de détails de maisons à louer comme s'il
pensait aux six mois à venir. Il a loué la maison Unter den Linden que
vous occupiez jadis. Elle est toute délâbrée, ayant été convertie en magasin

de tapissier pendant maintes années. Il faut donc la peindre et la mettre en état habitable ce qui durera jusqu'à la fin du mois de février au plus tôt, me dit-il, et avec des promesses d'ouvriers allemands cela pourra bien durer jusqu' à la mi-mars, je dois donc m'y rendre, alors, d'ici et lui de Londres où il compte faire un séjour de 2 mois & demi. En attendant je reste dans ma maison avec chiens, chevaux, domestiques &c., tout comme quand nous y étions ensemble, c'est pour moi un sujet presque de joie de pouvoir passer l'hiver tranquillement avec mes pauvres enfants & le savoir out of harm's way, comme nous disons, chez ses parents, et l'horrible Juive à Francfort, mais elle crie hautement qu'elle ira à Berlin chez deux tantes qu'elle a déterrées. Promettez-moi de vous informer & ne craignez pas que je casse les vitres, mais comment voulez-vous que je me laisse insulter comme à Baden après votre départ? Et comment voulez-vous que je permette à un jeune homme de seize ans d'être témoin de la conduite de son père? J'attendrai – mais si j'allais là je ferais plus de tort à sa réputation que si je le laissais avec sa maîtresse seul. Vous avez vu que femme et enfants étaient oubliés. J'irais donc dans ce cas affreux en Angleterre y attendre que l'ouragan soit passé, mais je ne ferais point d'éclat. Et en attendant j'ai le projet d'aller le rejoindre à Berlin au printemps quand ma maison sera prête. Voilà, ce me semble tout ce que je puis faire de plus froid & du calcul le plus anti-passionné. Personne ne pourra trouver extraordinaire qu'une femme et trois enfants ne voyagent pas vers le nord de l'Allemagne au milieu de l'hiver, pour aller se loger à l'auberge. Je reste donc avec *mon* établissement à Stoutgard, mon mari prépare *son* établissement à Berlin, pendant qu'il se prépare il passe en Angleterre.

Je suis, Dieu merci, beaucoup plus calme, la monotonie de ce lieu agit comme l'opium. Mon avenir est bien douloureux mais c'est à quoi il ne faut jamais songer – car on ne sait pas si on aura un avenir & je ferai tout au monde pour me résigner à mon sort tout en faisant tout au monde pour que cette vilaine intrigue cesse. . . . Le froid ici est incomparable, vous vous croiriez chez vous, c'est au reste un froid sec, Dieu merci, l'humidité me tue & m'abîme les nerfs. Si cet hiver avait été pluvieux & brumeux je me serais je crois suicidée. Adieu, ma très chère. Le roi ici m'a dit que vous iriez à Baden l'été prochain? Je ne sors pas du tout – même pas au spectacle qui était mon unique ressource l'année passée.

Schreiben Sie nur recht bald und oft!*

---

* 'Do write soon and often.'

Diplomacy

Duke of Bedford to Lord William Russell at Berlin [WPP]

Woburn Abbey, December, 24. 1835.

Your kind and affectionate letter has given me very great pleasure, and I assure you *de bon coeur*, that I look forward to seeing you here with real satisfaction, this is not *façon de parler*, or the mere compliments of the season, but written in perfect truth and sincerity. Whenever you arrive in London you have only to go to Belgrave Square and the housekeeper will prepare a warm room for you. You will find Wrio and Eliza (who I am sorry to say is in a very weak state of health) there, and Tav. and John, I hope you will find here. I assure you, you are quite wrong in supposing that the Duchess has not a very sincere affection for you. I trust you will be here soon, as towards the middle of January I go to the sea side, in hopes that the bracing air of the sea may continue the benefits which I unquestionably received from the highlands in the autumn – write to me soon, and believe me always my dear William,

Your very affectionate Father,

B.

Lord William set out from Berlin in bitter weather with snow falling, and stopped at Frankfort as he had when coming. He was in London on 1 January, and went next day to Woburn Abbey.

Despite Lord Grosvenor's 'near economy', his family proved a great resource to Lady William during the winter which she passed at Stuttgart. Lady Grosvenor wrote emphatically to her mother deploring Lord William's conduct, making it clear that he was a monster, his wife an angel, and the Jewess 'une infâme coquine'.

'The little dinners at Lady William's are very pleasant to us. She dines at three and we sit on talking afterwards, just ourselves and two or three guests and the children.' The Russell boys, she thought, were very nice. Celebrating the festival in German style, Lady William asked them all to her Christmas party, when they saw for the first time 'a Christmas tree, which is an upright pole with branches of spruce firs upon which are fastened innumerable bonbons and little lighted tapers'.

They found their hostess good humoured and agreeable in every way. 'She knows all the people who ever were born and all the books that ever were written, and yet has full value for utter nonsense.'[37]

LORD WILLIAM'S DIARY

1 Jan., 1836. To Woburn Abbey, full of people, 24 at table. What splendid luxury, what refinement, what comfort. The Duchess spoke to me on the subject of marriage kindly & sensibly; kindness & sense always makes an impression on me. Remained the whole month. Went to Panshanger. I delight in Lady Cowper.

After this visit Lady Cowper wrote to Madame de Lieven: 'William Russell has just left me. He spent two days here, but I can tell you nothing about the Jewess, although we talked on every subject. I was too discreet to broach the subject myself, and when he told me he was going to Berlin in a fortnight, I hoped it was to rejoin his wife. He looks very well but a little sad, and also a little shamefaced, as though he feared indiscreet questions. .'³⁸
Sir George Shee was Lord William's successor at Stuttgart.

Hastings Russell to Lord William Russell in London [WP]

[Stuttgart, January 1836]
His Excellency Shee brought your letter of the 6th last night – his arrival & the expectation of his arrival has caused the most extraordinary excitement – Wellesley – Erpf, cooks. I cannot describe all the events & conflicting elements – but I am going to write a fable after the fashion of Gay call'd the secretary, the minister & the two cooks which will give you some faint idea of our situation. – nothing was ready for him – he had no bed – no curtains – no stove no dinner – there never was a Dip in such a dilemma – in a few days his retinue arrives & he will appear in all his splendour.

I am sorry you reduce me to a rotten old worn out harness which cannot be tack'd together & for which tacking & tackling Erpf asks more than the whole concern new.

Mamma sends you word she is in despair at having written you what you call numerous & long letters but she says she has an antipathy to writing & yet when she gets a pen in her hand she cannot help writing much nonsense & hopes you will excuse her & she will let you digest what you have & not write for some time to you. She received no letter from you since the 22 from Berlin till the 2d. from London though you mention having written from Brussels but she never got it & she says you seem so gay with balls, masquerades, singing & shooting that it must be a perfect nuisance to have Mrs Wellesley's handsome brother at Woburn to put you in mind of dull Stuttgardt. I will not give your love to her for she has transferr'd her diplomatic affections to Shee – & before he came she said 'he really writes such nice letters, I am grown quite fond of him' – so when she has seen him one will not be able to sit in the room with them. She says her brother the captain makes up to aunt Georgy – is it so?

Diplomacy

... Mamma bids me tell you she implores you not to send any of our furniture to Berlin as she will not have a chair to sit on when she goes to England – & Berlin is so very precarious, the things would cost enormously & it is better to hire there: this is what she bids me say.

Arthur grows very tall & thin Odo is well & merry, it is very funny to hear him say the multiplication table in German. I grow tall & grow fat too, I suppose it is reading so much Greek. I am very well and very boisterous.

Scythian Slyboots & little Fontenay have had a tiff at whist, the whole town talked of it till Shee's arrival turned their thoughts but it was very grand – their passions strong & the ladies at the tea table nearly screamed with affright & let many stitches fall in their knitting so that there will be a rise in the price of stockings.

I wonder whether the arrival of Mendelssohn in London caused as much sensation.

Hastings Russell to Lord William Russell in London [WP]

[Stuttgart 1836]

I have bought the horse as you bid me, the ould rogue Münchingen as soon as he heard it was for you pretended it was all a mistake & wanted 80 then I said very sorry but that I could not go beyond 60 that the horses were going the next day & wish'd him goodbye; then he came down to 70 & then said again it was a mistake & took 65. . . .

The German greys will be easily sold as many people have ask'd about them the whole winter wishing for them in spring; I shall see after it & about the Carlsruhe match for the English greys &c &c. but I shall not employ Nicholson for he runs down horses so you never would sell them; he says he never see'd such an oss as the one you bought & that it is *ruinated* since it has been here – he always abuses horses as you know.

Meyendorff puffs your German horses continually since Baden & calls them *les hirondelles*. Nicky has fatted them up so that they are not as swift now as swallows, but they are never vicious except one of them in the stable, on the contrary I found the English kick at times in harness but never the Germans. . . .

Atty's mouth is horrible since you went, quite a crust & pains him he says. . . .

I am glad you saw I had progressed in Greek I feel it myself by reading

an ode of Pindar in Greek with Schwab offhand to my own surprize; I had
not been to him for some time I mean during the winter months, my hour
is 4 & I now return to it as it is daylight & no snow on the ground; after 3
months interruption with Schwab I felt my own progress, in a new author
& a difficult one.

I have begun the Bible in Hebrew this week & shall in one year do what
it takes 3 for in Greek.

I wish you would tell me what is to happen to me in the Guards you
said 18 was the latest age one could enter; supposing I should get my
commission sooner what am I to do? to leave my studies for St James's
Street or can you insure me till 18? pray answer me this.

Hastings Russell to Lord William Russell [WP]

[Stuttgart 1836]
As you disinherited me before I enjoyed even a particle of the fortune
you assured me I hope you will compensate by giving me by return of post
a harness for four in hand plain black & so as to be split in two. Wellesley's
comes to pieces & here they are bad & dear.

Expecting a thaw daily which never comes we skate unceasingly, on the
top of the hill *privatim* the whole race of Grosvenors & me, father, mother,
boys, girls, who cannot skate slides, & then in the Anlager *pro bono* with the
Crown Prince & his parasites. . . .

The brown horse is quite well & the poor old white was shot on the 23
of Dec. through the head; he fell without a struggle & his skeleton is to be
put in the museum as they have not yet got an Andalusian & lectures will
be read over him twice a year. I never saw anything so changed as he was,
his coat was all falling off & yellow, his hind quarters contracted, so that he
had not the use of his legs & all the hair off his head from rubbing it with
turpentine.

Mamma does not stir out for 9 days together & then takes a freak of
driving in the shut carriage with all the windows up a hot bottle at her feet
& covered with furs – which she calls air & exercise to make her sleep well.
She drives regularly round by the Ludwigsburg road & comes home by
Canstadt, & looks like Lady Elizabeth Lowther at Lausanne & at Tun-
brigewells. She has excused herself at the court circle on the plea of
chilblains as this year toothache won't do, nobody would believe her so
now the other extremities answer the purpose of pretexts for house-

keeping. I hear her friends have applied for a loan of her court trains in consequence. . . .

You must not expect me to write but on Sundays for I have no time even to shave if I had a beard, on week days I begin before Day break & work away till 12 then I skate till 3 then dine, digest till 5, & then begin again at Sophocles. At 8 I want to go to bed without washing then Mamma comes & scolds & I am obliged to soap & soak, brush & comb so that I don't get to bed till near 9 when I never wake till 6 with old Johann bringing in my clothes.

LORD WILLIAM'S DIARY

Jan. To London, saw John, Melbourne & Palmerston. Went to Brighton, long conversation with the King. Sir H. Taylor offered me the Guelph – which I refused.

2 Feb. Went to Dover where I passed three days with my father & the Duchess, who talked to me very frankly & kindly about F[rankfort] & R[ebecca].

Leaving the Duke and Duchess, he crossed over to France and spent ten days in Paris. He saw many friends but passed his time mostly with Madame de Lieven. Since his visit to Paris in November they had written to each other and she declared herself his most devoted friend. 'Vous me manquez à tout instant. J'aurais tant de choses à vous dire. Personne ne m'est d'une société si douce que vous.'[39] 'Je ne sais me plaire vraiment qu'avec un Anglais, mais je n'en aime comme je vous aime. I like you so much.'[40]

It is only from her letters to him that we can form some idea of his state of mind, for about now he laid aside his journal and did not take it up again for several years. The reproof she sent him soon after his first arrival in Berlin signifies how much he was troubled by his domestic situation.

'Je ne crois pas à la menace que vous me faites de vous jeter dans les bras de la bonne, car en supposant même que vous ayez à vous plaindre à Berlin, ce ne serait pas en vous avilissant que vous iriez vous venger, mais vous n'avez pas à vous plaindre, j'en suis sûre car vous ne serez pas grossier comme votre Chef* et vous ne ferez pas le *babe* qui a besoin d'une bonne. Vous ne me dites pas un mot de Lady William, et elle ne m'écrit pas. Je suppose qu'elle est avec vous, ou qu'elle va vous suivre. Je vous regrette tous les jours.'[41]

Lady William Russell to Princess Lieven [LP]

[Stuttgart] le 23 février [1836]

Ma chère amie, je n'ai point répondu à votre lettre parce que je me doutais bien parce que mon beau-frère m'écrivait que Lord William irait à

* Lord Palmerston.

Paris, en preuve de quoi il y a trouvé une lettre de ma façon que j'ai envoyée à l'Ambassade. Il m'a écrit trois fois de Paris, c'est toujours le même style, un état d'irritation frénétique sans dire pourquoi.

Enfin le temps et la patience voilà ce qu'il faut. Je reste ici jusqu'au mois d'avril, cela est convenu et raisonnable de toutes les manières. Il est parti je crois le 16 de Paris. Je voudrais bien avoir des détails & vous conjure de m'en donner. . . . J'ai eu une lettre de Fulda, de Madame Tamis assez consolante, elle avait appris des choses à son passage à Francfort dont elle m'a fait part pour me tranquilliser. La Juive ne va point à Berlin à moins qu'on ne l'enlève ou qu'elle ne s'évade. Ses parents et toute cette juiverie est au désespoir du scandale & désire que cela cesse. Les Juifs ont montré plus de nerf que les Chrétiens, car la pusillanimité de mes beaux-frères a été pitoyable. Ils sont fâchés de ce que j'aie été '*annoyed*'; vous connaissez ce terme qui ne veut pas dire ennuyé, ni chagriné, mais simplement contrarié!!! mais ils sont surtout désolés non pas tant que la chose soit arrivée mais que l'on en ait parlé!!!

Enfin ce sont des âmes de papier mâché.

Vous verrez je crois le Duc et la Duchesse à Paris. Son amant actuel n'est plus le peintre mais dit-on son valet de chambre suisse.* Si vous voulez connaître la généalogie de ce rapport Lord William me l'a dit, qui le tenait de Lord Essex, qui l'avait appris de Charles Greville à qui [*torn*] confiseur l'avait raconté – un Italien que Greville avait placé chez le Duc de B. et qui sortait de chez le Duc de York.

Voilà un fabliau – comme sa soeur la Duchesse de Manchester a quitté son mari pour un (*gamekeeper*) garde-chasse† – c'est dans le sang & irrésistible apparemment. Je deviens méchante, et acariâtre de désespoir je crois. Ayez pitié de moi, chère amie, mais mon bonheur a fait un terrible naufrage! Dites-moi si nous nous retrouverons cet été. Où irez vous? L'hiver ici est comme en Russie à ce que Meyendorff m'assure – nous gelons. Le roi m'a chargé de le rappeler à votre souvenir si tant y a que vous vous rappeliez de lui dans cette atmosphère. Voilà son expression. . . .

* Lady William described the Duchess of Bedford as 'coquette comme la lune', and her moral character perhaps never stood very high. Her liaison with the painter Landseer was public enough to allow *The Satirist* to write in 1833: 'The Duchess of Bedford has been suddenly taken ill in Ireland. Strong draughts were resorted to which relieved the patient. Edwin Landseer is her Grace's draughtsman!' And in the same year le Marchant wrote of her as 'a bold bad woman with the remains of beauty'. Aspinall (ed.), *Three Early Nineteenth Century Dairies*, p. 366.

† According to Mrs Smith, writing in 1812, 'The Duchess of Manchester left home years before with one of her footmen'. Lady Strachey (ed.), *Memoirs of a Highland Lady*, p. 151.

Je sors le moins souvent possible sans pourtant vouloir avoir l'air de me renfermer pour verser des larmes, car je n'ai nulle vocation pour le rôle de victime ni envie de jouer la Griséldis. Je m'efforce à faire ce qui me semble 'recht', mais j'ai le coeur tout à vous, ma bonne amie, & je ne saurais jamais vous dire combien je vous suis reconnaissante. Je voudrais bien pouvoir croire à notre réunion quelque part en Allemagne – mais on dit que vous allez en Angleterre. Adieu, ma bonne, je vous embrasse. Brûlez mes lettres, je vous en conjure & ne me délaissez pas! Ecrivez!

When Lord William left Paris in February Princess Lieven wrote: 'Nous nous occupons beaucoup de vous ici. Madame de Dino ne sait plus se promener sans vous. Adieu, my Lord, j'ai pleuré sincèrement votre départ. Je me suis trop habituée à vous.'[42]

Taking Frankfort on the way to Stuttgart, Lord William spent several days there and returned there after visiting his family. 'Saw my dear children, returned to F[rankfort] and saw the Baron, he has a soul of purest gold, I could pass my life with him but all goes wrong.' Lord William's visits to Frankfort, at this time and later, suggest that it was here that Madame de Haber was keeping house for her father, Baron Salomon von Haber, but it cannot be disregarded that 'the Baron' might possibly be Baron Amschel Mayer Rothschild whose family had long been established there.

Lord William arrived at Berlin on 8 March in time for a great costumed ball at the Duchess of Cumberland's, and he commented that he was 'intensely bored'. His visit to Stuttgart had given his wife a ray of hope for the future.

Lady William Russell to Princess Lieven [LP]

[Stuttgart] le 4 mars, 1836.

... Depuis que je vous ai écrit mon mari est venu ici de Francfort, y ayant laissé sa voiture & arrivant la nuit dans une petite calèche de poste. Il est resté 5 jours avec nous et sa conversation a été tout différente de ses lettres; il était embarrassé, gêné, mal à son aise, mais il faut qu'il ait été content de sa réception puisqu'il est venu pour 24 heures et qu'il a remis son départ de jour en jour pendant 5 jours de suite. Enfin j'ose espérer que la France et l'Angleterre ont bien agi sur lui & que j'ai quelque peu à espérer. Il m'a dit que vous iriez probablement à Baden & qu'il vous y avait promis une visite de quinze jours – qu'il m'en parlerait plus en détail après votre décision, qu'il saurait plus tard, et que nos projets d'été en dépendraient. Ainsi, chère, faites-m'en part. Il va loger à l'auberge à Berlin, son appartement n'étant rien moins que prêt; & le reste de la maison en tous cas ne serait que provisoirement préparée pour moi le mois prochain, & finalement achevée cet automne, c'est à dire que l'on y travaillerait pendant notre absence de Berlin en été. Dans tout ceci il n'y a rien de nouveau & mon départ pour Berlin ne devait en tout cas avoir lieu qu'au printemps – cela sera donc le commencement, le milieu, ou la fin mois d'avril selon. . . .

A few words must be said about Lord William's position and official life in Germany since the subject is scarcely touched upon in the ensuing letters. His diplomatic talents, as may be seen in his clear and temperate despatches to Lord Palmerston, were never severely tested during the six years he spent in Prussia.

'England stands as well as possible',[43] he wrote to his brother during the first weeks of his mission, and the satisfaction he expressed with his own position called forth a warning from Lord John not to rate his talents too high; but with Ancillon, the Prussian Foreign Minister, and his successor Baron Werther, Lord William dealt firmly and with spirit. The major problems occupying the attention of the governments of Europe at this time were: a civil war in Spain; the Holland–Belgium dispute; the revolt of Mehemet Ali against the Sultan, and the possibility of an attack on Turkey by Russia. Any one of these could have involved the Great Powers in a war. Lord William saw the Eastern Question as the most menacing.

'Why not persuade the Turks to fortify Constantinople?' He returned frequently to the subject, suggesting it could be done with Rothschild's money and the skilled aid of British engineers. 'I wish you would send me there. It is a post more fit for a military man than for a Sybarite.'[44]* The signing in 1840 of a treaty to settle the affairs of the Levant, between England, Russia, Austria and Prussia on the one hand and the Porte on the other, without the sanction of Louis-Philippe's government, did indeed nearly lead to war with France. A proposal of the King of Prussia's, that in the event of such a war the Duke of Wellington should be given command of the armies of the German Confederation, was submitted to the Duke through Lord William – an invitation his old general was pleased to accept, saying he was confident that his health was equal to the task.

'This gave great pleasure to the King,' wrote Lord William to Palmerston, 'and he said his intention was, should war break out, to give the Duke not only the command of the armies of the Confederation, but to write himself to the Emperors of Austria and Russia to give him the command of their armies at the same time.'[45]

At Berlin Lord William found a Court that was at variance with the Prussian people. The old King Frederick William III, whom he had known

* Sir John Ponsonby was ambassador at Constantinople.

Diplomacy

at Cambrai, ruled Prussia as an absolute sovereign, and was the father-in-law of the Emperor of Russia. He rarely saw his Ministers and did not speak to foreign diplomatists on public affairs. The mass of the nation whom Lord William described as 'the most enlightened people on the Continent, yet without a particle of civil liberty', leant towards England, while the Court favoured Russia. The press, he reported, was 'shackled and perverted'. Diplomatists lived in an artificial society and were excluded from moving among liberals. 'Do not', said one of these last to the English envoy, 'allow yourself to be misled by the apparent tranquillity of the country. Our Government sleeps, but there burns an underground fire which will one day burst forth.'[46]

Contending at the Court with the strong prejudice he suspected against 'my name, party and opinions', Lord William was gratified when the King's eldest son the Prince Royal, seized his hand and cried: "Old England for ever!' The Duke of Cumberland (after 1837 King of Hanover), having attempted to slight the English Minister, had been obliged to apologise, and was civil and guarded in his language to him, although it was not unusual to hear him abusing the English Government furiously in front of the Diplomatic Corps.

Lord William favoured his son, Prince George of Cumberland, as a husband for Princess Victoria, finding he had a quick intelligence and a sound heart, but feared there was no hope of recovery for his eyesight; he then transmitted a proposal that Prince Adelbert of Prussia might be considered; but a Coburg was preferred.

He kept the Foreign Secretary informed of the prodigious progress industry was making and how German products were contending with English goods in America and the Levant. He predicted that Prussia would dominate the Diet.

The visits of some English reformers to Berlin is evidence that the Prussian system was not held in high repute by these earnest people. In 1837 Lord William described in a despatch the aims of the socialist Robert Owen* who had been to see him. 'When he made known to me his ideas, which are no less than to do away with faith in the divine origin of the Christian religion, private property, marriage, money, monarchy and the institutions on which the social order is based, I told him it was useless to see the King, than whom no man living was more impressed with the necessity of preserving everything in its present state. . . . However as Mr Owen has rendered great services to mankind by his efforts to promote a better system of education for the lower classes . . . I presented him to some men of letters who discussed the question with him, tho none became converted to think his views practicable.'[47]

Three years later a deputation of Quakers arrived to inspect the prisons and to induce the King of Prussia (who had been endeavouring to unite

---

* Robert Owen (1771–1858), philanthropist, who put into practice some of his social theories.

13*   375

Lutherans and Calvinists in one church) to allow his Protestant subjects religious liberty. Mrs Fry and Mr Gurney were received with sympathy by the Royal Family but the King, not wishing to have the deficiencies of his prisons pointed out to him in person, refused to see them, saying he was ill. He died, indeed, two months later and was laid to rest by the side of his beautiful Queen Louise in a Grecian temple at Charlottenburg.

The Duchess of Dino was at Berlin that same summer. Meeting the English Minister at dinner she found him taciturn as ever – 'as a Russell should be', she wrote; 'he says he is not displeased with his position, and anything that separates him from Lady Russell always suits his taste'.[48] The loquacity of Baron Humboldt, * who was also present, made it easy for those who did not wish to speak to remain silent.

Taciturn, and so shy, according to a member of his staff, that it was infectious, Lord William had none the less friends and admirers among his fellow diplomatists. His secretary, Lord Augustus Loftus, recalled in his later life a dinner at which the host was the Turkish Minister. Kiamil Pacha, annoyed at being prevented from seating Lord William on his right, the French and Russian Ministers being present, placed him opposite saying: 'Les bons amis se regardent toujours en face.'[49]

Since there was no pressure of work, Lord William was at pains not to have a numerous staff. 'There is positively nothing to do here', he wrote to his brother. 'I am always at Potsdam shooting wild ducks.' And to his chief he expressed his reluctance to enlarge his mission. 'I am not in want of another secretary. I have three and scarcely work for one & when they are so numerous the Chancery becomes a sort of coffee house where the despatches are read and criticised like the newspapers. Besides some are the lovers of women, some drink, some gossip from vanity, & between their vices & their follies everything transpires. Lord Augustus Loftus has none of these faults and appears to be a very good lad.'[50]

Lord William's private life was inevitably the subject of scrutiny and gossip; Lady Charlotte Bury's scandalous memoirs having a part in spreading knowledge of it. In the United States of America Fenimore Cooper wrote that he heard the William Russells had a *mauvais ménage* and that Mrs Rawdon was spoken of as an *intrigante*. 'Lady William', he wrote, 'has gone to join her husband at Berlin, though he keeps the beautiful Jewess openly to the great scandal of the pious King and Queen.'[51] And Charles Greville wrote of 'the ostentatious infidelities of William Russell'.[52] Bresson, the French Minister at Berlin, kept the Duchess of Dino informed of his colleague's conduct: 'Lord William extends the area of his amusements more and more, he is now divided between three ladies, one of whom attracts him with some frequency to Mecklenburg.'[53]

When Lord William wrote a wounding letter to Augustus Loftus absent on leave, accusing him of spreading calumnious reports about his chief, the

---

* Alexander von Humboldt (1769–1859), the traveller and naturalist. He was notoriously talkative.

secretary answered with some spirit that he recollected 'when reference was made to the frequency of the dinners you gave to the Schlippenbachs,* I stated that nothing was more natural in the absence of your family than that you should form a *coterie* of friends about you. . . . I imagine this report may have been carried to you from either Bresson or Meyendorff, both of whom I believe would be happy could they do me an injury.'[54] Meyendorff had been transferred from Stuttgart to Berlin and wrote to Count Nesselrode that he was 'au mieux' with William Russell.[55]

In 1841 when Lord William was recalled from Berlin, Charles Greville who was staying at Woburn, wrote: '[William] is very angry at being recalled from Berlin, though so far from being angry, he ought to be ashamed of himself for not having resigned, for with his violent politicks and his bitterness against, and abuse of, the present Government, he ought not to have thought of staying there. Aberdeen has treated him with great civility, and has accompanied his recall with many expressions of regret and personal kindness, for which he ought to be grateful. Palmerston however had ordered all his diplomatic tribe to stick to their places, but William R. should have felt in his case it was impossible. The truth is he is poor, and the place suited his finances and was convenient for his *amour* with Madame de Haber.'[56]

Princess Lieven was a faithful correspondent during the spring. She chid Lord William for his bitterness and condoled when he was sad. She wrote him page after page of politics and complained that he did not impart to her the knowledge he must have.

Princess Lieven to Lord William Russell [WP]

Paris 22 jan. 1836

. . . vous ne me donnez pas l'embarras de répondre à des nouvelles intéressantes car vous ne me dites aucune. . . . Je crois que vous vous moquez de moi avec vos réticences. Vous ne me dites rien parce que vous ne savez rien. Voilà comment je rassure mon amour propre et ma curiosité – je voudrais un peu vous piquer.

Paris 5 mars 1836

Vous m'avez écrit de Stoutgard une lettre bien aigre, my lord – je ne sais pourquoi vous l'avez fait et qu'est ce qui vous inspirait. J'espère que

* During the short time that he kept a diary at Berlin, Lord William writes of seeing 'C' or 'Clo' and that he heard 'strange things of her'. 'But she is a vapour of vanity', it is therefore interesting to find in the Diary of Baron Philipp von Neumann a reference to a duel fought between Count Schlippenbach and M. Theodoki 'husband of the famous Lady Ellenborough. No one was hurt except the wife of the Count, who was the cause of the duel, and her wound was a moral one.' Count Otto Schlippenbach married in 1836 Clothilde von Arnim.

vos dispositions pour moi auront changé avec les lieux, et c'est dans l'espoir que vous avez cessé de vous moquer de moi que je vous adresse ceci à Berlin. . . .

Paris 27 mars 1836
. . . Je vois avec regret que vous n'êtes pas content de Berlin, patience, cela viendra, on aurait bien mauvais goût si on ne vous aimait beaucoup, et à cet égard n'allez pas écouter des commérages. . . . C'est que tout le monde vous aime, mais moi plus que tout le monde.

Paris 7 avril 1836
. . . je vois que Berlin ne vous divertit pas, car vous avez dans cette lettre l'esprit triste, frondeur. . . . Je pense à vous tous les jours et beaucoup, je vous regrette, je vous désire, enfin voilà une déclaration en règle, que je ne crains même pas de livrer à la curiosité de deux gouvernements.

Writing as she did to so many people, it was not surprising that some malicious gossip was repeated to William Russell and she defended herself from his attack with asperity.

Princess Lieven to Lord William Russell at Berlin [WP]

Paris. 13 avril, 1836.
Je viens de recevoir votre lettre du 5 et je réponds bien vite à l'article qui la termine. Je ne saurais jamais me fâcher contre vous, mais vous me gênez un peu cependant en me disant que vous avez été blessé par des commérages qui me regardaient, il me semble que leur réfutation se tourne tout naturellement dans toutes les preuves d'amitié que je vous ai toujours données. C'est de si bon cœur que je vous aime que vous devez croire à mon affection plus qu'à toutes les affections du monde. Il n'y a *pas un mot de vrai* en tout ce qu'on vous a dit, si j'ai jamais parlé de vous à Lord Grey dans une lettre c'est pour lui dire combien je vous aime, et quant à Madame Nesselrode je ne lui ai pas écrit une ligne; nous ne sommes point en correspondance du tout, et nous n'avons pas entendu parler l'une de l'autre depuis Baden. A Baden, mon cher Lord William, Madame Nesselrode a vu ce que tout le monde a vu; ce qu'elle a dit depuis, je n'ai pas à en répondre. Je vous prie de ne point me confondre avec elle. Je vous prie de ne point permettre à votre cœur d'être distrait

un moment de la pensée que vous avez en moi une amie bien fidèle, bien devouée. Tout passe dans le monde mais il me semblerait bien difficile que mon amitié pour vous passât jamais.

Voilà ma réponse à votre quatrième page. Elle m'a peinée et touchée en même temps car j'y ai vu de l'affection pour moi.

Lady William Russell to Princess Lieven [LP]

Stoutgard, 9 avril 1836

Ma bonne et chère amie, si je ne vous écris pas vous comprenez que c'est pour ne pas paraître trop ennuyeuse car mon existence est si monotone que je ne saurais vous mander quoi que que cela soit. Revenir sur le passé, des complaintes tout cela n'est pas ce que j'approuve, c'est inutile, c'est égoïste, cela lasse les meilleurs amis – enfin vous connaissez mon coeur & vous êtes indulgente pour ma tête. Je vous suis attachée, reconnaissante, confidante & le serai toujours. Je ne vais plus à Berlin, c'est à dire je n'y vais qu'au mois de septembre. Cet arrangement part de mon mari. Je n'en suis pas mécontente et je n'y vois rien de sinistre – suis-je aveugle ? Je n'en sais rien mais l'opium de l'existence de Stoutgard & cette manière de vivre au jour la journée remettant mon avenir à la Providence m'a, Dieu merci, calmée & j'attends. La maison, ou plutôt l'appartement, qu'il avait louée fort à la hâte pendant son séjour de dix jours cet hiver à Berlin ne convient pas – il en cherche une autre et il me mande formellement qu'il n'a pas de quoi me loger, qu'il quittera Berlin en été pour me rejoindre et que plus tard il m'indiquera l'endroit. Ce déplacement donc, c'est à dire aller à Berlin à la fin du printemps pour le quitter au commencement de l'été serait plus qu'inutile. Il m'a conseillée d'aller à Berlin ou de rester ici. J'ai pris un juste milieu & j'ai loué provisoirement pour le mois de mai une maison à Cannstadt, * le berceau de vos ancêtres que vous m'avez la première fois fait voir il y a 14 ans dans une promenade que nous avons faite ensemble de Stoutgard. Mon bail ici finit à cette époque et l'archiridicule Shee brûle de prendre possession de son *official residence*. Si vous saviez ce que c'est que cette residence !! Ce magnifique Hôtel de l'Ambassade d'Angleterre, vous comprendriez son ardeur. Il est rempli de procédés envers moi, je n'ai pas à me plaindre, mais de tous les sots que j'ai jamais vus certes mon Shee est la fleur des pois. J'abdique donc à la fin de ce mois, et je me rends à ma villa, à mon

* Cannstatt: a small watering place near Stuttgart.

Chiswick. Comme c'est très près cela m'est extrêmement commode pour tous les détails d'éducation et tout ira son *Schlendrian*.* L'air aussi y est meilleur qu'ici car c'est un gouffre. Au mois de juin donc je porterai mes pas là où l'on dira d'aller & je soupçonne que vous y serez pour quelque chose car je vous ai déjà dit ce que je sais sur Baden. Ne rétractez donc rien, mais tenez mois au courant. Je puis compter (sans aucune explication) sur ce que les horreurs de l'année passée ne se répéteront plus, car les parents de la Juive s'en sont mêlés et se sont comportés plus chrétiennement que les *nobles Normands* au delà de la Manche. Je reçois les lettres les plus amicales et les plus délicates de l'Angleterre. La bonne reine m'en a écrit deux toutes affectueuses et m'envoie un bracelet qui seront à propos de rien si cela n'était que je devine ce qu'elle veut me prouver. Enfin on est *bien bien* bon pour moi si cela pouvait consoler d'une peine aussi intime et aussi cuisante. La Cour ici me comble de politesse & d'attentions, roi, reine, princesses, chacun à sa manière & je me loue fort de Meyendorff. Cette année tout persiflage a cessé & il me témoigne un intérêt si suivi, si constant et avec tant de tact & de mesure et un ton si radouci & en même temps sans aucune exagération ni affectation, que j'en suis plus que contente. Je voudrais, chère amie, que vous lui fassiez parvenir l'expression de tous mes sentiments de reconnaissance indirectement et par plus d'une voie. . . .

The Duchess of Bedford's affection for her stepson was undoubtedly sincere. In the absence of his wife her warm feelings for him always asserted themselves, and William's submission of his intimate correspondence to her shows his confidence in her judgement.

Duchess of Bedford to Lord William Russell at Berlin [WPP]

Dover, April 11 [1836]

My dearest William,

According to your desire I return the letters. Had I followed my own inclinations, I should have put them into the fire. My giving you advice would be ridiculous, as you know perfectly well what is right. The only use I can be of is to be your physician and to prescribe for your disease, which I hope is not incurable, though I fear it will be a work of time before you get rid of its effects, without great care it might become fatal.

* *Schlendrian*: 'according to routine'.

You must strictly avoid everything that tends to weaken your determination to avoid everything that can let other people into your unfortunate state, keep that to yourself, and remember that your private conduct no one has a right to enquire into, but your official situation has placed you in a responsible and exalted state, and you must not allow yourself or others to tarnish the bright name of Russell.

. . . We have enjoyed two fine days; today, however, is a grey heavy cold day, makes one's nose red and one's eyes of the same colour. Your father is quite well, and I am always and ever shall be, my dearest William, though you have frequently behaved very ill to me,
your attached and affectionate
Georgy Bedford

Lord William Russell to Lord John Russell [PRO]

Berlin, April 20 1836

According to your letter just received, I owe my place here to pure nepotism, so if I fail the blame will fall upon you, however I will do my best. I know my talents are moderate & if I thought I was a mere pocketer of money I would resign tomorrow, still I think I can be of some use for I doubt if anyone of your great diplomatists is so intimately acquainted with the Continent as I am. I owe this to having a tolerable judgement & the extraordinary confidence that men of all parties place in me, merely because I do not betray them. . . . My wish was to urge, assist & promote the regeneration of Turkey, a deed that would illustrate your foreign policy for ever, which as yet has not been marked by any feature except that of wavering & indecision on every subject.

You doubt my diplomatic talents, you are right, I would not have you employ me on any difficult negociation, I should fail, but you may employ me where a firm & quick decision is necessary. The Prince of Orange would never have halted his victorious troops if I had not gone to him, Donna Maria would never have sat on the throne of Portugal if I had not been sent there, & Don Carlos would never have gone to Spain if I had not been sent away. These are my credentials. On a scene of action I can be of great use, in a passive scene like this I am not worth one straw. I know human character well & it is not easy to deceive me.

Here I am painted by myself – and I know myself. My services are at your disposal. I ask for nothing but leave to retire & wait your good pleasure, in the meantime employ me in any way you like.

Diplomacy

Hastings Russell to Lord William Russell at Berlin [WP]

Cannstadt, April 26. 1836

I delay'd writing to you till after the horse fair . . . thinking I should find a match for the white coachhorse & also to get some cheap & nasty pony for Nicholson to ride with the children; but there was nothing but small strong cart & plough horses & a few little showy slight Jew-dealer's beasts, so that it is impossible to get anything like a coachhorse in Wurtemburg.

I wish you would come & see us here at Caii Antonii Stativa where we have been ever since the 23 when we were turned out of Stuttgardt by Shee impatient of balls, messages & importunities.

The house is cheerful & clean the garden large & the weather bright & sunny; in summer it will be very dusty as you well know & not much shade.

I wish when you come that you would bring my, that is your pistols, & also a shooting gun as I am totally destitute of those indispensable articles as I only have a rifle, a blunderbuss & a pair of little holsters.

I think I never told you how I rode Jerome & Schönburg a race on the Rosenstein, how I beat them both & how Schönburg went to Vienna & Jerome to the lake of Constance.

The town is quite dull without these two heroes.

Goodbye mon cher Papa

Hastings Russell to Lord William Russell at Berlin [WP]

Canstadt. 4 of May 1836

This letter will reach you on your Birthday: Mamma has been so unwell these last two days that she is not able to write and wishes you many happy returns, as I also do. Here are two letters from the little boys for you on your birthday. I wish you were going to spend it here, we are so well lodged and comfortable.

All Stuttgardt turns out to come here, everyone who can muster carriage, gig or horse comes here. Jerome included who is return'd.

Mamma bids me tell you that she has not overeaten herself and is not ill of an indigestion but took a chill from the change of house and change of weather which has given her an inflammatory pain in her side as if a knife were stuck in it, she expects to be well tomorrow but can scarcely breathe.

Atty has one of his colds but it is only in his head.

We have had very fine and very foul weather. Nicky has the rheumatism, the horses are well and so am I.

What sort of place is Potsdam for us, whilst you are at Berlin? Mamma says she asked you and you never answered her.

Lady William Russell to old Lord William Russell [WP]

[Cannstatt] June 19, 1836.

... I have been waiting here till your nephew fixed his summer plans, he wrote me from Berlin a week ago, that he had sent for his leave of absence to England & should be at Baden-Baden on the 1st of July, I have accordingly taken a house there, it is a day's journey from Stuttgardt & I know every stone & tree on the road as I came backwards & forwards several times last year when we also passed the summer at Baden. I originally remained on at Stuttgardt, because we had the lease of our house for 6 months longer on our hands; that I had just got settled for the winter, that Hastings had begun his winter course of lectures, for here it is as in Edinburgh, lads live at home or at a Professor's house & attend the classes. A winter journey to the north of Germany was terrific – & your nephew was to go to England & Paris before he finally settled at Berlin; when he got there, where I was to join him in spring, he found that the apartment which had been hired for him, for it was not a whole house – would not contain his whole family, he therefore look'd out for a larger & better one, which he could not secure till autumn, this made me remain on here the spring, I mean May & June, beyond my original intention of Easter. I shall therefore with my boys go to Berlin next autumn & during the summer we shall wander & bathe & drink waters according to the German fashion – beginning by Baden, where I go in 4 days & where you might were you in luck catch your old friend Lady Westmorland who is on her way to Italy via Baden.

I have taken formal leave of the Court yesterday 18th, audience, dinner etc., etc., and paid all my Ppc visits. ... so I am dead to the world of Stuttgardt & given up to the Purgatory of packing & paying bills. I have been overwhelmed with attentions from the Court & German society during my *widowhood* here. The King has given Hastings as a parting souvenir a thoroughbred Arabian mare 6 years old – perfectly beautiful, bred in his Harar & never rode by mortal man yet except the *écuyer* who broke him for Hastings – it was a secret & a surprise as a *bonne bouche* on our departure. The Queen gave me her picture in a bracelet – she is a very amiable patient Grizzle & he a very clever well bred man, as you know – both old acquaintances of mine as the former's Russian Queen was. Sir Geo. Shee is your nephew's successor here, the greatest quiz & fool I ever saw & as vulgar as heart could wish.

So much for all you enquire about – now are you likely to come to Baden? – where you will find nephew & niece & great nephews all assembled. Hastings quite a young man, I quite an old woman; he is to go into the Guards in a couple of years & is on the lists of 3 household regiments. In the meanwhile he studies & meets with approbation & popularity. He has good health, good sense & good conduct, is 16, promises to be tall & is very like us both I am told. The other two are little boys with Russell faces, speaking French, German & *English*, one as well as the other; very good tempered & good hearted. My mother has just left Paris. . . .

Princess Lieven arrived at Baden in July where she found Lady William and her boys already established. The Princess awaited with mounting impatience William Russell's arrival. His visit was put off from week to week as he lingered on at a rival watering place, Wiesbaden; his excuses covering perhaps his reluctance to meet his wife and his disinclination to forgo the company of his mistress.

'I got yesterday your letter of the 1st', wrote the Princess. 'Je compte les jours et les heures, le 12 viendra bientôt, c'est demain en huit. Vous serez homme de parole, et moi je serai bien contente. Personne me plaît comme vous, et je ne veux même pas qu'on me plaise, parceque je prétends vous garder ma fidelité.'[57]

Two days later she wrote again to voice her impatience. 'Vos trois bains de vapeur de plus à Wiesbaden me mettent au désespoir, my Lord. Comment me plantez vous de la sorte? Je voulais partir samedi, maintenant je retards mon départ jusqu' à mardi, dans l'espoir que ce sacrifice vous disposera à venir me voir encore un moment. . . . deux lettres de moi vous attendent à Francfort. Je m'ennuye, je n'ai personne, je voudrais partir et ce n'est que pour vous que je reste.'[58] 'Je suis désesperée de rester si longtemps sans vous voir; il faut bien que j'accepte vos motifs mais vous me contrariez horriblement. Quand donc arrivez vous? Je suis bien souffrante.'[59]

When Lord William came he stayed but a short time, preferring to spend his leave at Frankfort.

Duchess of Bedford to Lord William Russell [WPP]

Brighton, Aug 25th, 1836.

Altho' you have never written to me since my medical letter from Dover, I return good for evil, dearest William, as I know you will be happy to hear that dear Louisa and her little girl are going on in every respect as well as possible, she is nursing, and that as yet succeeds.

I have the very best accounts of your father. Georgiana, Cosmo and Ally are with him, Georgy writes that he improved the moment he crossed the Tweed. I am going to join him, as soon as I can make up my mind to leave my dear child. . . . I have nothing to amuse you with, as there is not a soul here I ever heard of before. I have got a small house close to Louisa – and lead a most primitive life. Get up before six o.c., on a horse at 8 o.c., dine at two, sup at ten, and turn in soon after eleven. What are you doing? I heard of Lady William at Baden – write to me lazy old Billikins and believe me always

Affectionately yours

Duke of Bedford to Lord William Russell [WPP]

The Doune, Aug 29, 1836.

Here I am in my old Highland quarters, and for a worn out invalid, tolerably well. This morning's post brought a long letter from you, for which accept my best thanks. I will not delay to answer it, for there is much in it, which requires some reply, though you say nothing of Lady William and the bairns and I should have been glad to have heard something of them – the last account I heard in London was that they were at Baden – you at Wiesbaden. . . .

You are quite right as to my oaks. I am forming an *arboretum* at Woburn, which will of course include a *Quercatum* for the Monarch of the Woods. . . . When you next visit Woburn, you will I flatter myself find my garden establishment much improved. Many of your ideas for Woburn are good, and if I had £100,000 to throw away or make ducks and drakes with I would execute some of your Utopian schemes. Our orangeries in England are miserable compared with those of France and Germany. Whether from mismanagement, or our insular climate, I know not. I believe Hampton Court are the finest (poor enough!) and those at Mount Edgecumbe, which have been there 150 years and are still poor enough. It was *I* who carried the approach from the London entrance to the west front, assisted by Repton* – *hic adsum qui feci, in me convertite ferrum*! I will place you at the London entrance and defy you to construct a better approach to the west front, than I have done. Repton was a coxcomb, but he had infinitely more genius than one half of his critics and detractors.

* Henry Repton (1752–1818), landscape gardener.

Diplomacy

Evergreens hardly ever do well on the Continent – even at Paris common Portugal laurels will not grow – at Berlin, I am told they have the latter in tubs. All foreigners are struck with my evergreen plantations. What Talleyrand admired most at Woburn, was the Basin Pond, and he used to carry every one to the Saloon windows to look at it – *tenez, c'est beau*! he used to say to every one – *on ne peut pas disputer le goût*. Enough of grounds and gardening. . . .

By the time Lord William returned to his post at Berlin, where he began negotiating for a larger house that would take in his family when they should join him, his wife had laid her plans for the coming months, and although these did not include a winter residence at Berlin relations between husband and wife were cordial enough to admit of a project for the reunion of their households in the spring. Leaving Baden at the end of October, Lady William with her mother, her sons, the tutors, maids and menagerie (for she travelled with birds and dogs) made her way to Dresden, which was more than half-way to Berlin. The English Minister at Dresden was her cousin, being the son of her father's sister Lady Granard. The Hon. Francis Reginald Forbes represented his country at the Court of Saxony for nearly forty years 'petitement et sottement', according to a contemporary who found him 'aristocrate pour lui-même, jacobin lorsqu'il jugeait ceux que le sort avait placé au-dessus de lui, méchant dans ce propos, il ne disait de bien de personne, excepté de ses domestiques et plus encore de sa chienne'.[60] There were those, however, who found him clever and agreeable. The wife of George IV with her foreign accent used to call him 'Mr Fob', a name that was thought amusing and 'ludicrously appropriate'.[61] He was unmarried, and played the harpsichord very prettily. His sister, Lady Rancliffe, was one of Mrs Rawdon's intimate friends and the family connection could have been seen as an addition to the amenities of a winter at Dresden.

Lady William's determination not to return to England was never clearly stated to Woburn or to Wilton Crescent: indeed, from time to time she seems to have announced her arrival for the near future, but a tendency to plan one thing and to do another was a characteristic that increased with age and was never more apparent than when a decision had to be taken about a journey. She had suffered the humiliation of Lord William's infidelity at the most vulnerable time of her life, between her fortieth and fiftieth years; his affair was public and widely spoken of. Her resolve not to expose her woes in England may have been determined by a suspicion that, except for Lord John, she had never been very popular with her husband's family; and her hatred of hypocrisy would have made her loth to mix in a society that might say one thing to her face and another behind her back.

Studies, sightseeing and the social life of Dresden were interrupted by an epidemic of influenza which swept through the town with the onset of bad weather. Lady William, who was seriously ill, was not recovered enough to go with her family when they dined with the British Minister on Christmas Day.

Lord William Russell to Lady William Russell at Dresden [PRP]

[Berlin, November 1836]

Last spring when I was nearly dead with the heat, ennui & stink of Berlin I commissioned a man to find me a country house at Potsdam. He found none, but the other day, on returning from Dresden, I met my friend, who told me he had found one for next summer. I went to see it & it is an excellent house, excellent rooms as dry as a board, warmer than this house even without fires, large garden, opposite the Regal Garden & Palais de Marbre, farm, dairy with fresh milk & butter, on one side a Dutch colony, on the other a Russian colony – in short with various other *agréments*. So I have sent my man to enquire the price &c.,&c. – price of hiring furniture &c. & if it is reasonable I shall take it from the present time. It will be a sort of Cintra to you & you will go in and out. You have a good road – 3 hours and plenty of horses. The children will get fresh air, fresh milk & good walks – none of which are to be had in Berlin. Indeed I should not be surprised if you were to prefer passing the winter there to Berlin. *Vous verrez.*

You can if you like put in your Stutgart furniture, then it will not be mixed with mine. Beds I can hire & I will put in a maid who can roast & boil & keep the house so that at any moment you can order your carriage & run down there when you are out of humour with me. At all events in the spring you will find it a great resource. There are fencing masters & riding masters at Potsdam.

Hastings Russell to Lord William Russell at Berlin [WP]

[Dresden] Dec. 2d. 1836

My Mother desired me not to write to you & desired my Grandmother not to write to her constant correspondent Pauline [Neale] at Berlin whilst she was ill, which she solemnly promised not to do, as she did not wish you should be told of illnesses untill they were over, & as we are not in the habit any of us of daily letters we did not imagine that our silence would appear unusual, but she wrote yesterday to you & the letter was put into the post at the hour that was to ensure its arrival the next day, today, the day on which I get yours dated Wednesday.

My Mother and Arthur are recover'd but the weather is abominable against invalids and disagreable to people in health, gloomy & variable, frost & rain quickly following each other. The Doctor said last night we should be in travelling order in a fortnight. My Mother is grown extremely thin particularly in the face. Arthur picks up, but he had the same illness last year at Stuttgard and was liable after his recovery to constant recurrences of sharp pain in his groin and about his navel every time he walked out which obliged him repeatedly to come home & it lasted a couple of months which they say after inflammation in the bowels particularly in winter is common. Arthur's pains are & were call'd rheumatic inflammation.

My Mother was very ill indeed. I never saw her in fever before. It was a regular bilious fever.

I think I have made out my medical report as accurate as possible.

The horses are all very well & so is Nicky & his A.D.C. all but a sore throat he Nicky has now got well of.

Do you think we had better come away the middle of the month or remain it all out before we go to Berlin.

As I heard you advise my Mother before you went away; you & my Mother seven or eight times discussing the knotty point here & at Baden? Would it be better to get over a bad part of the winter here & have longer days & more daylight in Berlin when we come as we are fixtures here till middle of next month? Where are we to go at Potsdam? or are we to go straight to Berlin. Odo is well & has ailed nothing nor I either except that I hurt my foot & nearly lamed myself.

The Dowager Duchess of Richmond and her daughter Lady Sophia Lennox spent some months in Berlin during the winter and spring. 'Old Peg' or 'Peggy me dear', the name by which she was known at Woburn, was a sister of the Duchess of Bedford. Presuming on a relationship with Lord William, Sophia Lennox, after she had left Berlin, wrote to him in a flirtatious manner, signing herself 'Your, my dear Billy, very affecte Coz, Sophy', and she addressed her letters to 'Under der dear Linden'. To write in so saucy a way she must have received encouragement from Lord William.

'My dear Billy, you are much too bad to call me capricious and accuse me of behaving ill to "dear Billy". I am very much inclined to be greatly affronted and not answer your letters.' But the correspondence flourished and her tone became more pert.

'I am extremely obliged to you, dear Billy, for your amusing letter, and greatly flattered with your kind wish of having me at Berlin. By your account Berlin must be dull. Cannot you *pour passer le temps* get up at Berlin as well as Frankfort the beautiful opera 'La Juive' * which I hear you constantly attended during your last excursion to the mountains.'[62]

For an unmarried girl of twenty-four it was a bold jest.

Lord William came twice during the winter to see his family, while Girardet, the manservant, went backwards and forwards between Berlin and Dresden. In January he brought with him from the north a bunch of asparagus, and he was also the bearer of a letter from the King of Prussia's daughter.

Princess Frederica of Prussia, Grand Duchess of Mecklenburg-Schwerin, to Lady William Russell at Dresden [PRP]

Berlin, 6 janvier, 1837.

Lord William nous a fait espérer si souvent que vous arriveriez. Nous étions si sûrs de votre arrivée le jour avant Noël ou le jour même de la fête que sachant que vous coucheriez à Potsdam qui n'est qu'une promenade de deux heures – que Lord William qui nous a fait le plaisir de venir manger le mince pye chez nous, promit de vous persuader de venir nous joindre, sans toilette, même en costume de voyage. Malgré qu'il soit toujours le bienvenu chez nous, ce jour-là pourtant il nous inspire, au Duc et à moi, un regret bien vif en le voyant venir seul, et lui même avait l'air bien triste en nous disant '*it is again postponed*'.

Hastings Russell to Lord William Russell at Berlin [WP]

Dresden, Sunday. Jan 22. [1837]

I am very sorry that you took amiss my not writing sooner to you, but as my Mother was writing every day I thought it did not signify as a matter of punctilio whether I answered by return of post or not.

My Mother after having been five days well had a relapse of two days but is all right again, but every relapse weakens her, her cheeks are very high coloured & as she has been so long ill & lives on such spare food I do not know what it can be. She has no cough & has now no fever but the least thing quickens her pulse & heightens her colour.

The first fine day she is to drive out in an open carriage & I expect we

---

* An opera by Halévy.

shall go to Berlin in ten days if all goes on as at present. Odo has been & is still amiss with sharp pains in his bowels but he goes out every day as we all three do. The weather & climate are very dreary & everybody talks of the *grippe*; it has made its appearance amongst the lower orders, only chiefly the soldiers.

I ride when I can, drive sometimes, sometimes go in a sledge & take long walks every day. We are very crampily & darkly lodged as you may remember. . . .

Tear off this sheet for Girardet.

DADET!! . . . n'oubliez pas mon gros bidet, et les deux petits bidets pour mes petits frères. Ainsi que deux petits tables basses comme à Stoutgardt, Canstadt, Baden et partout ailleurs, pour leurs bassins douches, lave-mains et coetera.

Hastings Russell to Lord William Russell at Berlin [WP]

Dresden, 30 Jan. 1837

Odo has the *grippe* since last night and I begin to feel queer since this morning; little Drocourt is very bad indeed & likely not to be soon quit of it, Girardet keeps up & so does Arthur but it will go round we are told. The whole house & the whole town are very ill for the 2 Doctors say it is of a bad sort worse than the *grippe* of 5 years ago at Dresden.

Lord De La Warr was to give a ball tonight to the Royal Family, the King & Prince John both have the *grippe* & suddenly Lady Elizabeth West* too, so it is put off for a week. Our journey must be ditto, for the first is out of the question being the day after tomorrow.

Mother has no *grippe* but is in constant anxiety from her own long illness & seeing everybody round her sick & hearing of nothing but physick & fever. . . . the doctors look haggard. We have not seen Granny for near a week. German winters are not jolly, this is our third. You are as merry as May at Berlin with your Madeira climate & Lucullus banquets & intricate politics.

Lord William reappeared suddenly at Dresden for a few days early in March to urge his wife forward, and three weeks later the move to the north was made.

* Hastings's future wife.

The night on the way to Berlin was spent at Potsdam where he had hired a pleasant house to serve his wife as a retreat from the capital when she was 'out of humour' with him. The letter he sent by Girardet to meet her there was written in his driest manner and must have seemed discouraging, but the remembrance of past compliments paid to 'la belle Betzi Rawdon' by the King of Prussia and his brothers in London and at Cambrai, spurred Lady William on to complete the last lap of her journey, and on 22 March the heavy berlin in which she travelled drew up in front of her husband's house at 21 Unter den Linden.

Mrs Rawdon had remained at Dresden.

Lord William Russell to Lady William Russell at Dresden [PRP]

[Berlin, March 1837]

Girardet will make you his report & you will decide accordingly but

> How the world would stare
> If wife should dine at Edmonton
> And I should dine at Ware.

You have come so far, you must come a little farther. You should have gone to Paris or England & then you would have avoided all the annoyances that await you here.

The Court is so ungracious to the Corps Diplomatique, that although we, the Ministers, who are paid to submit, must submit to their rudeness, it is no reason why our wives should, & they have a fair excuse in saying they do not go to Berlin because the Court does not receive them. I was at Court last night & not one of the Royal Family asked me if you were coming or not. It is not worth while to get the toothache & the belly ache for such people. However you have come to the gates of Berlin & you must come *in*, with the best grace you can.

The education at the University may turn out very learned men, but it does not turn out gentlemen – that high bred, high spirited gentleman who comes out of the corruption of our schools & universities is not to be met with here, & I do not see one man young or old who I would wish to serve as a model for Hastings – certainly not the Princes, whose minds are of the lowest calibre. Gossip, slander, back-biting, horse-dealing, lying – with complete ignorance of the world constitute what is called society & we all of us wear a mask to cheat each other. However you may delight in it, so I will not prejudice you against the state of things, but I do not think it a place to be selected for Hastings.

Girardet is off and will explain every thing to you. Don't answer all this because your letters are read at the post, this moral government making no scruple to break the seal of a letter & pry into the secrets of another.

There is at this moment and for several years a marked reduction in the number of letters that passed (or that have been preserved) between the William Russells and their relatives in England, indeed the Duke was to complain that he had not heard from his daughter-in-law for over a year, and were it not for the journal of the boys' French tutor, which has remained in the possession of the Russell family, it would have been difficult to trace the course of Lady William's movements during the latter part of the time she spent in Germany with her sons.

Monsieur Drocourt, or little Trop-court, as the Duke of Bedford called him, was engaged as a tutor to go to Lisbon in 1832, and he remained with the family for fourteen years. His pupils were very fond of him and after he had left them and they were grown up they never went to Paris without going to see him. He appears to have been a young man of imperturbable cheerfulness and good humour, for he bore with equanimity being turned out of his own room to make place for others, and he would sit up all night, without complaining, to guard a carriage heavily loaded for an early morning start. He was simple and unassuming, for he dined at the table of Prince Metternich and with the Duke of Bedford, but was not above spending an evening at the theatre with the children's nurse, Mrs Butler. Of his enthusiasm there can be no doubt, for anxious to prove himself a companion to the boys as well as director of their studies, he took lessons in riding, driving and swimming, and the complacency with which he noted his success makes it clear that he was not previously much good at these occupations. He threw himself into the children's boyish pursuits, leading them about the German countryside, butterfly net in hand, vasculum hung from the shoulder, encouraging them in their study of botany and lepidoptery, and he did not recoil before their passion for snakes and other reptiles. Among his many qualities was an ability to stuff at need a newborn puppy or a toad, and he was an inveterate sightseer.

A letter of his has remained among the Russell papers addressed from Lisbon in 1833 to 'Mon cher Papa et ma chère Maman', part of which is written in the dialect of Picardy. The young tutor tells his parents of the English books that Milady has lent him, her hope that he will read English poetry and her advice to him to take some exercise 'pour ne pas devenir empâté; elle trouve que j'engraisse trop'. He adds: 'Depuis plusieurs jours j'ai changé de chambre et le maître d'allemand qui est ici depuis trois jours reste dans la mienne. Milady a demandé hier à un des petits enfants, s'il ne voulait pas m'avoir avec lui, et alors il a fallu aller.'[63] There can be no doubt that from the beginning he was a favourite with the boys. . . .

The journal which he began in 1836 was probably kept as part of a schoolroom ritual and shown in the evening to the boys' mother, for Lady William corrected with a red pencil and emphatic hand M. Drocourt's misspelling of aristocratic names, and underlined outstanding events, such as the visit she received at Potsdam from the Emperor of Russia.

He had the assistance of a German tutor called Siefert; but whether he was the same German who displaced M. Drocourt from his room at Lisbon remains unknown. The two men got on well together; they were both Catholics.

The Frenchman was always prompt to note a lapse from health, whether it were a bilious attack, an inflamed eye, a cold in the head, or the chill that often followed a bath. 'Mr Arthur est malade', he would write, or 'Mr Odo n'est pas bien', and at regular intervals we are told that 'Milady est indisposée.' In an age when cholera and typhoid were prevalent, *malaise* could presage serious illness.

In the manly arts the tutors were hardly rivals, for Mr Siefert never fired a gun or ventured on a horse, but he was far readier than the Frenchman to plunge into cold water. Drocourt's respect for the difference between his own situation and that of his employer's children was never relaxed. The boys were invariably referred to as Mr Russell, Mr Arthur and Mr Odo. The two latter might be mentioned collectively as 'les enfants' but individually the prefix was never omitted. It is possible to detect the pride he felt when his pupils associated with other boys of high rank. He had but one holiday in eight years and it is difficult to imagine him ever sitting still or reading a book. Through the eyes of this excellent, amiable and self-effacing man we are able to follow some of the events that succeeded the arrival in Berlin of Lady William and her sons, and over everything he wrote about he cast the aura of his cheerful temperament.

He eventually married a governess in the household of Prince Metternich.

Princess Frederica of Prussia, Grand Duchess of Mecklenburg-Schwerin, to Lady William Russell at Berlin [PRP]

mardi 28 [March 1837]

La mise pour la présentation chez la Princesse Royale est la même qu'il vous faudrait *for an evening party* à Londres, c'est à dire manches courtes, turban ou chapeau paré à plumes, très peu ou pas de diamants, corsage ou fermoir ou boucles d'oreilles, cela serait bien, mais *no display*, ainsi pas comme un jour de cercle etc,etc. Je suis sûre que vous êtes très bien fournie pour tous les genres de toilettes & que vous possédez tout ce qu'il y a de plus nouveau en chapeaux et turbans; moi, qui ne suis pas sortie depuis l'hiver passé je n'ai que très peu de ces beautés là, mais si vous le désirez, chère Lady William, je vous enverrai tout ce que je possède. . . . Je suis sûre aussi que si vous vous coiffiez en cheveux ce soir pour aller au Château vous en souffririez pour 15 jours.

The house in Unter den Linden to which Lord William had moved in order to accommodate his family had previously been lived in by Lord Minto when he was British Minister. The Russells occupied the *bel étage* and nine rooms on the upper floor. The other part of the house was inhabited by members of the Arnim family.

Room was also found for the Russell boys' many pets. As well as their dogs, Neptune and Vic, there were parakeets and hedgehogs. Vic had puppies every six months – 'Un des petits de Vic meurt, je l'empaille', wrote M. Drocourt – and the hedgehogs were also fruitful – 'Petits hérissons nés, six vivants, un mort'. For the children it was the beginning of a lifelong interest in animals, although the passion for reptiles which was so pronounced in later years was not yet in evidence.

Berlin was then a small town, and open drains ran through many of the streets, making it a disagreeable residence in hot weather; but the streets were wide and the buildings handsome; there were woods close at hand for walking, and boats plied on the many lakes in the neighbourhood. M. Drocourt carried out with enthusiasm the programme of sightseeing arranged by the boys' parents, leading them round the museums and palaces. He took them to the Arsenal and to the porcelain factory; to the Egyptian collections of Mr Passalaqua, and to the diorama of Gropius. He flagged a little while tramping in the heat over the sandy plain about Charlottenburg and wrote with feeling of a day spent at Tegel, the home of Humboldt the traveller. 'Un bon ¼ mille de sable profond à travers un bois clair fourmillant de papillons. La maison est charmante.' They went to the Botanical Gardens and to the races at Schönhausen, and they dined with the Duchess of Cumberland. The arrival of Colonel Hare on a visit was the occasion for an expedition to the famous Pfauen-Insel in the Havel, where the river widened into a lake on its course from Spandau to Potsdam.

Duchess of Bedford to Lord William Russell at Berlin [WPP]

Belgrave Square, May 9th [1837]

Forty-eight hours ago, Eliza was delivered safely of an enormous girl. . . . Isabella and her babe are quite well.

I hope Lady William and your young men are quite well. Many thanks for your offer of executing any commissions I may have. Lamb's wool is my want, for my present hobby is work. 'Good old Granny, with her specs upon her nose, working when she is not nursing the babies.'

Diplomacy

What an altered picture, the once lovely, charming etc. etc. Georgy Gordon, to become a darling old soul, who is now, ever,
Always affectionately yours,

Duke of Bedford to Lady William Russell at Berlin [PRP]

Woburn Abbey, May 10, 1837.
A short time ago I received your long and interesting letter from Berlin. I was glad to see your handwriting once more after so long a silence. The subject matter of your communication was deeply interesting as it related chiefly to Hastings' education and welfare. All you say on this subject is sensible and well considered, as everything that comes from you must be; and his intellectual education will I have no doubt be all that can be desired, but I have no wish to enter upon this, not considering myself as a competent judge. I want the elements of a German education in fact, and studied jurisprudence under the celebrated Professor Putten, but I do not know if I was ever a jot the better for it; but as I said before it is useless for me to enter into these theories and speculations. What I am most anxious about at this moment, is his moral character, *qui naturellement commence à ce moment à se developper*, and I still think it quite necessary on this account, he should enter into some profession, and mix with young men of his own age, and rank and station in life, for he is no longer a boy. I think him now fully capable of deciding what profession he would most prefer; and whether legal, military or diplomatick, I am confident that his talents fit him to distinguish himself in either. With reference to the other part of your letter, I can have no hesitation in saying that I wish the annual sum I pay towards his education, to remain where it is, quite confident that you will employ it to the best advantage for him. . . .

If the three months spent that summer in Berlin were a testing time for Lady William, strengthening her resolve not to live there with her husband, the frequent excursions to her house at Potsdam, sometimes for the day, sometimes for two or three, may be seen as joyous outings for the boys as much as retreats for herself from the annoyances of life in the capital; and Lord William was often in the party that rode or drove from Berlin to Potsdam in little more than two hours. Drocourt wrote of what he saw and of the occupations and amusements in which he and his pupils were included. The official life of his employers was beyond his vision and goes unchronicled. Callers at the house, however, could sometimes be observed, and we learn that Prince Radziwill and Alexander Humboldt came to see Lady William, and that she received visits from Dr Wolff, who must have been the well-known homoeopathic doctor, which would imply an acceptance of the system adopted by Lord Lynedoch and recommended by Lord William to Lady Holland.

No shadow of domestic disagreements appears in the journal and we might surmise that none existed were it not for the expressions of tender concern in the letters Lady William received from the Queen of Wurtemberg which denote anxiety for her well-being. 'Vous ne vous faites pas d'idée, ma chère amie, combien votre sort m'intéresse, et combien j'aimerais de le voir changer, de vous savoir heureuse, tranquille en jouissance du calme le plus parfait.' [64] The unhappy Pauline, herself a neglected wife, wrote mournfully of her own situation, of the King's unkindness, of her anxiety about her three children, and of the difficult character of her strong-minded stepdaughter.

'Si Dieu me fait la grâce d'éloigner Sophie! Au moins la paix rentrera un peu dans ces murs. Je suis sûre qu'alors bien des choses seront plus faciles à supporter!' [65] 'Adieu, ma chère, chère Lady William, conservez moi votre amitié et soyez sûre de celle que je vous ai vouée pour la vie. Votre dévouée Pauline.' [66]

From time to time Lord William went away from Berlin. He went perhaps to enjoy himself at Frankfort, but when he was at home he was assiduous in accompanying his family to their country retreat. Monsieur Drocourt describes such a visit in June. 'A Potsdam. Dîner. Pêche aux poissons et grenouilles. Mr Russell et moi nous faisons une excursion dans un petit bâteau. Milord veut entrer et la frêle nacelle menace de chavirer.' The clamour of boyish laughter must have sounded over the water of the Havel as Lord William displayed his clumsiness.

At Berlin the hot weather was made tolerable by bathing in the Spree and in the Plötzensee. Lady William, remembering the pleasure of sea bathing at Genoa long ago, ventured into the water too, but with dire results: 'Milady est malade. Trop longue natation.'

'I shall go and boil myself in some hot baths,' wrote Lord William to Palmerston at the end of July, 'probably Wiesbaden, to enable me to get thro next winter.' [67] He might have added that he had made arrangements for his family to go in the opposite direction to Carlsbad. From the correspondence of the Queen of Wurtemberg and Lady William it is evident that the King had made a similar resolution to pass the hottest time of the year apart from his wife. The Queen's communications are often full of innuendoes but this letter written in June makes clear Lady William's problems of policy.

'Je suis obligée', wrote the Queen, 'bien à contre-coeur d'aller à Carlsbad au mois de *juillet*, parce que je dois y aller *seule*!' She expressed a hope that she might meet her friend in Bohemia but added: 'J'aime mieux renoncer au grand plaisir de vous voir si cette absence donne lieu à un voyage à F . . . ! Je vous supplie, chère amie, de ne venir à Carlsbad qu'après que l'*on* vous aura quittée afin que l'*on* n'ait aucun prétexte de vous quitter et que l'*on* ne puisse pas par là se donner des excuses.'[68]

On 7 August Drocourt noted 'Milord part pour Wiesbaden. Nous revenons à Berlin.' Lady William showed a characteristic inability to make up her mind, and her own journey to the mountains was delayed. But at the end of the month they set out and, travelling by night, arrived at Carlsbad the next day. They were shortly joined by Mrs Rawdon.

As a child Bessy Rawdon had spent several summers at Carlsbad with her parents, and a long dormant passion for this hilly resort was now revived, as were her memories of the kindly French abbé who had been her tutor then, and who during their walks had implanted in her an early love of natural things; a fondness which, remaining undeveloped in herself, she was to pass on to her sons.

Situated in the old kingdom of Bohemia close to the frontiers of Germany and Austria and at an equal distance from Dresden and Prague, the little watering place lay in a narrow valley on the banks of a stream called the Tepl. Hot and cold springs gushed forth in the drinking and bathing establishments and the powerful waters of the most important source, the Sprudel, were ejected at a temperature not far below boiling point. Imbibed without caution, they could have disagreeable and even dangerous consequences. Polish Jews and middle-class Germans rubbed shoulders with the Russian and Austrian nobility. English visitors were becoming more numerous every year. While much was done to entertain the distinguished and fashionable society with balls, soirées and concerts in the public rooms, it was possible to lead a very simple life spent largely out of doors, and walking was part of the cure. The wooded hills that encircled the town were traversed in all directions by paths that offered a variety of walks from which the energetic and the infirm could make their choice according to their taste or strength. The summits of many of the hills were crowned with a seat or summerhouse, an obelisk or a temple, memorials of some former visitor or resident. In the years to come the Russells were to make their own contribution to these ornaments, and until recently Russell Weg and Russell Sitz figured on the maps of the environs of Carlsbad.

It was already late in the season when Lady William arrived, but a few friends were still in the town. She and Hastings dined with the King of Hanover, and they went *en soirée* to Count Chotek, a friend of Lady William's youth, and to Sir Frederick Lamb, the English ambassador at Vienna.

With their tutors the boys roamed the woods and scrambled to the tops of the hills. The Hirschensprung had a fine view, and the temple of Findlater commemorated the sojourn of a dissolute Scotch peer. Longer excursions were made in a carriage with Lady William and Mrs Rawdon. At the porcelain factory at Hammer they bought the china beakers used at the springs and other small pieces inscribed 'Karlsbad' in gold. 'Mr A. et Mr O. me font présent d'une tasse et d'une bénitier pour ma mère', wrote M. Drocourt.

Before they left in October a small pot was buried at Himmel auf Erden, and a tree frog was captured for the boys' collection. . . .

Well provided with travelling maps and anxious to show her sons a different part of Germany, Lady William devised a new route for their return to the north. A week was spent at Teplitz, another bathing place, allowing her to renew acquaintance with Prince Clary, the great landowner, who took Hastings out shooting and invited them to his private theatre. 'Promenade au Schloss, beaucoup de lièvres, multitude de perdrix. Mr Siefert saute pardessus une vache.' 'oct. 15. Partis de Teplitz. Arrivés à Dresde. Grenouille verte perdue.' Two days later they reached Potsdam where they found Lord William returned from a visit to England.

The house that was to be their home from October to the following July lay outside the town on the edge of the Heiligersee and opposite the Marble Palace. It was an enchanting residence for the boys. Potsdam, with its historical associations, was but a mile away. Having seen Sans Souci, Voltaire's room, and the clock that stopped at the moment of Frederick the Great's death, they were free to amuse themselves in boats on the great expanse of water that was a feature of the area and which lapped the shores of the meadow by their house. To sail or row from one to another of the many lakes that were linked to the river Havel by narrow waterways became a principal amusement for the children and their tutors, as it was for the people of the country. The nine months described in the diary of M. Drocourt can be seen as a happy time for the Russell boys, and the news reached England that things were going well with their parents too.

'The William Russells', wrote Lady Holland to her son, 'lead a singular and recluse life at Potsdam; from where she never stirs, and he only on post days for a few hours to Berlin always returning at night. The fine son Hastings is withdrawn from attending the lectures of a celebrated professor as the association with the young students might lead him into mischief.'[69]

She was not perfectly well informed, for Lord William often spent a night away, and the reason she gave for Hastings's withdrawal from lectures was not supported by the evidence, since Lady William liked her children to mix with all classes and many years later Odo congratulated her for having allowed him to associate with the tradespeople at Carlsbad, as in that way, he said, he gained an insight into the German character which he would not otherwise have had and which was useful to him in his profession.

When the English Minister went to Berlin to write and to receive despatches, his family occasionally went with him for one day or for several, and he was supported by the presence of his wife when he gave a large dinner at the Embassy in November. The modes of conveyance to the capital were various. Hastings and his father sometimes covered the eighteen miles on horseback, sometimes they rode only part of the way, being met by a carriage at Zehlendorf. A slow moving wagon transported boxes and those persons not in a hurry. There was, too, a pony carriage made of wicker, and a *calèche* that we hear of being re-upholstered in blue calico when the summer came.

Diplomacy

'A Berlin avec la berline', punned Drocourt, and he wrote with admiration of Hastings conducting a carriage drawn by five horses. While Nicholson, the English coachman, remained in charge of the stables at Berlin, a German, Freitag, was head groom at Potsdam. He was liable to go off duty with the key of the stables in his pocket. Lady Rancliffe, who came from Berlin to call on her cousins, was detained till half past ten at night with no means of being conveyed home until he returned. M. Drocourt and Mrs Butler were often sent to Berlin in the wagon to fetch a case of wine or a uniform, and they were closely associated when it came to packing. The hours of schoolroom work play no part in Drocourt's journal, it is of the pastimes we hear. The two tutors occupied their leisure making cartridges for the assault on the birds and animals that fell almost daily to Hastings's gun. Coots and moorhens, water snakes, owls, squirrels and tom tits were prey for the young sportsman, who found more worthy game when he was invited with his father to shoot wild boar in the Grünewald.

Duke of Bedford to Lord William Russell at Berlin [WPP]

London, Nov. 21, 1837

A thousand thanks for your letter. We are just getting into the carriage for Dover, *chemin faisant* to Paris and Nice, at which latter place, I sincerely hope we may have the pleasure of seeing you in the course of the winter – we will do all in our power to make you as comfortable as possible, and the southern sun will cheer you more than the cold, frosty atmosphere of Berlin. I am tolerably well at present for an old shattered fellow in his 72nd year, but I have a fancy that Nice will make me better. I heard of the veteran Lynedoch in his 91st, at Holkham the other day, shooting hares and pheasants *con amore.* . . .

Lord John Russell to Lady William Russell at Potsdam [PRP]

Wilton Crescent, Nov 22, 1837.

I am happy to hear that you mean to come to England. Altho' I do not much like Hastings going into the Army I think at his age, & seeing his station & family, he ought to be in this country the next two years.

I am now in the thick of the fight – Tories very strong, Radicals very quarrelsome. God help me.

The first snow fell in November. 'Nos hérissons dorment depuis deux ou trois jours. Ils sont roulés l'un près de l'autre dans le foin de la boîte.' The repetition of 'vent impétueux' and 'température désagréable' leaves a harsh impression of the rigours of a winter in North Germany. When the lakes froze they began to skate and it was possible to travel at speed where they had lately gone in boats and Lady William allowed herself to be conveyed in a *chaise glissante*. At Christmas there was half a foot of snow on the ground. 'Lanterne magique, spectateurs, Freitag, Koch. Snapdragon, bullet pudding. Je ramasse la balle de fusil avec les dents.

'5 jan. 1838. Milord revient de Berlin avec trois ponies qu'il a acheté à Berlin. Expédition sur la glace. Milord en traîneau avec les enfants tiré par une corde par le hussard et Freitag et dirigé par Mr Russell. Mr Siefert et moi en arrière. Moi je vais près de l'île des paons, je reviens du canal, j'attends, je vois revenir le traîneau et nous rentrons.

'7 jan. Milord retourne à Berlin. Mr Russell l'accompagne jusqu'à Zehlendorf et revient avec le hussard et Freitag en patinons depuis le Wannensee en 40 minutes.

'18 jan. Nous allons à la messe avec les trois ponies. L'église est glaciale.' It is the first mention of any religious observance, and attendance at a mass rather than at the Lutheran service shows perhaps a deference to M. Drocourt's sentiments, or is a sign of Lady William's predisposition towards the Catholic Church.

'6 fév. Je prends avec la chambre obscure une vue du Palais de Marbre et d'une maison blanche au but du lac depuis la chambre de Milady.

'7 fév. Le temps est magnifique. Grande bataille à coups de boules de neige dont Freitag fait partie. Les enfants prennent dès aujourd'hui du cacao pour déjeuner.

'8 fév. Grand vent toute la journée qui a abattue la neige des arbres. Milady et les enfants ont bu à ma santé. Milady m'a souhaité de la boire encore chez elle en 25 ans.

'11 fév. Milady est indisposée. Le coiffeur Adolphe vient de Berlin pour couper les cheveux.'

The 20th was Odo's birthday. He was nine years old. M. Drocourt noted 'Naissance de Voltaire 1694. Mort de Hofer 1810*. Anniversaire de Mr Odo. Temps magnifique. Les enfants vont en traineau, montent à cheval, s'amusent toute la journée. Milord retourne à Berlin. A dîner nous portons des toasts à Mr Odo. Milady lui porte une en lui disant, "Mon enfant, je préfère vous voir mourir comme Hofer que vivre comme Voltaire." Nous changeons de chambre pour arranger la notre pour Madame Rawdon.

'24 février. Madame Butler et moi nous allons dans le fourgon à Berlin chercher differentes choses. En revenant nous trouvons la chambre d'étude lavée et nettoyée; le soir elle est cirée et le lendemain frottée.'

Lord John Russell to Lord William Russell at Berlin [WPP]

Whitehall, February 24, 1838.

I supposed from what you said that you were anxious to go to Nice for your rheumatism, and to see my father. I did not suppose you were

* Tyrolean patriot, shot by order of Napoleon.

anxious, or even willing, to exchange Berlin for the *otium sine dignitate* of Naples, so I took no step upon that subject, and as you do not express any desire to make this inglorious exchange I shall do nothing about it.

I think the object to which you should look when you are to move again, is Constantinople rather than any other place – the interest is great – and your experience daily increases.

Lady William's wish to get her husband out of Germany and to live herself in a better climate led her to make suggestions to her brother-in-law for a post that would be more agreeable. Misunderstanding Lord John's reference to Constantinople, husband and wife were both nettled when he wrote that 'Constantinople is not vacant; nor likely to be', and that their hopes of promotion in the near future were not to be realised. But Lord William resigned himself to the disappointment and wrote to his brother: 'You are right, it would be foolish in me to go to Constantinople, but I had my old disease the spleen, and then I sigh for change of place. Thro the remedy of Frederick the Great – rhubarb & horse exercise I am better.'[70]

When the first signs of spring appeared in March he went off to see his father at Nice. Lady William had formed a plan to go to England, which like so many of her schemes was later to be given up.

The winter came to an end in an atmosphere of imminent change. Once the lakes were free from ice they took up old pursuits and went far afield again in boats.

When Lord William came back from Nice his family was in Berlin to meet him and returned with him to Potsdam where preparations for giving up the house and disposing of some of the animals were being made. An auction of chickens and fishing nets was held on the grass in front of the house, and the hedgehogs were liberated on one of the islands, but the peasants, knowing the boys' fondness for wild things, continued to bring them small captured animals and young birds, receiving money for their pains.

'Mr Odo achète une petite chèvre qu'il aime beaucoup.' It was difficult to reduce the menagerie.

Several events added momentum to their last weeks at Potsdam. The King of Prussia, the King of Wurtemberg and the Emperor and Empress of Russia arrived in the town. There was a row among the Russells' servants, and measles broke out on the eve of departure. Of Mrs Rawdon we hear little during this time. Drocourt records her arrival at Potsdam in February and her departure for Dresden at the end of June.

Lady William Russell to Lord John Russell [PRO]

[Potsdam 1838]

Never suppose I can be huffy at your not writing. I must know how much you have to do, so such an idea never crosses my brain. You seem to be quite a conquering hero, all bow down to you – *macte virtute*.

Constantinople was perhaps a mistake. I spoke to you of Naples knowing it might be had & as it was possible you might wish to extract your brother from Germany the notion of climate &c.,&c., seemed to me a reasonable pretext. However it appears you answered your brother 'Naples is *otium sine dignitate*, what do you say to Constantinople. Why don't you go to Nice?'

This was what he quoted to me in a note from Berlin to Potsdam, so I thought Constantinople was on the cards. To Nice he went & is come back.

The Czar and Czarina and Czarowitz – the King and Queen of Hanover and the King of Wurtemberg (who travels like a gentleman without his wife) arrive this week. I go to Carlsbad as if I cherished republican sentiments and flew from potentates and Oedi*poi* Tyran*noi*. I expect to go to England in autumn and have actually sent bales of goods to Rotterdam to await my passage whenever it may occur. Whenever you chuse to write to me direct Berlin as all will be sent on to me wherever I may be. My liver goes wrong – I grow old, my side aches on the right, my heart aches on the left, I put my shoulder to the wheel manfully, I push against destiny, we have a hard tussle but I have a stout heart tho' a sore one. I must keep up my health because of the boys who want me and so I must go to Carlsbad and goodbye to you. God bless you.

Lord Tavistock to Lord William Russell at Berlin [WPP]

May 31st 1838.

. . . I received your letter of ye 21st yesterday – and grieve at the low spirits in which you wrote, what you say about our poor mother is quite true. You may have inherited the disease from her, but I have often thought that we all inherit also, from her, the greater part of whatever virtues we possess – neither John nor I have low spirits by nature, but Russell has, and where they come from I know not, unless from his stomach, which has always been a very weak one. I know alas too well what it is to experience depression of spirits from that cause.

I am sorry for what you tell me about Nicholson. It is singular how unfortunate you have always been about your servants, but it seldom happens that their faults come to light till they are dead or absent. . . .

Diplomacy

Princess Sophia of Wurtemberg accompanied her father to Berlin. Her affections were divided between Lord William Russell and his wife. In the letters she wrote to Lady William till the end of her life there was often a passionate and sometimes a tragic urgency.

Princess Sophia of Wurtemberg to Lady William Russell at Potsdam [PRP]

Berlin, 31 May, 1838

When I came here my first thoughts were of you, my dear and excellent friend; the joy of finding you again was the warmest feeling I know, but the days passed and you did not arrive. Lord William had given me some hopes of your arrival & till yesterday I expected you; but your reasons are too good to suffer any contradiction, and I am grateful that you have not forgotten the two girls you saw in their first youth and who on their part ever preserved for you an attachment which time can only strengthen. During these two years I wrote you three letters, but never sent them away, they would only have tired you. Always anxious to receive news from you I was happy to hear you liked Berlin and its inhabitants. Amidst the hurry and bustle of my stay I enjoyed many things here *tout en désirant quelques fois du calme et du repos.* On Monday we depart, but as we are travelling slowly we stop at Potsdam to look at one of the places quite *entre nous,* with travelling dresses, and now I have a proposition, *can* you, *will* you give me a meeting there? Come in a *douillette* but only come, for I would depart with a deep regret if I could not see you. Years may pass before chance bears us together and I want to see again the most distinguished woman I ever knew in my life.

I have been interrupted. Not a moment of peace. Answer me as soon as you can and then I will tell you the time and the place. Now farewell *et j'ajoute au revoir! Je vous embrasse ma chère et parfaite amie; cette lettre est confuse, incompréhensible,* vous *me la pardonnerez, car avant tout je voulais vous parler et me flatte encore de l'idée de vous retrouver.*

Princess Sophia of Wurtemberg to Lady William Russell at Potsdam [PRP]

Saturday [Berlin, 2 June 1838]

I am returning home from a *déjeuner dansant* tired and over-heated. Madame de Spitzenberg gives me your letter and I read it whilst undressing. I relinquish an evening at the play to answer that kind dear letter and am again with you as in former days. I must tell you first that I have *not*

403

had the measles and that I am not at all afraid and if I were I would forget all to see you. There, our plans are rather altered, we come on Monday to Potsdam, but not to go away, we spend the day after to assist at a festival, something military. We start at eight and hope to be at Potsdam about 10 o'clock, it begins at eleven, then I have an hour for me to see you my kind friend. I have many things to tell you of these two years and you also; *mais je ne crois pas à votre vieillesse, c'est une fausse prétention. Moi j'ai vieilli, et dans ces huit jours j'ai décidé de mon sort, et mon avenir. Quand je vous reverrais dites-vous que je suis liée à jamais au fils d'un homme qui vous a beaucoup connue, du Prince d'Orange.* Gardez-moi le secret, chère amie, personne ici n'en est au court que ma tante de Wurtemberg et l'Empéreur. Quand nous nous reverrons ne m'en parlez pas, ces choses-là se portent dans le fond de l'âme, on ne saurait les détailler, mais Dieu donne toujours la force et le courage, qui redouble dans le silence. Je voulais donc l'écrire, mais je n'en saurais parler. Ne me blâmez pas de cette contradiction.* My confidence in you *is great*, in my own force it is *small*.

I had a bit of conversation with Lord William at the ball which was long and rather tedious. There are many interesting names around, names which took part in German history and they all have a kind of cleverness that is not to be found in our southern regions. We feel and reflect; they reason and talk, conversation and company are more animated, but for life our south is better. I have been very much interested here, rather than amused, it was too serious a time to admit or fancy frivolous enjoyment. Do not regret my stupid three letters, they were not worthy of you, as is also this scrawl, but it must go off as soon as possible, and I have in perspective a dress to finish and a supper at Lord William's. My bodily strength is at an end and I will be glad to find again my quiet room at Stuttgart and my books and *toutes mes habitudes qui acquièrent un double charme par la séparation. Au revoir donc, chère amie,* I rejoice to see you again, your bright eyes and kind smile, and am proud to have been told here I ressembled you.

Hastings Russell to Lord William Russell at Berlin [WP]

Potzdam, 2nd June 1838
... With regard to Girardet's accusations against Nicholson they rest solely with him and the twenty witnesses he told you in my presence in the

---

* In March 1839 the Queen of Wurtemberg wrote to Lady William: '... le départ de la S. est un grand bonheur; elle est plus méchante que jamais.... Elle déteste son future et cependant elle dit qu'elle veut un mari....'

drawing-room standing by the balcony were ready to come forward. It is all Berlin evidence and Berlin stories without any reference to the villages or hamlets in the neighbourhood that he may or may not have driven to. Girardet said all Berlin was crying out at having seen your coachman wearing your livery driving women of the town in and about Berlin and returning frequently late in the evening with the horses so overtired that they were off their feed for two days together. Out of the twenty witnesses in Berlin he, Girardet, named seven by name, five of whom are living in the same house you inhabit.

Whether Nicholson *is* or is *not* guilty of these things remains with him to prove, it is to be hoped he will be able to justify himself.

When the Berlin accusations are clear'd off it will be time enough to make questions at Potsdam, which is quite a secondary affair and in no way bears upon the Berlin stories.

These things by Girardet's account took place during the summer whilst we were all away, my Mother at Carlsbad, you at Wiesbaden and Girardet left in charge of the Berlin concerns. Nobody without any exception of persons either at Potsdam or at Berlin accused Nicholson; Girardet first wrote to me on the subject and as I took no notice his note was followed up by a long and detailed letter written and signed in German at his suggestion. I have kept the two documents.

You told me you had enquired of Sir George Hamilton and of Lord Augustus Loftus as to the truth of your carriage and horses having been seen as described in and about Berlin and that they both told you that they heard so and that it was publicly talked of.

When all this mass of Berlin evidence is got rid of and the innocence of the accusers and accused made out you can send down emissaries or have the people up by the coach paying their journeys from hence and back again.

But I again repeat that whether Nicholson came once to Potsdam or a dozen times or not at all it has no kind of reference to what Girardet says has happened in Berlin and what you say your two secretaries declare to have heard.

The men and women here will be very glad of a trip to Berlin so you will let me know when you choose to have them up for examination.

They are none of them in the service of your family, Koch the gardener, who has help'd John Evans, and the farmer's mother who kept the keys of the house.

Diplomacy

Lord William Russell to Lady William Russell at Potsdam [PRP]

[Berlin] Saturday 6 o'clock [2 June 1838]
The Emperor and Empress go to Potsdam this evening. He told me he should call upon you tomorrow morning, so if you think it wrong to receive him you must take the necessary steps to prevent his visit. The King of Hanover also goes to see you.

I am just come from Ribeaupierre's* breakfast – very handsome. The little W. girls were there & friendly as usual. They are dying to see you.

Tomorrow I am engaged in town. On Monday I am invited to the *fête* at the King's Palace at Potsdam & shall go straight there without calling at your house, but after the *fête* I shall come and sleep there & then put myself in quarantine, at least if it is necessary. So on Monday evening you may expect me. I have not mentioned to any one the measles.

Frederick William III of Prussia to Lady William Russell [PRP]

The New Palace, June 5 1838
Believe me it is with the *sincerest* and I may add the deepest regret that I dare not approach your house to take leave in person, but never having had the measles I own I should not like at my age to catch them. You say they are now going off and this is *precisely* the most catching moment of the malady.

DROCOURT'S DIARY

3 juin. L'Empéreur de Russie accompagné du Gen. Nostitz vient rendre visite à Milady.

4 juin. Je vais porter une lettre au Nouveau Palais pour la Princesse Sophie de Wurtemberg, et je vois une partie de la fête. Les enfants se lèvent. Milady va voir le Roi et la Reine de Wurtemberg.

6 juin. Mr Russell accompagne Milord jusqu'au bout du Wannensee où la voiture l'attendait. Schnitz et quatre de ses hommes ramaient.

7 juin. Les chevaux arrivent avec M. Girardet. Mr Russell est indisposé. M. Girardet va à Berlin.

9 juin. M. Girardet vient nous faire ses adieux. Il va en Suisse. Mr R. se met au lit.

10 juin. L'éruption commence chez Mr Russell.

* The Russian Minister.

406

Diplomacy

[The dismissal of Girardet after nearly ten years' service must signify the innocence of the coachman Nicholson.]

Lord William Russell to Lord John Russell [PRO]

[Berlin 1838] June 10.

Mr Spontini*, director of the Opera of Berlin & composer of *Cortes*, *the Vestal* & other operas well known to you, is going to London with the intention of bringing out a new opera, the scene of which is laid during the civil wars of Charles 1st. He wishes that the opera should be approved by you in your official capacity. I told him that the English Ministry did not, like the Prussians, meddle with operas & that you were no musician. *J'ai beau dire* – but in vain. He says he could never produce an opera here representing English history unless approved of by the English Government. So pray see him, & do what you can for him & get him introduced to the Queen, & beg Lady John to protect him, he is a man of great merit, talented, instructed, one of the greatest composers of the day & much esteemed by the King of Prussia. He is independent in fortune & seeks glory – not money. Get him invited to some good concerts & introduce him to people who can be of use to him.

M. Adolphe came for the last time to cut their hair and they made one more expedition to the Pfauen-Insel and to an island where there were hundreds of sandmartins' nests hollowed out of the sandy banks. 'Les enfants s'amusent avec les hirondelles. Promenade en bâteau pour la dernière fois. Nous revenons avec une petite brise et le clair de lune.'

On 1 July the *berline*, the *calèche* and the *fourgon* were packed up ready for leaving Potsdam. 'Le départ est remis à demain', wrote Drocourt, revealing again Lady William's reluctance to face a removal. While Mr Siefert and a groom took the *calèche* and four of the horses towards Dresden the others went to Berlin and Freitag, the German groom, went with them. 'Pleurs de Freitag. Sa pauvre grandmère.'

They stayed two weeks in Berlin. The British Minister twice gave dinner for twenty-four persons, and Prince Radziwill entertained the Russells and their eldest son. Hastings now emerges from Drocourt's journal as an adult. We hear of him riding with friends of his own age in the Tiergarten and giving them a dinner; and he competed in a shooting match and won it. The younger boys spent much time swimming in the Spree; the

---

* Gasparo Spontini (1774–1851), composer of numerous operas. '. . . . He hoped in the winter of 1838 to produce "Miltons Tod und Busse für Königsmord" (Milton's death and repentance for the King's execution.) He spent the summer of 1838 in England, studying historical, national and local colouring . . . but not a note of it has ever been heard.' *Grove's Musical Dictionary*.

Diplomacy

weather was very hot. 'Milady loue un bain de douches, nouvelle invention.' She was subscribing to her belief in a maxim that, written out in her bold hand, exists among her papers: 'Those who are afraid of improvement because it is accompanied by innovation may one day find that they have to submit to innovation which is not improvement.'

Carlsbad had been again chosen for a summer sojourn. The way there lay through Dresden where Mrs Rawdon once more attached herself to the party, and a detour was made in order to pass three days in the mountains at Schandau.

A Polish lady who met them in this corner of the Saxon Switzerland has left an account of Lady William in her middle age, and of her foolish, doting mother, that is vivid and ill-natured. Forming her opinion as much on hearsay as on observation, Countess Rzewuska recounts tales of Mrs Rawdon's own unhappy marriage, and accuses her of a share in embittering relations between Lord William and his wife by her complaints and interference. She tells of her petty meanness, her absorption in trivialities, and, since she had no permanent abode, her constant anxiety about the uncertainties of the morrow. An unwelcome companion on mountain walks, Mrs Rawdon was reluctant to relinquish any viewpoint, and despite her age clambered up the rocks, helped by servants, since she had not the use of her hands which were occupied in clasping miniatures of her beloved grandsons. Her strange manner, rattling talk, and the disturbance she caused, led others at the inn at Schandau to imagine that she was insane and being conveyed to a madhouse.

The Countess had heard of Lady William in time past at Vienna as 'la belle Betsi Rawdon'. At Schandau she describes her as being without grace, her prominent bones giving her an appearance of muscular strength that contrasted strangely with her delicate features. The beautiful brow was furrowed by three deeply marked lines, two caused, thought the Countess, by the sorrow of knowing that her husband was unfaithful, the third proceeding from a regret that a forehead once so smooth was now wrinkled and quite without serenity.

While Lord William went off by himself to another part of Germany, his family proceeded to Bohemia where he joined them in early autumn. They occupied that summer an entire lodging house at Carlsbad. It was on three floors and had fourteen rooms. Mrs Butler did the cooking. Mrs Rawdon took an apartment in another house. Lady William and her children began at once to drink the waters but Hastings found the effects so uncomfortable that he gave them up next day.

The boys took shooting lessons with Count Gorcy's *Jäger*, and were learning to fence. A German grenadier instructed them in drill. Part of each day was spent at the shooting range where Hastings competed with two men ten years older than himself, Walewski and Morny.* It was the

* Count Walewski (1810–68), natural son of Napoleon and Marie Walewska. Count Morny (1811–65), natural son of Charles de Flahault and Hortense de Beauharnais, wife of Louis Bonaparte, King of Holland.

height of the Carlsbad season. 'Soirée à la maison. Miss Kemble,* Comtesse Potowska et le bijoutier Wallnöpfer, chantent au piano.' Lady William's tea table was always well attended; Thomas Raikes was often there in the evening and describes in his diary a ball at which Princess Radziwill and Lady William did the honours of the *fête*.

Lady William also received a visit from the young woman who had flirted with Lord William in Berlin, Lady Sophia Lennox. She brought to call her middle-aged husband, Lord Thomas Cecil, to whom she had been married for one month.

Lord Tavistock to Lord William Russell at Berlin [WPP]

July 3rd, 1838.

I hope the Ministers of Foreign Powers especially of Prussia, Austria and Russia will report faithfully to their Courts the great national and political features of the Coronation. Never in this or in any other country was witnessed such a manifestation of popular feeling, tempered with loyalty and order – and it is most remarkable and quite unparalleled that on Saturday night after three days of festivity and such a fair in Hyde Park as never was held before, not one charge had been made at the police offices – not a single instance of riot or drunkenness – not 5/- worth of damage (as reported to the Office of Woods) done to the trees in the Park! Lord Tweeddale, who went with Lord Dalhousie in disguise to the Fair, and mixed in all the booths, dances etc. from 9 till 1 at night! and who has known low life since he was a boy, has just given me a most curious, and interesting account of the great change which he perceived in the morals and manners of the people. It must have astonished, and did astonish the foreigners to see all this done without the aid of troops except for show, the people acting on many occasions as one man, in support of the police in keeping off the crowd whenever the pressure was too great, for there was literally nothing else that made their assistance necessary. But the pleasant part in all this to you & me is that it is the fruit of seven years of liberal Government during which we have been incessantly told that our rulers were undermining the Throne, and destroying the aristocracy and with that all the best institutions of the Country. Contrast what took place on the three days of Coronation festivities, among the hundreds of thousands who were assembled from all parts of the kingdom with ye days of Toryism and George 4th and then tell your

* Adelaide Kemble (1816–68), opera singer, daughter of Charles Kemble. She spent 1837–9 in Germany.

Diplomacy

foreign friends of the Holy Alliance what has been the result. Lord Tweeddale says that altho' he and Lord D. took great pains to disguise themselves, they were detected as not belonging to the middle or lower classes and were treated better on that account. The Queen's own conduct was admirable but what has pleased me most was the great national scene which was exhibited to the foreigners and which must open their eyes if they choose to see and to speak the truth.

Duke of Bedford to Lord William Russell at Berlin [WPP]

London, July 28, 1838.

... Many thanks for your offer of buying 'beautiful things' for me at Dresden. I should not object to the white and gold plates at a guinea each, provided they are not attached to a service, but I do not want any more services of china, and I have enough of the dark blue handle knives and forks for my old Sevres service. In a former letter you asked me to give you all my books to give as a present to the King's Librarian at Berlin. Many of my privately printed books on botanical and other matters, which you dignify by the name of 'Works' are now out of print, but if you wish it I will collect together what I can, and send them to you for the King's Librarian. I suspect His Majesty has not looked at the 'Woburn Marbles', which accounts for his keeping it so long. *A propos* of these matters, pray tell Dr Waagen* when you see him, that I have read his travels 'Arts and Artists in England', and regret that my 'fat housekeeper clad in black silk' hurried him so unnecessarily thro' the rooms at Woburn, but I promise him this shall not occur again, should he ever renew his visit – he makes many mistakes, but this is not unusual to a foreigner who was so hurried 'through the rooms'. . . .

I congratulate you on your newly acquired dignity of G.C.B. You ought to have had it sooner, but better late than never.

Lord William, who had been at Frankfort, joined his family in September. Negotiations for Hastings's entry to the Army had been on foot for many months, and the appearance of a comet on the day he was nominated a lieutenant in the Scots Fusiliers was noticed with complacency by the tutor.

* G. F. Waagen, Keeper of the King of Prussia's pictures. He published in 1837 *Kunstwerke und Künstler in England und Paris*, appearing in translation in 1838 as *Works of Art and Artists in England*.

2 October was Lady William's birthday, a date never allowed to pass without some celebration. 'Naissance de Milady. Image de Ste Elizabeth encadrée et suspendue à la petite chapelle au bout de la Wiese. Les voitures sont emballées. Le fils de la maison monte la garde.' They left the next day, *fourgon* and carriages fording the river between Carlsbad and Eger. Leaving behind limpid streams and rocky woods, they passed through Ratisbon to reach Munich.

If Lady William led her husband to believe that it was here she meant to spend the winter, he was to learn otherwise on his return to Berlin. His wife was in a wandering mood; neither the attentions she received at Munich from the cosmopolitan society in which she felt so much at home, nor the presence of her girlhood friend Princess Polignac (who as Maria Parkyns had also been a ward of Lord Moira) could satisfy her for more than a few weeks. In December she had her belongings packed up again and with her mother, her children and her attendants, set out on the road to Vienna. During those autumn weeks their tutor had recorded an event of some importance to the Russell children. The museum at Munich accepted from the boys a mole found at Cannstatt and a marten from Baden, both presumably stuffed by M. Drocourt. It was the young Russells' first contribution to the study of animal species, and their interest in natural history was spurred by professional approbation.

Returning to his post Lord William addressed a private letter to Lord Palmerston: 'You might do me a favour, & one that will suit you as well as me. When I went thro Frankfort, I heard that Fox disliked it very much, & was not likely to return there. It is a place & a post that would please me, & Berlin is odious to me, so we might either change, or you could shuffle the cards, so as to give this to any one you wished to promote. The President of the Diet of Frankfort is a friend of mine & we should get on well together. Then the town is near the Baths my health requires & near England, where I shall now be obliged to go occasionally, as I have put my son in the Guards & must look after him & assist him. . . . It may as well remain *entre nous* until it is settled.' [71] His request met with an instant refusal.

Hastings Russell to Lord William Russell at Berlin [WP]

[Munich, November 1838]

The horses will be 15 days on the road the stableman has received all his wages and board wages up to Berlin that is one fortnight in advance the time he will be on the road; also an extra sum for the 4 horses & at Nuremberg and at Leipsic he is to touch two more sums for the furtherance of the horses (*he* being paid) as he took to Bavarian beer and the habit is not easily got rid of, I thought it as well not to trust him with the whole sum in advance but get the remainder on the road from bankers. . . . The man is hardworking and tolerably sober but the beer here is cheap, strong and delectable. . . .

A luminous thought. Make Görtz sleep in the stables – he always has.

Now I will tell you my reasons for sending my little mare a long journey to the north in winter although it is against my Mother's wish and advice. Her ultimate destination, the mare's, is England; if she goes to Italy she must go 80 miles & come back 150 (German miles N.B.) Berlin is so much on her road.

At Venice where we shall most likely be till you come I have no use for her when you come we shall go so rapidly to the south that she could not follow. All this would be anything but a rest which she wants for her wind galls increase much. At Berlin you were so good as to say 'you would lay her by' if you could give her a loose box for the winter; if your stables are not quite full a few boards are soon knock'd up.

I have told the hussar you would keep him in your stables if the horses came safe, if not that he would be sent back to Potsdam to pass the winter without his wife. . . .

Don't send her to England before me and when you ride her remember she wont bear much! . . .

[in Lady William Russell's hand]

I have received your letters & by this time you must have got all mine? We have fine weather *'il fera beau'* – I told you so.

We shall soon start.

Both the King & the Prince Royal go to Italy (separately) one in December the other in January – so I am not the only winter traveller.

Hastings Russell to Lord William Russell at Berlin [WP]

Munich, Nov. 22d. 1838

. . . I am going to a pigeon match at 12, it's now 10; the result of which I will tell you when I come back; the match is between Prince Gargarin the Russian secretary, Count Wittgenstein and Estherhazy and Prince Polignac, Count Deuxponts & Lieut Hastings Russell, Scots Fusilier Guards. Am I to put Lieut. H.R. S.F.G. or as you wrote it H.R. Lieut. or how? write me a treatise on the subject.

A few days ago I went to see the cuirassier barracks here it is *fort* remarkable that the King of Bavaria is going to arm them with Lances at the Emperor of Russia's advice; my plan if you remember. Their stables are well kept but their horses show no blood, all dunghill bred; they are larger than the Prussians. The men's rooms are dirty enough, old beds, 2 men to a bed; Why has my regiment marched to Brighton?

I have got you a pair of pistols which I am sure you will like, hair trigger &c &c. I shall send them by Winkelman, they were Bingham's, he is gone to England & sold them to me. He only used them once, as good as new, better looking than mine, English butts. I think you will like them. Winkel is delighted at being entrusted with fire arms it flatters his vanity and feeds his courage; I promised him you would give him the super-intendance of your armoury and a glass case to put the guns in; he can load and clean for I've taught him.

The pigeon match was no match at all an old blackguard General Deuxponts came, took the affair into his own hands, understood nothing; nobody lost, nobody won, I took no trouble, but killed one bird less than the best shot and came home to write you this.

[in Lady William Russell's hand]
I must just add however, that in conscience I have no great relish for Italy – but no even vague idea of wintering at Munich. I might at Vienna & so finish my survey of Germany but I never dreamt of Munich, the climate is detestable & a couple of months sufficed me for my survey of Bavaria, except the country part of it which I hope to see next spring. Read the continuation in my other letter.

Lord John Russell's wife died on 1 November, after giving birth to a daughter two weeks previously.

Lord Tavistock to Lord William Russell at Berlin [WPP]

Windsor Castle, Nov. 30th, 1838.
I got your two lines here yesterday to enquire about poor John. He was of course dreadfully afflicted at first. They had been so perfectly happy, that it is impossible to contemplate a greater shock than this sudden separation. However, he bears up like a man of courage and of virtue, and enters on his duties before him with all the heart and spirit he can muster. I went with him to the funeral, and passed some days with him at that time.

It is impossible not to admire the fortitude with which he has met his blow which it has pleased God to inflict upon him or not to perceive that a great struggle was passing in his mind under the first feelings of grief, between his own inclinations, and his sense of public duty and of what he owes to his friends. He could, however, decide nothing for himself, and put his case into my hands, which brought on a long correspondence with Melbourne with whom I trust I have now settled everything in a way that will be satisfactory to him. At present, however, he is not sanguine as to his powers of being able to get through his task in the House of Commons – but Parliament is not to meet till the 5th of February and before that I hope that time will have begun to exercise its never failing power. It has been gratifying amidst his affliction to receive the testimonies that have been paid to his character from all quarters – not only from his friends, public and private but also from many of his political adversaries especially Stanley and Graham, from whom I have received the kindest of sympathy and regard, I trust all this may tend in some degree to soften the asperities of political warfare. . . .

Lord William Russell to Lord John Russell [WP]

Berlin Dec 19. 38.
. . . My political position here is perfect. I doubt whether any English Minister ever stood so well at the Court of Berlin as I do. When I came here I had cruel uphill work to keep my ground. I am now at the top of the tree. This I owe partly to my own straightforward course, partly to the wise course of your Cabinet, & partly to my being your brother, for they have here the greatest admiration of your conduct on the various difficult questions you have had to meet. Eichhorn, the most enlightened of the Ministers here, told me, squeezing my hand, that Prussia had no wish beyond that of being on good terms with England. The Prince Royal sent to me to say the same. This is all very well & we will keep our influence asleep until the moment of exercising it arrives. . . .

Lady William Russell to Colonel Hare Clarges [PRP]

776 Wollzeile [Vienna] Dec 29 [1838]
. . . I really am very happy here. I do not walk round a corner of a street or walk up a staircase without two hands extended towards me. Don't you

know me, I am Jeanette. Don't you know me, I am Charles. Don't you know me, I am Paul. And such cordial looks & kind voices, that I am like Baron Munchausen's posthorn, all my tones melt & my tunes & I come forth melodiously & have a flow & thaw of words & ideas that I thought dead within me. All my old friends are so hearty to Hastings, you would be pleased – and the way in which the military sights are shown him quite astounds me. . . . He says wherever he goes, barracks &c. he finds them prepared to receive him & to show him all, & everybody civil & no gruff, surly, or forbidding looks or ways.

For the next twelve years Vienna was to be Lady William's home. Except for the eighteen months she spent in England after the death of her father-in-law she rarely left it but to go to Carlsbad or to the little resort of Baden, until she returned to England after she became a widow. She was received in Vienna with open arms; her ties with England were loosened and she was reabsorbed into the frivolous, generous, reactionary and predominantly Catholic society that had been her early background and to which by instinct she belonged. Returning to the scenes of her childhood, she sought compensation for the failure of her marriage, and found it in the company of the gay, good-natured people who had been her first friends. There were advantages in living at Vienna rather than at Berlin, not the least being that she was three hundred miles away from her husband: she was among affectionate friends, her anxious mother was able to be near her, and the welcome accorded to 'la belle Betzi Rawdon' was extended to her sons. Hastings was given every assistance to acquire practical knowledge of the Austrian Army, while the younger boys found themselves learning to dance and going to children's parties at foreign Embassies and at Court. A small cloud on the horizon – the eventual departure of Hastings to join his regiment in England – could still be ignored.

The kindness with which Lord William wrote to her at this time, urging her to live where she was happy, points to an absence of the rancour that had embittered their relationship three years ago. He was to see much less of his children in the future, but his love for Hastings was rewarded by the easy intimacy with which his eldest son wrote to him.

They reached Vienna in the early part of the winter season of 1838-9. 'Milady et Mr R. en soirée chez le Prince Metternich', Drocourt wrote the day after their arrival in the town. Lady William's friendship with the Chancellor's third wife, Mélanie, who had young children, ensured invitations for herself and her sons to the palace within the Hofburg that was Metternich's official residence. Lady William may have felt a perverse pleasure in knowing that the political opinions expressed in those gilded rooms were not ones that would have been acceptable to her Whig relatives.

Diplomacy

In the Hofburg, there reigned a feeble-minded but amiable monarch, the Emperor Ferdinand I. He was without children but his brother and his sister-in-law, the Archduchess Sophie, had youthful sons, Francis Joseph and Maximilian, and the Russell boys were duly bidden to the Court to make acquaintance with the Archdukes and to dance. 'Bal d'enfant à la cour. L'Impératrice mère fait demander Mr Arthur et converse avec lui.'

Among the well-known names recurring in M. Drocourt's journal, which are those of the people with whom Lady William passed her time, such as Zamoyski, Esterhazy, Liechtenstein, and Schwarzenberg, there are three others – Bombelles, Szechenyi and Czernin – which are of importance for it was with the sons of these families that Arthur and Odo grew up and formed lasting friendships.

Count Henri Bombelles* was 'Governor' of Francis Joseph and Maximilian, afterwards the Emperors of Austria and of Mexico; his wife was *Dame du Palais*. They had apartments in the Hofburg and at Schönbrunn, and the Russell boys spent much of their time with the Bombelles children. Count Szechenyi was *Grand Maître* to the Archduchess Sophie; he had two sons, Imre and Denès, who were the same age as Arthur and Odo. Count Czernin had a house near Carlsbad as well as in Vienna and Humbert Czernin was Arthur's particular friend. Hastings was sometimes asked to shoot with the two magnificent landowners, Prince Esterhazy and Prince Schwarzenberg, and Lady William had the use of their boxes at the Burg Theatre.

The drama in Vienna was in a flourishing condition and a week rarely passed without their visiting one or other of the many playhouses. It was a principal amusement. While M. Drocourt would sometimes go with Mrs Butler to the play or the opera when his pupils were otherwise engaged, Mr Siefert would accompany Pauline and Regina, the two maids who had been in the Russells' service since Stuttgart, to one of the theatres or to entertainments in the Prater.

Lord John Russell to Lady William Russell at Vienna [PRP]

Cassiobury, Jan. 7, 1839.

I was very glad to receive your letter this morning, I was anxious to hear something of you. Your proposed journey to Italy is, I think, the best thing that can be done till Hastings puts on his red coat.

I have been attending much to business, & tho it is no satisfaction to me, & worries me far more than it used to do, yet it passes the time, for which I am grateful. And all the children under my charge, to whom I am much

---

* Count Henri Bombelles (1789–1850) was one of the sons of the Marquis de Bombelles, see note p. 61. His wife was Sophia Fraser, related to Lord Saltoun. 'Quelques personnes la trouvent ennuyeuse, et l'accuse d'être trop occupée de ses enfants et de sa nursery.' Mrs Craven, *Lady Georgiana Fullerton*, p. 105.

attached, for they are all good and kind, are at present in health, which is the greatest mercy God can show me.

Give my love to your boys. May they be always a comfort to you.

Duke of Bedford to Lord William Russell at Berlin [WPP]

Woburn Abbey, January 25, 1839

... The 'fatted calf' shall immediately be killed and sent off to Berlin, or in other words I have directed the park keeper to kill the best and fattest doe he can find in the Park; but you German gastronomes are of course aware that Doe venison is not like buck or heavier* because the doe venison of Woburn Park is in England proverbially good. A friend of mine who was a complete John Bull and complained he could get nothing to eat at Berlin that was not Germanised, was invited to dinner at Court, where to his great joy he saw a smoking haunch of venison, and said to himself, 'At last I shall get something that I can eat'. He sent for some and the first mouthful that he got felt something crunch between his teeth, and behold the haunch was *piqué* with sugar candy! so don't forget to tell your cook that you like yours without sugar candy. . . .

Duchess of Bedford to Lord William Russell at Berlin [WPP]

Woburn Abbey, Jan 27, 1839

I cannot give a better proof of my affection for you, than that of accepting your magnificent present, for I never like receiving what I cannot return in the same scale, or laying myself under obligations, if I do not like the giver. I do like you, and feel very much pleased at your very kind remembrance of me, and the kind injunctions contained in your letter. Your health shall be drank, but the beautiful *cadeau* will adorn a table at Campden Hill, being much too pretty to be touched by an English servant. Your father is quite delighted with it.

. . . Lord Aberdeen arrived here yesterday. His eyebrows came off one morning when he was washing his face, his hair turned quite white and his eyelashes also. He has got a dark wig, and the change in his appearance is beyond all expression. I think very few people would know him. You will see in the papers Wriothesley's appointment to the Deanery of Exeter. It is disputed whether the appointment belongs to the Government or to the

---

* Heavier or havier: a gelded fallow deer.

Diplomacy

Dean and Chapter, which ever way it is decided, Wrio must refuse it, the salary being only £120 per annum, which would not pay the simple expense of moving his family there and back. . . . The Duke heard from Lady William from Vienna where she remains until next month, goes to to Triest, Venice, etc. . . .

When they were not studying, Drocourt showed his pupils the sights of Vienna. They found that butterflies could be chased on the ramparts on a fine day. He led them into the country to where the main stream of the Danube flowed, and they filled their pockets with gravel from its banks and drank of its un-cerulean waters. To their delight a steam boat floated on the river, and, further portent of a new age, a steam engine was to be seen at the Nord Bahn.

The land behind the station was found to be profitable ground for hunting frogs, and lizards could be caught on the banks of the canal. A tortoise was purchased, and the porter of their house gave them two tree frogs in a jar; Hastings added a small snake found in the hills while walking with Drocourt, and the Frenchman one day had the chance of stuffing a large toad brought him by Odo. Lady William's visitors were sometimes surprised to receive from her children, as a mark of their favour, the gift of a small frog.

The impetuosity of the wind claimed M. Drocourt's attention in Austria as it had done in Prussia, and spring seemed long in coming. He wrote with distaste of the melting snow that filled the streets of Vienna as late as April, and there was slush and mud in the Prater when he and Hastings took what he called 'une de nos promenades'.

A warm attachment had grown up between the little Frenchman and his handsome, ardent and manly pupil during the seven years that they had known each other. The young mind that Drocourt had been charged to cultivate was now able to stimulate his own. They were not far apart in age and were linked by many cares and interests. Hastings was not yet twenty, but in the absence of his father he shared with the tutor responsibility for the well-being of his mother, grandmother and brothers as well as for the servants and the horses. He and Drocourt were answerable to Lord William for sums of money disbursed to pay grooms and those masters hired to teach the boys extra subjects not undertaken by the French tutor or the German.

Quitting the society of women and children, they would set out on their long walks in happy anticipation of a free exchange of their thoughts, and hoping to find in the breezes of the Wiener Wald an antidote to the stuffy atmosphere in which each must pass his evening – in theatre or ballroom. Struggling against the wind and the rain and the mud, they sometimes got no further than the edge of the town, but on a fine day they would skirt the Danube as far as Nussdorf, or, taking a *fiacre* to Grinzing, they would go on

418

to climb the Leopoldsberg, returning the ten miles to Vienna on foot. Debating Hastings's coming departure for England to join his regiment, they spoke of his unknown future and possible high destiny, and of Drocourt's own modest aims. 'Mr Russell et moi, où serons-nous, que ferons-nous en 25 ans?'

Lord William Russell to Lady William Russell at Vienna [PRP]

Berlin. Ap. 15 [1839]

. . . As you like Vienna & Hastings is enabled to prosecute his Military studies in that Military Capital you cannot do better than remain on there until we can see a little clearer into the *avenir*. The journey here is long & expensive & the *séjour* of Berlin rather more detrimental than advantageous to Hastings. The human mind is at a low ebb, tittle tattle & silly lies are its most serious occupation, *manners are bad & morals worse*. I would rather at once launch him into the vortex of London where the mind & spirit & judgement & character are severely tried every day than let him twaddle & vegetate here where there is neither vice nor virtue.

As soon as I receive an answer from the Horse Guards as to Hastings leave I will write & tell you when you must be in England – till then remain in Vienna or its neighbourhood.

The story of poor Flora * is horrible. . . . I am told that it arose from a jealous feeling between the Courts of the Queen & her Mother, each priding itself on superlative chastity, & the Queen having some distrust of her Mother's virtue, which made her discard Conroy, but they played their cards ill, for I should say that if chastity was incarnated in the female form it was in Lady Flora. How Lady Tavistock could have dabbled in such nastiness I cannot imagine.

Melbourne has more difficulty to govern the Court than to govern the Nation. He very properly chose the most chaste Whig Ladies to place about our young virgin, but in seeking for chastity he forgot good sense, good feeling & other little virtues which adorn the female character, & it is

* Lady Flora Hastings (1806–39), eldest daughter of the 1st Marquess of Hastings, and first cousin to Lady William, was Lady of the Bedchamber to the Duchess of Kent. A change in her figure led to the suspicion among the Queen's ladies that she had been privately married. As head of the female part of the Royal Household Lady Tavistock informed the Prime Minister, Lord Melbourne, who did nothing to crush the scandal. Lady Flora was examined by the Court physician, Sir James Clarke, and another doctor, who certified that she was not and never had been pregnant. She died in July of a disease of the liver. The Queen was criticised for having shown little feeling for Lady Flora's situation.

Diplomacy

to be feared that the pedantry & prudery of Ultra Chastity will bring about the same disorders that have fallen on other Courts by want of Charity. So it is in religion, in politics, in physics &c &c – an excess of principle leads to the same disorder as a want of principle. Nature places Harmony in tolerance & forbearance.

Lord William Russell to Lady William Russell at Vienna [PRP]

[Berlin 1839]

I wish you would read the description of the school in Yorkshire in *Nicholas Nickleby*. It puts me so much in mind of the school I was at that the blows and starvation came back to my recollection most frightfully. Dickens (the author) is the modern Fielding & quite equal to him in many descriptions. Read also *Oliver Twist*.

. . . You need not pity me. I am very happy here. I have books, horses, & health. The duties of society are over for the season, & my life flows on like a calm stream thro a plain. That most dreadful of all disorders – ennui – has not yet attacked me tho it has my friend Bresson & I never saw a man suffer so cruelly. A great punishment for having said Berlin was the most agreable town in Europe. I have taken a line here which renders my life more easy if not more agreable; formerly I struggled to perform my social duties – to be popular. I gave dinners, concerts &c, in short bored & ruined myself *pro bono publico* & then learnt that I was abused for stinginess by some, for ostentation by others, for a fool by all. My own secretaries heading the abusive cry. *Là dessus je fis plus de réflexion que jamais*, & I looked about for a model – a man who steered the course without envy or censure obstructing his path, & I found the wisest of my colleagues to be Wheaton the Yankee. He has established his family at Paris & goes to visit them without ever asking leave. He lives here in a small lodging, keeps no carriage, never gives a glass of water to a soul, & dines with everybody. Everybody likes him, respects him & speaks well of him. He pockets his *quattrini* & laughs at the world. This fine man then I shall take as my model & grow rich & wise myself. . . .

In May a house was taken at the little spa of Baden near Vienna and they all went to stay there when the weather grew hot. Drocourt was sent back to fetch things that had been forgotten and to pack up more books for his employer. Floras and natural history books were indispensable since the children came in from their walks with their hands full of flowers, and the identity of captured caterpillar, chrysalis or reptile was eagerly sought in their manuals. M. Drocourt had been so long away from France that the German name for a flower came to him more easily than the French; on occasion he could produce a Latin name without reference to a book.

That summer Lady William was taken with a new fancy. Her study of the Scriptures had always been a source of pleasure to her, and since she was interested in comparative religions, her sightseeing programme, as she moved about Germany, often included a visit to a synagogue. She now decreed that they must all study Hebrew, and in a country with a large Jewish population it was not difficult to find a master. It was not just an educational whim for the lessons continued at Carlsbad, and Lady William added several books in Hebrew to her library.

Lord William Russell to Lady William Russell at Vienna [PRP]

[Berlin 1839]

I find Melbourne's letter too cold. Then I blame the Hastings family for sacrificing their daughter & sister to political purposes. Lord Hastings' letter is verbose & ill-written & published in the *Morning Post*, not to defend his sister, but to injure the Court & Lord Melbourne. There is little of the noble blood of the father in that youth. However as I began by saying, it is a sad & inexplicable story & I will say no more till I understand more.

Who was supposed to be Lady Flora's lover, or did the *St Esprit* operate the miracle – for Lady Flora pregnant otherwise than by a legitimate husband would be a miracle. . . .

Lord Tavistock to Lord William Russell at Berlin [WPP]

May 27th [1839]

You expressed yourself so strongly about the treatment Lady Flora Hastings had received, having been (I presume) informed thereupon by some of the Hastings family (for you surely would not give credit to the newspaper accounts), that I think I may as well send you some extracts from a letter I received lately from the Duke of Wellington on this subject. You are aware that he was consulted by the Duchess of Kent and knows the whole story. He says: 'The affair originated in an erroneous medical opinion, which was revised and immediately rectified. Everything was done to relieve the object of this erroneous opinion from its evil consequences; an apology was made to her, the Queen received her, she resumed the performance of her duties of honor in the Palace, and has continued to perform them to this moment.

In the course of these transactions the ladies of the Queen's Household must have had duties to perform, which varied in proportion as the original error has testified. I never heard of Lady Tavistock's name till long after the subject had been mentioned to me. I never thought that there was any trace of malice in these transactions. Under these circumstances I should have considered it most improper and unjust to have censured any individual, particularly a lady, without making previous enquiries, which considering the nature of the case, the nameless circumstances attending it, and the great names which must have been mentioned, would have been highly inexpedient, and injurious to the feelings, above all, of the innocent object of the original mistake.'

So much for the Duke of Wellington's opinion against yours, and you will not forget that he has heard both sides. I could not understand what you meant about Lady William being 'so angered'*. At first I thought it was against Mr Fitzgerald for his abominable letter, giving up ladies' names on what he had heard 'mentioned', but by your last letter it appears she is angry with someone else, although you do not say with whom.

I am engaged very deeply in political matters, and have been entrusted with the secrets of both camps. Indeed, so occupied was I for two or three days, that I'd not time even to read my letters.

Old Lynedoch is more wonderful than ever. On Friday he came from beyond Derby by the mail, occupied himself out riding the whole morning, dined with us, and went from our house to a ball in the Regent's Park!

Lord John Russell to Lady William Russell at Vienna [PRP]

Campden Hill, June 9, 1839.

I have received your letter from Vienna, & am glad that you like the society there. I daresay it is more like a capital than Stutgart, or Berlin, but for we who care about politics, not so interesting as London or Paris.

I have passed a wretched winter but now that the fine weather is come, I feel more revived. It seemed at one time as if we were quite out of our offices, but as matters stand now it is very difficult either to go on, or to

* In her journal for 12 June 1839, Queen Victoria wrote: 'I understand Lady William has played the deuce about it.'

Diplomacy

resign – however there seems no possibility of forming another ministry just at present.

I suppose when you come to London you will look out for a house. There is no one who can do this so well as you can do it for yourself – there are new quarters of the town since you were here, & many of them much pleasanter than the old streets & squares.

My father is remarkably well. I shall be very glad to see Hastings again.

Lord William Russell to Lady William Russell at Vienna [PRP]

[Berlin] July 8 [1839]

I send you another letter from Tavistock on the subject of Lady Flora. I shall now let the subject drop for it is impossible to penetrate the phalanx of lies that covers the truth. In the meantime poor Lady Flora is dying. I fear that there is no hope of recovery. Yet what can she do better than die, poor thing. This horrid story would have embittered her days, which were to be dragged out in the foolish, tiresome routine of a Court where she was not liked, without a hope, too, of ever finding consolation in the natural destiny of a woman – that of a mother – to be doomed to be an old maid, and to live at Court without the only honors an old maid can claim, those of chastity, appears to me to be the most sad of all the sad destinies to which poor mortals are doomed. No, she cannot do better than die. She has probably one of those high tempered spirits that appear to feel nothing until they break, too much steel in them to bend. She is her father in petticoats. Lord Hastings & his wife have behaved like fools in allowing themselves to be made the tools of the Tory party, whose object is to injure the Queen, & not to redress the injuries done to Lady Flora. He appears to be a weak, silly young man.

The chaste & virtuous Howard is astonished that a woman of your rigid moral principles should like Vienna, which he says is the most immoral town in Europe. He would not trust his chaste carcass there on any account. It is a curious thing that the chaste & virtuous women of Berlin find Howard too chaste. Explain to me this – why chaste women don't like chaste men, why virtuous women dislike their virtue. Hamilton, Howard & Loftus* are the three most unpopular men in Berlin. This puzzled me, especially as they all have different characters & are all gentlemanlike, so I tried to find out the cause, & I discovered that not one of them had ever

* His three secretaries.

423

Diplomacy

been known to have a *liaison de coeur* or a *liaison de corps* since they had been here, which the women look upon to be an affront to their sex, & as the women make the reputation of men they had revenged themselves by making a bad reputation to these three moral, virtuous men. This is a puzzling case & puts a man in the dilemma of being unpopular or immoral. Marriage, however, is a solution of the problem, but for a *gonzony** as Lady de Clifford says – it is a puzzler. So is human nature. The longer I live the less I understand it, but what formerly distressed me now amuses me. I sometimes see much weakness & hypocrisy in those who are honored, & such firmness & goodness in those who are reviled, that I lose all respect for human judgement. This is a misfortune for it is better to go with the herd.

Politics look black in England. The Ministry goes *clopin clopant*; John alone keeps it from sinking. The Tories grow more violent & more factious than ever. They wish to be as stupid & as dangerous as the ultra Carlists who overturned the throne of Charles X. As for me I will live & die where God has placed me – a Whig aristocrat. I value & love the people & honor the Monarchy, but I prefer my own class to either. So I will neither be a courtier nor a cotton spinner. If my sons turn Tories I shall break my heart.

I am glad you take the notion of going to London so reasonably. It appears to me that the preliminaries to a separation from Hastings could not take place on more comfortable ground. He will be like a young bird that gradually learns to fly, but like a bird as soon as he feels his wings strong – away he will go. Nature is nature treat her as you will. Adieu.

Although Mrs Rawdon went off to Carlsbad on 1 July 1839, it seemed as if Lady William's own departure from Vienna was in jeopardy. Indisposition figures daily in Drocourt's journal. 'L'abcès de Milady dans la bouche est crevé pendant la nuit passée. Emballage.'

They got off at half past eight at night and reached Prague after two days' travelling. Count Chotek, the Grand Burgrave of Bohemia, was their host at dinner and he took the boys and their mother to his box at the theatre. He followed them a few days later to Carlsbad with his family.

At Carlsbad the boys took up their fencing and shooting. Mrs Rawdon had the tattling company of the English Minister to Saxony and his sister, Lady Caroline Forbes, to help her through the day, and the Duke of Saxe-Coburg-Gotha, who had with him his sons Albert and Ernest, entertained Lady William. With Prince Schwarzenberg and Count Festertich, Hastings

* *Gonzo*: 'a blockhead'.

was a competitor in the shooting matches and as usual carried off the prizes. Though he was occupied with these aristocratic friends, he was not above a day's shooting with the burghers of Carlsbad, and he had time to walk with the little Frenchman, who on many days was resigned to taking more leisurely exercise with Mrs Butler and the children. 'Pluie continuelle. Mr R. et moi, après dîner, allons faire une promenade errante, triste et humide. En revenant Mr R. converse avec le poète Polonius (Mr Labenski).' *

Lady William was contemplating a project that summer, the fulfilment of which was to associate her name with Carlsbad for a hundred years. Belvederes, obelisks and summer-houses adorned the neighbouring hills and afforded resting-places with a view for the perambulating people of the town; but the little chapel of St Leonard on the way to Aich had fallen into ruins and it became her ambition to rebuild it. The first stones for its construction were carried there by her children in the middle of August, and the tiny building in a Gothic style, with shady arbours and seats on either side, was ready by 2 October, her birthday, to receive the image of St Anne. The installation was, however, marred by the behaviour of some rough and revolutionary descendants of John Huss, who happened to watch these Popish proceedings. 'Grossièreté et impertinence des tabliers bleus. Deux scieurs de bois en prison. Mr R. et moi chez le Bourgmestre, et les hommes sont mis en liberté.'

The reckless purchase of a quantity of pictures from an Italian dealer placed Lord William in an awkward financial predicament from which he was eventually saved by Lord Tavistock. Lord John wrote to him: 'I do not think you shine as a man of business in all this and that has been the source of all the difficulty.'[72]

Lord William Russell to Lady William Russell at Vienna [PRP]

Berlin. Au 17. [1839]

I write you a few lines by the post & now write by this Courier to repeat the same things, tho shortly, for your journey to Carlsbad appears to be yet undecided & you may be or you may not be in England.

First I thank you for your offer to come here, & if you do come I will make you as comfortable as I can in my narrow inconvenient habitation but I would rather advise you not to come here. There are 50 little reasons too small to put on paper, but all united will make one strong one. I mean that your presence here would not add much to my comfort, & I think that you would find Berlin a very disagreable residence for yourself, however

---

* Count Xavier Labenski (?1790–1855) was born in Poland; he published poems in French under the name of Jean Polonius.

do as best seemeth fit. As to the comments & interference of relations & friends that is nonsense. Mrs Wheaton & her children live at Paris & Wheaton lives here. I was at Corfu when you were at Rome, & at Lisbon when you were at London.

There is a report here that old Lamb * is grown into old Ram, that he is *perdu* since the gout seized his noble parts, & that he is *non compos* as a Minister, that he will retire, & that I shall succeed him. The report comes from Vienna & I believe from Metternich's salon. If so, you can join me at Vienna, but as you are so well with Palmy & wife you can learn the truth of this report in London. *En attendant* Paris & Italy are open to you for the winter & as I am able to spare money (as Odo says) living as I do, I will meet your wants as far as my purse will allow. However, mind I only give an opinion & decide nothing. With regard to the London house I give *carte blanche*, only begging you not to exceed the £2000 for the present, which ought to include the £374 paid to Mr Wing. I will endeavour to spare for the furniture &c.

The story you heard of Fumaroli† is true. Whether or not he is a rogue remains to be proved, probably he is. That I was a fool is certain. 'Now the name of the man was Nabel (me) and the name of his wife Abigail (you) & she was a woman of good understanding & beautiful countenance & the man was churlish & evil in his doings & he was of the house of Russell. Nabel is his name & folly is with him', but as Abigail took all the folly of Nabel on herself I hope you will be as generous as Abigail. However it is not yet certain that my folly is so great for I have all the pictures still in my possession, & they may be worth more, they may be worth less than I gave, but pictures are rising in value every day. What I learnt by my folly is this, that my brothers behaved like Jews & that if ever I am in want of bread it is not from them that I must ask it. This knowledge is not without its value.

You who know everything from the Cedar to the Hyssop tell me why ladies' maids are called Abigails.

I send enclosed an order for the money you paid for the table – is it in the house? I also send you a most beautiful collection of Elbe pearls‡, the best I have seen. I hope they will please you. They were sent from Stockholm to be sold & I bought them, I believe a bargain, but probably I am again like Moses & his pair of green spectacles. However dont fash

---

* Sir Frederick Lamb, ambassador at Vienna: created Lord Beauvale 1839.

† The picture-dealer mentioned below, p. 427.

‡ River pearls are found in fresh-water mussels in many parts of the world, and there were fisheries in Saxony.

yourself about money. If I die you will find stuff in the house to give me a splendid funeral & money to put in your pocket besides. I mean you will find property of various kinds which you may sell on the spot or transport to England. Such as pictures, books, china, table linen, furniture, curiosities &c. all of which is a resource to fall back upon should the day of pecuniary distress arrive. Remember I brought nothing to this house but all has been accumulated by my industry & penuriousness therefore grumble not.

Lord William Russell to Lord John Russell [WP]

Berlin August 28.39

. . . You urge me to go to England to take steps about a draft of mine on Child & Co & you say that 'neither my Father nor Tavistock are disposed to stir a step in the matter'. They are most kind – their kindness will never be forgotten by me. It is necessary that a man should occasionally get into a scrape to know the weight of his friends' hearts. I have committed an act of folly but the lesson I have received has been the severest & bitterest I ever received in my life. I must teach myself to live on bread & water that I may never again be so treated. What can I do in England, if neither my Father nor Tavistock are disposed to assist me. Nothing – but I may be arrested & clapt into prison. . . . You wish me to come to England to give an explanation, that can be given by letter as well as by voice. This is it.

There came here last winter an Italian picture dealer, who brought me a letter from Rome. He was not able to sell his pictures, & proposed some of them to me for what he called half their value. I thought, not only that the possession of the pictures would give me great pleasure, but that it would be a good investment of money, as I could sell them when in want. I thought also at the time that I could dispose of the sum without difficulty. I erred. I then proposed to the picture dealer to restore him his pictures – he refused. I then proposed to pay him £5 per cent untill I could pay the whole. He refused. I then asked Tavistock to be security for the sum. He refused. I endeavoured to borrow the money – every body refused & I then learnt that a man who has been 35 years his own master, living in an extravagant world, struggling to keep his position, & never owing a shilling, derives no credit whatever from his character.

I had intended to have taken Hastings to England to place him in his Regiment – but I cannot go there before this affair is settled. . . . By the solemnity of your letter one would think my draft was for £40,000, instead of £4000.

Lord William Russell to Lady William Russell at Carlsbad [PRP]

Berlin. Sep. 7 [1839]

I received by the courier your letter of the 28, in which there is a great deal of good sense, reason & judicious calm observation on men & things. I will endeavour to reply in the same spirit, & reciprocate (as the Yankees say) your *cupio omnia quae vis.*

I do not make out from your letter whether or not you come to Berlin & regret that you did not say positively yes or no, for I doubt whether it would be possible to cram into this house & I have now the offer of another, but if you don't come I should not give myself the trouble to move unless it were into a smaller & warmer house, for this is cold, dreary & large without convenience or comfort. However, should you come, I will put you up as well as I can, but I do not think that Berlin would be pleasant for you, or profitable for the boys. In my opinion nothing would be more profitable for the boys than to pass the winter at Paris & go thro a course of French literature, aided by other studies. And I think that if you were to renounce the pomps & vanities of fashionable society, & get amongst the French men of letters you would find pleasure & profit in Paris for yourself. I don't mean the Balzacs & Victor Hugos, but the men who devote themselves to ancient literature, the classics & the history of the middle ages. I can see by the books that Asher sends me to look at that the works of this sort are numerous & excellent.

I am now reading *La vie et l'histoire de la poésie d'Horace, par le Baron Walckenaer* which is full of interest. Hastings would collect a vast deal of military information at Paris, & amuse himself at the same time & in the course of the winter or spring I would run down & see you. However all this is a *projet en l'air* & I wish you to do what best pleases you.

I am glad the Elbes are to your taste, I may pick up some more in the course of time. Pray take great care of my snuff-boxes & the portfolio I left in London. The story of Hastings' silver mug is most curious. I suppose the thief was afraid to sell it, but how did John get hold of it? He is a queer fish with his vague notion. It is strange that he should be so distinguished in public life & in private life have so little knowledge of men & things. If I owe five shillings he writes me a long letter on the immorality of owing

428

money – at the same time, he drinks my wine at his Cabinet dinners, uses my linen, makes me pay for the furniture he hires, wears out my own furniture by which the debt of five shillings was increased. There is an inconsistency in all this which is incomprehensible.

Should Vienna become vacant I don't think they could pass me over again, even should John neglect to take my part. As for the house in London, I leave it in your hands, only put a stop to any more expenditure for the present. When we have spared we will begin again. . . .

I hope you have put the marble inlaid table into the house. I bought it of the rogue Fumaroli for my father, but he declined to take it, & sent me the bill for the carriage, custom house &c. which I paid. Tavistock laid claim to it but when he found it was mine, he ordered it out of the house. So much for having rich relations. The table was made a present of by the Pope to the Doge of Venice to commemorate the Christian League against the Turks. It has on it the Arms of Austria, Poland, Venice & Rome & is a curiosity, but too splendid for a *bicoque* like my house. However, when we are ruined we will sell it.

To give you an idea of Prussia, no human being has invited me or will allow me to kill a partridge on their estate, so I have been obliged to hire a manor – so much for Prussia. How different in Austria.

God bless you all.

Hastings Russell to Lord William Russell at Berlin [WP]

Carlsbad, Sept the 13th. 1839

I have had no other wish than being a soldier since I was 8 years old and I have never altered my purpose as you know; a year's leave is a long leave but as I was to expect two, and everybody I had met with had enjoyed the same I did not foresee a new regulation & only look'd to the event of a war to make me join my regiment any sooner than you originally settled: as I am very happy in my present state I cannot regret its being prolong'd but never at the expense of leaving my profession of course.

. . . I am not idling at a bath I am drinking and bathing & cleaning myself inside & out & reading & growing & getting a beard & everything quite proper as Nicky says. I hope we shall soon see you if you can tear yourself away from that Paradise.

I beg leave to state that dining with old Prussian Blue would be no allurement. I had dined with 3 Kings (not Caspar, Melchior & Balthasar but William, Frederic & Ernst) at their respective tables before I was 17 – King of England at Brighton, King of Wurtemberg at Stuttgardt & King of Hanover at Carlsbad – so except to make up the number of a pack of cards 4, I see no honor in eating noodles with your starch friend.

Lord William made a brief appearance during September. Although he had not seen his family for nearly a year, he only stayed four days. At Teplitz, where Lady William paused after leaving Carlsbad on her way to Dresden, he reappeared, returning almost at once to Berlin; by then they had agreed to meet in England. Hastings's prowess with firearms after a day's shooting with Prince Schwarzenberg was carried to exceptional lengths. 'Mr R. tue trois poulets au pistolet dans la cour', and two days later we hear that 'Mr R. tue une oie au pistolet dans la cour'.

Before the party moved on to Dresden the news came of the Duke of Bedford's death in Scotland. He had written to his daughter-in-law a few days before he died, and perhaps remorse for having kept his grandsons away from him prompted her to endorse the letter when it came: 'Last letter I received from the poor Duke at Teplitz in October 1839.'

Duke of Bedford to Lady William Russell at Teplitz [PRP]

The Doune N.B. Sept 21 1839

I received your letter from Carlsbad of the 8th ult. in due course (as the merchants say) since I have been here in this highland retreat, and am conscious that I ought to have answered it earlier, but I fear you must find me very remiss, and very unpunctual in answering letters, which used not to be the case with me formerly, but amongst the various infirmities of old age, those of incapacity of writing, of a sad deficiency of memory etc., amongst the very conspicuous – however, I must throw myself on your indulgence, and ask your forgiveness – I can do no more.

I trust you have all escaped the ravages of the Carlsbad waters better than I did – to use a vulgar phrase, 'they played the very deuce with me'! I am rejoiced to hear that Hastings is coming to England this month, and I trust with the military education that you have given him, that he will join his regiment an accomplished soldier, and be hereafter a Marlborough, or a Napoleon, serving his country.

Of course when the winter theatres are open, my boxes at Drury Lane and Covent Garden will be at your orders, whenever you may be pleased to apply for them. I am not likely to be in London till after Christmas as the Duchess is so anxious to be with Louisa during her confinement that I have made up my mind to cross over from hence to the north of Ireland,

Lady William Russell with her sons, Arthur, Hastings and Odo, from a
painting by Julius Schoppe

Lady William Russell with the drawings of her sons, from a lithograph by
Kriehüber

the beginning of November and we shall probably not be in England till after Christmas.

John seems to have taken upon himself the whole weight and responsibility and support of the Government, and all I can say to him is, God send him a good deliverance! He is now reposing from his House of Commons labours, at his villa near Windsor.

I have not heard from William for more than an age, nor do I know what is become of him. I have been expecting to hear from him for the last three months, respecting some Saxon china, Bohemian glass &c., which he sent to me from Berlin. I presume he is now there, but pray tell him to write to me.

You talk of my 'grouse shooting' on the hills here – all the recreations have been long over with me. I have not had a gun in my hand for the last four years, and am now only an old and miserable worn out invalid, but always your affectionate

Bedford

'Emballage' and 'Milady est indisposée' in Drocourt's journal suggest scenes of disorder and an access of indecision in the early days of November.

'Temps gris. Chargement des voitures. Mr S. et moi passons la nuit à emballer.'

'A 8¼ du matin nous quittons Teplitz et à 6h. moins ¼ nous arrivons à Dresde. A la montagne après Arbesau brouillard extraordinairement épais et très froid.'

The fog on the Erzgebirge was probably less thick and yellow than that which was shrouding the gas lamps of London when they reached London Docks at the end of November. They had travelled from Dresden as far as Leipzig on the new railway. Journeying across Germany to the Rhine in pouring rain, they went down the river from Mainz to Rotterdam by boat, and embarking in the steam-packet were carried in thirty-five hours across the North Sea and up the Thames. They had spent eleven nights on the way from Dresden.

Colonel Hare had lent the Russells his house in Mayfair and they were joined there by Lord William. Mrs Rawdon arrived from Germany a week later. Hastings became a soldier, living with his family in South Street or in barracks at St John's Wood, according to his military duties. His brothers were spectators the first time he mounted guard at St James's.

7th Duke of Bedford to Lord William Russell [WPP]

Woburn Abbey, November 15 1839.

I did not write to you after our poor father's death, because John told me that he had informed you of the sad event, and I had nothing more to say to you. I knew we should have the same feeling on the subject, and that we could condole with each other on the loss we have sustained.

There were, however, many circumstances attending both his life and death for which we ought to be thankful. The delays which have unavoidably occurred in the removal of his remains from Inverness by steam have been very distressing, and the last melancholy ceremony will not take place till tomorrow, four weeks (all but one day) since his death. . . .

We had no right to expect my poor father's life to be so long spared to us, and it is a comfort to think that he had long been prepared for the blow that took him from us, happily without pain or consciousness, but nevertheless I feel greatly shocked at it, and almost overpowered by the responsibility that is before me, and the anxious duties that are now cast upon me. I must try to do my best, but I can never expect, my dear William, to supply in any degree the loss you have had, although I hope to be a friend to you and your boys whenever you stand in need of my support. I can say no more.

. . . It will be necessary to shut up the old Abbey for a time.

7th Duke of Bedford to Lord William Russell [WPP]

Oakley, Dec 3rd, 1839.

Pray accept my very best thanks for your very sensible and right judging letter. There is as you say truly 'a medium in all things' and I must try to find it as well as I can. I did not mean to say that I should continue to limit myself to £12,000 a year, but that, by commencing with that income, I should be able to see my way, and to increase it according to circumstances in the meantime. I feel the utmost confidence in Russell. He never was in debt, and I am persuaded he never will be. When he was a little boy, he had a way of telling people that 'nothing was theirs until they had paid for it', and he has always acted up to that feeling. When he was at Oxford, he told me that if I wished him to keep out of debt, and not exceed his income, I had better take him away – on account of the extravagance he found established there and which it would be impossible for him to resist. . . . Therefore I feel the greatest security in Russell, and you will see that he deserves it. The rent roll of the Estate will increase, there is reason to expect – not in London, but in Beds, Devon and Cambridgeshire, when the buildings and repairs are finished and the new works in the Fens come into full operation – this on one hand, and a sinking fund on the other, will ensure (barring unforeseen events) a gradual diminution of charges, and a wholesome restoration of the family affairs – but it will require persevering and long continued rather than over severe economy, and forbearance. This is the task that has fallen upon me. There is great truth in all you say about my father – but he had not the power or resolution to hold his hand, whenever money was within his reach. Adam always saw and lamented this. It led him (thoughtlessly) to do things, that nothing but his high character, and confidence and affection could have enabled us to pass over. I once said to Adam in speaking of certain transactions – 'This is all very well, with my father. His character is high, and you know that nothing he can do will ever be noticed by me, except to yourself – but what should you say, if a person of more questionable character were to do what he is now doing, with your sanction. The Duke of Marlborough for instance.' 'I should say at once (replied Adam) that he was trying to cheat Lord Blandford.' You and I know that nothing could be further from my poor father's thoughts than to do or intend any thing unjust. I merely name the circumstance to show you how things were conducted and I do so in perfect confidence. I have never, till now, mentioned this to any body not even to John, or to Lady T. – or to Russell.

It is marvellous to me how the estate ever can have got so encumbered. Our great grandfather, John Duke of Bedford, was considered the richest man of his day, and is so spoken of by Junius. He died without debt, leaving my uncle with a minority of 18 or 19 years before him. What *his* fortune must have been therefore, free and unencumbered on coming to the title, can hardly be calculated on – yet after having been in possession only 15 years – having in that time sold the great family estates in Surrey and Hants, he died leaving a debt of more than £200,000, that debt was increased by his successor to more than half a million, and he has left encumbrances, the interest of which amount in a round sum to £40,000 a year. I know not how these things are done even with every allowance for extraordinary cheating. My uncle's ready money in coming to the title must have been considerable, when his grandfather died, and when he came of age, there was none of those great fortunes which have since sprung up with the times or been created with the war.

You encourage me to write openly and I have done so, tho' I have given you more time than I can afford.

During the first weeks in London Arthur and Odo with the two tutors pursued a course of sightseeing that took them from the Tower of London to the

British Museum and the Polytechnic Institute, and included a visit to the Industrious Fleas, while their evenings were often spent at the play when the ducal boxes at Drury Lane and Covent Garden were available. Lady William went about with her husband and together they introduced their fine eldest son to their friends. They were on a friendly footing with Holland House, Adelaide the Queen Dowager received them graciously at dinner, and old Lord Lynedoch, when he was in town, expected the whole family to dine with him on Sundays. When Lord William presented Hastings to his Sovereign, Queen Victoria expressed a wish to see also Arthur and Odo whom she remembered as children at Tunbridge Wells. Lady William, who had declared her unwillingness to go to Court after the cruel treatment of her cousin Lady Flora Hastings, obediently accompanied them to the Palace. They had had their hair cut by Truefitt in the Burlington Arcade.

In February Prince Albert arrived in London and two days later was married to the Queen. '10 fév. Pluie très forte. Milord et Milady dînent chez Lord Palmerston. La voiture met 1½ heure pour revenir prendre les enfants, Mr S., Regina et moi pour voir les illuminations, celles de gaz, surtout, qui sont belles. Nous mettons deux heures pour aller prendre Milady à cause de la foule de piétons et de voitures. Revenus à la maison à minuit moins ¼. Milord, Milady, Madame et Mr R. vont en soirée chez la Duchesse de Sutherland.'

At the beginning of March Lord William returned to Berlin by way of Paris. Princess Lieven reported his visit to M. Guizot: 'Lord Russell et Apponyi sont venus me voir. Le premier a tout bêtement de l'esprit et une bonté de cœur parfaite. Il me raconte peu à peu tout avec beaucoup de finesse.' And again next day: 'L'infaillible Lord William est encore venu hier pendant mon luncheon. C'est une excellente et douce créature, avec un esprit d'observation très fin.'[73] When Lord William had gone away she wrote to him, 'je vous remercie encore des bonnes paroles d'amitié de votre lettre, des bons moments que vous m'avez donnés ici. I miss you so much, parce qu'avec personne je ne parle à cœur ouvert comme avec vous. God bless you, dear Lord.'[74]

Before he left London, a house had been bought in Grosvenor Place; although it amused his wife to plan for carpets and furniture, she was never to occupy it for more than a few weeks and it was her husband who derived pleasure from it, and her eldest son who was troubled by it. The children with M. Drocourt were often in the house helping to unpack the cases which had come from Germany, and watching the disposal of the marble busts, some of which were of themselves, and some of ancient Greeks and Romans. Arthur and Odo appear to have made few friends in London. They were perhaps not quite at ease with English boys, but they renewed acquaintance with the family of Lord Grosvenor. They liked the eldest son, Lord Belgrave, well enough to visit him at Eton. Hastings, when not on guard, went out at night to balls and evening parties by himself or with his mother, and the rare chance of having him at home in the evening was seized on by his brothers to display high spirits: 'Avec Mr R. nous dansons et chantons jusqu'à dix heures; et alors Mr R. va au bal avec Milady.'

Arthur and Odo's taste for natural history was never repressed. The number of animals, both warm and cold blooded, that were accommodated in their schoolroom inspires respect for the tutors and for Mrs Butler. Their mother, too, seems to have shown no repugnance for any of their pets. As well as Vic, their dog, there were parrots, large and small; white mice and green lizards; tortoises, plain and striped, silkworms, snakes, toads and frogs of every size, and at the proper season frog's spawn and caterpillars too. Siefert and Drocourt accompanied the boys to the damper spots of Paddington, and they explored the ditches of St John's Wood. From Craven Hill they brought back newts, and St John's Wood yielded sustenance for the snakes, who seldom fed, but liked their food alive, and sentiment was not allowed to interfere with scientific study.

They introduced themselves to Dr Bell,* of the British Museum, and from time to time made presents to him of their reptiles and amphibians, dead and alive; and he for his part lent them books on natural history. Mr Gray,† his assistant, was always ready to help them with problems of zoology. Treated as pets as well as objects of study, the more sinuous of their animals and those with good acceleration were apt to escape while being handled: 'Nous perdons un de nos serpents et nous retrouvons le crapaud perdu.'

Lady William's toleration seems remarkable for these evasions were not always confined to the children's quarters: 'Le lézard qui était resté dans les rideaux du salon tombe vivant sur le journal que Mr R. lisait.' The escapade did it no good, for a week later 'le pauvre lézard est mort après plusieurs jours d'agonie'. Mr Gray accepted it, preserved in spirits of wine, for the British Museum.

Far more interesting to Arthur and Odo than a visit to the pantomime or the diorama was a walk to Cannon Street, where a collared viper could be bought, or one of those glass jars containing creatures preserved in alcohol, from which the semblance of reality and all colour has been drained. Near the Bank there was a taxidermist's shop where they could loiter and stare and choose additions to their collection of stuffed animals, now rapidly increasing, for many a captured frog or toad surplus to their needs was made to yield its skin to M. Drocourt's knife, and, skilfully stuffed, took its place on the schoolroom shelves with bottled eft and embryo.

A terrible event occurred in May. Old Lord William was murdered by his Swiss valet Courvoisier, in his house in Norfolk Street, not far from where Lady William was living. The servant knew he was about to be dismissed for unsatisfactory conduct and stated at his trial: 'My character was gone and I thought murdering him the only way to cover my fault.' He was convicted and hanged two months later.

---

* Dr Thomas Bell, F.R.S. (1792–1880), Vice-president of the Zoological Society.
† John Gray (1800–75), keeper of the zoological collections at the British Museum.

Diplomacy

Hastings Russell to Lord William Russell at Berlin [WP]

Friday. 8th. of May. 1840

Many happy returns of this day but few of them away from us and none of them with so dreadful an event so near to damp them.

I have many things to write, none of importance, but still such as might interest you at some other time; now I feel no wish to write them & you would feel little pleasure in reading them, so goodbye and God bless you and make us all meet again as well and happy as when we parted.

Hastings Russell to Lord William Russell at Berlin [WP]

Tuesday. May 26. 1840

You have written me several letters and sent me various things for which both I thank you, especially for the books and account of the firelock, but I did not answer each letter immediately & individually and in that *peccavi*: for by putting off what I had to say it either accumulated too much or was forgotten; nevertheless my time has been fully occupied though perhaps not always as profitably as I could wish.

We drill in the Park every morning except guard mounting or dismounting day from 8 till 11 a.m. and as we Parade in the barracks I have to walk down there & then march up with the battalion. I then go to Westmacott's who has ask'd me to sit for my ugly phiz in plaster as a study for him. I go home & dress and by the time one has paid a couple of indispensable visits or taken a small ride in the Park it is time to dress for dinner, dinner lasts till 11 and I never have courage to go any where after, or I should never be up at 7 for drill.

May 28th.

. . . You say my letter of the 8th. was short, the 8th. was your Birthday, I wrote to you on it & about it and nothing else, besides my uncle had just been murdered & I was not much disposed to write news. . . .

Adieu mon cher Papa.

Hastings Russell to Lord William Russell at Berlin [WP]

Tuesday June 16th 1840

. . . Those who say that they cannot see me are the young & the foolish, the inexperienced & the unwise, the thoughtless & the idle, those whose world is a ballroom, those with whom a crowded assembly is stuffed. My pursuits are of another kind, of a more solid nature, of a cast in which there is more forethought & more subsequent pleasure. The crowded ball has for me no attractions, the late opera, in summer, no charms. A pleasant dinner followed by a smoke and early party is all I require, is what I enjoy, & what I find in London.

Morning visits, seeing few of one's friends at once, & at moderate intervals when professional duties allow of daylight being spent in so doing is another rational & agreeable manner of employing the day. In the afternoon an hour's ride in the Park between 5 & 6 is enough of the world for me, enough of me for the world. This is the part I play in Society and as we now parade in barracks at ½ past 7, I always am glad to get to bed at an hour which ensures me at least 7 hours & a half sound sleep so that the next morning I find myself cool, fresh, strong, in good health & in good spirits.

Today Ascot week begins but I do not think I shall go down there, although I should have liked to have seen the course, yet as I have little interest in the race & do not belong to any party going there and that most of our officers wish to go, and that some of us must stay with the Battalion I shall remain in town and leave Ascot for some other year. Epsom I went to with old Hare & Lord Charles Manners, we rode down, & up again went over the fence & bilk'd the pike after Sutton and dined with Hare on our return.

Expeditions were made during the summer months by carriage and on horse-back to visit the Misses Berry at Petersham. Sometimes they stayed a night or two at the Castle Hotel in Richmond and drove with Miss Mary and Miss Agnes as far as Hampton Court. Samuel Rogers was the centre of an excursion to Putney in June. He had always found Lady William agreeable and he liked her younger children too. On occasion they were asked to appear in St James's Place at the end of a dinner to which their mother and brother had been invited, and the old gentleman would show them some of his treasures. Lady William, though widely entertained, was in an economical mood and received few guests at home. Lord Lynedoch and Colonel Hare were faithful visitors and often dined or drank tea with her and her sons. It would seem that Mrs Butler did the cooking as she had done it at Carlsbad, for it was noted when they moved to a house in Kensington after Christmas: 'Nous avons une cuisinière.'

The money saved on housekeeping was spent on portraits of herself and the children. A family group was commissioned from Schoppe,* a Berlin painter, and Lady William sat to a French artist, Valentini.

* Julius Schoppe (1797–1868). He was much employed by the Prussian royal family.

Diplomacy

Lady William Russell to Colonel Hare Clarges at Perth [PRP]

34 South Street
Wednesday, 19 August, 1840.

I have nothing on earth to tell you except that I am bored to death & have the fidgets & die to travel. . . .

Hastings is shooting grouse at Glossop near Sheffield & is to be back in a week. . . . We have hurricanes & deluges. London empty & all mournful & dreary, as one can use no exercise. I envy your voyage & your journey & your sojourn in Scotland. Tell Lord Lynedoch the family picture is beautiful as a picture but we are none of us like. Still it will be a pretty ornament & perhaps all the better for not being too like four ugly people. The figures and air will do to remind him of us & the whole thing is graceful & agreeable in composition. In sitting to Valentini I took a French post book, pink paper 1836 out of the library, for which I am accountable & left the deed recorded on a visiting card where the book stood. * The said book is a duplicate, the other being bound in calf & of the year 1838. I am planning journies, none of which I shall ever execute & am breaking my heart after Carlsbad. I think I will pass the winter there to make up for my loss. . . .

I have not heard of late from Berlin, so I conclude Lord William is touring, he remains absent till the middle of October. . . .

Hastings Russell to Lord William Russell at Berlin [WP]

September 4th 1840

As I have many things to ask, to answer and to say, and as I am not much of a quilldriver, and that time flies fast, I will divide my letter into Nos. not according to order but as they come into my head. So first I have got your letter of the 26th. of Aug. Your prescription of grouse shooting has done me much good, although it rained incessantly the whole week, I have seen the Peak of Derbyshire the moors which are beautiful, the grouse, the heather, the Yorkshire breakfasts, the course of the Derwent, Sheffield, Rotherham, Derby, Birmingham, Manchester, Glossop, Ashton and should have gone on to Liverpool had I been able to get a prolongation of leave. However, I am very sorry at having been the cause of depriving my Mother of Carlsbad this year which is necessary for her health and good for Odo. . . .

* She did not return it; it is among her books today.

438

Diplomacy

Hastings Russell to Lord William Russell at Berlin [WP]

South St. October 5th 1840

... Your horse started on the 3d. My Mother will let you know more about it as she undertook the sending. I bought him a pair of travelling trowsers & a ship halter which I will dun you for in due time. Besides these articles you will receive one saddle, one bridle, one Roller Blanket & breastplate and a hood & blanket of Hawkins's as there was not clothing enough. The man has travelled horses in Germany before & has taken horses to Jamaica so he must be accustomed to the sea. . . .

I went some days ago to the Horse Guards. Sir John Macdonald bids me tell you that you are the only friend he has, that every one else is against him, he looks very much harassed, this does not look like the eternal Peace you spoke of last March. Can't the Corps Diplomatic keep the gates of the Temple of Janus shut? Are we to have a war? Write & tell me something. You don't write often, or say much, it is an age since I have had a letter. This is not like a dutiful Father.

Another frequenter of the Russell house that summer was a naval officer, Hastings Henry.* He was popular with the boys and interested in their collections, relieving them of their grey parrot when he went to sea. In the autumn he was given the command of the *Salamander* and Lady William saw her chance of getting a passage to the Mediterranean for all the family. Strings were vigorously pulled and Lord Minto, First Lord of the Admiralty, sent a permit for her to embark in a warship. But in October the boys went sadly to look at the *Salamander* anchored at Woolwich, for Hastings Henry was being sent on a voyage to the Mediterranean without them. 'Notre départ est ainsi retardé.' Ten days later Admiral Parker, now serving as a Sea Lord at the Admiralty, called to bid Lady William hold herself ready for instant departure; but she did not leave London. She may, as usual, have changed her mind, or perhaps the destinations of Her Majesty's ships were altered to meet the political situation, since war with France was not improbable in view of the Eastern Question. On 16 October Hastings came of age, and a month later at Chenies, 'Mr R. communie le soir (première communion)'. A chapel attached to the parish church contains the monuments of the Russell family from the time of the first Earl of Bedford to the present day, and Lady William's brother-in-law, Lord Wriothesley Russell, was the rector; she was fonder of him and his wife than of her other in-laws and it could have been they who prevailed with her to have Hastings confirmed.

* Hastings Henry (1808–79), son of John Henry and Lady Emily Fitzgerald, daughter of the 2nd Duke of Leinster. He assumed the name of Yelverton when he married in 1845 the Dowager Marchioness of Hastings, Baroness Grey de Ruthyn.

15*

Hastings Russell to Lord William Russell at Berlin [WP]

South Street. October 30th 1840

Alfred Saits called here yesterday & claimed 3s. which I gave him, for lodging in Hamburg and boat fare on the Thames. I told [him] you were satisfied with the care he took of the horse & dog which latter I am sorry to see you do not seem pleased with, she was little Odo's getting, you had given him the commission, and he gave himself great trouble about it. I could not help him much as you know I am no great judge of dogs. . . .

You of course know how we have been disappointed in a passage to the Mediterranean so I need say nothing on that score. My leave is from Nov. 1st up to the 15th of March 1841. I hope I shall see you before it is out as you will then have been absent one whole year.

I expected a letter from you on my birthday and was much disappointed to see you had forgotten it.

You ask me about Lord Cardigan's court martial,* the whole army (I mean the officers) think like the court of course, and the civilians think like the newspapers. As to our men I have no means of knowing, seeing so little of them as we do in the Guards, but a corporal brought a man up before the orderly room for impertinent and abusive language & when he was ask'd by B. Drummond if it was very bad, he said, 'Yes, very bad, he said I was worse than Lord Cardigan.'

Lord William Russell to Lady Holland [HH]

Berlin Nov 1 [1840]

I have just heard of the death of your excellent distinguished husband,† & only write two lines to say how much I feel for you, my own grief can be nothing compared to yours. I have seen you so many years in the enjoyment of all the happiness this world can give, that I can scarcely imagine fortitude enough to bear up against this severe blow. My father & Lord Holland were two of the links that chained us to the endearment of life, & these two links are broken almost at the same moment. I hope that you will consider me amongst the friends that remain to you for I shall always be as I am now sincerely yours.

* A quarrel between Lord Cardigan and one of his officers arose from Lord Cardigan sending Captain Reynolds an insulting message at a great mess dinner. The Captain responded and was charged by Cardigan with writing an improper and intemperate letter. Captain Reynolds, to the astonishment of many, was dismissed the service.

† Lord Holland had died on 22 October.

Diplomacy

Lady Holland to Lord William Russell at Berlin [WP]

Dec. 8 1840

I have felt deeply all the truth & kindness of your expressions, but cannot touch upon the subject, beyond thanking you for your compassion. I am indeed a most wretched heartbroke creature. Miss Fox* has kindly promised to reside with me. We have not been separated since my overwhelming calamity. My house in South Street is too small to lodge her, I applied to Colonel Hare to let me have his adjoining house on lease, it being generally said by his friends that he will never inhabit it himself. It would be a most important accession & enable me to fix my abode, avoiding thereby all the distress & trouble of seeking another house. Neither my health nor spirits render me fit for such an exertion. It is Lord Duncannon's suggestion that I apply to you for your good services on my behalf with Colonel Hare, with whom Duncannon says he is sure you could prevail, all circumstances considered – of my forlorn, miserable condition, for I am, dear William, quite overwhelmed. If universal sympathy & sincere regret at the loss could assuage my grief, I certainly have it fully, never was a man more beloved, esteemed & admired. If others so feel, what must I do after 42 years of such a tender union! unclouded as you know, & always tenderly beloved – forgive me & if you can help me in my request I will pay my rent & restore the house as I find it, only get it as my refuge for the little time I am likely to want anything. My health is daily becoming worse. I dread lingering painful illness, but an acute one has no terrors at present for me. God bless you.

On Christmas Day Drocourt recorded that 'Milady donne un grand dîner pour toute la maison.' It seems likely that the mistress and her family sat down to a feast with her servants in bourgeois German fashion, but Drocourt was not there himself, for he left for Paris a few days before Christmas and was away for three weeks. It was more than six years since he had had a holiday.

Early in 1841 the Russells moved to a house in Hyde Park Gate. It belonged to Sir James Stephen and was nearly opposite the Kensington turnpike. The arrival and departure of the mails was a constant amusement to the children of Nassau Senior who lived next door, but it may be doubted if Arthur and Odo were stirred like them by the rattle of wheels and the sound of horns, for behind the house there was fresh scope for scientific study. Augustus Loftus, who was on leave in London, wrote to his chief in Berlin that he had seen Lady William several times: 'They have got a

* The Hon. Caroline Fox, Lord Holland's sister.

441

delightful house . . . with the rear windows looking into the country and the windows of the drawing room opening onto a nice lawn and garden.'[75]

From the fields and ditches near at hand it was easy to bring into the house innumerable frogs 'que nous mettons dans un bassin pour voir la ponte des œufs'. The boys' curiosity regarding the productivity of their captives was soon rewarded. 'Une de nos grenouilles a pondu 2486 œufs. Nous portons les œufs dans leur ruisseau natal.'

Drocourt led his pupils far afield to Hammersmith and Fulham and Westminster Cemetery; with Hastings he would walk to Putney and Battersea. Mrs Rawdon had a lodging in the New Road near Regent's Park.

7th Duke of Bedford to Lord William Russell at Berlin [WPP]

Woburn Abbey, Jan. 8, 1841.

. . . In justice to Hastings, I must say I did not expect him to write to me, or answer my letter till he could fix a time for coming to us, and I think I told him so.

You knew we were not in London, when he came over, but as soon as we settled there, we did our best to get him to come to us, and the Duchess wrote to his mother to ask her to bring him to dinner, and to fix her own day or days. I also asked and wished him to come to us at Oakley whenever he could get away for a day or two to shoot – and the moment our plans were fixed about coming here, he was the very first person I wrote to invite, and to tell him to come whenever he could. What more could I do? If he requires greater attention than this, it is probably because he has been a little spoilt, by the want of a public education. It is always in these little matters that the advantages of a public education are felt. With respect to elder and younger brothers, be assured that all positions in life have their due share of good and ill. Defoe, I think, says that the happiest are the middle class. I am quite sure it is not ye highest. 'Property has its duties as well as its rights.' You are little aware of the cares and worries – and the plagues I have had to go thro in ye course of the last year, and were it not that it would be wicked to complain of my lot, and not to be grateful for it, I should say that a man with fewer of these cares and responsibilities is a happier man. I know that the happiest days I have passed were at Oakley, free from all the duties and cares that have since fallen upon me.

When I felt it right to fix my own income at £12,000 and to devote myself to the care of the estate, a sensible friend observed to me, 'You are only a well paid agent, for those who have settlements, and mortgages on your estates.' This may be an exaggeration but there is some truth in it. If I could put you in my place, and take your income in place of my own, I am sure I should not be a less happy man – but it is wrong to complain of the lot which has been cast upon us by providence – be assured, however, that the means of happiness depend upon ourselves, and not upon our respective positions, except in as far as they bring greater cares and charges.

With respect to Russell, I wish he had taken Hastings by the hand but it is not his way, I wish it was. He never calls on any body. I try hard to get him to go now and then to Lady Bradford, but without success. Russell, I know, likes Hastings, but he must learn to take people as he finds them. Russell, like all of us, has his merits and demerits, his good and bad qualities – among the latter is a most extraordinary and morbid feeling of diffidence which makes him think that he cannot be useful or agreeable to any body. He would think that his society would bore Hastings, and that he would prefer that of younger and more lively and agreeable people – all this is wrong, but I cannot (tho' I try hard) drive it out of his head. If Hastings had mixed more with other boys, he would have understood better, and have allowed more for these peculiarities, and varieties of character and disposition in mankind. There has been nothing, I am sure, to make H. think that he could be only '*tolerated*' here, my invitations have been as cordial as my anxiety to see him here has been great. Lady T. and John will tell you that I was not only anxious to see him, but in a fidget from day to day, at his not coming.

Adieu. I have written all this in a great hurry, feeling anxious that you should not be led away by false impressions about our feeling towards your son. John, I am sure, feels the same. I think him a very nice youth. I like what I have seen of him and wish much to cultivate a further acquaintance with him.

Hastings Russell to Lord William Russell at Berlin [WP]

34 South Street
Friday. Jan 8th 1841

... Hatfield, Chevening, Buckhurst & other previous engagements prevented my going to Woburn. Not being in Town & my letters not being forwarded made it impossible for me to answer John by return of post, my Uncle Bedford's letter he wrote in November was to say that he should be at Woburn in December & that I might come when I liked. I could not read the name of the place it was dated from & he also told me in it not to answer him. His other letters I have answer'd the same day I received them. I am sorry to have been the cause of so much anxiety & regret to my uncle, but the advantage of making the acquaintance of people I already know does not seem an irreparable loss to me.

I doubt the possibility of my Mother's coming to Berlin this month as even the letters are obliged to go round by Calais which itself is block'd up with ice, but from your recommending the Hamburg passage so strongly & as I heard that you were there a short time ago, I thought it likely that you should have run over to see us and your house which you have been near a year absent from.

I myself shall remain with my Mother & go with her where ever she goes until my leave expires.

7th Duke of Bedford to Lord William Russell at Berlin [WPP]

Oakley, April 4, 1841.

I received your last letter at Belvoir Castle* where we passed 4 or 5 days very agreeably and I hope somewhat profitably to myself, in as far as I saw much of the interior management and economy of a most magnificent establishment conducted with a degree of order – and regularity – combined with the truest hospitality, that can be conceived. It is true that the Duke is there only from 3 to 4 months in the year, and that he has sacrificed his town residence as well as Cheveley, but while he *is* there, he lives like an English Duke. All you say about me and my affairs is true, and I already find that I must increase my means. Palfreman's accounts for the quarter ending at Christmas amount to nearly £4,000 altho' we were only 5 weeks at Woburn, and much away.... However my means *are* increasing and after another year or two of prudence, I shall have an ample income for everything I can require, and leave a bed of roses for my successors – but the old system was stopt just in time, to save the family estates, just as the Poor Law came into operation to save the landed property of the kingdom.

I will take care of your letters – some of them are very interesting. There is among them an admirable one in favour of public education, containing reasoning that is quite unanswerable. I wish Lady William could be induced to send your two boys now, if not too late for Arthur, to a public school, but I fear she is immoveable on that subject. Russell told me one day that he would not take £100,000 for what he gained by going to Eton – i.e. what he had gained in satisfaction to his own feelings....

* The seat of the Duke of Rutland.

Part 4

LAST YEARS
1841–1846

In May, Hastings, presumably granted further leave of absence from his regiment, went off in the *Salamander* to St Petersburg with Hastings Henry, who had been to the Mediterranean and come back. It was arranged that Hastings Russell should visit his father at Berlin and then go to meet his mother and brothers at Aix-la-Chapelle on their way to Carlsbad.

Lady William's home was once more charged with the air of removal. The books that had been unpacked to fill the shelves at Hyde Park Gate were put into cases again and sent to Tilbury's warehouse. Mrs Rawdon gave up her lodging and moved into her daughter's house. She went with her and her grandsons to say goodbye to the Misses Berry, and Samuel Rogers gave a dinner for Lady William and the boys. Two days before they were to leave, Lord John Russell announced his forthcoming marriage with a young woman twenty-five years his junior, Lady Frances Elliot, the daughter of the Earl of Minto. 'Emballage arrêté. Les chevaux viennent, le départ est retardé.'

In the years to come Lady William was to say many disagreeable things about her sister-in law and perhaps when, having made acquaintance with Fanny Elliot, she set off three days late for the Continent, she was already persuaded that Lord John's second wife was not a person she would ever care for.

Hastings Russell to Lady William Russell in London [PRP]

Berlin May 31st 1841

I received your letter of the 25th last night and saw the one of the same date to my Father this morning. You have foreseen my answer. I do not wish to come in immediately, altho' it has always been my *Augenmerk* for the future. *Noch bin ich es nicht gewachsen*, not full-fledged yet for such an undertaking. Any measure that would free me from family thraldom is indeed a godsend and you are my Political Providence in having made it serve at a future period. You misunderstood me if you thought I meant that the House and the duty of the Guards were too much work for me. It was the tenfold increase of expense which they mutually bring on that I

445

knew myself incapable of supporting and not a fear of not having enough time for idleness. My Father is so kind as not to take the expense into consideration – but at the same time he will not give me any advice on the subject. I hope that acting as I do I shall not meet his disapprobation. . . .

My detailing all the civility I met with during the 90 hrs I was at St Petersburg is useless. Everyone to whom *you* have given a firman to any place will be received in the same manner. When we meet at Aix la Chapelle on the 10th, 11th, or 12th of June, it will be *Hoff zum dunken*, besides I daresay you have seen Hastings, on his return, as you have without a doubt not started on the appointed day. . . .

Goodbye, my dear MM, God bless you and big Atty and little O. I hope that your recovery is not an invention of yours to keep me quiet, and I sincerely hope that Drocourt's convalescence is going on more rapidly than it was.

Lord William Russell to Lord John Russell [PRO]

Berlin, June 16.41

I wish you joy & hope it may bring you all the happiness you deserve. But you are a perfect salamander to live in such flames. You set fire to the country, & to a lady's heart at the same time, and you flourish in the general conflagration.

Lady William's party crossed the Channel in a steam boat to Ostend where the *berline* and the *calèche* were put onto the train that took them to Aix-la-Chapelle where they expected to meet Hastings, but he had given up waiting for them and they found him at Carlsbad ten days later. Mrs Rawdon joined them in July and Lord William came from Berlin for a week.

Hastings Russell to Lord William Russell at Berlin [WP]

Aix la Chapelle
Sunday. June 13th. 1841
Atty's Birthday

The little carriage has stood the journey very well.

My Mother is not here. I hope to God that it is only procrastination and not an accident which has kept her.

I leave this for Carlsbad tonight where I shall be on the 18th. and where I hope you will soon come to see me.

I arrived here yesterday at 5 p.m. Don't show my letters about like Granny.

Hastings Russell to Lord William Russell at Berlin [WP]

Carlsbad, Friday. 18th. June

Although I am convinced that my Mother's journey has been delayed by the weather or put off for some trivial cause, as usual, yet I cannot help feeling anxious, and imagining all kinds of improbable accidents that may have happened to them. If any letter for me has come to Berlin or you have heard from her, or of her, write me word here as soon as you can, for there are few things more disagreeable than incertitude & anxiety. Waiting at Aix was intolerable to me and almost equally uncertain as to her arrival. I should have gone over to England if you had not said I had better not. To come back to Berlin would have bordered on the ridiculous.

Why should not you come here? Your dislike to the place will go off when [you] see it again, I am certain. Exchange that whirlpool of gaiety Berlin for this little eddy of innocent amusement. You have no longer the excuse of a ministerial crisis and it is but a 48 hours' drive. Act like a dutiful father and come and see

Your indulgent & affectionate son.

... Tomorrow an answer to my Aix la Chapelle letter might reach Carlsbad if you answered immediately, which I hope you did for I am exceedingly anxious about my Mother & brethren.

Hastings Russell to Lord William Russell at Berlin [WP]

Carlsbad, June 20th. 1841

I send you my application for extension of leave which it is high time to forward. I have delayed it so long in hopes of hearing from you or my Mother about whom I am getting very uneasy. . . .

If you have any news of my Mother do not fail to let me know soon. I am much afraid some illness must have detained her in England, but still I could not risk going there without knowing even whether I should find her.

I found numbers of acquaintance here. The Palffys, Mr & Mrs Austin and of all the people in the world, Col. Eden, the Capt. of my Company.

447

The 5th. Company never muster'd so strong abroad since the peace.

Good bye, my dear Father. Write to me soon & put me out of this inquietude or come yourself which is still better.

When Lord John wrote to his brother proposing the Government of Bombay to him, Lord William answered: 'I decline Bombay. .... It is entering into a new service of which I know nothing, and all for money. Tell them I am much flattered by their obliging offer but to Bombay I go not.'[1]

Hastings Russell to Lord William Russell at Berlin [WP]

Carlsbad, 25 July. 1841

... You tell me to lighten the weight of time by writing, & so I do, and say, that time never hangs heavy on my hands, that I am sorry you think it does, that I am sorry you were ill on your way back to Berlin, sorry that I write so bad a hand & sorry that you have refused *Bumbay*. My Mother was never against your taking it, she said so in London before you knew of its being offered you and I think she would have preferred my going with you to my going alone, if I do go to the East Indies and now that I have said what I am sorry for I will say that I am glad at having so little to be sorry for and hope that the same absence of care may remain with me for many years, if I live many years, and hope that you may feel the same in Berlin the retreat you prefer to the *beatis gazis Arabune*.

7th Duke of Bedford to Lord William Russell at Berlin [WPP]

Woburn Abbey, Aug. 3rd, 1841.

Nothing could have gone off better than our Royal visit. I believe I received and entertained my Sovereign in a becoming manner. So at least I was told by all my guests, and no one among them expressed himself more strongly and warmly than the Duke of Wellington. I send you some reports from the county papers. They are not quite correct but may serve to amuse you at so great a distance. ...

Both the Queen and Prince were so kind and amiable that it was impossible not to be pleased with them and I felt what I did not expect, really sorry and gloomy when they left us. I have reason to believe from all I hear, as well as from their own expressions, that they were greatly pleased with their visit and with all they saw here.

Last Years

I did not mention John's marriage because I hardly knew what to say about it. He ought to know what is most likely to lead to his own happiness. Melbourne tells me that it is not a popular marriage among his political friends, and partisans. The family are not liked and are considered jobbers, but I hear a good report of her. I think John could have stood higher if he had not married. All the sentiment that centred about him, and his great charge, will be destroyed by it, and a third family, his wife having no money, will add greatly to his expenses. However, I expect he ought to be the best judge of his own happiness. . . .

Lord John Russell to Lord William Russell at Berlin [WPP]

Minto, Aug. 4 [1841]

You are quite mistaken in supposing that I had any hand in preventing Hastings coming into Parliament. He had a very good offer of a seat, but his mother, instead of consulting me, took the advice of Lord Abinger! and Baron Parkes!! and Rogers!!! When we afterwards found that Russell would not stand again for Tavistock, it was necessary to have some-one on the spot to canvas, and Hastings had gone to Petersburgh.

Melbourne and Hobhouse have decided on giving Bombay to Sir W. Macnaughten. I think you are quite right in not wishing for it.

The Russell family was now recognised as of consequence and merit at Carlsbad. They were on friendly terms with many of the bourgeois inhabitants who had known them for four consecutive summers. Lady William's kindness and charity was appreciated and her sons' prowess with firearms was admired. The Sharpshooters of the town paraded in front of Hastings who devised a shooting match for them, offering six pieces of gold as a prize. Soon after, he left for a visit to Italy and returned two months later driving a little carriage he had bought in the Tyrol. Mr Siefert went away to Baden and is not heard of again. There were benefit nights for poor families and *soirées musicales* in the public rooms. At home Odo entertained their friends with card tricks and conjuring.

The visitors from whose company Lady William derived most pleasure were Mr and Mrs John Austin.* Sarah Austin recalled twenty years later how Odo had taken trouble to please her on this visit. 'A day or two after we

---

* John Austin (1790–1859), jurist; he was professor of jurisprudence at London University in 1826. His wife was Sarah Taylor (1793–1867), well known for her translations from the German. They lived in Germany 1841–3.

449

Last Years

arrived at Carlsbad I met the little fellow walking alone. He was looking about for lodgings for us. *Quelle gentillesse* on the part of a young boy.'[2] She wrote now to her dearest friend, Harriet Grote.*

Mrs Sarah Austin to Mrs George Grote [Grote papers]

Alte Wiese [Carlsbad]

24 August, 1841

... His [John Austin's] audience here is of the feminine gender – Lady William Russell and Mlle Schopenhauer,† and, before we left, Mrs Hamilton Gray. Cummer dear, we are certainly looking up! These women have beaten all the men who have been here out of the field for general knowledge and powers of thought and conversation. It is true we have been unlucky in men. With the exception of my old friend General Leyser, and the most venerable of human beings the Archbishop of Erlau (who is my passion) we have had no very interesting men. Laube, the writer,‡ is clever, but 'jeune France', a 'genre' I do not like. Schelling § was here just when we returned, and Lady William had no rest till I made his acquaintance. He overwhelmed me with speeches, regrets, etc, but was going away the next day. *Que voulez-vous?* Neander, the author of 'Church History' is here, and we are only waiting till my husband is well, to make his acquaintance. . . . Miss Schopenhauer arrived only on Saturday, very poorly. . . . She and my husband, ill as they were, discussed the light questions of the 'existence of evil' and the 'eternity of the world', as soon as they met; and last night came Lady William to ask him to throw light on the Schelling and Hegel controversy, which *she* is looking into.

I cannot express the love and admiration this most noble woman has inspired me with. I spend part of every day with her. We walk or drive &c., and we go to her, or she comes to us of an evening. I see her as a mother, maintaining all her authority and as much loved as obeyed. With her, alone, I felt no want of society. Her knowledge of men and books is equally extensive, and the activity of her mind extraordinary, in her situation. . . .

---

* Harriet Grote (1792–1878), née Lewin, was the wife of George Grote, the historian of Greece.

† Adèle Schopenhauer (1797–1849) was the sister of Arthur Schopenhauer, the philosopher. She wrote several novels and had a great talent as a silhouettist.

‡ Heinrich Laube (1806–84), Liberal German writer.

§ F. G. J. Schelling (1775–1854), German philosopher who founded a system of subjective idealism.

450

Melbourne's ministry fell at the end of August and the Tories come again into power. It did not strike Lord William that his own position was in jeopardy, but he took up his diary again to mark his anxiety about the state of England.

'I suppose you will not leave Berlin on leave of absence', wrote Lord John, 'your doing so would be tantamount to a resignation.'[3] Having watched at Berlin the summer manœuvres of the Prussian Army, Lord William went into Silesia to see more of the troops, but the manœuvres ended before he ever found the horses he had sent on ahead, and the King and Court had moved on to another district. His leave began in the middle of September and without regard for his brother's caution he left Berlin and made his way to Prague, passing a day here and there with friends. His family were not as he expected at Prague, and he drove on after a week to Carlsbad and found them preparing for removal. 'The Grand Duke of Saxe Weimar and the Austins left – the last of the drinkers, but the weather is still beautiful; the leaves yellow but the sun bright. It is a pretty hole.'

It was his wife's birthday on 2 October, and on the next day he set out with Hastings to cover again the hundred miles to Prague. Lady William and the others followed.

The Jewish settlement in Prague was one of the oldest in Europe and it was fitting that the young students of Hebrew, as soon as they arrived, should be taken by Drocourt to see the ancient Jewish cemetery and to visit some of the synagogues where prayers were being read for the Feast of Tabernacles. In contrast to these solemn scenes, all the nobility of Bohemia with fine horses and handsome equipages had come to Prague for the races. Two other travellers were in the town whom Lord and Lady William found good company: Alexander Baillie and Knudtzon, the Dane.* 'The friendship of these two gentlemen is of European notoriety and admiration', wrote Lord William in his diary. This friendship must have been dwelt on with some emphasis, for Drocourt notes it also. 'Courses de chevaux. En y allant, Milady avec les enfants, Mr Baillie et son ami inséparable, tombent de la voiture qui se brise sous eux. Personne n'est blessé.'

After a week of entertainment the Russells moved on to Vienna. 'Les douaniers veulent ouvrir, Milord ne veut pas.' Lord William's obstinacy delayed them at the Customs for three hours, but there was soon a joyful reunion with the Bombelles family at Schönbrunn, and a more formal one with the Metternichs. A communication from the new Foreign Secretary, Lord Aberdeen, was already on its way to Berlin when Lord William left his family in Vienna to return to his post, but the news of his recall reached him before he got there. 'I went to Dresden where Forbes informed me that

---

* Jorgen von Cappelen Knudtzon (1784–1854) was a native of Trondheim, which town he represented for a time in the Swedish parliament. He travelled extensively and on a voyage to Jamaica in an English boat he met Alexander Baillie, who took a great liking to the young Norseman. Sharing antiquarian and artistic interests, and having independent means, they spent the rest of their lives together travelling about Europe and the Levant. Knudtzon was a patron of Thorwaldsen. Baillie was perhaps the son of James Baillie, who sat as M.P. for Horsham.

Last Years

Lord Burghersh had been gazetted to my post. What a brusque & ungracious way of turning me out.' A few days later he wrote an intemperate
despatch to Lord Aberdeen expressing his resentment at the manner of his
recall.

Lord Augustus Loftus to Lord William Russell at Vienna [WPP]

Berlin, October 1841.

Tho' I am daily expecting your return, I cannot refrain from sending
one line on the chance of this finding you still at Vienna.

It has hitherto been my good fortune to communicate intelligence of an
agreeable nature to your Lordship and I much regret that it is now my
irksome lot to convey to your Lordship the nomination of Lord Burghersh
as your successor at this Court. Allow me at the same time to convey to
your Lordship the assurances of my regret at an event which deprived the
Mission of its chief – the country of an able servant. For myself personally,
I shall ever recollect that it was under your Lordship's guidance that I first
entered the harness of diplomacy, and be assured that I shall ever be
sensible of the kind interest which your Lordship has so often expressed
for my welfare. And I trust that tho' the ties of service are now broken,
those of friendship will remain, that your Lordship will continue to me
the same feeling of regard, which you have hitherto entertained. . . .

Lord Aberdeen to Lord William Russell at Berlin [WPP]

Foreign Office, Oct. 13, 1841.

I am afraid that my communication will be unwelcome; and I should
be sorry if you thought that I made it without personal regret; but the
mission you fill is of so prominent a character that it is not improbable that
you may have anticipated a change, as the consequence of what has taken
place in this country. I hope you will believe that I should have had sincere
pleasure in requesting you to remain at Berlin, had the nature of the
mission, and the arrangements connected with the change of administration, rendered it possible for me to do so. Many reasons combine to increase my regret; and I can truly say that it is the most painful thing I have
had to do, since my return to this office. I must, however, inform you that
it is intended to send Lord Burghersh to Berlin; and I have only to hope
that his appointment, or that of some other substitute, may not have been
unexpected.

Last Years

Hastings Russell to Lord William Russell at Berlin [WP]

Vienna, October 30th 1841

I expect a letter from you before I leave Vienna . . . to tell me whether I shall find you at Berlin. . . . If not where I shall meet you, in short any orders you may have to give me. I write to remind you of this lest you should write too late or forget me altogether in the turmoil of affairs.

Good bye, my dear Papa. The weather has been fine & I hope your journey was not disagreeable.

[in Lady William's hand]

Successors now-a-days arrive rail-road pace; you will scarcely have time to button on your pea jacket.

I am glad the Burghershes get something – they have a large family – larger than ours; & the same income & habits of expence & luxury. So I don't grudge them their diplomatic tread-mill. Your colleague Beauvale did not wait for snow & the woodcocks to return to Vienna but came per rail to be off to Italy by the back door before Gordon drives under the *porte cochère – ainsi un clou chasse l'autre. You* ousted your friend Adair – Burghersh ousts you who are *his* friend – & Lord Beauvale asks me to dinner!!!! so much has adversity already softened his character! He heard by chance I was at Vienna. I told him I had never left it since 1839 when chance equally revealed my *séjour* to him – & that he had never found out I was here all along. He thought you & I tender turtle doves had taken wing together.

I hope we shan't have war with America? that is all I care about! – all the rest *m'est fort égal.* The Conservatives God bless them are turning Papists & the *Globe* is grown pious – shock'd at Sabbath breaking. 'Oh Scribes & Pharisees. Ye hypocrites!!!' as our divine Master said. The world was always the same, *Anno Mundi* and *Anno Domini* what you please. . . .

I feel sorry for your annoyance as to the sudden recall, it gives no time to pack & to pay! & you will be worried to death – unless you *did* attend to my constant warnings & got ready?

Burghersh will be at Berlin by the 3d. week in November.

LORD WILLIAM'S DIARY

27 Nov. From the beginning to the end of November when I left Berlin I received nothing but attention and friendly speeches from my colleagues & all

453

the society, expressed by dinners, parties, words &c., and by none more than by the King & Royal family. This consoled me for the spiteful conduct of Lord Aberdeen.

30 Nov. That great fool Lord Burghersh arrived, & threw himself into the hands of that fool and beast Sir George Hamilton; alas, poor England to be so represented.

[Hastings came from Vienna to join his father and they left Berlin together early in December and took a boat from Hamburg to England.]

6 Dec. Four days in a gale of wind. Heavens what misery.

9 Dec. Landed at the Tower where we found Hastings' regiment. Went to Mivart's.* From the misery of a ship to the luxury of Mivart's there is only a step, yet what a contrast.

[Dining with the widowed Lady Holland and with the Misses Berry, Lord William found himself made welcome by the old set and the sympathy he received on the circumstances of his recall soothed his wounded feelings.]

16 Dec. Went to Broadlands. I like Palmerston much, he is very agreable and has always been very civil to me, ay, more, kind. He says Aberdeen has behaved most indecorously to me. Lady P. very warm about it.

19 Dec. Heard from a good source that Lady Burghersh made the Duke of Wellington ask for Berlin for Burghersh, he being ruined and in immediate want of money. This is the old Tory system of managing things; first men, then the country, or rather the latter must pay for the vices of the former.

21 Dec. Went to Woburn Abbey, where I found the Duke of Sussex, the Duchess of Inverness & a large party. 30 at dinner.

23 Dec. Plays were got up by Mr Shelley & very well acted by himself, Charles, Edward, Lady C. Paget, Mrs Leicester Stanhope & others.

26 Dec. The Duke of Sussex went away and the party broke up, having spent a week gaily & agreably. The Duke is *facile à vivre* & requires no Royal attentions.

Lord William Russell to Lady Holland [HH]

Woburn Abbey, Wednesday [25 December 1841]

As you take an interest in everything that happens at Woburn Abbey, I send you the bill of the plays acted last night, & really admirably well acted. There was a scene between Charles & Mrs Stanhope that was perfection.

* Mivart's Hotel in Lower Brook Street was the precursor of Claridges Hotel.

You questioned me a good deal the last time I saw you, as to the style of living here, I can now answer you more learnedly than I was able to do then. In point of magnificence it is equal to the old days, & in point of comfort there is an evident improvement; that is, all that concerns the housekeeper's department is more *soigné*. We are 30 at table, great profusion, & an admirable *cuisine*, besides, repasts at every hour of the day. From 10 to 12 breakfast – from 2 to 3 luncheon, from 5 to 6 tea, at 7 dinner, & after balls & theatres hot suppers, otherwise cold. The Duke of Sussex appears delighted, passes the mornings in his room & is no *gêne* to any one. You will be glad to hear the old Abbey has come out of the fire of its purification with more splendour than ever, but pray consider this as a private communication for your own satisfaction & nobody else. Our party breaks up tomorrow & I shall probably return to town on Friday.

Hastings Russell to Lord William Russell at Woburn [WP]

[The Tower] Christmas Day 1841

I have little chance I fear of seeing Woburn, perhaps I should not be refused leave, but it would not be fair to ask it. . . .

I am passing my Christmas quietly alone in my quarters. The Governor asks us all to dinner today, all those on duty but I am malingering & mean to stay at home reading & writing this whole eveng.

I have had a letter from my Mother, what makes you think her bored at Vienna?

That d——d pain in my shoulder is beginning again but otherwise I am better. Good bye, my dear Father, God bless you. I wish you a merry Christmas and what is better a happy new year, tho' I am not very merry here yet I am perfectly happy & contented which is much better.

My Mother writes out of spirits, was that your reason for thinking her bored? Have you written to her for Christmas or to the little boys? . . .

Hastings Russell to Lord William Russell at Woburn [WP]

Tower, Tuesday Dec. 28th. [1841]

The reason you had not heard from me, my dear Father, was the Sunday and Christmas day interval, by this time you will have had 2 letters.

455

Last Years

I wish that your informer as to the healthy state of the Tower would pass the winter here for me. *I* am not well enough to dine with the Berrys, and out of 9 Officers present, staff included, 3 are well, 4 more or less indisposed & 2 very unwell.

I have changed my quarters for the better up stairs to the 1st. floor. My friend the Quartermaster sergeant brought the barrack rules & regulations to my assistance & proved that my junior had no right to keep it.

An old pensioner here is very anxious to see you. Senton, orderly to Fred Ponsonby, who says you will remember him well, that he crossed the Pyrennees with you. I promised to let him know if you ever came to the Tower again, poor old boy, you seem to put him in mind of all the fair days of his life. It is a sad thing to outlive oneself.

I have been all morning veryfying the Mess inventory which forced serious reflexions on me as to the horrors of housekeeping & establishment.

Write me a little line every day if you can. I am very glad to hear from you. Have *you* heard from my Mother & of the boys. I hope & trust they are all of them well. It seems to me as if we shall all be grown old before we meet again.

Don't let my Mother know that I have not been well. I shall be all right again before she could hear and it would only worry her uselessly.

Lord William's injudicious despatch to Lord Aberdeen was with the help of Charles Greville's good offices finally removed from the record in March. The letters he received from his eldest son were a solace to him when he was lonely and in poor health. Hastings in his spare time was active in getting Grosvenor Place ready for his mother's occupation should she choose to come to England; but she remained in Vienna.

She was often ailing during the winter and Drocourt's diary gives prominence to her indispositions. She may have missed her eldest son and found parties in crowded rooms tedious without him, and balls at Court less amusing. The strains of middle age allowed her to make her health an excuse for not going about as much as usual. She was sometimes received privately by the Empress and she dined with the French and the English Ambassadors, and with Esterhazy and Zamoyski, and even gave some dinners herself. Her prime concern was, as ever, the education and happiness of her sons. Masters came to teach them a variety of subjects, Hebrew always among them, and they got to know the scientific collections of Vienna and the men who looked after them. They still enjoyed hunting for toads in the suburbs of the town, and specimens were sometimes sent to Dr Bell at the British Museum. Arthur had riding lessons in the Spanish School in the Hofburg, and it was during this winter that Kriehüber* made his first drawings of the brothers. Their friendship with the children of Count Bombelles was a great resource and their mother was as fond of the parents as they were themselves of the sons. Since the Count was Governor to the Archdukes Francis Joseph and Maximilian, the Emperor's nephews, they got to know them well too. Accompanied by Baroness Lebzeltern and a tutor, the Abbé Mislin, the young Bombelles would dine with the Russells in Vienna as often as Arthur, Odo and M. Drocourt did at Schönbrunn. Lady William confessed to Princess Metternich that she found it comic that Russell children should live with Abbés and Archdukes but that she liked to think that the impression that remained would be ineffaceable.

Charles Greville to Lord William Russell in London [WPP]

London, Jan. 26, 1842.

I did not think you had been 'imparting your grievance to any one' but the complaints you have made to your intimate friends, are repeated to their intimate friends – others who sympathise with you re-echo them, and thus they reach the ears of those you complain of, replies and counter accusations are provoked, and in this way a hubbub is made and personal feelings are excited and embittered. I have heard what you complain of in a general way, and in an equally general way have heard the *per contra*, but I have never seen a line of the correspondence. I will own to you that, as at present informed, I cannot discover any ground of offence that Aberdeen has given you, but on the contrary the clearest evidence of his desire to do what he considers his publick duty in a manner not only the least offensive but the most amicable to you, and it is because it seemed to me that such could be the general opinion if the matter was sifted and made publick that I said what I did to Tavistock. I have no intimacy whatever with Aberdeen, and all my interest in the matter is with you and for you, and with the view I take of the matter I thought it much better that you should let it drop. There may, however, be circumstances with which I am unacquainted which would entirely alter my opinion if I knew them – at all events I am very sorry that anything should have occurred to wound your feelings, and to interrupt the social harmony which you say generally exists in spite of political differences.

* Josef Kriehüber (1800–76).

Last Years

Lord Aberdeen to Charles Greville [WPP]
Private

Argyll House, Feby, 6th, 1842.

I think you had better suggest to Lord William that he should write to request that his despatch might be cancelled. As the Queen has seen all that has passed on the subject, I should like to send her his letter, as the termination of the affair. Indeed, without the Queen's permission I could not properly abstract or cancel any despatch in the office. They are the property of the Crown and not mine.

Although, as I told you, I have already mentioned Lord William to the Queen, and expressed my belief that his impressions were much changed since he wrote the despatch in question, it would give me great pleasure to be able, by his own declaration, to remove any unfavourable opinion from her mind.

Having been under the necessity of adopting a course, which I am aware must have been disagreeable to Lord William, I have now really no other feeling than a desire to do whatever may be most kind and considerate; and he may be assured that I do not retain the slightest vestige of anger or ill will, in consequence of his hasty proceeding towards me.

Lord William Russell to Lord Aberdeen [WPP]
[*draft*]

Belgrave Square, Feb 7 [1842]

As I understand from Mr Greville that your Lordship has expressed to him your regret that the nomination of my successor at the Court of Berlin should have appeared in the Gazette before I could possibly have heard of my recall, I wish to be permitted to withdraw a despatch I wrote to your Lordship receiving this intelligence dated November – which I wrote under impressions that are now removed. I have therefore to request your Lordship to obtain the sanction of the Queen to cancel the despatch in question.

Charles Greville to Lord William Russell [WPP]

Council Office, Feb 9th, 1842.

To avoid all mistakes I have thought it better to put on paper exactly what passed (to the best of my memory) between Lord Aberdeen and me, and I only need add that it was impossible for any man to speak of another with [?more] expressions of personal esteem, and of respect for his character, than he did of you. He looks forward with great satisfaction to the restoration of your usual amicable relations, and will be most happy to see you whenever you like to call upon him and to present you to the Queen whenever H.M. shall be pleased to receive you. He wishes you to write to him your desire to have H.M.'s leave to withdraw your despatches of the 2nd Nov. as he has no authority to return it to you or to cancel it, without the Queen's permission.

Lord Aberdeen to Lord William Russell [WPP]

F.O., Feb 10th 1842.

I am very sorry that the mode of your recall from Berlin should accidentally have been such as to have produced an erroneous impression on your mind, under which you wrote your dispatch of 2nd Nov. 1841. You may believe me when I say that nothing could be further from my intention than to carry this decision into effect in any measure calculated to wound your feelings. My private letter must have been sufficient to prove to you how reluctantly I took that step at all, and how much I regretted it.

With respect to your dispatch, I shall with great pleasure obtain the Queen's permission that it should be cancelled and as far as I am concerned, every thing shall be as if it had never been written.

Charles Greville to Lord William Russell [WP]

Office, Friday, March, 1842

The despatch is committed to the flames and Aberdeen will be very happy to see you whenever you like to call at the F.O.

Hastings Russell to Lord William Russell [WPP]

Monday 20th March [1842]

The ironmonger from Russell Street is here cringing to the impervious Williams who has dragged a man from Sharpus with him laden with door handles which he insists upon applying in the most promiscuous manner. Gas pipes are winding themselves about everything in the house like snakes round the Laocoon. North is hammering lustily to simulate industry. Tyre

459

and Sidon, Manchester and Birmingham, the dockyards of Carthage are as churchyards compared with 35 Grosvenor Place. I forgot to mention several members of the horticultural Society loose in the gardens.

I enclose a letter from my mother, and Stephen's estimate in which neither shower bath nor fender irons are included. It would take him 3 weeks he says to put up the bath – one week to put up the grate. Williams will call on you on Wednesday morning and I entreat that you arm yourself against 2 horrible hall chairs he will attempt to try and stick into you.

	£	s	d		£	s	d
Tomlin	30			Tilburys	100		
North	10			Dow	60		
Stephens	60			Rade	50		
Slater	20			Hobson	?		

In imitation of my Mother I have filled up the blank space at the end of my letter with all the Bills due or estimates sent in, that I could possibly think of. I daresay I have forgot many but still there is enough to provoke reflection, as MM would say. If you will leave me an unlimited order on your Banker I will engage to procure the receipts, otherwise I am running short. Taglietti has brought in £14.17.6 pennyworth of wages due. In short our situation grows truly alarming and assumes the appearance of a hunting love affair.

Et valeo & ti amo

Lord William left England again in April, spending some weeks in Germany before he joined his wife at Carlsbad in May.

Hastings Russell to Lord William Russell at Vienna [WP]

Grosvenor Place
Monday. April 11th. 1842

. . . I wrote to Berlin 2 days after you sailed but did not send. I found my letter was too melancholy a production, I tore it up and waited till the blue devils went. I have had 3 letters from you and I thank you for wishing I was with you. God knows I wish it too that I might see my Mother and my brothers soon again. I have got several letters from my Mother. I see she wishes me to say, 'Come here to me as I can't go to you.' But like the boy whose guts the fox gnawed out, I will not sing out first lest she should say I brought her home against her wish. But I hope you will not let her stay in Vienna. They all want change of air and this malignant fever there has been alarms me very much for them – so take them any where for change of air & scene. Don't let them stay in Vienna. You must be there by now. . . .

Hastings Russell to Lord William Russell at Vienna [WP]

Grosvenor Place
Sunday. April 24th 1842

The reason you have not heard from me, my dear Father, is – that you said when starting, write straight to Vienna unless you write immediately to Berlin. It was not likely that a man out of place should find friends!? anywhere especially at Berlin – however I wish you joy of them. Popular Pappyo.

Lord Ludlow, as you know, is dead and has left you 5000. When Lady Holland heard it she was very glad but said, 'Alas! poor William. I'm afraid nothing can bring him straight.'

I hope she's wrong for I am running fast to ruin and expect £50 for the kitchen, another 50 I have spent upon the sundries in the house – of this you gave me 30. What my Mother saved for me is going, as you know, for you yourself said, 'Never mind.' So I look to you. For it is not fair to think my Mother is to save with the whole family upon her hands.

. . . The world is much astonished at your refusing employment* and the old officers repeat what they had said when first you took to Diplomacy. 'There is a good officer spoiled for the Army.'

Your *huffy* son

Hastings Russell to Lord William Russell at Berlin [WP]

Grosvenor Place
Wednesday April 27th 1842

I see by the Times that you have taken private lodgings at Berlin which had I known that you were about to do I would have written there, but having told me to write direct to Vienna unless I wrote immediately, of course you hardly can have expected a letter from me at Berlin. . . .

I have had another bout of low spirits. I see no pleasure in futurity –

* Lord William had been offered the command of the Plymouth District.

wrong at my age and with greater causes for happiness than almost any one. I suppose it's physical.

Time flies on very fast, you must soon let me know where I shall find you in July. . . . You have lived so much away from us of late that I miss you less, but I confess that I pine after my Mother and my brothers. My Mother writes in better spirits than she has done [*torn*] God keep her so. Good bye my dearest Father and may God bless you.

The garden is trimmed and gravelled, everything is in leaf, the weather hot & sunny and the house charming. My stables prosper. Gas burns over the door. I wish you all were here to see it. . . .

Hastings Russell to Lord William Russell [WP]

Grosvenor Place
Wednesday May 4th 1842

Tho' London is delightful at this time of the year & tho' I pass my whole day in amusement yet I long to see Mother & brothers above all else. Besides my *tin* is running to an end and I have had no news of those £50 I asked you for the kitchen. I have followed your advice, dismissed thoughts of *quid cras*, spared no expense and made the house delightful, kept myself, 2 horses and a groom in livery – in short while the money lasted made myself as comfortable as possible. I have read over your letters in the *nunc est bibendum* style on shortness of life and the necessity of present enjoyment and while I read I found they'd been exemplified by your poor brother Henry's death at Greenwich in a fit, yesterday morning. . . .

Good bye my dearest Father and may God keep death from us all for many a long day.

Your friends the Fitzroys cut me whenever they meet me. What have *you* done to them. My conscience acquits *me*.

Lord William Russell to Lady Holland [HH]

Berlin, Ap. 27, 42.

. . . I came here for a few days & by the kindness & hospitality of my friends have been induced to remain 3 weeks, during which time I have

Marmor Palais, opposite the Russells' house in Potsdam
Lady William Russell's room at Carlsbad, 1844–5, from an oil painting

Lord William Russell, Berlin 1839, from a drawing by J. Maguès

never once dined in my inn. I have frequently seen the King who always talks with pleasure of his visit to London. They were astonished that Lord Westmorland* should have accepted the post without occupying it. I tell them *besogna mangiare*,† and that he is a needy nobleman. Aberdeen's diplomacy does not stand high, they compare Gordon to Beauvale in a manner little flattering to the former. Nesselrode writes that Stuart is a 'cadavre ambulant'. From Paris they write that Cowley is in his dotage and Sir S. Canning‡ makes Ponsonby regretted, even by Austria. I hope your health and spirits are better than when I left you, wishing you a return of both.

Hastings Russell to Lord William Russell [WP]

Tilt Yard Guard, May 17th 1842

I had not forgotten your birthday and I dare say my Mother had not either. We have been too much in the habit of keeping ours and the boys' together. But you had ever paid so little attention to these puerilities of ours that I passed your birthday over without outward visible sign, thinking it best pleasing to yourself. Such were my reasons for not writing on the 8th. of May. . . .

I am sorry my dunning letter displeased. It is difficult to write aesthetically on housekeeping. But I thank you for your prompt transmission of the £50. . . .

My Uncle Bedford calls on me every day. He came the day before yesterday to ask me to dinner and yesterday again for the same purpose. I showed him the whole house, the stables & my stud. . . .

A case of rape interrupts me, I must finish when I can. N.B. The case is not mine but a Grenadiers of the 3rd. Battalion I enclose the report.

Hastings Russell to Lord William Russell at Carlsbad [WP]

Tilt Yard Guard
Sunday. May 22d. 1842

Do not imagine that I have not been relieved since the 17th. but believe that I have been in the treadmill of amusement with short intervals of sleep

---

* Lord Burghersh succeeded his father as Earl of Westmorland in December 1841.
† 'One must eat.'
‡ Sir Stratford Canning had succeeded Lord Ponsonby at Constantinople.

ever since, unable to write or read or hardly think. In the meantime your letter from Carlsbad has reached me. – And the first thing I see is, 'Did you go to Lord Ludlow's funeral?' I did. It was, thank God, the first funeral I have ever attended. My Uncle John very much affected. I had always thought his little heart as wizened as his face but even Sydney Smith would have recanted then.

You ask about my horse. I think I must have told you we keep 3 horses. Mount a friend. Pay visits with a groom, in short are quite the Herr Barons of Grosvenor Place.

The summer at Carlsbad that year followed the usual pattern. When Hastings arrived on leave he gave his little Tyrolean carriage as the prize in a shooting match, and it was won by the baker of Carlsbad. Arthur and Odo paid the first of many visits to Petersburg, near Liebkowitz, the home of Count Czernin, and their brother went away to shoot with Count Nostitz. Lord and Lady William had the company of Mr and Mrs Austin, and Knudtzon and Baillie were welcome visitors.

It will be seen that what Lady William said she was going to do rarely bore any relation to what she did. Her visit to Carlsbad lasted nearly six months; returning to Vienna in October, she was accompanied by her husband as well as by her three sons.

Lady William Russell to Lord Lynedoch at Milan [NLS]

Carlsbad, 25 May, 1842.

... I regret immensely your rheumatic ailments and losing this occasion of seeing you, but we must make it out yet, and we will continue one or two or all of us to visit you *là bas* in autumn; Hastings has been invited by Genl. Walmunden to the manoeuvres for a second time and will avail himself of it in September. So *he* will be with you – and perhaps and most probably his father will be induced to go with him. We go to Vienna from hence the end of June and Lord William means to see a little of Hungary. I shall settle myself at Baden where now a rail road takes you in half an hour, and shall pass July and August there. Our intention was to return to England by November but it is not impossible if you winter in Italy that we might be tempted to do the same. Happen what may, I beg of you write to me here Carlsbad all June – and to Vienna July and August, and tell me how you are and whether your rheumatism relents. Let me hear from you a few lines as often as you can – it will be a great pleasure to me. Arthur & Odo are growing & strengthening and fattening and I may say in full bloom, for Odo is much improved in looks & is less bilious & stouter. They both kiss your hands as we say in these parts & have never had such pleasant recollections as your Sunday dinners. I hope to see my dear Hastings in July.

Hastings Russell to Lord William Russell at Carlsbad [WP]

35 Grosvenor Place
Saturday 28th. 10½ p.m.

Today, after a week's inability to write, I have refused a dinner that I might finish this unhappy letter. One from you came . . . refusing to cooperate about my leave. I half expected it but thought it best to leave no stone unturned.

What you say of your dear friends the Fitzroys is novel and the opposite of what you said in London. For a most harmonious family which certainly we are when all together, we write most acrimonious letters to each other – but this enlivens correspondence.

The next letter I write I hope will not be so disjointed – such a week as the last cannot return – coming home from Stafford house at 6 a.m. riding to the Derby at 11 – home at 8 for dinner & not in bed till one – a field day the next morng. at ½ past 7. then inspections &c. home, dress for dinner & another full dress ball that takes me home at 5 o/c next morning. If I had a Father, Mother, little brothers to sit at home with I should not want all this – but as it is, it makes the time of separation fly past.

Good bye, dear Pappy & I hope soon to be able to join you spite your not helping me. . . .

Mrs Rawdon to Arthur Russell [PRP]

[?1842]

My darling dear Atty, you will receive this little letter upon your birthday, God bless and protect you and give you many, many happy 13 June and preserve and bless your dear dear brothers Baba and darling Odo. M. Drocourt never told me what book I could get for you for this day and so, love, I am forced to give you only a very ill worked purse with a silver gilt clasp which can be put from one purse to another, and two little seals. I have got you the gold pieces we used to talk about and have put them into your purse and also the same for darling Odo because I know that you like each to have the same and I have written about your magazines to London and I have written to Paris about your journal and the books I subscribed for but I wish to prevent mistakes that M. Drocourt would be so obliging as to send me the names and the dates of your books which I bought and had sent from Paris that the people may make no mistake. I hope love that you may have a very pleasant birthday and that your Mama and your dear brothers are all well. I wish I was near enough darling to give you a kiss and to wish you by word of mouth instead of by letter health and long life and happiness with your dear dear mammy and your 2 brothers. God bless you all.

Your old Granny

What's to be done? There's no use fretting
About the purse that I am netting
I've time enough methinks to net
This purse for my dear darling pet
'Tis for my Arthur's natal day
The month of June so bright and gay
My gentle child, my lovely boy
Your Mother's pride your brother's joy
May you pass birthdays long and happy
With Mammy Brothers and old Pappy

for 13 June 1842

God bless you my darling boy and grant you many happy birthdays. Amen, Amen.

Lady William Russell to Lord Lynedoch [NLS]

Carlsbad 28 June, 1842.

I have received two letters from you & Lord William has received one. I write now for fear of exaggerated reports reaching you as to his health. He is quite well again, having been ill from an imprudent use of these waters without medical advice and a sudden leaving them off in the very midst of their course *quand les humeurs étaient mises en mouvement*, to take a rapid & distant journey, at the end of which he rode hard to try young 4 year olds of which he bought two, and he lived well – whereas a strict regime is kept up. His attack gave way to cupping immediately and at the end of ten days he drove his gig himself, having ridden at the end of the week & gone out walking the 3rd day. Nothing could be more favorable or rapidly progressive than his convalescence. But as I have letters with the most sinister report I am anxious to spare so good a friend as you any anxiety. He never kept his bed nor even his rooms, only the house, which in this place is an event as one's life is spent out of doors. You may remember where you now are, the universally accredited story of Marshal Radetzky's having shot himself on account of his illness supposed incurable. So one may expect anything as to inventions of bad news. Arthur & Odo are growing & thriving & I expect soon Hastings, as his leave was to begin the 1st July. Always, dear Lord Lynedoch, your very affectionate friend

Lord John Russell to Lady William Russell at Carlsbad [PRP]

Chesham Place, July 12, 1842.

Hastings had told me before he went of William's illness, but it was a great consolation to me to have your account of his speedy recovery. His convalescence seems to show a good bottom of constitution. But this attack should teach him caution. Scampering about like a young aide de camp is not to be done with impunity at our age. The Carlsbad waters are, I fear, very dangerous to meddle with – they did some harm to my father, & contributed to his first attack.

Hastings is universally liked. I saw less of him than I wished, but his unaffected manner, & good sense are always agreeable. I hope he will be a good Whig and not a Radical or a Tory.

We are going to Scotland tomorrow, heartily tired of the fatigues of London, where pleasure is still harder labour than business.

7th Duke of Bedford to Lord William Russell [WPP]

Oakley, July [1842]

I do not find that 'I worry myself about things that can't be remedied', beyond the moment, but as I am not a piece of marble or stone or deal board, these worries have an effect upon me for a time. But I have so many other more important matters to think of that one succeeds another in rapid succession, and so drives the old worry away. The Duchess, I know, exists and flourishes upon grievances. She had them in the full career of her prosperity, and so we can't expect her to be without them now, but that is a very small and insignificant part of her conduct. If she could confine herself to them, there would be little to care about. You tell me to write directly to her. Can you for a moment suppose *that* would cure her? If you do I will tell you what happened last summer. She wrote to me to ask *me* to do something for Georgiana*. I answered her letter immediately, and sent Georgiana £200. But there was some expression in my letter (God knows unintended by me) at which she took offence. It was simply that she told me that she had done all she could afford to do, or rather what she *had* done for Georgiana, viz; having drawn out of the funds £1,000 for her trousseau and made her very poor. I answered that it was very magnificent on her part, and that it was more than I thought she was called upon to do, or something to that effect. She complained much of this remark of mine. Georgiana has since told my Duchess, that it was only £200 (I think) that she received from her mother (when she marrried) for her trousseau! You see therefore that my writing does no good. My letters are sure to be too cold, or to afford something to make a handle of. ... I have tried excess of kindness towards the Duchess and her sons, but have now got to the end of my tether in that direction. If I had not done so, I might have had reason to reproach myself, or have furnished them with ground for doing so. Now, I have given them no weapon but that of ingratitude.

Hastings and his father were both again in England when their correspondence was resumed. Lord William was living in his house in Grosvenor Place but was often at Woburn Abbey. He rightly suspected that Hastings was in love with Lady Elizabeth West, the daughter of Lord De La Warr.

Hastings Russell to Lord William Russell [WP]

Thursday Dec 15 [1842]

It gives me great pleasure to think that you miss me, my dear Father, and I am glad you tell me so for otherwise I confess I should hardly have thought it – had I thought so I certainly would have stayed till the afternoon tho' I should probably have had a less agreeable journey back. I regret not having done as you wished and beg your pardon for it. I am sorry that you say you will ask me no more favours – they are more agreeable than commands which I ought rather to expect. I hope you will un-think, unsay, and not do as you threaten. I enclose a letter from my

* Lady Georgiana Russell married Charles Romilly in January 1842.

mother which I beg you will either return me or take great care of as I keep them all carefully ticketed and docketed and should be very sorry to lose any one part of one of them. I hardly like trusting them out of my hands, but you will be anxious to hear details best seen in my mother's letter. Of course you will not show or read any part of it to anybody. . . .

Hastings Russell to Lord William Russell [WP]

[Buckhurst] Monday Dec 19th [1842]
Write to me here and tell me when you come to town that I may be there to receive you. I was coming back on Tuesday but they won't let me go till Thursday, if then. The direction is Buckhurst, East Grinstead, Sussex.* . . .

Hastings Russell to Lord William Russell [WP]

Queen's Guard. Friday 23rd Dec. 1842
I returned to Town this morning at 10 o'clock & found I was 2 days over leave, had been reported for missing one inspection parade by Colonel Taubman and one guard mounting duty. I met the relief marching off, a Captain carrying the colours – nevertheless I have been allowed to go on [*torn*] instead of arrest. All this is against my getting further leave, yet if I can I am going back to Buckhurst. But I have not yet seen the C.O. & till then I can know nothing. 3 of my Brother officers have said they would answer for my duty. They are good fellows one and all.

I am much obliged to the Duke for his kindness to me and wish you would tell him so.

On Christmas day I am engaged to Lady Mary Ross † and must not throw her over, she has always been very kind to me and my mother told me not to neglect her.

I enclose two letters from my mother one of which I read. I found them on my return not having had them forwarded. I will write again tomorrow when I know more of my fate and am less hurried. I do not like your jokes and jibes and am

Your affecte son

* The home of Lord De La Warr.
† Lady Mary Ross (1777–1842), daughter of the 2nd Duke of Leinster, married Sir Charles Ross, Bt.

On reading over my Mother's letter a second time I find nothing of immediate interest to you except that she says she is going to Venice and coming back to Vienna on April 1st 43.

Hastings Russell to Lord William Russell [WP]

Guards Club, Sat. Dec. 24th [1842]
I have been refused any further leave of course, & wigged sufficiently. I am going in consequence to Buckhurst tomorrow by the 2 P.M. train & stay till the 2d. of next year saving that I come up for inspection of necessaries on Thursday.

What I said about the impropriety of throwing over Lady Mary Ross in a former letter does not hold good naturally in this case.

Hastings Russell to Lord William Russell [WP]

Grosvenor Place.
Wed. Dec. 28th [1842]
I apprehend that 2 of your letters will not fall into my hands until I slip down by the rails tomorrow to Buckhurst. I slipped up an hour ago for tomorrow's peculiarly d——d inspection. I have received & written a letter from & to my Mother, by the former all's well & in the latter I enclosed your paternal from OOburn in which you say poor Mother!...

I never look on your letters as types of your intentions & feelings, my dear Papa, & if I could have persuaded my Mother of this it would have saved her bitter hours. If I did it would give me real pain to think I had embittered your Christmas 1842. But I do not think I have done so or given you cause to say so.

Now if I have said anything in this letter that displeases you – I beg your pardon for it. Letters I know are subject to more misinterpretation than words or actions & seem to have been given to man that his meaning might be misunderstood & dissension disseminated. I have always written as seldom & argued as little as I could for this reason. If in this letter I have departed from my rule in a manner you disapprove of I hope you will tell me so calmly & forgive your affectionate son.

Hastings Russell to Lord William Russell [WP]

Queen's Guard. St. James's Sat Dec. 31 [1842]
At 2½ o'clock this morning, my dear Papa, I being in my first sleep after dancing till 12, after shooting all day, after dancing the whole of the fore-

going night, after coming by rail & horseback from town, at $2\frac{1}{2}$ a.m. an *estafette* arrived sent by my admirable brother officers showing that one of our 3 duty Ensigns had broken his head in a gig & that the other was on a D.C.M. at the Tower consequently that I, No. 3, must be on parade Portman St. barracks by $9\frac{1}{2}$ a.m. – 7 hours to do 41 miles in, no postchaise nearer than 9 miles off, a night black as Erebus – wind in the S.W. & a steady little rain. Here I am, though, having had a full half hour to spare – here I am with a taught skin & a red eye, feverish & tired on the Queen's Guard & ready, as soon as relieved tomorrow, to return whence I came.

On Monday 2d. Jan. 43 you will find me in Grosvenor Place, come up by an early train. I have I regret to say accepted a dinner at Lady Mary Ross's at 6 on that day being uncertain as to your arrival.

I was agreably surprised by your letter of Wednesday, just received. I feared you had taken its subject far too seriously but your vein of pleasantry reassures me for I confess I was annoyed by your four last.

Till Monday then, ta ta, when I hope to explain things I am much too *riche en cautèle* to write.

LORD WILLIAM'S DIARY

1843. The first of the year found me at Woburn Abbey, a large party. I enter the new year at peace with all mankind, & thankful to God for all the blessing he has heaped on my unworthy head. My wife and boys are well, I am here in the enjoyment of health, my brother's society, and this delightful residence.

2 Jan. Went to London, & found my dear Hastings on his return from Buckhurst. He must be in love with Lady Elizabeth.

4 Jan. Dined at Lady Holland's, her table is always agreable, she has the talent to bring together the cleverest men in London.

9 Jan. Three days passed in the routine & pleasure of London life. Much dining out, much gossip, much nonsense talking, but diverting.

10 Jan. Went with Hastings to Windsor to see Wrio & his wife. He told me more gossip in three hours than one can hear in London in three weeks.

11 Jan. Dined with Lady Holland, Rogers, Luttrell, & all the wits.

12 Jan. Returned to Woburn Abbey, where a large party was assembled to meet the Duke of Sussex.

13 Jan. We sat down 32 at dinner. Duke of Sussex, Duchess of Inverness, a good natured, foolish little woman; Lord Scarboro', George & Lady Agnes Byng, Lord Uxbridge & two daughters, Edward & Alexander. Acting plays, charades,

16*

dancing, with all the amusements of an English country house. Beautiful weather.

16 Jan. Acted *The Follies of a Night.* I wrote the Prologue, John the Epilogue. Acting excellent, especially Mrs L. Stanhope & Colonel Keppel.

Lady Charlotte Guest, who was staying at the Abbey, also took part in the theatricals. She found she liked Lord William 'more and more every hour. He is very quiet, almost taciturn, but a most agreeable and highly informed man. He wrote the Prologue spoken tonight and Lord John wrote the Epilogue, both good but with all my partiality for everything Lord John does I liked Lord William's best.'[4]

Lord John Russell to Lady William Russell at Vienna [PRP]

The Grove, January 23, 1843.

I am very grateful to you for your congratulations. The mother & the little boy* are going on very well hitherto. I wish you would come to England to make acquaintance with your nephew. You would find your son making himself a good officer & liked in every society where he goes. So far our fears that he would not be an Englishman are falsified. Much is owing to his merit, as well as your motherly care. But now the solicitude of the world, which always takes so affectionate interest in other people's concerns, has turned its attention to Arthur. It is remarked that he is arrived at an age when he ought to be educated for some profession. I do not know what is intended for him, but I hope if he shows any capacity he will study for the law. It is an excellent profession in this country, & fits a man for a world of other occupations. But then he should go to Cambridge & fag at mathematics.

Having been thus liberal of my advice what to do, I trust the examples you have seen will prevent your sending any of your sons into what is called diplomacy. Something should be done to check that ridiculous mode of providing for young gentlemen. A man would be a far better secretary of Legation, if he were to start from Downing Street in that capacity, than he is likely to become by lounging some years in Paris & Vienna.

We have had a great party at Woburn, of which your husband & son will have given you an account. Here at Clarendon's, we have had C. Greville, and Lord Auckland; his successor in India has made himself so

* John Russell, later Viscount Amberley, born 10 December 1842.

ridiculous that it is thought he must be recalled. We go from here to Brocket, where we shall find Lord Melbourne tolerably well but unfit for any exertion at present. Lady Beauvale* is liked and admired by every body. She seems to have acquired at once an intimate knowledge of English habits and connexions.

LORD WILLIAM'S DIARY

26 Jan. Dining out every day. London life is very agreable if one has a good stomach & good health.

28 Jan. Breakfasted occasionally with Rogers, his breakfasts are good & gay, but the old man grows deaf & forgetful.

10 Feb. Went for two days to the Priory,† a delicious residence but dull, & its inhabitants good but without conversation.

12 Feb. My health is not good, swimmings & noises in my head. Cupped but not better.

17 Feb. Hastings is a dear boy & promises to make a good soldier.

22 Feb. Went to Cardington for a couple of days to see my old general Lord Lynedoch, he is very old, but full of warm feelings & the picture of an old soldier. Daily correspondence with the Duke of Bedford. I would not have all his fortune to be so worried with trifles as he is. I give him what encouragement I can.

1 March. Dined with that crazy being Lord Brougham. Lord Abinger & others there. Lady Holland would not come.

2 March. Dined with Lady Holland, with whom I dine 2 or 3 times a week. Sidney Smith &c. Her dinners are always agreable & instructive, learned men always being present.

3 March. Dined with poor old Lynedoch, where I met Dr Hume, a great fool but the Duke of Wellington's doctor.

4 March. A great dinner at Lord Palmerston's to meet the Duke of Sussex, & a party afterwards.

7th Duke of Bedford to Lord William Russell [WPP]

Oakley, March 7th, 1843

... As for gratitude or thanks, I never expect them. I know the Duchess's children, except for one or two, have no affection for any of us, and that they are glad to take the advantages of Woburn, for the sake of their

---

* The daughter of Count Maltzahn.
† Bentley Priory, Stanmore, belonging to Lord Abercorn.

own conveniences and not from any feeling they have towards us. All this is very vexatious, but this is a world of trial and trouble, and there are always two ways of looking at all these matters. I take what I consider the right way, rather than the pleasant way. I wish with all my heart, I could place you in my shoes, not only for six months, but for a much longer period. You would not manage the estate as well, but you would probably treat the Duchess and her belongings much more as they deserve. Charles has every quality that can make a man disagreeable, therefore, it can be no pleasure to me to have him settled under my Park wall, but I have persuaded myself that it was right. I do not wish to have any direct communication with the Duchess on money matters. . . .

Recollect how the Duchess's children have been brought up, self – self – self, nothing else, and no good feeling.

LORD WILLIAM'S DIARY

18 March. Days consumed in clubs, dinners, evenings chiefly at Lady Holland's & Miss Berry's; theatres, operas &c. In politics nothing interesting, Peel being in power has nothing to propose. This is always the way with the Tories, but public opinion forces them to do something, then comes the difficulty. Peel is a showy coxcomb, but no statesman, & vulgar, & low-minded. The Duke of Wellington is worn out, the rest stupid, excepting always Stanley & Graham, two rogues, excepting Lord Lyndhurst,* the worst man in England. John grows uxorious & idle, his wife encourages him in this.

1 April. I remained all this time in London, dining out so much my head got very bad again, was cupped & put myself on a regimen.

2 April. Had settled to go, but as it blew a storm, I put it off delighted to stay another day with my dear boy, having taken leave of everybody.

[He reached Paris on 6 April.]

Lord William Russell to Lady Holland [HH]

Paris, Palm Sunday [9 April 1843]

Out of sight out of mind is not always true & as I was always in your sight when I was in London enjoying your good and agreable dinners I

---

* John Singleton Copley, Baron Lyndhurst (1772–1863), three times Lord Chancellor.

wish to prove to you that you are not out of my mind, by writing you a gossiping letter, such as you like to receive at breakfast, that may be read with the Morning Post. I am now 3 days in Paris, & a more beautiful & agreable town for those who wish to see & hear & laugh & talk exists not on the earth. As I am only here for a few days & wish to have my fill of pleasure without losing a moment or a particle I took my hat on arriving & went off to the Palais Royal Theatre to take my chance of Déjazet*. *J'ai bien tombé.* Four pieces succeeded each other, one more comical than another, and one more indecent than another at which women laughed *à gorge déployée.* There was Déjazet & Paris in 1872 telling the stories of her youth. Then there was a parody of Victor Hugo's famous *trilogie* called *Les Burgraves.* The French appear to be sent into the world to laugh. But I must now take you into good society & respectable theatres. The next morning as soon as I thought Madame de Lieven could have made her *toilette* I knocked at her door, she received me, not as a fallen Whig, but as an old friend of 25 years' friendship. I never saw her in better health & spirits. Her *appartement* (Talleyrand's†) is beautiful. After I had admired the interior she took me to the window, there is the Hotel of the Invalides where repose the ashes of Napoleon, there the column that was acclaimed by Sesostris, there the Chamber of Deputies, there stood the guillotine; so much for souvenirs, now admire those beautiful fountains, those green fields, & the happy population basking, sauntering, enjoying life. Then she took me in her carriage to Suresnes to see the garden of Baron Rothschild, where nature is made to yield to money, & produce the fruits & flowers of summer in the spring. We passed through the Bois de Boulogne & saw the *beaux* & the *belles* of Paris lounging about, & were clattered past by the King & Queen so surrounded by officers & soldiers it was scarcely possible to see them, but the glimpse I had shewed the King in great health. In the evening I went with Madame de Lieven to the *Opéra Comique*, & the attentive Guizot attended her, leaving Europe to get on as it could, whilst he placed himself at the Scythian's feet. Today I am to dine with her to meet the Duchesse de Talleyrand‡ who is they say grown young & fat, the effects of a well spent life. But here my adventures cease, so I have nothing to relate but episodes that are without interest for you. I think the hatred of the English has subsided, & all notions of war are dead.

* Virginie Déjazet (1797–1875), the most amusing actress of her day.
† In the rue St-Florentin.
‡ After Talleyrand's death the Duchess of Dino's husband succeeded his uncle as Duc de Talleyrand.

Money is the ruling passion of the French; speculation of all sorts which would be disturbed by war. One might say of them what Jugurtha said of the Romans – the Nation is to be bought. *En attendant* they are very amusing, which is the whole of my affair. I think, however, that religion is creeping in. I went yesterday to the new church of La Madeleine (which is like a concert saloon) & saw women in all corners in abstracted devotion. The King & Queen are very devout, but *he* is never sincere.

Now I am *au bout de mon papier*, & if I have salted & sweetened your muffin, I have succeeded, so believe me

faithfully yours

Lord William's diary, for the month he remained at Paris, is a chronicle of visits and dinners. He dined with the King and Queen at the Tuileries, and Madame de Lieven, Lord Cowley, the Duc Decazes and his old flame, Baroness Delmar, entertained him. 'Curious conversation with Emily.' Lord Brougham was in Paris too, 'I met him constantly, very amusing, but it is sad to see such great talent so degraded.' He visited the Louvre with the portrait painter, Lehmann, and he sometimes met Madame Durazzo. He left Paris at the beginning of May.

LORD WILLIAM'S DIARY

6 May. Arrived at Stutgart, drank tea with Wellesleys, every thing in *statu quo*. Life appears a dream, when, after 8 years one returns to a place & finds everything in the same state. She has 4 more children & the same character; he discontented & ill. Sir G. Shee absurd as ever.

7 May. Invited to dine with the King. Had an hour's audience before dinner. A clever man, takes a *coup d'oeil* of Europe & its men & doings in a most masterly manner. Princess of Orange & Neipperg *. Sat between Taubenheim & Madame Spitzenberg. After dinner the Princess of Orange invited me to her room & talked. She is not happy, her husband don't suit her. With child 2nd time, has a fine boy. Clever, capable woman, should have married the Duke of Orleans. Talked again with the King, rather systematic & doctrinaire; arises from want of space for his talents.

8 May. My birthday, 53, the deuce how time flies, must make up my accounts, time approaches, feel old, but health better since I left London & Paris.

14 May. Arrived at Vienna.

16 May. Called at Metternichs, his birthday & his grandson died, ominous.

* Princess Marie of Wurtemberg married Alfred, Count Neipperg, in 1840.

Dined with Flahaults*; Shelburne,† who will probably marry Miss Flahault.

17 May. Great soirée at Princess Schönburg's, beautiful women, beautifully dressed. Conversation with Flahault about his daughter's marriage.

18 May. Bad cold in the head & unwell. Rode with Arthur to see the Emperor embark to open the Diet at Pressburg. Gordon & Flahault went there, *à quoi bon?*

19 May. Dreadful cold. What a w[oman]. Impossible, neither affection, kindness or accommodation. *Pazienza.* Horrible weather. Read the 1st vol. of *Dix Années de la France* by Blanc. Blanc, like all Frenchmen who write on national concerns, writes unfairly, wilful errors.

30 May. Gordon gave us a great breakfast at Eberstein where Richard Coeur de Lion was confined. Went in steam carriage with Princess Esterhazy, Lobkowitz, Pechtenstein &c., English & French Ambassadors. Horrible weather. Returned by water.

13 June. Dear Arthur 18 years old, is 14 in manner & knowledge. Gave him a dressing case.

A few days later Lord William made his way south by himself into Hungary, where he stayed with the family of Count Szirmay at Loposzlav and at Podgradje near Agram. From there he made a tour in Croatia with the Count, and at Dubitsa in Bosnia took coffee with a Turk. 'These days spent at Podgradje with my excellent lady and her daughters in all the charm of friendliness & retirement & beautiful scenery.' Returning to Vienna he found a letter from Hastings announcing his wish to marry Lady Elizabeth West. In July he made an excursion down the Danube with Count Bombelles and his sons. 'Embarked at 5 a.m. for Presburg & Pest. At Presburg took up the leader of the Hungarian opposition, a great talker', ‡ and at Pest he was shown by the engineer himself, Mr Clark, the stupendous new iron bridge.

Lord William Russell to Colonel Hare Clarges [PRP]

Vienna, July 30. [1843]

... We were to have gone to Carlsbad long ago, but the bad weather detained us & then Lady William's health, who has had a bad illness. She is still in bed but much better & soon we shall set out. I may, or rather she may, then have to go to England for Hastings wants to marry Lady Elizabeth, Lord Delaware's daughter, but he has no money, she has no

* The Comte de Flahault was French ambassador at Vienna.
† Henry Petty-Fitzmaurice, Earl of Shelburne (1816–66), son of the 3rd Marquess of Lansdowne. His first wife died in 1840; he married secondly Emily Flahault in November 1843.
‡ Presumably Louis Kossuth (1802–94), the Hungarian revolutionary leader.

money, & I have no money, that being the case I had recourse to the Duke of Bedford & he has no money, poor fellow. What a nasty necessity this same money is.

I have made some interesting excursions into Hungary. . . .

LORD WILLIAM'S DIARY

17 Aug. Went with Shelburne to Reichenau. Emily don't like the marriage, not surprised, girls should marry men, not footmen.

18 Aug. Wrote an angry letter to the Duke of B., because he behaves unfairly about Hastings' marriage. I don't want him to give money if he dislikes it, but I must have him fair, & not take back from me what he has given.

19 Aug. Wrote to John, & Lord Delawarr to give him a statement of my fortune.

21 Aug. Left Vienna.

22 Aug. Arrived at Prague; the beauty of the town always pleases me. Met Bacourt and drove about with him.

25 Aug. Carlsbad. Found Lady William and the boys in their old quarters, Couronne d'Angleterre.

26 Aug. Lord and Lady Ashley here, Prince Golytzin, governor of Moscow, Lomonsoff, Russian Minister in Brazil, Captain Trotter who commanded the fatal Niger expedition, & but few others.

27 Aug. Saw my doctor Hochberger who advised me to drink the waters.

30 Sept. The month of September was very beautiful, rather cold but sunny. Everybody gone, & the place dull enough for those who cannot live alone.

5 Oct. Great shooting match. Odo one of the four who shot the point 4th shot.

8 Oct. Violent rains. Nobody at the fountains but Mentem & Mlle Schopenhauer.

23 Oct. After fighting with a fractious horse, had a sort of attack of gout in the feet – delayed my journey.

[He left Carlsbad on 1 November and reached Paris in a week.]

10 Nov. Called on Madame de Lieven. Received me in her usual friendly way, met there Guizot. Says she is ill, an economical way to give no dinner.

21 Nov. Daily letters from Hastings. Won't come to see me. Quite in the hands of the Delawares. Dined with the Cowleys, that disgusting old woman Lady Aldborough* there, why do they receive her.

22 Nov. The weather fine & warm; bought some *aquarelles*.

* Cornelia Tandy married the 5th Earl of Aldborough in 1804. She was coarse in her conversation, and made herself ridiculous by the youthfulness of her dress.

23 Nov. Dined with James Rothschild. Very magnificent. Dinner given to the Bressons. She handsome – he vulgar.

26 Nov. Letter from Lady William from Frankfort. Good.

Two weeks after her husband had left Carlsbad, Lady William and her sons, starting at eleven o'clock at night in a snowstorm, followed in his steps as far as Frankfort. The journey was not without adventure: 'En descendant les montagnes, la berline, privée de lumière, est près de tomber dans un fond d'au moins 100 pieds.' Mrs Rawdon, travelling in her own carriage, reached Frankfort two days ahead of them. Going on to the Rhine, they embarked in the steam boat to Cologne, whence the new railroad carried them to Brussels. M. Drocourt counted twenty-four tunnels on the way.

Early in December Lord William came to see them there and Hastings followed, returning with his father to London after ten days. Lady Holland had written shrewdly of the proposed marriage when it was first spoken of: 'There is another alliance on the *tapis* which is not very promising, nor as yet quite certain, between Hastings Russell & Lord Delawarr's daughter, Lady Elizabeth West. The father is an easy going, weak man; the mother is reckoned scheming and interested; the whole family high Tory and Puseyites. These principles will not do with the domains and departed shades of Woburn. You will say the possible want of beauty does not concern others; yet it is a merit the less. No answer is come from Lord William. It is said Lady William is well disposed. Perhaps she would not object to what must annoy the family on that very score'.[5]

That Lady William had now changed her attitude becomes apparent, and the lack of feeling she showed in her conduct was to give Hastings much pain. He came again to Brussels to see his mother after Christmas and stayed till a few days before the wedding to which she did not go.

Lord John Russell to Lord William Russell [WPP]

Althorp, Dec. 20, 1843.

I am very glad to find you are arrived in merry England. I will tell you at once our plans. We stay here till Saturday, and then go to Woburn – we shall stay there till the middle of January, so I hope you will come then. It does not appear from your letter that Lady William is arrived. I suppose she will come for the marriage which the newspapers say is to take place in January. My wife sends her love.

Poor Lord Lynedoch!* you will be sorry not to have seen him once

* Lord Lynedoch died 18 December 1843, aged 93.

more – he has left no more gallant or honest heart than his own in the world.

7th Duke of Bedford to Lord William Russell [WPP]

W. Abbey, Dec. 22, 1843.
It is very proper in Lord and Lady Delawarr to think of asking us to the wedding – but we expect people here till after the middle of January, and our leaving here (except for one day when I have an engagement) is out of the question. You may tell them this, to save the trouble and compliment of an invitation. The only objection to lending Endsleigh for the honeymoon is that it is to be painted, but if I can stop it till February, I will do so.

LORD WILLIAM'S DIARY

15 Jan. Returned to town, dined with Lady Holland. Lady Davy, Luttrell &c. She told me John had said, a proverb was the wit of one and the wisdom of many, but it must be older than him.*
16 Jan. Prepared things for my dear boy's marriage.
17 Jan. Went with Hastings to Buckhurst. Signed the deeds, makes up £1000 a year. Lord & Lady Amherst,† Lord Liverpool, Lord Verulam, & a large party. Much pleased with his bride, not pretty, but lady like and dignified.
18 Jan. My dear boy's marriage. God bless him and make him happy. Everything went off admirably. Wrio the only one of the family who appeared. No present from the Duke, for shame.
19 Jan. Much pleased with the De La Warrs & the kindness of the Amhersts who lent Knole Park. Arrived in London. Letter from Hastings, & another from my good capricious wife, saying she would come over.

Hastings Russell to Lord William Russell [WP]

Knole Jan 19 [1844]
I wrote you one line yesterday telling you of our arrival.
... I wrote to my Mother this morning and if you would forward a

---

* '... a definition of a proverb which Lord John Russell gave one morning at breakfast at Mardock's, "one man's wit and all men's wisdom".' R. J. Mackintosh, *Life of Sir James Mackintosh*, ii, 473.
† Lady Amherst and Lady De La Warr were the daughters and co-heirs of John Frederick Sackville, 3rd Duke of Dorset.

letter of hers which must be in Grosvenor Place to Knole I shall get it on Sunday, the day before we leave this place, which bye the bye is beautiful. I had no idea from having seen it from the Tunbridge road, how large and quaint and queer the house was or how fine the park, and the *savoir vivre* of the Amhersts makes them well worthy of this house. The least things thought of for us, so unlike the dear Bedfords.

God bless you my dear Father, and make you live happy, many happy years with your affectionate son Hastings and daughter Bessie.

Hastings Russell to Lord William Russell [WP]

Knole Saturday Jan 20 [1844]

I wish I could come and make your house cheerful for you immediately. The honeymoon once over Bessie and I will try to make it so if you will let us.

My Mother's letter is very unlike the one you have from her. She talks of my marriage on the 18th and says that if I marry on the 25th I am to let her know that she may give me more commissions. I am heartily glad that my marriage is safe over, for one delay is ever followed by another. My Mother's arrival in England a week after the marriage she *could* not come to will have a fine moral effect on our wise friends who reason by induction so conclusively. In haste good bye. God bless you. I am glad you miss me. Glad and sorry.

Hastings Russell to Lord William Russell [WP]

Knole Sunday Jan. 21 1844

The constant change of plans that 'attacks your nerves' is what had so greatly shaken mine. You understand the cause *now* you will acknowledge it. I am at present beyond the reach of worry, it had been my companion for many months – its cessation is all I will remember. Not think of its return.

My poor dear Mother is a frightful prey to indecision. I wrote to her the 8th. 12th. 13th. 14th. 15th. & 16th. She has not lacked information, whence her surprise? I do not know.

It is right well that all is over. I have not fear of my Mother's want of satisfaction. After a few days' thought, first resignation & then approval will appear in her letters I am convinced. Amen.

481

We shall not be at the Peacock before 12 o'clock. I hope to see you there. Call your daughter Bessie – she sends you her duty & her love.

Thank you for writing to Lord Delawarr. I wish to show the Amhersts every gratitude I can from every quarter I can convey it to them. You have good cause to be ashamed of our family, they want good breeding sadly. . . .

God bless you my dear Father. It pleases me to think you loved me so well from your missing me so much but I trust our separation will be a very short one.

LORD WILLIAM'S DIARY

21 Jan. Alone in my pretty cheerful house, with a cheerful mind. I delight in occasional solitude, one gets one's scattered thoughts together & converts the too terrestial into better stuff.

22 Jan. Missed Hastings at the Peacock at Islington going to Bourn; 2 smoking post horses.

23 Jan. Furious letter from my good wife about the marriage settlements. Went to Woburn. Lord & Lady Cottenham, Palmerstons, Carrington, Standish, John, & many others.

24 Jan. These large parties are the type of idleness & gossip, very pleasant for a short time, but tiresome in the end.

26 Jan. Letter every day from my dear boy, very happy.

Hastings Russell to Lord William Russell [WP]

Bourn Hall,* Jan 26th. [1844]

It is a long time to be two days without a letter from you.

What does my Mother? *I* do not hear from her – do you?

I am afraid you have forgotten your first born in the festivities of Woburn.

I reckon on your coming here & I should say the sooner the better, if it suits you.

The calmness of all around me, even the weather, has quite restored me to myself. Irritability & anxiety are gone & what I wish is that you should see me happy 'cum placens uxor' before your departure, or the arrival of my Mother makes it impossible.

* Bourn Hall, Caxton, Cambridge; a property of the De La Warrs.

482

Last Years

Hastings Russell to Arthur Russell at Brussels [PRP]

Bourn Hall. Jan. 26. 1844

Eight days ago I renounced celibacy & now the eighth, I wish to tell you my adventures since that time – so listen, on the 17 I went to Buckhurst with Pappyo, we got there late, in time for dinner, after which I went to Withyham, the village, & slept there at the Rectory, close to the church. I did not close my eyes (which is so right to do the day before one marries) & the next morning I felt horribly frightened. At 11 o'clock a procession of every kind of carriage brought everybody from Buckhurst – amongst others – my wife that was to be.

The victims being ready, we marched into the church, which was crammed full of people – half the parish. Then the marriage service began & lasted quarter of an hour, during which we behaved very well & there was little piping: the service over, we marched back again into the Rectory to sign, as you see at the play – On our way there we were pelted with flowers & all the children yelled at us. The signing signed – we were carried back to Buckhurst & staid there till 3 o'ck. – at 3 we started off for Knole & as we started, the people who had come from the church to see us start, & waited at the door, – the people, at least 500 souls, all at once gave three cheers, & then for the first time Bessie burst into tears & so did Baba.

At 5 o'ck. we got to Knole, the Sevenoaks bells ringing for us enough to make one die of melancholy – you know how sad a peal of bells can make one – and they pealed away till 9 o'ck.

At the gates of Knole there was a crowd of women strewing flowers – & men with little bells – I never made out why? – and so we went in & found the dinner ready – and all about Knole & the ghosts that night, I must tell you next time.

Hastings Russell to Arthur Russell at Brussels [PRP]

Bourn Hall. Jan. 27. 1844

I continue my story – Knole is the most magnificent old house I ever saw. The cluster of towers you see from Tunbridge road can give you no idea of what it is, court after court, with towers, turrets, galleries, colonnades, corridors & winding staircases, great halls & chapels, greenhouses, orangeries, stables, courts & outhouses all running into, out of, right & left, & away from each other, covering 5 acres & all built of old grey stone.

The most striking thing about it though is the deep silence & the solitude.

The servants live, heaven knows where, & when you ring they come, but otherwise you never meet, or hear, or see them – at dinner they brought in the dishes & disappeared. Breakfast and luncheon we always found ready to the minute but no one sign of how it got there.

Well Atty Patty – at about half past 11 we went to bed & at about 12 o'clock we woke hearing something fall with a heavy thud on the floor above us, in some room over our own – after this, the noise continued till near 4 o'clock in the morning. This sort of *Boglerie* was a bore, but even if I had known my way up to the Black Boy's Passage (over us) & to the Devil's room, where some one once was murdered – even if I had known my way there, which being the first night in the house I did not, I should not have felt much inclined to run up in my nightshirt & in the dark to stop the thumping – so I laid still, when all on a sudden & without any previous warning, the handle of the door was sharply turned & a push made to open it – *I had bolted it* – without which I do not know what we should have seen – nor cared to see it.

The next night the thumping was almost the same but nothing else occurred & the third night when I sat up to try & catch him all was silent. *La suite à demain.*

Hastings Russell to Arthur Russell at Brussels [PRP]

Bourn Hall. Jan 29. 1844

I do not quite remember where I left off last, but I think I had finished with Knole.

On Monday 22nd. we came here posting all the way, there are no railroads yet in this northern direction which could be of any use to us.

We left Knole at 9 & went to Bromley, which you must remember, we did not stop in London but went through the Borough straight to the Peacock at Islington & thence to Waltham Cross &c. We grubbed at Wades Mill & got here at 7, in the dark, so dark I did not know where I had got to – we drove through about half a mile of wood after leaving the Caxton road & then I found myself in the middle of a crowd of people of all sorts & kinds, an immense band of music & a quantity of boys carrying lights – at the same time there was a peal of bells close to me though I could not distinguish where it came owing to the thick darkness.

When we got out the people cheered & my wife cried & I did not make out how I had got there. Then we were affable & went & stood out on the terrace & bowed & made ourselves popular by going down among the people who cheered & hollowed & the band blew & thumped & the bells rang & I felt a strong desire to run away & hide myself – this bobber had been so unexpected, & the darkness was so great, together with not knowing the place at all that I began to feel considerably frightened.

The next morning with the light I found myself in a very pretty old manor house with a thick yew hedge garden such as one sees in England only. The village church touches the Park & the village itself is scattered in single houses far beyond it.

The country is very flat but good for riding & we have got two horses here and Nap, who is with us, is delighted with the rabbit hunting. I wish Odo was here to shoot them with me.

Pappyo comes tomorrow from Woburn. I do not know how long he means to stay. Goodbye, my little Atty Patty. Now I have told you all my adventures. God bless you & dear MMyo & Odo. You never write to me but never mind provided you remember your affectionate BaBa.

LORD WILLIAM'S DIARY

27 Jan. [Woburn] Solitude, solitude, how I do love you.

28 Jan. Took a long walk with Rogers, a wonderful old man. Told me many anecdotes of Byron, Fox, Grattan & many others.

30 Jan. I think if all the hearts of all the Russells were put together, they would not yet make one good heart. Good God, how the Duke freezes one. I envy him not his possessions, & would not accept them, were I obliged to take his character with them.

31 Jan. Went by Bedford, St Neots, to Bourn. Rode with Hastings towards Cambridge. Snowstorms.

1 Feb. Hastings & his wife seem very happy & fond of each other.

2 Feb. Heavy snow. Elizabeth cold & close. Don't get on with her.

3 Feb. Left Bourn, hard frost; by coach to London. My house cheerful, & solitude always agreable to me.

4 Feb. Began the London life of morning visits, dinners & plays, agreable enough with health.

Hastings Russell to Lord William Russell [WP]

Bourn Hall Feb 4th [1844]

I missed you much on going to bed last night and almost went to the door of your room before I remembered it would be fireless and lightless.

I write only to tell you this and to remind you of my being. My goings out and comings in you can guess at knowing our mode of life.

Goodbye, God bless you. Write about my Mother, please.

I say to myself looking out of the window at the snow, 'I am glad to be neither travelling by land or by water, not a captive or a prisoner, a woman labouring of child or a young child.' You see I have been to church this morning.

Hastings Russell to Lord William Russell [WP]

Bourn Hall. Feb. 6th 1844

Thank you for your amusing letter, my dear Papa. By all means send me the Morning Chronicle and believe if there is any part in it I should shun more than the rest it is the Court circular, which never fails to raise my bile.

I do not envy your *Maréchale pâtés* nor your meretricious charge but I am glad to know you content.

18 Bills! horror. £100, amount, consolation in as much that it might be much worse.

The weather is bright clear & cold – so much the better, it is seasonable & this snow once gone we may expect the spring. I read aloud all evening and greater part of the morning also – at night I have a tussle with Morpheus as you know but I shall beat him by reading out loud & keep him off by my own noise – it is a painful imperfection & does not depend on too great repletion for I eat very sparingly at dinner & drink no wine. Towards evening I get hoarse reading the whole day long – that will go off.

I am sorry to finish *Paradise* today. I am delighted with *Rasselas*, when I first read him I could not then half understand his merit.

Hastings Russell to Lord William Russell [WP]

Bourn. Feb. 16. 1844

I am not grumpy. I only wish to enliven our correspondence with a little acrimony. 'La dispute est d'un grand secours. Sans elle on endormirait toujours.'

Two letters from MM reached me with yours this morning. She says

'Till you go into the Tower' (1st. June) instead of 'Till you go to Windsor' (1st. Sept.)

I am most grateful to her and to you for the loan of your house – most grateful – but I am sorry my Mother should keep away from England on that account. I had much rather she were in Grosvenor Place & ourselves houseless.

We both of us wish to avoid the London season and nothing takes us there till June 1st. Till then we can either remain here or go to Buckhurst as we like. Indeed Bessie says she had rather go to Paris than encounter this London season. If we could only stay here or at Buckhurst and I agree with her. As to the Army you know that I am decidedly & positively of opinion, that I ought to leave it, having married that I ought not to expose my wife to the discomfort & inconvenience it entails without sufficient reason, such as promotion & its profit, increase of income, would be. That there is no such object to be gained you were quite sure of when I last saw you. Indeed you thought it loss of time and I know it to be loss of money. This is my opinion but I should be very sorry to raise a hue & cry & interference that would annoy you. And I would not run counter to your wishes. Above all my Mother's approbation must be sought. At present she is decidedly averse to such a step, but I have too many proofs of her decision not being always final not to hope for her approval when she better understands the case.

I have tried to be very clear and dispassionate, my dear Father and I hope I have succeeded. Goodbye, God bless you.

The second bedroom floor in Grosvenor Place is the one alloted to us by MM whenever we go there.

Hastings Russell to Lord William Russell [WP]

Bourn feb. 17 1844

My means must circumscribe my plans, such as they are you have long known them. As well as my opinion that I ought to leave the Guards on marrying. Your disregard of pecuniary sacrifice to my fancy for the Army calls for my best thanks. It is very kind & handsome in you to humour me thus. But I should be sorry to indulge my whim for a redcoat at the expense of money which might be more usefully employed.

Besides you give me but faint hopes of getting on half-pay & you tell me there would be no advantage in it. In this your judgement must be my best guide, after all it is but a foolish fancy. On full pay it is disadvantageous to remain, decidedly.

The longer we can be *kept* and avoid London the better for us and I shall let this last as long as possible. I certainly prefer & wish to live in England & I will try my best to do so. If we cannot, why then we must live abroad.

I am ready to go to Paris to see my Mother if you will tell me that she wishes it & that you think it for the best. It will be a very expensive operation but if you think it *ought* to be, it shall be done. Going abroad for pleasure on a lark differs widely from journeying to settle in a cheap country. I cannot bear the thought of my keeping my Mother away from her home by occupying her house and if by saving *now* I could give myself a roof in London when obliged to go there – I should much like it. . . .

Hastings Russell to Lord William Russell [WP]

Bourn Feb. 23. 1844

Small beer, my dear Father, is one of the few things which Mammon cannot command in the metropolis – it is not to be had for money or love, in London can scarce procure it. There is one chance – The Clubs! *They* brew small beer. I could get some from the Guards were I in London. In general Clubs will send nothing *out*. But surely if Brooks's paid Sheridan's debts they will never refuse table beer to a Russell? Try Brooks's – or any other Club. Elsewhere, no table beer (not table ale) Porter & Ale *yes*! Smallswipes* – *No*! Should any one assert the contrary set him down as an Impostor.

I return MM's letter. I have received its twin saying 'write to Ostend'. Let me know as soon as you hear she is gone to Paris.

I heard today from Lord & Lady Delawarr. They wish us to stay at Bourn as long as possible. The longer the better. . . .

LORD WILLIAM'S DIARY

21 Feb. Went to the Chapel Royal. Made to pay 2d to enter!!!

24 Feb. Dined with Lord & Lady Palmerston. Melbourne there, talked of returning to power, quite unfit for it.

* i.e. inferior beer.

488

25 Feb. Dined with John. Macaulay there, whose head seems to be a repository of universal knowledge, which he brings out at will.

Hastings Russell to Lord William Russell [WP]

Saturday Feb 24th [1844]

De Castro & Dawson, Piccadilly, close to the White Horse cellar, are your teamen and grocers. Black tea 6/- lb, lump sugar 10d. And Richardson, Great Scotland Yard is the coal merchant's direction. You will find it more accurately on the chimney piece in your sitting room, in one of the French vases, I think. At all events amongst the bills or in your Book. . . .

Sunday Feb 25

I wish I could run up to Town to nurse you my dear Father. I will if your next letter leaves you still in bed, but I trust this will not be. Who would be your doctor if you needed one? . . .

Hastings Russell to Lord William Russell [WP]

Bourn Monday Feb 26 [1844]

I am very anxious about your cold, my dear Father. No post today and I cannot hear before tomorrow. I had hoped my Mother would be with you, but you tell me her final decision only comes today. Final? I still think England will be her next move whenever that takes place. It is very desirable she should come to England. I urge her to it continually and her mind changes according to whether the post brings your letter or mine.

Lord and Lady Delawarr come here on Thursday and stay one week. If you leave England what am I to do about the Army? Without your help I can do nothing but stay or sell.

Your being ill, alone, in London makes me very uncomfortable. If you are not well tomorrow I will come up to Town on Thursday, but I hope for better news tomorrow.

Hastings Russell to Lord William Russell [WP]

Bourn. Tuesday. feb. 27. 1844

Married or unmarried, my dear father, *you* should not have been ill in London and *I* well at Bourn.

489

I have a letter from my Mother. Coming – Mrs B. precedes, she says – I question? but coming, – disliking Paris (except in summer) and glad we don't leave Bourn.

All this is very satisfactory to me & further I am pleased with her saying she only objected to my leaving the Army 'on marrying, but after being married I am more fit to judge.'

Her disapprobation of this measure was the only thing that made me hesitate although I thought her wrong.

God bless you, my dear father & keep you well.

I give my benediction to the Holly & Poodle for their care of you.

LORD WILLIAM'S DIARY

28 Feb. Ill with influenza.

1 March. Lady W. announces her arrival one day & puts it off the next. Horrible weather.

6 March. I pass my time very agreably. The morning I read, then walk, go to Club & dine out.

Hastings Russell to Lord William Russell [WP]

Bourn Thursday 29th Feb [1844]

. . . If I hear one word about my Mother's coming Sunday – I will come up on Monday. If she delays again, on Wednesday. I wish to be there to receive her when I can be of use. I am very glad to know you about again. I too have had a severe cold. The weather has been damnable. Today the first spring day – beware of catching cold. I have seen you with heavy colds but never remember hearing you cough. God bless you, my dear Papa, and make you well.

Hastings Russell to Lord William Russell [WP]

Bourn Sunday March 3d. 1844

Joey* is bursting with health and a visit to his wife must have been almost necessary by this time to keep him straight in the paths of virtue. I will write him his instructions & not bother you with them, but pray continue the Morning Chronicle. Lord De La Warr delights in it, he asked me twice for it this very day.

* A groom.

The DLW return to town on Friday, so that I shall not be able to come up for MM when she comes – if she comes?

I had a letter from Lady John today, very kind & affectionate. Thank her from me, she answers for Uncle Ivan's warmth of feeling towards us. As Sydney Smith says, he conceals his feelings, which accounts for what you tell me of him at Holland House. Ha! Ha! Ha!

Hastings Russell to Lord William Russell [WP]

Bourn March 5 [1844]

Poor old Lynedoch   Barossa *

I too have had a double letter of wigging without one word of arrival or departure. Patienza! You are out of spirits, my poor Papa, the consequence of your influenza. If MM was not to be expected daily I should propose coming up wife and family to keep house for you and nurse you, but perchance this would bore you to death. As you say sons are as like each other from Terence down as fathers are, though in our case, I must say, your indulgence to me distinguishes you from most fathers as the paucity of my exigences does from most sons, I think. . . .

You would not pay us another visit? would you? If it did not bore you too much, the change of air would do you good.

Hastings Russell to Lord William Russell [WP]

Bourn March 7 Thursday [1844]

My ducal uncle and godfather is more severe than sensible in his stricture, more waggish than wise in his remarks. Lady Charles's dislike of country quarters is no reason for me to leave the Guards, to whose lot country quarters scarce ever fall. And as to Lord Harrington's much to be admired example, had he staid at home, tended his farms and educated his sons and daughters the former might not have been the disreputable scamps they are, and the ignorance and low minds of the latter would have been corrected by education. If the *Dook* had written the letter you enclose, to me, I should have called his attention to these matters which he has overlooked. . . .

* The day was the anniversary of the battle of Barossa in 1811, at which Lord William had fought under Lord Lynedoch.

491

Last Years

I am very glad to know you mending. Influenza hangs so long about one and damps the spirits so. I was afraid you would remain some time with cough and spleen.

Have you no news from MM?

LORD WILLIAM'S DIARY

10 March. A delicious wet Sunday. Read Bossuet. His variations too strong for us Protestants, but Protestantism is freedom, Catholicism slavery. This is the whole secret & never touched upon. God has nothing to do with it.

11 March. Presided at the Covent Garden Fund dinner.* Went off very well.

Hastings Russell to Lord William Russell [WP]

Bourn March 12 Tuesday [1844]

Preside at the Covent Garden Fund dinner! Bravo, *mon cher Papa.* Popular orator, ex-Dip, unemployed General. Famous! I expect 3 columns filled with abuse of Government in tomorrow's paper.

MM coming immediately? How much so? MM's *immediately* are adverbs of *time.* She does not write to me and *I*, not knowing when she would be off, have not written since the 6th.

The Bavarian beer sounds ambrosial food and I would my Mother were there to pass judgement on it. God grant she may come soon.

Goodbye, my dear Father, do not fail to let me know if you are less well; I will come up and nurse you on the spot.

Hastings Russell to Lord William Russell [WP]

Bourn Tuesday March 19 1844

You have answered me as I wished, but not as I expected, I thought you would say, 'You are too old & too idle to think of the law as a pursuit.' It was this fear & the fear of your telling Lady Holland & Co. of my scheme that

* More than a thousand people attended a banquet given to Daniel O'Connell in Covent Garden Theatre 'to show, on the part of Englishmen, the admiration entertained towards him for forty years' constant and consistent advocacy of the rights and privileges of Irishmen'.

made me sound you slightly before I told you that I think, being determined to leave the Army during this sempiternal peace and on my marriage and unwilling to be unoccupied, I shall find the study of the law a creditable and useful employment of my time. I do not, for that, see myself in possession of any one of the prizes of the profession, or even of a silk gown, but I escape the imputation of being a proud pauper of the west end who cannot dig & is ashamed to beg, and I employ my time profitably previous to Parliament which I still look to, as coming to me of necessity some day, perhaps on other interest than my family's.

I now regret having refused Lord Grosvenor's offers, though very young to have accepted, then, when they were made.

I apprehend MM will ridicule my project, her disappointment in my capabilities will lead her to it. I almost fear to write to her about it and I will wait until I see her to avoid an upbraiding answer which pains me more by letter than by word of mouth.

In the meanwhile I beg you not to mention my intention to anyone. I should gain no credit for planning such a course if I am afterwards unable to execute my meaning vigorously.

I may be of great use to my two brothers in starting them in their career though such instruction as I can gain before them and the life I must lead will free me from the trammels of a frivolous society which I abhor.

For fear you should mistake me & suppose me tired of one profession & anxious for another, as a pleasant change I will repeat that the Army is the profession of my constant affections and that it is necessity which drives me from it, for the many reasons I need not repeat. Reason alone leads me to embrace a different pursuit, not lassitude of service in the Army but predilection shall never influence my choice where reason speaks, neither shall it impede or weaken the execution of what I have once determined to be for the best.

You shall not by any means deprive me of the pleasure of reproaching you for having lured me into extravagance by paying for my brougham, nevertheless I thank you for the offer and still more so for the good humour with which you hear all my impertinencies.

In a few days I shall be able to speak with you about these things but do not be surprised if after all that I have said, of my firmness & of my conviction, you still see weakness in my adieus to the Army and a little lingering over the loss of bearskin caps & pipe clay belts, swords & sashes, red coats & blue coats. It is all very childish no doubt, but I cannot help it. . . .

Hastings Russell to Lord William Russell [WP]

[1844]

... yesterday you agreed with me in leaving the Army – today you alter your opinion. Let me hope that tomorrow will bring you back to your first mind.

Though I have no 'farms to look after, horses to rear, lands to let, houses to build, cotton to spin or mines to dig' yet I have a wife's welfare to consult and my own advantage.

If I were son of the Military Secretary & got a Colonelcy in India whilst in the Guards like Somerset then the Army might offer valid reasons for not being forsaken, but *I* can neither get employment, nor promotion. Unmarried no employment was to be found for me, married I shall get no promotion. I am an Ensign at 25. I have gained popularity in my corps by buffoonery. I am battalion wag. Popular Battalion wag and Ensign at 18 is charming – at 25, & married it is pitiable and what prospect of rising above these dignities have I by remaining in the Guards? ...

Hastings Russell to Lord William Russell [WP]

Bourn Saturday March 23 [1844]

My Mother's irritability is constantly fomented and increased by brooding over distant trifles. Bring her here and the occupation of some real business with the amusement of society, which she totally lacks at Brussels, will do more towards removing those morbid and melancholy and violent feelings which dictate such letters (as you say you have received and I am but too able to appreciate), than any compliance with wishes, which from their constant and rapid changes, it is impossible to keep pace with. I am convinced of this, and think you will agree with me.

It seemed to me next to impossible for us to stop in Grosvenor Place on our way through Town seeing there are no means of feeding in the house and scarcely means of sleeping – nevertheless if you should wish it we will stay with you. ... On Tuesday and on Wednesday please write to Temple Dinsley, Hitchin, Herts, and any of those days will find us ready to go to London instead of Buckhurst, MM will be annoyed at our preceding her in Grosvenor Place.

494

Last Years

Hastings Russell to Lord William Russell [WP]

Bourn Hall, Caxton. March 24th 1844

We will breakfast with you on Thursday 28th. at 11 o'clock coming from Temple Dinsley and if you wish us to stay with you, any number of days, we will do so provided you let us know on Tuesday morning. . . .

But you must get a cook, for Lady DLW will not be in town and the *Kuchelfrau* we have here must go to Buckhurst. And Bessie cannot dine at a club.

Our occupying Grosvenor Place before MM and without her leave & knowledge will displease her much but if you wish it we will come . . .

You say you are for keeping the people's noses to the grinding stone. You are a cold blooded aristocrat as Mr Austin says – but you add, 'If we can?' If we can satisfy them with what is called in Parliamentary language, *boons*, which means red hot half pence thrown to a beggar.

Hastings Russell to Lord William Russell [WP]

Buckhurst Park
Thursday April 4 [1844]

I wish you had staid here, my dear Father, instead of returning to Town to loneliness in crowds – your empty house & London vapours.

Tomorrow's Post *may* bring some tidings from MM. Do not leave London without writing – or leave me long without a letter if you go.

I grow every day more anxious about MM measures. . . .

LORD WILLIAM'S DIARY

6 April. Left London in the Antwerp steamer for Brussels.

7 April. Wife & boys gone to Calais. Found Mrs Rawdon.

Speculation regarding Lady William's next move may be seen to have occupied her husband and son since the beginning of the year. Monotonous entries in M. Drocourt's diary reporting the state of the weather tell us little of life in Brussels, nor what it was that kept them there. *'Variable'*, he put down day after day, and this could be as well taken as a comment on the indecisive mood of his employer as a record of sunshine and cloud. Drocourt's natural good spirits seem to have been quite subdued by Lady William's heartless treatment of her eldest son.

Lord William missed his family by four days at Brussels, but hurrying on he found them all at Calais, where his wife had perhaps placed herself expecting him to cross from England to that port. Paris was now her destination and they all travelled there together and stayed in the Rue de Rivoli. From this time on, the impulsive journeys of Lady William are recorded by another hand, for Arthur had begun to keep a journal too. The irregular and brief entries reflect the grave and dreamy nature of the unawakened adolescent, who on his eighteenth birthday had been judged by his father to be more like a boy of fourteen. In a beautiful and precise hand Arthur kept a diary to the end of his life, but unlike Lord William's journal it is rarely a record of emotion. Conscious that another was detailing events, M. Drocourt ceased for a time to recount the amusements and sightseeing that occupied the boys. They went often to the Jardin des Plantes with its caged animals and natural history collections, and the presence in Paris of Mr Gray, their friend from the British Museum, no doubt helped to effect an introduction to M. Bibron, the Director, with whose writings Arthur was already familiar. The boys often looked in on him, finding him ready to talk to them, and willing to let them see the boas take their food. They began again to buy small animals for themselves.

Since it now seemed likely that Arthur would study law and in order that he should see legal procedure, M. Ledru, a distinguished French lawyer, was induced to show him the Palais de Justice. Finding the English boys observant and intelligent, Ledru took them to see the funeral procession of Lafitte, who had played an active part in the revolution of 1830; and Arthur was able to note the presence of Marshal Soult,* Berryer,† Louis Blanc,‡ Thiers§ and Mignet.‖ On a subsequent occasion he heard Mignet lecture at the Académie des Sciences Morales et Politiques, and at a party given by Ledru, (a 'magnetic party') he was introduced to Louis Blanc and Eugène Sue.** These well-known names were entered in the journal, which there is evidence his parents were allowed to see. If the coarse novels of Sue were unread by his mother, she would not have been ignorant of the morals of George Sand. Twenty-five years later when he was over forty and a married man, Arthur was to slip away on Sunday afternoons without telling his mother for fear of her disapprobation, to visit George Eliot, that virtuous exponent of unmarried love; now, with the innocent frankness of youth, he recorded that when M. Ledru took him to see *Antigone* at the Odéon, he had introduced his young friend to George Sand. He also met one evening

* Nicolas Soult, Duc de Dalmatie (1769–1851), victor at Austerlitz.
† Antoine Berryer (1790–1868), distinguished lawyer.
‡ Louis Blanc (1811–82), revolutionary publicist.
§ Adolphe Thiers (1797–1877), statesman and historian.
‖ F. A. M. Mignet (1796–1884), historian.
** Eugène Sue (1804–57), novelist.

in Mrs Austin's rooms in Paris, Alfred de Vigny,* Barthélemy-Saint-Hilaire† and Alexis de Tocqueville;‡ with the two first he was in later years to become well acquainted.

Lord William went to London at the end of April but came back a week later. He saw Princess Lieven daily.

Hastings Russell to Lord William Russell [WP]

Buckhurst Park
April 23rd 1844 Tuesday

There is nobody here to leave Bessie with, or I should run up to Town today to see you instead of writing. See you I must before you return to Paris. Will you come here?

I would propose bringing Bessie to Grosvenor Place for a day if I did not fear displeasing MM. She wrote to Bessie today asking about my *grippe* & saying she had not heard since the 16th. Now, I have written almost daily to her, or you, or Odo. . . .

Lord William while in Paris noted on 9 May: 'Hastings arrived', and four days later, 'Hastings left; he passed these few days with us in good spirits.' It was the first time Hastings had seen his mother and brothers since his marriage. He did not bring his wife with him.

In June, Lord John wrote to his brother: 'I had some hopes that you would have kept to your intention of coming home before this. The best thing you can do is to come and live quietly in England for two or three years at least. Foreign travel is very well but foreign sojourn unsettles all the affections and habits, public and private.'[6] Leaving his family in Paris, Lord William went again to England in the middle of the month, and Princess Lieven wrote to him, as so often before: 'Je suis desolée de votre départ, je ne sais que devenir. Si vous étiez ici, si vous étiez encore garçon, je vous entraînerais à Versailles à Fontainebleau en succession, car voilà la vie que je vais mener.'[7] He remained two months in England, seeing much of Lady Holland, sometimes dining with Samuel Rogers or the Palmerstons, where he found Lord Melbourne 'very silent and broken'. With Hastings and Elizabeth he was entertained by the friendly De La Warrs. Madame de Dino was visiting London with friends, and he showed her party Westminster Abbey, St Paul's and the Mint, and took them for the day to Woburn Abbey.

* Alfred de Vigny (1797–1863), poet.
† Jules Barthélemy-Saint-Hilaire (1805–95), politician and philosopher.
‡ Alexis de Tocqueville (1805–59), political publicist.

On 17 July, M. Drocourt made a brief entry in his journal: 'Nous allons rester à Versailles à l'Hotel du Réservoir. Mr R. et sa femme arrivent le soir même de Londres.' 'Baba', wrote Arthur succinctly, 'arrived at 10½.' It is only a year later that we hear of the unhappy tension that marred the family party during the four weeks the young couple remained at Versailles, for Lady William could not conceal her dislike of her daughter-in-law.

Hastings Russell to Lord William Russell at Grosvenor Place [WP]

Versailles. July 21st 1844

You have indeed not been oblivious of my interests and I am very thankful.

My uncles require stimulus. When I return to England I will pay court to Lady Minto, she manages John & makes him take houses as you say Lady D L W manages me.

No doubt you must be dull alone in London.

What are your projects? Latterly you talked of Paris before we left it?

On our way to Folkestone last Monday we heard of an accident to one of the morning trains, but on the line they are always chary of details.

Tuesday was a fine morning – no wind & little swell – 3 hours passage. It rained during the afternoon until we reached Bernay at 8. It is a charming place. We slept there.

Wednesday was a long pull from 5 A.M. to 10 P.M. without a halt.

I think Atty grown, both boys look very well but Odo's stomach is swollen. MM is thinner than in May but better in health, I think, than I remember her for years.

Do you come to Paris?

Approaching one another from London and Versailles, the Russells brought off late in August, at Boulogne, one of those rendezvous they were fond of proposing but rarely successful in achieving.

LORD WILLIAM'S DIARY

17 Aug. Went to Dover. Weather too bad to cross. Crossed at 11 p.m., bad crossing.

18 Aug. Arrived at Boulogne at 3 a.m. Hastings and Elizabeth arrived at 10 [from Paris]. Breakfasted and dined with them. Letter from Lady William to say she would follow.

19 Aug. Lady William & the boys arrived. Went to Calais with them.

20 Aug. They all crossed to England. Violent west wind. Returned to Boulogne where I found Madame de Dino, Lady Atkinson etc.

Drocourt remained at Calais, perhaps seizing a chance to visit his family in Picardy. 'Milady', he wrote 'et les jeunes gens vont en Angleterre pour deux ou trois jours.' They did not, however, return for three weeks, when they were accompanied on their way to Carlsbad as far as Calais by Hastings, striving anxiously to regain his mother's favour.

Hastings Russell to Lord William Russell in France [WP]

Grosvenor Street*
Thursday August 22d. 1844

Abominable passage, cher PaPa, $3\frac{1}{2}$ hours blowing very hard & much swell tho' little sea. MM sick for the first time in her life & very much astonished. She said, 'Catch me a larking again without a maid', for we had to sleep at Dover, too late for the last train.

In the meantime she is pleased with the house & four years' grudge on that score are, I hope, effaced. . . .

The boys know their way about surprisingly, they are delighted with the house and like London at first sight notwithstanding its emptiness which is shocking at this moment. . . .

MM dislike to my wife which is consummate, tho' not unexpected as you know, forbids my looking forward with much pleasure to anything. . . .

Hastings Russell to Lord William Russell in Germany [WP]

Buckhurst Park, Sept. 13th. 1844

. . . I think MM was pleased with her three weeks' visit to England for she talked of returning with less horror, she seems reconciled to the house. I am very glad of it, she is constantly displeased with me. I am very sorry, but do not know how to regain her favour.

Carlsbad was reached on 19 September. Lord William found his wife living at the Gartenhaus, an annexe of the Goldene Schild, when he arrived. He had

* The De La Warrs' London house.

been travelling slowly towards Bohemia since they parted at Calais and had been well amused on the way. At Baden Baden he had fallen in with many old friends, and at the *table d'hôte* at the Badershof had found himself placed next to Lady Sophia Cecil and Lord Thomas. From Mannheim he made an excursion to breakfast at Herrnsheim, the castle of the Duke Dalberg*. 'They proposed me to stay. Stayed. Durazzos, Bathursts, de Mauley, Clarendons arrived. Drove to the Rhine. Magnificent, rowed in Leveson's Thames wherry.

'5 Sept. Took leave of the ladies going to church. Madame Durazzo's last word. Went thro Mayence to Frankfort. Lady W. not arrived.'

At Wiesbaden he found the Palmerstons and the Beauvales. 'Returned to Frankfort. No letter from Lady W.' Moving on, he passed ten days happily at Berlin. When he reached Carlsbad he found that Lord and Lady James Hay, with their lovesick daughter, were remaining, like his wife, beyond the end of the season. 'Miss Hay in love with and wants to marry Gudin the painter – the parents oppose' it on account of birth, but they had better and will consent.' He judged rightly; the Hay family went away in October and a month later the happily wed Monsieur and Madame Théodore Gudin returned to Carlsbad to spend their honeymoon.† But by then Lord William had gone back to England. Lady William stayed where she was and there she remained for the next fourteen months. She liked the frugal German middle-class life and cared very little if her sons spoke English with foreign accents. Inseparable for any length of time from their mother, nurse, and tutor, the boys, though now aged nineteen and fifteen, still led a happy 'nursery life', and, living as they did in a close domestic circle, their mother had no rival in their affection. Mrs Rawdon was absent.

Lord William Russell to Lady Holland [HH]

Carlsbad, Ocr. 20 [1844]

Perhaps I may make a letter acceptable to you by speaking of the Palmerstons; after various plans and repeated hesitations they decided to go to Vienna, and are now, I believe, at Prague. I had just returned from there when I got her letter announcing this decision, but the doubtful tone of her letter did not encourage me to re-return, the weather being bad. Palmerston had the greatest success at Berlin, one of my correspondents said his countenance united 'la finesse du renard et la force du lion'. There is a great reaction to the late Whig Government in Germany. Palmerston is

---

* The Duchess Dalberg was the sister of Madame Durazzo. Her daughter Marie, widow of Sir Richard Acton Bt, had married secondly, in 1840, Lord Leveson, later 2nd Earl Granville.

† Théodore Gudin (1802–80) wrote in his memoirs: 'Lady William Russell, femme très supérieure, a fait mon mariage.'[8]

contrasted to Aberdeen to the detriment of the latter, and Peel is looked upon as a clever and lucky charlatan.

We are all alone here. Every soul has fled from the cold & falling leaves, but we are in excellent health, & that is the best thing in the world. We have Eldon, Malmesbury and Arnold, 3 works of immense interest to help through the long evenings and now and then some discussions on German philosophy to enliven us, the English are children compared to them, in deep thinking and anilysing [*sic*] but *à quoi bon?* it leads to pantheism and materialism.

Lady William was much pleased with the glimpse she caught of you in London and the pleasant hours she passed with you. I shall leave this the end of the month for England, but whether by Paris or the Rhine is un-decided, & my first enquiry will be after you, hoping to find you in health & spirits. Lady William is not so easily put into motion, & she is too near her beloved Vienna to expect she can leave Austria without taking a peep into it, so, I don't answer for her. . . .

Hastings Russell to Lord William Russell at Grosvenor Place [WP]

Bourn Dec 4th [1844]

Cher Papa, Why no letter from you this morning? *Cher Papa*, I long to see you, *Cher Papa*, why tell me nothing of MM and the boysinhos. Till tomorrow *Cher Papa*. Goodbye and God bless you.

We leave Bourn at 11 o'clock tomorrow morning and journey by Potton, Biggleswade and Ampthill. I hope to be at Ooburn by 4 o'clock, you will leave Euston Square at 1 o'ck and we will both arrive at the same moment. *Cher Papa* I shall have great delight in seeing you again.

Lord John Russell to Lady William Russell at Carlsbad [PRP]

Unsted Wood, Dec. 15, 1844.

I was very glad to see your hand, and to learn that you were all well and thriving. We are not so fortunate. Fanny has had another mishap and has suffered from it more than usual. It was almost ten days ago, and she is still in her bed, and far from recovered. But the doctor says she is going on well, so I must be satisfied. . . .

I should be very glad if you would all come here in the spring in some interval of public business when we can all be happy here. And really your young men must not be Germans. Hastings has avoided it wonderfully, considering the time he spent abroad in his early youth. Arthur must come home and work at his law very soon. William told me he was not to go to a university, which on the whole I am sorry for. So many connexions and acquaintances are made there that a young man who has been at Oxford or Cambridge has great advantages over those who have not.

Have you read Dr Arnold's life? He was an excellent man – somewhat of a visionary in his projects for the state, but virtuous, practical and eminently useful in all relations of life. He was a friend of Niebuhr and still more of Bunsen.

I hope you will go on writing. William is in London, and I expect to see him in a few days. Indeed, when Fanny is better I hope he will come here. The little fair girl and the little black-eyed boy are very flourishing and the most loving of playmates. . . .

Hastings Russell to Lord William Russell at Grosvenor Place [WP]

Bourn House Dec 18th 1844

Do not contemplate O! Papa! any alteration in your house till you have heard what MM says on that score. . . .

I read Madame de Sévigné but I do not improve, my soil ungrateful to epistolary produce. I never felt the pleasure of writing for the sake of writing. It seems to me that Cadmus his invention is for the communication and transaction of business welfare. When I have gone beyond these it has been my luck to stir up mischief. But I have too deep a sense of being what MM so often tells me I am, viz: 'a poor concern', not to have a very shrewd suspicion that I may be wrong.

LORD WILLIAM'S DIARY

The first of the year found me at Woburn Abbey in tolerable health, but very weak & not able to walk far. A large party, the Dowager Duchess and Rachel acting charades.

13 Jan. Hastings & Elizabeth joined our party but he is not social & dislikes this merry making.

Lord John Russell to Lady William Russell at Carlsbad [PRP]

Unsted, Jan. 18, 1844 [?1845].

. . . I am glad you like so well your summer watering place in the middle of winter. It seems very odd to me that you should prefer it to Grosvenor

Place, but I was born a cockney and continue a cockney. In my view there is no country to compare with England, and no town to London. . . .

Do not suppose that I do not see the evils of an English university – the society – the habits of expense and luxury – the want of religious instruction &c. I am going to send Ribblesdale * to Oxford, and I have thought and trembled on this subject. But it is all over-balanced by the advantage of being put in a *campus martius* to strip and struggle with one's equals – and prepare for the still more manly and animating struggle for political liberty in a free assembly. This preparation makes our idle, luxurious, hunting and shooting nobility so far superior to the German counts and princes who consider their titles a privilege for ignorance. . . .

Princess Lieven to Lord William Russell at Grosvenor Place [WP]

Paris, 4 février, 1845.
You see I am unable to write to you myself. J'ai les yeux dans le plus triste état du monde. . . . je suis touchée de votre amitié, de votre bonne lettre, de cette visite infortunée à Baden. Elle m'avait eté au cœur. Mais où pouvais-je vous en adresser le témoignage. Comment imaginer que vous iriez vous enterrer à Carlsbad quand tout le monde le quitte? Vous avez bien fait de revenir en Angleterre. Vous feriez mieux encore de venir à Paris. Cela me consolerait un peu pour mes yeux. . . . Je voudrais bien être de vos petits dîners à Holland House que vous me décrivez si agréablement. Je suis reduite à mon couvert solitaire et dans les ténèbres. Mais ma chambre ne désemplit pas de monde. Mes amis me soignent bien – et les événements politiques assez animés me tiennent en curiosité et en haleine. Vous ne me parlez pas de Lady William. Où est-elle et que compte-elle faire? Si c'est à Carlsbad que vous l'avez laissée, je n'y vois vraiment d'autre plaisir que d'y attraper des crapauds.

Adieu, *dear Lord William.* Ecrivez moi – je vous en prie et aimez-moi toujours.

LORD WILLIAM'S DIARY
10 Feb. Went to pass a few days with Hastings.
14 Feb. The coldest weather I ever knew in England. Thermometer 14. Bitter cold easterly wind.
15 Feb. Dined with Lady Holland & went to Lady Palmerston's. Very cold. Gave

* His stepson.

Last Years

Panizzi for the [British] Museum Padre Pasquale's translation of Milton, *Paradise Lost* in Armenian.*

Hastings Russell to Lord William Russell at Grosvenor Place [WP]

Bourn Saturday March 1 [1845]

I hasten to accept your charming present. Our Carrier Elbourne of Bassingbourne will take the pony phaeton or fetch it where you may direct. I hope it hath an harness. If not I will do like the Swiss, who when I gave him one half crown asked for another, and beg you to add an harness to your gift. And finding you so generous I will say decidedly – another sealskin jacket – not repair the old one. To fit quite perfectly it might be a shade longer on the sleeves and the waist might fit a little tighter.

It is lucky I did not take the house you offered me for I have had two letters from M.M. today . . . dissuading in both from house and holding. I give up all intention of a house in London and 'Quid sit futurum cras fuge quaerere'. I will say 'Mors certa – Hora incerta' and live *au jour la journée en attendant*. But in the middle of my philosophy I remember you promised me a pair or two of Carlsbad socks – *extrafein* and I will presume thus far upon futurity to ask you for them. Whence the paper you sent me and I return? It reminds me of Uncle John's life of our acephalic ancestor which is in Grosvenor Place and which I wish to have. It is mine, an avuncular present from the author. Pray send it me. Poor Uncle (not Nunckey) B. His *insania* is not *amabilis*. If any *Rana esculenta* † are sent from the monastic marshes I will ascertain, pay and decline.

If I had Poodle's 7, and Georgy's 15 hundred a year put together, I would not give dinners with it and inasmuch might manage with it.

Je vous embrasse as the Franzouskis say.

Hastings Russell to Lord William Russell at Grosvenor Place [WP]

Bourn Thursday March 13. 1845

I too have had a large letter from MM – very amusing with a little infusion of gall. Not a word about movements. Pray tell me more of your letter. . . .

---

* Anthony Panizzi (1797–1879), Keeper of the printed books. The translation was dedicated to Lord William (cf. p. 60 n., above).
† i.e. edible frogs.

Please tell Uncle B. when you next write to him that Bessie & I returned enchanted with our visit to Oakley for he was enormously civil & kind to me & Aunty Bedford too. They are coming here on their way to Noo-market!!!!! You will have ascertained that the *Wellawares* are coming here on Monday next. I think of running up to Town to see you when they are here. I suppose they stay one week.

When will you come? The poneyshay, the poneyshay will you come down in him?

Bessie's jacket is beautiful & she has got it on. A beautiful skin & fits like wax, colour splendid, not to be torn and very warm.

Goodbye – my hands are frozen. Tomorrow you shall hear how I owe uncle B. £1,800.

Pray write, write, write to me. *Rusticus*! . . .

LORD WILLIAM'S DIARY

31 March. The month of March very cold with occasional sunny days, passed in London, the best place in bad weather.

4 April. Made a tour in the fens with Hastings and Elizabeth. First to Thorney, seeing the beautiful cathedral at Peterborough. The Duke's repairs to Thorney church not in good taste.* Head badly attacked. Saw the beautiful & interesting Cathedral of Ely.

11 April. Nasty cold easterly wind. 3 days in bed.

7th Duke of Bedford to Lord William Russell at Grosvenor Place [WPP]

W. Abbey, April 10, 1845

You have drawn inferences which are not correct, and which of course I did not intend. I have no objection (on the contrary) to *read* your letters, but when I tell you that I was detained in my room opening, reading and answering letters yesterday, and the day before, from half past six till half past one and even then several left unopened, because my hand and eyes and back ached, and I wanted fresh air and that this often happens to me, you will readily understand why I have not time for political discussions on the various topics of the day, as they arise. Not to notice your letters at all, as sometimes happens when I have not time to write in what they contain, appeared to me to require explanation, or to answer them

* Thorney was one of the Duke of Bedford's estates. The repairs to the church were carried out by Blore.

shortly and sharply to be equally or still more objectionable, therefore it seemed best and fairest to tell you why I could not enter into that sort of correspondence with you. I had to choose one of these three courses, and I took that which appeared to me to be the best, and the most intelligible to yourself. My letters relate chiefly to matters of business which I *must* attend to. Political letters, whether wise or not, are unnecessary, especially if there is any disagreement that calls forth a controversial correspondence – sometimes my political friends write the news of the day to me – but they all tell me they do not expect answers – with Tories I never correspond – except on matters which we are not likely to differ upon. Mr Heady* always wants me to have a secretary, and writes to urge it again today – but I should dislike that more than the trouble I now have. If you wish to hear any other objections which I have not stated, you have only to ask for it – otherwise I think I have said enough. . . .

Hastings Russell to Lord William Russell at Grosvenor Place [WP]

Bourn. Sunday. April 13. 1845

I am distressed by your letter today, as I always am when you speak of my misconduct to MM. I do not deserve what you say – indifference about my brothers. But I had rather talk with you than write to you about these matters.

Bessie desires me to thank you for the large present of garden seeds. The Duchess of B. brought us none, but we have had some perch from Thorney.

The Bedfords go away at half past nine tomorrow morning.

Hastings Russell to Lord William Russell at Grosvenor Place [WP]

Bourn. Friday. April 25. 1845

My bad writing is no show of 'independence' but an infirmity which constantly annoys me, & which I have struggled to overcome unsuccessfully during several years. Some days I am much less capable of writing than others, on which (such as today & yesterday) I feel a constant apprehension and anxiety. My hand is shaky and I write with great difficulty under a feeling of irritation. At this moment I am doing my best

---

* The Duke's agent.

to write well and yet find myself leaving out words & letters in every line, besides an incapacity to form the letters.

I assure you I lament my deficiency and have no idea of showing spirit by writing a bad hand.

You must forget that you told MM not to write to you again in London, when you say you 'wait anxiously for a letter from her'.

I send you a sketch of MM, A. & O. sledging. Pray send it me safe back, with Granny's letter.

If I am of no use to you in London for a few hours & can be of use by staying the night over I will come up the day before you go & see you off. . . .

LORD WILLIAM'S DIARY

22 April. The proposal to augment the grant to Maynooth, has roused a Protestant demonstration in England, such as has astonished Peel & everyone, but he has impudence for anything.

23 April. Went to the *levée*, Queen very gracious.

28 April. Went with H. to Newmarket.

29 April. Returned from Bourn, where Hastings lives an idle life but apparently very happy.*

4 May. Went to the Queen's ball.

6 May. Went back to Bourn. Very cold.

8 May. 55 alas, alas. Hair grey, teeth decaying, strength diminishing, memory failing & all the symptoms of old age; time to die.

10 May. Brought H. & E. to town who went on to Buckhurst.

12 May. Sir R. Peel proposed 3 new colleges for Ireland, without Christian education. Everybody approves but it won't do, there must be a reaction.

13 May. Sir Robert Inglis declares Peel's plan a gigantic system of godless education, so it is.

14 May. Saw much of the Duke, violent against Peel's plan.

15 May. Dined at Richmond with Lady Holland, St Aulaire & Broglie, *père et fils*.

17 May. Hastings came to town to take leave of me, an affectionate boy.

Lord William left England for the last time on 18 May, embarking in the Thames in a boat that carried him to Holland. At The Hague he had an audience with

---

* Hastings left the army in 1844 and led an idle life until he entered parliament in 1847.

his old comrade-in-arms, the King. At the Castle of Loo he was received by the Prince and Princess of Orange. 'Dined & supped with them. Hawking with Mr Newcomer. Long walk & talk with Princess Sophia.' She sent him next day a present 'with a pretty letter' and gave him a note to take to Lady William with whom she had corresponded as with a dearest friend since 1838.

Hastings Russell to Lord William Russell in Germany [WP]

Grosvenor Street, May 22 1845

I had watched the night & thought you sure of a good passage. However I am glad your spirits are the better for the voyage. Spirits are happiness.

I took the chair for John at the dispensary dinner yesterday & made my first attempt at speaking. I am glad to find myself able to address a multitude without fear – & my voice is better than I expected. I will write you the particulars another time & only wish to give a sign of life to you at Frankfurt within the week as you directed me.

Lord William Russell to Lady Holland [HH]

Castle of Loo [1845]

I don't know how I can better express my sense of all your kindness to me than by writing to you, & I know you like a letter. I was punished for leaving London so abruptly by a long and stormy passage. My chief object in taking this road was to pay a long promised visit to my old yet young friend the Princess of Orange, a charming person, clever, instructed, lively, amiable, living in this historic Château with all the simplicity & absence of *gêne* & etiquette, that Royal persons like occasionally to indulge in. Her kindness to me is unbounded & I enjoy myself much in the walks & drives of Loo, built by our William 3d, & the scene of many diplomatic negotiations. Lord Malmesbury speaks of his interview with the Queen here. At the Hague I paid my *devoirs* to the King & was received by him like an old friend, so, up to the present moment, my journey has been one of great pleasure & interest, for the Dutch are an interesting people, & I must say, to the shame of England, one must leave it to find countries well-governed & people without grievances. Protestants & Catholics here live in perfect harmony, Free Traders & Agriculturists without a Corn Law, & poor without a Poor Law. I fear we are great bunglers in legislation.

Last Years

I have had no news from England since I left, but suppose Maynooth still occupies the public mind. Foreigners look on us with pity. The weather is very cold & wet, but yesterday we took advantage of a fine evening to go out hawking, like a Wouverman picture, I never saw the sport before.* The Princess asked much about you and Lady Palmerston which gave me an opportunity of making the eulogium of two such dear friends. I hope your health is good & that I shall see you in July.

A blank in the journal leaves us, as usual, ignorant of the persons with whom Lord William passed his time at Frankfort, where he spent some days. His belief in the power of mineral waters to cure most ills led him from Frankfort to the baths of Homburg, Kissingen and Alexandersbad, staying long enough to observe the amenities of each place, meaning perhaps to return some time in search of health. He reached Bohemia in June.

During the year spent at Carlsbad the young Russells became wholly identified with the life of the town, and after the end of the season, when all the visitors to the springs had gone away, their only society was that of what Drocourt called 'les premiers bourgeois', or 'la jeunesse de Carlsbad', and of necessity the amusements of their contemporaries were their own. Archery helped the marksmen of the summer season to keep their eye in until the shooting matches began again in May. Riding and driving parties were made up of young and old, and Lady William, tempted out by fine weather from her library, might be seen in a carriage on the road to Aich or Schlackenwerth with Dr Hochberger as her companion, while youthful cavaliers cavorted in attendance.

The aristocratic English woman, who gave herself no airs and allowed her children none, was held in high esteem by the people of Carlsbad. The clever doctors Mannl, Sorger and Hochberger were her friends, and she accepted without prejudice for herself and her sons invitations from bureaucrats and tradespeople. Two visitors from the fashionable world, Prince Löwenstein and his daughter, Princess Camille de Rohan, who passed through Carlsbad during the dead season, called on her and were fortunate enough to find her at home. She might well have been out, and they would have been surprised to learn that she was at a soirée given by the Inspector of the Postal Service, or at a reunion of the Musikverein 'pour souhaiter la fête à Joseph Labitzky'. Labitzky was a professional musician, the master

---

* C. A. Disbrowe describes in *Old Days in Diplomacy* (p. 313) a hawking party with Queen Sophie in the 1840s. 'The time was always chosen when the herons went home with food for their young.' The riders loosed the hawks and then 'followed at tremendous speed to save the herons' lives. They took a particular feather from the birds' heads, placed a ring marked with the name of the place and date on their legs and let them fly.'

509

of the town band that played during the season at the fountains, and some-times favoured distinguished persons with a serenade below their windows. He was perhaps in charge of Odo's musical education, for he was given a tie pin by Lady William, 'une grosse chrysoprase entourée de diamants'.

Since Arthur had put aside his journal it is from the Frenchman that we hear of three damsels, denoted by him as 'les inséparables', who were for a time the boys' companions out of doors and their partners in the evening when they met at the Goldene Schild for dancing, games and song. They were the daughters of the proprietor of the Schild and of the doctors.

When the snow fell in January and the fir trees were bowed down with the weight of it, the cracking noise of whips shook the windows of Carlsbad as the sleighs ran about the town. Lady William, wrapping herself in a fur-lined green velvet cloak, went on her errands in a blue sleigh, her little groom, Johan, perched behind her flourishing his long *Schlittenpeitsche* over the brown and grey brabazons. As many as twenty sleighs, the horses hung with little bells, would career in parties about the countryside, making rendezvous in the villages to eat cakes and drink coffee, beer and punch: 'En traîneau; les jeunes gens, Labitzky et moi. Mr Odo, perdant la route, nous verse doucement sur la neige près de Donawitz.' Toboggans were dragged up the mountains and brought the merry young people down at speed. 'Les gens sont aux fenêtres pour nous voir arriver.'

At Christmas Lady William gave a party when one hundred and forty people accepted invitations to 'une soirée magique'. The honest burghers were readily amused with a magic lantern, and Odo's conjuring and card tricks. The same people, no doubt, filled the church when a solemn mass was sung to celebrate the crowning of the victor in the shooting competitions. Odo, whose musical talent was developing, had composed a four-part song for the occasion, and another of his works, a Miserere, was heard one day in the church immediately after the sermon.

But for the Russell boys, science competed with the arts, and they expended much energy in their efforts to send up a gas-filled balloon. 'Le grand ballon est tenu par 7 ou 8 personnes; il s'élève droit et majestueux, traverse des nuages bas, et nous le perdons de vue.' But more distant persons, alerted by gunfire, 'le voient au-dessus des nuages et le perdent de vue par sa petitesse. Nous apprenons que notre ballon est tombé à Falkenau, 6 lieues de Carlsbad.'

While the spa was little frequented in the winter months, in the New Year the springs were blessed, and in March Odo began to bathe at home in water carried from the Sprudel. His mother followed suit, but again it was evident that the cure did not agree with her, for she was soon applying leeches to remedy her condition.

A period of heavy rain coincided with the spring thaw and the Tepl's course through the town was blocked with trees and branches borne down from the mountains by the flood. From his window M. Drocourt watched the *débâcle*. The wild transition from winter to spring was followed by 'des journées de toute beauté', and at the beginning of May Lady William changed her lodging – perhaps on account of expense, or because the approach of summer demanded a different aspect for her rooms. A week after her removal to Madame Kugler's establishment Labitzky and his band set up their music stands beneath her windows and honoured her with a serenade. The fête of St John Nepomuk, patron saint of Bohemia (when all the springs were wreathed with flowers) and the opening of the shooting matches in May, emphasised the corporate and traditional life of the town that was about to assume the character of a fashionable watering place.

'Journée magnifique. Ouverture du tirage; les tireurs vont chercher leur roi, viennent présenter leurs hommages à Milady (les jeunes gens se sont esquivés pour échapper à la réprésentation) puis vont ouvrir le tir; une grande foule se réunit, jeu de boule, danse etc.' Some days later Drocourt wrote: 'Milady et les jeunes gens dînent en société au Sächsische Saal.' The fashionable world had arrived.

Labitzky's band greeted Lord William with a serenade when he arrived in June. 'Le soir les tireurs viennent à $9\frac{1}{2}$–$10\frac{1}{2}$ pour Milord. Foule pressée sous nos fenêtres. Milady donne aux musiciens un tonneau de bière.' 13 June was Arthur's birthday. 'Mr Arthur a aujourd'hui 20 ans. Compliments, verres, couronne de fleurs, gateaux abondent. Nous allons prendre le café chez Mlle Stark au Schild.' Lord William noticed that his son 'received presents from the whole town, he is a gentle sweet boy, and much beloved'.

The height of the season brought many friends to the baths and there were balls and illuminations for visiting royal persons, but Lord William found his wife as difficult to live with as ever. 'Sad scenes, melancholy.' Provoked and despondent, he wrote a wounding letter to his son in England that determined Hastings to join his parents as soon as possible.

Lord William Russell to Hastings Russell at Bourn [PRP]

Carlsbad. 1 July 1845

I have just received your letter of the 22d. You say mine was not *exhilarating*, do you expect it to be like a bottle of Champagne? You say your passion is to pay bills – an excellent passion – *mine is to scold – chacun à sa manière*, but why be affronted. Men are made of all sorts of stuff, but the art of living is to take the stuff as you find it, if my letters don't exhilarate it is because I am of a melancholy nature, but they are not intended to offend. Lady Holland always says I am the most dutiful father she ever heard of, but you are not satisfied with a father's duty to his son, this is hard on your poor father, however let that pass but don't exact duty from your Mother, she is made of sterner & harder stuff than I am & you will break yourself to pieces if you try to bend her. She is still smarting under your conduct to her at Versailles, & Lady De La Warr's ill-judged &

insolent letter, the brother's arrival to watch you, & your taking part with strangers against her. She does not again wish you to make the painful sacrifice of coming abroad to see her, but if you were to come, with good will, unexpectedly, with affection in your heart, & attention in your manner & promises for the future, she would be the happiest of Mothers. Her feelings are now deeply wounded, her hopes blighted, but intense love for you is at the bottom of her heart; this it is in your power to revive, consequently I can feel no pity for you, knowing that it is in your power to repair the misunderstanding that exists. Can you think the love of a mother & such a mother worth no sacrifice, look back to your younger days & think how she loved you & does that love deserve no return in riper years? but I have long written in this strain without effect so will say no more, for you do not or will not understand me – God help you!

Your brothers are going off today – a neat post wagon trotting in to Petersbourg – without the Saint – to see Atty's friend Czernin, & sleep out two nights, this is a great step, as it is breaking thro' the terrible nursery life which annoys & frightens me. They are charming boys, the sweetest tempers, & very intelligent & well mannered but poor Atty is very idle, more from constitution than ill will to learn. He takes much interest in subjects that interest him especially Natural History & Theology. I want him to be a clergyman, the idlest of professions in our Church, but he says he could not conscientiously subscribe to the 39 Articles, & who can? Old Austin, with a lawyer's subtlety, says they are only a form, but Atty is too conscientious to submit to form in such a disguise.

Odo is sharper but more worldly & will be exposed to all the temptations of the world, but I hope his principles which are sound & his judgement which is excellent will guide him through the dangerous labyrinth. They have been too long in this place & I am anxious to get them to England. . . .

Hastings Russell to Mrs Rawdon [WP]

Bourn. August 19. 1845.

From what you have heard from MM I make no doubt that she will wish you to come out with me, and we will go by Frankfort if you please, and you shall pay anything you like in London. It is only on the road I bargain to be paymaster, – and at the end of our journey I insist on paying such part of the expense as I shall think fit – without any objection on your part. These are my stipulations. . . .

In August Lord William was taken ill. 'Loss of feeling. Sent for Hochberger. 16 cups.' His illness left him weak and lame. 'Wrote to Hastings to encourage him. Scenes, worse and worse. Out alone – beautiful evening. Sad, sad.' He recovered enough strength to make a little tour with Arthur and M. Drocourt, going to Dresden, Leipzig and Berlin. Returning to Carlsbad, he began a course of Marienbad waters that were available for patients who found local ones unsuitable.

Hastings reached Carlsbad in September and was followed a week later by Mrs Rawdon, who may have stayed to rest and see her cousin Forbes at Dresden on the way. It was the last time they were to be all together.

Encouraged by his father to break out of the 'nursery life' and to pursue an interest he found increasingly absorbing, Arthur went away with Dr Hochberger to join a meeting of naturalists at Nuremberg. In his absence Odo showed himself again a distinguished marksman, carrying off prizes for shooting. It was the custom for visitors to Carlsbad to provide the prizes for these contests and the *Karlsbad Kalender* recorded the contributions made by the Russell family to the awards for this popular regional sport. In one season Lady William gave a grandfather clock, a silver cup, a silver tobacco box, a large meerschaum pipe, a cigar holder, a sugar bowl and six coffee spoons, a silver fruit basket and a table centrepiece with glasses.

'Birthday', wrote Lord William tersely on 2 October. 'All this time passed happily with my dear boys – it is a pleasure to see them together.' He left next day with Hastings and parted from his son at Frankfort. His own destination was Homburg, where he remained a month taking the cure. 'The baths strengthen me but I am very weak', he wrote. 'They have done me much good but my health is shaken.'

By Aschaffenburg, Wurzburg and Anspach he made his way to Donauworth, from whence the railway took him to Munich: 'No letter, sadly perplexed.' He pottered about the picture galleries enjoying the fine weather, waiting for the letter from his wife that did not come. 'No letter, determined to go.' At Innsbruck he waited for the mail: 'No letter.' 'Up the Brenner, no snow, dust flying on the south side. Slept at Botzen, and into Italia. Took the new road by the pass, the one which Napoleon marched to Bassano. Magnificent scenery described by Beckford. To Bassano, to Padua. By the railroad, two hours to Venice. Beautiful weather. Called on Small, the Consul. On taking up Galignani was shocked to read Lady Holland's death. I had seen much of her all winter, she was a superior woman & invariably kind to me. Aged 74. The end of the famous Holland House society, the most brilliant ever seen in London.'

Hastings Russell to Lord William Russell in Germany [WP]

B.hurst, Oct. 15 1845

I found Elizabeth recovering from a long & painful miscarriage. On my arrival here on Sunday 12th. she had come downstairs for the first time, yesterday & the day before (beautiful days) she has been out & is much stronger. . . .

As soon as Bessie can bear the journey we shall return to Bourn. We never can regret having lived there, while we could, & till I know what climes you, MM & my brothers will pass more than six months in I cannot spend my time better, (I think) than there 'Inveni Portum' – as long as it lasts. I should not have been discontented had you let me stay at Homburg with you – unless I had heard of Bessie's illness. Then to be sure I must have wished myself here. I was spared much anxiety on the road by not having heard of her illness.

God bless you, my dear Father – what more can I say? I know as much of what my family will do this winter as I did 6 weeks ago before that I left England.

Hastings Russell to Lord William Russell in Germany [WP]

Buckhurst Park, Oct. 26 1845

I have had a crusty letter from Uncle B. in which his Grace allows me to tell you that I am to be put up for Lichfield in case of Lord Granville's death. I foresee such a detestable time of it, if ever I am brought into Parliament, that I am in no hurry, though I will not refuse to venture anything, because inactivity is not good for man & because at least there is experience to be gained. And I am in no trepidation partly from the number of false alarms I have met with & partly from ignorance of what I am going *at*.

Uncle B. says he does not write to you because you desired him not. From the tenor of his letter a medical man would say he had the piles. . . .

MM in her last letter says never a word about her movements so you give me news (if I could believe it) when you say she is going to Vienna directly. . . .

God bless you, my dear PP & give you health to endure your brothers when you come to England.

Lady William moved herself, her mother, sons, and attendants to her old quarters in Vienna at the end of October. Astonishment at each other's change of plans was an emotion she shared with her husband, and they were never to learn that what the other said was unlikely to bear any relation to what was actually done.

Last Years

Lady Holland left Lord John Russell for his life a considerable estate in Kennington.

Lady William Russell to Lord John Russell [PRO]

Vienna 3 December 1845

I see . . . Lady Holland has left you an annuity . . . of 2 thousand a year. I hope it may be so, & not 2 thousand legacy once told, for you want it & deserve it & it will add to your comfort & not to your luxury. You are the only Englishman I know (I daresay there are many I don't know) who lives virtuously on your income in that vicious island of ours. I mean addicted to the Plutus vices to the highest degree, & it requires strength of mind to resist pecuniary torment. So I really am glad. Her death must have affected you. She was maternal to you in *her* maternal way & it is a huge blank in social intercourse & dear recollections to you in particular. Your elder brother lost Lord Spencer – also a blow. We are now in those evil days of regrets & apprehensions after having got over the days of sharp moral pains & deep disappointment. Altogether this life is a curious piece of business.

I am here on my way to winter in Italy (Rome). Write to me there, old Torlonia's. To my immense surprise your brother *dévancé* me. He went to Homburg, where he was to remain all October – and then go to London and Paris & thence either join me in Italy or I join him in England – whichever way his health and feelings led him after Homburg, London & Paris. In the meanwhile I was to amuse myself at Vienna (from Carlsbad). '*Figurez vous* my surprise *et imaginez mon étonnement*' as Prince Lieven used to say every time his wife was with child – when I receive a letter from Munich to tell me [he] has altered his *marche-route* & given up London & Paris.

From Hastings I hear rumours of Parliament. I shall be glad he does *something* & regret the army as I think it was the only thing he was fit for. He is quite lost to me, 'but I suppose it is *all right*' as you say when things go wrong.

Dearest John, God bless you & make your wife well & your children good. Don't forget old Bettina in this weary world. I wanted to put on a black gown for Lady Holland but Flahault prevented me, saying he knew she was no relation. He, Flahault is very thriving here. He is liked & cherished & has overcome all their anti-Gallican feelings, which St Aulaire could not in thrice the time with treble the means. Don't quote me, but our country is at an immense discount & there is an affected commiseration for our coming woes casting their shadows before that puts me in mind of Mrs Candour. 'All the world is a stage.'

Goodbye *frater vita amabilior*. Arthur & Odo are tall, bearded & strong. One of these days I will bring them home, when the income tax & the Corn Laws are abolished.

Hastings Russell to Mrs Rawdon at Vienna [WP]

Bourn. Dec. 6th. 1845.

I thank you for your legible letter, without any date, from Vienna & am very sorry to hear of poor Butty's accident and of your smashed carriage. It was lucky that you were close to Vienna where you could get it repaired.

Nineteen drops of laudanum contain one grain of opium, and four grains of opium are the lowest fatal dose that can be taken by a full grown person. A child may be poisoned much cheaper. But pray, dear Granny, do not play any tricks with your opium pills. Of course you know that ten minims, by measure, of laudanum is equal to 15 drops of laudanum and that ten drops of laudanum are equal to seven and half minims only – and so on.

Lady Holland has left Uncle John an estate value 1500 a year.

God bless you. I wish you were all coming here.

LORD WILLIAM'S DIARY

28 Nov. Left Venice by rail.

30 Nov. Remained at Verona in hopes of a letter from Vienna, got none.

1 Dec. Most beautiful day, the scenery of the Lago di Garda seen in perfection, the residence of Catullus who describes it. Brescia, where I saw the newly discovered temple of Mars & subscribed for the work on it. Thick fog all day, very cold. Arrived at Milan. Sent to post, no letter.

5 Dec. Dined with General Walmoden, sat next to Madame Garcia, engaged at the Scala.

10 Dec. The climate of Milan foggy, damp, cold and disagreable, I was never well there. My great pleasure was to go every morning to the Cathedral, today it was all day full; St Ambrose, the patron saint of Milan.

11 Dec. Took leave of Walmoden, having a letter from Lady William to say she would be at Milan the 19th.

12 Dec. Set off for Genoa in search of a better climate. Slept at Voghera. On my way visited the famous Certosa of Pavia. I never saw so many precious stones, marbles, bronzes, pictures in so small a space. The architecture is beautiful, the whole magnificent and well preserved.

13 Dec. The students of Pavia all in the streets. What can be the career of all these fine looking young men, they must *déborder* the social limits. Horrible roads, immense traffic, rice and colonial produce. Arrived at the Croix de Malte, Genoa.

14 Dec. Fine sunshine, keen air. Walked all over my old reminiscences. Genoa made more carriageable don't improve it. Thriving in spite of the Sardinian Government.

16 Dec. Found Abercromby* & Lady Mary here for her health. Abercromby went to Turin for Christmas duties. How glad I am to have done with diplomacy & its shallow useless forms.

17 Dec. My head never right, leg better, tried fasting. Three old letters from Lady William, on the 7th at Vienna, but talks of being at Milan 15th or 20th. Patience!

18 Dec. Galignani brought in the news that the Peel Cabinet had resigned on account of the Corn Laws. This must be to shake off the trammels. John cannot make a Cabinet, he has no men, unless he takes Cobden's party. A Tory ministry cannot last, Peel must come back, he is an artful dodger.

20 Dec. John came back from Windsor & called his old Tory colleagues round him, he might as well attempt to stop a leak in a ship with blotting paper.

Hastings Russell to Mrs Rawdon at Vienna [WP]

Bourn. Dec. 21st. 1845.

God bless you on your birthday & may I soon see you all in England. I know nothing of any of you. . . .

Uncle John has failed in forming a ministry & Peel is in office again & for some time, probably.

I cannot tell you how worried I am when I do not hear of you all regularly. One dread constantly haunts me, which is that of a carriage accident with those overloaded carriages, & MM is so careless of that danger.

God keep you all in health & safety.

I prophesy that MM will dislike Italy. – if she goes there.

* Ralph Abercromby, later 2nd Baron Dunfermline (1803–68), English Minister at the Sardinian Court. His wife was a daughter of Lord Minto and sister to Lady John Russell.

Last Years

21 Dec. Walked round Genoa with Sir Frederick Adam. Beautiful day, he dined with me and then sailed for Leghorn. Adam settling the new ministry sends me to Ordnance!!

25 Dec. Christmas Day & Lady William who was to have been in Rome for Christmas not yet left Rome [*sic*], at least I suppose not for I have no letter.

27 Dec. Bad cold and cough. 5th day of starvation & not weakened by it. Letter from Lady William at Vienna!!!!!

28 Dec. Whilst writing to H. a letter came from Lady Mary Abercromby to say John was out & Peel with the Queen. I am glad of it, the pear is not ripe for John.

31 Dec. Weather still warm & beautiful. Lady William on the 20th still at Vienna.

Lord William's health declined rapidly during the last months of his life. He was subject to pains and confusion in his head and his doctor treated his frequent colds and bilious attacks with blue pills and black doses. Ill and lonely, he was exasperated by his wife's characteristic indecision which delayed her leaving Vienna. Sometimes she spoke of setting out at once, sometimes of coming in a month or two. He wrote to her nearly every day urging her to declare her plans, and noted wryly her equivocations.

In January he took an apartment in the Palazzo Pallavicini, a noble house standing high above Genoa in the Peschiera. It was approached by cobbled lanes through orange and lemon groves, and had a wide view over the town. Delighted with the situation, he took a three months' lease and bought the outgoing tenant's horses. He had friends among the Genoese, and the Abercrombys, in whose drawing-room he sat much, were very kind to him, but they were concerned at his loneliness and lack of purpose. Lady Mary wrote to her brother-in-law, Lord John, that they were so glad to have Lord William near them. 'He is so calm and far seeing in his views and so really liberal and honest, and on other subjects too besides politics he is so agreeable. He has not yet heard from Lady William when she is to leave Vienna.'[9]

Hastings Russell to Lord William Russell at Genoa [WP]

Buckhurst, January 1st. 1846

... I have written you 13 letters from England in last year, since I left you at Homburg, all directed care of Kock & Gogel, which I thought the safest direction as long as you were bounding about Europe.

I must put in a protest when you say, 'you are accustomed to ill usage from your wife & children and obliged (God forbid) to fix your affection

518

upon strangers', & pass on to politics. You now know that John failed & you will look upon this failure as the work of his guardian angel, preserving him from worse defeat. . . .

Lord John Russell to Lady William Russell at Vienna [PRP]

Edinburgh, Jan. 14, 1846

I have received your letter some time ago, but was then engaged in cabinet making, which not turning out very successful, I have returned to my wife and family. I am now going again to London to see what we shall see. I expect a great revolution in parties, and a strange battle between the friends of 'the bread tax' and its enemies. My part is tolerably clear.

Fanny is still only in her way to recovery. But I am assured that in a month she will be well. Similar cases have almost uniformly ended in a complete cure. And nothing has occurred to show that hers will be an exception. Indeed I feel very sanguine, though not quite happy till I know she is really well.

I went to Glasgow the other day and was very well received. The old popularity of the Reform Bill seems coming back.

William has been making [*torn*] movements on the map of Europe. We heard of him at Genoa with [*torn*] Mary Abercromby taking a very kind interest in my proceedings. . . . Your staying abroad on account of cheapness is ridiculous. By living in Grosvenor Place, you will save house rent, and hotel bills, and when our Corn Laws are abolished, every thing will be at a moderate price. . . .

Hastings Russell to Lord William Russell at Genoa [WP]

Woburn Abbey, January 18th 1846

I am at Woburn in the midst of a large political party. (I enclose a list of it.) You see, all the old lot – ungrateful to Lord Grey (for having saved them) but determined to support Peel in all liberal measures he may propose this season. The nature of one of these measures we are to know on Thursday (meeting of Parliament.) It cannot fail to be a most interesting session and I look forward to it with great attention. Ireland, though lost sight of at this moment, occupies me most. I am sorry a man of so little truth is governor of England but I see no present hope of the country receiving good rule at other hands.

John's animosity is undiminished, he neither asked after you nor my Mother. He looks ill, ugly & unclean.

We return to Bourn tomorrow – there to stay till Fate drives us farther. MM writes to me from Vienna (date Jan 1st.) thinking you gone to England. I hope Mrs Denton may live on till your return without firing the house, she was so fuddled when I paid her last, that we could scarcely settle accounts.

Lord John Russell	Sir John Hobhouse
Lord Bessborough	Lord Minto
Lord Clarendon	Mr Ellice (Bear)
Lord Cottenham	Mr Tufnell

Besides these six topsawyers & 2 under-strappers there are their wives & children & other people besides.

Hastings Russell to Lord William Russell at Genoa [WP]

Bourn, Jan 26. 1846

Since my return to Bourn on ye 19th. I have received three letters from you. In your *brief* of the 12th. you tell me to write to Rome. Rome! True, '*Tout chemin mène à Rome*', but your going there seems so problematic if it depends on MM and then you say 'direct Rome' rather in an airy way. So I would not give the Pope a chance of opening my letters in your absence & enclosed one line for you to MM Vienna, to say I would not write again till I got a safer direction, but now on receipt of your *favor* of the 17th (as Tilbury calls a letter, when he encloses your Bill to me for 1845 – amount £31. 7. –) on receipt of your favor my itching to write is so great that I pen these pages & send them under cover to Ralph the Rover through Johnny Biddywell F. O. thinking they cannot go very wrong & reckoning on your *status quo* lasting some time longer. How long will it last? I wonder! I heard from MM (day before yesterday date Jan. 15, saying she should be at Rome at Easter! Now Easter day is the 12th. of April so the engagement is not imminent – and you tell me you shall be in England early in April, so I calculate MM will stay at Vienna & you at Genoa till ye 1st. of April, at least, & think it safer to write to Toorin than to Room.

However, 'a truce to this melancholy jesting', I will lay aside family matters to dip my pen into political ink & begin another sheet. –

Dear Peel has not yet told us what his cornplaster is to be - we are to know tomorrow.

He should drop the P. & call himself Eel – you have read his speech on Thursday, he said to the Whigs, 'come in & pass this measure, please.'

John said, 'What measure were you going to propose?'

Peel said, 'Ah! that's the secret.' John framed a measure & sent it to Peel, asking if he would support it. Peel said, 'Call Parliament & you shall see.' Could the Whigs come in on that? No!

Mine uncle of Bedford writes me – there are to be resignations tomorrow when the dear old Tory Pories in office find out what Peel's ideas are. How surprised they will be!

It is rumoured at Cambridge that I am to stand for the county. The Whigs of the shire look up to me as their representative & leader. If I had *quatrini* I would be a HELL of a fellow but in this country *bisognia* tin, – or else more talent than I can boast of. Destiny has destined my destiny to be circumscribed within this duty, – not to spend more than 1,000 a year & I by no means complain. I only say there is more to be bought for money in England than in any other country in the world.

God bless you. I wonder you should like to be out of England at so interesting a moment.

Hastings Russell to Lord William Russell at Genoa [WP]

Bourn, February 8th. 1846

I think you will absolve me from the blame you give me in your letter of the 25th Jan. when you recollect that I had scarcely sent my first letter to you through the F.O. (on your telling me to write under cover to Abercromby) when I heard from you desiring me to direct to Rome which I have luckily not done but ventured another letter through F.O. Altogether it is surprising you should have heard so often from me when you consider that whilst I was writing to you at Homburg I suddenly had a letter from you dated Munich, bidding me direct to Venice which I fortunately did not do since I find my Mother's letters were not forwarded to you from thence when you were found to be at Genoa. You must have overlooked my telling you some time back that the Lichfield idea was at an end – some one – I know not whom – having been found with better claims upon the borough.

Albertus Parvus sent for Wiltshire & said to him, 'Mine teer

Fintchester you shall pee mine Kroom off te stuhl,' who said the place did not suit him – so Albert is in a fix as he won't take anything cheaper than a Marquis.

. . . It is wretched suspense not knowing what you are going to do, although MM says what you choose to do is no business of mine.

Hastings Russell to Mrs Rawdon at Vienna [WP]

Bourn. February 12th. 1846.

Thanks, very many thanks, dearest Granny, for your letter. MM so seldom writes to me & says so little about herself & my brothers when she does that it is a great godsend to me to hear something about them.

I am sorry your money has been mis-sent to Rome. I had some apprehension about your journey thither & my Mother's on account of the length of the way & travelling through Italy not being as comfortable as German travelling, especially without good servants. But now I feel tolerably assured that MM will no more go to Italy this year 46 than she has any of the preceding years from 1835. I only pity the poor lady who is to be confined in May for I doubt your having started for Carlsbad then. I heard from PP today. He says he is well & happy at Genoa this time. In his former letter he was not so well pleased – and does not say much else, the cast of his letter being political.

God bless you, dearest Granny.

Hastings Russell to Lord William Russell at Genoa [WP]

Bourn, Feby. 15. 1846

. . . I should pity the forlorn situation you describe, my dear Father, were I not assured that you, as well as I, were as certain as human probability can make one that M M would winter in Vienna, & no more go to Italy this year than any of the preceding ten years that she has talked of it. I therefore must look on your journey to Homburg, Munich, Venice, Milan & Genoa as a pleasure tour gratuitously undertaken. I am very sorry you should put yourself out of ye reach of every part of your family when your health is not as good as I could wish & my only consolation for it is your repeated assertion of your love of solitude & being better when alone. . . .

Hastings Russell to Lord William Russell at Genoa [WP]

Bourn. February. 22d. 1846

'Tout vient à point nommé pour qui sait attendre,' is my obliged consolation for many things, MM's absence from England, my own nullity &c &c.

Do not regret having written often to me, my dear Father. It is my very greatest pleasure to see your hand writing & MM's, even when you find fault with me. I regret being unable to write so as to please you. It is not from laziness, but because I do not know how to set about it. I doubt your reading (or receiving) all my letters for I have often answered the questions I last meet with in your letter of the 9th. Feby. (last received).

The Duke of Bedford will not return the china and has so much home correspondence on politics that he says he cannot undertake to write to you on that subject now. He said of a person abroad (not yourself), 'If he gratuitously puts himself at a distance from home, he ought not to be offended at not hearing as regularly as if he were in England, at the moment of a political crisis, when events pass so rapidly that they must be unintelligible to one not on the spot.'

You may remember that I used not to be much afraid of the Duke of Bedford and if you think my intimacy with him too great (tho' I can assure you it is not excessive) it was your own wish & will & making. . . .

Hastings Russell to Lord William Russell at Genoa [WP]

Bourn, February 26. 1846

I am glad you say I don't fib, (MM always tells me I lie like Hell.) It is true I only told Uncle B. *orally* where you were (which he knew) when I gave him your messages, but surely that was enough. He said he had too much to write about then at home (Whig cabinet formation) to write abroad on politics. . . .

MM is quite right, the Army is my trade, but I grew ashamed of myself in the Guards & when I found, after 3 years' begging, that you would neither procure me exchange nor employment – what could I do? The Pagets could get what they wanted – Marsh (my junior) could be put on half pay. – Wood (half an idiot) could get command of the 80th. – & I was to rot in the Guards. If I was 50, & not a cripple, I would serve again, if I had a chance of promotion or employment – but I cannot regret having left the Guards when I did.

Why did you send me a bit of my own ugly writing?

Last Years

Hastings Russell to Lord William Russell at Genoa [WP]

Bourn, Ash Wednesday 1846

Eastern news must reach you sooner than it reaches me & you know that Fitzroy Somerset has lost a son in India. It is not my fault that you have not done the same – I did my best in 42 to go to India. Sir H. Harding seems to have been taken by surprise. . . .

February went by and Lord William got no better. The weather was wet and cold.

LORD WILLIAM'S DIARY

3 March. Wrote to Vienna. 3 letters.

4 March. Wrote to Vienna.

5 March. Wrote to Vienna complaining and despairing.

6 March. Wrote to Vienna.

On 7 March he got into a steamboat which took him to Naples in four days.

LORD WILLIAM'S DIARY

11 March. Sic transit tempus, from Lady Holland's room to the Chiaia of Naples is only a step. She is gone and I am going. Mr Brockhausen who asked me to dine to meet the Duchesse de Sagan, Lichnowsky, Schellenberg, Putbus and others. Teaed at Madame de Solthurm.

13 March. Dined with Knudtzon and Baillie. Went to Pompei, cold terrible.

Two days later he re-embarked in the ship that had brought him and was carried back to Genoa. The excursion had been unwise, for shortly after-wards he was taken ill in Lady Mary Abercromby's drawing-room and Dr Duff was sent for who physicked and bled him. He was much weakened by this attack and appealed anew to his wife to join him, but she sent no satisfactory communication.

Hastings Russell to Lord William Russell at Genoa [WP]

Bourn, March 5th. 1846

Poor old Lynedoch!   Barossa

. . . You give me too much credit for my politics. I only write you my political opinions because you have so long & constantly scolded me for

524

not doing so, otherwise I should scruple to load a letter with such useless stuff.

I am always grateful when you tell me I may find shelter under your roof and if you will obtain MM's permission for my availing myself of yours I should wish for nothing more. . . .

You would not have been cold here this winter – it has not been like the last – indeed I hardly think you can have been warmer at Genoa. However you would have been bored & that is worse.

I am much obliged to you for the scrap of MM's letter & not affronted at being called Anglomane. Why should I?

This last letter of yours (of February 20, Odo's birthday) is not written in the same good spirits that you have hitherto seemed in at Genoa. I hope & trust your health is not the cause. I do not like to think of you alone – though you say you prefer it.

Granny writes me from Vienna, – she says never a word about moving. Indeed I do not suppose any move is likely till the annual change of quarters, to Carlsbad in June, takes place.

God bless you, my dear Father. I wish I could think I was to see you soon.

Hastings Russell to Lord William Russell at Genoa [WP]

Bourn. March 7. 1846

I have heard from John saying I might come in for Westminster in June if I could come to live in London now, and have no dislike to ballot.

I have answered that *I* have no dislike to ballot, & that I will take a lodging in London on hearing from him again but that my main reliance must be in his advice. I enclosed my answer to the Duke of Bedford for inspection & approbation.

I have heard from old Hare asking much after you & have told him what I could, – which is not much – I wish you were in England.

You say something about my reading in one of your last letters. I have just finished the last volume of Fielding's works. I am very glad to have read them – but very sorry to have no more of them to read. At this moment I am reading Lyttelton's *Henry II*, Sir Humphry Davy's *Salmonia* for the 2d. time, a German & a French work, besides odds & ends.

The d——d papers take so many hours to read. I get up from them every morning in a cold sweat and seldom regain equanimity during the day.

Do not think me apathetic about representation but I have all but represented so many places already that I can no longer get up excitement on short notice at the mention of a new place. . . .

Hastings Russell to Lord William Russell at Genoa [WP]

Bourn, March 15. 1846

. . . I cannot yet think that you expected MM in Italy. Solitude & a mild winter is what I thought you sought, & found, & with them better health I trust. . . .

I have got the *grippe* and am writing under the influence of the influenza which you know blue devils one as much at least as blue pills, but I fight against low spirits & fight against them still. – Though the thought that I shall never come to a right understanding with MM, that no pardon-begging, no admission of error will attain forgiveness from her, chagrins me very deeply & very constantly.

I have now been ill one week. At first I fought against it but these last days it has almost confined me to my bed. Still I fight against depression.

I have read Sir H. Davy's Salmonia in bed & Izaak Walton & been very much delighted by them both & chiefly by Salmonia. You have got Ranke's Popes – I think? I wish I had them here. . . .

[appended to the above letter]

March 13th.

I got your letter yesterday at the same time with one from MM. Your praise of me in two of your last letters is undeserved – and so is (I think) MM's censure in this letter (postage 4/10d) I want encouragement & not rebuffs. Without a little vanity (self esteem) nothing would be done in this world and to be constantly told by one's own Mother that one is an Idiot, a coward & a liar is very disheartening. . . .

Hastings Russell to Lord William Russell at Genoa [WP]

[1846]

. . . When you can tell me anything of my chance of ever seeing you or MM & my brothers again I beg, pray & beseech you to let me hear. You must feel how very much I wish for such intelligence.

I did not make you the cause of my leaving the Army but I gave you some of the causes for which I left the Army when you twitted me with not being in India at this time. I am very thin skinned about having left the Army & MM always taunts me with it – and I do not think it was my fault if I did not serve in India – or elsewhere than in the Guards. . . .

Hastings Russell to Lord William Russell at Genoa [WP]

Bourn, March 18. 1846

My council of Uncles or *Punt* as the Sikhs call it, have decreed that I shall not stand for W[estminster] I do not yet know what Borough I am to make the next feint at. When I do you shall hear. . . .

I heard yesterday from MM date March 8th which added to being *gripped* has made me *hipped*. I wish *you* at least were coming home.

March 19th.

Today's post brought me a letter from Granny three sides of paper & not one word about Mother, brothers, movements, plans. It is true that I know MM will go to Carlsbad about August & return to Vienna about December. Still I had rather hear any improbability than be told nothing. . . .

Hastings Russell to Mrs Rawdon at Vienna [WP]

Bourn. March 27th. 1846.

I write to answer your letter . . . dear Granny and to tell you that I have got the talisman, and further that you must not expect to hear from me again after you receive this letter. I find my writing makes mischief & messes & historics & squabbles and I think it is best, and determine not to write again.

You ask me why I do not go to London? I have no house to go to there – and the reason I have not a house in London is that MM advised me *not* to take a house because I should find myself involved in greater expense than I could meet. Otherwise I should have housed myself before now, since it has always been my wish to have a house of my own in London. And it is so still, if I can manage it without getting into debt, – and now that I have had two years' experience in housekeeping (thanks to MM's advice) I think myself almost able to take a house in London.

And now, dear Granny, I think I have answered this question that you have asked me in many letters, accurately & minutely.

I wish you told me more of MM and my brothers.

Hastings Russell to Lord William Russell at Genoa [WP]

Bourn, April 5th. 1846

I thank God I know you better by your letter of the 24th. March. If I thought you wished it I would set out tomorrow to join you, though I believe you will be well again long before this letter reaches you, yet I do not like your being so far from MM or my brothers or myself when you are liable to illness. I am afraid you are not cautious enough, not careful enough of your diet.

I am more inclined to think of you than of Cromwell but since you wish it I will tell you what I know of him, which I collect from old maps & books here at Bourn. Carlyle's style is so disagreeable that I did not read him. *The Examiner* & *Liberal Review* praised him exorbitantly so I suppose I am wrong. Besides the collection of letters were worth reading for their own sake and first.

It was an ancestor of a Sir Richard Williams of high degree, who was a connection of Thomas Cromwell Lord Essex of low degree, who first took the name of Cromwell in honour of him & to him was given Hinchinbrooke at the dissolution of ye monasteries. By the Bye, Thomas Cromwell not only was the maker of the Russells, as you say, but when he was serving in Italy under Bourbon, helped John Russell esq. out of Bologna where he was in danger. . . .

Hastings Russell to Lord William Russell at Genoa [WP]

Bourn, April 9th. 1846

Thank God, my dear Father, I have news of you today, only 10 days old.

You tell me not to leave England or I would not wait for your sanction, but if you have the least wish, or rather no repugnance, to my setting out for Genoa to travel home with you let me hear & I shall be with you a week after. If you really leave Genoa on the 17th. when you say your house is up, of course I cannot get there in time – but I can meet you on the road if you wish it.

The thought of seeing you has brightened me up. . . .

. . . I should have set out for Genoa long ago – but you told me in one

& the same letter of your illness and intention to leave Genoa – so that I had no fair chance of finding you there. I now get more anxious finding you do not leave Genoa & think I ought to be off – still I should wish to hear from you in answer to my letter of the 5th. before I start.

M.M. & my brothers are nearer you than I am, surely they are with you by this time. If I set out before I get a letter, I put myself beyond the possibility of hearing for near ten days, therefore I ought to wait & be directed by your next letter. I am ready to start at a moment's notice & you will know whether I have done so by the tenor of your own letter to me.

God bless you, my dear Father. I trust you will not run away from all of us again.

Hastings Russell to Mrs Rawdon at Vienna [WP]

Bourn. April 14. 1846.

MM bids me write to you – and so I will – and tell you how much it worries me that MM should stick for ever at Vienna. My brothers have got foreign accents, of that there is no doubt – & if they were to come to England for a short time it surely would not prevent their going abroad again whenever it suited MM.

This winter has been wretchedly passed. My Father in one place, MM, my brothers & yourself in another, – myself in a third and I can see no reason why this should ever cease. Vienna, Carlsbad will go on for ever.

When you write to me you are always so cautious that I hear nothing of MM, brothers, yourself, Butty, Mr Drocourt, Macaw, Vic or anything that I most wish to know such as projects – length of stay &c &c.

My Father tells me he is about to leave Genoa for England on the 15th. which I am glad of. I had written to ask him whether I should go out to him.

What MM will do I am afraid I know well enough – go to Carlsbad in August & back to Vienna in December.

Hastings Russell to Mrs Rawdon at Vienna [WP]

17 Upper Grosvenor Street.
April 18. 1846.

I have to thank you for a kind letter but I cannot consent to your calling my writing to you 'kindness', all I wish for & most ardently is peace

529

& harmony in my family & no squabbles & huffs & misunderstandings & if my writing to you or *not* writing to you or anything else in the world could bring that about – God knows how willingly I would do it.

I am very anxious about my Father & you do not even name him in your letter – yet MM must have heard of his illness by the 7th.? I would have gone out to him if he had not talked of leaving Genoa in every letter, and at this moment if I hear from him where I may meet him I shall set out immediately. He writes in the worst spirits. I hear of him through Uncle John & Ralph Abercromby and am grievously disappointed at not hearing of him from Vienna, as I expected long before this.

I cannot tell you how much I long to see you again and that we should all be near together or how little hope I have of it. My Father at least talks of coming to England and says he wishes it – his project was to go by sea from Genoa to Havre de Grâce, which I hope he will not do.

He was to sail on the 15th. – but he writes very wildly. I wish to God that Peace were possible amongst us & that we might all live together *anywhere.*

Hastings Russell to Lord William Russell at Genoa [WP]

17 Upper Grosvr. St.
April 23d. 1846

I have made every preparation to be off at a moment's notice, have got £200 in circulars, a passport from Pollon, and only wait for your answer to my letter of the 5th. asking where to find – or meet you (if you wish to see me) – to be off.

I shall come *post* by Boulogne-sur-mer, Chalon-sur-Saône, Chambéry, Mont Cenis &c. for I have not time to get the malleposte & the other ways are uncertain. By this time I hope, MM & my brothers must be with you. . . .

Hastings Russell to Lord William Russell at Genoa [WP]

17 Upper Grosvr. Street.
April 25. 1846

I have received your letter of the 14th. answering mine of the 5th. & telling me not to set out for Genoa & that you are going to Florence. My passport & circulars were ready & I keep them in case you should change your mind, when my knapsack would soon be packed – for my own kit is not large.

MM not sending A. or O. or not coming herself when you were ill, is so incomprehensible that I feel there is something unexplained about it. It is so unlike her precepts to me.

The relief your letter was to me is not to be told, for an anxious journey of 10 days is no joke & Elizabeth made herself very unhappy. The Duke of Bedford & John were for my going out to you so that I almost accuse myself of remissness at not having started when your affectionate brothers thought I ought to go.

Pray, my dear Father, do not put yourself at such a distance from all of us again. I have been very anxious about you. . . .

God bless you & bring you safe home & soon.

Hastings Russell to Lord William Russell at Genoa [WP]

17 Upper Grosvr. Street
April 26. 1846

I did not hear from you yesterday – but when I look at your last letter and see you talk of Florence – change of air & scene – I feel confident that your health is not such as to require my leaving England – although John still wishes me to set out.

I have been very much frightened about you but your last letter has set me right again and I am sure that on joining you I should have found you well, and Atty or Odo, or MM, A. & O. with you where ever you might be, yet I am sorry to hear you speak of Florence for that will be going further from us all – the thing I most dread, & would beg you not to do again.

MM does not write to me & I have not heard one word about your illness from Vienna *yet*. There is something in this unexplained to me I am certain, but which I expect to have cleared up in my next letter.

I wish that you were coming home. If frugality is all you want & you could bear with us – I am sure our table is sufficiently frugal & our habits sufficiently domestic for a sick man. I fear that they are too much so – you told me you could live with all but bores – once – leaving Bourn – & that is an arrangement, I fear, quite beyond my control. Still I return to my prayer that you will put yourself near MM and my brothers or myself until your health is better. . . .

Hastings Russell to Lord William Russell at Genoa [WP]

Rectory, Withyham. May 3d. 1846

I have received your letter of the 24th., my dear Father, and remember to have answered it by anticipation. I thought you would forget that early in April you forbade my writing until I got a new direction from you. Since you wrote this you will have been 'assomméd' by my letters.

I am glad you go to Turin – it is so much less distance between us. You say you do not hear from MM – no more do I – for nearly one month I have not had a line from her and an occasional illegible letter from Granny is all I get from Vienna.

Next Friday is your birthday and I did hope we should pass it together. Ten days later you will have been out of England one year without returning. (You sailed on the 18th. of May 45 from the St. Catherine's Wharf.)

I have found a house at low rent which will not be to be had till Christmas next. I do not know yet whether it will do – but I shall keep my eye on it in case of Parliament – in the meanwhile I shall stick on at Bourn.

Remember I have no sort of wish to go abroad this summer for my amusement but only in the hope of being of use to you or MM or agreeable to either, would I go.

Hastings Russell to Mrs Rawdon at Vienna [WP]

Withyham. May 8th. 1846.
PP's birthday.

I have this day received 3 letters from you, one without date. . . .

I wish that anything that I could say would make you believe that I do *not* grudge postage & that I wish most ardently to hear *of* MM & my brothers since I do not hear *from* them. I beg & beseech you to write large characters on wide paper & not to *cram* or write so small.

Pray write to me direct – not minding the postage, & write to Grosvenor Place (I think MM can have no objection.) My letters are forwarded from there to wherever I may be, & no time whatever is lost.

I was afraid I had offended MM without knowing how – but I see by your letter that it was by saying, in answer to a proposal of MM's, that I should set out on the 1st. of March for Rome to meet her (MM) there, (it is lucky that I did not do so!) that I was afraid it would prove another

Aix-La-Chapelle – which it would have done – but I am very sorry that allusion displeased MM. I always try to say as little as possible in all my letters.

With respect to my Father he certainly has been very ill, and *this* time he seems to me to have a perfect right to say he was left in the lurch by his family – although it usually is the other way.

At Carlsbad in October MM urged PP to go to Italy, because it was good for his health & she wished to go to Rome. I do not believe he ever expected MM would go to Italy any more than I did – & only went there for his own pleasure, still what he says receives colour from the foregoing fact.

MM's course is quite clear, she must take her own steps without reference to my Father, with whom no combined movements can be made, but she must not make my Father's style of writing an excuse for staying at Vienna because she likes it – and it would have been better not to say she was going to winter in Italy when she was going to winter at Vienna.

I am doing all I can to get my Father to join MM – or come to England – it is not fair on us to put himself at such a distance when his health is such. As to MM's coming to England this year – I no more believe it than I did when you were in Ireland writing to me daily that she was coming. I wish it was likely because the only chance I see of my ever being allowed to live in harmony with my family seems to depend on that. I have tried it on the Continent & will not try it again.

I quite understand my Father's letter being such as to prevent any one from setting out to join him, for I myself (though at a greater distance) should have started for Genoa had he not always written that he was about to leave it – but that does not affect the previous winter arrangements – and yet P.P. tells me distinctly that he wrote for Atty or Odo.

The 8th of May was Lord William's fifty-sixth birthday. 'Another year nearer the grave', he wrote. Gaining a little strength and his restlessness increasing, he set off again by boat to Naples where he passed three days with his friends, and when he left he was accompanied to Civita Vecchia, the first port of call on the way back, by Knudtzon and Baillie. At Leghorn he found letters, and from Genoa he took up again his daily appeal to his family. His letter to Arthur is so gentle and unassertive that his son may be forgiven for not reading in it the urgent call his father was making for the presence of his wife and sons. He wrote to them all again, and to Mrs Rawdon as well, pressing for their early arrival, but in the end it was Hastings who went to him.

Last Years

Lord William Russell to Arthur Russell at Vienna [PRP]

Genoa, May 24 [1846]

My dearest Atty,

There is to be a meeting of Italian *scavans* * here in August, like the one you went to at Nuremberg, but I don't propose to you to come to this, because it would be too hot. They are to live in the house I live in now, very cool and a garden full of fountains. Your friend Berzelius† is coming.

I shall set off from this as soon as I can and go over the Alps to England, I wish you would come and make the journey with me, it would do us both good, the fine air of the mountains, now just passable, but don't come without Mama's leave. Tell Odo I have got many more drawings for him, and to buy some at Vienna.

I am better, *much better*, but not strong enough to make the long journey to Vienna or I would join you, tell me where you are going, and I will join you as soon as I am able.

At night my garden is like Vauxhall, it is illuminated by millions of fire flies and they fly into the great hall, and save me the expense of oil.

Give my love to Mama and Odo.

Your affectionate father

who wants much to see you.

Hastings Russell to Mrs Rawdon at Vienna [WP]

Genoa. June 7. 1846.
Trinity Sunday.

I write that you may not be one day without a letter, but I direct care of Arnstein for fear this should fall in MM's hands.

The Doctors still give hope – but I have very little.

I wish MM was here.

Hastings Russell to Mrs Rawdon at Vienna [WP]

June 9th. 1846.

Thank God my Father is better today.

The Doctors will not pronounce him out of danger, but still I have not the horrible certainty of MM's not finding him which I had. . . .

* i.e. *savants.*
† J. J. Berzelius (1779–1848), a Swede; one of the founders of modern chemistry.

534

He is always calling me & I cannot write more.

The quantity of medicine he has taken has destroyed his stomach – a drop of gruel brings on violent hiccup.

Hastings Russell to Mrs Rawdon at Vienna [WP]

June 10th. 1846.

My Father has had a bad night and is worse today. I again begin to doubt MM's arriving in time. She might arrive on the 15th. but that is only just possible. I trust she lost no time.

Hastings Russell to Mrs Rawdon at Vienna [WP]

Genoa. June 13. 1846.

My Father is now out of all danger & my anxiety is about MM's arrival. Sometimes I look on it as certain & at others I doubt. When I remember that my marriage could not bring her to England – when there was no reason to prevent her, I am not sure of even my Father's deathbed to bring her to Genoa. If at least I only knew she was *not* coming I should then act for myself. But till I hear this I leave every thing for her to settle & there is much to be done.

According to my reckonings I must hear on the 16th. since I wrote on the 4th. Till then I shall pass anxious time.

Today Atty comes of age! The almanack says so but I can hardly believe it. It is six years since I passed a birthday with him.

God bless you. The heat is frightful.

I always write to you that you may have news of my Father if MM has left Vienna & if she is still there, I trust not, she will have news thro' you.

Hastings Russell to Mrs Rawdon at Vienna [WP]

Genoa. June 16. 1846.

Today 16th. is the *twelfth* day since I wrote about my Father's danger. And *NO* answer yet. I am afraid MM must have left Vienna.

The Doctors now say he should not stay here another hour – although it appears impossible to move him.

On the 20th. (if I do not hear from MM on that day) I shall decide upon removing my Father without waiting any longer. I think four days is the most I ought to wait for MM when the Doctors are so urgent for his departure.

Hastings Russell to Mrs Rawdon at Vienna [WP]

Genoa. June 19. 1846.

Thank God, dearest Granny, I have at last got a letter from you and one of the same date from MM, Trieste, where she was detained by the steamer to Venice having sailed before she could get there. I think she would have come better by Innsbruck. However now I know her so near my heart is light for PP is recovering fast. I only hope the hot journey will not have hurt MM.

Elizabeth is here with me & I do not know what I should have done without her, – poor thing – she has had a hard time of it.

The heat is tremendous.

I have got an excellent apartment ready for MM – high rooms & cool.

Lady William with Arthur and Odo had left Vienna on 12 June. The journey to Genoa took seven days.

Hastings Russell to Mrs Rawdon at Vienna [WP]

Genoa. June 20th. 1846.

Thank God, dearest Granny, MM & the boys got here safe & sound last night – without headaches or any distress from the heat.

PP gets better daily & the only question will be about his removal – as soon as possible.

MM will now write to you so do not expect to hear from me again.
In haste.

Arthur Russell to Mrs Rawdon at Vienna [WP]

26. June 1846.

Papa is going on every day better, since the Italian physician has been treating him; his mind is perfectly clear now, but his body is so weak that he must be helped to everything like a little baby & he is attended on day & night.

We inhabit one of the most beautiful palaces in Genoa, situated on a hill at the back of the town, surrounded by terraces of orange & lemon trees, with a magnificent view over the sea & neighbouring mountains; if there is any air in Genoa we feel it.

God bless you, my dear Granny, I am just in time for the post.

Hastings Russell to Mrs Rawdon at Vienna [WP]

Genoa. July 1st. 1846.

I find you have written to Gibbs the banker to know why you do not hear regularly from Genoa. The reason is simply that since MM & my brothers arrived I have not thought it necessary to write to you daily, as I used – and it appears they are not as regular correspondents as I was. As to Gibbs' care of letters – nothing can be greater & I have received all yours punctually. If anything has remained unanswered in them – it is owing to my being unable to read more than a few lines in each.

My Father has not had as good a night as usual, but he is making up for it this morning by sleeping soundly. . . .

MMyo & the boys are all very well.

I trust my Father may soon be able to move and that we shall all meet somewhere a short time hence.

Lord William died on 16 July. Although it might be thought that the reunion of his wife and eldest son at his bedside would herald better relations between them, it was otherwise, and for the time being the breach was wide.

Lady William and her younger sons left Genoa the day after her husband died, and travelled slowly by Innsbruck back to Vienna, where she spent the first months of her mourning. They went to Carlsbad in September and remained there for nearly two years. Arthur and Odo sometimes went away for a few days to see their friends the Czernins at Petersburg near by, and in the summer of 1847 and the following spring M. Drocourt, now in the service of the Duc de Beaufort-Spontin, came to see them from Petschau. But Lady William had little society but that of the Carlsbad doctors until she returned to Vienna during the revolution of 1848.

Last Years

Lord John Russell to Lady William Russell at Genoa [PRP]

July 22, 1846.

My dear Sister,

I have just heard from a telegraphic dispatch the melancholy news of my poor brother's death. It was too much to expect that he should survive the many severe attacks he has lately had. May God have mercy upon him – and you and all his dear children!

I hope you and Hastings and Elizabeth in this sad trial will seek some comfort in helping, and loving one another. There is some satisfaction to you in having been with him, and doing every thing to the best of your judgement to preserve his life.

Hastings and his wife should come home as soon as possible. I do not know what you will think best to do. Your health may have suffered from the anxiety and watching, added to the climate. But God, if we allow it, turns these afflictions to our benefit, and makes us endeavour to please him better than in our prosperity we ever could.

Yrs very affly

J.R.

Hastings Russell to Mrs Rawdon at Vienna [WP]

35 Grosvenor Place, Augt. 3d. 1846.

I . . . scratch off one line in a great hurry to you – for I find very much to be done in England.

I heard from MM at Innsbruck but by this time you are all together.

I reached Chenies in the middle of the night of the 26th. & thanked God I had reached my journey's end – for I had a great wish that he should lay at Chenies. I was also very thankful to have been able to spare Mmyo much misery by enabling her to leave Genoa as soon as she did and it is a great comfort to me to think I was allowed to nurse my Father during the whole 46 days of his illness & to pay him the last duties as I have done – tended him in sickness & washed him after death, seen him laid in his coffin & travelled safely eleven hundred miles with it & lastly & at last gone down into the vault with him & seen him placed where I hope one day to lay beside him.

God bless you, my dear Granny. I have written in great haste this time but a few days hence I hope to be able to write you more leisurely.

Lady William Russell to Lord John Russell [PRP]

Vienna, 3 Aug, 1846.

My beloved John,

You too have gone thro' a similar affliction. I feel most bitterly my cruel disappointment for till within 2 hours of his death I did not expect to lose him! The comfort my two younger sons give me is most rational and above their years – that *he* would not have borne old age or prolonged sickness. His social disposition, great activity and habits (military for my father was the same) of locomotion. Everything was against his resignation to years coming on, and an invalided state, and that he was 4 weeks, when we nursed him day and night, cheerful, full of hope, sanguine – indeed certain of going to where he felt sure of a cure. I will show you his letters and explain to you all you were urged to blame – for you wrote me a cruel and unjust letter, being *blinded* and also torn to pieces by public business, so I made every allowance but was sadly cut up by the style and contents, so contrary to your constant friendliness for me during 30 years. But remember I will decidedly clear up all. You ought to know how upright I am? The tenderness my poor husband showed me the whole time and the joy at seeing me and the reliance on all he expected me to do for him were most touching and consolatory and Arthur and Odo witnessed every word and have hearts and heads sufficient to appreciate and remember every word.

As you ask me about my eldest son I will tell you and it remains between you and I alone that you *must* repress his excessive arrogance, he does not understand his situation and I am most serious in what I say and earnest that you should attend to it without mentioning me at present. He has erroneous notions of being heir apparent and is overbearing to a degree quite painful and that might have serious consequences. Rely on what I say. He is quite altered, exceedingly insolent, and what you must prevent, is his interfering and acting as padrone in matters he has *no* authority. I am obliged to advert to this and have told him to leave all in *status quo* in Grosvenor Place till I arrive. What I bid him do is, to settle all bills due by his father in Genoa and in London – to pay out of the £1000 I gave him as a wedding present for which loan I will pay him interest till I repay the sum which will be as soon as possible. He had kept the money for his future London house outfit, so he will not lose one penny by it – beyond *that* he is not to go as to my affairs – for he does not know where to stop and has shown great indelicacy. Remember I have facts and not opinions. Your elder brother *meant* well, but show'd great want of tact in sending

539

money and a servant without my participation, neither being, thank God, wanted, and in what he called 'backing' Hastings. He will be shocked when he sees into what he has done without I am sure *intending* to insult me. But suspend your judgement and keep your counsel till we meet. I will answer for justifying what I say.

I shall of course come home and have not the most remote intentions of settling abroad; tho' I shall every year drink Carlsbad and so must Odo, whose liver complaint is beyond all doubt, and who is positively benefited by Carlsbad. So on that score there is no shadow of turning on my part being the deepest conviction. He is just now in an uncomfortable state – from a pain in his heart (new). The last day of his father's existence he *ran* himself in the scorching sun to fetch him a blister and brought it back climbing in great haste . . . since which he has incessantly suffered. I have seen my doctor here who hopes it is muscular (a strain) but cannot yet decide. He is a youth with talent & sensibility. Arthur is very studious & both are intellectual beyond their years & are my guardian angels. The delicacy, affection, & rationality of their soothing conduct is really admirable. My poor old Mother is here & sincerely grieved. He sent her repeatedly thro' her 2 grandsons most kind messages & had even written to her to come to him when he fancied (as a sick fancy) that neither Hastings or I would.

I had left here my apartment, servants, carriages, effects & unpaid bills. The town is empty, I have but one poor friend whose husband died 2 days before mine! & who is in sad affliction with a good and only son to console her.

Try without mentioning me to prevent Hastings taking possession of Grosvenor Place & all in it & about it. Repress his violence & right of conquest & take him down a little – *mettez le à sa place*. You will render him & all of us an essential service. I speak from experience remember . . . & beseech you to believe and be silent, acting as from yourself. I desired him to pay immediately so as to destroy the false & painful notion the silly letters he wrote produced in England & in Italy. *I* remunerated the English & Italian Doctors & the man-servant who nursed him; you are aware that I have for many years had a separate allowance, preferring it to a limited credit which my poor husband had proposed. I always lived within it so as to have a couple of hundred pounds for exigencies – knowing that *he* always lived *beyond*. I have his honour and his credit at heart and Hastings compromised both by ill-temper and covetousness. I pay all and everything.

God bless your wife and children and be assured that I am sincere and affectionate towards you in all things – so let nothing interrupt our 30 years of friendship.

This is in answer to your brotherly letter of 22d July.

Hastings Russell to Mrs Rawdon at Vienna [WP]

Bourn. August 25th. 1846.

I have not been able to make out a dozen words of your letter. If you would but believe that I do not grudge postage & not cramp your letters so – I should be so, so much obliged to you. Pray, pray, when you have such a subject as my poor Mother's health to write about – write legibly. She never mentions herself when she writes to me & my only means of hearing something of her is from you. So let me beseech you to write to me again about MM & to write largely & legibly. I do not *indeed* grudge postage. What can I say to make you believe me, often as I have said it!

God bless you & pray write to me about my MMyo.

Hastings Russell to Mrs Rawdon at Vienna [WP]

Woburn Abbey.
September 15th. 1846

I . . . feel as anxious as you can that MM should get to Carlsbad & not give way to that procrastination which works so much harm & misery.

Her letters have long been directed to Carlsbad and it is evident to me from the manner in which she misunderstands that she has never had them forwarded.

It is of great importance, I am sure, to her quiet & satisfaction & consequently to her health, that she should come to England, after Carlsbad, and see everything settled there & understand why it should be so, & I beg you most earnestly not to keep her from setting out as is your usual habit to attempt when the time of departure draws near.

It is evident that the health of all has suffered from so long a sojourn at Vienna & I think on this account a return there would be far from desirable. Pray urge & do not retard MM's coming to England this next November.

Hastings Russell to Mrs Rawdon at Carlsbad [WP]

Bourn. October 16th. 1846.

I write you one line on my birthday to say God bless you, & may we be together on yours.

I am naturally very anxious to know what chance there is of your coming to England before Christmas. MM has never alluded to it in her last letters but Aunt Margaret writes from Skelton that she is soon going to London in order to meet you. If there is anything in this pray write it me. It would be very desirable that MM should come to England soon for she has taken such a perverted view of everything & writes me such abusive letters that I am much pained by both, & see no better remedy than coming here to see things as they are. I hope you will put no obstacle in the way of her coming home, for by doing so you will be prolonging a painful misunderstanding between mother & son which has lasted much too long already.

Hare has not yet sent your talisman but he has promised to send it soon.

Hastings Russell to Mrs Rawdon at Carlsbad [WP]

Bourn. November 12th. 1846.

I have two letters to thank you for. I promise you I will take care that MM shall not see my servant when she comes to England & I am much obliged to you for reminding me of this. He may possibly be no longer in my service then for I think of taking a house in London in January & then I shall have to reduce my servants.

I am very much annoyed at the thoughts of your going to Wisbaden when MM comes here – so much so that I beg you to reconsider such a decision. I have been looking forward to seeing you all & it will be a grievous disappointment to me if you should not come. I shall write strongly to MM to dissuade you from doing such a thing.

I am very glad to hear from you that you do not dissuade her from coming to England for it is most desirable that she should come for business sake, instead of cavilling at what I want to do at a distance & writing unfair & violent letters which give me much pain.

I cannot tell you how much I long to see you & if it were not for the unforgiving and mistaken harshness & violence of my poor MM I should certainly be with you all now.

If there is any chance of MM's coming home at any time – pray do not leave me without intelligence of it longer than necessary.

I am very sorry that Vicky should have died just now for I am sure it has upset MM much. I have been saddened by her death poor beastie ever since I got your letter.

MM tells me Atty & Odo ride the old brabazon horse now; I am very much afraid that he will come down with them. Atty rides carelessly & there is nobody to say the horse is unsafe. This has worried me since I heard of it.

Hastings Russell to Mrs Rawdon at Carlsbad [WP]

Buckhurst Park.

December 21st. 1846.

I write today to bid God bless you on your Birthday which I am very sorry you should pass away from me & out of your own country. I wish I could hope to see you soon but now that winter has set in MMyo will scarcely move from Carlsbad. I only hope that when she does move – that you will come with her & give up the idea of stopping at Wiesbaden.

I have had a sharp attack of *grippe* or I should have thanked you before now for your letter. I am heartbroken at MM's relentlessness but I see no way to soften it. I think that she is throwing away her own happiness by driving those most attached to her away. It has marred mine, but I have said as much & perhaps more than a son ought to say to his Mother about this without attaining anything. Nothing I can say or do, depend upon it my dear Granny, will conquer MM's aversion. I can only [? hope] for a mild word which will always bring me back to my MM whenever she shall be tired of scaring me away.

This is a sad subject, dearest Granny & one you are more likely to make worse than better I fear. However that may be, I shall always remain your very affectionate grandson.

Lady William Russell to Lord John Russell [PRP]

[Carlsbad] 23 Jany, 1847.

. . . I remain here till April. I am snowed up & I do not regret it – for I am quiet and have a home here, which you sybaritical Britons would despise. . . . 8 years return have like a snowball roll'd up a mass of habitable commodities & I pride myself on the books of reference accumulated. My sons are occupied *intra* & *extra muros* – and I sit expecting my husband every posthorn I hear. I can quite understand such a thing becoming a fixed idea. They have taken more colds & yet this winter is not so severe a one as 1845, tho we enjoy 10 & 14 degrees of cold . . . deep snow and good sledging (our sport, as foxhunting is in England). I am getting too full of blood, am ordered to be cupp'd – am leech'd – & so on, as at my age & with my constitution is to be expected. I am not red at all, but heavy of limb & drowsy, & that you may not say prosy too, I give you all my blessing. . . .

I hear the bells of the sledge so I am going to immerse myself in my furs & whisk out of my rocks onto the hills & cut along the Prague road going over ditches & fields 'right across the country'. Our valley is many degrees warmer from the warm springs & the high rocks, Carlsbad being in a *cul de sac*.

It is my Patmos.

Pressure from the Duke of Bedford and Lord John Russell secured the return of Arthur to England in 1849, and he was appointed private secretary to his uncle who had been Prime Minister for three years. Odo was attached to the Embassy at Vienna and transferred to Paris the next year. Lady William came back to England in 1850 and bought a house in Mayfair. She rarely moved from the sofa in her drawing-room after she had broken her leg in Rome in 1862. With her gift for making friends her circle of acquaintance grew large. She counted Robert Browning, the Carlyles, Lord Houghton and Sir Anthony Panizzi among her friends. Poets and *savants*, as well as aristocratic ladies, politicians, travellers, diplomats, crowned heads, and her son's friends were eager to pass an evening in her company in the ancient house in Audley Square where she spent the last twenty-five years of her life. She was received into the Roman Catholic Church in 1860.

SOURCES AND BIBLIOGRAPHY

Unpublished Sources

WPP   *Letters to Lord G. William Russell.* 3 vols, privately printed 1915–1920.

WP   Woburn Abbey papers.

PRP   Private Russell papers.

PP   Palmerston papers.

PRO   Public Record Office, London:

Russell papers. PRO 30/22/1b, 2a, 2b, 2d, 3b, 3c, 4a, 4e, 5a, 10, 17.

Granville papers. PRO 30/29/8/1, 30/29/17/1–2, 30/29/17/4, 30/29/17/13.

FO 63/384, 63/389, 63/397, 64/205–6, 64/210–11, 64/214, 64/222, 64/228.

ADM 1. 375.

British Museum:

HH   Holland House papers. Add. MSS 51667, 51668, 51674, 51676, 51681.

LP   Lieven papers. Add. MSS 47376, 47399, 47400.

(These papers are in course of arrangement. References date from 1969.)

NLS   National Library of Scotland:

Lynedoch papers 3617, ff. 196; 3618, f. 6; 3619, f. 37; 3623, f. 111, f. 163.

Museo civico, Bassano, Italy. MSS Canoviani, VIII–847.

Books Consulted

Acton, Harold: *The Last Bourbons of Naples, 1825–1861.* London 1961.

Apponyi, Rodolphe: *Vingt-cinq ans à Paris, 1826–1850.* 4 vols. Paris 1913–26.

Aspinall, Arthur (ed.): *Three Early Nineteenth Century Diaries.* London 1952.

Atkinson, R. H. M. Buddle & G. A. Jackson (eds.): *Brougham and his Early Friends. Letters to James Loch, 1798–1809.* 3 vols. London 1908.

Badcock, Lovell: *Rough Leaves from a Journal kept in Spain and Portugal, during the years 1832, 1833, & 1834.* London 1835.

Béraud, Edmond (ed.): *Souvenirs du Baron Gudin, peintre de la marine, 1820–1870.* Paris 1921.

Bickley, Francis (ed.): *The Diaries of Sylvester Douglas (Lord Glenbervie).* 2 vols. London 1928.

Brett James, Antony: *General Graham: Lord Lynedoch.* London 1959

Brougham, Henry, Lord: *Life and Times, Written by Himself.* 3 vols. London 1871.

Broughton, Lord (John Cam Hobhouse): *Recollections of a Long Life.* 6 vols. London 1909, 1911.

Bury, Lady Charlotte: *Diary illustrative of the Times of George the Fourth.* 4 vols. London 1838, 1839.

Castle, Egerton (ed.): *The Jerningham Letters, 1780–1843.* 2 vols. London 1896.

Sources and Bibliography

Clayden, P. W.: *Rogers and his Contemporaries.* 2 vols. London 1889.

Cooper, James Fenimore: *Letters and Journals.* Edited by J. F. Beard. 6 vols. Harvard 1960–8.

Craven, Mrs Augustus: *Lady Georgiana Fullerton, sa vie et ses œuvres.* Paris 1888.

Disbrowe, C. A.: *Old Days in Diplomacy.* London 1903.

Edgcumbe, Richard (ed.): *The Diary of Frances Lady Shelley, 1787–1817, 1818–1873.* 2 vols. London 1912, 1913.

Engel, C.-E. (ed.): *Mémoires du chevalier de Gramont.* Paris 1958.

Erskine, Mrs Steuart (ed.): *Anna Jameson: Letters and Friendships, 1812–1860.* London 1915.

Fremantle, Anne (ed.): *The Wynne Diaries, 1789–1820.* 3 vols. Oxford 1935–40.

Gore, John: *Nelson's Hardy and his Wife.* London 1935.

Grant Duff, Sir Mountstuart: *Notes from a Diary, 1851–1872.* 2 vols. London 1897.

Granville, A. B.: *The Spas of Germany.* London 1843.

Granville, Castalia, Countess (ed.): *Private Correspondence of Lord Granville Leveson Gower, 1781–1821.* 2 vols. London 1916.

Grenier, G. C. (ed.): *Mémoires de la Comtesse Rosalie Rzewuska, 1788–1865.* 2 vols. Rome 1939.

Grote, Harriet: *Posthumous Papers of George Grote.* Privately printed, 1874.

Guest, Lady Charlotte: *Extracts from her Journal, 1833–1852.* Edited by the Earl of Bessborough. London 1950.

Guizot, François: *Lettres de François Guizot et de la princesse de Lieven.* Edited by Jacques Naville. 3 vols. Paris 1963.

Hare, Augustus: *The Story of My Life.* 6 vols. London 1896–1900.

Haydon, Benjamin: *Autobiography and Memoirs, 1786–1846.* 2 vols. London 1926.

Head, Sir Francis Bond: *Bubbles from the Brunnens of Nassau, by an Old Man.* London 1834.

Hoetzsch, Otto (ed.): *Peter von Meyendorff. Politischer und Privater Briefwechsel 1826–1863.* 3 vols. Berlin 1923.

Hood, Thurman L. (ed.): *Letters of Robert Browning.* Collected by Thomas J. Wise. London 1933.

Huxley, Gervas: *Lady Elizabeth and the Grosvenors: Life in a Whig Family, 1822–1839.* Oxford 1965.

Hyde, H. Montgomery: *Princess Lieven.* London 1938.

Ilchester, Earl of (ed.): *Chronicles of Holland House 1820–1900.* London 1937.

—— *Elizabeth, Lady Holland, to her Son, 1821–1845.* London 1946.

—— *The Journal of the Hon. Henry Edward Fox, 1818–1830.* London 1923.

Le Strange, Guy (trans.): *Correspondence of Princess Lieven and Earl Grey.* 3 vols. London 1890.

Leveson Gower, Hon. F. (ed.): *Letters of Harriet Countess Granville 1810–1845,* 2 vols. London 1894.

Locker Lampson, F.: *My Confidences.* London 1896.

Loftus, Lord Augustus: *Diplomatic Reminiscences, 1837–1862.* 2 vols. London 1892.

Macaulay, Rose: *They went to Portugal.* London 1946.

Mackintosh, R. J.: *Memoirs of the Life of Sir James Mackintosh.* 2nd edition. 2 vols. London 1836.

Sources and Bibliography

Maxwell, Sir Herbert (ed.): *The Creevey Papers*. 2 vols. London 1903.

Morgan, Lady: *Italy*. 2 vols. London 1821.

Moore, Thomas: *Memoirs, Journals and Correspondence*. Edited by Lord John Russell. 8 vols. London 1853–6.

Neumann, Philipp von: *Diary, 1819–1850*. Translated and edited by E. Beresford Chancellor. 2 vols. London 1928.

Origo, Iris: *The Last Attachment*. London 1949.

Palmerston, Lord: *Selection from Private Journals of Tours in France in 1815 and 1818*. London 1871.

Peel, Lady Georgiana: *Recollections*. London 1920.

Prothero, R. E. (ed.): *Letters and Journals of Lord Byron*. 6 vols. London 1898.

Radziwill, Princess (ed.): *Memoirs of the Duchesse de Dino, 1836–1840*. 3 vols. London 1909–10.

Raikes, Thomas: *Journal 1831–1847*. 4 vols. London 1856–7.

Robinson, L. G. (ed.): *Letters of Dorothea, Princess Lieven, during her residence in London, 1812–1834*. London 1902.

Ross, Janet: *Three Generations of English Women*. 2 vols. London 1888.

Simpson, M. C. M.: *Many Memories of Many People*. London 1898.

Smith, Nowell C. (ed.): *Letters of Sydney Smith*. 2 vols. London 1958.

Spectator, 7 March 1891: Benjamin Jowett, article, 'The late Duke of Bedford'.

Strachey, Lady (ed.): *Memoirs of a Highland Lady*. London 1898.

Strachey, Lytton, and Fulford, Roger (eds.): *The Greville Memoirs 1814–1860*. 8 vols. London 1938.

Sudley, Lord (trans.): *The Lieven–Palmerston Correspondence, 1828–1856*. London 1943.

Ticknor, George: *Life, Letters and Journals*. Edited by G. S. Hilliard. 2 vols. Boston 1909.

Trollope, Frances: *Vienna and the Austrians*. 2 vols. London 1838.

Walpole, Spencer: *Life of Lord John Russell*. 2 vols. London 1891.

Wilson, Harriette: *Memoirs*. 2 vols. London 1909.

Woodham-Smith, C.: *The Reason Why*. London 1953.

Zamoyska, Priscilla: *Arch Intriguer : A biography of Dorothea de Lieven*. London 1957.

Zeitschrift für Geschichte des Oberrheins, 109 (1961): Heinrich Schnee, article, 'Hofbankier Saloman von Haber als badischer Finanzier'.

REFERENCES

PREFACE, INTRODUCTION *pp*. xiii–xvii ; 1–17

1. Russell papers, PRO 30/22/2b (92)
2. PRP: Moira to J. Rawdon, 30 Jan. 1797
3. PRP: E.A.R. to Lady Duff Gordon (?1871)
4. Moore, *Journal*, i. 283
5. Locker Lampson, p. 379
6. *Granville Letters*, i. 34
7. PRP: E.A.R. to Lady Duff Gordon (?1871)
8. 'Beppo', LXXXIII and LXXXIV
9. Locker Lampson, p. 377
10. E.A.R. to Mrs Herbert, Sept. 1869
11. Locker Lampson, p. 377
12. PRP: E.A.R. to Lady Duff Gordon (?1871)
13. PRP: E.A.R. to Laura Russell, 17 Oct. 1865
14. Holland to Fox, p. 7
15. Broughton, i. 148
16. PRP: Capecelatro to E.A.R., 1816
17. *Granville Letters*, i. 100
18. ibid., i. 88
19. ibid., i. 100
20. *Shelley Diary*, i. 70
21. Broughton, i. 157
22. HH add. MSS 51674 (552): Dss of Bedford to Lady Holland
23. WP: W.R. to J.R., Jan. 5, 1812
24. PRP: E.A.R. to Laura Russell, 22 May 1866
25. Holland to Fox, p. 54

FAMILY AND FRIENDS *pp*. 18–34

1. Ticknor, i. 270
2. Granville papers, PRO 30/29/5: Lady Sutherland to Lady Gower 13 Dec. 1785
3. *Greville Memoirs*, iv. 209
4. ibid., i. 86
5. WPP ii. 56: Bedford to W.R.
6. WP: Bedford to W.R., 28 April 1822.
7. Broughton, iii. 112
8. HH add. MSS 51668 (877): Bedford to Lady Holland, 1828
9. ibid. (253): Bedford to Lady Holland, 13 Nov. [1826]
10. PRO 30/22/10: Bedford to J.R.
11. PRP: E.A.R. to Laura Russell
12. *Letters of Sydney Smith*, p. 425
13. Moore, *Journal*, iii. 283

References

14. Holland to Fox, p. 184
15. Broughton, iii. 166
16. WPP i. 290: Tavistock to W.R., 8 March 1839
17. WPP iii. 313: Bedford to W.R., 8 Jan. 1841
18. ibid., iii. 310: Bedford to W.R., 14 Sept. 1840
19. ibid., iii. 326: Bedford to W.R., 27 April 1841
20. PRO 30/29/6: Leveson to Granville, 14 July 1837
21. Guest, *Journal*, p. 109
22. WPP iii. 314: Bedford to W.R., 8 Jan. 1841
23. Grey to Lieven, 20 Oct. 1834
24. PRO 30/22/3a: Lord Russell to Tavistock, 8 Feb. 1838
25. WPP i. 351: Bedford to W.R., 2 Sept. 1842
26. Haydon, ii. 254
27. Smith, *Works*, iii. 233
28. *Letters of Sydney Smith*, p. 482
29. Holland to Fox, p. 89
30. PRO 30/29/7/13: Byng to Granville
31. PRO 30/29/17: Leveson to Lady Granville
32. *Wynne Diaries*, iii. 311
33. PRO 30/29/8/1/38: Canning to Granville
34. WPP i. 128: Dss of Bedford to W.R.
35. Gore, p. 75
36. ibid., p. 129
37. WPP i. 284: Dss of Bedford to W.R., 20 Dec. 1838
38. PRP: E.A.R. to Laura Russell.
39. Janet Ross, ii. 143
40. PRP: Bedford to A.R.
41. PRP: A.R. to O.R., 1876
42. *Browning Letters*, p. 282: 14 Jan. 1888
43. FO 918/84: O.R. to A.R., 21 Feb., 21 June 1854
44. *Granville Letters*, i. 299
45. PRP: Moira to J. Rawdon, 29 March
46. *Granville Letters*, i. 127
47. PRO 30/29/17: Lady Granville to H. Stewart, 1 Feb. 1823
48. Lady Holland, *Journal*, p. ix
49. *Letters of Sydney Smith*, p. 108
50. PRO 30/22/6: Bulwer to Lady Granville, 20 Feb. 1843
51. Holland to Fox, p. 51
52. Brett James, p. 122
53. Broughton, ii. 174
54. Brett James, p. 103
55. *Shelley Diary*, i. 49
56. Brett James, p. 324
57. *Greville Memoirs*, i. 73

1. BILLIKINS AND BETTINA *pp.* 35–112

1. *Granville Letters*, i. 127
2. Palmerston, *Journals*, p. 48
3. MSS Canoviani, VIII – 847
4. ibid.

5. Ticknor, i. 268
6. HH add. MSS 51667: Bedford to Lady Holland
7. *Granville Letters*, i. 196 et seq.
8. *Glenbervie Diaries*, i. 289
9. Fox, *Journal*, p. 37
10. HH add. MSS 51667: Bedford to Lady Holland [?1820]
11. PRO 30/29/17/4, No. 12: Lieven to Lady Granville
12. ibid., No. 14: Lieven to Lady Granville
13. Fox, *Journal*, p. 159
14. ibid., p. 169
15. HH add. MSS 51681 (402): E.A.R. to Lady Holland
16. ibid. (401): E.A.R. to Lady Holland
17. HH add. MSS 51676 (370): W.R. to Lady Holland

2. MILITARY YEARS *pp.* 113–244

1. WPP i. 30b: Bedford to W.R., 14 April 1824
2. Holland to Fox, p. 34
3. PRP: Lieven to E.A.R., 9 Sept. 1824
4. Spencer Walpole, *Life*, i. 137
5. HH add. MSS 51668 (877): Bedford to Lady Holland
6. Part printed in Walpole, *Life*, i. 137
7. Fenimore Cooper, i. 405: Cooper to E.A.R.
8. *Granville Letters*, ii. 99
9. Moore, *Journal*, vi. 207
10. PRO 30/22/17: Bedford to J.R.
11. PRP: Bedford to E.A.R., 16 Nov. [1831]
12. WP: Fox to W.R.
13. WP: Adair to W.R., 21 Oct. [1831]
14. ibid., 10 Feb. 1832
15. ibid., 2 March [1832]
16. ibid., 30 March 1832

3. DIPLOMACY *pp.* 245–444

1. PP: Palmerston to W.R. (private), 18 June 1832
2. ibid., 30 June 1832
3. WP: H.R. to W.R. [1832]
4. Holland to Fox, p. 138
5. ADM. I, 375: W.R. to Capt. Hillyar, 15 Oct. 1832
6. FO 63/397: Hillyar to W.R., 15 Oct. 1832
7. ibid. (no. 10): Hillyar to W.R., 16 Oct. 1832
8. *Chronicles of Holland House*, p. 27
9. PP: W.R. to Palmerston, 9 July 1833
10. WPP i. 207: Byng to W.R., 26 Sept. 1833
11. PP: Hoppner to Palmerston, 2 Aug. 1833
12. *The Age*, 15 Sept., 20 Oct. 1833
13. WP: J.R. to W.R., 13 Nov. 1833
14. Lieven–Palmerston letters, p. 49, 18 Nov. 1833
15. WP: J.R. to W.R., 6 Nov. 1833
16. PP: W.R. to Palmerston, 18 Dec. 1833

17. *Dino Memoirs*, i. 116
18. *Greville Memoirs*, iii. 33
19. *Creevey Papers*, ii. 285
20. WPP i. 849: J.R. to W.R., 27 Aug. 1834
21. Gore, p. 176
22. PRP: Meaghers to W.R., 5 July 1834
23. WP: J.R. to W.R., 6 Aug. 1834
24. WP: Wellesley to W.R., 5 May 1834
25. PRP: Palmerston to E.A.R., 30 Oct. 1833
26. WPP i. 234: J.R. to W.R., 18 Jan. 1835
27. Spencer Walpole, *Life*, i. 240
28. Holland to Fox, p. 156
29. WP: Lieven to W.R., 16 mai 1835
30. HH add. MSS 47399, 31 mai/11 juin 1835; 11/23 juin 1835
31. ibid., 10 juillet 1835
32. ibid., 2/14 juillet 1835
33. ibid., 4/16 juillet 1835
34. ibid., 1 août 1835
35. WPP iii. 150: Mrs Wellesley to W.R., 20 July 1835
36. WPP iii. 152: Bedford to W.R., 21 July 1835
37. Huxley, p. 150 et seq.
38. Lieven–Palmerston letters, p. 111
39. WP: Lieven to W.R., 25 oct. 1835
40. ibid., 6 déc. 1835
41. ibid., 8 jan. 1836
42. ibid., 27 fév. 1836
43. PRO 30/22/2a: W.R. to J.R., 16 March 1836
44. PRO 30/22/2a: ibid., 9 March 1836
45. PP: W.R. to Palmerston (private), 20 Jan. 1841
46. FO 64/206: W.R. to Palmerston, 15 March 1837
47. FO 64/211: ibid., 10 Dec. 1837
48. *Dino Memoirs*, ii. 201
49. Loftus, i. 51
50. PP: W.R. to Palmerston (private), 23 Jan. 1838
51. Fenimore Cooper, v. 80
52. *Greville Memoirs*, v. 41
53. *Dino Memoirs*, ii. 311
54. WP: Loftus to W.R., 13 Feb. 1841
55. Meyendorff, i. 144
56. *Greville Memoirs*, iv. 434
57. WP: Lieven to W.R., 4 août 1836
58. ibid., 6 août 1836
59. ibid., 21 août 1835
60. Rzewuska, ii. 383
61. Bury, i. 22
62. WP: Lennox to W.R., 19 June 1837
63. PRP: Drocourt to his parents, 4 mai 1833
64. PRP: Pauline to E.A.R., 24 oct. 1837
65. ibid.
66. ibid.
67. PP: W.R. to Palmerston (private), 26 July 1837

68. PRP: Pauline to E.A.R., 2 juin 1837
69. Holland to Fox, p. 166
70. PRO 30/22/3d: W.R. to J.R.
71. PP: W.R. to Palmerston (private), 14 Nov. 1838
72. WPP i. 299: J.R. to W.R., 10 Sept. 1839
73. Lieven to Guizot, ii. 24, 10 mars 1840
74. WP: Lieven to W.R., 19 avril 1840
75. WP: Loftus to W.R., March 1841

4. LAST YEARS *pp.* 445–544

1. PRO 30/22/4b: W.R. to J.R., 20 July 1841
2. PRP: Sarah Austin to Laura Russell, 1 Jan. 1866
3. WPP iii. 333: J.R. to W.R., 31 Aug. 1841
4. Guest, *Journal*, p. 144
5. Holland to Fox, p. 209
6. WPP iii. 366: J.R. to W.R., 10 June 1844
7. WP: Lieven to W.R., 19 jan. 1844
8. Gudin, p. 196
9. PRP 30/22/5a: Lady M. Abercromby to J.R., 10 Jan. 1846

INDEX AND
LIST OF LETTERS PRINTED

555

Index

556

Index

Index

Index

Index

LIST OF LETTERS PRINTED

List of Letters Printed

Mrs Rawdon to—
Arthur Russell: 465.

6th Duke of Bedford to—
Lord William Russell: 35, 45, 59, 62, 79–80, 90, 97, 116–17, 119, 130, 133, 136, 138–9, 144, 148, 167, 173, 176, 182, 185, 191, 203, 207, 211–12, 223, 230–1, 235, 242–3, 266–7, 269, 271–2–3, 277, 279, 284–5–6–7–8, 317, 362, 367, 385, 399, 410, 417; Lady William Russell: 73–4, 153, 171, 173, 196, 219, 226, 228, 257–8, 283, 285, 288, 299, 334, 395, 430; Lady Holland: 117, 121.

Duchess of Bedford to—
Lord William Russell: 103, 107, 190, 232, 380, 384, 394, 417; Lady William Russell: 103.

Marquess of Tavistock to—
Lord William Russell: 175, 179, 198, 214, 220, 326, 331, 402, 409, 413, 421, 431–2, 442, 444, 448, 467, 473, 480, 505.

Lord John Russell to—
Lord William Russell: 118, 141, 165, 174, 179, 184, 202–3, 212, 239, 257, 264, 281–2, 284–5, 289, 325, 336, 400, 449, 479; Lady William Russell: 40, 119, 121, 140, 147, 152, 158, 160, 187, 190, 199, 201, 211, 215, 222, 225, 259–60, 266, 268, 270, 273, 279–80, 323, 329, 399, 416, 422, 467, 472, 501, 519, 538; Lord Palmerston: 348.

Princess Lieven to—
Lord William Russell: 377–8, 503; Lady William Russell: 363; Prince Lieven: 338–9–40–41–42, 344, 346, 351, 362.

Lord Holland to—
Lord William Russell: 53, 98, 185, 188, 302, 307; Lady William Russell: 308.

Lady Holland to—
Lord William Russell: 62, 146, 188, 195, 219, 241, 337, 441; Lady William Russell: 298.

Lord Palmerston to—
Lord William Russell: 256, 263, 271, 274, 278, 280, 282–3, 291; Lady William Russell: 297.

Letters addressed by others to Lord William Russell
Lord Aberdeen: 452, 459; Lady Bath: 142; Sir E. Disbrowe: 292; Charles Greville: 457–8–9; Capt. Hillyar, R.N.: 262; Lord A. Loftus: 452; Mrs H. Seymour: 93.

Letters addressed by others to Lady William Russell
Princess Frederica of Prussia: 389, 393; Frederick William III of Prussia: 406; Lord Lynedoch: 275; Princess Sophia of Wurtemberg: 403.

Other Letters
Lord Aberdeen to Charles Greville: 458; General Cordova to Viscount Santarem: 310–11; Mrs Austin to Mrs Grote: 450.